ISBN 978-1-331-52048-1
PIBN 10201101

English
Français
Deutsche
Italiano
Español
Português

www.forgottenbooks.com

Mythology Photography **Fiction**
Fishing Christianity **Art** Cooking
Essays Buddhism Freemasonry
Medicine **Biology** Music **Ancient
Egypt** Evolution Carpentry Physics
Dance Geology **Mathematics** Fitness
Shakespeare **Folklore** Yoga Marketing
Confidence Immortality Biographies
Poetry **Psychology** Witchcraft
Electronics Chemistry History **Law**
Accounting **Philosophy** Anthropology
Alchemy Drama Quantum Mechanics
Atheism Sexual Health **Ancient History**
Entrepreneurship Languages Sport
Paleontology Needlework Islam
Metaphysics Investment Archaeology
Parenting Statistics Criminology
Motivational

THE GREVILLE·MEMOIRS

(THIRD AND CONCLUDING PART)

A JOURNAL OF THE REIGN

OF

QUEEN VICTORIA

FROM 1852 TO 1860

BY THE LATE

CHARLES C. F. GREVILLE, Esq.

CLERK OF THE COUNCIL

EDITED BY

HENRY REEVE

REGISTRAR OF THE PRIVY COUNCIL

NEW YORK
D. APPLETON AND COMPANY
1887

PREFACE

TO THE THIRD PART OF THIS JOURNAL.

IT appears to be unnecessary and inexpedient to delay the publication of the last portion of these papers, which contain some record of the events occurring between the year 1852 and the close of the year 1860, a period already remote from the present time, and relating almost exclusively to men of the last generation. I have little to add to the notices prefixed by me to the two preceding portions of this work, but I am grateful for the length of days which has enabled me to complete the task confided to me by Mr. Greville three and twenty years ago, and to leave behind me a record of that delightful company to which I was bound by the closest ties of intimacy and friendship. On looking back upon the first half of the present century, I believe that we were too unconscious of the exceptional privileges we enjoyed, and that we did not sufficiently appreciate the remarkable gifts of the statesmen, the orators, the historians, the poets, and the wits who shed an incomparable lustre on the politics, the literature, and the social intercourse of those years. Of these personages some traces are to be found in the preceding volumes and in these pages.

Nor am I less grateful for the reception this publication has met with from the world, which has far surpassed the modest expectations of the author, and has at last conveyed to the reader a just estimate of the integrity and ability with which these Journals were written. They bear evident marks of the changes which are wrought in a man's character and judgments by the experience of life and the course of years; and they fall naturally into the three periods or divisions of Mr. Greville's life which I was led from other causes to adopt. In the first part he appears as a man of fashion and of pleasure, plunged, as was not inconsistent with his age and his social position, in the dissipation and the amusements of the day; but he was beginning to get tired of them. In the second part he enters with all the energy of which he was capable, though shackled by his official position, upon the great political struggles of the time—the earnest advocate of peace, of moderation, of justice, and of liberal principles —regarding with a discriminating eye and with some severity of judgment the actions of men swayed by motives of ambition and vanity, from which he was himself free. This was the most active period of his life. But years advanced, and with age the infirmities from which he had always suffered withdrew him more and more from society, and deprived him of many of those sources of intelligence which had been so freely opened to him. Hence it is possible that the volumes now published contain less of novelty and original information than the preceding portions of the work. But, on the other hand, the events recorded in them are of a more momentous character—the re-establishment of the French Empire, the Imperial Court, the Crimean War, the Indian Mutiny, and the Italian War are more interesting than the rise or fall of a Ministry; and it is curious to note precisely the effect produced at the time on the mind of a contemporary observer. No one was more conscious of the incompleteness of these Journals, and of a certain roughness, due to the impromptu character of a manuscript hastily written down, and rarely corrected, than the author of them. He was more disposed to underrate their merit, as appears from his concluding remarks, than to exaggerate their importance. But the public have judged of them more favorably; and if he entertained a hope that he might contribute some pages to the record of his times and the literature of his country, that hope was not altogether vain.

· HENRY REEVE.

January, 1887.

CONTENTS

CHAPTER I.

CHAPTER II.

CHAPTER III.

CHAPTER IV.

CHAPTER V.

CHAPTER VI.

CHAPTER VII.

CHAPTER VIII.

CHAPTER IX.

CHAPTER X.

CHAPTER XI.

CHAPTER XII.

A JOURNAL

REIGN OF QUEEN VICTORIA,

FROM 1852 TO 1860.

CHAPTER I.

Divisions of the Liberal Party—Lord Lansdowne as Head of a Liberal Government—Hostility of the Radicals—National Defences—Lord John Russell's Literary Pursuits—The Queen's Speech—The Peelites—Protection abandoned—Duke of Wellington's Funeral—Mr Villiers' Motion—Disraeli's Panegyric on Wellington—Death of Miss Berry —The Division on the Resolution—Disraeli's Budget—Lord Palmerston's Position—The Division on the Budget—Lord Derby resigns—Liberal Negotiations—Formation of Lord Aberdeen's Government—Lord St. Leonard's – Tone of the Conservatives—Lord Clanricarde and the Irish Brigade - Violence of the Tories—Lord Palmerston agrees to join the Government—The Aberdeen Cabinet – First Appearance of the New Ministry—Irritation of the Whigs

October 22d, 1852.—As usual, a long interval, for since the Duke's death I have had nothing to write about. The distribution of his offices and honors has not given satisfaction. The appointment of Fitzroy Somerset would have been more popular than that of Hardinge to the command of the army, especially with the army; but I have no doubt the Court insisted on having Hardinge, who is a great favorite there.

Matters in politics remain much as they were. There has been a constant interchange of letters between Lord John Russell and his leading friends and adherents, and conversations and correspondence between these and Palmerston, the result of the whole being a hopeless state of discord and disagreement in the Liberal party, so complete that there appears no possibility of all the scattered elements of opposition being combined into harmonious action, the consequence of which can hardly fail to be the continuance in office of the present Government. The state of things may be thus summed up : Lord John Russell declares he will take no office but that of Premier, considering any other a degradation ; but he says he does not want office, and if a Liberal Government can be formed under anybody else he will give it his best support.   He resents greatly the expressed sentiments of those who would put him by and choose another Prime Minister, and this resentment his belongings foster as much as they can.   Palmerston professes *personal* regard for Lord John, but declares he will never again serve *under* him, though he would *with* him, and his great object has been to induce Lord Lansdowne to consent to put himself at the head of a Government (if this falls) under whom he would be willing to serve, and he would consent to Lord John's leading the House of Commons as heretofore.   This he communicated to the Duke of Bedford in conversation at Brocket, and he afterward wrote a detailed account of that conversation to Lansdowne himself, which was an invitation to him to act the part he wished to allot to him.   Lord Lansdowne wrote him an answer in which he positively declined to put himself at the head of a Government, stating various reasons why he could not, and his conviction that John Russell was the only man who could be at the head of one hereafter. With regard to other opinions, Graham is heart and soul with Lord John, and decidedly in favor of his supremacy. The Whig party are divided, some still adhering to him ; others, resenting his conduct in the past Session and distrusting his prudence, are anxious for another chief, but without having much considered how another is to be found, nor the consequences of deposing him.   The Radicals are in an unsettled and undecided state, neither entirely favorable nor entirely hostile to Lord John ; the Peelites are pretty unanimously against him, and not overmuch disposed to join with the Whig party, being still more or less deluded with the hope and belief that they may form a Government themselves.   Graham has always maintained (and, as I thought, with great probability) that it would end in Palmerston's joining Derby, and at this moment such an arrangement seems exceedingly likely to happen.   There were two or three articles not long ago in the " Morning Post " (his own paper), which tended that way.   I have just been for two days to Broadlands, where I had a good deal of talk with him and with Lady Palmerston, and I came away with the conviction that it would end in his joining this Government.

He admitted it to be a possible contingency, but said he could
not come in *alone*, and only in the event of a remodelling of
the Cabinet and a sweep of many of the incapables now in it.
Sidney Herbert, who was there, told me he had talked to
him in the same tone, and spoke of eight seats being vacated
in the Cabinet, and as if he expected that nobody should *certainly* remain there but Derby, Disraeli, and the Chancellor.
It is evident from this that it depends on Derby himself to
have him, and if he frames measures and announces principles such as would enable Palmerston with credit and consistency to join him, and if he will throw over a sufficient
number of his present crew, he may so strengthen his Government as to make it secure for some time. It may, however, be a matter of considerable difficulty to turn out a great
many colleagues, and not less so for Palmerston to find people to bring in with him ; for though he is very popular, and
can excite any amount of cheering in the House of Commons,
he has no political adherents whatever, and if Derby was to
place seats in the Cabinet at his disposal he has nobody to
put into them, unless he could prevail on Gladstone and
Herbert to go with him, which does not seem probable.[1]

November 3d.—Since writing the above, circumstances
have occurred which may have an important influence on
future political events. John Russell, whether moved by
his own reflections or the advice or opinions of others I know
not, has entirely changed his mind and become more reasonable, moderate, and pliable than he has hitherto shown
himself. He has announced that if it should hereafter be
found practicable to form a Liberal Government under Lord
Lansdowne, he will not object to serve under him, only re-
serving to himself to judge of the expediency of attempting
such an arrangement, as well as of the Government that
may be formed. The letter in which he announced this to
Lord Lansdowne was certainly very creditable to him, and
evinced great magnanimity. He desired that it might be
made known to Palmerston, which was done by Lord Lansdowne, and Palmerston replied with great satisfaction, saying, "for the first time he now saw daylight in public
affairs." Lord Lansdowne was himself gratified at Lord
John's conduct to him, but he said that it would expose him
to fresh importunities on the part of Palmerston, and he

---

[1] [A list of the members of Lord Derby's Administration will be found in
the second volume of the Second Part of this Journal, p. 547.]

seems by no means more disposed than he was before to take the burden on himself, while he is conscious that it will be more difficult for him to refuse. He has been suffering very much, and is certainly physically unequal to the task, and *le cas échéant* he will no doubt try to make·his escape ; but, from what I hear of him, I do not think he will be inexorable if it is made clear to him that there is no other way of forming a Liberal Government, and especially if Lord John himself urges him to undertake it.

The other important matter is a correspondence, or rather a letter from Cobden to a friend of his, in which he expresses himself in very hostile terms toward John Russell and Graham likewise, abuses the Whig Government, and announces his determination to fight for Radical measures, and especially the Ballot. This letter was sent to Lord Yarborough, by him to the Duke of Bedford, and by the Duke to Lord John. He wrote a reply, or, more properly, a comment on it, which was intended to be, and I conclude was, sent to Cobden ; a very good letter, I am told, in which he vindicated his own Government, and declared his unalterable resolution to oppose the Ballot, which he said was with him a question of principle, on which he never would give way. The result of all this is a complete separation between Lord John and Cobden, and therefore between the Whigs and the Radicals. What the ultimate consequences of this may be it is difficult to foresee. but the immediate one will probably be the continuation of Derby in office. Lord John is going to have a parliamentary dinner before the meeting, which many of his friends think he had better have left alone. He wrote to Graham and invited him to it. Graham declined, and said he should not come up to the meeting. To this Lord John responded that he might do as he pleased about dining, but he assured him that his absence at the opening of the Session would give great umbrage to the party and be injurious to himself. Graham replied that he would come up, but he has expressed to some of his correspondents his disapproval of the dinner. Charles Villiers agrees with him about it, and so do I, but the Johnians are very indignant with Graham, and consider his conduct very base, though I do not exactly see why.

The question of national defence occupies everybody's mind, but it seems very doubtful if any important measures will be taken. The Chancellor told Senior that the Government were quite satisfied with Louis Napoleon's pacific assurances, and saw no danger. It is not clear that John Russell partakes of the general alarm, and whether he will be disposed (as many wish that he should) to convey to Lord Derby an intimation that he will support any measure he may propose for the defence of the country, nor is it certain that Derby would feel any reliance on such assurances after what passed when he came into office. On that occasion Derby called on Lord John (who had just advised the Queen to send for him) and said, on leaving him, "I suppose you are not going to attack me and turn me out again," which Lord John assured him he had no thoughts of, and directly after he convoked his Chesham Place meeting, which was certainly not very consistent with his previous conduct, nor with his engagement to Derby.

London, November 11th, 1852.—I passed two days at The Grove with John Russell the end of last and beginning of this week, when he was in excellent health and spirits, and in a very reasonable composed state of mind. There were Wilson, Panizzi, George Lewis, and the Duke of Bedford; very little talk about politics, except in a general way. Lord John has been engaged in literary pursuits, as the executor of Moore and the depositary of Fox's papers, and he is about to bring out two volumes of Moore and one of Fox, but in neither is there to be much of his own composition; he has merely arranged the materials in each.

There has been great curiosity about the Queen's Speech, and a hundred reports of difficulties in composing it, and of dissensions in the Cabinet with regard to the manner in which the great question should be dealt with. As I know nothing certain on the subject, I will spare myself the trouble of putting down the rumors, which may turn out to be groundless or misrepresented. A great fuss has been made about keeping the Speech secret. They refused to communicate it to the newspapers, and strict orders were given at the Treasury to allow nobody whatever to see it. Derby, however, wrote to Lord John that as he had always sent it to him, he should do the same, and accordingly Lord John received it, and read it at his dinner, but those present were bound on honor not to communicate the contents of it. Lord John and his friends have been all along determined, if possible, to avoid proposing an amendment.

There was a Peelite gathering at a dinner at Hayward's

the day before yesterday, at which Gladstone, Sidney Herbert, Newcastle, Francis Charteris, Sir John Young, and others were present; and Hayward told me they were all united, resolved to act together, and likewise averse to. an amendment if possible; but from the manner in which they have dealt with Free Trade, it is very doubtful whether Cobden at least, if not Gladstone, will not insist on moving an amendment. A very few hours will decide this point.[1]

November 12th.—The question of Protection or Free Trade, virtually settled long ago, was formally settled last night, Derby having announced in terms the most clear and unequivocal his final and complete abandonment of Protection, and his determination to adhere to, and honestly to administer, the present system. His speech was received in silence on both sides. There has not yet been time to ascertain the effect of this announcement on the various parties and individuals interested by it.

November 16th.—I went yesterday to the lying in state of the Duke of Wellington; it was fine and well done, but too gaudy and theatrical, though this is unavoidable. Afterward to St. Paul's to see it lit up. The effect was very good, but it was like a great rout; all London was there strolling and staring about in the midst of a thousand workmen going on with their business all the same, and all the fine ladies scrambling over vast masses of timber, or ducking to avoid the great beams that were constantly sweeping along. These public funerals are very disgusting *med sententiâ*. On Saturday several people were killed and wounded at Chelsea; ye e d everything was orderly and well conducted, and I heard of no accidents.

Charles Villiers' motion, after much consultation and debate, whether it should be brought on or not, is settled in the affirmative, and was concocted by the Peelites at a meeting at Aberdeen's, Graham present. Nothing could be more moderate, so moderate that it appeared next to impossible the Government could oppose it. Yesterday morning there was a Ministerialist meeting in Downing Street, when Derby harangued his followers.

November 21st.—I saw the Duke's funeral from Devonshire House. Rather a fine sight, and all well done, except the car, which was tawdry, cumbrous, and vulgar. It was

[1] [The new Parliament was opened by the Queen in person on November 11.]

contrived by a German artist attached to the School of Design, and under Prince Albert's direction—no proof of his good taste. The whole ceremony within St. Paul's and without, went off admirably, and without mistakes, mishaps, or accidents; but as all the newspapers overflow with the details. I may very well omit them here.

Now that this great ceremony is over, we have leisure to turn our thoughts to political matters. I have already said that Villiers proposed a mild resolution which was drawn up by Graham at Aberdeen's house, and agreed to by the Peelites.[1] Then came Derby's meeting, where he informed his followers that he must reserve to himself entire liberty of dealing with Villiers' resolution as he thought best, but if he contested it, and was beaten, he should not resign. He then requested that if any one had any objection to make, or remarks to offer, on his proposed course, they would make them then and there, and not find fault afterward. They all cheered, and nobody said a word; in fact they were all consenting to his abandonment of Protection, many not at all liking it, but none recalcitrant. After this meeting there was a reconsideration of Villiers' resolution. Cobden and his friends complained that it was too milk and water, and required that it should be made stronger. After much discussion Villiers consented to alter it, and it was eventually put on the table of the House in its present more stringent form. Lord John Russell was against the alteration, and Gladstone and the Peelites still more so; but Charles Villiers thought he could not do otherwise than defer to Cobden, after having prevailed on the latter to consent to no amendment being moved on the Address. There is good reason to believe that the Government would have swallowed the first resolution, but they could not make up their minds to take the second; and accordingly Disraeli announced an amendment in the shape of another resolution, and the battle will be fought on the two, Dizzy's just as strongly affirming the principle of Free Trade as the other, but it omits the declaration that the measure of '46 was " wise and *just*." At this moment nobody has the least idea what the division will be,

---

[1] [On November 23, Mr. Charles Villiers moved Resolutions in the House of Commons, declaring the adherence of Parliament to the principles of Free Trade and approving the Repeal of the Corn Laws. Mr. Disraeli moved an amendment, not directly adverse. But this amendment was withdrawn in favor of one more skilfully drawn by Lord Palmerston. On this occasion Lord Palmerston rendered an essential service to Lord Derby's Government.]

nor how many of the most conspicuous men will vote, nor what the Government will do if they are beaten. Moderate men on the Liberal side regret that the original resolution was changed, deprecate the pitched battle, and above all dread that the Government may resign if they are beaten, which would cause the greatest confusion, nothing being ready for forming a government on the Liberal side, and the Government would go out with the advantage of saying that they were prepared with all sorts of good measures which the factious conduct of their opponents would not let them produce. Things have not been well managed, and I expect the result of all these proceedings will be damaging to the Liberal interest, and rather advantageous to Lord Derby.

An incident occurred the other night in the House of Commons, which exposed Disraeli to much ridicule and severe criticism. He pronounced a pompous funeral oration on the Duke of Wellington, and the next day the " Globe " showed that half of it was taken word for word from a panegyric of Thiers on Marshal Gouvion de St. Cyr. Disraeli has been unmercifully pelted ever since, and well deserves it for such a piece of folly and bad taste. His excuse is, that he was struck by the passage, wrote it down, and, when he referred to it recently, forgot what it was, and thought it was his own composition. But this poor apology does not save him. Derby spoke very well on the same subject a few nights after in the House of Lords, complimenting the authorities, the people, and foreign nations, particularly France. It is creditable to Louis Napoleon to have ordered Walewski to attend the funeral.[1]

On Saturday night, about twelve o'clock, Miss Mary Berry died after a few weeks' illness, without suffering, and in possession of her faculties, the machine worn out, for she was in her 90th year.[2] As she was born nearly a century ago, and was

---

[1] [Count Walewski, then French Ambassador in London, expressed some reluctance to attend the funeral of the conqueror of Napoleon I., upon which Baron Brunnow said to him, " If this ceremony were intended to bring the Duke to life again, I can conceive your reluctance to appear at it ; but as it is only to bury him. I don't see you have anything to complain of."]

[2] [Miss Mary Berry was born at Kirkbridge, in Yorkshire, on March 16, 1763 ; her sister Agnes, who was her inseparable companion for eighty-eight years, fourteen months later. Her father, Robert Berry, was the nephew of a Scotch merchant named Ferguson, who purchased the estate of Raith, in Fifeshire. William Berry, the brother of Robert, and uncle of these ladies, succeeded to this property, and took the name of Ferguson. The Miss Berrys first made the acquaintance of Horace Walpole in 1788, when he was seventy years

the contemporary of my grandfathers and grandmothers, she was already a very old woman when I first became acquainted with her, and it was not till a later period, about twenty years ago. that I began to live in an intimacy with her which continued uninterrupted to the last.   My knowledge of her early life is necessarily only traditional.   She must have been exceedingly good-looking, for I can remember her with a fine commanding figure and a very handsome face, full of expression and intelligence.   It is well known that she was the object of Horace Walpole's octogenarian attachment, and it has been generally believed that he was anxious to marry her for the sake of bestowing upon her a title and a jointure, which advantages her disinterested and independent spirit would not allow her to accept.   She continued nevertheless to make the charm and consolation of his latter days, and at his death she became his literary executrix, in which capacity she edited Madame du Deffand's letters. She always preserved a great veneration for the memory of Lord Orford, and has often talked to me about him.   I gathered from what she said that she never was herself quite sure whether he wished to marry her, but inclined to believe that she might have been his wife had she chosen it.   She seems to have been very early initiated into the best and most refined society, was a constant inmate of Devonshire House and an intimate friend of the Duchess, a friendship which descended to her children. all of whom treated Miss Berry to the last with unceasing marks of attention, respect, and affection. She had been very carefully educated, and was full of literary tastes and general information, so that her conversation was always spirited, agreeable, and instructive ; her published works, without exhibiting a high order of genius, have considerable merit, and her "Social Life in England and France" and "The Life of Rachel, Lady Russell," will always be read with pleasure, and are entitled to a permanent place in English literature ; but her greatest merit was her amiable and benevolent disposition, which secured to her a very large circle of attached friends, who were drawn to her as much by affectionate regard as by the attraction of her vigorous understanding and the vivacity and variety of her conversational powers.   For a great many years the Misses Berry were among the social celebrities of

of age, and they became the objects of his devoted attachment and regard. See "National Biography," vol. iv. p. 397.]

London, and their house was the continual resort of the most distinguished people of both sexes in politics, literature, and fashion.   She ranked among her friends and associates all the most remarkable literary men of the day, and there certainly was no house at which so many persons of such various qualities and attainments, but all more or less distinguished, could be found assembled.   She continued her usual course of life, and to gather her friends about her, till within a few weeks of her death, and at last she sank by gradual exhaustion, without pain or suffering, and with the happy consciousness of the affectionate solicitude and care of the friends who had cheered and comforted the last declining years of her existence.   To those friends her loss is irreparable, and besides the private and individual bereavement it is impossible not to be affected by the melancholy consideration that her death has deprived the world of the sole survivor of a once brilliant generation, who in her person was a link between the present age and one fertile in great intellectual powers, to which our memories turn with never-failing curiosity and interest.

December 4th.—Last week the House of Commons was occupied with the "Resolutions," the whole history of which was given by Graham, and which need not be repeated here.[1] The divisions were pretty much what were expected, and the only interesting consideration is the effect produced, and the influence of the debate on the state of parties.   Palmerston is highly glorified by his small clique, and rather smiled on by the Tories, but he has given great offence to both Whigs and Radicals, and removed himself further than ever from a coalition with John Russell and the Liberal party.   Lord John himself, who made a very good speech, rather gained reputation by his behavior throughout the transaction, and is on better terms both with Cobden, Bright, and his own party, than he has been for some time past.   Disraeli made a very imprudent speech, which disgusted many of his own adherents, and exposed him to vigorous attacks and a tremendous castigation on the part of his opponents, by Bernal Osborne in the coarser, and Sidney Herbert in more polished style.   The Protectionists generally cut a very poor

---

[1] [After three nights' debate, the Resolutions moved by Mr. Villiers were negatived by 256 to 236, and the motion adroitly substituted for them by Lord Palmerston in favor of " unrestricted competition " was carried by 468 against 53, being accepted by the Government.]

figure, and had nothing to say for themselves. "If people wish for *humiliation*," said Sidney Herbert, "let them look at the benches opposite." But all the dirt they had to eat, and all the mortification they had to endure, did not prevent the Derbyites from presenting a compact determined phalanx of about three hundred men, all resolved to support the Government, and to vote through thick and thin, without reference to their past or present opinions. The Ministerial papers and satellites toss their caps up and proclaim a great victory, but it is difficult to discover in what the victory consists. It certainly shows that they are strong and devoted if not united.

After the division there was a good deal of speculation rife as to Palmerston's joining the Government, which his friends insist he will not do. I am disposed to think he will. Since that we have had Beresford's affair in the House of Commons, and Clanricarde's folly in the Lords. Cockburn produced a strong *primâ facie* case against Beresford, and the committee has been appointed on his case, and proceeds to business on Monday.[1] Clanricarde chose *de son chef* to propose a resolution like that of the Commons, which Derby refused to take and offered another in its place, which Clanricarde has accepted. He gave Derby the opportunity he wanted of setting himself right with his own party, who, albeit resolved to support him, are smarting severely under his complete abandonment of Protection, and the necessity to which they are reduced of swallowing the nauseous Free Trade pill. He will make the dose more palatable by soothing their wounded pride. Clanricarde went to Lord Lansdowne and told him what he proposed to do. Lansdowne objected, but Clanricarde said he did it individually and would take all the responsibility on himself, on which Lansdowne very unwisely ceased to object. His purpose is to take no responsibility on himself.

December 6th.—Ever since the termination of the "Resolutions" debate the world has been in a state of intense curiosity to hear the budget, so long announced, and of which such magnificent things were predicted. The secret was so well kept that nobody knew anything about it, and not one of the hundred guesses and conjectures turned out to be correct. At length on Friday night Disraeli produced his

---

[1] [This related to proceedings with reference to the recent election at Derby.]

measure in a house crowded to suffocation with members
and strangers.   He spoke for five and a half hours, much
too diffusely, spinning out what he might have said in half
the time.   The budget has been on the whole tolerably well
received, and may, I think, be considered successful, though
it is open to criticism, and parts of it will be fiercely attacked, and he will very likely be obliged to change some
parts of it.   But though favorably received on the whole,
it by no means answers to the extravagant expectations that
were raised, or proves so entirely satisfactory to all parties
and all interests as Disraeli rather imprudently gave out that
it would be.   The people who regard it with the least favor
are those who will be obliged to give it the most unqualified
support, the ex-Protectionists, for the relief or compensation
to the landed interest is very far from commensurate with
their expectations.   It is certainly of a Free Trade character altogether, which does not make it the more palatable to
them.   He threw over the West Indians, and (Pakington,
their advocate, sitting beside him) declared they had no
claim to any relief beyond that which he tendered them,
viz., the power of refining sugar in bond—a drop of water
to one dying of thirst.   I think it will go down, and make
the Government safe.   This I have all along thought they
would be, and every day seems to confirm this opinion.
They have got from three hundred to three hundred and
fifteen men in the House of Commons who, though dissatisfied and disappointed, are nevertheless determined to swallow everything and support them through thick and thin,
and they have to encounter an opposition, the scattered
fractions of which are scarcely more numerous, but which is
in a state of the greatest confusion and disunion, and without any prospect of concord among them.

The Duke of Bedford came to me yesterday, and told
me he had never been so disheartened about politics in his
life, or so hopeless of any good result for his party, in which
he saw nothing but disagreement and all sorts of pretensions
and jealousies incompatible with any common cause, and
Aberdeen, whom I met at dinner yesterday, is of much the
same opinion.   The principal object of interest and curios-
ty seems now to be whether Palmerston will join them or
not.   On this the most opposite opinions and reports prevail.   Just now it is said that he has resolved not.   At all
events, if he does, he will have to go alone, for he can take

nobody with him, as it certainly is his object to do.   But it does not appear now as if there was the least chance of Gladstone or Sidney Herbert joining him.   The Duke of Bedford told me that both Derby and Palmerston were in better odor at Windsor than they were, and that the Queen and Prince approve of Pam's move about the Resolutions, and think he did good service.   Aberdeen also thinks that though the Whigs and Radicals are angry with Lord Palmerston, and that his proceeding was unwarrantable, he stands in a better position in the country, and has gained credit and influence by what he did.   Abroad, where nobody understands our affairs, he is supposed to have played a very great part, and to have given indubitable proof of great political ower.

p   *December 9th.*—Within these few days the Budget, which was not ill received at first, has excited a strong opposition, and to-morrow there is to be a pitched battle and grand trial of strength between the Government and Opposition upon it, and there is much difference of opinion as to the result. The Government have put forth that they mean to resign if beaten upon it.   Derby and Disraeli were both remarkably well received at the Lord Mayor's dinner the night before last, and this is an additional proof that, in spite of all their disreputable conduct, they are not unpopular, and I believe, if the country were polled, they would as soon have these people for Ministers as any others.   Nobody knows what part Palmerston is going to take.

December 18th.—The last few days have been entirely occupied by the interest of the Budget debate and speculations as to the result.   We received the account of the division at Panshanger yesterday morning, not without astonishment ; for although the opinion had latterly been gaining ground that the Government would be beaten, nobody expected such a majority against them.[1]   Up to the last they were confident of winning.   The debate was all against them, and only exhibited their weakness in the House of Commons.   It was closed by two very fine speeches from Disraeli and Gladstone, very different in their style, but not unequal in their merits.

Panshanger, December 19th.—I went to town yesterday

---

[1] [The division on the Budget took place on December 16 after five nights' debate, the numbers being—for the Government, 286 ; against, 305 ; adverse majority, 19.]

morning to hear what was going on.   Lord Derby returned
from Osborne in the middle of the day, and the Queen had
sent for Lords Lansdowne and Aberdeen.   She had been
gracious to Derby, and pressed him to stay on, if it were
only for a short time.   I saw Talbot, and from the few
words he let drop I gathered that they have already resolved
to keep together, and to enter on a course of bitter and determined opposition.   Not that he said this, of course, but
he intimated that he had no idea of any new Government
that might be formed being able to go on even for a short
time, and that they would very speedily be let in again.
The language of the Carlton corresponds with this, and I
have no doubt they will be as virulent and as mischievous
as they can.   It remains to be seen, if a good Government
is formed, whether some will not be more moderate, and
disposed to give the new Cabinet a fair trial.

Clarendon writes me word that the meeting at Woburn
between John Russell, Aberdeen, Newcastle, and himself
has been altogether satisfactory, everybody ready to give and
take, and anxious to promote the common cause, without
any selfish views or prejudices.   Newcastle is particularly
reasonable, disclaiming any hostility to John Russell, and
only objecting to his being at present the nominal head of
the Government, because there is rightly or wrongly a prejudice against him, which would prevent some Liberals and
some Peelites joining the Government if he was placed in
that position ; but he contemplates his ultimately resuming
that post, and he (Newcastle) is ready to do anything in
office or out.   There is no disposition to take in Cobden
and Bright, but they would not object to Molesworth.

I went over to Brocket just now, and found the Palmerstons there.   He is not pleased at the turn matters have
taken, would have liked the Government to go on at all
events some time longer, and is disgusted at the thought of
Aberdeen being at the head of the next Ministry.   This is
likewise obnoxious to the Whigs at Brooks's, and there will
be no small difficulty in bringing them to consent to it, if
Lansdowne refuses.   Beauvale said if Palmerston had not
been laid up, and prevented going to the House of Commons, he thinks this catastrophe would not have happened,
for Palmerston meant to have done in a friendly way what
Charles Wood did in an unfriendly one, and advised Disraeli
to postpone and remake his Budget, and this advice so

tendered he thinks Dizzy would have taken, and then the issue would have been changed and deferred till after the recess. But I don't believe this fine scheme would have taken effect, or that Dizzy would or could have adopted such a course. Beauvale says he is pretty sure Palmerston will not take office under Aberdeen's Premiership; on the other hand, Aberdeen has no objection to him, and will invite Palmerston, if the task devolves upon him. Ellice fancies Lansdowne will decline, and that Aberdeen will fail, and that it will end in Derby coming back, reinforced by Palmerston and some Peelites. The difficulties are certainly enormous, but by some means or other I think a Government will be formed. The exclusions will be very painful, and must be enormous. Lord Derby met Granville and others at the station on Friday, and he said he calculated the new Cabinet could not consist of less than thirty-two men, and many then left out. It will be a fine time to test the amount of patriotism and unselfishness that can be found in the political world.

London, December 21st.—I came to town yesterday morning, and heard that the day before (Sunday) a very hostile feeling toward Aberdeen had been prevailing at Brooks's, but no doubt was entertained that the Government would be formed. In the afternoon Clarendon came to me on his way to the House of Lords, and told me all that had passed up to that time. On receiving the Queen's summons, a meeting took place between Lansdowne and Aberdeen at Lansdowne House, at which each did his best to persuade the other to accept the commission to form a Government. Lansdowne pleaded absolute physical inability, and his friends seem to be quite satisfied that he really could not undertake it. Accordingly Aberdeen gave way, and departed for Osborne on a reiterated summons, and, after telling the Queen all that had passed between Lansdowne and himself, undertook the task. Nothing could be more cordial all this time than the relations between himself and John Russell; but as soon as it became known that Aberdeen was to form the new Government, certain friends of John Russell set to work to persuade him that it would be derogatory to his character to have any concern in it, and entreated him to refuse his concurrence. These were David Dundas and Romilly, and there may have been others. This advice was probably the more readily listened to, because it corresponded

with his original view of the matter and his own natural disposition, and it produced so much effect that yesterday morning he went to Lansdowne and told him that he had resolved
to have nothing to do with the new Government.   Lansdowne was thunderstruck, and employed every argument he
could think of to change this resolution.   It so happened
that he had written to Macaulay and asked him to call on
him to talk matters over, and Macaulay was announced while
Lord John was still there.   Lansdowne told him the subject
of their discussion, and the case was put before Macaulay
with all its pros and cons for his opinion.   He heard all
Lansdowne and Lord John had to say, and then delivered
his opinion in a very eloquent speech, strongly recommending Lord John to go on with Aberdeen, and saying that, at
such a crisis as this, the refusal of his aid, which was indispensable for the success of the attempt, would be little short
of treason.   Lord John went away evidently shaken, but
without pronouncing any final decision.   Clarendon then
called at Lansdowne House, and heard these particulars, and
Lansdowne entreated him to go and see Lord John and try
his influence over him.   Clarendon had the day before given
him his opinion in writing to the same effect as Macaulay.
He went, saw him, and repeated all he had before written.
Lord John took it very well, and, when he left him, said,
" I suppose it will be as you wish," and when I saw Clarendon he seemed reassured, and tolerably confident that this
great peril of the whole concern being thus shipwrecked *in
limine* had passed away.   After the House of Lords, where
I heard Derby's strange and inexcusable speech, we again
discussed the matter, when he said Lord John had raised
another difficulty, for he said he would not take the Foreign
Office, alleging, not without truth, that it was impossible for
him or any man to perform the duties of so laborious an
office and lead the House of Commons.   Lord John also
signified to Clarendon that he should insist on *his* being in
the Cabinet, which Clarendon entreated him not to require.
Newcastle, who was there, suggested that Lord John might
take the Foreign Office for a time, and if he found the two
duties incompatible he might give it up, and Clarendon
seemed to think this might be done, and at all events he
means to persuade Lord John (as no doubt he will) to make
up his mind to take it, for his not doing so would certainly
be very inconvenient.   Should Lord John prove obstinate

in this respect, I have no doubt Clarendon will himself be put there.

We talked about the Great Seal, and Senior had been with Lord Lansdowne, who appears to incline very much to getting Lord St. Leonards[1] to stay if he will, but Senior thinks he will not ; certainly not, unless with the concurrence of his present colleagues, which it is doubtful if Derby in his present frame of mind would give. The Chancellor was at Derby's meeting in the morning, which looks like a resolution to go out with them. It will be a good thing if he will remain, but it will do good to the new Government to invite him, whether he accepts or refuses. We talked of Brougham, but Clarendon, though anxious to have Brougham in as President of the Council, thinks he would not do for the Woolsack, and that it will be better to have Cranworth if Lord St. Leonards will not stay. There is a great difficulty in respect to the retiring pension. There can only be four, and Sugden's will make up the number, so that a fresh Chancellor could have none except at the death of one of the others. The worst part of the foregoing story is, that Lord John will not join cordially and heartily, and it is impossible to say, during the difficult adjustment of details, what objections he may not raise and what embarrassments he may not cause.

There was a meeting at Lord Derby's yesterday morning, at which he told his friends he would continue to lead them, and he recommended a moderation, in which he probably was not sincere, and which they will not care to observe. Lord Delawarr got up and thanked him. Nothing can be more rabid than the party and the ex-ministers, and they are evidently bent on vengeance and a furious opposition. I fell in with Lord Drumlanrig and Ousely Higgins yesterday morning, one a moderate Derbyite (always Free Trader), the other an Irish Brigadier. Drumlanrig told me he knew of several adherents of Derby who were resolved to give the new Government fair play, and would not rush into opposi-

---

[1] [Sir Edward Burtenshaw Sugden was one of the most eminent equity lawyers of the day, distinguished as an advocate in the Court of Chancery and by his important legal writings. He was twice Lord Chancellor of Ireland under the two Administrations of Sir Robert Peel, and he received the Great Seal of England on the formation of Lord Derby's Administration in 1852, with a peerage under the title of Baron St. Leonards. But he owed his celebrity and his promotion to his eminence as a lawyer far more than to his activity as a politician.]

tion, and Ousely Higgins said he thought the Irish would be all right, especially if, as the report ran, Granville was sent to Ireland ; but there is no counting on the Irish Brigade, whose object it is to embarrass every Government.   If they could be friendly to any, it would, however, be one composed of Aberdeen, Graham, and Gladstone, the opponents of the Ecclesiastical Titles Bill.

December 22d.—On going to The Grove yesterday afternoon, I found a letter Clarendon had received from Lansdowne in bad spirits enough.   He had seen Aberdeen, who had received no answer from John Russell, and Aberdeen was prepared, if he did not get his acceptance the next morning, to give the thing up.   Lansdowne was greatly alarmed and far from confident Lord John would agree, at all events, that he would not take the Foreign Office, in which case Lansdowne said he (Clarendon) must take it. Nothing could look worse.   This morning Clarendon received a letter from Aberdeen announcing that Lord John had agreed to lead the House of Commons, either without an office or with a nominal one, and asking Clarendon to take the Foreign Office.   We came up to town together, he meaning to accept unless he can prevail on Lord John to take it, if it be only for a time, and he is gone to see what he can do with him.   He told me last night that when he was at Woburn last week, the Duke informed him that he had had a confidential communication from Stockmar, asking for his advice, whom the Queen should send for if the Government was beaten and if Derby resigned.   He had just received this letter, and had not answered it, and consulted Clarendon what he should say.   Clarendon advised him to recommend Lansdowne and Aberdeen, and he wrote to that effect.   The very morning after the division, just as they were going hunting, the hounds meeting at the Torr, a Queen's messenger arrived with another letter, requesting he would communicate more fully his sentiments at the present crisis.   The messenger was ordered to keep himself secret, and not to let his mission transpire.   The Duke, under Clarendon's advice, wrote a long letter back, setting forth in detail all that had, not long ago, passed about Palmerston and Lansdowne, and his notions of the difficulties and exigencies of the present time.   He said that it was evident Lord John could not make a Government, and that he was himself conscious of it.

December 23*d*.—It appears that on Tuesday (21st) Aberdeen went to Palmerston, who received him very civilly, even cordially, talked of old times, and reminded him that they had been acquainted for sixty years (since they were at Harrow together), and had lived together in the course of their political lives more than most men. Aberdeen offered him the Admiralty, saying he considered it in existing circumstances the most important office, and the one in which he could render the greatest service to the country, but if he for any reason objected to that office,* he begged him to say what other office he would have. Palmerston replied that he had no hostile feeling toward him, but they had for so many years been in strong opposition to each other, that the public would never understand his taking office in Aberdeen's Government, and he was too old to expose himself to such misconceptions. And so they parted, on ostensibly very friendly terms, which will probably not prevent Palmerston's joining Derby and going into furious opposition. In the course of the day yesterday both Clarendon and Lansdowne called on Palmerston, and he expressed great satisfaction at Clarendon's appointment to the Foreign Office.

In the afternoon I called on Lady Clanricarde, who gave me to understand that Clanricarde was likely to become a personage of considerable influence and power (and therefore worth having), inasmuch as the Irish Band had made overtures to him, and signified their desire to act under his guidance. She said this was not the first overture he had received of the kind from the same quarter; that for various reasons he had declined the others, but she thought at the present time he might very well listen to it that they were very anxious to be led by a gentleman, and a man of consideration and station in the world. All this, to which I attach very little credit, was no doubt said to me in order to be repeated, and that it might impress on Aberdeen and his friends and colleagues the importance of securing Clanricarde's services and co-operation ; and I am the more confirmed in this by receiving a note from the Marchioness in the evening, begging I would not repeat what she had told me.

There was nothing new yesterday in the purlieus of Whiggism, but I think somewhat more of acquiescence, and a disposition to regard this combination as inevitable. The Derbyites quite frenzied, and prepared to go any lengths.

Lonsdale told me the party were delighted with Derby's intemperate speech in the House of Lords, which seems to have
been rehearsed at his own meeting the same morning ; and
the other day twenty ruffians of the Carlton Club gave a
dinner there to Beresford, to celebrate what they consider
his acquittal ! After dinner, when they got drunk, they
went upstairs, and finding Gladstone alone in the drawing-
room, some of them proposed to throw him out of the win-
dow. This they did not quite dare to do, but contented themselves with giving some insulting message or order to the
waiter, and then went away.

Hatchford, Friday, 24th.—The great event of yesterday
was Palmerston's accession to the Government. Lord Lansdowne had called on him the day before, and had, I suspect,
little difficulty in persuading him to change his determination and join the new Cabinet. He said he would place
himself in Lord Lansdowne's hands, and yesterday morning
I heard as a secret, though it was speedily published, that
he had agreed to take the Home Office. The next thing
was Lord John's consent to take the Foreign Office. This
he was persuaded to do by Clarendon, who engaged to help
him in the work, and relieve him by taking it himself the
moment Lord John should find himself unequal to it, and
on these conditions he consented. It was settled that Gladstone should be Chancellor of the Exchequer, but Delane
went to Aberdeen last night for the purpose of getting him
to change this arrangement on the ground of the difficulty
there would be about the Income Tax.

The important part of forming the Cabinet is now done,
and nothing remains but the allotment of the places. It
will be wonderfully strong in point of ability, and in this
respect exhibit a marked contrast with the last ; but its very
excellence in this respect may prove a source of weakness,
and eventually of disunion. The late Cabinet had two paramount chiefs, and all the rest nonentities, and the nominal
head was also a real and predominant head. In the present Cabinet are five or six first-rate men of equal or nearly
equal pretensions, none of them likely to acknowlege the
superiority or defer to the opinions of any other, and every
one of these five or six considering himself abler and more
important than their Premier. They are all at present on
very good terms and perfectly satisfied with each other ; but
this satisfaction does not extend beyond the Cabinet itself ;

murmurings and grumblings are already very loud. The Whigs have never looked with much benignity on this coalition, and they are now furious at the unequal and, as they think, unfair distribution of places. These complaints are not without reason, nor will it make matters better that John Russell has had no communication with his old friends and adherents, nor made any struggle, as it is believed, to provide for them, although his adhesion is so indispensable that he might have made any terms and conditions he chose. Then the Radicals, to judge from their press, are exceedingly sulky and suspicious, and more likely to oppose than to support the new Government. The Irish also seem disposed to assume a menacing and half hostile attitude, and, having contributed to overthrow the last Government, are very likely (according to the policy chalked out for them after the election) to take an early opportunity of aiding the Derbyites to turn out this. Thus hampered with difficulties and beset with dangers, it is impossible to feel easy about their prospects. If, however, they set to work vigorously to frame good measures and remove practical and crying evils, they may excite a feeling in their favor in the country, and may attract support enough from different quarters in the House of Commons to go on, but I much fear that it will at best be a perturbed and doubtful existence. Such seems the necessary condition of every Government nowadays, and unfortunately there is a considerable party which rejoices in such a state of things, and only desires to aggravate the mischief, because they think its continuance and the instability of every Government will be most conducive to the ends and objects which they aim at.

London, December 28th. — The remonstrances against Gladstone's being Chancellor of the Exchequer were unavailing, but he says he is not tied up by anything he said about the Income Tax. This will nevertheless be a great difficulty, for Graham and Wood, though not perhaps so much committed as Gladstone, are both against the alteration, which the public voice undoubtedly demands. Last night the new Ministers took their places on the Treasury bench, and the Tories moved over to the opposite side. Aberdeen made his statement, which was fair enough and not ill received, but it was ill delivered, and he omitted to say all he might and ought to have said about Lord Lansdowne, nor did he say enough about John Russell. He said, on the other hand, more than enough about foreign policy, and gave Derby a good opportunity of attacking that part of his speech. Derby was more moderate and temperate than on the first night, and made a pretty good speech. He was wrong in dilating so much on what had passed in the House of Commons, and he made very little of the case of combination ; he was severe on Graham and his speech at his election at Carlisle, and Graham heard it all. Nobody else said a word.

The Government is now complete, except some of the minor appointments and the Household. It has not been a smooth and easy business by any means, and there is anything but contentment, cordiality, and zeal in the confederated party. The Whigs are excessively dissatisfied with the share of places allotted to them, and complain that every Peelite without exception has been provided for, while half the Whigs are excluded. Though they exaggerate the case, there is a good deal of justice in their complaints, and they have a right to murmur against Aberdeen for not doing more for them, and John Russell for not insisting on a larger share of patronage for his friends.[1] Clarendon told me last night that the Peelites have behaved very ill, and have grasped at everything, and he mentioned some very flagrant cases, in which, after the distribution had been settled between Aberdeen and John Russell, Newcastle and Sidney Herbert, for they appear to have been the most active in the matter, persuaded Aberdeen to alter it and bestow or offer offices intended for Whigs to Peelites and in some instances to Derbyites who had been Peelites. Clarendon has been all along very anxious to get Brougham into the Cabinet as President of the Council, and he proposed it both to Lord John and Aberdeen, and the latter acquiesced, and Clarendon thought it was going to be arranged that Granville should be President of the Board of Trade, and Brougham President of Council ; but Newcastle and Sidney Herbert not only upset this plan, but proposed that Ellenborough should be President of Council, and then, when he was objected to, Harrowby. They also wanted that Jersey should remain Master of the Horse, Jonathan Peel go again to the Ordnance, and Chandos continue a Lord of the Treasury. With what object they wished for

---

[1] [It was, however, Lord John who prevented Mr. Cardwell, the President of the Board of Trade, from having a seat in the Cabinet, on the ground that there were already too many Peelites in it.]

these appointments I have not an idea, but the very notion of them is an insult to the Whigs, and will be resented accordingly.

Lord Lansdowne seems to have taken little or no part in all this. He hooked Palmerston, and, having rendered this great service, he probably thought he had done enough. The Whigs at Brooks's are very angry, and Bessborough told me that he thought his party so ill used, that he had implored Lord John to withdraw even now rather than be a party to such injustice. Lord John seems to have been very supine, and while the Peelites were all activity, and intent on getting all they could, he let matters take their course, and abstained from exercising the influence in behalf of his own followers which his position and the indispensability of his co-operation enabled him to do. This puts them out of humor with him as much as with Aberdeen and his friends.

We had a great reunion here (at Lord Granville's) last night, with half the Cabinet at dinner or in the evening. I told Graham what the feelings of the Whigs were. He said they had a very large and important share, the Chancellors of England and of Ireland, etc., and he defended some of the appointments and consequent exclusions on special grounds. They have made Monsell, an Irish Catholic convert, Clerk of the Ordnance, together with some other Irish Catholic appointments, and he said that these were necessary in order to reconquer in Ireland what had been lost by the Ecclesiastical Titles Bill, and that it was of more consequence to conciliate that large part of the Empire than to provide for the Ansons and the Pagets; and on the same ground he justified the appointment of St. Germans instead of Lord Carlisle as Lord Lieutenant. All this may be very true, but the Whigs to be left out to make room for these substitutes will not be convinced or pacified by the political expediency which Graham sets forth, nor will such appointments be at all popular here. If, however, they really should be the means of rallying the Irish Brigade to the support of the Government, it may be patronage well bestowed. But this makes it a disagreeable start, and may be hereafter productive of serious consequences. Nothing can be more shortsighted, as well as unfair, than the conduct of the Peelites in trying to thrust their own people instead of Whigs into the offices, for they can only hope to keep their places at all by the zealous support of the whole Whig force, themselves bringing next to nothing in point of numbers, and to encounter such a numerous and compact Opposition will require the zealous co-operation of all who wish well to the Liberal cause, and who are against Derby. Newcastle talked to me last night about Aberdeen's speech, acknowledged its deficiencies, and said he had told Aberdeen what he thought of it. Aberdeen acknowledged it all, said he was so unaccustomed to make such statements, that he had forgotten or overlooked it, and wished he could have spoken it again to repair the omission. They all seem *at present* very harmonious in their intercourse.

After dinner last night John Russell and Charles Wood went off to meet Aberdeen, for the purpose, I believe, of settling some of the arrangements not yet fixed. Clarendon told me that Charles Wood had been of use in stimulating John Russell to interfere and prevent some of the proposed changes which the Peelites wished Aberdeen to make in the list as originally settled between him and Lord John, and it is very well that he did. It is impossible not to see that Lord John himself, though now willing to co-operate and do his best, has never been hearty in the cause, nor entirely satisfied with his own position ; and this has probably made him more lukewarm, and deterred him from taking a more active and decided part in the formation of the Government. We are just going down to Windsor, the old Government to give up seals, wands, etc., the new to be sworn in. They go by different railways, that they may not meet. It is singular that I have never attended a Council during the nine months Lord Derby was in office, not once ; consequently there are several of his Cabinet whom I do not know by sight—Pakington, Walpole, and Henley. With my friends I resume my functions.

December 29th.—I went down to the Council yesterday at Windsor with the *ins*, and we saw nothing of the *outs*, who went by another train and railway. Palmerston was there, looking very ill indeed. They all seem on very cordial terms. Graham told me he had had a very friendly conversation with Palmerston, and was greatly rejoiced at being again united to his old colleague. He acknowledged that it was a great mistake in Aberdeen to have offered the Mastership of the Horse to Lord Jersey. Aberdeen has now proposed the Lord Steward's place to Carlisle, which he will probably not take, and possibly be offended at the offer. I suppose Aberdeen has been subjected to pressure from various quarters, but might have made a better selection and distribution than he has done.

January 5th, 1853.—The elections are all going on well, except Gladstone's, who appears in great jeopardy. Nothing could exceed the disgraceful conduct of his opponents, lying, tricking, and shuffling, as might be expected from such a party. The best thing that could happen for Gladstone would be to be beaten, if it were not for the triumph it would be to the blackguards who have got up the contest; for the representation of Oxford is always an embarrassment to a statesman, and Peel's losing his election there in 1829 was the most fortunate event possible for him. The only speech of the new Ministers calling for special notice is Palmerston's at Tiverton, which appears to me to conceal an *arrière-pensée.* He spoke in civil, even complimentary, terms of the Derby Government, so much so, that if any break-up or break-down should occur in this, and Lord Derby return to office, there appears no reason why Palmerston should not form a fresh coalition with him; and it looks very much as if he was keeping this contingency in view, and putting himself in such an attitude as should enable him with some plausibility to join the camp of such a restoration.

The Cabinet of Lord Aberdeen's Administration consisted of the following Ministers ·

Earl of Aberdeen	First Lord of the Treasury.
Lord Cranworth .	Lord Chancellor.
Earl Granville .	Lord President of the Council.
The Duke of Argyll	Lord Privy Seal.
Mr. Gladstone .	Chancellor of the Exchequer.
Viscount Palmerston	Home Secretary of State.
The Duke of Newcastle .	Secretary for Colonies and War.
Lord John Russell (and later the Earl of Clarendon) .	Foreign Secretary.
Sir James Graham	First Lord of the Admiralty.
Mr. Sidney Herbert .	Secretary at War.
Sir Charles Wood . . .	President of the Indian Board.
Sir William Molesworth . .	First Commissioner of Works.

The Marquis of Lansdowne without office.

CHAPTER II.

A Royal Commission on Reform—M. de Elahault on the Emperor Napoleon—Lord John's Blunder—Disraeli's Negotiation with the Irish Members—Lord Beauvale's Death—Lady Beauvale's Grief—Napoleon III. and Mdlle. de Montijo—Parliament meets—The Emperor's Marriage—Disraeli's Attack on Sir C. Wood—Dislike of Mr. Disraeli—Lord John Russell leaves the Foreign Office—Lord Stanley's Liberal Votes—Disraeli's Opinion of his Colleagues—The Government in Smooth Water—England unpopular abroad—Massimo d'Azeglio—The Austrians in Italy—The Bishop of Lincoln—The Duke of Bedford's Papers—Lord Palmerston leads the House—Social Amenities—Rancor of Northern Powers against England—Friendly Resolution of the Emperor Napoleon III.—Difficulties at Home—The India Bill—The Eastern Question—The Czar's Proposals—Russian Assurances—The Royal Family.

Bowood, January 12th, 1853.—I came here on Monday to meet the Cannings, Harcourt,[1] and Lady Waldegrave, the Bessboroughs, Elphinstone, Senior, and the family. Senior talked to me about the Government and Reform, and the danger of their splitting on the latter question and propounded a scheme he has for obviating this danger. He wants to have a Royal Commission to inquire into the practice of bribery at elections and the means of preventing it, or, if possible, to have an inquiry of a more extensive and comprehensive character into the state of the representation and the working of the Reform Bill. We talked it over, and I told him I thought this would not be a bad expedient. He had already spoken to Lord Lansdowne about it, who seemed not adverse to the idea, and promised to talk to Lord John Russell on the subject. Senior, when he went away, begged me to talk to Lord Lansdowne also, which I attempted to do, but without success, for he seemed quite indisposed to enter upon it.

Beaudesert, January 19th.—To town on Saturday and here on Monday, with the Flahaults, Bessboroughs, Ansons, my brothers, and the family. Lord Anglesey and M. de Flahault talk over their campaigns, and compare notes on the events of Sir John Moore's retreat and other military operations, in which they have served in opposing armies. Flahault was aide-de-camp to Marshal Berthier till the middle of the Russian campaign, when he became aide-de-camp to Napoleon, whom he never quitted again till the end of his career. His accounts of what he has seen and known are curious and interesting. He says that one of the Emperor's

---

[1] [George Granville Harcourt, Esq., M. P., eldest son of the Archbishop of York, and third husband of Frances, Countess of Waldegrave.]

greatest mistakes and the causes of his misfortunes was his habit of ordering everything, down to the minutest arrangement, himself, and leaving so little to the discretion and responsibility of his generals and others that they became mere machines, and were incapable of acting, or afraid to act, on their own judgments.   On several occasions great calamities were the consequence of this unfortunate habit of Napoleon's.

London, January 24th.—The Duke of Bedford called here this morning.   I had not seen him for an age ; he was just come from Windsor with a budget of matter, which as usual he was in such a hurry that he had not time to tell me. I got a part of it, however.   I began by asking him how he had left them all at Windsor, to which he replied that the state of things was not very satisfactory.   The Queen disapproved Lord John's arrangement for giving up the seals of the Foreign Office on a given day (the 15th February) which had not been previously explained to her Majesty, as it ought to have been.   She said that she should make no objection if any good reason could be assigned for what was proposed, either of a public or a private nature, any reason connected with his health or with the transaction of business, but she thought, and she is right, that fixing beforehand a particular day, without any special necessity occurring, is very unreasonable and absurd.   Then they are all very angry with Lord John for an exceeding piece of folly of his, in announcing to the Foreign Ministers, the day he received them, that he was only to be at the Foreign Office for a few weeks. This, as the Duke said, was a most unwise and improper communication, particularly as it was made without any concert with Aberdeen, and without his knowledge, and, in fact, blurted out with the same sort of levity that was apparent in the Durham letter and the Reform announcement, with both of which he has been so bitterly reproached, and which have proved so inconvenient that it might have been thought he would not fall again into similar scrapes.   The Foreign Ministers themselves were exceedingly astonished, and not a little annoyed.   Brunnow said it was a complete mockery, and they all felt that it was unsatisfactory to be put in relation with a Foreign Secretary who was only to be there for a few weeks.

The Queen is delighted to have got rid of the late Ministers.   She felt, as everybody else does, that their Govern-

ment was disgraced by its shuffling and prevarication, and
she said that Harcourt's pamphlet (which was all true) was
sufficient to show what they were.[1] As she is very honorable and true herself, it was natural she should disapprove
their conduct.

Yesterday Delane called on me, and gave me an account
of a curious conversation he had had with Disraeli. Disraeli
asked him to call on him, which he did, when they talked
over recent events and the fall of the late Government, very
frankly, it would seem, on Disraeli's part. He acknowledged
that he had been bitterly mortified. When Delane asked
him, "now it was all over," what made him produce such a
Budget, he said, if he had not been thwarted and disappointed, he should have carried it by the aid of the Irish
Brigade whom he had *engaged* for that purpose. Just before
the debate, one of them came to him and said, if he would
agree to refer Sharman Crawford's Tenant Right Bill to the
Select Committee with the Government Bill, they would all
vote with him. He thought this too good a bargain to miss,
and he closed with his friend on those terms, told Walpole
what he had arranged, desired him to carry out the bargain,
and the thing was done. No sooner was the announcement
made than Lord Naas and Sir Joseph Napier[2] (who had
never been informed) came in a great fury to Disraeli and
Walpole, complained of the way they had been treated, and
threatened to resign. With great difficulty he pacified or
rather silenced them, and he was in hopes the storm had
blown over, but the next day he found Naas and Napier had
gone to Lord Derby with their complaints, and he now
found the latter full of wrath and indignation likewise ; for
Lord Roden, who had heard something of this compromise
(i. e., of the Tenant Right Bill being referred to Committee),
announced his intention of asking Lord Derby a question in
the House of Lords. Added to this, as soon as the news
reached Dublin, Lord Eglinton and Blackburne testified the
same resentment as Naas and Napier had done, and threatened to resign likewise. All this produced a prodigious

---

[1] [Mr. William Harcourt published a pamphlet at this time on "The Morality
of Public Men," in which he censured with great severity the conduct of the
late Ministers.]

[2] [Lord Naas was Chief Secretary for Ireland, and Sir Joseph Napier Attorney-General for Ireland, in Lord Derby's Administration of 1852. Lord Eglinton was Lord Lieutenant of Ireland, and the Right Hon. Francis Blackburne
Irish Lord Chancellor.]

flare-up.   Disraeli represented that it was his business to
make the Budget succeed by such means as he could, that
the votes of the Brigade would decide it either way, and
that he had made a very good bargain, as he had pledged
himself to nothing more, and never had any intention of
giving any *suite* to what had been done, so that it could not
signify.   He did not succeed in appeasing Lord Derby, who,
a night or two after in the Lords, repudiated all participation in what had been done, and attacked the Irishmen very
bitterly.   Disraeli heard this speech, and saw at once that
it would be fatal to the Budget and to them, as it proved,
for the whole Brigade voted in a body against the Government, and gave a majority to the other side.   He seemed in
pretty good spirits as to the future, though without for the
present any definite purpose.   He thinks the bulk of the
party will keep together.   Delane asked him what he would
have done with such a Budget if he had carried it.   He said
they should have remodelled their Government, Palmerston
and Gladstone would have joined them (*Gladstone* after the
debate and their duel!); during the intervening two or
three months the Budget would have been discussed in the
country, what was liked retained, what was unpopular altered, and in the end they should have produced a very good
Budget which the country would have taken gladly.   He
never seems to have given a thought to any consideration of
political morality, honesty, or truth in all that he said.
The moral of the whole is, that let what will happen it will
be very difficult to bring Lord Derby and Disraeli together
again.   They must regard each other with real, if not
avowed, distrust and dislike.   Disraeli said that Derby's position in life and his fortune were so different from his, that
their several courses must be influenced accordingly.   It is
easy to conceive how Lord Derby, embarked (no matter how
or why) in such a contest, should strain every nerve to succeed and fight it out; but the thing once broken up, he
would not be very likely to place himself again in such a
situation, and to encounter the endless difficulties, dangers,
and mortifications attendant upon the lead of such a party,
and above all the necessity of trusting entirely to such a colleague as Disraeli in the House of Commons without one
other man of a grain of capacity besides.   As it is, he will
probably betake himself to the enjoyment of his pleasures
and pursuits, till he is recalled to political life by some fresh

excitement and interest that time and circumstances may throw in his way; but let what will happen, I doubt his encountering again the troubles and trammels of office.[1]

January 30th.—Yesterday morning Frederic Lamb, Lord Beauvale and Melbourne, with whom both titles cease, died at Brocket after a short but severe attack of influenza, fever, and gout. He was in his seventy-first year. Lady Palmerston thus becomes a rich heiress. He was not so remarkable a man in character as his brother William, less peculiar and eccentric, more like other people, with much less of literary acquirement, less caustic humor and pungent wit; but he had a vigorous understanding, great quickness, a good deal of general information; he was likewise well versed in business and public affairs, and a very sensible and intelligent converser and correspondent. He took a deep and lively interest in politics to the last moment of his life, was insatiably curious about all that was going on, and was much confided in and consulted by many people of very different parties and opinions. He never was in Parliament, but engaged all his life in a diplomatic career, for which he was very well fitted, having been extremely handsome in his youth, and always very clever, agreeable, and adroit. He consequently ran it with great success, and was in high estimation at Vienna, where his brother-in-law, Palmerston, sent him as Ambassador. He was always much addicted to gallantry, and had endless liaisons with women, most of whom continued to be his friends long after they had ceased to be his mistresses, much to the credit of all parties. After having led a very free and dissolute life, he had the good fortune at sixty years old, and with a broken and enfeebled constitution, to settle (as it is called), by marrying a charming girl of twenty, the daughter of the Prussian Minister at Vienna, Count Maltzahn. This Adine, who was content to unite her May to his December, was to him a perfect angel, devoting her youthful energies to sustain and cheer his valetudinarian existence with a cheerful unselfishness, which he repaid by a grateful and tender affection, having an air at once marital and paternal. She never cared to go anywhere, gave up all commerce with the world and all its amusements and pleasures, contenting herself with such society as it suited

[1] [A singularly unfortunate prediction! The alliance of Lord Derby and Mr. Disraeli remained unbroken, and continued long enough to enable them (after a second failure) to bring the Conservative party back to power.]

him to gather about them—his old friends and some new ones—to whom she did the honors with infinite grace and cordiality, and who all regarded her with great admiration and respect. In such social intercourse, in political gossip, and in her untiring attentions, his last years glided away, not without enjoyment. He and his brother William had always been on very intimate terms, and William highly prized his advice and opinions ; but, as Frederic was at heart a Tory, and had a horror of Radicalism in every shape, he was not seldom disgusted with the conduct of the Whig Government, and used sorely to perplex and mortify William by his free and severe strictures on him and his colleagues. He nominally belonged to the Liberal party, but in reality he was strongly Conservative, and he always dreaded the progress of democracy, though less disturbed than he would otherwise have been by reflecting that no material alteration could possibly overtake him. His most intimate friends abroad were the Metternichs and Madame de Lieven, and his notions of foreign policy were extremely congenial to theirs. Here, his connections all lying with people of the Liberal side, he had nothing to do with the Tories, for most of whom he entertained great contempt. Brougham, Ellice, and myself were the men he was most intimate with. He was very fond of his sister, but never much liked Palmerston, and was bitterly opposed to his policy when he was at the Foreign Office, which was a very sore subject between himself and them, and for a long time, and on many occasions, embittered or interrupted their intercourse ; but, as he was naturally affectionate, had a very good temper, and loved an easy life, such clouds were always soon dispersed, and no permanent estrangement ever took place. He was largely endowed with social merits and virtues, without having or affecting any claim to those of a higher or moral character. I have no doubt he was much more amiable as an old man than he ever had been when he was a young one ; and, though the death of one so retired from the world can make little or no sensation in it, except as being the last of a remarkable family, he will be sincerely regretted, and his loss will be sensibly felt by the few who enjoyed the intimacy of his declining years.

February 8th.—Yesterday I went to see the unhappy Lady Beauvale, and, apart from the sorrow of witnessing so much bodily and mental suffering, it is really a singular and

extraordinary case.   Here is a woman thirty-two years old,
and therefore in the prime of life, who has lost a husband of
seventy-one, deprived of the use of his limbs, and whom she
had nursed for ten years, the period of their union, with the
probable or possible fatal termination of his frequent attacks
of gout constantly before her eyes, and she is not merely
plunged in great grief at the loss she has sustained, but in a
blank and hopeless despair, which in its moral and physical
effects seriously menaces her own existence.   She is calm,
reasonable and docile, talks of him and his illness without
any excitement, and is ready to do everything that her
friends advise ; but she is earnestly desirous to die, considers
her sole business on earth as finished, and talks as if the pro-
longation of her own life could only be an unmitigated evil
and intolerable burden, and that no ray of hope was left for
her of any possibility of happiness or even peace and ease
for the future.   She is in fact brokenhearted, and that for a
man old enough to be her grandfather, and a martyr to disease and infirmity ; but to her he was everything ; she had
consecrated her life to the preservation of his, and she kept
his vital flame alive with the unwearied watching of a Vestal
priestess.   She had made him an object and an idol round
which all the feelings and even passion of an affectionate
heart had entwined themselves, till at last she had merged
her very existence in his, and only lived in, with, and for
him.   She saw and felt that he enjoyed life, and she made it
her object to promote and prolong this enjoyment.   "Why,"
she says, "could I not save him now, as I saved him heretofore ?" and not having been able to do so, she regards her
own life as utterly useless and unnecessary, and only hopes
to be relieved of it that she may (as she believes and expects)
be enabled to join him in some other world.[1]

February 9th.—Yesterday Clarendon told me a curious
thing about the Emperor Napoleon and his marriage, which
came in a roundabout way, but which do doubt is true.
Madame de Montijo's most intimate friend is the Marchioness of Santa Cruz, and to her she wrote an account of what
had passed about her daughter's marriage and the Emperor's
proposal to her.   When he offered her marriage, she expressed
her sense of the greatness of the position to which he proposed to raise her.   He replied, "It is only fair that I should

---

[1] [She lived, however, and married Lord Forester, *en secondes noces*, in
1856.]

set before you the whole truth, and let you know that if the position is very high, it is also perhaps very dangerous and insecure." He then represented to her in detail all the dangers with which he was environed, his unpopularity with the higher classes, the *malveillance* of the Great Powers, the possibility of his being any day assassinated at her side, his popularity indeed with the masses, but the fleeting character of their favor, but above all the existence of a good deal of disaffection and hostility in the army, the most serious thing of all. If this latter danger, he said, were to become more formidable, he knew very well how to avert it by a war ; and though his earnest desire was to maintain peace, if no other means of self-preservation should remain, he should not shrink from that, which would at once rally the whole army to one common feeling. All this he told her with entire frankness, and without concealing the perils of his position, or his sense of them, and it is one of the most creditable traits I have ever heard of him. It was, of course, calculated to engage and attach any woman of high spirit and generosity, and it seems to have had that effect upon her. It is, however, curious in many ways ; it reveals a sense of danger that is not apparently suspected, and his consciousness of it ; and it shows how, in spite of a sincere wish to maintain peace, he may be driven to make war as a means of self-preservation, and therefore how entirely necessary it is that we should be on our guard, and not relax our defensive preparations. I was sure from the conversations I had with M. de Flahault at Beaudesert, that he feels the Emperor's situation to be one of insecurity and hazard. He said that it remained to be seen whether it was possible that a Government could be maintained permanently in France on the principle of the total suppression of civil and political liberty, which had the support of the masses, but which was abhorred and opposed by all the elevated and educated classes. The limbs of the body politic are with the Emperor, and the head against him.

February 11th.—Parliament met again last night. Lord Derby threw off in the Lords by asking Lord Aberdeen what the Government meant to do, which Aberdeen awkwardly and foolishly enough declined to give any answer to. The scene was rather ridiculous, and not creditable, I think, to Aberdeen. He is unfortunately a very bad speaker at all times, and, what is worse in a Prime Minister, has no readiness whatever. Lord Lansdowne would have made a very pretty and dexterous flourish, and answered the question. Lord John did announce in the House of Commons what the Government mean to do and not to do, but they say he did it ill, and it was very flat, not a *brilliant* throw-off at all.

February 16*th.*—Yesterday Cowley arrived from Paris. He called on me, and gave me an account of the state of things there and some curious details about the Emperor's marriage and his abortive matrimonial projects. He confirms the account of Louis Napoleon's position set forth in Madame de Montijo's letter. The effect of his marriage has been very damaging everywhere, and the French people were not at all pleased at his calling himself a " parvenu," which mortified their vanity, inasmuch as they did not like to appear as having thrown themselves at the feet of a parvenu. For some time before the marriage was declared, Cowley, from what he saw and the information he received, began to suspect it would take place, and reported it to John Russell. Just about this time Walewski went to Paris, and when Cowley saw him he told him so. Walewski expressed the greatest surprise as well as mortification, and imparted to Cowley that a negotiation had been and still was going on for the Emperor's marriage with the Princess Adelaide of Hohenlohe, the Queen's niece, at that time and still with the Queen in England. This was begun by Lord Malmesbury, and the Emperor had regularly proposed to her through her father. A very civil answer had been sent by the Prince, in which he said that he would not dispose of his daughter's hand without her consent, and that he had referred the proposal to her, and she should decide for herself. The Queen had behaved very well, and had abstained from giving any advice or expressing any opinion on the subject. They were then expecting the young Princess's decision. This being the case, Cowley advised Walewski to exert his influence to stop the demonstrations that were going on between the Emperor and Mlle. de Montijo, which might seriously interfere with this plan. The next day Walewski told Cowley that he had seen the Emperor, who took him by both hands, and said, " Mon cher, je suis pris," and then told him he had resolved to marry Mlle. de Montijo. However, on Walewski representing the state of the other affair, he agreed to wait for the Princess Adelaide's answer, but said, if it was unfavorable, he would conclude the other affair, but if the Princess accepted him he would marry her.   The day following the answer came : very civil, but declining on the ground of her youth and inexperience, and not feeling equal to such a position.   The same day the Emperor proposed to the Empress.   Cowley says he is evidently much changed since his marriage, and that he is conscious of his unpopularity and the additional insecurity in which it has involved his position.

February 19*th.*—Lord Cowley told me something more about the marriage. He saw the Queen on Thursday (17th), who told him all about it.   The first step was taken by Morny, who wrote to Malmesbury, and requested him to propose it, stating that the Emperor's principal object in it was to "resserrer les liens entre les deux pays."   Malmesbury accordingly wrote to the Queen on the subject.   She was annoyed, justly considering that the proposal, with the reason given, placed her in a very awkward situation, and that it ought not to have been mentioned to her at all.   The result was what has been already stated, but with this difference, that the Queen set her face against the match, although the girl, if left to herself, would have accepted the offer.   However, nobody knows this, and they are very anxious these details should not transpire.   The two accounts I have given of this transaction seem to me to afford a good illustration of the uncertainty of the best authenticated historical statements.   Nothing could appear more to be relied on than the accuracy of Cowley's first account to me, and if I had not seen him again, or if he had not imparted to me his conversation with the Queen, that account would have stood uncorrected, and an inaccurate version of the story would have been preserved, and might hereafter have been made public, and, unless corrected by some other contemporaneous narrative, would probably have been taken as true.   The matter in itself is not very important, but such errors unquestionably are liable to occur in matters of greater moment, and actually do occur, fully justifying the apocryphal character which has been ascribed to almost every historical work.[1]

The Queen seems to be intensely curious about the Court of France and all details connected with it, and on the other hand Louis Napoleon has been equally curious about the

[1] [Further details with reference to the marriage of the Emperor will be found in Lord Malmesbury *Memoirs*, vol. i. pp. 374 and 378, which confirm Mr. Greville's narrative.]

etiquette observed in the English Court, and desirous of assimilating his to ours, which in great measure he appears to have done.

Last night there was the first field day in the House of Commons, Disraeli having made an elaborate and bitter attack on the Government, but especially on Charles Wood and Graham, under the pretence of asking questions respecting our foreign relations, and more particularly with France.[1] His speech was very long, in most parts very tiresome, but with a good deal of ability, and a liberal infusion of that sarcastic vituperation which is his great forte, and which always amuses the House of Commons more or less. It was, however, a speech of devilish malignity, quite reckless and shamelessly profligate; for the whole scope of it was, if possible, to envenom any bad feeling that may possibly exist between France and England, and, by the most exaggerated representations of the offence given by two of the Ministers to the French Government and nation, to exasperate the latter, and to make it a point of honor with them to resent it, even to the extent of a quarrel with us. Happily its factious violence was so great as to disgust even the people on his own side, and the French Government is too really desirous of peace and harmony to pay any attention to the rant of a disappointed adventurer, whose motives and object are quite transparent.

February 20th.—Disraeli's speech on Friday night was evidently a political blunder, which has injured him in the general opinion, and disgusted his own party. It is asserted that he communicated his intention to his followers, who disapproved of it, but he nevertheless persisted. The speech itself was too long; it was dull and full of useless truisms in the first part, but clever and brilliant in the last; and his personalities were very smart and well aimed; but there was not a particle of truth and sincerity in it; it was a mere vituperation and factious display, calculated to do mischief if it produced any effect at all, and quite unbecoming a man who had just been a Minister of the Crown and leader of the House of Commons, and who ought to have

---

[1] [Sir Charles Wood, President of the Board of Control, made a speech to his constituents at Halifax on February 3, in which he commented in severe language on the despotic character of the Imperial Government of France. The speech was thought to be unbecoming in the mouth of a Cabinet minister, and Sir Charles apologized for it. But Mr. Disraeli made it the subject of a fierce attack in the House of Commons.]

been animated by higher motives and more patriotic views. This was what the more sensible men of the party felt, and Tom Baring, the most sensible and respectable of the Derby-ites, and the man of the greatest weight among them, told me himself that he was so much disgusted that he was on the point of getting up to disavow him, and it is much to be regretted, as I told him, that such a rebuke was not administered from such a quarter. It does not look as if the connection between Disraeli and the party could go on long. Their dread and distrust of him and his contempt of them render it difficult if not impossible. Pakington is already talked of as their leader, and some think Disraeli wants to shake them off and trade on his own bottom, trusting to his great abilities to make his way to political power with somebody and on some principles, about neither of which he would be very nice. Tom Baring said to me last night, "Can't you make room for him in this Coalition Government?" I said, "Why, will you give him to us?" "Oh, yes," he said, "you shall have him with pleasure."

Lord John Russell has taken leave of the Foreign Office, and has had an interview with the Queen and Prince, satisfactory to both. She has been all along considerably annoyed at the arrangement made about his taking the Foreign Office only to quit it, and his leading the House of Commons without any office, which she fancies is unconstitutional, and the arrangement was announced in the newspapers without any proper communication to her. The consequence has been some little soreness on both sides, but this has now been all removed by explanations and amicable communication. The Queen attacked him on the constitutional ground, but here *elle l'a pris par son fort*, and he easily bowled over this objection.[1] Then she expressed her fear lest it should be drawn into a precedent, which might be inconvenient in other cases, to which he replied that he thought there was little fear of anybody wishing to follow the precedent of a man taking upon himself a vast amount of labor without any pay at all. Then she said that a man independent of office might consider himself independent of the Crown also, and postpone its interests to popular re-

---

[1] [The objection taken by Her Majesty was to Lord John Russell's proposal that he should retain his seat in the Cabinet and the leadership of the House of Commons without holding any special office in the Government. But in fact, as a Privy Councillor of the Crown, a Minister, with or without office, is under precisely the same obligations to the Sovereign and to Parliament.]

quirements ; which he answered by saying that he did not think any Minister, as it was, thought very much of the Crown as contradistinguished from the people, and that he was not less likely to take such a part as she apprehended by holding an office of £5,000 a year, from which a vote of the House of Commons could at any moment expel him. He appears to have satisfied them both, and to be satisfied himself, which is still more important.

February 25th.—The Jew question and the Maynooth question have been got over in the House of Commons without much debate, but by small majorities. The most remarkable incident was young Stanley[1] voting with the majority in both questions, and speaking on Maynooth, and well. As he is pretty sure to act a conspicuous part, it is good to see him taking a wise and liberal line. Disraeli voted for the Jews but did not speak, which was very base of him. Last night I met Tomline at dinner, who is a friend of his, and told me a great deal about him. He has a good opinion of him, that is, that he has a good disposition, but his personal position perverts him in great measure. He says he dislikes and despises Derby, thinks him a good " Saxon " speaker and nothing more, has a great contempt for his party, particularly for Pakington, whom they seem to think of setting up as leader in his place. The man in the House of Commons whom he most fears as an opponent is Gladstone. He has the highest opinion of his ability, and he respects Graham as a statesman. Tomline told me that his system of attacking the late Sir Robert Peel was settled after this manner. When the great schism took place, three of the seceders went to Disraeli (Miles, Tyrrel, and a third whom I have forgotten), and proposed to him to attack and vilify Peel regularly, but with discretion ; not to fatigue and disgust the House, to make a speech against him about once a fortnight or so, and promised if he would that a constant and regular attendance of a certain number of men should be there to cheer and support him, remarking that nobody was ever efficient in the House of Commons without this support certain.[2] He desired twenty minutes to consider

[1] [The present Earl of Derby, who succeeded his father as fifteenth Earl in 1869. He entered public life as Under Secretary of State for Foreign Affairs in 1852.]

[2] [This anecdote is related on the authority of Mr. Tomline as stated in the text. It was mentioned in the lifetime of Lord Beaconsfield, and in justice to him it must be said that he altogether denied the truth of the story.]

of this offer, and finally accepted it. We have seen the result, a curious beginning of an important political career.
now they dread and hate him, for they know in his heart he
has no sympathy with them, and that he has no truth or
sincerity in his conduct or speeches, and would throw them
over if he thought it his interest.

March 1st.—The Government seem upon the whole to be
going on prosperously. They have at present no difficulty
in the House of Commons, where there is no disposition to
oppose their measures, and an appearance of moderation
generally, which promises an easy Session. John Russell
has spoken well, and seems to have recovered a great share
of the popularity he had lost. Aberdeen has done very well
in the House of Lords, his answers to various "questions"
having been discreet, temperate, and judicious; in short, up
to this time the horizon is tolerably clear. On the other
hand the divisions have presented meagre majorities, and the
Government have no *power* in the House of Commons, and
live on the good-will or forbearance of the several fractions
of which it is composed. John Russell is in his heart not
satisfied with his present position, and not animated with
any spirit of zeal or cordiality, though he is sure to act honestly and fairly the part he has undertaken. There is still a
good deal of lurking discontent and resentment on the part
of those who were left out, and of the Whig party generally,
who are only half reconciled to following the banner of a
Peelite premier; of the malcontents the principal are Carlisle and Clanricarde, who are both in different ways very
sore; Normanby is dissatisfied, Labouchere, Seymour, and
George Grey not pleased, but except Clanricarde none have
shown any disposition to withhold their support from the
Government, or even to carp at them. Aberdeen seems to
have no notion of being anything but a *real* Prime Minister.
He means to exercise a large influence in the management
of foreign affairs, which he considers to be the peculiar, if
not exclusive, province of himself and Clarendon. Palmerston does not interfere with them at all, but he must do so,
if any important questions arise for the Cabinet to decide,
and then it is very likely some dissension will be the consequence. There are four ex-Secretaries for Foreign Affairs in
this Cabinet, all of whom will naturally take part in any discussion of moment. Argyll began rather unluckily, running
his head indiscreetly against Ellenborough on an Indian pe-

tition.   He is burning with impatience to distinguish himself, and broke out too soon, and out of season ; but he was
not unconscious of his error, and it will probably be of use
to him to have met with a little check at his outset, and
teach him to be more discreet.   He spoke again last night,
and very well, on the Clergy reserves, when there was a
brilliant passage of arms in the Lords, in which Lord Derby
and the Bishops of Exeter and Oxford distinguished themselves.

News came by telegraph last night that the dispute between Turkey and Austria is settled, which will relieve us
from a great difficulty.   If it had gone on, we should have
had a difficult part to play, and unluckily the good understanding that was reviving between us and Vienna has all
been upset by the late attempt on the Emperor's life,[1] which
has thrown the Austrians into a ferment, and renewed all
their bitter resentment against us for harboring Kossuth and
Mazzini, to whom they attribute both the *émeute* at Milan
and the assassination at Vienna severally.   They are no doubt
right about Mazzini and wrong about Kossuth, but fortunately for us the first is not in England and has been abroad
for some time, and it will probably be impossible to bring
any evidence against Kossuth to connect him with the Hungarian assassin.   But these troubles and attempts, the origin
of which is attributed to men residing here, and, though
neglected by the Government, more or less objects of popular favor and sympathy, render all relations of amity impossible between our Government and theirs, and the disunion
is aggravated by our absurd meddling with such cases as the
Madiai and Murray at Florence and at Rome, which are no
concern of ours, and which our Government does in compliance with Protestant bigotry.   What makes our conduct the
more absurd is that we do more harm than good to the objects of our interest, for no Government can, with any regard
to its own dignity and independence, yield to our dictation
and impertinent interference.   The Grand Duke of Tuscany
said that the Madiai would have been let out of prison long
ago but for our interference.   John Russell's published letter on this subject, which was very palatable to the public,

---

[1] [The Emperor of Austria was stabbed in the neck on February 18, by
Joseph Lisbeny, on the ramparts of Vienna, fortunately without serious consequences. The assassin had not the remotest connection with anyone in this
country.]

was as objectionable as possible, and quite as insolent and presumptuous as any Palmerston used to write.

Last night the Marquis Massimo d'Azeglio came here. He was Prime Minister in Piedmont till replaced by Count Cavour, and is come to join his nephew, who is Minister here. He is a tall, thin, dignified-looking man, with very pleasing manners. He gave us a shocking account of the conduct of the Austrians at Milan in consequence of the recent outbreak. Their tyranny and cruelty have been more like the deeds in the middle ages than those in our own time ; wantonly putting people to death without trial or even the slightest semblance of guilt, plundering and confiscating, and in every respect acting in a manner equally barbarous and impolitic. They have thrown away a good opportunity of improving their own moral status in Italy, and completely played the game of their enemies by increasing the national hatred against them tenfold. If ever France finds it her interest to go to war,[1] Italy will be her mark, for she will now find the whole population in her favor, and would be joined by Sardinia, who would be too happy to revenge her former reverses with French aid ; nor would it be possible for this country to support Austria in a war to secure that Italian dominion which she has so monstrously abused.

March 3d.—Lord Aberdeen has gained great credit by making Mr. Jackson, Rector of St. James's, Bishop of Lincoln. He is a man without political patronage or connection, and with no recommendation but his extraordinary merit both as a parish priest and a preacher. Such an appointment is creditable, wise, and popular, and will strengthen the Government by conciliating the moderate and sincere friends of the Church.

The Duke of Bedford writes to me about his papers and voluminous correspondence, which he has been thinking of overhauling and arranging, but he shrinks from such a laborious task. He says : "With respect to my political correspondence, it has been unusually interesting and remarkable. I came so early into public life, have been so mixed up with everything, have known the political chief of my own party so intimately, and of the Tory party also to a limited extent, that there is no great affair of my own time I have not been well acquainted with." This is very true, and his

---

[1] [Remarkable prediction, verified in 1859.]

correspondence, whenever it sees the light, will be more interesting, and contribute more historical information, than that of any other man who has been engaged in public life. The papers of Peel and of the Duke of Wellington may be more important, but I doubt theirs being more interesting, because the Duke of Bedford's will be of a more miscellaneous and comprehensive character ; and though his abilities are not of a very high order, his judgment is sound, his mind is unprejudiced and candid, and he is a sincere worshipper of truth.

For the last few days John Russell has been kept away from the House of Commons by the death of the Dowager Duchess of Bedford, when Palmerston has been acting as leader, taking that post as naturally and undoubtedly belonging to him, and his right to it being entirely acquiesced in by his colleagues of both camps. They say that he has given great satisfaction to the House, where he is regarded with the same favor and inclination as heretofore, and *personally* much more acceptable than Lord John. Cobden dined with John Russell the other day, and, what is more remarkable, Bessborough told me he met Roden at dinner the other day at the Castle at Dublin, St. Germans and he on very good-humored terms. These are striking examples of the compatibility of the strongest political difference with social amenities. Cobden, however, is not in regular opposition to the Government, but in great measure a supporter.

March 10*th*.—I met M. de Flahault last night, just returned from Paris. He said that he found there a rancor and violence against us among the Austrians, and Russians and Prussians no less, quite inconceivable. He talked to them all and represented to them the absurdity of their suppositions and exigencies, but without the slightest effect ; he found the Emperor, however, in a very different frame of mind, understanding perfectly the position of the English Government, and completely determined to maintain his alliance with us, and not to yield to the tempting cajolery of the Continental Powers, who want him to make common cause with them against us. Such is their madness and their passion, and such the necessity, real or fancied, in which they are placed by the revolutionary fire which is still smouldering everywhere, and their own detestable misgovernment (at least that of Austria, which the others abet), that they are ready to co-operate with France in coercing and weakening us, and to sacrifice all the great and traditional policy of Europe, in order to wage war against the stronghold and only asylum of constitutional principles and government.

Flahault said that the Emperor has had an opportunity of placing himself in the first year of his reign in a situation which was the great object of his uncle's life, and which he never could attain. He might have been at the head of a European league against us, for these powers have signified to him their willingness to follow him in such a crusade, the Emperor of Russia and he being on the best terms, and a cordial interchange of letters having taken place between them. But Napoleon has had the wisdom and the magnanimity to resist the bait, to decline these overtures, and to resolve on adherence to England. Flahault said that he had had an audience, at which he frankly and freely told the Emperor his own opinion, not being without apprehension that it would be unpalatable to him, and not coincident with his own views. While he was talking to him, he saw him smile, which he interpreted into a sentiment that he (Flahault) was too *English* for him in his language and opinions, and he said so. The Emperor said, "I smiled because you so exactly expressed my own opinions," and then he told him that he took exactly the same view of what his true policy was that Flahault himself did. Flahault suggested to him that, in spite of the civilities shown him by the Northern Powers, they did not, and never would, consider him as one of themselves, and they only wanted to make him the instrument of their policy or their vengeance; and he reminded him that while England had at once recognized him, they were not only in no hurry to do so, but if England had not recognized him as she did, he would not have been recognized by any one of those Powers to this day, all which he acknowledged to be true.

The prevailing feeling against England which Flahault found at Paris has been proved on innumerable occasions. Clarendon is well aware of it, and does his best, but with very little success, to bring the foreign Ministers and others to reason. Madame de Lieven writes to me in this strain, and even liberal and intelligent foreigners like Alfred Potocki, who has been accused of being a rebel in Austria, writes that we ought to expel the refugees. At Vienna the people are persuaded that there is some indirect and undefinable participation on the part of the British Government

in the insurrectionary and homicidal acts of Milan and
Vienna, and they have got a story that the assassin Libeny
had a letter of Palmerston's in his shoe. Unreasonable as
all this is, we ought to make great allowance for their excited feelings, for they have a case against us of a cumulative
character. It goes back a long way, and embraces many
objects and details, and is principally attributable to Palmerston, partly to his doings, and perhaps more to his sayings.
They can not forget that he has long been the implacable
enemy of Austria, that he advised her renunciation of her
Italian dominions, and that he and his agents have always
sympathized with, and sometimes aided and abetted, most of
the revolutionary movements that have taken place. Then
there was the Haynau affair, and the lukewarmness and indifference which the Government of that day, and Palmerston particularly, exhibited about it ; then the reception of
Kossuth, the public meetings and his speeches, together
with the speeches at them of Cobden and others of which
no notice was ever taken, and finally the transaction about
Palmerston's receiving Kossuth and his famous answer to the
addresses presented to him from Finsbury and Islington.
All these things satisfy the foreign Governments that we are
not only politically but nationally their enemies, and that
we harbor their rebellious subjects out of hatred to them,
and that we regard with sympathy and a secret satisfaction
the plots which they concoct in safety here and go forth to
execute abroad. And when they are told that our laws
afford these people an asylum, which no Government has
the power to deny them, and that Parliament and public
opinion will not consent to arm the Government with the
powers of restraint or coercion they do not possess, they only
explode the more loudly in denunciations against that free
and constitutional system which is not only a perpetual reproach, but, as they think, a source of continual danger to
their own. So much for foreign affairs.

At home, while the political sky is still serene enough,
there are some rocks ahead, and I think the Government in
peril from more than one cause. First and foremost there
is the Indian question. There is something ominous in the
conjunction between a Coalition Government and an India
Bill, and if they don't take care, they will get into a scrape.[1]

[1] [The Charter of the East India Company being about to expire, Sir Charles
Wood, the President of the Board of Control, introduced in an elaborate speech

The Opposition is broken and disorganized, and at present there is no disposition on the part of the extreme Liberals to join in any strong measures against the Government; but this is a question on which all the scattered fractions might be made easily to combine, and there are already symptoms of a possible combination *ad hoc* in the Indian Committee of the House of Commons. Lowe is very much dissatisfied with Charles Wood, and with the intentions of Government, and even talks of resigning; and the "Times" is going into furious opposition on the Indian question, and is already attacking the Government for their supposed intentions. This, therefore, is assuming a serious aspect. There is besides the Budget and the difficulty of the Income Tax, and these two questions are enough to put them in great perplexity.

March 19*th.*—The question of Indian government and the renewal of the Charter is every day increasing in importance and attracting more and more of public attention. It is a matter of great difficulty for the Government to deal with. They are threatened by enemies, and pressed by friends and half friends, who want them to postpone any measure for another year or two years. They, on the contrary, stand pledged, and think they ought to propose something this year. It presents a field on which the various fractions of hostility and semi-hostility to the Government may meet and combine, and perhaps place them in great difficulty. The Committees are going on taking evidence with the knowledge that the Government will probably not wait for their several reports before proceeding to legislation. Granville has got the management of the Government measures in the House of Lords, and is working very hard at Indian affairs. Yesterday I met at dinner at Ellice's two able men just arrived from India for the purpose of giving evidence, a Mr. Halliday and a Mr. Marchmont. They are for maintaining the present system, but with many reforms and alterations; they spoke highly of Lord Dalhousie as a man of business.

March 24*th.*—As I never see Clarendon now, who is entirely absorbed in the duties of his office, he engaged me to go and dine with him alone yesterday, that we might

a Bill for the future government of India by the Company, which changed the Constitution and limited the patronage of the Court of Directors. The Bill was finally passed on July 28.]

have a talk about all that is going on, and he told me a great deal of one sort or another. I learned the state of our relations with France and Russia in reference to the Turkish business, and he gave me to read a very curious and interesting despatch (addressed to John Russell) from Seymour, giving an account of a long conversation he had had with the Emperor Nicholas about Turkey and her prospects and condition, and his own intentions and opinions, which were amicable toward us, and very wise and moderate in themselves, contemplating the dissolution of the Turkish Empire, disclaiming in the strongest terms any design of occupying Constantinople—more than that, declaring that he would not do it—but supposing the event to happen, not thinking the solution of the problem so difficult as it is generally regarded. He threw out that he should have no objection, if a partition was ever to take place, that we should appropriate Egypt and Candia to ourselves. He seems to have talked very frankly, and he said one curious thing, which was that Russia was not without a revolutionary substratum, which was only less apparent and less menacing than in other parts because he possessed greater means of repression, but nevertheless that the seeds were there. It is lucky Dundas is a prudent man, and refused to carry his fleet up to the vicinity of the Dardanelles at Rose's invitation, or mischief might have ensued. As it is, we disapprove of Rose's proceedings and have approved Dundas's, at the same time ordering him not to move without express orders from home, and moreover Clarendon refused to give Stratford Canning any discretionary authority to send for the fleet (though it was afterward given), which he had asked to be entrusted with. Clarendon is much dissatisfied with the conduct of the French Government, who were in a great hurry to send off their fleet, and they sent orders to sail on the mere report of what Rose had done, and without waiting to learn the result of his application to the Admiral ; and they did this, although they knew the despatches were on the road, and that a very few hours would put them in possession of the actual state of the case. Moreover, Cowley moved heaven and earth to induce Drouyn de Lhuys to withdraw the order to sail, but without effect. They persisted in it, after they knew we were not going to stir, and Cowley could not see the Emperor, who he says was evidently avoiding any communication with him. Still very friendly language continues to pass between us, and our Government are inclined to attribute this unwise proceeding to the vanity of the French, their passion for doing something, and above all the inexperience and want of *savoir faire* in high matters of diplomacy of the Emperor and his ministers.   There is not one among them who is fit to handle such delicate and important questions, the Emperor, who governs everything by his own will, less than any ; and Drouyn de Lhuys, who has been for many years engaged more or less in the Foreign Office, is a very poor and inefficient minister.

Clarendon told me he had seen Brunnow, and after recapitulating to him all the various causes for alarm, resting on facts or on rumors, especially with regard to Russia and her intentions, he said that our Government had received the word of honor of the Emperor that he had no sinister or hostile intentions, and disclaimed those that had been imputed to him, and that on his word they relied with such implicit confidence that he had not the slightest fear of disquietude. Brunnow was exceedingly pleased, and said that was the way to treat the Emperor, who would be excessively gratified, nothing being dearer to him than the confidence and good opinion of this country, and he said he would send off a courier the next day, and Clarendon should dictate his despatch. The instructions given to Menschikoff have been enormously exaggerated, the most serious and offensive parts that have been stated (the nomination of the Greek Patriarch, etc.) being totally false.[1] I asked what they were, and he said nothing but

---

[1] [While these pacific assurances were given in London, Prince Menschikoff arrived in Constantinople on March 2, and commenced that arrogant and aggressive policy which led in the course of the year to hostilities between Russia and the Porte. It has, however, only recently transpired, by the publication of Lord Malmesbury's "Memoirs" (vol. i. p. 402), that when the Emperor Nicholas came to England in 1844, he, Sir Robert Peel, then Prime Minister, the Duke of Wellington, and Lord Aberdeen, then Foreign Secretary, drew up and signed a Memorandum, the spirit and scope of which was to support Russia in her legitimate protection of the Greek religion and the holy shrines, and to do so without consulting France. To obtain this agreement was doubtless the object of the Emperor's journey. It bore his own personal signature. The existence of this Memorandum was a profound secret known only to the Queen and to those Ministers who held in succession the seals of the Foreign Department, each of whom transmitted it privately to his successor. Lord Malmesbury received the document from Lord Granville, and on leaving office in 1853 handed it to Lord John Russell. This fact, hitherto unknown, throws an entirely new light on the causes of the Crimean War. The Emperor of Russia naturally relied on the support of the very ministers who had signed the agreement and were again in power, while Lord Aberdeen was conscious of having entered into an engagement wholly at variance with the course of policy into which he was reluctantly driven.—H. R.]

a string of conditions about shrines and other ecclesiastical trifles. Walewski seems to have done well here, condemning the conduct of his own Government, and not concealing from them his own opinion, and entirely going along with us. It was on Saturday night that the courier arrived with Rose's and Dundas's despatches, and a few of the Cabinet met on Sunday at the Admiralty to talk the matter over. Clarendon sent for John Russell from Richmond, and he thought it advisable to summon Palmerston to this conciliabule, to keep him in good humor, which it had the effect of doing. There were himself, Palmerston, John Russell, Aberdeen, and Graham. He had written to Lord John on Saturday night, and sent him the despatches ; he got an answer from him, full of very wild talk of strong measures to be taken, and a fleet sent to the Baltic to make peremptory demands on the Emperor of Russia. This, however, he took no notice of, and did not say one word to Aberdeen about it, quietly letting it drop, and accordingly he heard no more about it, nobody, he said, but me, knowing what Lord John had proposed. I asked him what were Palmerston's views. He replied that he did not say much, and acquiesced in his and Aberdeen's prudent and reserved intentions, but he could see, from a few words that casually escaped him, that he would have been ready to join in more stringent and violent measures if they had been proposed. His hatred of Russia is not extinguished, but as it was, there was no expressed difference of opinion, and a general agreement. He said he had had a prejudice against Gladstone, but he now liked him very much, and Granville had already told me the same thing. Aberdeen likes his post and enjoys the consciousness of having done very well in it. He is extremely liberal, but of a wise and well-reasoned liberality. As it has turned out, he is far fitter for the post he occupies than Lansdowne would have been, both morally and physically.

The Queen is devoted to this Government, and expressed to Aberdeen the liveliest apprehension lest they should get themselves into some scrape with the India Bill, and entreated he would run no risks in it. Aberdeen, in announcing this one day to the Cabinet, said that the best thing for them to do was to bring forward a measure of so liberal and popular a character as to make any serious opposition impossible. Clarendon agreed in this, and I told him that this had long been my own idea, and that what they ought to do was to throw open the civil and military appointments to competition, and to grant appointments after examination to qualified candidates, just as degrees are given at the universities. We passed the whole evening together, talking over all matters of interest, and he told me everything he knew himself.

April 4th.—I went to Althorp last week, and returned for a Council on Friday. After it Graham and I stayed behind, when he talked about the Government and their prospects, which he thought pretty good ; they were going on in great harmony, and the greater, he thought, because they had originally had such diversities of opinion. This led to a disposition to mutual concession, and feelings of delicacy toward each other. The Queen is extremely attached to Aberdeen, more than to any minister she had ever had. Lord John's position anomalous and unsatisfactory, and always a question whether he would not become disgusted and back out. Graham said that Clarendon was doing admirably —better than he had anticipated.

Lady Lyttelton, whom I met at Althorp, told me a great deal about the Queen and her children ; nothing particularly interesting. She said the Queen was very fond of them, but severe in her manner, and a strict disciplinarian in her family. She described the Prince of Wales to be extremely shy and timid, with very good principles, and particularly an exact observer of truth ; the Princess Royal is remarkably intelligent. I wrote this because it will hereafter be curious to see how the boy grows up, and what sort of performance follows this promise, though I shall not live to see it. She spoke in very high terms of the Queen herself, of the Prince, and of the simplicity and happiness of her private and domestic life.

3

CHAPTER III.

London, April 21st, 1853.—I have had such a bad fit of
gout in my hand, that I have been unable for some time past
to write at all, though there has been plenty to write about.
The Government has been sustaining defeats in the House
of Commons on detached questions of taxation, much to
their annoyance and embarrassment, and which were more
serious from the inference to be drawn from them than
for their intrinsic importance.   They were caused by the
meddling and absurd crotchets of some of their friends, and
the malignity and unprincipled conduct of their enemies :
the first bringing forward motions for reduction of certain
items, merely to gratify clients or constituents, and the
Tories joining with the Radicals in voting for things which
they opposed when they were themselves in office, reckless
of consistency or of consequences.   But the whole affair
was unpleasant, as it displayed strikingly how little authority the Government has over the House of Commons, and
the difficulty, if not impossibility, of carrying on the service
of the country.

These little battles were, however, of little moment compared with the great event of Gladstone's Budget, which
came off on Monday night.   He had kept his secret so well,
that nobody had the least idea what it was to be, only it
oozed out that the Income Tax was not to be differentiated.
He spoke for five hours, and by universal consent it was one
of the grandest displays and most able financial statement
that ever was heard in the House of Commons ; a great
scheme, boldly, skilfully, and honestly devised, disdaining

popular clamor and pressure from without, and the execution of it absolute perfection.   Even those who do not ad-
mire the Budget, or who are injured by it, admit the merit
of the performance.   It has raised Gladstone to a great
political elevation, and, what is of far greater consequence
than the measure itself, has given the country assurance of
a *man* equal to great political necessities, and fit to lead
parties and direct governments.

April 22d.—I met Gladstone last night, and had the pleasure of congratulating him and his wife, which I did with
great sincerity, for his success is a public benefit.   They
have been overwhelmed with compliments and congratulations.   Prince Albert and the Queen both wrote to him, and
John Russell, who is spitefully reported to have been jealous,
has, on the contrary, shown the warmest interest and satisfaction in his success.   The only one of his colleagues who
may have been mortified is Charles Wood, who must have
compared Gladstone's triumph with his own failures.   From
all one can see at present, it promises certain success, though
many parts of the Budget are cavilled at.   It will be difficult, if not impossible, to find any common ground on which
Radicals or Irish can join the Derbyites to overthrow it, and
the sanguine expectations which the latter have been entertaining for some time, of putting the Government into some
inextricable fix, have given way to perplexity and despondency ; and they evidently do not know what to do, nor how
to give effect to their rancor and spite.   Lord Derby had a
great meeting not many days ago, at which he recommended
union, and cheered them on in opposition, of course for form's
sake, talking of *moderation* and *principles*, neither of which
he cares a fig for.   Mischief and confusion, vengeance against
the coalition, and taking the chance of what may happen
next, are all that he and Disraeli are bent upon.   I met the
latter worthy in the street just before the Budget, a day or
two previous.   He asked me what I thought of the state of
affairs, and I told him I thought it very unpleasant, and it
seemed next to impossible to carry on the Government at all,
everybody running riot in the House of Commons, and following his own fancies and crotchets ; nor did I see how it
could be otherwise in the present state of parties and the
country ; that since Peel's administration, which was a strong
Government, there had been and apparently there could be
none.   The present Government was not strong, and they

were perpetually defeated, on minor points, indeed, but in a
way that showed they had no power to work through Parliament. I said of course they would dissolve if this continued,
but that Gladstone's Budget might make a difference one
way or the other. Disraeli scouted the idea of a dissolution,
by which, he said, they would certainly gain nothing. Why,
he asked, did not the Peelites join us again, as they might
have done, and got as good terms as they have now, and then
there would have been a strong Government again? As I
don't want to quarrel with anybody, I restrained what it was
on my lips to say—" You could not possibly expect them to
join you "—but I did tell him that, even if the present Government could not maintain itself, of all impossible things
the most impossible was the restoration of his Government
tale quale, to which he made no reply. To be sure, the Protectionist seceders from Peel have now drunk the cup of
mortification, disgrace, and disaster to the very dregs. They
are a factious and (as I hope) impotent Opposition, under the
unprincipled guidance of men, who, clever and plausible
though they be, are totally destitute of wisdom, sincerity,
and truth. They have not only lost all the Protection for
the maintenance of which they made such struggles and
sacrifices, but they have likewise brought upon themselves
the still heavier blow to the landed interest which is going
to be inflicted in the shape of the legacy duty. Had they
possessed more foresight, and been less violent and unreasonable, this would not have happened to them ; for if Peel's
original Government had held together, and they had been
content to accept his guidance, no Budget would have contained this measure. Schemes might have been devised to
lighten their burdens, or to increase the compensations they
really have obtained in other ways ; but, be this as it may,
they would certainly have been saved from this direct im-
post, which I doubt if Peel himself ever contemplated, but
which he would certainly have spared them if they had not
deserted him, nor would his successors have departed from
his policy in this respect. But from first to last their conduct has been suicidal in every respect.

May 3d.—The Government is going on very flourishing-
ly. A capital division in the House of Lords on the Canada
Clergy Reserves Bill,[1] on which occasion there was a scene

---

[1] [This was a Bill abolishing the title of the Protestant Clergy to certain portions of waste lands in the Colony.]

between Derby and Clarendon, in which both were, to my mind, in the wrong. The whole affair appears in all the newspapers, but what does not appear is the rather absurd termination of it, when, after much excitement and strong language interchanged, the belligerents ended by drinking each other's healths in water across the table. The victory in the Lords has been followed up by one still more important in the House of Commons on the Income Tax, which was carried by 71, a great many of the Opposition voting with Government, much to the disgust of their friends. These divisions have filled the Derbyites with rage and despair, and nothing can exceed their depression and their abuse of the Budget and its authors. What vexes and provokes them so much is the ascendency and triumph of the Peelites. They could endure it in the Whigs, but their hatred of the name and party of Peel is inextinguishable.

May 15th.—At Newmarket last week, during which the Budget was making its way very successfully through the House of Commons, where Gladstone has it all his own way. The Speaker told me he was doing his business there admirably well. While I was at Newmarket came out the strange story of Gladstone and the attempt to extort money from him before the police magistrate.[1] It created for the moment great surprise, curiosity, and interest, but has almost entirely passed away already, not having been taken up politically, and there being a general disposition to believe his story and to give him credit for having had no improper motive or purpose. Nevertheless it is a very strange affair, and has not yet been satisfactorily explained. It is creditable in these days of political rancor and bitterness that no malignant attempt has been made to vilify him by his opponents or by the hostile part of the press. On the contrary, the editor of the " Morning Herald " wrote him a very handsome letter in his own name and in that of the proprietor, assuring him of their confidence in his purity and innocence, and that nothing would induce them to put anything offensive to him in the paper, and they had purposely inserted the police report in an obscure part of the paper. It is very fortunate for Gladstone that he was not intimidated and tempted to give the man money, but had the courage to face

---

[1] [An attempt had been made to extort money from Mr. Gladstone on a spurious charge, which he met by instantly giving the delinquent into custody and meeting the case at a police office.]

the world's suspicions and meet the charge in so public a manner.

The Stafford Committee has at length closed its proceedings, after exposures of the most disgraceful kind, which are enormously damaging not only to Augustus Stafford himself but to Lord Derby and his Government. The Duke of Northumberland comes clear out of it as to corruption, but cuts a wretched and ridiculous figure, having failed to perform the duties or to exercise the authority of a First Lord while he was at the Admiralty. Disraeli's evidence was nothing but an attempt to shirk the question and involve it in a confusion of characteristic verbiage which only excited ridicule. This affair has done great harm to them as a party, and served to make them more odious and contemptible than they were before.[1] They are now irretrievably defeated, and though they may give much trouble and throw difficulties and obstructions in the way of the Government, it is all they can do. Every day adds to the strength and consistency of the Government, both from their gaining favor and acquiring influence in the country, and from the ruin in which the Tory party is involved, and the total impossibility of their rallying again so as to form another Government. This latter consideration has already produced the adhesion of some moderate and sensible men who take a dispassionate view of affairs and who wish for a strong and efficient Government, and it will produce still greater effects of the same kind.

May 22d.—I met in a train a day or two ago Graham and the Speaker, not having seen Graham for a long time. Since my friends have been in office I have hardly ever set eyes on them or had any communication with them. Graham seemed in excellent spirits about their political state and prospects, all owing to Gladstone and the complete success of his Budget. The long and numerous Cabinets, which were attributed by the "Times" to disunion, were occupied in minute consideration of the Budget, which was there fully discussed, and Gladstone spoke in the Cabinet one day for three hours, rehearsing his speech in the House of Commons, though not quite at such length. Graham again said Clarendon was doing admirably. Palmerston he

---

[1] [Charges of misconduct in the department of the Admiralty were brought against Mr. Augustus Stafford, who had held office under the late Government. They were investigated by a Select Committee of the House of Commons.]

thinks much changed and more feeble, his energy much less, and his best days gone by. He thinks Lord John's position without office an unfortunate one, and regrets he did not stay at the Foreign Office or take another; he thinks his influence impaired by having none. He talked of a future Head, as Aberdeen is always ready to retire at any moment, but it is very difficult to find any one to succeed him. I suggested Gladstone. He shook his head and said it would not do; and he was for John Russell, but owned there were difficulties there too. He considered Derby and the Tories irretrievably ruined, their characters so damaged by Stafford's Committee and other things; he spoke of the grand mistakes Derby had made. Gladstone's object certainly was for a long time to be at the head of the Conservative party in the House of Commons, and to join with Derby, who might, in fact, have had all the Peelites if he would have chosen to ally himself with them instead of with Disraeli; thus the latter had been the cause of the ruin of the party. Graham thought that Derby had committed himself to Disraeli in George Bentinck's lifetime in some way that prevented his shaking him off, as it would have been his interest to do. The Peelites would have united with Derby, but would have nothing to do with Disraeli. Bad as the cases were that had come forth at the election committees, that of Liverpool was worse than any of them, and would create a great scandal. Forbes Mackenzie could not face it, and would probably retire; but it is doubtful if this would prevent an inquiry and exposure, and when boundless corruption appeared at such a place as Liverpool, with its numerous constituency, it was a blow to the representative system itself, and showed the futility of attempts to destroy bribery and improper influence.

May 30*th.*—Great alarm the last two or three days at an approaching rupture between Russia and Turkey, as, if it takes place, nobody can pretend to say what the consequences may be. Vast indignation of course against the Emperor of Russia, who certainly appears to have departed from the moderate professions which he made to Seymour a short time ago, and the assurances that were given to us and France. But Clarendon, whom I saw yesterday, is rather disposed to give him credit for more moderate and pacific intentions than his conduct seems to warrant. He says that he is persuaded the Emperor has no idea of the view that is taken of his proceedings here, and that he thinks he is requiring no more than he is entitled to ; and it is only the other day that Nesselrode congratulated Seymour on the prospect of everything being satisfactorily settled, having no doubt of the Turks accepting the last proposals made to them, a copy of which Nesselrode showed him.   Still, though matters look very black, Clarendon is not without hopes of war being averted and some means found of patching up the affair, the Emperor having promised that he will in no case resort to *ulterior measures* without giving us notice of his intention. The difficulty for him now is to recede with honor, as it would be to advance without danger.   He has once before receded after to a certain degree committing himself, and he may not choose to do so a second time.   Then he is naturally provoked with the French, who are in fact the real cause of this by their intrigues and extortions about the holy places ; and we suspect that he is, besides this, provoked at the Montenegrin affair having been settled by Austria without his having a finger in that pie.   All these considerations combined make great confusion and difficulty.   Brunnow is in mortal agony, dreading above all things the possibility of his having to leave this country.

The Government continues to go on very well ; the Opposition got up a debate on the legacy duties in the House of Lords the other night, which only served to prove how entirely Derby's influence has declined even there.   They had thought themselves sure of beating the Government, but not only were they defeated, but accident alone (people shut out and absent) prevented their being defeated by a considerable majority.   The Cabinet is going on in the greatest harmony, and the men who were strangers up to the time of its formation have taken to each other prodigiously. Aberdeen unfortunately wants the qualities which made Lord Lansdowne so good a leader, and is rather deficient in tact and temper in the House of Lords as he used to be formerly, when he attacked Lord Grey's Government and Palmerston's administration of foreign affairs always with too much asperity ; but in spite of these defects he has not done ill even there, and in the Cabinet he is both liked and respected, being honest, straightforward, and firm, very fair, candid, and unassuming.   Granville tells me that of the whole Cabinet he thinks Aberdeen has the most pluck, Gladstone a great deal, and Graham the one who has the least.   He speaks very well of Molesworth, sensible, courageous, and conciliatory, but quite independent and plainspoken in his opinions.

June 1st.—John Russell made an imprudent speech the night before last on the Irish Church, giving great offence to the Irish and the Catholics.   He could not help, as leader of the Government, opposing a proposition having for its object the destruction of the Irish Church, but he might have done it with more tact and discretion, and not in a way to elicit the cheers of the Tories.   The Tail will pay him off for this whenever they can.   *Quantum mutatus ab illo,* who broke up a Government for the sake of an appropriation clause.

Last night Macaulay reappeared in the House of Commons, and in a speech of extraordinary power and eloquence threw out the Judges' Exclusion Bill.[1]   It was the first time he had spoken, and though his physical strength is impaired he showed that his mental powers are undiminished.

Senior called on me a day or two ago, just returned from Paris, where he has been living and conversing with all the notabilities (principally of the Liberal party), and he tells me there is but one opinion among them, that this Empire can not last, and they only differ as to the time it may last. Most of them think it will be short.   Thiers gives it only a year, Duchâtel alone thinks it will go on for some years. The unpopularity of Louis Napoleon increases and his discredit likewise, and as soon as the unpopularity shall extend to the army, it will be all over with him.   The Opposition which had sprung up, which has increased rapidly and will increase still more in the Corps Législatif, is deemed to be very important and significant, and they think it will be impossible for him to go on with such a body so constituted and disposed, and he will have to decide upon suffering the embarrassment it will cause him, or having recourse to a *coup d'état,* a measure which would be hazardous.   There are no fresh adhesions to the Court beyond the half dozen men of rank or name who have already joined it, and who are hated and despised for having done so.   While such is the opinion of the people of mark at Paris, they are never-

[1] [A Bill was before Parliament which would have excluded the Master of the Rolls from the House of Commons, he being the only Judge who could sit there.   The Judge of the Admiralty Court had already been excluded.   Macaulay opposed the Bill with such force and eloquence that he changed the opinion of the House, and defeated the measure.   An unusual occurrence.]

theless sensible of the danger which would accompany a
counter-revolution, and of the uncertainty of what might
follow, what influences might prevail, and what form of
government be adopted ; but they seem generally to think
that while in the first instance there would be a succession
of provisional arrangements and fleeting transitory governments, it would end in the restoration of the monarchy
under Henri V., but that this would not take place by the
acceptance and triumph of any divine hereditary right, but
must be adopted by the nation and ratified by a national
vote.

June 5th.—I saw Clarendon on Friday morning for a
few minutes ; he takes a very gloomy view of the Russo-
Turkish question, and is greatly disgusted at having been
deceived by the Emperor ; he says he is harassed to death
with the whole affair, and with the multiplicity of business
he has besides ; he has a difficult task to perform, taking a
middle position in the Cabinet between the opposite opinions of those who are for more stringent measures and those
who, like himself, are for patience and moderation.   Palmerston, in whom his ancient Russian antipathies are revived,
is for vigor, and as in former times "leading John Russell
by the nose," Clarendon and Aberdeen for moderation ; but
he is beset by different opinions and written suggestions and
proposals, and all this worries him exceedingly.   I asked him
how the Court was, and he said very reasonable, their opinions being influenced, of course, by Aberdeen.

He talked with great disgust of John Russell's speech on
the Irish Church, how unfair it was as well as unwise, and
how reckless of the damage it caused to the Government,
and the embarrassing and awkward situation in which he
thereby placed many of their supporters.   These are the
general sentiments with regard to that speech, which was
neither more nor less than speaking the Durham letter over
again, and, considering what that famous letter cost him,
he might have been expected to steer clear of such a scrape.
But he is more than ever the creature of impulse and of
temper, and he seems to have lost a great deal of his tact
and discretion, and certainly he is no longer fit to be either
head of a Government or leader of the House of Commons,
and perhaps the latter position in such a Government as this
suits him still less than the former would.   When I came
to town yesterday morning I found that several of the Irish

Roman Catholic members of the Government occupying subordinate offices (Messrs. Keogh, Monsell, and Sadleir), had
resigned in consequence of Lord John Russell's speech, but
an hour afterward I learned that they had been induced to
remain by an assurance from Lord Aberdeen that Lord John
did not express the sentiments of the Government on this
subject.

Charles Wood brought on the India Bill on Friday night
in a speech of unexampled prolixity and dulness.   There is
not yet time to ascertain how the plan is likely to be received,
but I suspect it will meet with a great deal of opposition,
although, as it is more favorable to the existing interests than
was expected, it will very likely pass, as, if Leadenhall Street
was to go further, it would certainly fare worse.

St. Leonards, June 7th.—I am here for Ascot, a lovely
place and divine weather. The affair with the Irish has ended
as harmlessly as anything so awkward could do.   Mr. G. H.
Moore asked some rather impertinent questions in the House
of Commons on Monday, which Lord John answered in an
easy, nonchalant, jesting manner.   The House laughed,
nobody said anything, and there it ended, but the Brigade
will probably seek opportunities of showing their teeth and
of revenging themselves on Lord John.   It has been rather
mortifying for him, but he has taken it very quietly, and
Aberdeen's letter to Monsell was shown to him and received
his assent.   The French are behaving very well about the
Eastern question, and I begin to think that it will in the
end blow over, as diplomacy will probably hit upon some
expedient for enabling the Emperor of Russia to do what
his real interests evidently point out.

June 13th.—I came back from Ascot on Friday, having
met Clarendon on Thursday on the course, who gave me an
account of the state of affairs.   On Saturday I met Walewski
at dinner, and had much talk with him, and yesterday I saw
Clarendon again.   The great event has been the sailing of
our fleet from Malta to join the French fleet at the mouth
of the Dardanelles, to the unspeakable satisfaction of the
French Government, who desire nothing so much as to ex-
bibit to all Europe an *entente cordiale* with us ; and Walewski
said to me that, however the affair might end, this great advantage they had at all events obtained.[1]   The Emperor of

[1] [Orders were sent to Admiral Dundas on June 2 to sail for the Dardanelles, and the fleet proceeded to Besika Bay, together with the French fleet.]

Russia will be deeply mortified when he hears of this junction ; for besides that it will effectually bar the approach of his fleet to Constantinople, if he ever contemplated it, there is nothing he dislikes and dreads so much as the intimate union of France and England.   His Majesty is now so greatly excited that nothing can stop him, and he told Seymour the other day that he would spend his last rouble and his last soldier rather than give way.   Still he professes that he aims at no more than a temporary occupation of the Principalities, and renounces all purpose of conquest.   The Russian army will therefore certainly march in, and it will be the business of the other Governments to restrain the Turks and prevent a collision, which Walewski thinks they can certainly do.

Austria holds the same language that we do, but will not act.   Clarendon sent for Count Colloredo on Saturday (who never hears from Buol), and set before him in detail all the dangers with which Austria is menaced by the possibility of war breaking out in the East, and above all by that of France being brought into the field in hostility with Austria.   In such a case the French would be quite unscrupulous, and excite all the revolutionary spirit, which, though now repressed, is thickly scattered over every part of the Austrian Empire, from Milan to Hungary.   Colloredo acknowledged the truth of the representation, and promised to report textually to Buol what Clarendon said.

All now depends on the Emperor Nicholas himself.   If he adheres to his determination not to advance beyond the Principalities, time will be afforded for negotiations, and some expedient may be found for enabling him to recede without discredit, and without danger to his own *prestige* at home.   The French and English feel alike on this point, and are conscious that the Emperor has gone too far to recede.   He is pushed on by an ardent and fanatical party in Russia, and is not entirely his own master.   Both Governments are therefore willing to make allowance for the exigencies of his position, and to assist him to the uttermost of their power in getting honorably out of the scrape into which he has plunged himself and all Europe.

June 22d.—The Opposition papers (especially the "Morning Herald" and the "Press," Disraeli's new journal) have been making the most violent attacks on Aberdeen and Clarendon, calling for their impeachment on the ground of

their conduct in this Eastern quarrel, particularly charging
them with having been cognizant of and approved of Menschikoff's demands, which have occasioned all the hubbub.
At last it was thought necessary to make a statement in reply, which was done by the "Times" on Thursday last.   The
article was a good one, but contained an inaccuracy, about
which Brunnow wrote a long but friendly letter of complaint
to Clarendon.   The day after this, another article was inserted to set the matter right, with which Brunnow was
quite satisfied ; but the explanations of the "Times" failed
to stem the torrent of abuse, and the Tory papers only repeated their misrepresentations with greater impudence and
malignity than before,   It was thought necessary a stop
should be put to this, and it was proposed to Clarendon to
let discussions come on in both Houses, moved by Layard in
the Commons, and Clanricarde in the Lords, which would
afford an opportunity for the only effectual contradiction,
Ministerial statements in Parliament.   Last night I met
him at the Palace, when we talked the matter over.   He is
still of opinion that it is essential to delay the explanations
and put off all discussion till the matter is decided one way
or another.   He thinks so in reference to the case itself,
leaving out of consideration the convenience of the Government ; he thinks that any discussion in the House of Commons will elicit a disposition for peace à *tout prix*, which
would seriously embarrass affairs, and only confirm Russia
in the course she is pursuing.   I do not think so, but his
opinions are founded on what he hears Cobden has said, and
on the *animus* of the peace party.   He told me again what a
task his is in the Cabinet, standing between and mediating
between Aberdeen and Palmerston, whose ancient and habitual ideas of foreign policy are brought by this business
into antagonism, and he says the difficulty is made greater
by Aberdeen's unfortunate manner, who cannot avoid some
of that sneering tone in discussion which so seriously affects
his popularity in the House of Lords.   He is therefore
obliged to take a great deal upon himself, in order to prevent any collision between Palmerston and Aberdeen.   It
appears that Palmerston proposed on Saturday last that the
entrance of the Russians into the Principalities should be
considered a *casus belli,* in which, however, he was overruled
and gave way.   The Cabinet did not come to a vote upon it,
but the general sentiment went with Aberdeen and Claren-

don, and against Palmerston.   He seems to have given way
with a good grace, and hitherto nothing has occurred of a
disagreeable character ; on the contrary, both Clarendon and
Granville tell me Palmerston has behaved very well.   Clarendon thinks (and in this I concur) that the country would
never forgive the Government for going to war, unless they
could show that it was absolutely necessary and that they
had exhausted every means of bringing about a pacific solution of the question, and nobody here would care one straw
about the Russian occupation of Moldavia and Wallachia.

That all means have not been exhausted is clear from
this fact.   The Austrians, who are more interested than anybody, have moved heaven and earth to effect a settlement,
and the Emperor of Russia has himself asked for their "*bons
offices*" for that end.   They have entreated the Turks on the
one hand to strike out some *mezzo termine* compatible with
their dignity and with their previous refusals of Menschikoff's terms, promising that they will urge its acceptance on
the Emperor with all their force, and on the other hand they
have implored the Emperor to delay the occupation of the
Principalities, so that by temporizing, mediation, and a joint
action and a judicious employment of diplomatic resources
and astuteness, it is still possible some mode may be hit
upon of terminating the quarrel.

July 9th.—For the last fortnight or three weeks little
has occurred which is worth noting.   The Eastern Question
drags on, as it is likely to do.   Aberdeen, who ten days ago
spoke very confidently of its being settled, now takes a more
desponding view, and the confidence he has hitherto reposed
in the Emperor of Russia is greatly shaken.   Clarendon has
long thought the prospect very gloomy, but they are still
endeavoring to bring about an accommodation.   The question resolves itself into this : what are the real wishes and
views of the Emperor ?   If his present conduct is the execution of a long-prepared purpose, and he thinks the time
favorable for the destruction of Turkey, no efforts will be
availing, and he will listen to no proposals that we can possibly make.   If, on the contrary, he is conscious that he
has got into a dilemma, and he wishes to extricate himself
from it by any means not dishonorable to himself, and such
as would not degrade him in the eyes of his own subjects,
then, no doubt, diplomatic astuteness will sooner or later hit
upon some expedient by which the quarrel may be adjusted.

Which of these alternatives is the true one, time alone can show.   Meanwhile the expense to which the Turks are put in the wretched state of their finances will prove ruinous to them, and, end how it may, the fall of the Turkish dominion has been accelerated by what has already taken place. There has been a great deal of discussion about bringing on debates on the Eastern Question in both Houses, but all the leading men of all parties have deprecated discussion, and it was finally determined last night that none should take place.   Disraeli alone, who cares for nothing but making mischief, tried to bring it on, but in the House of Lords Derby took a different and more becoming course, and recommended Clanricarde to give it up.   Disraeli urged Layard to persevere.   Granville told me yesterday that while he lamented that Aberdeen was not a more judicious and conciliating leader in the House of Lords, and was so inferior in this respect to Lord Landsdowne, he liked him very much, thought he was a very good Prime Minister, and, above all, anything but deficient in political courage, in which respect he was by no means inferior to Palmerston himself.

The Government have been going on well enough on the whole.   Their immense majority on the India Bill was matter of general surprise, and showed the wretched tactics of Disraeli, as well as his small influence over his party, for he could not get one hundred of the Tories to go with him.   A few small holes have been made in Gladstone's Budget, but nothing of consequence.   Tom Baring, however, told me he thought Gladstone had made some great mistakes, and that Graham would have been a better Chancellor of the Exchequer ; but this I much doubt.   Popularity is very necessary to a Chancellor of the Exchequer, and Graham would never have been so persuasive with the House as Gladstone.

July 12th.—The "Times" newspaper, always famous for its versatility and inconsistency, has lately produced articles on the Eastern Question on the same day of the most opposite characters, one warlike and firm, the next vehemently pacific by some other hand.   This is of small importance, but it is indicative of the difference which exists in the Cabinet on the subject, and the explanation of the inconsistency of the "Times" is to be found in the double influence which acts on the paper.   All along Palmerston has been urging a vigorous policy, and wished to employ more peremptory language and stronger measures toward Russia, while Aberdeen has been very reluctant to do as much as we have done, and would have been well content to advise Turkey to accept the last ultimatum of Russia, and so terminate what he considers a senseless and mischievous quarrel. Clarendon has had to steer between these two extremes, and while moderating the ardor of Palmerston, to stimulate Aberdeen, and persuade him to adopt a course congenial to public opinion in this country, which, however, inclined to peace and abhorrent of war, is not at all disposed to connive at the aggrandizement of Russia, or to submit to the insolent dictation of the Emperor. The majority of the Cabinet have supported Clarendon, and approximate more nearly to the pacific policy of Aberdeen than to the stringent measures of Palmerston. When the two articles appeared in the "Times," to which I particularly allude, Clarendon approved of the first, and found great fault with the other, while Aberdeen wrote to Delane and expressed his strong approbation of the second, and his conviction that the public would sooner or later take the views therein set forth. Clarendon tells me that he has no doubt Aberdeen has on many occasions held language in various quarters that was not prudent under the circumstances, and was calculated to give erroneous impressions as to the intentions of the Government, and he thinks that the Emperor himself has been misled by what he may have heard both of the disposition and sentiments of the Prime Minister, and of the determination of the House of Commons and the country at large to abstain from war in every case except one in which our own honor and interests were *directly* concerned.

I had a long talk with Clarendon on Sunday, when he told me that the chances of peace were a little better than they had been, inasmuch as there seemed to be a disposition at St. Petersburg to treat, and the Austrian Government was now in earnest bringing to bear all their influence on the Emperor to accept reasonable terms of accommodation. Colloredo brought him the copy of a despatch to St. Petersburg, which he said was excellent, very frank and free in its tone. Austria seems more fully sensible of the danger to herself of any war, which would inevitably let loose the revolutionary element all over the world. Clarendon has drawn up the project of a Convention which embraces all the *professed* objects of the Emperor, and which the Turks

may agree to ; he sent it to Paris, whence Drouyn de Lhuys
has returned it, with the full concurrence and assent of the
French Government, and it went to Petersburg yesterday.
The reception of this proposal will determine the question
of peace or war.

July 14th.—G—— said to me this morning that Palmerston is beginning to stir up matters afresh.   I saw him
yesterday morning at Holland House in close confabulation
with Walewski, with whom I have no doubt he interchanged
warlike sentiments, and complained of the lukewarmness of
Aberdeen and Clarendon.   It is evident that he is *at work,*
and probably, according to his ancient custom, in some underhand way in the press.   His flatterers tell him that a
majority of the House of Commons would support *him* and
a warlike policy, and though he may wish to believe this, and
perhaps does, he will hardly go the length of trying to break
up this Cabinet, with the desperate hope of making another
Government himself, based on the policy of going to war.
Certain newspapers are always asserting that the Cabinet is
divided and in dissension, and at the same time accusing it
of timidity and weakness, urging strong measures, and asserting that, if we had employed such long ago, Russia would
have been frightened, and never have proceeded to such
lengths.   But the Government are resolved, and wisely, to
avoid war as long as they can, and if driven on to it, to be
able to show the country that they had exhausted all means
of preserving peace.

July 18th.—At last there appears a probability of this
Turkish question being amicably settled.   On Saturday I
was told that despatches were just come from Sir Hamilton
Seymour of a more favorable character, and representing the
Imperial Government as much more disposed to treat, with a
real disposition to bring the negotiations to a successful issue.
My informant added that Palmerston predicted that none of
the projects and proposals which have emanated from the
different Courts would be accepted at Petersburg, which he
thought they all would.   Yesterday I saw Clarendon, and
found matters even in a still more promising state.   After
the Cabinet Walewski went to him, and communicated to
him very important news (of a later date than Seymour's
letters) from St. Petersburg, which to my mind is decisive
of the question of peace.   It appears that both France and
Austria have been concocting notes and projects of a pacific

tendency to be offered to the Emperor.   There have been
several of these, some framed at Constantinople, others at
Paris.   A short time ago the French Government prepared
one, which it submitted to ours ; Clarendon thought it
would not answer, and told them so.   They asked whether
he had any objection to their sending it off to St. Petersburg
and Vienna and making the experiment.   He replied, none
whatever, and though he did not think it would succeed, he
should rejoice if it did, as, provided the affair could be settled, it did not matter how.   In the meantime he drew up
his own project of a Convention, which went to Paris, and
received the cordial approbation of the Emperor ; and this
document is now on its way to Petersburg.   In the meantime the French project was sent there, Castelbajac took it
to Nesselrode, who read it very attentively, and said that he
liked it very much, but that he could give no positive answer
till he had submitted it to the Emperor.   The same afternoon
he saw the French minister again. and told him that he had
laid the project before the Emperor Nicholas, and that His
Majesty was not only satisfied, but grateful for it, "non
seulement satisfait, mais reconnaissant," and that the only
reason he did not at once close with it was that his ally, the
Emperor of Austria, had also submitted a proposal, and he
did not like to take another from another Court exclusively
without previous communication with him.   Clarendon
thinks that his proposal will be still more agreeable to the
Emperor than the French one, and that he will probably
end in taking it ; nor will there be any difficulty in this,
because ours is so fully concurred in by France as to be in
fact hers as much as ours.

July 31*st.*—Having been at Goodwood the last week, I
have not troubled myself with politics. either home or foreign,
nor have any events occurred to excite interest.   The most
important matter here has been the division in the House of
Lords on Monday last on the Succession Duties Bill, on which
the Opposition were signally defeated.   For a long time the
Government were very doubtful of obtaining a majority, but
their whippers-in were more sanguine at last.   Great exertions were made on both sides, the Derbyites whipped up all
the men they could lay their hands on, and the Government
fetched their ministers from Paris and Brussels, and the
Lord Lieutenant of Ireland.   The majority was greater than
either side expected, and Derby and his crew were exceed-

ingly disconcerted, and Derby himself much out of humor.
When Bessborough went over to him after the division, and
said, "Lord Aberdeen wants to know if you will object to the
Bill being read a third time on Thursday next," he pettishly
replied, "The Bill may go to the devil for all I care; I shall
take no further trouble about it."

August 1st.—I saw Clarendon as usual yesterday (Sunday), when he read to me a letter from Sir Hamilton Seymour, giving an account of his delivering to Nesselrode the
Convention which Clarendon sent over, as well as reading to
him Clarendon's private letter, which was a stinging one,
but very good. Nesselrode said of all the projects he liked
that the best, and if it was tendered to them *from Vienna*,
he thought it might do as the basis of an arrangment, but
he could give no positive answer till he had submitted it to
the Emperor. At the Cabinet on Saturday Clarendon read
Seymour's letter, when his colleagues begged they might see
the private letter of his which was alluded to, and he produced and read that likewise. It was generally approved of,
but the next day Palmerston wrote a note to Clarendon, in
which he expressed the warmest approbation of his note,
and added that he had only refrained from saying all he
thought of it at the Cabinet lest *his* approval might make
others think it was too strong. He added that he rejoiced
that the management of our foreign affairs was in such able
hands, and that, in fact, he (Clarendon) could do and say
what Palmerston himself could not have done. It was a
very handsome letter, very satisfactory both to Clarendon
personally, and as showing that there is no disagreement on
the Eastern Question in the Cabinet, or at least between
Palmerston and Clarendon, which is the essential point.
Their union and friendship are remarkable when we recollect
their past antagonism and Palmerston's jealousy of Clarendon, and the persuasion of both himself and Lady Palmerston
that Clarendon was always waiting to trip up his heels and
get his place. All these jealousies and suspicions were, however, dissipated when Clarendon refused the Foreign Office
last year, since which time they have been the best of friends,
and Palmerston was quite satisfied at his having the Foreign
Office. With regard to the chances of a pacific settlement,
the assurances from St. Petersburg are all very favorable,
but the acts of the Russian generals in the Principalities are
quite inconsistent with them, and between these conflicting

manifestations Clarendon is in no small doubt and apprehension as to the result.

London, August 8th.—Ever since last Monday, when Clarendon made a speech in the House of Lords on which a bad interpretation was put in reference to the question of peace or war, there has been a sort of panic, and the public mind, which refused at first to admit the possibility of war, suddenly rushed to the opposite conclusion, and everybody became persuaded that war was inevitable. The consequence was a great fall in the funds, and the depreciation of every sort of security. So matters remained till the end of the week. On Saturday afternoon I met Walewski, who told me he had that day received a letter from Castelbajac (the French Ambassador at St. Petersburg), informing him that the Emperor had signified his willingness to accept the proposal which was then expected from Vienna, and last night fresh news came that the proposal had arrived, and he had said he would take it, if the Turks would send an ambassador with it, exactly as it had been submitted to him. This I heard late last night, and Granville considered it conclusive of an immediate settlement. But this morning I went to the Clarendon and found him not so sure, and not regarding the pacific solution as so indubitable; there still remain some important matters of detail to be settled, though certainly the affair wears a much more favorable aspect, and there is every reason to hope it will all end well. But while this proposal was concocted at Vienna, the Cabinet here (last Saturday week) made some small verbal alterations in it, so that ultimately it will not be presented for the Emperor's formal acceptance word for word the same, and if he wants a pretext to back out of his present engagement, he can therein find one, as he only agreed to take it if it was word for word the same. Then it has not yet been submitted to the Turks, and it is by no means sure they may not make difficulties, or that Stratford Canning may not raise obstacles instead of using all his influence to procure their agreement, so that Clarendon does not consider that we are *out of the wood*, though he expects on the whole that it will end well. If it does it will be the triumph of diplomacy, and a signal proof of the wisdom of moderation and patience. Granville says it will be principally owing to Aberdeen, who has been very staunch and bold in defying public clamor, abuse, and taunts, and in resisting the wishes and advice of Palmerston, who would have adopted a more stringent and uncompromising course.

August 9th.—At Court yesterday Aberdeen was quite confident of the settlement of the Eastern affair, and Brunnow, who was there with the Duchess of Leuchtenberg to see the Queen, very smiling. Clanricarde interrupted Clarendon in the House of Lords, and made a violent speech. Clarendon answered very well, without committing himself. The Government are in high spirits at the prospect of winding up this prosperous Session with the settlement of the Eastern Question ; nothing else is wanting to their success.

August 11th.—I saw Clarendon yesterday. Nothing new, but he said he fully expected Stratford Canning would play some trick at Constantinople, and throw obstacles in the way of settlement. This seems to me hardly possible, unless he behaves foolishly as well as dishonestly, and it can hardly be believed that his temper and Russian antipathies will betray him into such extravagant conduct. It is, however, impossible to consider the affair as " *settled.*"

Yesterday all the world went to the great naval review at Portsmouth, except myself. It appears to have been a fine but tedious sight, for Granville set off at 5.30 A. M., and only got back at one in the morning.

August 27th.—Since the 11th I have been absent from town, at Grimstone for York races, then at Hatchford, and since that gouty. While at York the Session closed with *éclat* by a speech of Palmerston's in his most flashy and successful style. John Russell gave a night at last for the discussion of the Turkish question, and made a sort of explanation, which was tame, meagre, and unsatisfactory. After some speeches expressive of disappointment and disapprobation, Cobden made an oration in favor of peace at any price, and this drew up Palmerston, who fell upon him with great vigor and success. The discussion would have ended languidly and ill for the Government but for this brilliant improvisation, which carried the House entirely with it. It was not, however, if analyzed and calmly considered, of much use to the Government as to their foreign policy, for it was only an answer to Cobden, and Palmerston did not say one word in defence of the policy which has been adopted, nor identify himself with it, as he might as well have done. Though there was nothing in it positively indicative of dissent and dissatisfaction, any one might not unfairly draw the inference that, if Palmerston had had his own way, he would have taken a more stringent and less patient course. However, nothing has been made of this, and on the whole his speech did good, because it closed the discussion handsomely, and left the impression of Palmerston's having cast his lot for good and all with his present colleagues, as is really the case.

The Session ended with a very flourishing and prosperous speech from the Throne, and nothing was wanting to the complete success of the Government but the settlement of the Turkish question, which, however, seems destined to be delayed some time longer; for the Turks have refused to accept the Vienna note, except with some modifications, though these are said to be so immaterial that we hope the Emperor will not object to them. But all this is vexatious, because it reopens the whole question, causes delay and uncertainty, and keeps the world in suspense and apprehension. Granville told me that what had occurred showed how much more sagacious Aberdeen had been as to this affair than Palmerston, the former having always maintained that there would be no difficulty with the Emperor, but if any arose it would be from the Turks; whereas Palmerston was always sure the Turks would make none, but that the Emperor would refuse all arrangements.

August 28th.—It seems the Turks, after a delay of ten days from receiving the proposition, sent it back to Vienna, asking for some not important alterations; but immediately afterward they required a stipulation for the evacuation of the Principalities, and guarantees that they should not be occupied again. It is very improbable that the Emperor will listen to such conditions. Nesselrode has all along told Seymour that they (the Russians) mean in fulfillment of their pledges to evacuate the Principalities, as soon as they have got the required satisfaction, but that it must not be made *a condition*, and entreated him to abstain from any demand which might give an air of compulsion to the act, much in the same way as we have told Nesselrode he must not attempt to make any stipulation about the withdrawal of our fleet. Clarendon thinks that the Emperor is certain to reject the Turkish terms, and that the Turks are very capable of declaring war thereupon; for in their last communication they said that they were prepared for " toutes les éventualités," and he suspects that Stratford has not

bond fide striven to induce them to accept the proffered
terms.   Their rejection is the more unreasonable because
the proposal is a hash-up of Menschikoff's original Note,
and that which the Turks proposed in lieu of it, but in
which the Turkish element preponderates, so that not only
are their honor and dignity consulted, but in refusing they
recede from their own original proposal.

The Queen is gone to Ireland, and Lord Granville with
her, who is afterward to attend her to Balmoral.   This is
new, because hitherto she has always had with her either the
Premier or a Secretary of State.   Granville is to be relieved
when circumstances admit, but at present there is no other
arrangement feasible.   Aberdeen and Clarendon are both
kept in town till the question is settled.   Newcastle got
leave to go to Clumber for his boys' holidays, and Her
Majesty does not desire to have the Home Secretary.

But Charles Villiers told me last night that Lord
Palmerston's influence and popularity in the House of
Commons are greater than ever, and if this Government
should be broken up by internal dissension, he would have
no difficulty in forming another, and gathering round him a
party to support him.   This is what the Tories are anxiously
looking to, desiring no better than to serve under him, and
flattering themselves that in his heart he personally dislikes
his colleagues, and in political matters agrees with themselves.   They pay him every sort of court, never attack
him, and not only defer to him on all occasions, but make
all the difference they can between him and the rest of the
Government ; nor does he discourage or reject these civilities,
though he does not invite them, or say or do anything inconsistent with his present position, but he probably thinks
the disposition toward him of that large political party
enhances his value to his own friends and increases his power,
besides affording to him a good alternative in case anything
should happen to break up the present Government or
separate him from it.

September 2d.—For the last week the settlement of this
tedious Turkish question has appeared more remote than
ever, and Clarendon was almost in despair when I saw him
a few days ago, and the more so because he suspected that
Lord Stratford was at the bottom of the difficulties raised
by the Divan.   However, according to the last accounts, it
would seem that Stratford was not to blame, and had done

what he could to get the Turks to comply with the terms of
the Conference. At this moment the affair wears rather a
better aspect, and my own belief is that it will be settled.
It is a great bore that it drags on in this way, creating
alarm and uncertainty, shaking the funds, and affecting
commerce.

The Duke of Bedford, of whom I have seen nothing for
a long time, called on me a few days ago, and talked over
the present state of affairs, and the position of Lord John
Russell. He said Lord John was now quite satisfied with it,
and rejoiced at his own comparative freedom, and his immunity from the constant attacks of which he used to be the
object ; and he is now conscious that, by the part he has
acted in waiving his own pretensions, he has not only not
degraded himself, but has greatly raised himself in public
estimation and acquired much credit and popularity. besides
rendering the country a great service. He is very well with
his colleagues, and gratified at the deference shown him,
and the consideration he enjoys in the House of Commons.
There, however, I know from other sources, all the popularity is engrossed by Palmerston and by Gladstone, and Lord
John has foolishly suffered Palmerston to take his place as
leader very often, because he chose to stay away at Richmond, and not come near the House.

The Duke took this opportunity of telling me what is
now a very old story, but which he said he thought he had
never told me before, and I am not sure whether he did or
not. It was what happened to him at the time of the formation of this Government last year, of which he was evidently
very proud. Just before the Derby Government broke down,
and before that reunion at Woburn of which so much was
said, the Prince gave him to understand that they should
look to him for advice if anything occurred, which they were
every day expecting. The Duke was at Woburn, and one
morning when the hounds met there and half the county
was at breakfast in the great hall, word was brought him
that a messenger had come from Osborne with a letter for
him. He found it was a letter from the Prince, in which he
informed him that this was despatched by a safe and trust-
worthy hand, and nobody was to know of its being sent;
that the Derby Government was at an end, and the Queen
and Prince were anxious for his opinion on the state of
affairs, the dispositions of public men, and what course they

had better take. The Duke had recently been in personal communication with all the leaders, with Aberdeen and Lord John, Newcastle, Clarendon, Lansdowne, Palmerston, and others, and he was therefore apprised of all their sentiments and in a condition to give very full information to the Court. He sat himself down and with the greatest rapidity (his horse at the door to go hunting) wrote four or five sheets of paper containing the amplest details of the sentiments and views of these different statesmen, and ended by advising that the Queen should send for Lords Lansdowne and Aberdeen—as she did. Lord John had already told him he did not wish to be sent for. After this of course he could not resent the advice the Duke gave; and happily Lord John was firm in resisting the advice of some of those about him, and acted on the dictates of his own conscientious judgment and the sound advice of his friends.

September 3d.—I dined last night *tête-à-tête* with Clarendon, and heard all the details of the state of the Turkish question, and read the interesting correspondence of Cowley, with his accounts of his conversations with the Emperor, and many other things. Clarendon is very uneasy because he thinks the Emperor Nicholas's pride will not let him accept the Note as modified by *the Turks*, though he would have accepted the same Note if it had been presented originally by the Conference. This is one danger. The next is one at Constantinople, where there is a strong bigoted violent party for war, disposed to dethrone the Sultan and replace him by his brother. This brother (of whom I never heard before) is a man of more energy than the Sultan, and is connected with the fanatical party. The Sultan himself is enervated by early debauchery and continual drunkenness, and therefore in great danger should he by any unpopular measures provoke an outbreak from the violent faction. Clarendon thinks that Stratford has encouraged the resistance of the Divan to the proposals of the Conference, and that he might have persuaded the Turks to accept the terms if he had chosen to do so and set about it in a proper manner; but Clarendon says that he has lived there so long, and is animated with such a personal hatred of the Emperor, that he is full of the Turkish spirit; and this and his temper together have made him take a part directly contrary to the wishes and instructions of his Government. He thinks he wishes to be recalled that he may make a

4

grievance of it, and come home to do all the mischief he can. Westmorland wrote word the other day that Stratford's language was very hostile to his Government, and the Ministers of all the other Powers at Constantinople thought he had actually resigned, and reported the fact to Vienna.

The most important question now pending is what to do with the fleets. They cannot remain much longer in Besika Bay, and must either retire to Vourla or enter the Dardanelles. The Emperor Napoleon wishes they should enter the Dardenelles, but only a little way, and not go on to Constantinople; and Clarendon takes the same view, proposing a *mezzo termine*. The Emperor professes an earnest desire for a peaceful solution, and the strongest determination to act in concert with England to the end, and his views seem very sensible and proper. But, notwithstanding this disposition, in which he probably is sincere, there is reason to believe that he is all the time keeping up a sort of secret and underhand communication with Russia, and the evidence of this is rather curious. It appears that he has recently written a letter to the Duchess of Hamilton, in which he says that he believes the Russians will not evacuate the Principalities, and that he does not care if they stay there. This letter the Duchess showed to Brunnow, and he imparted it to Aberdeen, who told Clarendon, but none of the other Ministers know anything of it. Clarendon wrote word of this to Cowley, and told him to make what use of it he thought fit. In the first instance he said something to Drouyn de Lhuys of the Emperor's entertaining views different from ours, which Drouyn repeated to the Emperor, who spoke to Cowley about it, and protested that he had no separate or different objects, when Cowley, without mentioning names, told him what he had heard of his having written. The Emperor made an evasive answer to this, but gave many assurances of his determination to act with us heartily and sincerely. This incident seems to have made a great impression both on Cowley and Clarendon, particularly as both know something more. Cowley says he knows that the Emperor has a private correspondence with Castelbajac, of which Drouyn de Lhuys is ignorant, and Seymour writes to Clarendon that he has observed for some time past a great lukewarmness on the part of the French Minister in pressing the Russian Government, and an evident leaning to them. As the Duchess of Hamilton has no intimacy with Brunnow,

it appears very extraordinary that she could communicate
to him a letter of the Emperor's, and such a letter, which
would be a great indiscretion unless he had secretly desired
her to do so ; and all these circumstances taken together
look very like a little intrigue between the Emperor and the
Russian Court, which would also be very consistent with his
secret, false, and clandestine mode of conducting his affairs.
It is probable enough that he may wish to keep on good
terms with Russia and at the same time maintain his intimate connection with England.   That he is bent on avoiding
war there can be no doubt, and for very good reasons, for
France is threatened with a scarcity, and he is above all
things bent on keeping the people supplied with food at low
prices; and for this object the French Government is straining
every nerve and prepared to make any amount of pecuniary
sacrifice ; but the necessity for this, which absorbs all their
means, renders it at the same time particularly desirable to
maintain peace in Europe.

There never was a case so involved in difficulties and
complications of different sorts, all the particulars of which
I heard last night ; but the affair is so tangled that it is impossible to weave it into an intelligible and consistent narrative, and I can only jot down fragments, which may hereafter
serve to explain circumstances connected with the *dénouement*, whenever it takes place.   John Russell and Palmerston
are both come to town, so that a little Cabinet will discuss
this matter.   Palmerston is extremely reasonable, does not
take the part of the Turks, but on the contrary blames them
severely for making difficulties he thinks absurd and useless,
but is still for not letting them be crushed.   He is on the
best terms with Clarendon, and goes along with him very
cordially in his policy on this question.   Both Palmerston
and Lord John seem to agree with Clarendon on the question
of the disposal of the fleet better than Aberdeen, who is always for trusting the Emperor, maintaining peace, and would
be quite contented to send the fleet to Vourla or Tenedos,
and would see with regret the more energetic course of entering the Dardanelles.   However, there is no chance of any
material difference on this score, and I have no doubt, if the
question is not settled before the end of the month, the fleets
will anchor within the Straits and there remain.

I was glad to find that the Queen has consented to let
Palmerston take his turn at Balmoral, and Aberdeen has in-

formed him that he is to go there. It was done by Aberdeen speaking to the Prince at Osborne, who said he thought there would be no difficulty. The Queen acquiesced with the good sense she generally shows on such occasions, being always open to reason, and ready to consent to whatever can be proved to her to be right or expedient.

September 4th.—I went to Winchester yesterday, and fell in with Graham in the train, so we went together and had a great deal of talk, mostly on the Eastern Question. He thinks the Emperor of Russia will not accept the Turkish alterations, and he is very hot against Stratford, to whom he attributes all the difficulties. He has heard that Stratford has held language hostile to the Government, and he is inclined to think not only that he has acted treacherously toward his employers, but that proofs of his treachery might be obtained, and he is all for getting the evidence if possible, and acting upon it at once, by recalling him ; he thinks the proofs might be obtained through the Turkish Ministers, and if they can be, he would not stop to inquire who might be displeased, or what the effect might be, but do it at once. He acknowledges, however, that it would not do to act on surmises or reports, and that nothing but clear proofs of Stratford's misconduct, such as will satisfy Parliament, would render such a step justifiable or safe. . With regard to the fleets, he says there is no reason why they should not remain in Besika Bay, and it is a mistake to suppose they could not, and he is very decidedly against their entering the Dardanelles in any case, because it would be contrary to treaty and afford the Emperor of Russia a just *casus belli ;* and he maintains that his having (contrary to treaties and international rights) occupied the Principalities, affords no reason why we should infringe them in another direction. When this question comes to be discussed, his voice will evidently be for not entering the Dardanelles, though he acknowledges that we cannot retreat while the Russians remain where they are. He talked a great deal about Palmerston, of whom he has some distrust, and fancied he has been in communication with Stratford, and that he would concur with him in his proceedings, and he expressed great satisfaction when I told him that Palmerston and Clarendon were on the most cordial and confidential terms, and that the former entirely disapproved of the conduct of the Turks (which is that of Stratford) in regard to the Note. He thinks Palmerston looks to being Prime Minister, if anything happened to Aberdeen, but that neither he nor John Russell could hold the office, as neither would consent to the elevation of the other. On the whole, he inclines to the opinion that Palmerston has made up his mind to go on with this Government and his present colleagues, that he means to act fairly and honestly with and by them, and has no *arrière pensée* toward the Tories, though he is not sorry to have them always looking to him, and paying him, as they do, excessive court. It insures him great support and an easy life in the House of Commons, where, however, he says Palmerston has done very little this year, and he does not seem much impressed with the idea of his having gained very considerably there, or obtained a better position than he had before.

September 8th.—I saw Clarendon on Sunday. There is nothing new, but he said he would lay two to one the Emperor does not accept the modified Note ; it will be a contest between his pride and his interest, for his army is in such a state of disease and distress that he is in no condition to make war ; on the other hand, he cannot, without extreme humiliation, accept the Turkish Note. What will happen, if he refuses, nobody can possibly divine. The four Ministers met to discuss the matter, and were very harmonious ; Palmerston not at all for violent measures, and Clarendon said he himself was the most warlike of the four. I told him of my journey with Graham and all that he had said. He replied that he knew Graham was very violent against Stratford, but that it would be impossible to make out any case against him, as he certainly had read to the Turkish Minister all his (Clarendon's) despatches and instructions, and he gave the most positive assurances, which it would be difficult to gainsay, that he had done everything in his power to induce the Turkish Government to give way to the advice of the Conference, and whatever his secret wishes and opinions might be, there was no official evidence to be had that he had failed in doing his duty fairly by his own Government ; therefore it would be out of the question to recall him.

September 20th.—At Doncaster all last week ; I found Clarendon yesterday very much alarmed at the prospect in the East. He thinks it will be impossible to restrain the Turkish war party ; he told me that the Conference at Vienna had imparted their Note to the Turkish Ambassador there, and both he and his dragoman had expressed their entire approbation of it. They had considered this to afford a strong presumption that it would not be unpalatable at Constantinople, but it was not sent there because this would have occasioned so much delay, and it was desirable to get the Russians out of the Principalities as speedily as possible. The Russian generals had actually received orders to prepare for the evacuation, which the Emperor would have commanded the instant he heard that the Turks were willing to send the Vienna Note. The Emperor Napoleon has again given the strongest assurances of his determination in no case whatever to separate his policy from ours, his resolution to adhere to the English alliance, and to maintain peace *à tout prix*, which he frankly owns to be indispensably necessary to the interests of his country. The Austrians are already beginning to hang back from taking any decided part in opposition to Russia, and, while still ready to join in making every exertion to maintain peace, they are evidently determined if war breaks out to take no part against Russia, and this disposition is sure to be improved by the interview which is about to take place between the Emperors of Russia and Austria.

September 26th.—I have been at Hatchford all last week. I saw Clarendon on Thursday before I went there, and heard that two ships of each fleet were gone up the Dardanelles,[1] and that the rest would probably soon follow, as the French were now urging that measure. He was then going to Aberdeen to propose calling the Cabinet together, the state of affairs becoming more critical every hour, and apparently no chance of averting war. The prospect was not the brighter from the probability of a good deal of difference of opinion when they do meet. He showed me a letter from Palmerston, in which he spoke very coolly of such a contingency as war with Russia and Austria, and with his usual confidence and flippancy of the great blows that might be inflicted on both Powers, particularly alluding to the possible expulsion of the Austrians from Italy, an object of which he has probably never lost sight. Meanwhile the violence and scurrility of the press here exceed all belief. Day after day the Radical and Tory papers, animated by very dif-

---

[1] [The British vessels were steamers, the " Retribution " and another. There was at that time only one line-of-battle ship in each fleet having steam-power; all the other vessels of the line were sailing-ships.]

ferent sentiments and motives, pour forth the most virulent
abuse of the Emperor of Russia, of Austria, and of this
Government, especially of Aberdeen.

———◆◆◆———

CHAPTER IV.

The Conference at Olmütz—The Turks declare War—Lord Palmerston's Views—Lord
Palmerston lauded by the Radicals and the Tories—Failure of the Pacific Policy—
Lord Aberdeen desires to resign—Lord John to be Prime Minister—Obstacles to Lord
John's Pretensions—Danger of breaking up the Government—Lord John's Wilfulness
and Unpopularity—Alliance of the Northern Powers defeated by Manteuffel—Conflict
of the two Policies—Meeting of Parliament discussed—French Refugees in Belgium—
General Baraguay d'Hilliers sent to Constantinople—Mr. Reeve returns from the East
—Lord John's Reform Bill—The Emperor of Russia writes to the Queen—Sir James
Graham's Views on Reform, etc.—Opponents of the Reform Scheme—Abortive Attempts at Negotiation—The Four Powers agree to a Protocol—Lord Palmerston
threatens to secede.—Lord Palmerston resigns on the Reform Scheme—Lord Palmerston opposed to Reform—Effects of Lord Palmerston's Resignation—Conciliatory
Overtures—Lord Lansdowne's Position—Lord Aberdeen's Account—Lady Palmerston makes up the Dispute—Lord Palmerston withdraws his Resignation—Baraguay
d'Hilliers refuses to enter the Black Sea—War resolved on—Review of the Transaction.

October 4th.—I went to The Grove on Saturday, and
spent great part of the afternoon on Sunday reading the
Eastern Question despatches, printed in a Blue Book to be
laid by-and-by before Parliament.   On Sunday came Westmorland's account of his interviews with the Emperor of
Russia and Nesselrode at Olmütz, which sounded very satisfactory, for the Emperor was very gracious and pacific, and
Nesselrode in his name disclaimed in the most positive terms
any intention of aggrandizing himself at the expense of Turkey or of claiming any protectorate, or asserting any claims
inconsistent with the sovereignty and independence of the
Sultan, and moreover signified his willingness to make a
declaration to that effect in such form and manner as might
be hereafter agreed upon.   All this was very well, and
served to confirm the notion that, if some sensible men,
really desirous of settling the question, could be brought together, the accomplishment would not be difficult ; but the
distance which separates the negotiating parties from each
other, and the necessity of circulating every proposition
through so many remote capitals, and the consequent loss
of time, have rendered all conferences and pacific projects
unavailing.
   Yesterday morning a messenger arrived, bringing the

telegraphic despatch from Vienna, which announced the determination of the Turks to go to war, and that a grand Council was to be assembled to decide on the declaration, news which precluded all hope of adjustment;[1] and yesterday afternoon the further account of the decision of the Council was received. Such of the Ministers as are in town met in the afternoon, and it was decided that all the rest should be summoned, and a Cabinet held on Friday next.

It will be no easy matter to determine what part we shall take, and how far we shall mix ourselves up in the quarrel as belligerents. It will be very fortunate if the Cabinet should be unanimous on this question. Palmerston has hitherto acted very frankly and cordially with Clarendon, but the old instincts are still strong in him, and they are all likely to urge him to recommend strong measures and an active interference. Granville told me last night he thought Palmerston was not at all displeased at the decision of the Turks, and as he still clings to the idea that Turkey is powerful and full of energy, and he is quite indifferent to the danger to which Austria may be exposed, and would rejoice at her being plunged in fresh difficulties and threatened with fresh rebellions and revolutions, he will rather rejoice than not at the breaking out of hostilities. He will not dare to avow his real propensities, but he will cloak them under other pretences and pretexts, and give effect to them as much as he can. He has been speechifying in Scotland, where, though he spoke very handsomely of Clarendon, he did not say one word in defence of Aberdeen, or anything calculated to put an end to the notion and repeated assertions that he and Aberdeen had been at variance on the Eastern Question. I find Aberdeen feels this omission very much, and it would certainly have been more generous, as well as more just, if he had taken the opportunity of correcting the popular error as to Aberdeen, after having been reaping a great harvest of popularity at his expense.

Palmerston's position is curious. He is certainly very popular, and there is a high idea of his diplomatic skill and vigor. He is lauded to the skies by all the Radicals who are

[1] [The declaration of the Turkish Council or Divan, held on October 3, was to the effect that, if the Principalities were not evacuated in fifteen days, a state of war would ensue. To this the Emperor of Russia responded on October 18 by a formal declaration of war. War being declared, the Straits were opened, and, at the request of the Sultan, the allied fleets entered the Dardanelles on October 22.]

the admirers of Kossuth and Mazzini, who want to renew the scenes and attempts of 1848, and who fancy that, if Palmerston were at the head of the Government, he would play into their hands. On the other hand, he is equally an object of the flattery and praise of the Tories, who cannot get over their being succeeded by a Peelite Prime Minister, and they cling to the belief that there can be no real cordiality, and must be complete difference of opinion, between Aberdeen and Palmerston, and they look forward to the prospect of their disunion to break up this odious Government, and a return to office with Palmerston at their head. These are the political chimeras with which their brains are filled, and which make them take (for very different reasons) the same part as the Radicals on the Eastern Question. My own conviction is that both parties reckon without their host. Palmerston is sixty-nine years old, and it is too late for him to look out for fresh political combinations and other connections, nor would any object of ambition repay him for the dissolution of all his personal and social ties. He will, therefore, go on as he does now, accepting such popularity as is offered him as a means of enhancing his own importance in this Cabinet ; and, in the event of any accident happening to it, of making his own pretensions available.

October 6th.—Delano was sent for by Lord Aberdeen the night before last, when they had a long conversation on the state of affairs, and Aberdeen told him that he was resolved to be no party to a war with Russia on such grounds as the present, and he was prepared to resign rather than incur such responsibility. This was the marrow of what he said, and very important, because not unlikely to lead to some difference in the Cabinet, and possibly to its dissolution.

October 7th.—Clanricarde called here yesterday morning ; he is very strong against the Government and their policy, and maintains that if we had joined France and sent the fleet up when she did. the Emperor of Russia would then have receded, as his obstinacy was entirely caused by his conviction that France and England would never remain united, and that nothing would induce the latter to make war on Russia. He said this idea had been confirmed by the language of Aberdeen, who had continually spoken of his determination to avoid war to Brunnow and others, and in his letters to Madame de Lieven—*la paix à tout prix*. Clanricarde, however, himself said he would not declare war against

Russia, and we might defend Turkey without going that length. I went and told Clarendon all he had said (in greater detail), and he owned that it was more than probable that Aberdeen had held some such language as was attributed to him ; indeed, he had more than once had occasion to remonstrate with him upon it. Clarendon was very uneasy at the prospect of the discussion about to take place, and contemplates as extremely probable the breaking-up of the Government on the question of war. Palmerston has been very reserved, but always on the same friendly terms with his colleagues, and Clarendon in particular ; but Lady Palmerston as usual talks *à qui veut l'entendre* of the misconduct of the whole affair, and affirms that, if Palmerston had had the management of it, all would have been settled long ago. As matters have turned out, it is impossible not to regret that we were perhaps too moderate and patient at first ; for as the course we have adopted has not been successful, it seems unfortunate we did not try another, which might have been more so. But this is judging *après coup*, and nothing is so easy as to affirm that, if something had been done, which was not done, success would have attended it.

October 8th.—The Cabinet went off very well yesterday, no serious difference of opinion about anything, and a good concurrence both as to what had been done and what ought to be done hereafter. Lord Aberdeen is well pleased.

Newmarket, October 12th.—This morning I met the Duke of Bedford on the heath, who told me he wanted very much to speak to me about certain communications he had received which made him extremely uneasy, and full of apprehension of coming difficulties, threatening the very existence of the Government. It seems that a short time ago Lord Aberdeen imparted to John Russell his wish to resign, and to place the Government in his hands. He said that he had only taken his present post because his doing so was indispensable to the formation of the Government, and had always contemplated Lord John's eventually succeeding him, and he thought the time was now come when he might very properly do so. He did not anticipate any insurmountable opposition in any quarter, and he should himself speak to Gladstone about it, who was the most important person to be consulted, and he was in fact only prevented doing so, as he had intended, by not being able to go to Scotland, where he had expected to meet Gladstone. Whether Aberdeen had

spoken to Gladstone since his return to London, the Duke
of Bedford did not know. No steps appear to have been
taken with regard to Palmerston, nor does it appear that
any progress was made in accomplishing this change. The
Queen had been apprised of Aberdeen's intentions. Such
was the state of things when a short time ago the Duke received a letter from Lord John, in which he said that matters could not go on as they were, and that there must be
some changes; and that very soon he could no longer act
without being primarily responsible for the policy of the
Government—in other words, without resuming his post of
Prime Minister. This is all the Duke knows, as Lord John
entered into no explanations or details, and he is in total
ignorance of the grounds of his brusque determination, and
of what can have occurred to produce it. He sees, however,
all the difficulties and embarrassments that in consequence
of it are looming in the distance, and how very possible it is
that the Government may be broken up. All this we very
fully discussed, but without either of us being able to guess
what it all means, or what the result will be of Lord John's
putting his intentions into execution.

October 16*th*.—I came to town yesterday morning, and in
the afternoon went to the Foreign Office, and saw Clarendon,
to whom I imparted what the Duke of Bedford had told me.
He said he knew it all, Aberdeen having told him what had
passed between John Russell and himself; but having made
Clarendon give his word of honor that he would not say a
word of it to anybody, so he said, "I would not mention it
even to you, to whom I tell everything." He then, however,
went into the whole question, and told me what had passed,
which did not exactly agree with the Duke's story. According to Clarendon, Lord John went to Lord Aberdeen before
Parliament was up, and told him he could not consent to go
on in his present position, to which Aberdeen replied, "Very
well, you only meet my own wishes, and you know I always
told you that I should be at any time ready to resign my
place to you."

Nothing more seems to have taken place at that time,
nor till lately, when Lord John went again to Aberdeen, and
repeated his determination not to go on; but this time the
communication does not seem to have been received by Aberdeen with the same ready acquiescence in the proposed
change, and some plain speaking took place between them.

I infer, but as Clarendon did not expressly say so I put it
dubiously, that Aberdeen had spoken to Gladstone and ascertained that he would by no means agree to the substitution
of John Russell, and should go with Aberdeen if he retired.
At all events, while Aberdeen told him that he was prepared,
if he wished it, to broach the matter to his colleagues, he
intimated to him that it was evident he wanted to turn him
out, and put himself in his place, but that he (Aberdeen)
could not agree to retire at this moment, and before Parliament met, and that Lord John had better well consider the
step he was about to take, as it would in all probability
break up the Government, and asked him if he was prepared
to encounter the odium of doing so, more especially as he
must remember that he had only consented to form this
Government on Lord John's own assurance to him that he
was himself unable to form one.   He asked him if he was
secure of Palmerston's concurrence in the change he proposed, and he replied that he did not expect to find any
difficulty in that quarter.   This was the substance of what
passed between them, Aberdeen being evidently a good deal
nettled, and thinking Lord John is behaving very ill.   This
is Clarendon's opinion also, and he thinks, if Lord John
persists, the Government will be inevitably broken up, for a
considerable part of the Cabinet will certainly not consent
to have Lord John again placed at the head of the Government.   Clarendon does not believe a word of Palmerston's
being a party to it, and he knows that both Gladstone and
Newcastle would resign.   Graham he is not sure of, but
inclines to think he would retire with Aberdeen, especially
if Aberdeen has any compulsion or ill-usage to complain of.
For the moment, however, this storm has blown over, as
Lord John has signified to Aberdeen that he does not mean
to press the matter again for the present.   The Queen, when
it was mentioned to her, was anything but approving of or
consenting to the change.

In all this matter there is little doubt that Lord John has
been instigated by his connections, and they none of them,
Lord John himself included, have sense enough to see that
the course he is adopting is quite suicidal, and would be not
less fatal to his own reputation and popularity than to the
Government he belongs to.   He failed as Prime Minister,
and no credit attended his Administration, and no regret his
fall.   The popularity he lost, he in good measure regained

by his conduct on the formation of this Government, when
he waived his own pretensions, and for the public good
consented, after having held the first place, to accept the
second ; but the world does not know how reluctantly and
grudgingly he did this, and how sorely his pride and vanity
suffered on that occasion.   The position he occupied of leader
of the House of Commons without an office was anomalous,
and many thought it objectionable, but he himself insisted
on it, and it proved successful.   The House of Commons
not only accepted it, but were pleased to see a man so
eminent eschewing office with its functions and emoluments,
and gratuitously devoting · himself to the service and the
business of Parliament.   He became popular again in the
House, and would have been more so if he had not chosen
to quit the Treasury Bench early every afternoon, and go
down to Richmond, leaving Palmerston to do his work, and
ingratiate himself with the House.   Aberdeen reminded Lord
John that this position, which he now found intolerable, was
one he had chosen to make for himself ; that he had not only
declared he could not form a Government, but that every
office had been at his disposal, and he had been invited to
take the greatest offices, or, if he preferred it, any smaller
one, but that he had insisted on holding none.   Aberdeen is
quite right not to resign now, or before Parliament meets,
where he must appear as Minister to defend his own policy.

I expect that Lord John will not renew his demands for
some time, if at all ; but if he does, this is what will probably take place · The Government will be broken up, Lord
John will try to form one and will fail, and the Government
will again be constituted minus Lord John.   Nobody would,
I think, go out with him.   This is supposing (which I think
certain) that Palmerston would not make common cause with
him, but prefer to remain with the rest.   There would then
remain the great difficulty of the lead of the House of Commons and the part Palmerston would play ; but, dangerous
as it would be, it would probably be found necessary to trust
him with the lead, most distasteful though it would be both
to Aberdeen and to the Queen.

October 18*th.*—The Emperor of Russia moved heaven and
earth to bring about a new Holy Alliance between himself,
Austria, and Prussia, in which he would have succeeded if
it had not been for the wisdom and firmness of Manteuffel,[1]

[1] |Count Manteuffel was the Prussian Minister for Foreign Affairs, and the

who was proof against all his seductions. Austria consented, but only on condition that Prussia did likewise. The King of Prussia would have given way with his characteristic weakness, but Manteuffel would not hear of it, and contrived to keep his master straight. In an interview of two hours between the Emperor and Manteuffel *tête-à-tête*, the Emperor employed all the means he could think of to prevail on the Prussian Minister, but all in vain ; he refused positively to allow Prussia to depart from her neutrality. This had the effect of keeping Austria neutral also, and that of making the Emperor more inclined to peace ; but the Turkish declaration of war and peremptory summons to him to quit the Principalities leave him no alternative but that of taking up the gauntlet thus thrown down.

November 2d.—All last week at Newmarket, during which nothing of moment occurred but the renewed attempts at negotiation, and the consent of the Turks to defer the commencement of hostilities. I saw Clarendon the day before yesterday, who told me how matters stood, and showed me a despatch just received from Vienna with a copy of a very moderate and pacific Note from Nesselrode to Buol, showing that there is every disposition at St. Petersburg to patch matters up. Clarendon told me that he was heartily sick of the whole question, in which the double trouble and difficulty were cast upon him of reconciling the Russians and the Turks, and of preserving agreement in the Cabinet, where Aberdeen was always opposing measures of hostility toward Russia, and Palmerston for pushing them forward. He said he steered between the two, and that he and John Russell were more nearly agreed than any of the others ; he told me at the same time a characteristic trait of Palmerston. The Turks having determined to plunge into war against the advice of their protectors, especially against ours, and it having been made known to us that the Sultan and his Ministers were not disinclined to be guided by us, but that they were themselves overruled and driven to this extreme course by the Grand Council, it became necessary in Clarendon's opinion to notify to the Turkish Government that, since they had thought fit to take their own independent

leading member of the Prussian Cabinet. He was accused of sacrificing Prussian interests to those of Austria at the Conference of Olmütz ; but in fact he succeeded in defeating what would have been a very formidable confederacy of the German Powers with Russia.]

course, we should reserve to ourselves the right of acting
according to our own discretion, and not consider ourselves
bound to be dragged into a war at the heels of the Grand
Council, which is an assembly of ruffians and fanatics, by
whom it would be utterly inconsistent with the dignity of |
our Crown that our policy should be governed and influenced.
It seems too that this is a point on which the Queen feels
very strongly, and is exceedingly anxious that the honor
and dignity of the Crown should not be compromised.   Accordingly Clarendon drew up a despatch to this effect, to
which the Cabinet acceded, and Palmerston also, though
with some reluctance.   However, he not only saw the proposed despatch, but he made some alteration in it with his
own hand, thereby of course subscribing to it.   Just after
this Clarendon went to Windsor, and submitted the despatch
to the Queen and the Prince ; they objected to it that it was
not strong enough in their sense, but Clarendon prevailed
upon them to waive their objections, and, as it had been
agreed to in the Cabinet, to let it go.   But before it was
gone Clarendon received a letter from Palmerston, strongly
objecting to the despatch altogether, and desiring Clarendon
to inform Lord Aberdeen that he would be no party to such
a communication.   This was extremely embarrassing.   Clarendon spoke to Aberdeen, and afterward (at Aberdeen's
suggestion) informed the Queen what had occurred.   Her
Majesty said, "I advise you not to attach much importance
to this communication.   I know Lord Palmerston from much
experience, and it is probably only an attempt to bully, which,
if you take no notice of it, you will hear no more of."   The
result justified the Queen's sagacity, for Clarendon sent off
the despatch, and at the same time wrote word to Palmerston that he had done so, giving him sundry reasons why he
could not do otherwise, to which he received in reply a very
good-humored letter, merely saying that, as it was gone, it
was useless to say any more about it, and probably it would
do no harm.

There has been talk abroad and discussion in the Cabinet
about the meeting of Parliament.   Lord John and Lord
Aberdeen both wished Parliament to meet, the first because
he is always hankering after the House of Commons, the
latter because he wished Parliament to decide on the question
of peace or war, so that in the one alternative his hands
might be strengthened, or in the other he might have a

pretext for resigning. But both Clarendon and Palmerston were much against it, and now that there is a fresh prospect of peace, it is rendered more unnecessary and undesirable.

King Leopold is here, still uneasy (though less than he was) upon the subject of his *démêlés* with the Emperor of the French. The cause of them is the libellous publications of the French refugees in Belgium. They compose the most outrageous attacks of a personal nature on him and the Empress, which they have printed in Belgium, and get these papers smuggled into France, and disseminated among the lower classes, and particularly the troops. This naturally gives the Emperor great offence, and Leopold would afford him redress if he could ; but the Constitution was made by journalists, and the unrestrained liberty of the press is so interwoven with the Constitution, that the Legislature itself has no power to deal with the case, nor any power short of a Constituent Assembly. All this Leopold has submitted to his powerful neighbor, and their relations seem to be more amicable ; for very civil letters have passed between the two monarchs, through the Prince de Chimay, whom Leopold sent to compliment the Emperor when he went lately to Lille.

November 10*th.*—All attempts at settling the Eastern Question by *Notes* have been rudely interrupted by the actual commencement of hostilities. Meanwhile the Notes sped their way, but at Vienna it was deemed no longer possible to settle it in this manner, but that there must now be a regular treaty of peace, the terms of which the Allies might prescribe, and there is now a question of having a Congress or Conference here, to carry on the affair, It is, however, difficult to make out what the French are at, and. with all our intimacy, we must keep on our guard against all contingencies on the part of our Imperial neighbor. Nobody knows what is his real motive for sending Baraguay d'Hilliers to Constantinople. Francis Baring, when I told him of this appointment, said it could be only for the purpose of quarrelling, for he was the most violent of men, and was certain to quarrel with whomsoever he had to deal. If this be so, his quarrelling with Lord Stratford is inevitable, and it is by no means improbable that Louis Napoleon is tired of playing second fiddle to us, and sends this General there for the express purpose of counteracting our superior influence, and, by the tender of military counsel and aid, to substitute his own for ours.

Reeve is just returned from the East, having spent some time at Constantinople, and he came home by Vienna. Lord Stratford treated him with great kindness and hospitality, and talked to him very openly. He says that Stratford exercised a great but not unlimited influence and control over the Turkish Government, and of course is very jealous of the influence he possesses ; for example, he boasted to Reeve that he had carried a great point, and had procured the appointment of the candidate he favored as Greek Patriarch, an interference which, if it had been made by the Emperor of Russia, whose concern it is much more than ours, would have excited in us great indignation. Such an exercise of influence and in such a matter, of which the Russians are well aware, is calculated to exasperate them, and it is not unnatural that the Emperor should feel that, if any foreign influence is to prevail in Turkey, he has a better right than any other Power to establish his own. Reeve has a very poor opinion of the power, resources, and political condition of Turkey, and does not doubt the military success of the Russians. He says that the corruption is enormous—everybody bribes or is bribed. The Greek Patriarch whom Stratford got appointed had to pay large sums to Redschid Pasha and his son. The whole State is rotten to the core.

November 12th.—This morning John Russell breaks ground on the Reform plan, by referring his scheme to a Committee of the Cabinet, which is to meet at his house, consisting, besides himself, of Granville, Newcastle. Graham, Charles Wood, and Palmerston. I am afraid he will propose a lower franchise, probably 5*l.*, in spite of many warnings and the signs of the times, which are very grave and alarming—nothing but strikes and deep-rooted discontent on the part of the working classes. I am in correspondence with Ellesmere on the subject, and have sent his letters to John Russell, who does not appear disposed to admit the force of his reasoning against lowering the franchise. This Committee will probably be on the whole favorable to a democratic measure, Lord John from old prejudices and obstinacy, Graham from timidity, Newcastle because he has espoused Liberal principles ; Granville will be inclined to go with Lord John, and Palmerston alone is likely to stand out against a democratic scheme, unless Charles Wood should go with him, of whose opinions on the question of Reform I know nothing. Aberdeen is himself a Reformer, but I hear he is resolved not to consent to a 5l. franchise. I confess to great misgivings about this project in the present state of the country, and dread the further progress of democratic power. The success of the great Reform Bill and the experiences of twenty years without any of the apprehensions of the anti-Reformers having been realized, are now in my opinion sources of danger, as they create an opinion that progress, as it is called, is not only necessary, but perfectly safe. It consoles me for growing old that I shall not live to see the confusion in which this well-ordered State is likely to be involved, the period of peril and suffering it will have to go through, and the reaction, which will restore order and tranquillity at the expense of that temperate and rational freedom, which we alone of all the nations of the earth are in possession of. I see no reason why, if we choose recklessly, and without any cause, to cast away the good we enjoy, we should be exempted from paying the penalty which our folly and wickedness would so richly deserve. The above question in all its ramifications is infinitely more important than the Russian and Turkish quarrel, but there is no saying how the former may be indirectly and consequentially affected through the latter by means of the political differences which may arise out of it. Everything now looks black in the political horizon, and the war which has begun between the principals can hardly fail to extend itself sooner or later to the collateral parties.

November 15th.—Yesterday morning having met Clarendon on the railway, he from Windsor, I from Hillingdon, I got into the carriage and went home with him. He told me all he had to tell of what he had to go through with the conflicting proposals of Palmerston and Aberdeen in the Cabinet : the latter as averse as ever to any strong measures, and always full of consideration for the Emperor ; the former anxious for war, and with the same confidence and rashness which were so conspicuous in him during the Syrian question, insisting that nothing will be so easy as to defeat Russia, and he now goes the length of urging that none of the old treaties between her and the Porte should be renewed. All this *jactance*, however, does not go much beyond words, for he evinces no disposition to separate from his colleagues or to insist on any course which the majority of the Cabinet object to.

The Emperor of Russia has taken the unusual step of
writing an autograph letter to the Queen.   Brunnow, who
was rather puzzled, took the letter to Aberdeen, and asked
what he was to do with it.   Aberdeen told him to take it to
Clarendon, who sent it to the Queen.   She sent it to him to
read, and he suggested certain heads of an answer, but did
not communicate the letter, nor the fact of its having been
received, to any one but Aberdeen.   The Queen wrote an
answer in French, and he says a very good one.

Cowley has sent him an account of a conversation he
lately had with the Emperor Napoleon, in which he said
that the condition of France and the rise in the price of provisions, so deeply affecting the working classes, made him
more than ever bent upon preserving peace, and he proposed
that the Powers should be invited to concur with England
and France in drawing up a scheme of pacification and
arrangement, which should be tendered to the belligerents,
and whichever should refuse to accept it should be treated
as an enemy.   Clarendon said that there were many objections to this plan, but he seemed to believe in the sincerity
of the Emperor's desire for peace, in spite of the opposite
presumption afforded by Baraguay d'Hilliers' mission, and
its accompaniment of French officers.   He attributes that
mission to the wounded vanity of France, and the determination of the Government to send some man who shall
dispute the influence of Stratford, and assert that of France.
The character of Stratford had been fully explained to Baraguay d'Hilliers, and he went, ostensibly at least, with instructions and an intention to act with him in harmony, but
this the character of the two ambassadors will probably render quite impossible.

The Queen told Clarendon an anecdote of Palmerston,
showing how exclusively absorbed he is with *foreign* politics.
Her Majesty has been much interested in and alarmed at the
strikes and troubles in the North, and asked Palmerston for
details about them, when she found he knew nothing at all.
One morning, after previous inquiries, she said to him,
"Pray, Lord Palmerston, have you any news?"   To which
he replied, "No Madame, I have heard nothing; but it
seems certain *the Turks have crossed the Danube.*"

In the afternoon I called on Graham at the Admiralty,
and had a long talk with him about the Government and its
prospects, and the disposition and intentions of John Russell

and of Palmerston. He is, contrary to custom, very cheerful and sanguine on these points ; he was apprised of all that Lord John has said and done, but except on one occasion, just about the time of the prorogation, has had no communication with Lord John himself on the subject. He is now satisfied that Lord John has abandoned his designs, and has made up his mind to go on as he is, and he infers this from his frank and friendly conduct about the Reform Bill, which he has not kept to himself, but submitted to a Committee for the purpose of bringing it before all his colleagues in a very good spirit, and quite willing to have Palmerston on this Committee, from whom the greatest opposition was to be expected. Graham said their first meeting had gone off very pleasantly, and Palmerston had urged much less objection than he had expected ; he thinks therefore that his own reflections and his knowledge of the difficulties which would oppose themselves to his purpose have determined Lord John to acquiesce in his present position, nor is he afraid of Palmerston separating himself from this Cabinet, thinking that at his age he will not speculate so deeply for the chance of greater power and a higher place, to be purchased at the certain sacrifice of all his social relations and personal connections, and he therefore expects Palmerston will conform to the general sentiments, and decisions of his colleagues, both as to foreign policy and to Reform. Graham said he approved entirely of Lord John's scheme, and thought his proposed measure good and safe.

November 27th.—Council at Windsor on Friday 25th. The Queen was afflicted by the Queen of Portugal's death, though they never saw each other but once when they were children. I heard the particulars of the Reform Bill, which (if there is to be one at all) seems as little mischievous as can be. It seems to have encountered little or no opposition in the Cabinet, and Lord John considers it as having been accepted and settled there. Lord Lansdowne has not pronounced himself positively ; but though, no doubt, he dislikes it exceedingly, they think he will not retire upon it, and up to the present time he has indicated no such intention. Graham, who is always frightened, told me on Friday he was very uneasy lest Lansdowne should decline to be a party to it.

Palmerston has written a letter to Lord John, strong in the beginning, denouncing the measure as unnecessary and unwise, and complaining of his having originally committed his colleagues to it, by declaring his own opinion without any previous consultation and concert with them.   Then after criticising the Bill (ably, as I am told), he ends by announcing that he shall consent to it.   He sent copies of this letter to Aberdeen and to Lansdowne.

I brought Clarendon from the station to Downing Street, when he told me that he had begun some fresh attempts at renewing negotiations.   The proposal of the Emperor Napoleon to force terms on the two parties would not do, but he had sent a proposal of some sort (I could not exactly make out what), which, contrary to his expectation, Buol had agreed to ; but he did not seem very sanguine about any result from this beginning.   He said nothing could exceed the difficulties of the case, nor the embarrassments of his own position.   The Turks are now indisposed to agree to anything, or to make any concessions whatever, and of course the Emperor of Russia neither will nor can make peace and withdraw, without some plausible satisfaction.   Then at home the difficulty is just as great between Palmerston, who is all for going ahead, and wants nothing less than war with Russia, and Aberdeen, who is in the other extreme—objecting to everything, and proposing nothing.   John Russell is very reasonable, and agrees almost entirely with Clarendon ; but whenever he thinks he is going to be outbid by Palmerston, is disposed to urge some violent measures also.   He said he had a regular scene with Aberdeen the other day. After this Note (or whatever it was) had been discussed and agreed to in the Cabinet, and all settled, Aberdeen came into his room, and began finding fault with it, and raising all sorts of objections, when Clarendon, out of all patience, broke out : "Really, this is too bad.   You come now, after it has all been settled in the Cabinet where you let it pass, and make all sorts of objections.   And this is the way you do about everything ; you object to all that is proposed, and you never suggest anything yourself.   What is it you want ? Will you say what you would have done ?"   He declares he said all this with the greatest vivacity, being really exasperrated.   Aberdeen had nothing to say, and knocked under. The truth seems to be that the attacks upon him in the newspapers (though they don't know it) are pretty well justified, and very little exaggerated ; nor is the idea of Palmerston's real inclination much mistaken.   They have by accident very nearly hit upon the truth. Aberdeen, it seems, objects particularly to have any Conference *here*, and if there is to be anything of the kind, it seems likely to take place at Vienna, where, however, somebody would be sent to assist, if not to supersede, Westmorland.

December 10*th.*—The Protocol just signed at Vienna brings the four Powers together again, and Austria not only signed it with alacrity, but Buol told Westmorland if the Emperor of Russia was found unmanageable, "Nous irons avec vons jusqu'au bout." The Turks are now desired to say on what terms they will make peace, and I expect they will reply that they will not make peace at all till the Principalities are evacuated. It seems very doubtful whether this fresh opening will lead to any result between two Powers so impracticable as the belligerents.

The Duke of Bedford has been endeavoring to persuade Lord John to reconsider the franchise in his Reform Bill, and Lord John tells him not to be afraid of its going too low, and that there is more chance of its appearing too niggardly. Aberdeen said it was not yet settled. Meanwhile, the Bill is drawn and privately printed. Lord John considers it to have been accepted by the Cabinet, and that he is sure of the acquiescence of the two principal dissentients—Lansdowne and Palmerston. The former went out of town, only saying that he hoped the landed interest would have its due share of influence. Palmerston's letter I have already mentioned; but the other day Lady Palmerston held forth to the Duke against the Bill, and said that it was not settled at all, but was still under the consideration of the Cabinet; from which he infers that Palmerston is still making or prepared to make objections and difficulties. Between Reform and the Eastern Question, I think this Government would infallibly be broken up but from the impossibility of another being formed. I am still persuaded Palmerston will not try a new combination, and break with all his old friends and associates for the purpose of putting himself at the head of some fresh but unformed combination. Great as his ambition is, he will not sacrifice so much to it, and risk so much as this would oblige him to do.

December 12*th.*—I begin to think that I am after all mistaken as to Palmerston's intentions, and that his ambition will drive him to sacrifice everything and risk everything, in spite of his age and of all the difficulties he will have to

encounter.   I have said what passed between the Duke of
Bedford and Lady Palmerston about Reform.   This morning the Duke of Bedford came here and told me he had
called on Clarendon on Saturday, when he said to Clarendon
that he was very uneasy about Palmerston, and thought he
was meditating something, though he did not know exactly
what he was at.   Clarendon interrupted him—"Certainly,
he is meditating breaking up the Government; in fact, he
told me so."   At this moment it was announced that two
or three foreign Ministers were waiting to see him, when
he abruptly broke off the conference, and they parted.   I
said, "Depend upon it, what Clarendon alluded to was not
the Reform Bill, but the Eastern Question; and it is on
that that Palmerston is making a stir."   The Duke said he
thought so to; indeed, he was sure of it, because Clarendon
did not trouble himself about Reform, and he had already
told him more than once what excessive trouble and annoyance he had had between the widely opposite views and
opinions of Aberdeen and Palmerston, and that he had only
been able to go on at all from the agreement between Lord
John and himself.   However, Lord John is to see Aberdeen
this morning, and his brother afterwards; and before the
day is over we shall learn something more of this disagreeable matter.   My belief is that the differences between Aberdeen and Palmerston have arrived at a height which throat-
ens a break up, and that, with reference to this occurring,
Palmerston is also going back on the Reform Question; that
if he does separate from the Government, he may reserve to
himself to work *both* questions.   But I refrain from further
speculations, as in a few hours they will be resolved into certainty of some sort.

    Panshanger, December 14th.—It turned out that Palmer-
ston had *struck* on account of Reform, and not (ostensibly,
at least) about foreign affairs.   John Russell was indignant,
and inveighed to his brother against Palmerston in terms of
great bitterness, saying he was absolutely faithless, and no
reliance to be placed on him.   Of this fact these pages contain repeated proofs, but I own I am amazed at his making
this flare up on the question of Reform.   But his whole
conduct is inexplicable, and there is no making out what he
is at.   The news of the Turkish disaster in the Black Sea is
believed, but Government will do nothing about it till they
receive authentic intelligence and detailed accounts of the

occurrence.[1] So Clarendon told Reeve on Monday, but he is disposed to take a decisive part if it all turns out to be true ; and yesterday Delane had a long conversation with Aberdeen, who owned that if the Russians (as they suppose) attacked a convoy of transports at anchor, it is a very strong case, and he thought war much more probable than it was a few days ago, and he did not speak as if he was determined in no case to declare it. This does not surprise me, in spite of his previous tone ; for he has gone so far that he may be compelled in common consistency to go farther.

London, December 17th.—Yesterday morning the news of Palmerston's resignation was made public. It took everybody by surprise, few having been aware that he objected to the Reform measure in contemplation. I received the intelligence at Panshanger, and as soon as I got to town went to Clarendon to hear all about it. He had been quite prepared for it, Palmerston having told him that he could not take this Bill. Clarendon says Palmerston behaved perfectly well, and in a very straightforward way from first to last. When he was invited to join the Government, he told Aberdeen and Lansdowne that he was afraid the Reform Bill would bring about another separation between them. When the time arrived for discussing the Bill, and John Russell proposed to him to be on the Committee, he said that he accepted, because, although he saw no necessity for any Reform Bill, and he entirely disapproved of John Russell's having committed himself to such a measure, he would not (as matters stood) absolutely object to any measure whatever, but would join the Committee, discuss it, state all his objections, and endeavor to procure such alterations in it as might enable him to accept it. Finding himself unable to do this with the Committee, he still waited till the measure had been brought before the whole Cabinet ; and when he found that his objections were unavailing, and that the majority of his colleagues were resolved to take Lord John's scheme, nothing was left for him but to retire. He said he might have consented to a smaller measure of disfranchisement, and the appropriation of the disposable seats to the

---

[1] [The Russian fleet in the Black Sea attacked and destroyed the Turkish squadron in the harbor of Sinope on November 30. This decisive event, which was at variance with the previous declarations of the Emperor of Russia, compelled the British and French Governments to order their fleets to enter the Black Sea and occupy it. The Russian fleet withdrew within the harbors of Sebastopol.]

counties, but to the enlarged *town* representation, and especially to the proposed franchise, he could not agree ; and
moreover he said he was not prepared, *at his time of life,*
to encounter endless debates in the House of Commons on
such a measure. The first time, Clarendon said, he had ever
heard him acknowledge that he had *a time of life.* Clarendon showed me a very friendly letter Palmerston had written to him, expressing regret at leaving them, and saying he (Clarendon) had a very difficult task before him,
and, "as the Irishman said, I wish yer Honner well through
it." He has never hinted even at any dissatisfaction as
to foreign affairs as forming a part of his grounds for resigning.

Clarendon said he thought it would ere long be the
means of breaking up the Government, and I thought so
too ; but, on reflecting more deliberately upon the matter, I
am disposed to take a different view of the political probability, and of the part which Palmerston will play. As I
have been so constantly opposed to him, and have both
entertained and expressed so bad an opinion of him on a
great many occasions, I feel the more both bound and inclined to do justice to his conduct upon this one, in which,
so far as I am informed, he really has been irreproachable.
The first thing which seems to have suggested itself to everybody is that he has resigned with the intention of putting
himself at the head of the opponents of Reform, of joining
the Derbyite party, and ultimately coming into office with
Derby, or forming, if possible, a Government of his own. I
doubt all this, and judge of his future conduct by his past.
If he had been actuated by selfish and separate objects of
ambition, and really contemplated transferring himself from
the Whig to the Tory party, or setting up an independent
standard, instead of breaking with this Cabinet on the question of Reform, he would certainly have done so upon the
Turkish war, as he easily could. He would then have gone
out amid shouts of applause ; he would have put the Government into an immense difficulty, and he, would have reserved to himself to take whatever course he thought fit
about Reform. He has acted much more honestly, but less
cunningly for his own interest, supposing that he has the
views and projects that are attributed to him. Lord Lansdowne is placed in great embarrassment, for he agrees entirely with Palmerston ; and if he acts consistently on his

5

own convictions, he will retire too—that is, cease to form a part of the Cabinet.   Clarendon expects he will do so.

Hatchford, December 21st.—On Monday when I came to town from Goodwood, where I went on Sunday, I found a letter from Lady Palmerston, very friendly indeed.   She said her son William had told her what I had said to him about Palmerston and his resignation, which had gratified her.   She then went on to explain why he had resigned, and why at this moment instead of waiting longer ; she said he would have accepted a Reform Bill, but wanted Lord John's to be altered, had proposed alterations, and written to Aberdeen to urge them, and upon Aberdeen's reply that his suggestions could not be taken, he had no alternative but to resign, and he had thought it fairer to the Government to do so at once, and give them time to make their arrangements, than to put it off till the last moment, when Parliament was on the point of meeting.   I confess I think he was right in so doing, and I was greatly provoked with the "Times" for attacking him, twitting and sneering at him, and finding fault with him for his desertion ; so provoked that I wrote a letter to the "Times," which appeared on Tuesday, with my opinion thereupon.

On Tuesday morning I was surprised at receiving a letter from Lord Lansdowne, entreating I would tell him what was said, and what was the state of public opinion about Palmerston's resignation, giving me to understand that he was as yet undecided what course he should adopt, and should not decide at all events till he had seen the Queen next Friday ; he also said that he had been greatly surprised at this happening "*so soon*, whatever might have been the case later, having occurred (marvellous to say) before there had been any decision taken by the Government as such on the whole matter, or any ground for me at least to think that issue would be joined upon it without that apparently essential preliminary." I wrote to him in reply all I had heard of the reports and notions floating about, and said I hoped his determination would eventually be not to withdraw, and I sent him Lady Palmerston's letter to me, which I said seemed to me somewhat at variance with his statement, in as much as Palmerston evidently considered that the matter was settled.   I don't understand, however, why he wrote to Aberdeen, if the question was still before the Cabinet, and not yet definitively settled.   Assuming Lord Lansdowne's statement to have been correct, Palmerston ought to have disputed the matter in the Cabinet, and if overruled there, he might have resigned, and not till then.

Delane went to Aberdeen, and asked him for his version of the affair, when he said at once he had no hesitation in saying that the Eastern Question was the cause and the sole cause of Palmerston's resignation; that he had all along been opposing what was done, and might have resigned upon it any time for months past, and that but for that question he would have swallowed the Reform Bill. Delane observed, if this was true, Palmerston had acted a very high-minded and disinterested part. It has been imprudent of the Government papers to insist so strenuously that Palmerston resigned solely on account of Reform, and that there was no difference on foreign policy, because this elicited a violent article in the "Morning Post," insisting in turn that the Eastern Question was the real cause of his retirement, and everybody will believe that this was inserted or dictated by himself. It is strange to find myself the advocate and apologist of Palmerston, when the preceding pages are brimful of censure of his acts and bad opinion of his character; but, whatever prejudices I may have or have had against him, they never shall prevent my saying what I believe to be true, and doing him ample justice, when I think that he is acting honorably, fairly, and conscientiously. This letter of Lord Lansdowne's has a little shaken my convictions, but still I am struck with the fact of his having refrained from resigning on the Eastern Question, when by so doing he might have damaged the Government immensely, and obtained for himself increased popularity and considerable power if these were his objects.

London, December 22d.—I went to town this morning, called on Lady Palmerston, found her in good spirits and humor, and vastly pleased at all the testimonies of approbation and admiration he has received. She exclaimed with exultation, "He is always in the right in everything he does," a position I could not confirm, and which I did not care to dispute. We then talked of the present crisis, when to my no small amazement she said that she saw no reason now why it should not be made up, and he should not remain, that he left the Government with regret, liked his office, and had no wish to quit his colleagues, but could not consent to such a measure as Lord John had proposed. She then recapitulated what she wrote to me, and complained of Aberdeen's having replied to Palmerston's note in such a style of peremptory refusal ; if he had only expressed regret at the difference, and proposed a fresh reference to the Cabinet, it might have been avoided. Still, she thought if they were disposed to be reasonable it was possible to repair the breach. Palmerston had never had any answer to his letter of resignation, no notice had been taken of it, nor had the Queen's acceptance of his resignation ever been conveyed to him. She talked with bitterness of the articles in the "Times," and of his resignation having been so hastily published, and said he had all along been very much dissatisfied with the conduct of the Eastern Question, and convinced that, if his advice had been taken at first, we should not be in our present dilemma and embarrassing position, and he had only consented to stay in the Government, when overruled in his suggestions, because he thought he could nevertheless effect some good by remaining, and tender essential aid to Clarendon. I expressed the strongest desire that the matter might be patched up, and entreated her to try and bring it about. Palmerston was gone out, so I did not see him.

I then went to the Office, and directly wrote to Graham, who was at the Cabinet, begging him to see me, and telling him I had reason to believe Palmerston was not disinclined to stay. Meanwhile Bessborough called on me, and told me all the reports from Marylebone and other parts of the metropolis, as well as the country ; all represented Palmerston's popularity to be immense, great enthusiasm about the Eastern Question, and profound indifference about Reform ; and he said there was a report that Palmerston was not unlikely to stay in, and that it was of the greatest importance that he should. He also said that Hayter declared there was no chance whatever of their carrying the Reform Bill in the House of Commons, especially if Palmerston headed the opposition to it.

He was hardly gone when Graham came to me. I told him all that had passed between Lady Palmerston and me, and entreated him to see if something could not be done. He said he himself should be too happy to bring it about if possible, and he had no personal ground of complaint, but he did not know how Lord John might be disposed, particularly as Palmerston in one of his letters had spoken in very uncourteous terms of him and Aberdeen. He said it was wonderful how Palmerston, quite unlike most men, was often intemperate with his pen, while he was always very guarded in his language. In reply to some of the things Lady Palmerston had said, he told me that the difficulty was that Palmerston's objections went to the *principle* of the measure, and though the details might still be open to discussion, it was impossible they could concede the principles of the measure without dishonor, and this was not to be thought of. That with regard to fresh reference to the Cabinet, Palmerston had stated all his objections to the Cabinet, when they had been considered and overruled, therefore another reference to the *Cabinet* would have been useless. He asked me if Palmerston was prepared to give up his objections. I said I presumed not, but he must understand that I did not know what he was prepared to concede or require, only what I had repeated, that he was not disinclined still to remain if the matter admitted of adjustment. He said the office was still open, and that the Cabinet then going on was not about filling it up, but entirely on the Eastern Question. After a good deal of talk we parted, he promising to see what could be done to bring about a compromise and reconciliation.

I then wrote to Lord Lansdowne telling him what had passed, and suggested that, as he is to see the Queen to-morrow, he should invoke her assistance to settle this affair, and so the matter stands. I am satisfied that at this moment Palmerston would prefer staying where he is to anything else, present or prospective, and he does not wish to embark in fresh combinations ; but it is impossible to say what he may not do under fresh circumstances, and if he is exposed to all the attractions of excessive flattery and the means of obtaining great power. If this Government should be overthrown, I see no other man who could form one. Derby is in such a deplorable state of health that I do not think he could possibly undertake it, and though Palmerston's difficulties would be great, they would not be insurmountable, and the very necessity of having a Government, and the impossibility of any other man forming one, would give him great facilities, and draw a great many people from various parties to enlist under him. It is, therefore, of immense importance that there should be a compromise now, for I am strongly of opinion that if there is not the Government will not be able to go on. What I fear is that, if a negotiation should be begun, the parties will not come to terms, and neither be disposed to make sufficient concessions. Lady Palmerston hinted at Aberdeen's going out, which she said he had always professed his readiness to do, but I gave her to understand that if he did, Lord John would insist on taking his place, which would not, I apprehend, be more palateable to Palmerston than the present arrangement.

December 24th.—I went to town this morning to hear what was going on. I found Granville who told me there was a negotiation on foot, conducted by Newcastle, who had been to Palmerston yesterday and discussed the matter. Palmerston was to give his answer at twelve to-day; Granville did not think any concessions about Reform were to be made to him, and nothing more than an agreement that the whole question should be reconsidered. He was to write a letter, saying there had been "a misunderstanding," said he was evidently dying to remain, full of interest in foreign politics, and could not bear to be out the way of knowing and having a concern in all that is going on, and probably by no means insensible to the difficulties of another position, that of being the leader of an Opposition, and still more to the having to form and carry on a Government should that Opposition be successful. All this I think was exceedingly probable. I then went to Clarendon, where I learned that Palmerston had given his answer, and that he meant to stay. He had written a letter, not exactly such a one as they could have wished, but which must do; and though it was not yet formally settled, it had gone so far that it could not fail now. Both Clarendon and Granville told me John Russell had behaved admirably, which I was glad to hear. Granville thinks Palmerston has no *rancune* against Aberdeen, but a good deal against John Russell. Granville said I had made a bad selection in writing to Graham on Thursday about Palmerston's staying in, as of all the Cabinet he was the man most against him, and most opposed to his return ; but Clarendon said for that very reason he was very glad I had addressed myself to Graham, and that I had since written him a strong letter, as I did yesterday, setting forth as forcibly as I could the expediency of a reconciliation and the danger of Palmerston's separating himself from them, and the infallible consequences thereof.

Walewski has been making a great flare up about the article in the "Times," stating that Dundas wanted to pursue the Russian fleet after Sinope, and that Baraguay d'Hilliers put his veto on the operation. Clarendon assured him the statement was inserted without his privity, and he had nothing to do with it. Walewski then asked him to authorise a formal contradiction in the "Globe," or to let it be officially contradicted in the "Moniteur." Clarendon declined the first, and advised against the latter course. I offered to speak to Delane about contradicting it in the "Times," which I afterward did. He said the fact was true, and he had received it from various quarters, and it was useless to contradict it; but there was no reason the "Moniteur" should not do so if they liked, so I sent him to Clarendon to talk it over and settle what was to be done to smooth the ruffled plumage of the French.

On Thursday at the Cabinet the resolution was taken which amounts to war. The French sent a proposal that the fleets should go into the Black Sea, repel any Russian aggression, and force any Russian ships of war they met with to go back to Sebastopol, using force in case of resistance. We assented to this proposal, and orders were sent accordingly. This must produce hostilities of some sort, and renders war inevitable. It is curious that this stringent measure should have been adopted during Palmerston's absence, and that he had no hand in it. It will no doubt render the reconciliation more agreeable to him. This incident of his resignation and return, which has made such a hubbub not only here but all over Europe for several days, is certainly extraordinary, and will hardly be intelligible, especially as it will hereafter appear that he has withdrawn his resignation with hardly any, or perhaps no, conditions. On looking dispassionately at it, it seems to me Palmerston and Aberdeen have both been somewhat to blame. Lord Lansdowne left town ten days or a fortnight ago, with a distinct understanding, as he affirms, that the question of the Reform Bill was not to be definitively settled till after Christmas, and though he was aware of Palmerston's objections, he had no idea he would take any decisive step till then. A few days after he was gone to Bowood, Palmerston wrote to Aberdeen, a most unnecessary and ill-judged act. Aberdeen—instead of referring in his answer to the above-named understanding, and giving no other answer, replies that he has consulted John Russell and Granville, who think that nothing can be proposed that will remove his objections, and that he agrees with them, on which Palmerston sends in his resignation in a letter described to be brief and peremptory in its tone. All these letters were wrong, and none of them ought to have been written. I see they (his colleagues or some of them) think Palmerston never had really any intention of quitting his post, but *more suo* tried to bully a little, not without hopes that he might frighten them into some concessions on the Reform Bill, and meaning, if he failed, to knock under, as he has so often done upon other occasions. I am much inclined to suspect there is a great deal of truth in this hypothesis, being struck by Lady Palmerston's mildness and abstinence from violence and abuse, and the evident anxiety of both of them for a reconciliation, and again by the very easy terms on which he has been induced to stay. There has been no exaction or dictation on his part, but, so far as appears at present, something very like a surrender.

CHAPTER V.

Lord Palmerston's Return—The Czar's Designs—Uncertain Prospects—A Dinner of Lawyers—Preparations for War—The Reform Scheme modified—Russian Preparations for War—Entry of the Black Sea—Intrigues of France with Russia—Attacks on Prince Albert—Virulence of the Press—Attitude of Russia—Reluctance on Both sides to engage in War—Prince Albert's Participation in Affairs of State—Opening of Parliament—Vindication of Prince Albert—Offer of Marriage of Prince Napoleon to Princess Mary of Cambridge—Publication of the Queen's Speech—The Hesitation of Austria—Justification of the War—The Blue Books—Popularity of the War—Last Efforts for Peace—The Emperor Napoleon's Letter—Lord John's Reform Bill—Difficulties arising—The Greeks—Objections to the Reform Bill—Postponement of the Reform Bill.

Bowood, December 26th.—I came here to-day through town, where I saw *en passant* Granville and Clarendon; received a letter this morning from Graham, telling me everything was arranged and Palmerston would stay, which of course I knew long before. Clarendon thought Newcastle had managed it exceedingly well, inasmuch as by this mixture of conciliation and firmness he had got Palmerston to write and withdraw his resignation, without any conditions; indeed, Clarendon considers that Palmerston has virtually acceded to all the provisions of Lord John's Bill to which he had objected. Whether his actions correspond with this idea we shall see hereafter. The letter he has written they say is "artful and cunning," but Aberdeen does not appear dissatisfied with it ; and as it is a considerable concession in him to write any letter at all, they are right not to quarrel about the expressions.   On the whole, I am now of opinion that Palmerston will be damaged by this proceeding.   Nothing could justify his resignation at such a crisis but a case of urgent necessity, and if he really was urged to it by such a necessity, he clearly could not be justified in recalling his resignation five or six days afterward, finding himself exactly in the same situation as he was in before it.   It seems to me that he is certainly on the horns of this dilemma, that he was either wrong in resigning or wrong in returning.   I told Lord Lansdowne so, but he did not say much in reply ; and I find the language of this place is all favorable to Lord Palmerston, which I presume to be from their sympathizing in his objections to Reform ; and they throw most of the blame on Aberdeen for writing to him the letter he did, in which no doubt he erred.   However, they are all very glad it is made up, and justly think that the less that is said about it hereafter the better.   I think now that some steps had been taken towards a reconciliation even before the Thursday when Lady Palmerston spoke to me, and the Queen knew on Thursday that the reconciliation was highly probable ; for she wrote to Lord Lansdowne that evening, and told him he need not come to Windsor on Friday, which letter he received just as he was going to set off.   The Tories and the Radicals are equally puzzled, perplexed, and disgusted, and do not know what to say.   They accordingly solace themselves with such inventions and falsehoods as it suits their several purposes to circulate.

Clarendon received a letter from Cowley while I was with him, in which he said he sent him a paper tending to show that the Emperor of Russia was bent upon the destruction of Turkey, and prepared to run every risk, and encounter any enemy, in the pursuit of that object.   This is, I think, very likely ; and what is equally likely that, *per damna per cædes,* and with much danger and damage to himself, he will accomplish the ruin of the Turk.   But all speculation must be vague and fallacious as to the results of such a war as is now beginning.

January 3d, 1854.—I returned from Bowood on Saturday, having had no conversation whatever on politics with Lord Lansdowne—and of course I sought none.   News came there that the Turks had accepted the proposal of the Allied Powers to enter into a negotiation, and we are now waiting to see what the Emperor of Russia will be disposed to do; but almost everybody thinks he will refuse to treat, and certainly he will never admit, as the preliminary condition of negotiation, that no former treaties shall be revived. The Cabinet meets to-day for the purpose, I conclude, of resuming the consideration of the Reform Bill. The only thing Lord Lansdowne did say to me was, that he had had several conversations with John Russell when he was at Bowood, and that he thought he had made an impression on him; he evidently expected that Lord John would make concessions in his Bill which might satisfy, or partly so, him and Palmerston.

January 5th.—I dined on Tuesday with the Chancellor, Lord Cranworth: an array of lawyers, the Chancellor of Ireland (a coarse, vulgar-looking man, with twitchings in his face), Lord Campbell, Alderson, Coleridge, and the Solicitor-General (Bethell); besides these Aberdeen, Graham, and one or two more men.

I sat next to Graham and had much talk. He said the Cabinet that morning had gone off easily, and he thought matters would proceed quietly now. Palmerston is quite at his ease and just as if nothing had happened, which was exactly like him. Graham thinks the Emperor of Russia is determined on war, and will not consent to negotiate; he said he had been as anxious as any man to maintain peace, but if we were driven to go to war, he was for waging it with the utmost vigor, and inflicting as much injury as we could on Russia, and that we might strike very severe blows. It was commonly supposed Sebastopol was unassailable by sea, but he was not satisfied of that, as they are not in possession of sufficient information to be at all sure about it, but that he did not know what a powerful fleet with the aid of steam could not accomplish. He was inclined to believe that such a fleet might force the entrance to the place and destroy the Russian fleets, but that it would probably cost many ships to effect such an operation. In discussing the probability of Russia and Turkey being brought to terms we agreed that the conditions accepted by the Turks should prove a sufficient basis. When I asked him whether this would not satisfy even Palmerston, and whether he would not be desirous of peace if it could be so brought about, he said he thought

not, that Palmerston's politics were always personal, and
that nothing would satisfy him now but to *humiliate* the
Emperor.

Yesterday afternoon I saw Clarendon at the Foreign
Office. He said the Cabinet went off smoothly enough, and
Palmerston did not appear dissatisfied ; confirmed what
Graham said of his easy manner—no awkwardness or reserve. Aberdeen had written to him in answer to his letter
recalling his resignation, saying he wondered he should have
thought the matter of the Reform Bill *final ;* and John Russell, when it was all over, called on him. The alterations in
the Reform Bill were principally these : to extend somewhat
the disfranchisement and to give more of the seats to the
counties (which was what both Lord Lansdowne and Palmerston wished), and to reduce the county franchise from 20
to 10, taking Locke King's plan, the town franchise to be
6*l.*, with three years' rating, as originally proposed. This
is intended to admit the working classes ; as Clarendon said,
the *principle* of the last Reform Bill having been to *exclude*
them, and this to *admit* them. It seems now that Lansdowne and Palmerston will not dissent from this plan,
though they do not like it. The various propositions were
put to the vote *seriatim* in the Cabinet and carried *nem.
diss.*, so that, instead of everything having been conceded to
Palmerston (as the lying newspapers proclaimed), nothing
has been ; and he has, on the contrary, knocked under.

Clarendon showed me the Note submitted to the Turkish
Government with the proposals as the basis of negotiations,
to which we have not yet received a formal answer ; but
from a confused telegraphic message they think the Turks
have accepted them. These terms will then have to go to
St. Petersburg. But meanwhile the notification to the Emperor of the orders to our fleets was to reach St. Petersburg
this day, and Clarendon thinks it exceedingly likely this will
produce an immediate declaration of war on his part. His
warlike preparations are enormous, and it is said that the
Church has granted him a loan of four and a half millions to
defray them. I told Clarendon what Graham had said to
me of Palmerston's disposition. He said he did not know,
but it was not unlikely, and quite true about personal motives always influencing his conduct ; and that he had always
pleased himself with the reflexion that the downfall of Louis
Philippe might be traced to the Montpensier marriage, which

had really been the remote cause of it.   Graham had told
me that Stratford was now really anxious for peace, for he
began to see the possibility of war bringing about the substitution of French influences at Constantinople in place of
Russian, and of the two he infinitely preferred the latter.
Clarendon confirmed this.

January 6th.—All going on very amicably in the Cabinet, and Pam and Johnny the best friends possible, cutting
their jokes on each other, and Palmerston producing all his
old objections to the Reform Bill just as if it was discussed
for the first time.   From what has been settled in regard to
the fleets at Constantinople I think we are running an enormous risk of some great catastrophe.[1]   It appears that
Admiral Hamelin declared it was impossible to enter the
Black Sea with safety, and Baraguay d'Hilliers agreed with
him.   Dundas was of the same opinion, but said he was ready
to go if ordered.   Stratford was not convinced of the danger
as Baraguay d'Hilliers was.   Before the opinion of the French
Admiral could reach Paris orders were sent out for the fleets
to enter, and though some discretion is left to the Admirals,
the orders are so precise that it is extremely probable they
will obey them in spite of the danger, great as it is ; for the
Black Sea is so dark they can take no observations, and so
deep it cannot be sounded, perpetual fogs (which make the
darkness), and no harbor where the fleets can take refuge.
If the fleets should meet with any serious disaster, the indignation and clamor here would be prodigious, and the most
violent accusations would be levelled at the Government.   It
would be said that they would not let the fleets go during
the summer and safe seasons, when they could have done
anything they pleased ; but, having allowed the Sinope affair
to take place, and failed to bring about peace, they now send
the fleets when they can do no good and prevent no mischief,
and only expose them to damage or destruction.

Broadlands, January 8th.—I came here on Friday ; nobody is here but the Flahaults and Azeglio ; I walked with

[1] [On November 30 the Russian fleet from Sebastopol attacked the Turkish
squadron in the harbor of Sinope and destroyed it.   It was this violent action
on the part of Russia that at once decided the British and French Governments
to occupy the Black Sea with their fleets.   The Russian ships withdrew within
the harbor of Sebastopol, which they never left again.   I believe that Admiral
Dundas and Admiral Lyons proposed to enter the Black Sea at once and inter-
cept the Russian vessels before they could reach Sebastopol, but this proposal
was overruled by the French officers, who were disinclined to act until they received peremptory orders from the Emperor.]

Palmerston yesterday and talked of the Turkish question. He thinks the Emperor will not declare war on receiving news of the orders to the fleets, but send some temporizing answer. He said that if these orders had been sent four months ago, the whole thing would have been settled, which may or not be true ; he is very confident of the success of our naval operations, and of the damage we may do to Russia ; he has never alluded to Reform or anything connected with it, and is in very good humor.

January 15th.—I have never yet noticed the extraordinary run there has been for some weeks past against the Court, more particularly the Prince, which is now exciting general attention, and has undoubtedly produced a considerable effect throughout the country. It began a few weeks ago in the press, particularly in the " Daily News " and the " Morning Advertiser," but chiefly in the latter, and was immediately taken up by the Tory papers, the " Morning Herald " and the " Standard," and for some time past they have poured forth article after article, and letter after letter, full of the bitterest abuse and all sorts of lies. The " Morning Advertiser " has sometimes had five or six articles on the same day all attacking and maligning Prince Albert. Many of these are very vague, but the charges against him are principally to this effect, that he has been in the habit of meddling improperly in public affairs, and has used his influence to promote objects of his own and the interests of his own family at the expense of the interests of this country ; that he is German and not English in his sentiments and principles ; that he corresponds with foreign princes and with British Ministers abroad without the knowledge of the Government, and that he thwarts the foreign policy of the Ministers when it does not coincide with his own ideas and purposes. He is particularly accused of having exerted his influence over this Government to prevent their taking the course which they ought to have done with regard to Turkey, and of having a strong bias toward Austria and Russia and against France. Then it is said that he is always present when the Queen receives her Ministers, which is unconstitutional, and that all the papers pass through his hands or under his eyes. He is accused of interfering with all the departments of government, more particularly with the Horse Guards, and specifically with the recent transactions and disagreements in that office, which led to the retirement

of General Brown, the Adjutant-General. Then he and the
Queen are accused of having got up an intrigue with foreign
Powers, Austria particularly, for getting Palmerston out of
office last year ; that she first hampered him in the Foreign
Office, by insisting on seeing his despatches before he sent
them off, and then that she compelled John Russell to dismiss him on the ground of disrespectful conduct to herself,
when the real reason was condescension to the wishes of Austria, with which Power the Prince had intimately connected
himself. Charges of this sort, mixed up with smaller collateral ones, have been repeated day after day with the utmost virulence and insolence by both the Radical and the
Tory journals. For some time they made very little impression, and the Queen and Prince were not at all disturbed by
them ; but the long continuance of these savage libels, and
the effect which their continual refutation has evidently produced throughout the country, have turned their indifference
into extreme annoyance. I must say I never remember anything more atrocious or unjust. Delane went to Aberdeen
and told him that immense mischief had been done, and that
he ought to know that the effect produced was very great
and general, and offered (if it was thought desirable) to take
up the cudgels in defence of the Court. Aberdeen consulted
the Prince, and they were of opinion that it was better not
to put forth any defence, or rebut such charges in the press,
but to wait till Parliament meets, and take an opportunity
to repel the charges there. One of the papers announced
that a Liberal member of Parliament intended to bring the
matter forward when Parliament meets, but I do not expect
he will make his appearance. At present nobody talks of
anything else, and those who come up from distant parts of
the country say that the subject is the universal topic of discussion in country towns and on railways. It was currently
reported in the Midland and Northern counties, and actually
stated in a Scotch paper, that Prince Albert had been committed to the Tower, and there were people found credulous
and foolish enough to believe it. It only shows how much
malignity there is among the masses, which a profligate and
impudent mendacity can stir up, when a plausible occasion
is found for doing so, and how "the mean are gratified by
insults on the high." It was only the other day that the
Prince was extraordinarily popular, and received wherever
he went with the strongest demonstration of public favor,

and now it would not be safe for him to present himself anywhere in public, and very serious apprehensions are felt lest
the Queen and he should be insulted as they go to open Parliament a fortnight hence. In my long experience I never
remember anything like the virulence and profligacy of the
press for the last six months, and I rejoice that Parliament
is going to meet and fair discussion begin, for nothing else
can in the slightest degree check it, and this, it may be
hoped, will.

January 16th.—The attacks on the Prince go on with
redoubled violence, and the most absurd lies are put forth
and readily believed. It is very difficult to know what to
do, but the best thing will be a discussion in the House of
Commons—if possible, in both Houses. It is now said that
Sir Robert Peel is going to raise one. Clarendon told me
yesterday that he should not be surprised if the Emperor of
Russia were to recall Brunnow and not Kisseleff, as he is
more particularly incensed against England, knowing very
well that we have acted consistently and in a straightforward
direction throughout, while the French have been continually vacillating, and have kept up a sort of coquetry with
him ; for example, Castelbajac congratulated the Emperor
on the Sinope affair, and said he did so as a Minister, a
soldier, and a Christian. A pretty Government to depend
on, and which our stupid and ignorant press is lauding to
the skies for its admirable and chivalrous conduct as compared to ours !

January 21st.—For some days past the Tory papers have
relaxed their violence against the Court, while the Radical
ones, especially the "Morning Advertiser," have redoubled
their attacks, and not a day passes without some furious
article, and very often five or six articles and letters, all in
the same strain. It is not to be denied or concealed that
these abominable libels have been greedily swallowed all
over the country and a strong impression produced. The
press has been infamous, and I have little doubt that there
is plenty of libellous matter to be found in some of the
articles, if it should be deemed advisable for the Attorney-
General to take it up. There can be little doubt that the
Tory leaders got alarmed and annoyed at the lengths to
which their papers were proceeding, and have taken
measures to stop them. The Radical papers nothing can
stop, because they find their account in the libels ; the sale

of the "Advertiser" is enormously increased since it has begun this course, and, finding perfect immunity, it increases every day in audacity and virulence. One of the grounds of attack (in the "Morning Herald" and "Standard" principally) has been the illegality of the Prince being a Privy Councillor. In reply to this I wrote a letter (in my own name) showing what the law and practice are, but incautiously said the argument had been advanced by a member of the *Carlton Club*, whereas it was in fact a member of the *Conservative*, and I had imagined the two Clubs were the same. This mistake drew down on me various letters, attacking and abusing me, and for several days the "Morning Herald" has been full of coarse and stupid invectives against me, supplied by correspondents, who, from the details in their letters, must be persons with whom I live in great social intimacy. They are, however, of a very harmless description, and too dull to be effective.

January 25th.—I wrote a letter in the "Times" (signed Juvenal), showing up the lies of the "Morning Advertiser," and how utterly unworthy of credit such a paper is. I find Palmerston and Aberdeen have come to an understanding as to what shall be said in the way of explanation, which is a good thing. It is not to be much, and they will tell the same story. · One faint ray of hope for peace has dawned. The Emperor on receiving our Note has not recalled Brunnow, but ordered him to ask for explanations, and he is only to withdraw if the answer is of a certain tenor. Clarendon told him he could not give him an answer at the moment, and Seymour had said in the P. S. to his last despatch, "For God's sake don't give Brunnow any answer for three days." It is clearly one of two things—the Emperor meditates making peace, or he wants to gain time. The fact is, *he has got the answer*, for our instructions to the Admirals (which were communicated to him) explain our intentions. In a few days more we must receive his reply to the pacific overture.

January 29th.—Brunnow has not received his answer, but is to have it on Tuesday, when I imagine he will announce his departure. Kisseleff has not had his either, and there is some disagreement as to the answers between us and the French Government. Clarendon has sent to Paris the answer he proposes to give, but the French wish not to give Kisseleff any answer at all. nor even to tell him what it is, but to send their answer through their Ambassador at Petersburg, to which Clarendon strenuously objects. This is only for the purpose of delay, the Emperor Napoleon being so reluctant to go to war, and anxious to put off the evil day as long as he can. It is not wonderful, for the accounts of the distress in France, the stagnation of trade, and the financial embarrassments, and the consequent alarm that prevails as well as suffering, make it very natural that the Government should shrink from plunging into a war the duration of which is doubtful, but the expense certain. Colloredo told me the other day that he thought Orloff's mission to Vienna afforded a good prospect of peace, because he was sure Orloff would not have accepted the mission unless he had really expected to bring it to a successful issue, but Clarendon told me last night that Orloff is only empowered to propose the same conditions which the Emperor originally insisted on, and that his real object is to detach Austria and Prussia from the alliance, by any means he can and by offering them any terms they please.

The attacks on the Prince are subsiding, except from the "Morning Advertiser," which goes doggedly on in spite of its lies being exposed. John Russell told me the other day that soon after the Queen's marriage she asked Melbourne whether the Prince ought to see all the papers and know everything. Melbourne consulted him about it, and he thinks that he consulted the Cabinet, but is not quite sure of this. However, Melbourne and Lord John (and the whole Cabinet if he did consult them) agreed that it was quite proper she should show him and tell him everything, and that was the beginning of his being mixed up in public affairs. Why he did not then begin to be present at her interviews with her Ministers I do not know, but that practice began when Peel came in, and Lord John said he found it established when he came back, and he saw no objection to it. He told me last night that the Queen had talked to him about the present clamor, which of course annoyed her, and she said, if she had had the Prince to talk to and employ in explaining matters at the time of the Bedchamber quarrel with Peel, that affair would not have happened. Lord John said he thought she must have been advised by somebody to act as she did, to which she replied with great candor and naïveté, "No, it was entirely my own foolishness." This is the first time I have heard of her acknowledging that it was "foolishness," and is an avowal creditable to her sense. Lord John said, when Lord Spencer was consulted on the matter he replied, "It is a bad ground for a *Whig* Government to stand on, but as gentlemen you can't do otherwise."

February 1st.—Parliament met yesterday, a greater crowd than usual to see the procession. The Queen and Prince were very well received, as well as usual, if not better ; but all the *enthusiasm* was bestowed on the Turkish Minister, the mob showing their sympathy in his cause by vociferous cheering the whole way. The night went off capitally for the Government in both Houses. In the Lords Derby made a slashing speech, but very imprudent, and played into Aberdeen's hands, who availed himself thereof very well, and made a very good answer, which is better to read than it was to hear. Derby afforded him a good opportunity of vindicating the Prince, which he did very effectively, and then Derby followed him and joined in the vindication, but he clumsily allowed Aberdeen to take the initiative. Clarendon answered Clanricarde, who was hostile, but not very bitter ; the former showed how much he suffers from want of practice and facility. I thought he would have failed in the middle, but he recovered himself and went on. Derby was put into a great rage by Aberdeen's speech, and could not resist attacking *me* (whom he saw behind the Throne). He attacked my letter (signed C.), in which I had pitched into the Tories for their attacks on the Prince. I saw his people turn round and look toward me, but I did not care a fig, and was rather pleased to see how what I wrote had galled them, and struck home. In the Commons the Government was still more triumphant. The Opposition were disorganized and feeble ; all who spoke on that side took different views, and very little was said. John Russell made a very good speech, and took the bull by the horns about the Prince, entered at once on the subject, and delivered an energetic vindication of and eulogium on him in his best style. It was excellent, and between his speech and Aberdeen's and all those who chimed in, that abomination may be considered to be destroyed altogether, and we shall probably hear no more of it.

This evening —— told me a secret that surprised me much. I asked him casually if he knew for what purpose Prince Napoleon was gone to Brussels, when he told me that he was gone to try and get King Leopold to use his influence here to bring about his marriage with the Princess Mary, the Duke of Cambridge's sister ; that for a long time past Palmerston had been strongly urging this match with the Queen, and had written heaps of letters to press it, having been in constant communication about it with Walewski and the Emperor himself.   They had made such a point of it that the Queen had thought herself obliged to consult the Princess Mary herself about it, who would not listen to it.   The negotiator did not make the proposal more palateable, and he did not recommend himself the more, by suggesting that such a match was very preferable to any little German prince. It is incredible that he should have mixed himself in an affair that he could hardly fail to know must be very disagreeable to the Queen, besides that the Princess is not likely to sacrifice her country and her position for such a speculation, so hazardous and uncertain at best, and involving immediate obligations and necessities at which her pride could not fail to revolt.

February 2d.—The above story, put together with some other things, leads to strange conjectures about Palmerston, which seem to justify the suspicions and convictions of the Court and others about him.   I have before alluded to his intimate connection with Walewski, and the notorious favor with which he is regarded by the Emperor, who considers him as his great *appui* here.

Before proceeding I must, however, refer to another matter, which seems to have no connection with it.   There is always great anxiety on the part of the press to get the Queen's Speech, so as to give a sketch of it the morning of the day when it is made, and those who do not get it are very jealous of those who do.   There has been great bother about it on some former occasions, once particularly, because one of the Derbyites gave it to their paper, the "Morning Herald," it having been communicated in strict confidence, and according to recent custom, to the leaders of the party.   The other day Aberdeen refused to give it even to the "Times," and of course to any other paper, and he begged Palmerston not to send it to the "Morning Post," which is notoriously his paper.   Nevertheless, the Speech appeared in the "Times," and what seemed more extraordinary, in the "Morning Advertiser," the paper which has been the fiercest opponent of the Government, and the most persevering and virulent of the assailants of the Prince.   How these papers got the

Speech nobody knows, but as there were four dinners, at which at least a hundred men must have been present, it is easy to imagine that some one of these may have communicated it.   Delane has friends in all parties, and he told me that he had no less than three offers of it, and therefore he had no difficulty.   But how did the "Morning Advertiser" come by it?   It is politically opposed to both the Ministry and the Derbyites; but it must have got the Speech from some person of one or the other party, with whom it has some community of interest or object.   The run upon the Prince was carried on equally by the "Morning Herald" and the "Morning Advertiser" till within ten days of the meeting of Parliament, when the former was stopped; the latter never ceased.   I have heard it surmised more than once that these attacks proceeded from Paris, and were paid for by the Emperor Louis Napoleon, but I never could believe it.   The other day I met M. Alexandre Thomas at dinner at Marble Hill, and we came to town together.   He told me he had no doubt the abuse of the Prince was the work of the Emperor, and paid for by him.   It did not make much impression on me at the moment; but now, putting all these things together, I cannot help partaking in the opinion that the whole thing has been got up, managed, and paid for by Louis Napoleon, Walewski, and another person here.

Brunnow received his answer yesterday, with many civilities and regrets, *de part et d'autre*.   Orloff as we hear has failed in his mission to cajole the Austrian Government, but *non constat* that Austria will act a firm part against Russia. If she would only announce her intention to do so, the matter would probably be settled; for Russia would, as we believe, certainly come to terms, if she was sure of Austria acting against her, so that, in fact, Austria holds the decision in her own hands, and the greatest service she can do to Russia herself would be to compel her to surrender, as she may still do with an appearance of credit and dignity.

February 9th.—Nobody now thinks of anything but of the coming war and its vigorous prosecution.   The national blood is up, and those who most earnestly deprecated war are all for hitting as hard as we can now that it is forced upon us.   The publication of the Blue Books has relieved the Government from a vast amount of prejudice and suspicion.   The public judgment of their management of the Eastern Question is generally very favorable, and impartial people applaud their persevering efforts to avert war, and are satisfied that everything was done that the national honor or dignity required. I have read through the thick volumes, and am satisfied that there is on the whole no case to be made against the Government, though there are some things that might perhaps have been better done ; but what is there of any sort, or at any time, of which as much may not be said when we have been made wiser by experience and events ? These Books are very creditable in the great ability they display. As Lord Ellenborough said in the House of Lords, the case had been most ably conducted, both by Government and its agents. Clarendon's despatches are exceedingly good, and in one respect greatly superior to Palmerston's when he was at the Foreign Office : they are very measured and dignified, and he never descends to the scolding, and the taunts, and sarcasms in which the other delighted. Palmerston always wrote as if his object was to gain a victory in a war of words, and have the best of an argument ; Clarendon, on the contrary, keeps steadily in view a great political object, and never says a word but with a view to attain it. Stratford's despatches are very able, and very well written, but they leave the impression (which we know to be the truth), that he has said and done a great deal more than we are informed of ; that he is the real cause of this war, and that he might have prevented it, if he had chosen to do so, I have no doubt whatever. His letters have evidently been studiously composed with reference to the Blue Book, and that he may appear in a popular light. I find he has been all the time in correspondence with Palmerston, who, we may be sure, has incited him to fan the flame, and encourage the Turks to push matters to extremities. I should like to know what Palmerston would have said, when he was at the Foreign Office, if one of his colleagues had corresponded with any one of his Ministers abroad, in a sense differing from that in which he himself instructed him. The wonderful thing is the impunity which he continues to enjoy, and how, daring and unscrupulous as he is, and determined to have his own way, he constantly escapes detection and exposure. The good case which the Government has put forward, and the approach of war, have apparently extinguished or suspended all opposition, and the Session, which everybody expected to be so stormy and dangerous, bids fair to be as easy as possible. Great difference of opinion exists as to the wisdom of committing our Baltic fleet to Charles Napier. It was, however, decided at the Cabinet yesterday that he should have it,[1] and we have got a very powerful squadron ready. The war is certainly very popular, but I don't think its popularity will last long when we begin to pay for it, unless we are encouraged and compensated for our sacrifices by some very flattering successes.

February 15th.—Several days ago there was a short discussion in the House of Lords, in which the Government did not cut a good figure. Aberdeen made a declaration in favor of peace, saying "war was not inevitable," which produced an explosion against him, and it was so imprudent *in him*, and so calculated to mislead, that Clarendon insisted on his rising again and saying that no negotiations were going on, threatening to do so himself if Aberdeen did not. He complied, but the whole thing produced a bad effect, although there are no negotiations to which we are a party. Austria is making a new attempt with the Emperor, to which she was encouraged by Orloff before he went. We are satisfied with the conduct of Austria, but though she has rejected the Russian overtures, she will not engage to join us against Russia in certain contingencies. If she would do this, it would most probably settle the affair, and make the Emperor agree to reasonable terms.

This morning appears in all the newspapers the autograph letter of the Emperor Napoleon to the Emperor Nicholas, which has been so much talked of. If the Emperor of Russia at once closes with it, he will place us in a great dilemma, but it may produce peace. On Sunday Clarendon told me all about this letter. The Emperor took it into his head to write it, and sent a copy here for the approval of our Government. Clarendon made many objections, particularly to the suggestion of a simultaneous withdrawal of the Russian troops and the allied fleets, and to the separate negotiation of Turkey, two points we had all along laid great stress upon. Walewski returned the letter with the objections raised by us, and soon after informed Clarendon that the letter had been altered according to our suggestions, and the objectionable parts omitted ;

---

[1] [There was a question of appointing Lord Dundonald, a far abler man; but he was seventy-nine, and besides he made it a condition that he should be allowed to destroy Cronstadt by some chemical process of his own invention.]

but he did not bring him the amended letter. Clarendon wrote to Cowley, and said what had passed, and that he was glad the alterations had been made, but was surprised the letter, as altered, had not been shown to him. Cowley told Drouyn de Lhuys, who said they had sent the letter to Walewski, and he could not think why Clarendon had not seen it, and he wrote to Walewski desiring him to take it to Clarendon. He did so, when, much to his annoyance as well as surprise, he found that they had only made a few verbal alterations, and left the really objectionable parts nearly the same as before. This may put us in a very awkward position. If the Emperor Nicholas agrees, we must either agree also to what we entirely disapprove, or disavow the French, and perhaps separate from them ; and it will be very embarrassing if the Government are asked in Parliament whether they were a party to this letter and its proposals. Clarendon told me this was only one of many instances in which the conduct of the French had been very *louche* and insincere. He thinks this more attributable to Drouyn than to his master, and Walewski has behaved with great loyalty and straightforwardness ; but hardly a week had passed that he has not had to complain of something done by the French Government in a separate or clandestine manner, or of some proposal which they ought not to make, ans this makes one of the difficulties of the position of which nobody is aware—a fine prospect to be married to such a people on a great question but what can be expected from the Government of such a Sovereign and such Ministers ? It confirms my long settled opinion, that we are always in extreme danger of being thrown over by them. With regard to the whole question (and omitting these details) the Emperor Napoleon has behaved well enough to us ; for he has adhered steadily to the joint policy, though it is his interest to maintain peace, and public opinion in France runs as strongly that way as here it runs in the opposite direction.

The day before yesterday John Russell introduced his Reform Bill, having resisted the most urgent representations and entreaties to postpone it. His speech was very tame, and nothing could be more cold than its reception. The few remaiks that were made were almost all against it, or particular parts of it, and it has excited no enthusiasm in any quarter. ·The prevailing impression is that it will not pass

if it is persisted in.   If any Reform Bill were to be proposed
at all, this does not seem to be a very bad measure, and some
points in it are good ; but nobody wanted any measure, and
the few Radicals who do, do not care for the particular
measures Lord John proposes, and ask for other things
which he will not hear of, so that he offends and alarms the
Conservatives without conciliating the Liberals, and he dis-
gusts and provokes his own adherents by his refusal to defer
his Bill.   Palmerston and his clique are sure to abuse it, and
to employ all the underhand means they can to stir up oppo-
sitiou to it.

February 20*th.*—John Russell answered the questions put
in the House of Commons about the Emperor Napoleon's
letter very dexterously, telling the truth, but in a way not
offensive to the Emperor.   He also made an excellent speech
on the debate on the Blue Books, brought on by Layard in
a bitter speech very personal against Clarendon.   The
House of Commons as well as the country are so execs-
sively warlike that they are ready to give any number of
men and any amount of money, and seem only afraid the
Government may not ask enough.   I expect we shall have
had quite enough of it before we have done with this question, and that our successes and the effect produced on
Russia will not be commensurate with the prevailing ardor
and expectation here.   The most serious of all difficulties
seems to be rapidly coming, the insurrection of the Greek
population ; and this is a matter which has already caused a
good deal of difference of opinion and debate in the Cabinet,
one half wanting to assist in putting down the Greeks, the
other half opposing this scheme.   The danger of attacking
the Greeks is, that we should thereby throw them at once
into the arms of Russia, whereas the true policy is to persuade
them if possible to be quiet, and induce them to look up to us
for protection and future support.   It is an element in the
question of great importance, and very difficult to deal with.
It is disgusting to hear everybody and to see all writers
vying with each other in laudation of Stratford Canning, who
has been the principal cause of the war.   They all think that,
if he had been sincere in his desire for peace, and for an
accommodation with Russia. he might have accomplished it,
but on the contrary he was bent on bringing on war.   He
said as much to Lord Bath, who was at Constantinople.
Lord Bath told him he had witnessed the fleets sailing into

the Black Sea, when he replied, "You have brought some good news, for that is *war*. The Emperor of Russia chose to make it a personal quarrel with me, and now I am revenged." This Lord Bath wrote to Lady Ashburton, who told Clarendon. I asked John Russell yesterday why he sent Stratford back to Constantinople. He said when he sent him the quarrel was between France and Russia, and only about the Holy Places ; they knew nothing there of Menschikoff's demands, and nobody was so qualified as Stratford to assist in settling the original affairs.

February 25th.—Last night Clarendon made a capital speech in the House of Lords, far superior to any he ever made before, and the best that has yet been made in defence of the Ministerial policy. He has got on wonderfully since the Session began, each of his speeches being much better than the preceding one, till at last he has made one of very great merit and power, as all admit. It was spirited, diguified and discreet. I began to fear he would never get over the misfortune of his want of early practice, and never excel as a speaker ; but this speech was so good, that I now hope he will, having acquired confidence and facility, speak up to the level of his ability. The rage for this war gets every day more vehement, and nobody seems to fear anything, but that we may not spend money and men enough in waging it. The few sober people who have courage enough to hint at its being impolitic and uncalled for are almost.hooted down, and their warnings and scruples are treated with indignation and contempt. It does now appear as if Austria had made up her mind to act with us, and that we may depend upon her. The French made known to the Austrian Government some time ago that, in the alternative of her taking a hostile part, she must expect to be attacked in Italy, and Clarendon early in the business pointed out to Colloredo all the serious consequences his Government had to apprehend in all parts of her dominions if she abetted Russia. With a war so popular, and supported cordially by Parliament, and a flourishing revenue and trade, Government would look round on a cloudless horizon, if it were not for the Reform Bill, which is a matter replete with uncertainty, difficulty, and danger. Nobody has an idea whether it will be carried in the House of Commons ; almost all the friends of Government want Lord John to withdraw it, and the Cabinet is divided on the subject, Lord John, Graham, and Aberdeen

6

being strongly in favor of pressing it on at all hazards, Palmerston violently against. He has now reproduced all his own objections and arguments against the Bill itself, as well as against forcing it on now, quite justified in the latter, but unjustifiable in the former course. Having once knocked under, and come back to office, consenting to swallow it, however reluctantly, it is too late to cavil at the Bill itself ; but he may consistently and properly unite his voice with the voices of all prudent and moderate men, and strenuously resist its being persevered in at this moment against a feeling and opinion which are all but universal. On the whole, I rather expect (but with much doubt) that Lord John will yield to the general sentiment, and consent to postpone it.

February 27th.—We are on the very verge of a Ministerial crisis. John Russell will listen to no reason about his Reform Bill, he insists on going on with it, and will have it that his honor and character demand that he should, and he says, "When the honor of public men is preserved, the country is safe." Clarendon dined here yesterday, and told me he thought Lord John would break up the Government. It is, in fact, a political duel between Lord John and Palmerston. —— thinks, and probably he is right, that at the last moment Palmerston will give way, but in the meantime he himself and all his followers and admirers are moving heaven and earth to defeat the measure, and to set up opposition to it—none more active than Hayter, Secretary to the Treasury, whose borough is one of those to be disfranchised. Everybody thinks Sir Edward Denny's motion will be carried, and if it is that Lord John will retire. If it were not for the difficulty about leading the House of Commons, this would not signify. I do not see how any arrangement is possible but that Palmerston should take the lead, but I do not know if this will not lead to other resignations. Clarendon is indignant at the state of things brought about by Lord John's obstinacy. He told me that Graham supported Lord John vehemently, but that Aberdeen took no strong part, and had behaved very well. Having accepted Lord John's Reform measure, and pledged himself to it, he was ready still to abide by that pledge. There never was such a *mess* as it all is. Clarendon is now very hot on this war, which he fancies is to produce great and uncontemplated effects. He says for very many years past Russia has been the great incubus on European improvement, and the real cause of half the calamities that have afflicted the world, and he thinks a great opportunity now presents itself of extinguishing her pernicious influence, and by liberating other countries from it, the march of improvement and better government will of necessity be developed and accelerated, and in this way civilization itself may be the gainer by this contest.   The Emperor Napoleon has earnestly pressed that our contingent should be put under the command of the French Marshal, to which we have altogether objected, and he has acquiesced, though reluctantly.   We have agreed on a sort of *mezzo termine*, viz. that, in the event of a battle in which both forces are engaged, they should be under one Commander-in-Chief, who must be the Frenchman.   Clarendon lamented that he had got no better Minister at Vienna than Westmorland just now, who though well meaning is nearly useless, as Colloredo is here, who will take nothing on himself.   He says Castelbajac at St. Petersburg has really not represented the French Government at all, nor acted in any way in conjunction with Seymour, but been all along a base courtier of the Emperor Nicholas.   Clarendon has again and again remonstrated through Cowley with Drouyn de Lhuys on this inconsistency, and Drouyn has always replied that he is quite aware of it, and has been at least as much annoyed at it as we could be, but that the Emperor would never allow him to be recalled.   I asked Clarendon whether, now that war really was inevitable, Aberdeen was more reconciled to it, and he said not at all ; he yielded to the necessity, but very sulkily, and in the discussions relating to it in the Cabinet he took no part, and evinced a total indifference, or rather disgust. However, he expressed great admiration of Clarendon's speech, which he said was the best he ever heard.   Lord John has sent to his brother to come to town, telling him a crisis is at hand.   Granville, who is all with Lord John, personally and politically a Reformer, and highly approving of this Bill, is going to him to-day to see if he can prevail on him to give way to the general opinion, and at all events to put him in possession of what is said and thought on the subject.

March 6th.—After a great struggle John Russell was persuaded to put off his Reform Bill, but only till the end of April, so that in a few weeks the same embarrassment will begin again.   The satisfaction at its being deferred at all is great and general, and everybody thinks that some expedient will be devised for putting it off again, when the time comes, and so that we shall be rid of it for this year. All the Cabinet was for putting it off, except Graham and Aberdeen. The former has devoted himself to Lord John, and goes heart and soul with him. Why Aberdeen took that view I cannot imagine, unless he wished to bring about a crisis, and to make his escape by favor of it. My own opinion at present is, that on April 27 Lord John will insist on bringing it on, and abide the consequences. The tenor of his speech, and still more that of Aberdeen, the same night, lead me to that conclusion. The Radicals with old Hume at the head of them, approved of the course Lord John took, but expressly with the understanding that he really meant and would bring it on at the period to which it was postponed ; and as he is sure to be incessantly urged on by his *entourage* to be firm when the time comes, and he will be very reluctant to encounter the indignation and re-proaches of his reforming friends and adherents, the chances seem to me to be in favor of the battle taking place. I think his speech on putting it off was not at all good, nor what he ought to have said. He laid himself open to an attack from Disraeli, which was very just, and he could not answer it. It was quite absurd to ground the postponement on the war and its exigencies, and it was moreover not the real and true reason. He put it off because he was impor-tuned by everybody to do so, because Hayter proved to him that he would infallibly be defeated, and because there was no other way of preventing a break-up of the Government. He might have anticipated Disraeli's philippic by reverting to what he had before said, repeating his own conviction that the war afforded no reason for not going on with the Bill ; but that he found so many of his own friends and such a general concurrence of feeling in the House of Commons on the other side, added to great indifference in the country, that he had thought it right to defer to those opinions, and give up his own to them. Such a defence of his conduct as this would have been more effective and more consistent with the truth, but it would have involved something like an acknowledgement of error, from which it is probable that his pride and obstinacy revolted, so he made what I think was a very bad speech. If he does bring it on again in April, I expect he will be defeated, and then retire. In any case his retirement will lead to Palmerston's elevation, as

leader of the House of Commons if Lord John goes alone, as
Prime Minister if Graham and Aberdeen go with him, and
there seems no alternative, unless Lansdowne can be induced
to replace Aberdeen, which some think not impossible, though
it would only be for a short time.

CHAPTER VI.

Dinner to Sir Charles Napier—A Ministerial Indiscretion—Doubts as to the Reform Bill—
Discontent of Lord John Russell—The Secret Correspondence with Russia—War de-
clared—Weakness of the Government—Mr. Greville disapproves the War—Divisions
in the Cabinet—Withdrawal of the Reform Bill—Blunder of the Government—The
Fast Day - Licenses to trade in War—Death of the Marquis of Anglesey—Mr Glad-
stone's Financial Failures—Dissolution of Parties—Mr. Gladstone's Budget—Lord
Cowley's Opinion of the Emperor's Position—The House of Commons supports the
War—Disraeli attacks Lord John Russell—A Change of Plans—Lord John Russell's
Mismanagement—Attacks on Lord Aberdeen—Popularity of the War—Government
Majority in the Lords—Attitude of the German Powers—A Meeting of the Liberal
Party—An Appointment cancelled—Expedition to the Crimea—English and French
Policy united in Spain—Close of the Session - The Character of Lord Aberdeen's Gov-
ernment—Effect of the Quarrel with Russia—Lord Palmerston's Resignation—Way-
wardness of the House of Commons.

London, March 13th, 1854.—The only event of recent
occurrence was the dinner given last week to Sir Charles
Napier at the Reform Club, with Lord Palmerston in the
chair. Everybody disapproves of the whole proceeding,
which is thought to have been unwise and in bad taste.
The only Ministers there besides Palmerston were Graham
and Molesworth, and the former made an excessively foolish,
indiscreet speech, which has been generally censured, and
to-night he is to be called to account for it in the House of
Commons. It is marvellous that a man of mature age, who
has been nearly forty years in public life, should be so rash
and ill-judged in his speeches.[1] There seems now to be a
better chance of John Russell's again putting off his Reform
Bill next month. There are not two opinions, except
among the extreme Radicals, of the expediency of his doing
so, and his best friends (including his brother) greatly regret

---

[1] [At this dinner at the Reform Club, Sir James Graham made an intemperate speech in which he said: "My gallant friend (Napier) says that when he
goes into the Baltic he will declare war. I, as First Lord of the Admiralty, give
my free consent to do so. I hope the war may be short, and that it may be
sharp." Sir Charles Napier's subsequent performances in the Baltic did not
at all o   p   to this heroic language, and did not add to his former reputation.]c rres ond

he did not put it off *sine die* instead of to another fixed day.

March 20th.—There has been a little episode, not very important, but which being entirely personal caused some noise in the world. About a week ago, or perhaps more, appeared the Petersburg "Gazette" with a sort of manifesto, complaining bitterly of the conduct of the British Government, which was said to be the more inexcusable as a confidential correspondence had taken place between the two Governments, and we had been all along informed of their views and intentions. The "Times" published this (as did all the other papers), and with it a peremptory denial of its truth, stating that John Russell, then Foreign Secretary, had sent an indignant refusal to the proposals made to us. Derby took this up in the House of Lords, complaining of State secrets having been imparted to the "Times," and insinuating his belief that Aberdeen had communicated them. Aberdeen denied the imputation with some resentment, and said that a flagrant breach of confidence had been certainly committed, and he had reason to believe that the culprit was a man formerly in the Foreign Office as clerk, though now out of it, who had been appointed by Lord Malmesbury. On this Malmesbury flared up, and desired to know his name, which Aberdeen said he did not know. On a subsequent night Malmesbury again took the matter up, and challenged Aberdeen to give the name and produce his proof. Aberdeen said he had received the information in a way which left no doubt on his mind of its truth, and he was willing to leave the matter to the gentleman himself, and if he denied it, he would acknowledge that he was mistaken and had been misinformed. By this time everybody was aware that a young man of the name of Astley was the accused party. He wrote a letter to Malmesbury denying the charge, but his letter was not very distinct. However, Malmesbury read it in the House, and called on Aberdeen to retract the charge, which he immediately and completely did, and there the matter ended ; but though the man is thus acquitted, and the Opposition papers abuse Aberdeen (who in fact was very imprudent to mention it), there seems no doubt that he really did babble about this matter, though it is very certain it was not from him the "Times" got its information.[1] The story

[1] [The indiscretion, such as it was, appears to have been that of Lord Aberdeen himself, and Lord Malmesbury quoted with a good deal of wit and *à propos*,

told is this : Astley talked of the correspondence to some person in a railway carriage. That person told it to Lady Ashburton, who repeated it to Clarendon. When thus talked of, it might easily get to the "Times;" and the only wonder is, it did not get into many other papers besides.

Lord John Russell continues in a very perplexed and uncertain state about his Reform Bill, and hesitates whether to bring it on or not next month. On one hand he is urged to do so by his little knot of domestic adherents, by Graham vehemently, and to a certain degree by Aberdeen ; on the other he is entreated and argued with by all the rest of his colleagues, by his brother, by Hayter, and by an immense majority of his political friends and supporters. Still he hesitates. He has got a notion, and others tell him so, that his character is concerned in bringing it on, and that he is bound to risk everything to maintain it. Graham is quite inconceivable ; always rash at one moment and cowardly at another, he is now, and on this question, in his rashest mood, and he has persuaded himself, and tries to persuade Lord John, that if he perseveres and is beaten (which he cannot disguise from himself is probable, if not certain) he will only have to go out in order to return in triumph as Prime Minister. If a dissolution is proposed, and the Cabinet consent to it, he fancies a new Parliament will give him everything ; if the Cabinet will not dissolve, Lord John, Graham and Aberdeen would retire, the Government be broken up, and Lord John would have Parliament and the country with him in forming another. All this I believe to be pure delusion. By persisting in his course he may, and probably would, break up the Government, but he would destroy himself, he would never be forgiven by his party or by the country at large for breaking up the Government at such a moment as this, and all his visions of success and power would soon be dispersed. Whatever else might happen, he would be excluded from office, probably forever. His discontent with his present position the more inclines him to take this hazardous step, because he wants a change of some sort.

The Duke of Bedford came to me the other day to tell me Lord John was determined no longer to go on as he now is, and it seems that he is moved principally by pecuniary

in the House of Lords, Sancho Panza's saying, "that a cask may leak at the top as well as at the bottom."]

considerations.[1] He is poor and has a large family. While he is in office he is obliged to incur expenses by giving dinners and parties, and this additional expense is defrayed by the Duke, but in a very unsatisfactory way. Lord John sends him a sort of estimate or account of his extra expenses, and the Duke pays the money. It is not surprising that Lord John dislikes such assistance as this, and though he never complains, he is probably mortified and provoked that his brother does not once for all give him a sum of money or a large annuity. Everybody else is amazed that he does not do this ; but though he is much attached to Lord John, admires and is proud of him, his love of money is so great that he cannot bring himself, even for his brother, to do a generous thing on a great scale. His colossal fortune, which goes on increasing every day, and for which he has no use, might well be employed in making his brother easy, and in buying golden opinions for himself ; but the passion of avarice and the pleasure of accumulation outweigh all such considerations, and he falls in readily with Lord John's notion of taking an office for the sake of its emoluments. The present idea is to have this matter settled before Easter, to turn out Mr. Strutt from the Duchy of Lancaster, and put Lord John in the place with an increased salary during his occupation of it. Nothing, however, is settled about it yet.

The publication of the secret correspondence with Russia has excited great interest, and does great credit to the Government, but it increases the public indignation against the Emperor, because it exposes the extreme duplicity of his conduct ; and as he must have been aware that such would be the inevitable result of publicity, it is difficult to conceive what induced him to provoke it, unless Walewski's conjecture is the true one. He thinks that the Emperor thought it would make bad blood between us and France, faneying that we had not imparted the correspondence to the French Government, in which he was mistaken, as we had done so.

March 29th.—The die is cast, and war was declared yesterday. We are already beginning to taste the fruits of it. Every species of security has rapidly gone down, and everybody's property in stocks, shares, etc., is depreciated already from twenty to thirty per cent. I predict confidently that,

[1] [Lord John at this time had a seat in the Cabinet and led the House of Commons without any office in the Ministry and without any salary.]

before many months are over, people will be as heartily sick
of it as they are now hot upon it.   Nobody knows where
our fleets and armies are going, nor what they mean to
attempt, and we are profoundly ignorant of the resources
and power of Russia to wage war against us.   As the time
for action approaches, Austria and Prussia grow more reluctant to engage in it.   The latter has proclaimed her neutrality, and unless some events should make a change in her
policy, I do not believe the former will ever be induced
to *act* with us and against Russia.   The Government here
are in a very weak unsatisfactory state.   They are supported
in carrying on war, but in every other respect they are
treated with great indifference, and appear to have very
little authority or influence either in Parliament or in the
country.   Nobody seems to have risen in estimation, except
perhaps Clarendon, who has done his work well and got
credit for it.   Palmerston and Graham have positively disgraced themselves by their dinner to Napier, and the foolish
speeches they made both there and in the House of Commons
afterward.   I do not know what Palmerston's popularity
might turn out to be if it should be tested by some change
which brought him forward, but he certainly has greatly lost
ground this year by his whole conduct from his resignation
down to this time.   Gladstone, the great card of the pack,
has forfeited by the failure of his financial schemes a good
deal of the credit he had obtained.   John Russell has offended everybody by his obstinacy about his ill-timed Reform
Bill, so that the Government does not stand very high, and
is only strong in the weakness of all other parties.   They
are constantly beaten on small matters in the House of Commons, which produces a bad effect.   Up to this moment
nobody knows what John Russell means to do about the
Reform Bill ; if he puts it off again, he ought to do so to-
morrow, when the discussion will take place about the declaration of war.

April 2d.—The debates in both Houses were marked by
great bitterness on the part of the Opposition, by Derby in
one House, and by Disraeli and Layard in the other.   The
war fever is still sufficiently raging to make it impossible
for any man who denounces the war itself to obtain a patient hearing.   Nobody ventures to cry out against it but
Bright in the House of Commons, and Grey in the House of
Lords, but already I see symptoms of disquietude and alarm.

Some of those who were most warlike begin to look grave, and to be more alive to the risks, difficulties, and probably dangers of such a contest. I can not read the remonstrances and warnings of Bright without going very much along with him ; and the more I reflect on the nature of the contest, its object, and the degree to which we are committed in it, the more uneasy I feel about it, and the more lively my apprehensions are of our finding ourselves in a very serious dilemma, and being involved in great embarrassments of various sorts. Among other misfortunes, one is the discredit into which Gladstone has fallen as a financier. Notwithstanding his extraordinary capacity, most people who are conversant with the subject of finance think he has greatly mismanaged his affairs, and suffered his notions or crotchets to get the better of his prudence, and consequently that he has prepared for himself as Chancellor of the Exchequer very great difficulties. His Budget last year was so popular, and his wonderful readiness and skill in dealing with everything relating to finance excited so much admiration, that his reputation was prodigious, and he was not only the strength of the Government, but was marked out as the future Prime Minister whenever changes took place. All this *prestige* is very much diminished ; and although his failures are in great measure attributable to accidents over which he had no control, many who are not unfriendly to him think he has been rash, obstinate, and injudicious, and no longer feel the same confidence in him which they did a short time ago.

April 3d.—The Duke of Bedford has just been here, as uneasy about the state of affairs and as disgusted and alarmed at the war as I am. He does not know what Lord John will do about the Reform Bill, but fears rather than hopes as to his intentions. Aberdeen had desired that there should be a Cabinet before Easter, and that Lord John should *then* determine what he would do, but Palmerston requested that the final decision should only be made on the 26th, the day before that on which it is to come on. What his object is they do not know. The Duke, in talking to Lord John, suggested the certainty of his breaking up the Government by bringing on his measure, and the enormous evil this would be, to which Lord John replied that if he knew what the internal state of the Government was, he would perhaps not think the evil of the dissolution so great.

The fact is that, when the Opposition, as is their wont, taunt
the Government with their internal disagreement and want
of cordiality and union, they are much more right than they
themselves are aware of.   The Duke told me that the Queen
told him the other day that she had herself written to Lord
John urging him to give up bringing on his Bill.   Not long
ago the Queen was in favor of proceeding with it, but circumstances were very different at that time.

April 15th.—This has been a week of excitement.   It
had been settled that on Monday last John Russell should
announce his intention with regard to the Reform Bill.   His
uncertainty still prevailed, and he got into such a state of
mind about it that it made him ill.   He could not sleep, and
was in a terrible state of vexation and perplexity.   Aberdeen
then proposed to him to give up the Bill, but to obtain from
the Cabinet a unanimous consent to his pledging them to
go on with it hereafter at some indefinite time.   On Saturday
there was a Cabinet, at which he made this proposal, but
Palmerston and Lansdowne both refused their consent, and
Lansdowne was in conversation with his friends very vehement about it.   Graham appears to have been reasonable at
this Cabinet, and ready to adopt the course proposed to Lord
John.   It was eventually settled that he should announce the
abandonment of the Bill, and make the best statement he
could, not pledging the *whole* Cabinet as he had intended ;
but before this he urged them to accept his resignation,
which they refused, and then Palmerston begged he might
resign, which they refused equally.   So matters stood on
Saturday night, and everybody believed it was settled.   On
Sunday Lord John's doubts and fears returned, his mind
became unsettled again, and he was inclined to withdraw
from his agreement and to go on.   To the surprise of the
whole House of Commons, when Monday came, Lord John
only said he would make his statement the next day.   Everybody saw something was wrong, and the curiosity and excitement were very great.   All Monday and Tuesday morn-
ings were passed in conferences and going backward and
forward, the Duke of Bedford being called in to work upon
Lord John.   He did his best, and at last on Tuesday morning he and others finally persuaded Lord John to adhere to
what had been determined and withdraw his Bill.   This he
did in a very good speech, full of an emotion and manifestation of sensibility which succeeded completely with the

House, and he was greeted with prodigious cheering and compliments and congratulations on all sides.   Nothing could in fact go off better, or in a way more gratifying to him, and the Government appears to have been strengthened by the operation.   His emotion was sincere because he is no actor, but it was in my opinion totally uncalled for ; and as there is but a step between the sublime and the ridiculous, it might just as well have appeared ridiculous ; but fortunately for him his audience were disposed to take it *au grand sérieux*.   Even his brother, partial as he is to him, takes the same view of this that I do, and has written to me that as Lord John has often been abused when he did not deserve it, so he has now been overpraised.

April 24th.—When this Government was formed, its principal merit was supposed to be its great administrative capacity, and the wonderful way in which the business of the country was to be done.   It has turned out just the reverse of what was expected, for they commit one blunder after another, and nothing can be more loose, careless, and ignorant than the way in which their business is conducted. All sorts of mistakes and embarrassments are continually occurring in the House of Commons, and I have had occasion to see ample proofs of what I say, in all that has been done and is doing about licences and trade permissions, consequent on the recent declarations and Orders in Council.[1] Now another matter has occurred, discreditable from the carelessness which has been evinced.   When it was thought necessary to order a fast day for the war, the Queen set her face against it.   She thought it very absurd (as it is) and objected *in toto*.   Aberdeen with some difficulty overcame her objections, setting forth that it had been done by George III., and that the religious part of the community would make a clamor if it were not done.   So she gave way, but still insisted it should not be a "fast," so they settled it should be a day of "humiliation."   The Archbishop of

1 [On the outbreak of the war a Committee of Council was summoned to consider and frame divers Orders with reference to the prohibition of the export of military and naval stores, the detention of Russian ships, and questions of trade in Russian produce. Dr. Lushington, the judge of the Admiralty, was a member of this Committee, besides several Cabinet Ministers. The French Government proposed to revert to the old system of licences to trade with the enemy ; but this proposal was not agreed to by Great Britain. The Russian trade was left open, except when stopped by blockade. Licences were issued by the Privy Council for the export of military and naval stores to neutral Ports.]

Canterbury fully concurred, and the proclamation was issued accordingly. But the other day the merchants took alarm, and represented that, as the word "fast" was omitted, the case would not come within the provisions of Masterman's Bill, and that bills of exchange, &c., would be payable on the day itself, and not the day before as provided by that Act, and that all sorts of confusion would arise. The Bank of England took the Solicitor General's opinion, who thought that such would be the law. A great difficulty arose, for time pressed. The Chancellor thought the case would stand, and was for taking the chance, but the Cabinet on Saturday decided that it would be safer to correct the error even thus late. Aberdeen went to the Queen and told her, and this afternoon there is to be a Council to turn the "day of humiliation" into a "fast day," in order that "merchants" bills may be presented on one day instead of another, and that banking operations may not be deranged. The ridicule this throws on the religious part of the question is obvious, and the effect it ought to have is to discontinue these preposterous observances, which all sensible people regard as a mockery and a delusion. But all this ought to have been provided for, and the law officers ought to have foreseen the consequences and advised accordingly. In Peel's time this never would have happened ; but with a nominal Premier, a Home Secretary who will give himself no trouble about the details of his office, and an Attorney General who does nothing, knows nothing of law, and won't attend to anything, it is no wonder that such things and many others occur.

To return to the question of trading licences. When we went to war, the Government, I believe very wisely, resolved to relax belligerent rights and give all possible latitude to trade, with no more restrictions and reservations than were essentially necessary for carrying on the war. But this resolution involved a revolution of the old system and the necessity of completely constructing a new one, and as they long ago knew war was inevitable, they ought to have well considered all this, and framed their regulations before they issued their orders. But not a bit of this was done, and the consequence was a state of unparalleled confusion and embarrassment, applications from all sides, and hosts of petitions for leave to export goods of different descriptions. The Government at last set to work to deal with these cases, but in a very irregular, unbusinesslike way. Some two or

three of them met in Committee at the Council Office, and
with the help of Cardwell, President of the Board of Trade
but not in the Cabinet, and Dr. Lushington, who has nothing
to do with the Government, they have contrived to scramble
through the business ; but the *laches* and indifference of those
who ought to be most concerned, and the loose way of proceeding, have been very striking.   Some would not come at
all, some came for a short time, different people attended on
different days, so that different opinions prevailed, and no
regular system was established.   The other day, on Cardwell's
saying these questions would be taken up as soon as Parliament met and Government called to account, I suggested to
—— that, such being the case, he ought to get Lord John
Russell to attend the Committee.   He said he would ask him,
" but John Russell could not bear details ; he doubted if he
would come, and, if he did, would be of no use, as he would
be sure to go to sleep ; " and this is the way business of the
greatest importance is transacted.

May 3d.—The death of Lord Anglesey, which took place
a few days ago, has removed one of the last and the most
conspicuous of the comrades of the Duke of Wellington, who
all seem to be following their commander very rapidly.   I
have lived with Lord Anglesey for so many years in such
intimacy, and have received from him such constant kindness, that I cannot pass over his death without a brief
notice.

A more gallant spirit, a finer gentleman, and a more honorable and kindhearted man never existed.   His abilities
were not of a very high order, but he had a good fair understanding, excellent intentions, and a character remarkably
straightforward and sincere.   In his youth he was notoriously
vain and arrogant, as most of his family were, but as he advanced in age, his faults and foibles were diminished or softened, and his virtues and amiable disposition manifested
themselves the more.   He distinguished himself greatly in
the command of the cavalry in Sir John Moore's retreat,
but was not employed in the Duke's army during the subsequent years of the Peninsular war.   In the Waterloo campaign he again commanded the cavalry, not, as was supposed,
entirely to the Duke's satisfaction, who would have preferred Lord Combermere in that post.   He lost a leg at the
battle of Waterloo ; for this wound Lord Anglesey was entitled to a very large pension, of which he never would take

a shilling. He was a great friend of George IV., and exposed himself to unpopularity by taking the King's part in the Queen's trial; but their friendship came to an end when Lord Anglesey connected himself with the Whig party, and when he went to Ireland as Lord Lieutenant he deeply offended the King by his open advocacy of the Roman Catholic cause in 1829. The Duke of Wellington, then Minister and about to give up the Catholic question, quarrelled with Lord Anglesey and recalled him. For some years past they had not been on very friendly terms. Lord Anglesey was jealous of the Duke, and used to affect to disparage his capacity both as a general and a statesman, and this political difference completed their mutual estrangement. These hostile feelings did not, however, last long; Lord Anglesey had a generous disposition, and was too fair and true to do permanent injustice to the Duke. I do not know how the reconciliation between them was brought about, but their temporary alienation was succeeded by a firm and lasting friendship, and the most enthusiastic admiration and attachment entertained by Lord Anglesey toward the Duke. For many years before the death of the latter, the two old warriors were the most intimate friends and constant companions, and every vestige of their former differences and antipathies was effaced and had given way to warm sentiments of mutual regard. When the regiment of Guards became vacant, King William sent for Lord Anglesey and announced to him that he was to have it; he of course expressed his acknowledgements; but early the next morning he went to the King and said to him that he felt it his duty to represent to him that there was a man worthier than himself to have the regiment, that Lord Ludlow had lost his arm at their head, and that he could not bear to accept that to which Lord Ludlow was so justly entitled. This remonstrance, so unselfish and honorable, was accepted, and the regiment was conferred on Lord Ludlow.[1]

May 7th.—The failure of Gladstone's Exchequer Bill scheme has been very injurious to the Government, and particularly to him. The prodigious applause and admiration with which he was greeted last year have given way to distrust and apprehension of him as a finance minister, and

[1] [George James, third Earl of Ludlow in the peerage of Ireland, and created a baron of the United Kingdom in 1831, was born December 12, 1758, and died April 16, 1842, when the titles became extinct. He served with distinction in the army, and was colonel of the 38th regiment of foot.]

the repeated failures of his different schemes have in a very short time materially damaged his reputation, and destroyed the prestige of his great abilities.   All practical men in the City severely blame him for having exposed himself to the risk of failure, and reproach him with the folly of trying to make too good a bargain, and by so doing exposing himself to the defeat he has sustained.   The consequences will not probably be serious, but the Government is weakened by it, and the diminution of public confidence in Gladstone is a public misfortune.

Next in importance to the financial difficulty is the Oxford Bill, with which Government have got into a mess, and they are struggling through the measure with doubtful and small majorities, having been beaten on an important point, and now quite uncertain if they shall be able to carry it.   I fell in with Graham yesterday, and spoke to him about these things, when he replied that Gladstone's failure was very unfortunate, but he had no doubt he would make a great speech in his own defence on Monday night.   With regard to Oxford, he said it was quite true that they could not depend on carrying the clauses of their bill, but that was because in the present state of the House "they could not carry a turnpike bill," they were absolutely without power, and "it was a state of things that could not go on."[1]   Last night I had a talk with Charles Wood on the same subject, and he said that the truth was, a revolution had silently been effected.   Parties were at an end, and the House of Commons was no longer divided into and governed by them ; and that the predicament in which this Government is placed would be the same with every other, and business could no longer be conducted in Parliament in the way it used to be. All this is in my opinion quite true, and what has long struck me.   Whether the extreme elasticity of our institutions, and the power of adaptation to circumstances which seems to pervade them, will enable us to find remedies and resources, and that the apparent derangement will right itself, remains to be seen.   But it is a condition of affairs full of uncertainty, therefore of danger, and which makes me very uneasy whenever I think of it.   It is evident that this Government is now backed by no great party, and that it

---

[1] [Lord John Russell introduced a bill to make further provision for the good government of the University of Oxford and the colleges therein, which passed both Houses, with some amendments, in the course of the session]

has very few independent adherents on whom it can count. It scrambles on with casual support, and its continuing at all to exist is principally owing to the extreme difficulty of forming any other, and the certainty that no other that could be formed would be stronger or more secure, either more popular or more powerful.

May 7th.—It is scarcely a year ago that I was writing enthusiastic panegyrics on Gladstone, and describing him as the great ornament and support of the Government, and as the future Prime Minister. This was after the prodigious success of his first Budget and his able speeches, but a few months seem to have overturned all his power and authority. I hear nothing but complaints of his rashness and passion for experiments; and on all sides, from men, for example, like Tom Baring and Robarts, one a Tory, the other a Whig, that the City and the moneyed men have lost all confidence in him. To-morrow night he is to make his financial statement, and intense curiosity prevails to see how he will provide the ways and means for carrying on the war. Everybody expects that he will make an able speech; but brilliant speeches do not produce very great effect, and more anxiety is felt for the measures he will propose than for the dexterity and ingenuity he may display for proposing them. Parliament is ready to vote without grumbling any money that is asked for, and as yet public opinion has not begun to waver and complain; but we are only yet at the very beginning of this horrible mess, and people are still looking with eager interest to the successes they anticipate, and have not yet begun to feel the cost.

May 10th.—Gladstone made a great speech on Monday night. He spoke for nearly four hours, occupying the first half of the time in an elaborate and not unsuccessful defence of his former measures. His speech, which was certainly very able, was well received, and the Budget pronounced an honorable and creditable one. If he had chosen to sacrifice his conscientious convictions to popularity, he might have gained a great amount of the latter by proposing a loan, and no more taxes than would be necessary for the interest of it. I do not yet know whether his defence of his abortive schemes has satisfied the monetary critics. It was certainly very plausible, and will probably be sufficient for the uninformed and the half-informed, who cannot detect any fallacies which may lurk within it. He attacked some of his opponents with great severity, particularly Disraeli and Monteagle, but I doubt if this was prudent. He flung about his sarcasms upon smaller fry, and this certainly was not discreet. I think his speech has been of service to his financial character, and done a good deal towards the restoration of his credit.

May 12th.—Cowley called on me yesterday, when we talked over the war with all its etceteras. He said the Emperor had been most reluctant to go into it, but was now firmly resolved to pursue it vigorously, and not to desist till he had obtained fair terms of peace ; above all things he is bent on going on with us in unbroken amity. Cowley thinks his political position as secure as any position can be in France, and certainly the country seems satisfied with his rule. His social position is unimproved and rather worse ; his marriage was a fatal measure ; he would have done far better if he could have married the Hohenlohe girl, who was dying to be Empress, and Cowley thinks the Queen was wrong to prevent the match. In that case the Court might have been very different. In the beginning, after his marriage, he attempted to purify it as well as he could, and to get rid of all the disreputable women about it ; but by degrees they have all come back again, and now they are more *encanaillées* than ever.

The French Government have given a strong proof of their goodwill to us by recalling Baraguay d'Hilliers from Constantinople, and not sending another ambassador, as they find none can possibly live on good terms with Stratford. Cowley says the war might have been prevented, he thinks, and particularly if Stratford had not been there. The Emperor would have made greater concessions if Stratford had not been at Constantinople, and another ambassador would have striven to preserve peace instead of being, as he was, bent on producing a war.

Edward Mills tells me Gladstone's recent speech has immensely raised him, and that he stands very high in the City, his defence of his measures very able, and produced a great effect ; he said he lately met Walpole, who told him he had the highest admiration of Gladstone, and thought he had more power than ever Peel had even at his highest tide.

May 28th.—I have been so much occupied with the very dissimilar occupations of preparations for Epsom races in the shape of trials, betting, &c., and the finishing and correction of an article in the "Edinburgh Review" on King Joseph's Memoirs, that I have had no leisure to think of politics, or to record what has been going on in the political world, nor in truth has much material been furnished either by domestic or foreign transactions. The last fortnight in Parliament has been going on much in the way in which the present Government always goes on, and Gladstone, whom I met at dinner the other day, repeated to me very much what Graham had said some time before, about their utter inability to carry their measures in the House of Commons. There is, however, one important exception to this rule, and that is one of vital importance. On everything which relates to the war, and on all questions of supply, they can do whatever they please, and have no difficulty, and encounter no opposition. Tom Baring's motion on Monday last exhibited a striking proof of this; he introduced it by an able speech, and he mustered all the support that could be got, and yet he was defeated by above 100. I met Disraeli in the street the next day, when he said, "Your Government is very strong." I said, the war which was supposed to be their weakness turns out to be their strength. They can carry everything which appertains to that, and nothing else. And so it is; no sooner do they get a great majority on some important question than they find themselves in a minority, perhaps more than one, on something else. John Russell got beaten on his Oaths Bill the other night, a victory which was hailed with uproarious delight by the Opposition, though leading to nothing, and only mortifying to John Russell personally. These defeats, however, do not fail to be morally injurious to the Government, and to shake their credit. It was an ill-advised measure, which drew down upon itself those who are against the Jews and those who are against the Catholics. Palmerston has been showing ill-humor in the House of Commons, and has ceased to be so very popular as he used to be there. They have great difficulty in getting on with the University Bill, and Gladstone told me the other night he was very doubtful if they should be able to bring it to a successful end. All the Tories and High-Churchmen are against it of course, and the Dissenters regard it with no favor because it does not do for them what they desire; so it is left to the support of the friends of Government and those who sincerely desire a good measure of reform for those bodies.

June 5th.—I was at Epsom all last week. In the beginning
of it or the week before there was a great passage of arms in
the House of Commons between John Russell and Disraeli,
not a very creditable exhibition, but which excited greater
interest than more important matters. Though Disraeli began the attack, Lord John threw the first stone of offence.
which he had better have let alone. In reply to this Disraeli
broke out with inconceivable violence and made the most
furious assault upon John that he could, saying everything
most offensive and provoking. Lord John made a rejoinder,
and was followed by Bright, whose speech was very hostile
and spiteful, and much more calculated to annoy Lord John
than that of Disraeli, though much less vituperative. Disraeli seems inclined to have recourse to his old tactics
against Peel, and to endeavor to treat John Russell, and
Gladstone, when he can, in the same way, hoping probably
to re-ingratiate himself with his own side by giving them
some of those invectives and sarcasms against their oppo-
neuts which are so congenial to their tastes. This course
will not raise him either in the House or in the country, and
he will not find in Lord John a man either so sensitive or so
vulnerable as Peel, and he can make out nothing against a
man who refuses place, patronage, and emolument, and gives
his gratuitous services at a great personal sacrifice because
he thinks it his public duty to do so. There is nothing new
in the condition of the Government ; they are very firmly
seated in their places, the House of Commons supporting
them by large majorities in all their great measures and
those which involve a question of confidence ; but having no
dependable majority on miscellaneous questions, nor even
knowing whether they can carry any measure or not, it is
idle to twit them with being a Government on sufferance
and Lord John with not "leading" the House of Commons.
A revolution has taken place in the conditions of the political existence of governments in general and their relations
with Parliament, and there is at present no likelihood that
any government that can be formed will find itself in different circumstances, or that the old practice by which a government could command the House of Commons on almost
everything will ever be restored, Whether the new system
be better or worse than the old may be doubtful, but governments must make up their minds to conform to it for the
present at least. In the course of the next few days the

division of the Colonial from the War Department will take place. There seems little doubt that Newcastle will elect to take the War Department, and Clarendon told me yesterday he thought he would be the best man for it, warmly praising his energy, industry, and ability, and his popular and conciliatory qualities. Their great object is to prevail on Lord John to take the Colonial Office, which I expect he will eventually do, but not without much reluctance and hesitation. Granville tells me he is in a dissatisfied state of mind, in which he will probably long remain, especially as his *entourage* will always do their best to foment his discontent.

June 11th.—Yesterday and the day before the world was made acquainted with the recent arrangements and appointments, which have been received with considerable disapprobation.[1] Nobody can understand what it all means, and why John Russell, if he was to take office, was to insist on so strange an arrangement, and such a departure from the invariable practice of putting a peer in the office of President of the Council. Nothing can be more ungracious than the air of the whole proceeding : he turns out Granville to make room for himself, and turns out Strutt to make room for Granville. It seems that they wanted him to be Colonial Secretary, but this he would not hear of on the score of his health, and as it is now admitted as an axiom that the leader in the House of Commons has enough to do, and can not efficiently discharge the duties of a laborious department, it was reasonable enough that Lord John should decline the Colonies ; but there seems no sufficient reason for his not taking the Duchy of Lancaster, for the more completely the office is a sinecure, the more consistent his taking it would appear. , However, he would be President of the Council or nothing. I have been amazed at his indelicacy and want of consideration toward Granville, who deserved better treatment at his hands. Granville has always been his steady and stout adherent, defending his Reform Bill, holding himself his especial follower in the Coalition Cabi-

---

[1] [Lord John Russell insisted on taking the office of Lord President of the Council, which has always been held by a peer, and to effect this change Earl Granville was removed from the higher office of Lord President to that of Chancellor of the Duchy. The Right Honorable Edward Strutt, who had been Chancellor of the Duchy with a seat in the Cabinet, was dismissed from office, but he was subsequently raised to the peerage with the title of Lord Belper. This transaction reflected no credit on the author of it, who consulted nothing but his own dignity and convenience.]

net, and ready to support him or go out with him if ncces-
sary.   It was therefore particularly odious to insist on foist-
ing himself into Granville's place, and inflicting on him the
mortification of going downstairs.   Granville behaved very
well about it, with great good humor, only anxious to do
whatever was best for the general interest, and putting aside
every personal consideration and feeling ; and his conduct is
the more meritorious, because he dislikes the arrangement
of all things.   Aberdeen behaved very kindly to him, and
told him, if he objected to the change, he would not consent
to it, and, cost what it might, would tell John Russell he
could not and should not have the place.   Granville proposed
to go out, at least for a time, but Aberdeen said he could
not spare him, and nothing could be more flattering than all
he expressed of his usefulness in the House of Lords, and of
the value of his services.   Personally, therefore, he loses
nothing ; for though he preferred the Council Office to the
Duchy, his conduct has raised him in everybody's estimation, and he will play a part even more prominent than he
did before.

One reason why Lord John should not have come to the
Council Office was the embarrassment he will be sure to find
himself in about questions of education, his reputation and
his antecedents, as well as his political connections, making
him peculiarly unfit to be at the head of the Education Department ; and I am inclined to agree with Vernon Smith,
who said to me the other day that it would infallibly end in
Lord John's bringing in next year an impracticable Education Bill and withdrawing it.   George Grey's coming into
office will be of use to the Government.   Newcastle's being
War Minister is sure to be attacked, and all the Palmerstonians are indignant that Palmerston is not in that place,
which never was offered him, nor was he consulted about the
arrangement.   I think there is still a considerable opinion
that he would make a good War Minister, though everybody
is aware he makes a very bad Home one, and the *prestige*
about him and his popularity are greatly worn out.   They
have been obliged to go back to the reign of Henry VIII. to
find a precedent for a commoner being President of the
Council, when they say there was one, but I don't know
who he was.

June 21st.—At St. Leonards last week for Ascot races,
where I got wet, and have been ever since confined with the

gout. The "Times," though by way of supporting the Government, went on violently attacking John Russell about the recent changes. Lord John was very well received in the City at his election, and at the opening of the Crystal Palace he was more cheered than anybody. This morning the Duke of Bedford came here and told me he had had a good deal of conversation with his brother about this business, to which he (the Duke) had been a stranger while it was going on. Lord John said that when the Government was formed he had proposed to Aberdeen that he should be President of the Council, but Aberdeen had objected on the score of its being so unusual, therefore he was only going back to his original design. He had an invincible repugnance to taking the Duchy of Lancaster or any inferior office. Both when the Government was formed and now, he would have much preferred to have kept aloof, and to have led in the House of Commons that section of the Whig party which would have followed him, but he found this impossible, and as the Government could not have been formed without him, and could not now go on without him, he was obliged to sacrifice his own inclination. I said I could not conceive why he could not go on as he was till the end of the session, and then settle it ; that his pushing out Granville had a very ungracious appearance, and he would have done much better to take the sinecure office of the Duchy, it being quite absurd to suppose that he could be degraded by holding any office, no matter what. The Duke owned it would have been better to wait till Parliament was up before anything was done, and he regarded the question of the particular office much as I do.

There was a discussion in the House of Lords on Monday night on the war, when Lyndhurst made a grand speech, wonderful at his age—82 ; he spoke for an hour and a quarter with as much force and clearness as at any time of his life : it was greatly admired. Clarendon spoke well and strongly, and elicited expressions of satisfaction from Derby, after whom Aberdeen rose, and imprudently spoke in the sense of desiring peace, a speech which has been laid hold of, and drawn down upon him a renewal of the violent abuse with which he has been all along assailed. I see nothing in his speech to justify the clamor, but it was very ill judged in him with his antecedents to say what he did, which malignity could so easily lay hold of.

June 25th.—There never was such a state of things as that which now exists between the Government, the Party, and the House of Commons. John Russell made such a hash of it last week, and put himself and his Government in such a position, that nothing but the war, and the impossibility which everybody feels there is of making any change of Government in the midst of it, prevents the immediate downfall of this Administration. Last week John Russell opposed the motion for the abolition of Church rates in a flaming High Tory and Church speech. The motion was rejected by a slender majority, but his speech gave great offence to the Liberal party and his own friends. Immediately afterward came on the motion in the University Bill for admitting Dissenters to the University. This John Russell opposed again, although in his speech he declared he was in favor of the admission of Dissenters, but he objected to the motion on various grounds. The result was that he went into the lobby with Disraeli and the whole body of the Tories, while the whole of the Liberal party and all his own friends and supporters went against him and defeated him by a majority of 91. He took with him six or seven of his colleagues, and two or three of the underlings. Molesworth, Bernal Osborne, and some more stayed away, and some others voted in the majority. In the majority were found Christopher and a few Tories besides, who, however, only voted with the object and hope of damaging the bill itself and procuring its rejection in the House of Lords. Never was man placed in so deplorable and humiliating a position as John Russell, and nothing can exceed his folly and mismanagement in getting himself into such a scrape. The indignation and resentment of the Liberals are boundless, and I think he has completely put an extinguisher on himself as a statesman and as the leader of a party; they never will forgive him or feel any confidence in him again. There was a capital article on him and his proceedings in the "Times" yesterday, which was not acrimonious, like some others on him, and was perfectly just and true.

The victorious Liberals managed their affairs very ill. Instead of resting satisfied with a victory which must have been decisive (for after all the House of Commons had affirmed the principle of admitting the Dissenters by so large a majority, neither the House of Lords nor the University would have ventured to oppose it), they imprudently pressed

on another division [1] in which they were beaten, though by
a small majority, and this of course does away with a good
deal of the effect of the first division. Between the recent
changes which were universally distasteful, and his extraordinary maladroitness in these questions, Lord John is fallen
prodigiously in public favor and opinion, and while he is, or
has been till very recently, dreaming of again being Prime
Minister, it is evident that he is totally unfit to be the leader
of the Government in the House of Commons even in a subordinate post. He communicates with nobody, he has no
confidence in or sympathy with any one, he does not impart
his intentions or his wishes to his own political followers, and
does not ask to be informed of theirs, but he buries himself
at Richmond and only comes forth to say and do everything
that is most imprudent and unpopular.

The House of Commons is in a state of complete anarchy,
and nobody has any hold on it ; matters, bad enough through
John Russell, are made worse by Aberdeen, whose speech the
other night has made a great, but I think unnecessary clamor;
and Layard, who is his bitter enemy, took it up in the House
of Commons, and has given notice of a motion on it which
is equivalent to a vote of censure. Almost at the same moment Aberdeen, with questionable prudence and dignity,
gave notice in the Lords that on Monday he should explain
the speech he made the other night. Layard's design can
hardly be matured, because they never can permit a speech
made in one House of Parliament to be made the subject of
a motion and debate in the other. It is, however, incontest-
able that clamor and misrepresentation have succeeded in
raising a vast prejudice against Aberdeen, and that he is exceedingly unpopular.

The people are wild about this war, and besides the general confidence that we are to obtain very signal success in
our naval and military operations, there is a violent desire to
force the Emperor to make a very humiliating peace, and a
strong conviction that he will very soon be compelled to do
so. This belief is the cause of the great rise which has been
taking place in the public securities, and all sorts of stories
are rife of the terror and dislike of the war which prevail in
Russia, and of the agitation and melancholy in which the

[1] [It seems it was Mr. Walpole who insisted on the second division, which
he did for the express purpose of neutralizing the effect of the first, hoping to
get a majority, which he did, and it was rather dexterously done.]

Emperor is said to be plunged.　But the authentic accounts from St. Petersburg tell a very different tale.　They say, and our Consul just arrived from St. Petersburg confirms the statement, that the Emperor is calm and resolute, that his popularity is very great, and the Russians of all classes enthusiastic in his cause, and that they are prepared to a man to sacrifice their properties and their lives in a vigorous prosecution of the war.

July 9th.—It is remarkable that the Government are unquestionably stronger in the House of Lords than in the House of Commons, as has been clearly proved by the result of the Oxford University Bill.　Derby endeavored to alter it, and was completely defeated.　There were several divisions, in all of which the Government obtained large majorities, and at last Derby said it was evidently useless to propose any alterations, as the Government could do what they pleased in that House.　The session is drawing to a close ; that is, though it will last a month longer, all important business is over.　The Government will end it much in the same condition as they were in at the beginning of it, only that their weakness and want of popularity have been manifested in a thousand ways during the session.　Aberdeen's explanatory speech and the publication of his despatch of 1829 have given rather a turn to the current against him ; for though his violent opponents still snarl at him and abuse him, the impartial people begin to think he is not so bad as he has been represented, and the excessive absurdity of the charges with which he has been assailed begins to strike people.　There is still, however, a strong prejudice against him, particularly among the extreme Liberals, and I saw a long letter from Sir Benjamin Hall to the Duke of Bedford setting forth the discontent of the Liberal party and vehemently urging that the Government should be immediately modified, Aberdeen retire, and Lord John Russell again be Minister, with Palmerston as War Minister—perfectly absurd and impracticable, but showing what the notions are of the ultra-Radicals.　The Tories, agreeing in nothing else, concur with the Radicals in hating Aberdeen because he represents the Peel party, and is Minister as the successor of Sir Robert Peel, for whose memory their hatred is as intense as it was for his person when he was alive.　The war goes on without any immediate results, and without, as far as can be seen, a probability of the attainment of any signal or important successes. The foolish public here, always extravagant and impatient, clamor for attacks upon Sebastopol and Cronstadt, and are very indignant that these places are not taken, without knowing anything of the feasibility of such operations.   We now begin to believe that Austria is going to side actively with us, but we do not feel certain of it, nor shall we till she actually enters on the campaign.

July 19*th*.—Within a few days everything is changed. In respect to Austria, the intrigues of Russia with Prussia, and the determination of the King to do everything that he can or that he dares to assist his imperial brother-in-law, have had the effect of paralyzing the Austrian movements, and suspending the operation of her Treaty with Turkey. She cannot venture to declare war against Russia and to march her army into the Principalities while there is a large Russian force on the borders of Galicia, and the Prussians are in such an ambiguous attitude and disposition, that she can not only not depend upon Prussia to execute their defensive Treaty by protecting her dominions in the event of their being attacked by Russia, but she cannot depend upon not being taken in flank by Prussia as the ally of Russia. Clarendon told me on Sunday that it was impossible to make out what Austria was about, or what she really means to do. There is no doubt about Prussia, and he still inclines to believe that Austria's disposition to act with us is unchanged, but that she is compelled to act a cautious and dilatory part by her uncertainty as to Prussia.

On Monday John Russell convoked his supporters and quasi-supporters to a gathering in Downing Street, when he harangued them on the state of affairs and the difficulties of the Government, intimating the necessity of being better supported if the Government was to go on at all.   There are differences of opinion as to the way in which the meeting went off, and whether it was on the whole satisfactory.   The principal speakers were Bright, Vernon Smith, and Horsman, the two latter bitter enough against the Government. Bright, rather hostile, spoke well and alluded to Aberdeen in a friendly spirit, as did Hume.   The meeting gradually melted away, so that Lord John had no opportunity of making a reply, which was a pity, as he might have answered the objectors.   The best proof, however, that on the whole it was successful, was afforded by the fact that there was neither debate nor division on the War Secretary's estimate

moved for by Lord John that night.   All went off with the
greatest ease.   I am in hopes, therefore, that the Government
is somewhat in better plight than it was.

August 4th.—I have been out of town for the greater
part of the time since the 19th ultimo, at Goodwood, nearly
ten days.   Nothing very important has occurred in politics.
As the session has drawn toward a close, the Government
have, on the whole, done rather better in Parliament, that
is, the Opposition have been quite incapable of striking any
blows or doing them any injury.   The points that were
expected to be made against them entirely failed, and, with
the exception of one personal matter, they have had no difficulties or annoyances to vex them.   This matter was the case
of ——, the *dénouement* of which took place two days ago ;
after being Gladstone's private secretary for two years, this
gentleman was appointed by Newcastle, just before he gave
up the Colonies, to be Governor of South Australia.   The
appointment was criticised, but about ten days ago it was
called in question by the House of Commons, and at the
same time rumors were rife that he had been gambling in
the funds and had lost money ; he denied, and authorized
his friends to deny the imputation, but some of the Carlton
runners got scent of his transactions and followed it up with
such perseverance that he became alarmed, and thought himself obliged to prevent the shame and odium of detection by
confessing the fact.   The consequence was that the appointment was cancelled, and the whole matter explained and
discussed on Thursday night in the House of Commons,
when George Grey made a long statement.   The discussion
upon it was very creditable to the House, for there was no
personal animosity and no coarseness or inhumanity displayed, but, on the contrary, forbearance and good nature
toward the individual.   Any expectation of being able to
wound Gladstone through him has quite failed.   He is a
clever fellow enough and well educated, but he has been
very imprudent, and contrived at once to lose his place of
private secretary, his government, his seat in Parliament,
his character, and his money.

At last it does now appear as if Austria was going to join
us completely against Russia, and the invasion of the Crimea
is about to take place in complete ignorance of the means
of resistance and defence possessed by Russia, and whether
it will be a nearly impossible or comparatively easy enterprise.

Clarendon, when I saw him last Sunday, expressed great alarm at the state of affairs in Spain, from the weakness of Espartero, the difficulty of any cordial union between the military chiefs, so long rivals, and above all from the republican element which is so rife in Spain, and which may produce effects extending far beyond that country. He said that the French Government were acting in complete harmony and concert with us ; the Emperor is much alarmed at the state of Spain, but resolved to go with us in the policy of non-interference, and to take no part but such as we should take also. If he adheres to this wise course, it will cement the alliance between the countries, and bind us to him more than anything that could happen, and it will form a great and happy contrast to the policy of Louis Philippe and the conduct of Palmerston and Guizot.

August 14*th*.—The session closed on Saturday, and, all things considered, the Government wound it up tolerably well. Clanricarde, true to the last to his spiteful opposition, gave Clarendon an opportunity of making a parting speech on foreign affairs, of which he acquitted himself very successfully, and placed himself and the Government in a very good position as respects our diplomacy and the conduct of the war. But though all immediate danger is removed from the Government, and, unless they fall to pieces during the recess by any internal dissensions, they will probably go on unscathed, the state of affairs is very unsatisfactory, and pregnant with future troubles and difficulties. The Government in its relations with the House of Commons throughout the past session has been extraordinary, and I believe unprecedented. From the Revolution to the time of the Reform Bill, that is during 150 years, the system of Parliamentary government had been consolidating itself, and was practically established ; the Sovereign nominally, the House of Commons really, appointed the ministers of the Crown, and it was settled as an axiom that when the Government was unable to carry its measures, and was subjected to defeats in the House of Commons, its resignation was indispensable— not indeed that any and every defeat was necessarily fatal, because governments have often been beaten on very important questions without being ruined or materially weakened, but it was supposed that repeated defeats and Government measures repeatedly rejected implied the withdrawal of the confidence and support of Parliament so clearly that in the aggregate such defeats were equivalent to an absolute vote of want of confidence, which is in itself a sentence of political death. In former times the Crown was a power, and the House of Commons was a power, generally blended and acting harmoniously together, but sometimes resolving themselves into their separate elements, and acting independently, perhaps antagonistically, toward each other. In modern times, and more entirely in our own, this separate and independent action ceased, the Crown became identified with the majority of the House of Commons, and no minister, when he could no longer command that majority so as to be certain of carrying out all, or nearly all, his measures of government and legislation, could continue to be minister, and was obliged as a matter of course to surrender office to those who were in possession of, or could count upon, that command. The ministers were taken from the ranks of the Parliamentary majority, and when once appointed it was considered indispensable and certain that the same majority would place confidence in them, accept at their hands all the measures they should concert and propose, and support them against all hostile attacks, the spirit of party and combination suppressing all individual prejudices, crotchets, fancies, and partial or local influences. The Government and the party were bound by a sort of mutual allegiance to each other, and supposed to be, and usually were, animated by the same spirit and a communion of opinion and interest. Such were the general relations and such the normal state of things, liable to occasional variations and disturbances, bringing about various political changes according to circumstances. But the system was complete, and practically it worked well, and conduced to the prosperity and progress of the country.

When the great measure of Reform in Parliament was introduced in 1831, apart from all question of party struggles there was the still greater question considered by many reflecting people, whether the new Parliamentary and electoral system would be found compatible with the old practice of government by means of party and steady Parliamentary majorities. The Duke of Wellington in particular expressed his apprehension that it would not, and he put the question which has so often been quoted and referred to, "How is the King's Government to be carried on?" He did not, so far as I remember, develop his thoughts at the time, and argue the matter in detail, but it is very evident that what he anticipated was some such state of things as that at which we now appear to have arrived. For a long time his apprehensions appeared to be groundless, and certainly they were not realised by the course of events. In consequence of political circumstances which I shall not stop to specify and explain, notwithstanding all the changes which were effected, the governments contrived to go on without any insuperable difficulties, and without any striking difference from the way in which governments had been previously conducted. The popularity of the Reform Bill Administration supported them for a few years, and the Tory reaction, together with the great abilities of Sir Robert Peel, supported the Conservative Government for a few years more. Matters went on better or worse, as might be, till the great Conservative schism in 1846, which completely broke up that party, and produced a final separation between the able few and the numerous mediocrity of the party. Ever since that time the House of Commons has been in a state of disorganisation and confusion : the great party ties had been severed. After the repeal of the Corn Laws and the establishment of Free Trade it was difficult to find any great party principles which could be converted into bonds of union, and every day it became obviously more and more difficult to form any government that could hope to be strong or permanent. John Russell succeeded on the fall of Peel, but the Peelites warmly resented the conduct of the Whigs in Peel's last struggle, and, though they hated Derby and his crew much more, never gave Lord John's Government a cordial support.

Next came the quarrel between Palmerston and Lord John and the fall of the Whig Government. Many people, and Graham especially, were of opinion that a Derby Government *for a time* was an inevitable but indispensable evil, and after one abortive attempt at length a Derby Government was formed. From the beginning nobody thought it could last ; the wretched composition of it, its false position, and the mixture of inconsistency and insincerity which characterized it, deprived it of all respect, authority, and influence, and it was the more weak because divided and dissatisfied within, and because all the more honest and truthful of the party were disgusted and ashamed of the part they were playing. Thus feeble and powerless, despised by the public and detested by the Court, the first moment that the different parties and sections of parties combined to overthrow them, their destruction was inevitable, and after enjoying office for one year they fell.

It was easier to turn them out than to find a good and strong government to replace them. It was obvious that neither the Whigs nor the Peelites could form a government, still less Palmerston or the Radicals, and it became a matter of absolute necessity to attempt a coalition, which, whatever objections there might be to coalitions, would at least have the advantage of filling the several offices with able men.

When the Queen had a short time before, in anticipation of the event, consulted the Duke of Bedford as to whom she should send for when Derby resigned, he had advised her to send for Lord Lansdowne and Lord Aberdeen, being himself conscious that Lord John could not again form a government, at least not at that time. She did send for them, and each of them very sincerely and earnestly endeavored to persuade the other to accept the post of Prime Minister, and the task of forming a Government. Lansdowne was ill at the time, and while it is very doubtful whether anything would have induced him to come forward, his attack of gout was enough to insure his peremptory refusal, and nothing remained but that Aberdeen should make the attempt. The task was difficult and unpleasant, for it was impossible not to make many people discontented and mortified, inasmuch as places could not be found for all who had previously been in office, or who aspired to it, and it was no easy matter to decide who should be taken in, and who left out. Aberdeen resolved to make the coalition very comprehensive, and as much as possible to form a government which should represent the Opposition which had turned Derby out, but he put almost all the Peelite leaders into good offices, and the exclusions were principally on the Whig side. For a long time it was very doubtful whether John Russell would enter the Government at all, but Aberdeen was so well aware that he could not do without him that he announced his determination to throw up the Government unless Lord John consented to join. After much hesitation, and a struggle between his family and some malcontent hangers on who wished him to keep aloof, on one side, and the wisest of his political friends and colleagues who urged that it was his duty to come forward on the other, Lord John consented to lead the House of Commons, but without an office. He proposed indeed to take the Presidency of the Council, to which Aberdeen

objected, but gave him the choice of every other office.   He
said that if he could not be President of the Council he
would be nothing at all, and so it was settled.   Next came
the negotiation about Palmerston, who first refused, and
afterward, at the pressing solicitation of Lansdowne, agreed
to join.   Molesworth came in to represent the Radicals;
Monsell and Keogh (not in the Cabinet) represented the
Irish, and so the Coalition Government was completed.

Very strongly composed, it never, however, was so strong
as it looked.   The Ministers, Aberdeen, John Russell, Palmerston, having consented to act together, were too sensible,
too gentlemanlike and well-bred, not to live in outward good
fellowship with each other, but their respective and relative
antecedents could not be forgotten.   There could be no real
cordiality between Palmerston and Aberdeen, or between Palmerston and John Russell, and both the latter all along felt
uncomfortable and dissatisfied with their respective positions.
Lord John fancied he was degraded, and his flatterers endeavored to persuade him he was so, by joining a government of which he was not the head, and by serving under
Aberdeen.   Palmerston could not forget the long and bitter
hostility which had been carried on between himself and
Aberdeen upon foreign policy, and still less his having been
turned out of the Foreign Office by John Russell.   The
Whigs were dissatisfied that the Peelites, who had no party
to bring to the support of the Government, should have so
large a share of the offices, and above all the great bulk of
the Whig party could not endure that a Peelite should be at
the head of the Government, and of all the Peelites they most
particularly disliked Aberdeen, so that they yielded a reluctant allegiance, and gave a grudging and capricious support
to the coalition.

Nevertheless, the first session of Parliament was pretty
well got through, principally owing to Gladstone's successful Budget, the great ability he displayed in the House of
Commons, and the efficient way in which the public business was done, while the numerous measures of improvement which were accomplished raised the reputation of the
Government, and gave them security if not strength.   The
Session of 1853 closed in quiet, prosperity, and sunshine, but
during the recess clouds began to gather round the Government ; they were beset with internal and external difficulties.
John Russell became more and more discontented, and at

last he announced to Aberdeen that he was resolved not to meet Parliament again in his present position, and intimated his intention to be once more Prime Minister or to quit the concern.   In the meantime the Turco-Russian quarrel had begun, the hostile correspondence with Russia was in full activity, the public mind in a high state of excitement, the press bellowed for war and poured forth incessant volleys of abuse against the Government, but more particularly against Aberdeen, who was singled out as the object of attack, and the persevering attempts to render him unpopular produced a certain amount of effect.   The Cabinet became divided as to the mode of carrying on the dispute and the negotiations, some being for what were called vigorous measures, that is, for threats and demonstrations of force which could only lead to immediate war, while others were for exhausting every attempt to bring about an accommodation and preserve peace.   Something was known or suspected of these divisions, they were published and commented on with enormous exaggerations and the most unscrupulous violations of truth, and the Tory and Radical newspapers vied with each other in the violence of their denunciations of Aberdeen, and in a less degree, of Clarendon.

When this fury was at its height, the world was startled and astounded by the news of Palmerston's resignation.   It is needless to state here the history of that affair, which I have already recorded in ample detail.   It was in vain that the "Times" proclaimed that it was the Reform Bill and not the Eastern Question which was the cause of it.   The statement was scouted with the utmost scorn, and the public incredulity was confirmed when the "Morning Post," which was notoriously devoted to Palmerston, asserted the direct contrary.   Everybody imagined that the Government would go to pieces, that when Parliament met there would be prodigious revelations, and that the Eastern Question with its supposed mismanagement would prove fatal to the Coalition Cabinet.   The Derbyites were in raptures, and already counted on Palmerston as their own.   Great as had been the public surprise and the exultation of the Carlton Club at Palmerston's resignation, greater still was that surprise and the mortification and disappointment of the Carlton, when a few days afterward it was announced that Palmerston had changed his mind and was not going to resign.   Nobody could comprehend what it all meant, and ample scope was afforded to every sort of conjecture, and to all the statements and inventions that anybody chose to circulate. But as about the same time the Eastern affair progressed a step or two, and some energetic measures were adopted, the most plausible explanation was, that Palmerston had resigned because enough was not done, that the Government had been frightened into doing what he had before advised, and that, on their adopting his suggestion, he had consented to remain. In process of time the truth began to ooze out, but it never was completely known till Parliament met, and even then many people continued to believe that though the Reform Bill was the pretext, the Eastern Question was the real cause of Palmerston's conduct.

These threatening clouds cleared away. Aberdeen told Lord John nothing should induce him to resign after all the attacks that had been made on him, and he would meet Parliament and defend himself. Lord John gave up his demands, and consented to go on leading the House of Commons. Palmerston agreed to swallow the Reform Bill, and at length Parliament met. Everybody was ravenous for the Blue Books, which as soon as possible were produced. Their production was eminently serviceable to the Government, and though some criticisms were made, and there were some desultory attacks in both Houses, and the press continued to be as scurrilous and abusive as ever, the general impression was extremely favorable. Clarendon's despatches were highly approved of, and all fair and candid observers, including many who had found fault with the Government before, declared that they were perfectly satisfied that our policy had been wise and proper, and the whole of the negotiations very creditable to all who had been concerned in carrying them on. So little did the event correspond with the general expectation, that the Eastern Question, which had been considered to be the weak part of the Government, turned out to be its greatest strength; and the war which eventually broke out has been the principal cause of their being able to maintain themselves in power. It is now the fashion to say that if it were not for the war, they would have been turned out long ago. It is certainly true that their power in the House of Commons has been limited to all that concerns the war, in respect to which they have had no difficulty to contend with. The estimates have been granted without a semblance of opposition, and they

have received hearty and unanimous support in every measure and every demand requisite for carrying on the war,
nor, though exposed to some adverse criticism, have they
been seriously assailed with regard to their diplomacy or
their warlike preparations.

But while this, which is the most essential, has also been
their strongest point, on everthing else, without exception,
they have been almost powerless, and the House of Commons
has run riot with an independence and waywardness and a
caprice of which it would be impossible to find an example.
The Government has had no majority on which it could
depend, and it has never brought forward any measure
which it could count upon carrying through. Obliged to
withdraw many measures altogether, and to submit to the
alteration of others till they became totally different from
what they originally proposed, their defeats have been innumerable, and nobody seems to have the smallest scruple in
putting them in a minority upon any occasion; at the same
time it was very evident that the House of Commons was
determined that they should continue in office, for whenever any vital question arose, or any vote which could be construed into a question of confidence, and therefore involved
the existence of the Government, they were always sure of a
majority, and the Derbyite opposition, while they were able
to worry and insult them by partial defeats and by exposing
their general weakness, found themselves miserably baffled
whenever they attempted anything which had a tendency to
place the Government in serious embarrassment. The whole
conduct of the Session, and the relations of the Government
with the House of Commons, presented something certainly
very different from what had ever been seen before in the
memory of the oldest statesman, implied a total dissolution of
party ties and obligations, and exhibited the Queen's Government and the House of Commons as resolved into their separate
elements, and acting toward each other in independent and
often antagonistic capacities.   Disraeli was always reproach-
ing the Government with holding office on what he termed
the unconstitutional principle of not being supported by a
majority of the House of Commons, and of living from hand
to mouth ; but though this was a plausible topic, he knew
very well that no other government could be formed which
could exist otherwise, and that the House of Commons, while
it buffeted the Government about *au gré de ses caprices*, was

cept Dundas who gives credit to it. They are impatient for
the termination of Dundas's period of service, which will be
in December, when Lyons will command the fleet.

September 11*th.*—I went to The Grove on Friday, but
was brought up on Saturday by gout, and detained in London ever since. We had much talk about a variety of things.
The Prince is exceedingly well satisfied with his visit to the
Emperor. The invitation to Windsor appears to have been
publicly given in an after dinner speech. Clarendon said a
great deal about the Government, its prospects and its difficulties, and of the conduct and dispositions of different men
in it, that the Peelites had all behaved admirably, and he
has a very high opinion of Newcastle, who is able, laborious,
and fair. He does not see so much of Aberdeen as he did
last year while the question of peace or war was still pending. He and Aberdeen do not very well agree, and therefore Aberdeen does not come to the Foreign Office as he used
to do. I asked him in what they differed, and what it was
Aberdeen now wanted or expected. He said that Aberdeen
was quite of opinion that a vigorous prosecution of the war
afforded the best chance of restoring peace, and that he was
as eager as anybody for the expedition of Sebastopol, but he
was out of humor with the whole thing, took no interest in
anything that was done, and instead of looking into all the
departments and animating each as a Prime Minister should
do, he kept aloof and did nothing, and constantly raised objections to various matters of detail. In the Cabinet he
takes hardly any part, and when differences of opinion arise
he makes no effort to reconcile them, as it is his business to
do. In short, though a very good and honorable man, he is
eminently unfitted for his post, and in fact he feels this himself, has no wish to retain it, but the contrary, and only
does so because he knows the whole machine would fall to
pieces if he were to resign. John Russell Clarendon thinks
a necessity as leader of the House of Commons, but he is
disgusted with his perpetual discontent and the bad influence
exercised over him by his confidants, and he thinks he has
not acted a generous part toward Aberdeen in suffering him
to be attacked and vilified as he has been by his (John's)
followers and adherents, who endeavor to make a distinction
between him and Aberdeen, which is equally unconstitutional
on principle and false in fact. The same thing applies to
Palmerston, and they have neither of them stood forward as

health of both armies and of the prevalence of cholera both abroad and at home.   The French particularly, who have lost the most, are said to be completely demoralized and disheartened, and to abhor the war which they always disliked from the beginning.   My present impression is that we shall come to grief in this contest ; not that we shall be beaten in the field by the Russians, but that between the unhealthy climate, the inaccessibility of the country, and the distance of our resources, Russia will be able to keep us at bay, and baffle our attempts to reduce her to submission.

September 4th.—At The Grove for a couple of days, where I had much talk with Clarendon, and he showed me a great many papers about different matters : a very good letter written by Prince Albert to the King of Prussia, who had written to him a hypocritical letter, asking where the English and French fleets were going to winter, and whether he might depend on them in case he was attacked by Russia in the Baltic, which Clarendon said was a mere artifice to obtain knowledge of our plans, that he might impart them to the Emperor Nicholas, as he well knew he was in no danger of being attacked by Russia.   The Prince wrote an excellent answer, giving him no information, and entering into the whole question of Prussian policy without reserve. He starts to-day to Boulogne, invited by a letter from the Emperor himself, beginning "Mon cher frère," replied to very well and civilly by Prince Albert who began, "Sire et mon cher frère."   Clarendon said Aberdeen was as hot as any one upon the Crimean expedition.

They are not at all satisfied with Lord Raglan, whom they think oldfashioned and pedantic, and not suited to the purpose of carrying on active operations.   They wanted him to make use of the Turkish light cavalry, Bashi-Bazouks, who under good management might be made very serviceable, but he would have nothing to say to them ; and still more they are disgusted with his discouragement of the Indian officers who have repaired to the army, and who are, in fact, the most efficient men there are.   They look on General Brown as the best man there, and have great expectations of Cathcart.   It is very curious that neither the Government nor the commanders have the slightest information as to the Russian force in the Crimea or the strength of Sebastopol.   Some prisoners they took affirmed that there were 150,000 men in the peninsula, but nobody believes that, ex-quite determined to keep it alive, and not to allow any other to be substituted for it.   At present it is difficult to see how this state of things is to be altered, and time alone can show whether great parties will again be formed, and governments be enabled to go on as in times past, powerful in a consistent and continual Parliamentary support, or whether a great change must be submitted to, and governments be content to drag on a precarious existence, taking what they can get from the House of Commons, and endeavoring to strengthen themselves by enlisting public opinion on their side.

With regard to the prospects of this Government, much depends on the progress of the war ; for though they have done their part and are not responsible for failure of success, they are sure to be strengthened by success or weakened by failure.   But much depends also upon what passes in the Cabinet.   John Russell, whose mind is in a state of chronic discontent which was suspended for a time, is again becoming uneasy and restless, and will soon begin making fresh difficulties.   Then his Reform Bill, which he gave up so reluctantly, is still in his thoughts, and he will most likely insist upon bringing it forward again, a proposition which is sure to produce dissension in the Cabinet.

<hr/>

CHAPTER VII.

August 29th, 1854.—I have been out of town since the above was written ; at Grimston for York races, where Lord Derby was in high force and spirits, carrying everything before him at the races, and not a word was ever uttered on politics.   There is no news, but dreadful accounts of the

they ought to have done in Aberdeen's defence, and claimed
a joint responsibility with him in every act of the Government.   We talked over what could possibly be done if Aberdeen did retire, and I suggested that he (Clarendon) might
take his place, and that the rest would be more willing ·to
accept him for the head of the Government than any other
man.   He expressed the greatest disinclination to this idea,
to which he never could consent, but owned his present
office was extremely agreeable to him and deeply interesting.
Nevertheless, I do not think, if the case occurred and the
place was offered to him *consensu omnium,* that his scruples
would be insurmountable.

So certain are they of taking Sebastopol that they have
already begun to discuss what they shall do with it when
they have got it.   Palmerston wrote Clarendon a long letter
setting forth the various alternatives, and expressing his own
opinion that the Crimea should be restored to the Turks.
Clarendon is dead against this, and so, he told me, is Stratford.   At Boulogne the Emperor and Newcastle agreed that
the best course will be to occupy the Crimea and garrison
Sebastopol with a large force of English and French, and
hold it *en dépôt* till they can settle something definitive ; and
Clarendon leans to this arrangement, which will at least be
a gain of time.

London, September 19th.—At The Grove again last week,
where as usual I heard a great deal of miscellaneous matters
from Clarendon and read a great many despatches from
different people.   I asked him what the Prince had told him
of his visit to Boulogne, and what his opinion was of the
Emperor.   He said the Prince had talked to him a great deal
about it all at Osborne, and this is the substance of what
he said as far as I recollect it :   The Prince was very well
satisfied with his reception ; the Emperor took him in his
carriage *tête à tête* to the great review, so that they conversed together long and without interruption or witnesses.
The Emperor seems to have talked to the Prince with
more *abandon* and unreserve than is usual to him.   The
Prince was exceedingly struck with his extreme apathy and
languor (which corresponds with what Thiers told me of
him) and with his ignorance of a variety of matters which it
peculiarly behoved him to know.   He asked the Prince a
great many questions about the English Constitution and its
working, relating to which the Prince gave him ample and

detailed explanation, and Clarendon said that all that he repeated as being said to the Emperor was as good, sound, and correct as it possibly could be. The Emperor said that he felt all the difficulties of his own position, and enlarged upon them with great freedom, particularly adverting, as one of them, to the absence of any aristocracy in France. The Prince, in reply to this, seems to have given him very judicious advice ; for he told him that any attempt to *create* an aristocracy in France resembling that of England must be a failure, the conditions and antecedents of the two countries being so totally dissimilar ; that he might confer titles and distinctions to any amount, and so surround himself with adherents whom he had obliged, but that he had better confine himself to that and not attempt to do more. When they parted, the Emperor said he hoped it would not be the last time he should have the pleasure of seeing His Royal Highness, to which the Prince replied that he hoped not, and that he was charged by the Queen to express her hope that he would pay her a visit at Windsor, and give her an opportunity of making the Empress's acquaintance, to which the Emperor responded " he should be very glad to see the Queen at Paris." This *insouciant* reception of an invitation which a few months before he would have jumped at is very unaccountable, but it meant something, for it was evidently a *mot d'ordre*, because when the Prince took leave of Marshal Vaillant, he said he hoped he would accompany the Emperor to Windsor, where, though they could show no such military spectacle as the Emperor had shown him, they would do what they could, to which Vaillant replied, " We hope to see Her Majesty the Queen and Your Royal Highness at Paris." There seems no disposition at present to give him the Garter which is supposed to be the object of his ambition, and which Walewski is always suggesting.

Clarendon is extremely disgusted at the conduct of Austria and her declaration of neutrality, and he said that the complaints of the doings of the Austrians in the Principalities were not without foundation. Drouyn de Lhuys spoke very openly to Hübner on the subject, and pitched into the Austrian Government without stint or reserve, and Cowley sent a despatch in which all he said was detailed, with the addition that it was Drouyn de Lhuys' intention to embody it in a formal despatch to Bourqueney to be communicated to the Austrian Government.

September 22d.—The army has landed in the Crimea without opposition. It is difficult to conceive that the Russians should have been so utterly wanting in spirit, and so afraid to risk anything, as to let the landing take place without an attempt either by land or sea to obstruct it. They have a great fleet lying idle at Sebastopol, and though, if it had come out, its defeat and perhaps destruction would have been certain, it would have been better to perish thus, *vitam in vulnare ponens,* and inflicting damage on its enemy as it certainly might have done, than to remain ingloriously in harbor and wait to be taken or destroyed, as it infallibly will be when the town itself shall fall. Great indignation is expressed at the prospect of Napier's returning from the Baltic without making any attempt on Cronstadt, or to perform any exploit beyond the Bomarsund affair. He is detested by his officers, and they one and all complain that he has been so little adventurous, and maintain that more might have been done. The justness and correctness of this, time will show.

October 2d.—At The Grove on Saturday, where I generally pick up some scraps of information from Clarendon on one subject or another. On Saturday came the news that Sebastopol had been taken, which we did not believe a word of, but after dinner the same evening we got the telegraphic account of the victory gained on the 20th on the heights above the Alma, and yesterday Raglan's telegraphic despatch was published. It is nervous work for those who have relations and friends in the army to hear of a "desperate battle" and severe loss, and to have to wait so many days for the details and casualties. The affair does not seem, so far as we can conjecture, to have been very decisive, when only two guns and a few prisoners were taken. If it had depended on St. Arnaud, the expedition would have put back even after it had sailed; while actually at sea, St. Arnaud, who stated himself to be ill and unable to move, summoned a council of war on board the "Ville de Paris." The weather was so rough that it was determined that it would not be safe for Raglan to go, as with his own arm he could not get on board; so Dundas went, and General Brown, and some other officer deputed by Raglan to represent himself, together with the French Admiral. A discussion took place which lasted several hours. St. Arnaud strongly urged that the expedition should be put off till the spring, and he objected to all that was proposed as to the place of landing—in short, threw every obstacle he could in the way of the whole thing. Dundas and all the English officers vehemently protested against any delay and change of plan, and represented the intolerable shame and disgrace of putting back after having actually embarked, and their opposition to the French general's proposal was so vehement that he ended by giving way, rose from his sick bed, and consented to go on. He declared that he only agreed to the place proposed for landing in consequence of the urgent representations of his allies, and this he wrote home to his own Government. He is a very incapable, unfit man, and Clarendon told me that his own army recognized the great superiority of Raglan to him, and that the French were all delighted with the latter.

It seems that there was some misunderstanding as to the invitation given by the Prince to the Emperor at Boulogne, and the latter gives a very different account of what passed from that given by the Prince. The Emperor says that when he took leave of the Prince, he said, "I have not been able to give you such a reception as I could have wished, but you see I am only occupying an hotel; if you will come to Paris, where I should be delighted to receive the Queen, I could give her and yourself a more fitting reception;" and then, he says, the Prince invited him to Windsor, which he only seems to have taken as a civility unavoidable under the circumstances. It is impossible to say which account is the true one, but I rather believe that of the Emperor to be correct. Clarendon wrote this to the Queen, whose answer I saw; she said the intention was to make the invitation something between a cordial invitation and a mere civility, which the Emperor might avail himself of or not, according to his convenience. However, Her Majesty says she thinks the matter stands very well as it is, and she desires it may be notified to the Emperor that the most convenient time for his visit, if he comes, will be the middle of November.

The Duke of Cambridge and Prince Napoleon have both been strongly opposed to the Crimean expedition; the latter, they say, does nothing but cry, and is probably a poor creature and a poltroon. I am surprised the Duke should be so backward; however, I hope to hear he has done his duty in the field. The clamor against Dundas in the fleet is prodigious, and the desire for his recall universal, but he

will stay out his time now, which will be up in December.
It is the same thing against Napier in the Baltic; he will
come away as soon as the ice sets in, and next year Lyons
will be sent in his place, as the war will then be principally
carried on in the north.

I think a storm will before long threaten the Government
from the quarter of John Russell, who has been for some
time at Minto. He wrote to Clarendon the other day, and
alluded to the necessity of having an autumn session, to
which Clarendon replied that he was not so fond of Parliament as Lord John was, and deprecated very much any such
measure. To this Lord John sent as odious and cantanker-
ous an answer as I ever read, and one singularly illustrative
of his character. He said that he was not fonder of Parliament than other people, and his own position in the House
of Commons had not been such as to make him the more so,
and that it had been rendered more disagreeable by the fact
of the two morning papers which professed to support the
Government being always personally hostile to him; but, he
went on, if we were fortunate enough to obtain a complete
success in the Crimea, he did not see why he should not be
at liberty to retire from this, which he thought the very
worst government he had ever known. Of course, if there
was any failure, he must remain to bear his share of the responsibility of it. Clarendon was immensely disgusted, but
wrote back a very temperate answer. He said that it was
equally difficult to go on with him and without him, for the
Whigs, though often very angry with him, would follow him
and would not follow anybody else. He thinks, however,
that he is in a state of mind to create all sorts of embarrassments, and particularly that he will propose to bring forward
his Reform Bill again, the consequences of which nobody
can foresee. He says Palmerston has behaved much better,
for though he might complain, having been disappointed in
certain objects he had (such as being War Minister), he has
made no difficulties, and been very friendly. Clarendon
confirmed what I had heard, that Aberdeen is in a state of
great dejection and annoyance at the constant and virulent
attacks on him in the press; his mind is dejected by the illness of his son, whom he never expects to see again, and this
renders him sensitive and fretful, and he is weak enough to
read all that is written against him instead of treating it
with indifference and avoiding to look at the papers whose

columns are day after day full of outrageous and random abuse.

October 8th.—The whole of last week the newspapers without exception (but the " Morning Chronicle" particularly), with the "Times" at their head, proclaimed the fall of Sebastopol in flaming and triumphant articles and with colossal type, together with divers victories and all sorts of details, all which were trumpeted over the town and circulated through the country. I never believed one word of it, and entreated Delane to be less positive and more cautious, but he would not hear of it, and the whole world swallowed the news and believed it. Very soon came the truth, and it was shown that the reports were all false. Anybody who was not run away with by an exaggerated enthusiasm might have seen the probability that reports resting on no good authority would probably turn out untrue, but the press took them all for gospel, and every fool follows the press. When the bubble burst, the rage and fury of the deluded and deluding journals knew no bounds, and the "Times" was especially sulky and spiteful. In consequence of a trifling error in a telegraphic despatch they fell on the Foreign Office and its clerks with the coarsest abuse, much to the disgust of Clarendon.

October 20th.—At Newmarket all last week ; very successful on paper, but won very little money. I am every day more confirmed in my resolution to get rid of my racehorses, but shall do it gradually and as opportunities occur, and then confine myself to breeding. The two objects I now have in view are this, and to get out of my office. I want to be independent, and be able to go where and do what I like for the short remainder of my life. I am aware that "man never is, but always to be blest," and therefore when I have shaken off racing and office I may possibly regret both ; but my mind is bent on the experiment, and I fancy I can amuse myself with locomotion, fresh scenes, and dabbling in literature *selon mes petits moyens.* Of politics I am heartily sick, and can take but little interest in either governments or the individuals who compose them ; with the exception of Clarendon I am on intimate and confidential terms with no one.

Ever since the news came of the battle of the Alma, the country has been in a fever of excitement, and the newspapers have teemed with letters and descriptions of the events that occurred. Raglan has gained great credit, and

his march on Balaklava is considered a very able and judicious operation.   Although they do not utter a word of complaint, and are by way of being fully satisfied with our allies
the French, the truth is that the English think they did very
little for the success of the day, and Burghersh told some
one that their not pressing on was the cause (and not the
want of cavalry) why the Russian guns were not taken.   The
French, nevertheless, have been well disposed to take the
credit of the victory to themselves.

Burghersh tells two characteristic anecdotes of Raglan.
He was extremely put out at the acclamations of the soldiers
when he appeared among them after the battle, and said to
his staff as he rode along the line, in a melancholy tone, "I
was sure this would happen."   He is a very modest man,
and it is not in his nature any more than it was in that of
the Duke of Wellington to make himself popular with the
soldiers in the way Napoleon used to do, and who was consequently adored by them.   The other story is that there were
two French officers attached to headquarters—very good fel-
lows—and that the staff were constantly embarrassed by the
inveterate habit Raglan had of calling the enemy "the
French."   He could not forget his old Peninsular habits.

In this war the Russians have hitherto exhibited a great
inferiority in their conduct to that which they displayed in
their campaigns from 1807 to 1812, when they fought the
battles of Eylau and Borodino against Napoleon.   The position of Alma must have been much stronger than that of
Borodino, and yet how much more stoutly the latter was
defended than the former.   Then their having allowed the
allies to land without molestation is inconceivable, and there
is no doubt that they might have attacked Raglan with
great effect as he emerged from the wood on his march to
Balaklava, but all these opportunities they entirely neglected.
I expect, however, that they will make a vigorous defence at
Sebastopol, and that the place will not be taken without a
bloody struggle and great loss of life.

Within the last few days a very important question has
arisen, the decision of which is a very difficult matter.   It
has been found that the commerce of Russia has not been
materially diminished, as their great staples (hemp, etc.) have
passed regularly through the Prussian ports, being brought
there by land, and it is now desired to devise some means of
putting an end to this exportation.   Clarendon has written

to Reeve about it, and Granville has obtained returns of the amount of hemp and linseed imported from Russia in past years and in the present, from which it appears that though there is a diminution it is not a very considerable one. The effect produced is only the inevitable consequence of the policy that was adopted deliberately and after great consideration at the beginning of the war; and how that policy is to be adhered to, and the consequences complained of prevented, is the problem to be solved. A blockade of the Prussian ports in the Baltic has been suggested—a measure, as it seems to me, very questionable in point of right and political morality, and certain to be attended by the most momentous consequences. Such a measure may not be without precedent, or something resembling precedent; but no Power with anything like self-respect or pride could tamely submit to such an outrage and such an insult, and as it would certainly afford a *casus belli*, Prussia could hardly, without abandoning all claim to be considered a great Power, abstain from declaring war *instanter;* and, whatever may be the sentiments of the Prussian nation and of the Germans generally with regard to Russia, it is by no means unlikely that such an arbitrary and imperious proceeding would enlist the sympathies and the passions of all Germans without exception in opposition to us, and to France if she became a party to it.

Newmarket.—Granville told me on Saturday morning that he was much alarmed at the disposition evinced by John Russell, and he expects an explosion sooner or later.

London, October 30th.—I returned last night and found a meeting of the Committee of Council settled for to-day, to consider the question of stopping Russian trade. Wilson has drawn up a paper in which he discusses the various modes of accomplishing this object,' and recommends that the Queen should forbid all trade with Russia, and prohibit the importation of Russian produce, and require certificates of origin for tallow, hemp, etc. John Russell writes word that he cannot attend the meeting, but is ready, though reluctant, to vote for Wilson's proposal. Granville and Cardwell are both dead against it, after a discussion at the Council Office at which the majority were against the proposal.

November 4th.—At The Grove from Wednesday to Saturday; the Walewskis, Lavradios, Granvilles, Azeglio, and Panizzi were there, a pleasant party enough. Walewski

told me a curious thing which he said he knew to be true.
We were talking of Nesselrode, and I asked if he knew what
his present position was with the Emporor. He said he
had been out of favor, but latterly had resumed all his influence and was very well at Court; that although in the beginning of the quarrel he had done his best to moderate the
Emperor and to preserve peace, it was nevertheless true that
he was perhaps the immediate cause of the war, which had
turned upon the acceptance or refusal of the Turkish modifications of the Vienna Note; that when they arrived the
Emperor was inclined to accept them, and that Nesselrode dissuaded him from doing so, advising him to adhere to the unaltered Note, not to listen to the modifications,
and insisting that, if he did so, the allies would compel the
Turks to waive their demands and to accept the Note in its
original shape. Walewski also said that the Emperor was
exceedingly incensed when the fatal circular, which made
the Vienna Note an impossibility, was published. He said
it was never intended for publication, and he found great
fault with the document itself, insisted on knowing by whom
it had been composed, and ordered the author to be brought
before him. The man (whose name I forget) was not to be
found, and events which pressed on drove it out of His Majesty's mind.

In the "Times" of yesterday appeared a very able letter
of Bright's with his view of the war, and the faults committed by our Government in respect to it, which letter as
nearly as possible expresses my own opinion on the subject.
I have never agreed with those who fancy that by mere blus-
ter we might have averted the war, but I think by more
firmness toward not only Russia but toward Turkey, and
still more toward the press and the public excitement here,
together with a judicious employment of the resources of
diplomacy, we might have prevented it. However, we are
in for it, and I not only see no chance of getting soon out
of it, but I do not feel the same confidence that everybody
else does, that we are certain to carry it to a successful
end.

London, November 13th.—At Worsley all last week; nothing was thought of but the war, its events and vicissitudes.
The tardiness of intelligence and the perplexity and agitation caused by vague reports and telegraphic messages drive
everybody mad; from excessive confidence, the public, al-

ways nose-led by the newspapers, is fallen into a state of alarm and discouragement. There is no end to the mischief which the newspapers and their correspondents have done, are doing, and no doubt will continue to do. There does not seem at this moment more reason to doubt that we shall take Sebastopol than there ever was, but the obstinate defence of the Russians indicates that its capture will not be effected without a tremendous struggle and great sacrifice of life. On the other hand, the Russians, instead of despairing of being able to hold the place, are full of confidence that they will be able to protract their defence, till our losses, and still more the weather, will compel us to raise the siege, and then they expect to compel us to abandon the Crimea altogether, and to make our re-embarkation a dangerous and disastrous operation. It is to be hoped that such a calamitous result is not in store for us, but there is no disguising from ourselves that we have got a much tougher and more difficult job on our hands than we ever contemplated, and that our success is by no means such a certainty as we have all along flattered ourselves that it would be ; for supposing we succeed in entering the place by storm, our work will then be not nearly done. Sebastopol is not invested, and when the Russian garrison finds itself no longer able to hold the place, there is nothing to prevent its evacuating it on the other side and effecting a junction with the main Russian army. We shall then have to reduce the forts on the northern side, to put the place in a state of defence, and commence a fresh campaign against Menschikoff in the centre of the Crimea. All this presents an endless succession of difficulties, demanding large supplies and resources of all sorts which it will be no easy matter to afford. We are now talking of sending every soldier we possess to the scene of action, and expending our military resources to the last drop, leaving everything else at home and abroad to take care of itself, a course which nothing but an extreme necessity can justify, while at the same time it can not be denied that having gone so far we can not stop halfway, and having committed so large a part of our gallant army in this unequal contest, we are bound to make the greatest exertions and sacrifices to prevent their being overwhelmed by any serious disaster. But this very necessity only affords fresh ground for condemning the rashness with which we plunged into such a war and exposed ourselves to such enormous

8

dangers, and incurred such large sacrifices for so inadequate an object.

It is not very easy to ascertain what the feeling is in Russia about the war, but there is reason to believe that the nobles are getting very sick of it, and are very discontented with the Emperor, not so much for having engaged in it as for the manner in which it has been carried on. At St. Petersburg there prevails an intense hostility to us, and great wrath against Austria, and instead of yielding, or any thought of it, the notion is that they mean to redouble their efforts next year, and bring into the field far greater forces than they have yet done. I perceive that the question of the disposal of the Crimea (when we get it) is still undecided. Some fancy that we ought to hold it, as a great advantage to have the power of offering it back to Russia when the question of peace arises. I am more inclined to the other view, of destroying the place, and if possible the harbor, and, after carrying off· or destroying all the ships, to abandon the peninsula and leave the Russians to reoccupy it if they please. This would be very consistent with the object with which the war was professedly undertaken, and the Crimea, without Sebastopol and without a fleet, would be no longer formidable to Turkey for many a year to come ; but no doubt there would be difficulty in this as in any arrangement, and much difference of opinion, not unlikely to produce dissension, among our allies and ourselves. There is good reason to believe that our late naval attack on the forts was a blunder, and that it did no good whatever. If Lyons had been in command, he probably would have declined to make it, and he could have ventured to exercise his own discretion, which Dundas could not. Then it was very badly arranged, and this was the fault of the French Admiral, who at the last moment insisted on altering the plan of attack, and (contrary to the advice of all his officers) Dundas gave way to him. In this, however, it is not fair to blame the English Admiral, who may have acted wisely ; for his position was delicate and difficult, and he had to consider the alliance of the countries and the harmonious action of the two fleets, as well as the particular operation.

November 14th.—Yesterday morning we received telegraphic news of another battle, from which we may expect a long list of killed and wounded. The affair of the 25th, in which our light cavalry was cut to pieces, seems to have been the result of mismanagement in some quarter, and the blame must attach either to Lucan, Cardigan, Captain Nolan who was killed, or to Raglan himself. Perhaps nobody is really to blame, but, if any one be, my own impression is that it is Raglan. He *wrote* the order, and it was his business to make it so clear that it could not be mistaken, and to give it conditionally, or with such discretionary powers as should prevent its being vigorously enforced under circumstances which he could not foresee, or of which he might have no cognizance.

It is evidently the plan of the Russians to wear out the allied armies by incessant attacks and a prolonged defence, sacrificing enormous numbers of men which they can afford, but considering that they gain on the whole by the disproportionate, but still considerable, losses they inflict upon us. It is quite on the cards, if they can keep up the spirit of their men, who show great bravery though they cannot stand against our's, that they may *cunctando restituere rem*, and compel us at last to raise the siege, and at St. Petersburg they are very confident of this result. Here, though people are no longer so confident and elated as they were, no human being doubts of our ultimately taking the town.

Yesterday we had rather an amusing scene in the Court of Exchequer at the nomination of sheriffs, which does not often supply anything lively. The Head of Caius College, Cambridge, and this year Vice-Chancellor, was on the list, and Judge Alderson vehemently protested against his remaining there. A long discussion ensued, in which almost everybody took part, whether his name should be kept on or not, and if he should be struck off the roll. At last Alderson moved he should be struck off, to which somebody moved as an amendment (a course I suggested) that he should be omitted, but not struck off. It was to be put to the vote, when I asked if Alderson himself could vote, whether it was not a meeting of the Privy Council, at which the judges *attended* to give in names for sheriffs, and that Privy Councillors only could vote as to the choice of them. Alderson vehemently denied this view, and asserted that it was no meeting of the Privy Council, the proof of which was that the Chancellor of the Exchequer took precedence of the Lord President, and that the puisne judges had a right to vote. They then desired to see the Act of Richard II., which the Chancellor examined and read out, and afterward he gave it as his opinion

that the judges could vote, and this opinion was acquiesced
in by the rest.   Ultimately they all agreed, Alderson included, to accept the course I had proposed, and the Doctor's name was omitted from the list, but not struck off the
roll.

November 15*th.*—The Duke of Bedford tells me that Lord
John is in a better frame of mind than was apprehended not
long ago, by no means satisfied with his own situation, and
complaining of much that appertains to the Government, but
conscious that his position can not be altered at present, and
not at all disposed by any captious conduct to break up or
endanger the Government itself.   With regard to Reform
he is extremely reasonable, feeling the difficulty of his own
antecedents in regard to the question ; he is ready to conform
himself to the necessities of the case, and does not think of
urging anything unreasonable and impracticable.   He is
naturally enough very anxious that the Government should
manage their affairs in Parliament better this year than last,
and not expose themselves to so many defeats and the mortification of having their measures rejected or spoilt, and his
notion seems to be that they should introduce and announce
fewer measures, only such as are urgent and generally desired, and such as they may reasonably expect to carry, and,
having taken that course, to stand or fall by them ; this is
the wisest and most becoming course, and I hope it will be
adhered to and succeed.   Its success depends very much on
Lord John's own conduct, and the way in which he treats
the Whig and Liberal party.   I hear nothing of the intentions and expectations of the Opposition, but Lyndhurst
tells me he considers them extinct as a party and in no condition to get into power.   He spoke very disparagingly of
Disraeli, and said his want of character was fatal to him,
and weighed down all his cleverness.

November 16*th.*—A telegraphic despatch arrived from
Raglan with account of the battle of the 5th,[1] from which
we learn only that we were entirely successful in repulsing
the Russian attack, but that our loss was very great.   Another long interval of suspense to be succeeded by woe and
mourning ; but besides the private misery we have to witness, the aggregate of the news fills me with the most dismal
forebodings.   Raglan says the Russian force was even greater

---

[1] [The battle of Inkerman was fought on November 5.]

than at Alma, and vastly superior to his own. Menschikoff says that he is assembling all his forces, and preparing to take the offensive, that their numbers are very superior, and he confidently announces that he shall wear us out, and that our army *cannot escape him*. I do not see how the siege is to be continued by an army itself besieged by a superior force and placed between two fires. The reinforcements cannot possibly arrive in time, and even if they were all there now, they would not be sufficient to redress the balance. I dread some great disaster which would be besides a great disgrace. Whether every exertion possible has been made here to reinforce Raglan, or whether anything more could have been done, I cannot pretend to say ; but if matters turn out ill there will be a fine clamor, and principally from those rash and impatient idiots who were so full of misplaced confidence, and who insisted on precipitating our armies on the Crimea, and on any and every part of the Russian territory, without knowing anything of the adequacy of our means for such a contest. To overrate the strength and power of the allies, and to underrate that of Russia on her own territory, has been the fault and folly of the English public, and if they find themselves deceived in their calculations and disappointed in their expectations, their rage and fury will know no bounds, and be lavished on everybody but themselves. In the height of arrogance few exceptions were found to those who imagined it would be quite easy to crumple up Russia, and reduce her to accept such terms as we might choose to impose upon her. All the examples which history furnishes were disregarded, and a general belief prevailed that Russia would be unable to oppose any effectual or prolonged resistance to our forces combined. When the successes of the Turks at the beginning of the war became known, this confidence not unnaturally became confirmed, and boundless was the contempt with which the Russians were treated ; and the bare idea of granting peace to the Emperor except on the most ruinous and humiliating terms was scouted. We now see what sort of a fight the Russians can make ; and though the superhuman valor and conduct of our troops still inspire confidence and forbid despair, it is evident that we have rashly embarked in a contest which from the nature of it must be an unequal one, and that we are placed in a position of enormous difficulty and danger.

November 23d.—Last week at Savernake and at The

Grange ; came back on Tuesday ; and yesterday morning arrived the despatches with an account of the furious battle of Inkerman, in which, according to Raglan's account, 8,000 English and 6,000 French resisted the attack of 60,000 Russians, and eventually defeated and drove them back with enormous loss, our own loss being very great. The accounts of Raglan and Canrobert do not quite agree as to the numbers engaged, but, admitting that there may be some exaggeration in the estimate of the numbers of the Russians and of their loss, it still remains one of the most wonderful feats of arms that was ever displayed ; and, gallantly as our troops have always behaved, it may be doubted if they ever evinced such constancy and heroism as on this occasion—certainly never greater. My brother lost his youngest and favorite son in this battle—a boy of 18, who had only landed in the Crimea a few weeks before, and who was in a great battle for the first and last time. This is only one of innumerable instances of the same kind, and half England is in mourning. It is dreadful to see the misery and grief in which so many are already plunged, and the universal terror and agitation which beset all who have relations engaged in the war. But the nation is not only as warlike as ever, but if possible more full of ardor and enthusiasm, and thinking of nothing but the most lavish expenditure of men and money to carry on the war ; the blood that has been shed appears only to animate the people, and to urge them to fresh exertions. This is so far natural that I, hating the war, feel as strongly as anybody that, now we are in it, and our soldiers placed in great jeopardy and peril, it is indispensable to make every possible exertion to relieve them ; and I am therefore anxious for ample reinforcements being sent out to them, that they may not be crushed by overwhelming force.

In reading the various and innumerable narratives of the battle, and the comments of the " correspondents," it is impossible to avoid coming to some conclusions which may nevertheless be erroneous ; and I have always thought that people who are totally ignorant of military matters, and who are living at ease at home, should not venture to criticise operations of which they can be no judges, and the conduct of men who cannot explain that conduct, and who are nobly doing their duty according to their own judgment, which is more likely to be right than any opinions we can form. With this admission of fallibility, it still strikes me that there was a lack of military genius and foresight in the recent operations. It is asserted that our position was open and undefended, that General Evans had recommended that precautions should be taken and defences thrown up, all of which was neglected, and nothing done, and hence the sad slaughter which took place. This was Raglan's fault, if any fault there really was. It is admitted that no tactical skill was or could be displayed, and the battle was won by sheer courage and firmness. Then Cathcart seems to have made a false and very rash move which cost his own life and 500 men besides. These are melancholy reflexions, and the facts prove that we have no Wellingtons in our army now.

November 26th.—Government have determined to call Parliament together on the 12th of December, though it stands prorogued to the 14th. This is done under the authority of an Act, 37th George III. ch. 120. In the present state of affairs they are quite right, and it is better for them to have fair Parliamentary discussion than clamor and the diatribes of the press out of doors. The "Times," as usual, has been thundering away about reinforcements, and urging the despatch of troops that do not exist and cannot be created in a moment. I had a great battle with Delane the other day about it, and asked why he did not appeal to the French Government, who have boundless military resources, instead of to our's who have none at all, and accordingly yesterday there was a very strong article entirely about French reinforcements.

In the course of our talk he did, I must confess, make some strong charges against the Government, and particularly Newcastle. He complained that after the expedition was sent to the Crimea they remained idle, and made no attempt to form an army of reserve or to send continual reinforcements to supply the casualties which everybody knew must occur, and this is true. Again, when he returned from the East[1] he went to Newcastle and urged him to make an immediate provision of wooden houses against the winter, which would in all probability be required, and he suggested that this should be done at Constantinople, where, all the houses being built of wood and the carpenters very skilful, it might easily be done at a comparatively small expense, and whence the conveyance was expeditious and cheap. His

---

[1] [Mr. Delane had gone to the theatre of war in the autumn, and was there with Mr. Kinglake, the brilliant historian of the Crimean War.]

advice was not taken ; nothing was done, and now that the winter is come, and the troops are already exposed to dreadful suffering and privation, the work is begun here, where it will cost four times as much and, when done, will require an enormous time to convey the houses to the Crimea, besides taking up the space that is urgently required for other purposes. I was obliged to confess that this was inexcusable negligence and blundering, and I repeated what had passed to Granville last night, who could make no defence, and only said that Newcastle, with many merits, had the fault of wishing to do everything himself, and therefore much was not done at all ; and that the fact was, nobody ever imagined we should be reduced to such straits, and there was a universal belief that all would have been over in the Crimea before this, and that such things would not be required. I am afraid Newcastle, who is totally ignorant of military affairs of every sort, is not equal to his post, and hence the various deficiences : nor is Sidney Herbert much better—very well both of them in ordinary times, but without the ability or the resource necessary to deal with such an emergency as the present.

I saw a letter yesterday from Charles Windham, a Q.-M.-General on poor Cathcart's staff, with an account of the battle, and he says that if, directly after the march on Balaklava, Sebastopol had been assaulted, it must have been taken. This corresponds with the reports of Russian deserters, who declare that there were only 2,000 men in the place after the battle of Alma. There is always so much difference of opinion and fault finding in such affairs that it is not easy to come to a sound conclusion thereupon.

November 29th.—My surviving nephew arrived from the Crimea yesterday morning. He gave me an account of the battle, and denies that General Cathcart ever refused, or was ever offered, the aid of General Bosquet, as has been stated. He says that Cathcart was not in command, and it was not therefore to him that the offer would have been made, and that Cathcart did not go into action till he was sent for by General Pennefather, when he got his Division out, and went on the field. He was killed quite early, about twenty minutes after he reached the field of battle. My nephew confirms what has been said about the non-fortification of the position, which seems to have been an enormous blunder, against which most of the Generals of Division remonstrated. He says Cathcart was opposed to the expedition to the Crimea, not thinking they were strong enough, and he strongly advised, and in opposition to Raglan, that the place should be attacked immediately after the battle of Alma, while the Russians were still panic struck, and before they had time to fortify the town on the south side. He says he left the army in good health and spirits, but not expecting to take Sebastopol this year. Their sufferings had not been very great, though it was a hard life—plenty to eat, but mostly salt meat. He thinks, though the French behaved very gallantly and their arrival saved the army, that they might have done more than they did ; and a body of them that came late on the field actually never stirred and did nothing whatever.

In the evening I met Clarendon at the Travellers', and had a long talk with him about all sorts of things. He has been much disturbed at the "Times," especially as to two things—its violent abuse of Austria and its insertion of a letter from the Crimea, reflecting severely on Prince Napoleon. With regard to Austria it is peculiarly annoying, because we are now on the point of concluding a tripartite Treaty which is actually on its way to Vienna, and in a day or two it will be decided whether she signs it or not ; and nothing is more calculated to make her hang back than such articles in the "Times." Then as to Prince Napoleon, it has annoyed the Emperor and all his family beyond expression, and to such a degree that Drouyn de Lhuys has written an official letter to Walewski about it—a very proper and reasonable letter, but still expressing their vexation, and entreating that such attacks may, if possible, be prevented for the future.

We talked over Lord Raglan and his capacity for command, and we both agreed that he had given no proofs of his fitness for so mighty a task. Clarendon said he was struck with the badness of his private letters, as he had been from the beginning by those from Varna, showing that he had evidently not a spark of imagination, and no originality. We both agreed that it would never do to hint a doubt about his merits or capacity, and at all events that he is probably equal to anybody likely to be opposed to him. His personal bravery is conspicuous, and he exposes himself more than he ought. It is said that one of his aides-de-camp remonstrated with him and received a severe rebuff, Raglan telling him to mind his own business, and if he did not like the fire to go to the rear. Clarendon says there is no chance of taking Sebastopol this year, nor of taking it at all till we have an army strong enough to drive the Russians out of the Crimea. For this, 150,000 men would be required to make it a certainty; but with this force, no Russian army, however numerous, could resist the allies, and then the place would fall. This is a distant prospect. I expressed my wonder at the Russians being able to obtain supplies, and he said they got them from the Don and from Kertch.

December 5th.—I was at Middleton on Saturday and returned yesterday. There I saw a letter from Stafford, who is at Constantinople tending the sick and wounded, writing for and reading to them, and doing all the good he can—a very wise and benevolent way of re-establishing his reputation and making his misdeeds at the Admiralty forgotten.[1] He says he had heard so much of the sufferings and privations of the soldiers, and of the bad state of the hospitals, that he resolved to go there and judge for himself of the truth of all that had been written and asserted on the subject; that he did so, and found the very worst accounts exceeded by the reality, and that nothing could be more frightful and appalling than it all was. It had greatly improved, but still was bad enough. The accounts published in the "Times," therefore, turn out to be true, and all the aid that private charity could supply was no more than was needed. I believe there has been no lack of zeal and humanity here, but a great deal of ignorance and inexperience, and, above all, culpable negligence on the part of Lord Stratford, who had *carte blanche* from the Government as to expense, and who, after having done his best to plunge us into this war, might at least have given his time and attention to provide relief for the victims of it ; but it seems that from some fit of ill-temper he has chosen to do nothing, and evinced nothing but indifference to the war itself and all its incidents ever since it broke out. This I am assured is the case. His wife has been very active and humane, and done all she could to assist Miss Nightingale in her mission of

[1] [Mr. Augustus Stafford had been Secretary to the Admiralty under Lord Derby's first Administration, where he was supposed not to have done well; but when the accounts arrived of the sufferings and privations of the army in the dreadful winter of 1854-'55, Mr. Stafford was one of the first persons to go out and endeavor to relieve the deplorable condition of the troops.]

benevolence and charity.   But to return to Stafford's letter.
He says that while nothing could exceed the heroism of our
soldiers, the incapacity of their chiefs was equally conspicuous, and that the troops had no confidence in their leaders ;
he adds, it is essential to give them a good general if the
war goes on.   This, and much more that I have heard, confirms the previous impression on my mind that Raglan is
destitute of military genius or skill, and quite unequal to
the command of a great army.   It does not appear, however,
that the enemy are better off than we are in this respect, and
we do not know that in England a better general would now
be found.   The man, Stafford says, in whom the army seem
to have the greatest confidence is Sir Colin Campbell.   All
this is very serious, and does not tend to inspire a great expectation of glorious results.   From what Clarendon said to
me it is evident that *he* does not think much of Raglan, but
it would never do to express any doubt of his ability or of
his measures in public.   Delane told me yesterday that he
had received letters without end in this sense, and that he
entertained the same doubts that I did, but should take care
not to give utterance to them in the "Times."   This reserve
is the more necessary and even just because, after all, the
opinions may not be well founded ; and, as it is impossible
to change the command, it is very desirable not to weaken
the authority and self-confidence of the General by casting
doubts upon his conduct of the war.

December 11*th*.—For the last week the Austrian Treaty
has occupied everybody's thoughts, though, as the exact
terms of it are not yet known, people do not very well know
what to expect from it.   The great question that lies behind
it is, whether Prussia will follow in the wake of Austria, and
the rest of Germany with her.   If all Germany joins the
Allies it seems absolutely impossible that Russia should offer
any effectual resistance to such a combination of forces ; and
it will then be to be seen what impression can be made on an
Empire which, with many political deficiencies, nature has
made so strong for defensive purposes, and, if the contest
continues, whether the opinions and object of the Allies will
not diverge and ultimately break up the alliance.

Bright has published his letter in a penny form (or somebody has done it for him) with *pièces justificatives* extracted
from the Blue Books and from other sources, and in my
opinion he makes out a capital and unanswerable case.   He

does not, indeed, prove, nor attempt to prove, that the Emperor of Russia is in the right absolutely, but he makes out that he is in the right as against England and France, and he shows up the conduct of the Western Powers very successfully.   But in the present temper of the country, and while the war fever is still raging with undiminished violence, all appeals to truth and reason will be totally unavailing. Those who entertain such opinions either wholly or in part do not dare to avow them, and all are hurried along in the vortex. I do not dare to avow them myself ; and even for holding my tongue, and because I do not join in the senseless clamor which everywhere resounds, I am called " a Russian."   The progress of the contest has changed the nature of public opinion, for now its principal motive is the deep interest taken in the success of our arms and the safety of the band of heroes who have been fighting in the Crimea.   This is, of course, right and patriotic, and a feeling which must be common to those who have been against, and those who have been for the war.

Panshanger, December 14*th.*—The debates on Tuesday night were on the whole satisfactory, and not bad for the Government.   Derby made a slashing, effective philippic on the text of " Too late," asserting that the fault of the Government had been that they had done everything too late. Newcastle answered him, but was dull and feeble, totally unequal to meet Derby in debate. His case was not bad, but he could not handle it with effect. Government did better in the Commons, where Sidney Herbert made a capital speech, and produced a very good case in a very complete and satisfactory manner. He proved that reinforcements had been sent out month after month, and that they had never folded their hands and stood still as Derby charged them with having done. All the rage for the war which is apparent in the country was manifested in both Houses. According to present appearances, there will be very little done on the part of the Opposition against the Government during this short session.

December 17*th.*—These smooth appearances were deceitful, for the Government met with an unexpected and violent opposition to their Foreign Enlistment Bill. and only carried the second reading by a majority of 12.   Ellenborough, puffed up with conceit and soured by disappointment and the nullity of his position, commenced a furious attack on this bill in an able speech replete with bitterness and sarcasm.   Derby, too happy to join in any mischief, brought the support of his party, and a debate ensued, in which, as usual, the speaking of Ellenborough and Derby gave them the advantage, but the Government got a majority enough for their purpose.   The bill itself is very unpopular, nobody can tell why, except that all sorts of misrepresentations were made about it the first night, and people have not yet been undeceived.   I doubt if it was worth while to bring in such a bill, but it is certain if they had not done so, and immediately, they would have been furiously reproached by those who oppose them now, and above all accused of being "too late."   The imprudent speech which John Russell made about Austria the first night elicited a violent attack on him in the "Times," which is sure to have put him in very bad humor.   The speech and the attack were equally unjustifiable and mischievous.   I have no idea why he said what he did, unless it was for the sake of appearing to fall in with the vulgar prejudice against Austria.

December 18th.—The dislike of the Foreign Enlistment Bill is very general, but nobody can give any reason for their opposition to it.[1]   It is, however, so great that it is not certain that it can be carried through the House of Commons, and so little is the Government cared for that I doubt many being found who will incur the resentment of their constituents or give an unpopular vote to save them.   If they should be beaten, I think they must go out.   John Russell is in a bad disposition of mind, as may be gathered from his *entourage,* who are in rabid opposition.   Lord John, however, will probably do what he can to make this measure go down, as I find he is himself the author of it; but I much doubt if he would care for the Government being broken up, and he is not unlikely to regard such a catastrophe as the event best calculated to restore him to the post he so much covets.   It is certainly possible that Derby, conscious he could not make a Government himself, would offer to support the Whig section of this Cabinet with all the Peelites eliminated from it, and that an attempt might be made to form a Government with Lord John, Palmerston, and per-

[1] [The object of the Foreign Enlistment Bill was to enable the Government to enlist 15,000 foreigners in the British army to be drilled in this country.   It was denounced and opposed especially in the House of Lords as a dangerous and unconstitutional measure, but it eventually passed, and a considerable number of Germans were enlisted under it.]

haps Ellenborough.   However, all this is vague speculation,
and not worth following out.

December 20th.—Government got a majority of 39, better
than was expected.   Lord John threatened to resign if he
was beaten.   The debate will not do them much good when
it is read, nor serve to render their measure more popular.
Everybody thinks the whole affair has been grossly mismanaged, and that, instead of making a mystery of their intentions, they ought to have thrown out such intimations of
them as would have elicited public opinion ; but the truth
is, not one of them had the least suspicion that the measure
would meet with any resistance or even objection, nor would
there have been any if Ellenborough had not started the
hare, and then Derby and his party joyfully availed themselves of the opportunity to do mischief, and joined in the
cry.   When the bill was announced, Derby never dreamt of
opposing it.   The arguments against the measure seem to
me very plausible, except the constitutional one, which is all
stuff, and in which none of those who urge it are sincere ;
on the other hand, the former precedents do not apply in
this case.   The best argument for it is, that Raglan wants
trained men as soon as possible, and complains that they
send nothing but boys, who are of little use at first, and who
die in great numbers under the hardships and privations the
climate and the operations inflict on them.   Not only were
the Government totally unconscious of the opposition they
should encounter, but, when they found the steam was getting up, they neglected to enter into such explanations and
make out such a case as might, if well done, have extinguished dissension in the beginning.   All this displays a
want of prudence and foresight, for in a matter of such importance it is not enough to say that they did not expect any
fault to be found with their proposal, and they ought to have
employed some means to see what was likely to be thought
of it before they committed themselves to it.   They ought
to have ascertained how it was to be carried into effect, and
if they could count upon its success, and to be able to give
Parliament some assurance of it, instead of saying they had
taken no initiative steps out of affected deference to constitutional scruples, and knew not how they were to get the
men they are asking for.   It seems the general opinion of
their own friends that they have mismanaged their case, and
plunged into a difficulty they might have avoided.   The best

way of avoiding it would have been to raise a regiment or
two without applying to Parliament at all, mustered and
arrayed them at Malta or at Heligoland, or wherever they
pleased out of England, and sent them off as an experiment
to the Crimea.   Then, if they had done good ·service, and
Raglan had expressed his satisfaction and asked for more,
they might have raised any number and landed them here
without cavil or objection ; but to have adopted this course
they must have seen the necessity of feeling their way, which
not one of them did.   The great complaint now is the want
of organisation and good arrangement in the Crimea, and
generally at and about the seat of war, the confusion that
has taken place in forwarding and distributing supplies, and
the want of all expedients for facilitating the service in its
various branches.   There is much truth in all this, but the
responsibility for it rests upon Raglan, who, if he had been
of a prompt and energetic character, would have looked to
these things, seen what was wanting, and have taken care to
provide everything and set the necessary machinery in motion.   He had *carte blanche* from the Government as to
money and everything else, and, if he had concerted what
was necessary with Stratford, and insisted on his exerting
himself, I believe none of the complaints would have been
made, and none of the deficiencies have been found.   This
is what the Duke of Wellington would have done, and his
despatches are full of proofs that it is what he was always
doing.

December 24th.—The third reading of the Enlistment Bill
carried by 38, after a very fine speech from Bright, consisting of a part of his letter with its illustrations.   In
my opinion this speech was unanswerable, and no attempt
was made to answer it.   He was very severe on both Lord
John and Palmerston.   It is impossible that such reasoning
as Bright's should not make *some* impression in the country ;
but I do not think any reasoning however powerful, or any
display of facts however striking, can stem the torrent of
public opinion, which still clamors for war and is so burning with hatred against Russia that no peace could be
deemed satisfactory, or even tolerable, that did not humble
Russia to the dust and strip her of some considerable
territory.   Yesterday the "Times" ventured on an article
against Raglan as the cause of the disorder and confusion
and consequent privations which prevail in the army.

Delane wrote to me about it, and said he was aware he should be bitterly reviled for speaking these truths. I agree entirely with what he said, and see no reason why the saddle should not be put upon the right horse.

The Grove, December 31st, 1854.—The last day of one of the most melancholy and disastrous years I ever recollect. Almost everybody is in mourning, and grief and despair overspread the land. At the beginning of the year we sent forth an army amidst a tumult of joyous and triumphant anticipation, and everybody full of confidence and boasting and expecting to force the Emperor Nicholas in the shortest possible time humbly to sue for peace, and the only question was, what terms we should vouchsafe to grant him, and how much of his dominions we should leave him in possession of. Such presumptuous boasting and confidence have been signally humbled, and the end of this year sees us deploring the deaths of friends and relations without number, and our army perishing before the walls of Sebastopol, which we are unable to take, and, after bloody victories and prodigies of valor, the Russian power hardly as yet diminished or impaired. All last week I was at Hatchford with Lord Grey, when we did nothing but talk over the war, its management and mismanagement, Raglan, etc. Grey's criticisms are clever and not unfair, far from favorable to the Government, but detesting Derby, of whom he has the worst opinion, formed from a very ancient date and upon long experience of his character and conduct. Grey's idea is that there has been much mismanagement here and still greater on the spot, and that Raglan is quite incompetent and, as far as we can see, nobody else any better. The opinion about Raglan appears to be rapidly gaining ground, and the Ministers have arrived at the same conclusion.

I came here yesterday to meet Cowley, come over for a few days from Paris, and to have a talk with him and Clarendon. Cowley says that the alliance between the two countries is very hollow, and in fact there is nobody in France really friendly to us except the Emperor, Persigny, and perhaps Drouyn de Lhuys. The Emperor is bent on pursuing the war with vigor, and is sensible of the importance to himself of the French flag being triumphant. I asked him what they thought of our armies and our generals; he said from the Emperor downward they had the highest admiration for the wonderful bravery of the troops, but the greatest contempt for the military skill of the commanders, and for all our arrangements and *savoir faire*. He told us the following anecdote as a proof of the blundering way in which our affairs are conducted. Newcastle wrote to him lately to beg he would ask the French Government to give us a model of certain carts their army used in the Crimea, the like of which our people there had applied to him for. The French Minister replied that he could give drawings, but had no model ; but at the same time he advised us not to think of having similar ones, as these carts are so ill adapted for the purpose that they had discarded them, and had ordered others and better ones to be made, which were now in course of construction *at Malta.* So that we propose to get these machines without finding out whether they are suitable or not, while the French supply themselves with the proper article *in our own territory.*

I find from Clarendon that he is not only fully alive to Raglan's inefficiency, but has all along suspected it, and now the Government seem to have the same conviction; still they can take no step in the matter, for he has done nothing and omitted nothing so flagrantly as to call for or justify his recall, and if they were to recall him they do not know where to look for a better man to replace him. The war has bitherto failed to elicit any remarkable abilities or special aptitude for war, except in one instance, that of Captain Butler, the defender of Silistria, a young man of remarkable promise who, if he had lived, would probably have done great things and have risen to distinction.

Canrobert writes to his Government that he hopes soon to attempt the assault, but the Emperor and M. Vaillant by no means approve of it, and have sent him orders not actually prohibiting it, but enjoining caution in such a manner as will most probably effectually deter him from doing anything. They all think that the capture of the place could only be achieved (if at all) at a great cost of life, and that the captors could not hold it for many hours, as they would be pounded from the Northern forts which entirely command the place.

We discussed Austria and what she will do when the Russian answer comes to the last communication of the Conference at Vienna, and what she can do. Even if she recalls her ambassador from St. Petersburg and declares war, Cowley thinks she will never cross bayonets with the Russians or fire

a shot unless attacked ; and he believes, on what appear good
grounds, that if any fighting takes place between the Austrians and the Russians, the former will get beaten, and that
the Russian army is much the best of the two.   This is the
reverse of the general notion, but it seems that the Austrian
officers themselves are of that opinion.   It is no wonder,
therefore, that they have no mind to go to war and to encounter this danger to accommodate us, whom they still cordially hate on many accounts, but especially for the Haynau
affair, which still rankles in their hearts and in which they
think their uniform was insulted. *A propos* of this, Clarendon
told me that the Queen was talking to him very lately about
this affair, and told him that she had entreated Palmerston
at the time to write some expression of regret to the Austrian
Government, but that nothing would induce him to do it,
and he never did.

I asked Clarendon what was Palmerston's present tone
about the war.   He said he was very uneasy about the army
and its condition, but just as confident as ever as to the final
result of the war, and as lofty in his ideas of the terms of
peace we should exact from Russia.   He is all for restoring
the Crimea to Turkey, and, what is more, he has persuaded
the Emperor Napoleon to embrace that opinion.   As usual,
he never sees any difficulty in anything he wishes to do.   I
told Cowley and Clarendon what Grey said—viz. that he
agreed entirely with Bright's letter, and that the war might
have been avoided by either of the two courses—to have told
the Emperor of Russia in the beginning we would make war
on him if he persisted, and compelled to understand that
we really meant it, or to have forced the Turks to accept
the Vienna Note ; and, in either case, war would have been
avoided, but that the Cabinet itself being divided, everything was done in a spirit of compromise, and a middle
course adopted which led to all the mischief.   Cowley answered the first alternative and Clarendon the second.   Cowley said that one of the great difficulties of the British Government was to secure concert with the French, and to explain their own conduct without hurting the susceptibility of
their allies or divulging what passed between the two Governments.   The French were perpetually blowing hot and
cold, with a false air of vigor superior to our's at one moment, and at another wanting to do what our Ministers
would have been torn to pieces for consenting to.   For in-

stance, in spite of us they would send their fleet to the Dardanelles to support the Turks, and afterward they proposed to send the two fleets to Constantinople to compel the Sultan to sign the Vienna Note.   Cowley told me this war in its present shape and with these vast armaments had gone on insensibly and from small beginnings, nobody could well tell how.   In the first instance, the Emperor told Cowley he had no intention of sending any land forces to the East, and when we proposed to him to despatch there a small corps of 5,000 English and 10,000 French, he positively declined. Soon after Sir John Burgoyne was sent to examine and report on the state of the country and he gave an opinion that it would be desirable to send such a force to occupy a fortified position at Gallipoli in case of the Russians making a sudden attack with their fleet on Constantinople, in which case our fleets might be in some danger.   Cowley took him to the Emperor, to whom he told his story.   The Emperor said he thought his reasons good, and this was a definite and tangible object, and he would send the troops.   When Raglan was offered the command of the forces we were to send out, he said he would not go with less than 20,000 men ; and when we agreed to send this force, the French said if we sent 20,000 they must send 40,000, and so the expedition began, and it has since swelled to its present magnitude— our's in consequence of the clamor here and pressure from without, and their's to keep pace with our's in relative proportions.   With regard to the Vienna Note, Clarendon said Stratford never would have let the Turks sign it, and if they had recalled him the Cabinet here would have been broken up, Palmerston would have gone out, Stratford would have come home frantic and have proclaimed to the whole country that the Turks had been sacrificed and betrayed, and the uproar would have been so great that it would have been impossible to carry out the intention.   I think the first answer is more weighty than the last, and that the popular clamor and Palmerston's secession ought to have been encountered at whatever hazard rather than persist in the fatal course which could hardly fail to lead, and did eventually lead, us into this deplorable war.

CHAPTER VIII.

January 2d, 1855.—I received yesterday a letter from the Duke of Bedford relating to the views and position of Lord John Russell. He had talked over his position with the Duke, disclaimed any wish to be again Prime Minister, but desired Lord Lansdowne should be in the post; that he liked personally both Aberdeen and Newcastle, but thought them unfit for the emergency. He had proposed that Palmerston should be War Minister but was overruled, and now (the Duke asks) what is he to do if a vote of censure on the management of the war is proposed in the House of Commons, thinking as he does that it has been mismanaged? He would willingly break up this Government, which he really thinks a very bad one (what he wrote to Clarendon being his deliberate opinion), if he could see a chance of a better being substituted, and if he thought Derby could carry on the war more efficiently, which he does not. This letter is a complete reply to the objection Clarendon urged against Palmerston's being War Minister, for if Lord John himself wished it, nobody else could well object. He ought to have insisted on it, and, if he had, it must have been done.

Nothing can wear a gloomier aspect than affairs do at home and abroad—the Government weak, unpopular, dispirited, and divided, the army in the Crimea in a deplorable state, and the prospects of the war far from brilliant, no confidence in the commanding officers there, and no likelihood of finding more competent ones, everybody agreeing that till we have 150,000 men in the Crimea we cannot count on taking Sebastopol, and the difficulty of ever assembling such a force appearing very great. So far as I can collect, the

violent articles which the "Times" emits day after day have
excited general resentment and disgust. They overdo everything, and, while they are eternally changing their course,
the one they follow for the moment they follow with an
outrageous violence which shocks everybody. But as those
who complain most of the "Times" still go on reading it,
the paper only gets more rampant and insolent, for as long
as its circulation is undiminished it does not care what anybody thinks or says of it.

January 4th.—I wrote the Duke an answer with my
opinion on Lord John's position and obligations, which has
elicited another from him this morning. He says that it was
a few weeks ago that John made a formal proposal to Aberdeen that Palmerston should replace Newcastle at the War
Department. Aberdeen desired time to consider, and then
refused. Subsequently the matter was renewed, when Palmerston himself objected, and then it necessarily ended. The
Duke thinks that Lord John will not now stir it again, and
will make up his mind to go on, and to defend his Government in the House of Commons. He consulted Sir George
Grey, Lord Lansdowne, and Panmure, and they all advised
him not to resign. It is strange that while this is imparted
to me "very confidentially," and I had heard nothing of it
before, it is currently reported, and stated positively in the
"Morning Herald," that Lord John and others, mentioned
by name, have insisted on Newcastle's being turned out.
That some part of what has occurred has got out is clear,
and I incline to think that some of his satellites have set to
work, and that, by way of assisting Lord John's object, they
have given notice of what was going on to some of the Derbyites. There is a mysterious allusion to some impending
event in the "Press" on Saturday last, which looks very
like this.

The "Times" goes on against Raglan with greater vehemence every day, and will not be restrained by any remonstrances. Evans has put himself in communication with
Delane (though certainly having no hand in these attacks)
and has sent him an account of his having addressed a letter
to Canrobert many days before the battle of Inkerman for
the purpose of getting him to assist in taking precautionary
measures to resist the attack he was persuaded the Russians
would make, and Canrobert's answer, in which he says that
his means are curtailed by the necessity of providing for the

defence of Balaklava, and of extending his line and making dispositions "dans l'intérêt de la situation commune," but that he has ordered Bosquet to move nearer to Evans' division, and to be in readiness if anything should happen. There was a passage omitted in the printed letter of Evans to Raglan in which he alludes to the neglect of the precautionary measures he had recommended.

Gortschakoff has declared the Emperor of Russia will accept the first, second, and fourth articles of the four points, and will consider of the third. This may mean that he really wishes to make peace, or only be done for the sake of Austria, and to give her a pretext for not declaring against him. Clarendon is satisfied with Usedom, but not at all with his proposals. He says the King of Prussia has sent him to try and make a treaty with France and England entirely out of jealousy and mortification at Austria having made one, but he does not propose one similar to the Austrian Treaty, only a *defensive* one. Clarendon says the King in his heart hates Russia and winces under the influence he submits to, that he is indignant at the insults which have been heaped on him by his Imperial brother-in-law, and the contumely with which he has been treated, but, being physically and politically a coward, he has not energy to shake off the yoke he has suffered to be imposed on him.

Aldenham, January 6th.—I came here to-day. I saw Cowley yesterday, who has been to Windsor, and tells me that he finds by conversations he has had with Stockmar that the Queen is much softened toward Palmerston and no longer regards him with the extreme aversion she did. On the other hand, she is very angry with John Russell, and this is, of course, from knowing what he has been doing, and resentment at his embarrassing and probably breaking up the Government. This relaxation in her feelings toward Palmerston is very important at this moment, and presents the chance of an alternative which, if this Government fails, may save her from Derby and his crew, whom she cordially detests. I hear Newcastle is very low, as well he may be, for no man was ever placed in so painful a position, and it is one from which it is impossible for him to extricate himself. When the Government goes to pieces, as I am persuaded it will, the Queen is very likely to send for Palmerston, and he and Ellenborough, as War Minister, might make a Government that would probably stand during the war, and which

in present circumstances the House of Commons and the
country could not but support. My notion is that Lord
John would not take any office, but would support Palmerston, and advise all his friends and followers to do so. I
know no reason why Ellenborough should not act with anybody, and many of the present Government might stay in,
and certain changes be made which would let in more Whigs,
and so conciliate that party, while the Conservatives would
abstain from supporting any Government which did not contain Aberdeen and Newcastle. Gladstone might be a difficulty; Clarendon would be none, for he and Palmerston
have pulled very well together, and I have no doubt Palmerston would be very happy to keep him. This opens a new
prospect, and one very preferable to having Derby and his
friends in office again.

I asked Cowley about Canrobert's confidential letters to
his Government on the state of our army of which I had
heard. He said it was very true, and he had seen several of
these letters, in which Canrobert said that nothing could
exceed his admiration of the British soldiers, but he was
convinced the army would disappear altogether, for their
organization and management were deplorable; and he entreated his Government, if they possibly could, to interpose
in the interest of the common cause to procure some ameli-
oration of the organization, without which nothing could
save the army from destruction. The Emperor, Cowley
said, never mentioned our troops or commanders to him
except in terms of respect and with expressions of his admiration, but he knew that to others he spoke in a very
different tone, and said that our army was commanded by
an old woman.

January 12th.—I returned to town last night. The
Emperor of Russia's acceptance of the four points, as interpreted by us, of course excites hopes of peace, but I think
few people are sanguine as to the result. It is suspected to
be only a dodge to paralyze the action of Austria, but unless
there was some secret concert with Austria, which is not
likely, I cannot see what Russia is to gain by accepting
conditions which she does not really mean to abide by.
Such conduct could only deceive the Allies for a short time,
and, as there is no question of any suspension of military
operations, nothing would be gained in that respect, while
as soon as some decisive test of the Emperor's sincerity was

applied, his real meaning must be made manifest, and then not only would the *acharnement* of the Western Powers be increased, but it would be quite impossible for Austria not to join the Coalition, and to act verily and indeed against Russia. These reasons would induce me to put faith in the Russian announcement; on the other hand, it is barely credible that the Emperor should consent to the sacrifice of Sebastopol in the present state of the campaign, and with the almost certainty that we cannot take it for many months to come, if at all.

John Russell is gone to Paris, not for any political object, but merely to see one of his wife's sisters; but his journey there and conversations with the Emperor may not be without some consequences. I hear almost daily from the Duke of Bedford on the subject of John's conduct, the conduct of the war, and the state of the Government. For the present he appears to desist from doing anything to make an explosion. The curious thing is that the public, and particularly the Derbyite, newspapers should be so well informed as they are of what is going on. Though the immediate danger of a break up seems to be over, I still think the *animus* Lord John exhibits, the manifold difficulties of the Government, and their undoubted though unjust unpopularity, will before long break them to pieces.

January 14th.—I met Clarendon last night and had a talk about affairs at home and abroad. John Russell at Paris is satisfied with his conversation with the Emperor, who agreed that we could make no peace but one which would be glorious for us. Clarendon does not believe the Emperor of Russia really means to sacrifice Sebastopol, and thinks when he sent his acceptance of the four points he was not apprised of what had passed in the Conference, which was merely verbal. Gortschakoff, in a passion, said, "I suppose you mean to limit our naval force, or to dismantle Sebastopol, or both;" to which they replied, "Yes"; but nothing was put in writing to this effect. This makes a great difference, but I do not despair. There is a great question about a negotiator, and the Queen and Prince want Clarendon himself to go. He refused point blank; he does not like to leave it to Westmorland alone. I suggested Canning, but he thought Canning had not had experience enough, and that it ought to be a Cabinet Minister, and asked, "Why not Palmerston?" I objected the difficulty

of relying on him, his hatred of Austria, and the terror he
would inspire; and I said Granville might do, but that I
saw no reason why he should not go himself if he had reason
to think it was likely to succeed, though I would not go
merely to return *re infectd.* We then talked of Lord John
and of Newcastle. He said that Newcastle is exceedingly
slow, and has a slow mind, but that there is no case whatever for turning him out, and he cannot be blamed for the
failures in matters of detail, and as for the great measures
the responsibility belongs alike to all. Lord John never is
and never will be satisfied without being again Prime Minister, which is impossible. I said the Duke of Bedford assured me that his brother did not *now* want to be Prime
Minister. "What does he want then?—to retire altogether?" "Yes," said Clarendon, "that is his intense selfishness; utterly regardless of the public interests, or of
what may happen, he wants to relieve *himself* from the responsibility of a situation which is not so good as he desires,
and to run away from his post at a moment of danger and
difficulty. If we had some great success—if Sebastopol were
taken, for example—we should hear no more of his retirement." As matters are, however, Clarendon thinks very ill
of them abroad and at home. This disposition of Lord
John's keeps the Government in constant hot water, and
no confidence can be placed in Raglan, while it is impossible
to find anybody who would, as far as we can judge, do any
better.

The Court are exceedingly annoyed and alarmed at
Raglan's failure; the Prince showed Clarendon (or told him
of) a letter from Colonel Steele, who said that he had no idea
how great a mind Raglan really had, but that he now saw
it, for in the midst of distresses and difficulties of every kind
in which the army was involved he was perfectly serene and
undisturbed, and his health excellent! Steele meant this
as a panegyric, and did not see that it really conveyed a
severe reproach. The conviction of his incapacity for so
great a command gains ground every day; he has failed in
those qualities where everybody expected he would have succeeded best, even those who thought nothing of his military
genius. But, having learned what he knows of war under
the Duke, he might at least have known how *he* carried on
war, and have imitated his attention to minute details and a
general supervision of the different services, seeing that all

9

was in order and the merely mechanical parts properly attended to on which so much of the efficiency as well as of
the comfort of the army depended.[1]

January 19*th.*—We are still uncertain as to the real intentions of the Emperor of Russia, and whether he means
to accept the terms offered by the Allies ; but my own impression is that he will not accept them *in our sense,* and that
he never will consent to the sacrifice of Sebastopol till we
have taken the place and destroyed the fortifications, thereby
rendering its dismantling a *fait accompli.* There is certainly nothing in the present state of our affairs which war-
rants our lofty pretensions, and the proposal of terms so
humiliating to the Emperor.   The only possible grounds that
can be imagined for his acceptance are, his own knowledge
of the state of his own country and of the resources he can
command for carrying on the war, and a dispassionate and
farsighted calculation of the disposition and of the resources
of his opponents.   It is not impossible that he may foresee
that he must eventually succumb in a contest so unequal and
in which the number of his enemies increases every day.   He
may deem it better to make certain sacrifices now, with the
view of being able before long to retrieve his losses, than to
expose himself to the chance and great probability of being
obliged to make much greater sacrifices hereafter, and such
as it will be more difficult for him to repair.   The Duke of
Bedford tells me that Aberdeen and Clarendon are both
hopeless of peace, and that Lord John and Palmerston do
not consider it so absolutely hopeless ; Aberdeen says the
negotiations will not last half an hour.

The accounts from the army are as bad as possible ;
one third of it is in the hospitals, and the quays of Balaklava
are loaded with enormous stores of every kind, which it was
impossible to transport to the camp.   Very intelligent people therefore entertain the greatest apprehension of some
catastrophe occurring whenever the severity of the winter,
which has hitherto been comparatively mild, sets in.   The
best security is in the equally distressed state of the
Russians, and in fact nothing but this can account for their
having left us alone so long.

[1] [It may be proper to remark that a different and far more favourable view
of Lord Raglan's capacity as a General will be found *infra* at the beginning of
Chapter XII. of this Journal, upon the evidence of Sir Edmund Lyons, who was
entirely in the confidence of the Commander-In-Chief.]

The Duke of Bedford and I talked over the state of affairs here, and the political possibilities in the event of this Government falling to pieces or being compelled to resign. We both desire any arrangement rather than another Derby Government, and we agree in thinking that on the whole the best would be for Lord Lansdowne to undertake the formation of a Government, if he can be persuaded to do so, which does not appear wholly impossible.   This would satisfy Lord John, who would then remain in his present office, half a dozen of the present Cabinet would go out, some Whigs might replace them, and the thing would undoubtedly go on for a time.   It is impossible for Newcastle to continue to conduct the war, with the universal clamor there is against him and the opinion of his own colleagues (at least of such of them as I know the opinions of) that he is unfit for the post.   He has two very great faults which are sufficient to disqualify him : he is exceedingly slow, and he knows nothing of the qualifications of other men, or how to provide himself with competent assistants ; nor has he any decision or foresight.   He chose for his under-secretaries two wholly incompetent men who have been of no use to him in managing and expediting the various details of the service, and he has a rage for doing everything himself, by which means nothing is done, or done so tardily as to be of no use.   Then all the subordinate Boards are miserably administered, and the various useless, inefficient, or worn out officers have been suffered to remain at their posts, to the enormous detriment of the service.   The genius of Lord Chatham or the energy and will of the Duke of Wellington would have failed with such a general staff here, and with such a Commander-in-Chief as Hardinge, and with the *fainéantise* of Raglan.

January 20*th.*—It is only by degrees one can unravel the truth in political affairs.   John Russell told me last night that Austria has never given in her adhesion to our condition of making the destruction of Sebastopol a *sine quâ non* of peace.   She joins us in insisting on the "faire cesser la prépotence," but the means of accomplishing this remain to be discussed.   This is very different from what I had imagined, and makes it anything but certain that she will join her forces to ours, if the negotiations fail in consequence of our demands.   We are now endeavoring to bring the Court of Vienna into an agreement with us as to the conditions to be required, and it is no easy matter to get the Cabinet to agree upon the wording of the communications we make to her. This arises from the necessity of looking to the effect of what will appear in the Blue Books. Blue Books, Parliamentary discussions, and the Press tie up the hands of a Government, fetter its discretion and deliberate policy, and render diplomatic transactions (especially with Governments whose hands are more free) excessively difficult. Granville told me yesterday morning that the course of Russia had been more straightforward than that of England and France, and this morning he reminded me of having said so, and added that we were in a great diplomatic mess, France always finessing and playing a game of her own ; and I infer from what he said that, having got all she can out of us, she is now coquetting with Austria, and disposed to defer to her wishes and objects, and to be less *exigeante* toward Russia. This is only of a piece with what Clarendon has often said to me about France and her way of dealing with us ; however, if France will only insist on making peace on plausible terms, and with the semblance of its being an honorable and consistent peace, we cannot do otherwise than acquiesce in her determination, and if we only follow the lead she takes, the public here must needs be satisfied. This is Granville's own idea, as it is mine, and God grant that affairs may take this turn, and so we may get out of the tremendous scrape we are in, the escape from which will be cheaply purchased by the fall of the Government—a consequence that is almost certain if it does not happen before anything can be done.

Day after day the accounts from the Crimea represent a more deplorable state of things, entirely confirmative of Canrobert's statements to his own Government, and it is difficult to read them and not apprehend some fatal catastrophe. We know nothing of the state of the Russians either within or without Sebastopol, and this ignorance is not one of the least remarkable circumstances in this war, but we must conclude either that their condition is as bad as ours and that they are unable to attack us, or that their policy is to let the winter do its work, and that they do not think it necessary for them to fight sanguinary battles with very doubtful results when disease is ravaging the allied army and producing effects as advantageous for them as the most complete victories could do, as surely, only more gradually.

January 22d.—Every day one looks with anxiety to see and to hear whether the chances of peace look well or ill, and at present they look very ill. Clarendon seems to set his face against it—that is, he considers it hopeless; and it is not promising that the negotiations should be under the management of one who has no hopes of bringing them to a successful issue, and whose despair of it evidently arises from his determination to exact conditions that there is no chance of obtaining. I hear, too, this morning, that the instructions to Bourqueney are to be as *exigeant* as possible—not very wise pretensions anyhow, but they rather indicate the tone adopted by England than the real intentions of France, for it is one thing to make great demands and another to persist in them. It is, however, idle to speculate on the progress of a negotiation which must be so largely influenced by the operations and events of the war. Parliament meets to-morrow, and I think a very short time will elapse before the fate of the Government is decided by some vote about the conduct of the war. I think the Government themselves desire it, and, conscious of the state of public opinion and of the deplorable state of affairs, and most of them thinking there has been great and fatal mismanagement, they wish the question to be decided, would not be sorry to be driven out by an adverse vote, and consider that it would be a better and more respectable way of ending than by those internal dissensions, which, like a cancer, are continually undermining them. John Russell sees nothing but difficulties in the formation of another Government of a Whig complexion including a large portion of the present Ministers, and says that he does not think Lord Lansdowne *would*, or that he or Palmerston *could* accomplish it. He means now to stand by his colleagues, to accept his share of responsibility, and defend what has been done.

January 23*d.*—Parliament meets to-day, and probably no time will be lost in attacking the Government, but it is impossible yet to know whether they will be harassed by a continual succession of skirmishes and bitter comments on details, or whether some grand and decisive assault will be made. The general impression is that the War Department cannot remain in Newcastle's hands, and if he cannot be got rid of without the whole Ministry going to pieces it must so end. I think this is pretty much the opinion of the Ministers themselves; and though I believe they all, or most of them, personally like him, they seem, so far as I can see, to be agreed that he is unequal to his post.

With regard to peace, the prospect looks anything but
bright. The negotiations will not begin till we receive positive information as to the meaning of the Emperor of Russia
in accepting the four points. Some weeks ago Clarendon
wrote a despatch to Westmorland, in which he stated ex-
plicitly the meaning we attached to the four points, but this
has never been put officially before the Emperor, that we
know of. Buol acquiesced, as I understood, in our explanation, but John Russell distinctly told me that Austria had
never signified her concurrence in making the demolition of
Sebastopol a *sine quâ non* condition. Now, however, some
fresh communication has been made by Austria to Russia,
and we will not begin the negotiation until Austria shall
have signified to us that the Emperor's acceptance is such as
will warrant us in negotiating. I am not sufficiently acquainted with all the details to form a conclusive opinion,
but, as far as I can see, we have been hanging off from being
perfectly explicit, and have never yet come to a complete
understanding with Austria, much less with Russia, and I
am afraid of our Ministers committing themselves in Parliament by some declarations and professions of intentions
which may make peace impossible and break up the negotiations at once, for as to Russia consenting to dismantle Sebastopol, I look upon it as impossible, and absurd to expect
it. I earnestly hope that Bourqueney may be instructed to
come to an understanding with Austria, and that, if we insist
on terms impossible to obtain, our two Allies may compel us
to give way, or leave us to fight the battle alone. The only
thing quite certain is that we are in a state of the utmost
doubt, danger, and perplexity at home and abroad, all of
which is owing to our own egregious folly and unskilfulness,
and the universal madness which has pervaded the nation.

January 24th.—The Government is at an end, or at least
it probably will be before the end of the day. The Duke of
Bedford has just been to me to tell me that last night, after
returning from the House of Commons, Lord John wrote a
letter to Aberdeen to resign his office, and he will not attend
the Cabinet to-day. Nobody knows it but Aberdeen himself, and I am not permitted to tell Granville even, but it
will be announced to the Cabinet this morning. The immediate cause of Lord John's resignation is Roebuck's motion,
of which he gave notice last night, for a Committee to inquire into the conduct of the war ; it is intended as a hostile

motion, and would have been turned into a vote of censure
and want of confidence.   Besides this, it seems Hayter had
told Lord John that the aspect of the House was bad, and
members of the Government party disinclined to attend.
Accordingly, he said he could not and would not face the
motion ; Graham and Sidney Herbert might defend the conduct of the war, but *he* could not. · Heaven only knows what
will occur.   Lord John took no time to consider, but sent
his resignation at once, the moment he returned from the
House.   I told the Duke that I thought he had made himself obnoxious to very just reproach, running away from
such a motion, and explaining (as he must do) that he could
not defend the conduct of the war. ·He will naturally be
asked how long he has been dissatisfied with its management, and why he did not retire long ago.   The Duke said
he was aware of this, but he endeavored to make out that
the case bore some analogy to that of Lord Althorp in 1834,
when he resigned in consequence of a motion of O'Connell's.
But this was altogether different.   Nothing can, in my
opinion, justify Lord John, and his conduct will, if I am
not mistaken, be generally condemned, and deprive him of
the little consideration and influence he had left.   It has
been vacillating, ungenerous, and cowardly, for after all, in
spite of errors and mistakes, the conduct of the war admits
of a defence, at least as to many parts of it, and it would
have been far better to stand up manfully and abide the result of the battle in Parliament, than to shirk the fight and
leave his colleagues to deal with the difficulty as best they
may, trying to escape from the consequences of a responsibility which nothing he can say or do can enable him to ʾ
shake off.

January 26th.—Yesterday morning the Cabinet met, and
after some discussion they resolved unanimously not to resign, but to encounter Roebuck's motion.   Aberdeen went
down to Windsor, and there is another Cabinet this morning.   I saw John Russell in the afternoon, and told him in
very plain terms what I thought of his conduct, and how
deeply I regretted that he had not gone on with his colleagues and met this attack with them.   He looked astonished and put out, but said, "I could not.   It was impossible for me to oppose a motion which I think ought to be
carried."   I argued the point with him, and in the middle
of our talk the Duke of Bedford came in.   I asked him if

he did not think the remaining Ministers were right in the course they have taken, and he said he did. I then said, "I have been telling John how much I regret that he did not do the same," when John repeated what he had said before, and then went away. After he was gone the Duke said, "I am very glad you said what you did to John." The town was in a great state of excitement yesterday, and everybody speculating on what is to happen, and all making lists of a new Government according to their expectations or wishes ; most people place Palmerston at the head. In the House of Lords Derby asked me what it all meant. Clarendon came up while we were talking, and gave Derby to understand that he would probably have to take office again, expressing his own eagerness to quit it. I now hear that Lord John has been leading the Cabinet a weary life for many months past, eternally making difficulties, and keeping them in a constant state of hot water, determined to upset them, and only doubting as to what was a fit opportunity, and at last taking the worst that could be well chosen for his own honor and character. He is not, however, without countenance and support from some of his adherents, or from those who were so impatient for the destruction of this Government that they are satisfied with its being accomplished, no matter how or by whom or under what circumstances ; and as he has been long accustomed

to sit attentive to his own applause

from a little circle in Chesham Place, so he will now be told by the same set that he has acted a very fine and praiseworthy part, although such will not be the verdict of history, nor is it, as far as I can see, of the best and wisest of his own contemporaries. Nobody entertains a doubt of Roebuck's motion being carried by a large majority against the Government.

January 30th.—For the last three days I have been so ill with gout that I could not do anything, or follow the course of events. John Russell made a cunning and rather clever speech in explanation of his resignation, George Grey a good one and strong against Lord John. Opinions fluctuated about the division, some, but the minority, fancying Government would have a majority because the proposed Committee is so excessively difficult and in all ways objectionable ; but when it became known that the Derbyites meant to vote in a body for the motion, no one doubted the result, and it became only a question of numbers.[1] Lord John seems to have felt no regret at what he has done, and at exciting the resentment and incurring the blame of all his colleagues; and he goes so little into society, and is so constantly patted on the back at home, that the censure of the world produces no effect on him. They tell me he is in high spirits, and appears only to be glad at having at last found the opportunity he has so long desired of destroying the Government. Everybody appears astonished at the largeness of the majority. Gladstone made a very fine speech, and powerful, crushing against Lord John, and he stated what Lord John had never mentioned in his narrative, that he had been expressly asked in December whether he still wished the change to be made which he had urged in November, and he had replied that he did not, that he had given it up. This *suppressio veri* is shocking, and one of the very worst things he ever did.

Aberdeen went down to Windsor this morning to resign. It is thought that the Queen will send for Lansdowne, and ask him if he can make a Government, or will try, and, if he declines, that he will advise her to send for Palmerston; if Palmerston fails, then she can do nothing but take Derby. It seems likely now that we shall have either a Whig or a Derbyite Government, and that the Peelites will be left out altogether. The difficulties are enormous, and though everybody says that at such a crisis and with the necessity of attending to the war, and the war only, no personal prejudices or antipathies should prevent anybody from taking office if their services can be of use, men will not be governed by motives of such pure patriotism; and, whoever may make the Government, I expect there will be many exclusions and many refusals to join. Some say that, if Derby comes in, and with the same or nearly the same men as before, he ought to be kicked out at once, but I do not think so, and, much as I should abhor another such Government, I think in present circumstances it must be allowed the fairest play, and be supported unless and until it commits some flagrant errors.

January 31st.—The division was curious: some seventy or eighty Whigs, ordinary supporters of Government, voted

[1] [Mr. Roebuck's Motion for a Committee of Inquiry was carried on the 29th of January by a majority of 157 in a House of 453 members present.]

against them, and all the Tories, except about six or seven who voted against the motion ; Cobden and Bright stayed away. John Russell's explanation, had he spoken the truth, would have run in these terms : "I joined the Government with great reluctance, and only at the earnest entreaty of my friends, particularly Lord Lansdowne. From the first I was disgusted at my position, and I resolved, unless Lord Aberdeen made way for me, and I again became Prime Minister, that I would break up the Government. I made various attempts to bring about such a change, and at last, after worrying everybody to death for many months, I accomplished my object, having taken what seemed a plausible pretext for doing it."

February 1st.—Contrary to general expectation, the Queen did not send either for Lansdowne or Palmerston, but at once for Derby. He went directly to Palmerston, who declined to join him. He is trying to form a Government, and I see the Whigs are chuckling over the probability of his failing and being obliged to give it up, when they evidently flatter themselves that it will fall again into the hands of John Russell. Rather than this should occur, I would prefer that Derby should succeed, and if he can get no foreign aid, that he should reconstitute the wretched Government he had before. My disgust at the conduct of my Whig friends is intense. Although they were to the last degree indignant at the conduct of John Russell, they have, ever since the interregnum began, been dancing attendance on him, evincing every disposition to overlook the enormity of his conduct and to reform the party with a view of carrying him again to the head of affairs and making another pure Whig Government. I confess I thought that nobody could refuse to serve at the present crisis, and, if the Queen sent for Derby, Palmerston, if invited, could not help joining, and taking the War Department ; but I was wrong. I see in no quarter, as far as I have been able to observe and judge, any disposition to discard prejudices, antipathies, and personal feelings and interests, and to make every consideration yield to the obligations which the present emergency imposes. However, the game is not half played out yet. Meanwhile we are exhibiting a pretty spectacle to Europe, and I don't think our example will tempt other nations to adopt the institutions of which we are so proud ; for they may well think that liberty of the Press and Parliamentary government, however desirable they may be when regulated by moderation and good sense, would be dearly purchased at the expense of the anarchy and confusion which they are now producing here.

February 2d.—The Queen herself decided to send at once to Derby, and the result proves how wise her decision was, for she is relieved from the annoyance of having him, and he is placed in such a position that he cannot embarrass her new Government when it is formed. Derby went to Palmerston, invited him to join and to bring Gladstone and Sidney Herbert with him. On their declining he gave it up, and Her Majesty then sent for Lord Lansdowne.

Last night the Duke of Newcastle defended himself in the House of Lords against John Russell, and replied to his statements in the House of Commons, and did it very successfully, carrying the House with him. The whole affair, as it is gradually evolved, places John Russell in a disgraceful and odious light, and ought to demolish him as a public man, for he has shown himself to be actuated by motives of pique, personal ambition, and mortified vanity, and to have been insincere, vacillating, uncandid, and untruthful. The Duke's statement was crushing and appears to me not to admit of a rejoinder. It ought to cover him and his wretched clique with confusion ; but they will probably attempt to brazen it out, and doggedly to insist that John was justified in all he did. The discussion last night was very characteristic of Derby. If ever there was an occasion in which seriousness and gravity seemed to be required of a man in his position, it would seem to be that of last night ; but his speech was nothing but jeering at the late Cabinet and chaffing Newcastle ; it was really indecent, but very smart and funny, if it had not been so unbefitting the occasion.

February 4th.—No one can remember such a state as the town has been in for the last two days. No Government, difficulties apparently insurmountable, such confusion, such excitement, such curiosity, everybody moving about craving for news, and rumor with her hundred tongues scattering every variety of statement and conjecture. At last the crisis seems to be drawing to a conclusion. The Queen has behaved with admirable sense of her constitutional obligations. When Aberdeen took down his resignation, she told him she had made up her mind what to do, that she had looked at the list of the division, and found that the majority which

had turned out her Government was composed principally of
Lord Derby's adherents, and she should therefore send for
him.   Aberdeen said a few words rather discouraging her ;
but she said, though Lord Palmerston was evidently the
popular man, she thought, according to constitutional practice, Lord Derby was the man she ought to send for.   It
has been seen how Derby failed ; then she sent for Lord
Lansdowne, whom she desired to consult different people
and see what their opinions and inclinations were, and report
them to her.   This was on Friday.   He did so and made
his report, after which, on the same principle which had
decided her to send for Derby, she resolved to send for John
Russell, his followers having been the next strongest element
of the victorious majority.   Accordingly, on Friday night
or early yesterday morning, she placed the formation of a
Government in his hands.   He accepted it, and began by
applying to Palmerston, offering him any office he chose to
take.   Palmerston did not refuse, but his acquiescence
seems to have been of a hesitating and reluctant kind, and
nothing was definitely settled between them.   Gladstone and
Sidney Herbert, and afterwards Graham, decidedly refused ;
Clarendon desired to have some hours to consider of it.   However, the result of his applications was so unfavorable that
last night he considered his attempt virtually at an end,
though he had not actually given it up this morning, and
some further communication was taking place between him
and Clarendon, which was to be decisive.   As soon as this is
over, the Queen will play her last card, and have recourse to
the man of the people!—to Palmerston, whom they are crying
out for, and who, they fondly imagine, is to get us out of all
our difficulties.   From all I hear, I think he will make a
Government, because he really wishes and is determined to
do it, and many of the most important who would not join
John Russell will join· him.   In the course of to-day I
imagine it will all be settled.   The impression made by
Newcastle's speech against Lord John has been prodigious,
far greater and more general than I imagined, and it is confidently affirmed that, if he had taken office and stood again
for the City, he would have been beaten.   He still shows
fight against Newcastle, and intended to have answered him
and vindicated himself in the House of Commons yesterday,
if he had not been detained so long by the Queen that the
hour was up when he got there.   He means to return to the

charge to-morrow. In the course of all these transactions he urged Lansdowne himself to take the Government, and offered to continue at the Council Office and lead the House of Commons, or to take no office at all, and give him independent support in the House of Commons, or to go to the House of Lords and give him his best assistance there; but Lord Lansdowne declined all these offers.

February 5th.—I have often had occasion to remark on the difficulty of avoiding making false or erroneous statements in affairs like those I am treating of, for the reports which we hear from different people generally vary considerably, and sometimes the same thing repeated by the same person varies also; not that there is any intention to misrepresent or mislead, but circumstances apparently trifling are narrated differently according as the narrator has been impressed by, or remembers them, and thus errors creep in and accumulate, and at last it becomes difficult to reconcile statements that have become conflicting by degrees. However, I can only jot down what I hear, and reconcile the accounts afterward as well as I can. Yesterday afternoon I saw Clarendon, who confirmed his refusal to join Lord John, but with some slight difference as to the details. He said he had spoken very openly to him, but so gravely and quietly that he could not take offence, and he did not. It was not till he received Clarendon's final refusal that he wrote to the Queen and threw up his commission.

Her Majesty had seen Palmerston the day before, and told him if Lord John failed she should send for him, and accordingly she did so yesterday evening. Palmerston had told Lord John, as soon as he received the commission he should go to him. At present he has only invited Clarendon and Charles Wood (Whigs) to join him. Clarendon of course is ready, but Charles Wood demurs, and insists that unless Lord John will take office in the Government he cannot join, and that the whole thing will be a failure. Lord John is very averse to take office, and the more averse because he must then go to the House of Lords, for of course he cannot remain in the Commons, not leading it. The Duke of Bedford has been here in a grand quandary, seeing all sorts of difficulties, and in fact they spring up on every side. He agrees with Lord John, but was shaken by the arguments of Wood, which are backed up by George Grey and Panmure. I argued vehemently against Wood's view, and strongly ad-

vised Lord John's not taking office, and I convinced the
Duke, who is gone back to Lord John to talk it all over with
him again. On the other hand, the Peelites want the Government to be restored, with Aberdeen again at the head of
it, and it is very questionable whether they will join at all,
and, if they do, not without much difficulty and negotiation,
which will at least consume valuable time. In short, at this
moment the formation of a Palmerston Government, which
was to be so easy, is a matter of enormous difficulty. The
Queen wrote a civil and even kind answer to Lord John's
note giving the task up.

February 6th.—Great disappointment and dismay yesterday, the Peelites having refused to form part of Palmerston's
Government. Graham, Gladstone, and Sidney Herbert all
declined unless Aberdeen formed a part of it. Sidney Herbert was very willing to join, but would not separate himself
from Gladstone, who was deaf to all entreaties and remonstrances. It is believed that Graham is the one who has persuaded Gladstone to take this course. Aberdeen is anxious,
or pretends to be so, that they should join, and Newcastle
certainly is. What Gladstone says is, that unless Aberdeen
is in the Cabinet he can have no security that his (Aberdeen's) principles will be acted on, and that he may not be
called upon to be a party to measures, relating either to war
or peace, of which he disapproves. However, I have only
heard second hand what he says in conversation with others.
It has been in vain represented to him that there will be an
explosion of indignation against them all in the country for
refusing their aid at such a crisis, and their conduct will
never be forgiven. All this, he says, he is aware of, but his
objections stand on too high ground to be shaken. Palmerston means not to be baffled, and, failing the Peelites, to turn
to the Whigs and make the best Government he can. His
popularity, which is really extraordinary, will carry him
through all difficulties for the present. It was supposed that
his popularity had been on the wane, but it is evident that,
though he no longer stands so high as he did in the House
of Commons, and those who know him can easily see he is
not the man he was, in the country there is just the same
fancy for him and sanguine opinion of him as ever. John
Russell made a rejoinder to Newcastle in the House of Commons last night—a plausible speech enough, and it served to
set his friends and the Brooks's Whigs crowing again, and

saying he had made out a complete case ; but I do not see that it made his case a bit better than before. All who are at all behind the scenes are aware of the fallacies and deceptions in which his statements abound, and that they are of a nature that may not be exposed.

February 7th.—Yesterday Aberdeen and Newcastle, particularly the latter, renewed their endeavors to prevail on Gladstone to give up his scruples and to join the Government, and at last they succeeded, and in the evening Palmerston was able to announce that he had accomplished his task and the Government was formed. John Russell, on his side, pressed all his Whig friends to unite with Palmerston, and by these means the difficulties were gradually overcome. Lord Lansdowne would not take the Council Office, but agreed to be the organ of the Government in the House of Lords, though he seems afraid this should be thought to have committed him to more trouble and responsibility than he is inclined to take, and it is only a sort of quasi-leadership that he will own to. I find the Queen did propose to him to form a Government, and under certain conditions he was not unwilling to undertake it, but of course he much prefers the present arrangement. It is admitted on all hands that both Aberdeen and Newcastle have behaved very well, and done all in their power to facilitate Palmerston's arrangements. It is, however, much to be regretted that these Peelites have acted in concert and *as a party*, and I see from the fact a vast deal of embarrassment and opposition to the Government in prospect. Already the Derbyites are sulky and angry to the greatest degree, and the Whigs not a little indignant that so much anxiety has been shown to get Gladstone and his friends, and such a high price paid for them ; and the fact of their forming so large and important a part of the Government will secure the fierce hostility of the Derbyites, and make the support of the Whigs very lukewarm. The latter, too, will be influenced by John Russell, who, in spite of his present professions of amity and promises of support, is sure to be very soon a *frondeur*, and then in open and direct opposition. He told Clarendon "he meant to give his best support to the Government." Clarendon said, "You do ; well, at what do you think I value your support ?" "What ?" he asked. "Not one sixpence." *At first* Palmerston will meet with no opposition to signify ; if he does, he has only to dissolve, and the country will give

him a majority.   But opposition will gather about him soon
enough ; extravagant expectations are raised of the good he
is to do and the great acts he is to perform, all of which will
only lead to disappointment and mortification.   If the luck
which for many years accompanied him should do so still,
and some unexpected success crown his administration, he
may thus gain a great position ; but it is idle to depend on
the chapter of accidents and, according to all human probability, he is destined to carry on a disastrous war or to make a
peace (the wisest thing he can do) which will be humiliating,
because so wholly incommensurate with our extravagant expectations and ridiculous pretensions.   However, if any man
can make such a peace it is Palmerston, and it is much better that Aberdeen should have no concern in the Government, for it would be much more difficult if he was in the
Cabinet, and supposed to have any hand in it [1]

February 8th.—Now that all is settled, there is a momentary lull, and people are considering what sort of an arrangement it is, and how it is likely to succeed.   Many of those
who know better what Palmerston really is than the ignorant
mob who shout at his heels, and who have humbugged themselves with the delusion that he is another Chatham, entertain grave apprehensions that the thing will prove a failure,
and that Palmerston's real capacity will be exposed and his
prestige destroyed.   Some wish for a dissolution while his
popularity is still undiminished, fancying it will give him
a sure majority and will protect him against any change of

[1] [The Administration formed by Lord Palmerston was composed as follows:

First Lord of the Treasury	Viscount Palmerston.
Lord Chancellor	Lord Cranworth.
Lord President	Earl Granville.
Lord Privy Seal	Duke of Argyll.
Home Secretary	Sir George Grey.
Foreign Secretary	Earl of Clarendon.
Colonial Secretary . . .	Right Hon. Sidney Herbert (and, on his resignation, Lord John Russell).
Secretary at War . .	Lord Panmure.
Chancellor of the Exchequer	Mr. Gladstone (and, on his resignation, Sir G. Cornewall Lewis).
Board of Control . .	Sir Charles Wood.
First Lord of the Admiralty	Sir James Graham (and, on his resigna-tion, Sir Charles Wood, who was re-placed at the Board of Control by Mr. Vernon Smith).
Board of Trade . .	Right Hon. E. Cardwell (and, on his res-ignation, Lord Stanley of Alderley).
Postmaster General . .	Viscount Canning.
Lord Lieutenant of Ireland	Earl of Carlisle.
Woods and Forests	Sir Benjamin Hall.]

opinion ; but, unless the Derbyites give him an opportunity by some vexatious opposition, he can hardly dissolve, and if he did, though he would gain by it for a time, any change of opinion that might take place would be found no less in the House of Commons than in the country.

February 13th.—The political wheel turns rapidly round, and strange events occur, none more remarkable than John Russell's career during the last month, and the unexpected positions in which he successively appears. A few weeks ago breaking up his own Government, deeply offending col leagues and friends, and making himself generally odious, then trying to form a Government and finding nobody will ing to act with him ; he appeared to be in the most painful position of isolation, and everybody expected that his anomalous and unsatisfactory state would render him mischievous and soon conduct him into a troublesome opposition to the Government.   Very differently have matters turned out. He began by evincing a good and friendly spirit, and scarcely is the Government formed, when Clarendon proposes to him to go to Vienna as Plenipotentiary to treat for peace, and John at once accepts the offer, and yesterday morning his mission was publicly announced.   It was a happy stroke of Clarendon's in all ways, and it was wise in Lord John to accept it, for it has all the appearance of a patriotic and unselfish act, will cause his recent misdeeds to be forgotten, and replace him in the high situation from which he was fallen.   It is a very good thing for him to be thus withdrawn from Parliament for a time.   There he is always in danger of saying and doing something foolish or rash, and it will leave his followers in a condition to attach themselves to the Government without abandoning their allegiance to him, which will relieve all parties from embarrassment.[1]

[1] [The Conference of the Great Powers which was to open at Vienna, to which Lord John Russell was sent as British Plenipotentiary, had been convoked for the purpose of negotiating on the basis of the four points which contained the demands of the belligerent Allies and had been accepted as a basis of negotiation by the Emperor of Russia.   These points were as follows:

1. That Russia should abandon all control over Moldavia, Wallachia, and Servia.

2. That Russia should relinquish her claims to control the mouth of the Danube.

3. That all Treaties calculated to give Russia a preponderance in the Black Sea should be abrogated.

4. That Russia should renounce the claim she made to an exclusive right to protect the Christians in the Ottoman Dominions.

It was on the third of these points that the principal difficulty of the negotiation arose, and that the Conference failed to conclude a peace.]

February 17th.—Palmerston presented himself to the House of Commons last night for the first time as Minister, and not apparently with a very brilliant prospect of success. He made a tolerable speech, giving a rather meagre account of the formation of his Government, with the usual promises of vigor. The great point he had to handle was the disposal of Roebuck's Committee, which he is determined, if he can, to get rid of. The success of this, his first great operation, seems very doubtful. One man after another got up and declared he should vote for its going on. Roebuck insists on it ; and Disraeli announced his determined opposition to any attempt to quash it. If Palmerston fights the battle and is beaten, he must try what a dissolution will do for him ; and I think the success of it would be very doubtful, for, in spite of all the clamor that was raised by his name, and his apparently vast popularity in the country, it looks as if it was of a very shadowy, unsubstantial kind, and would very likely be found wanting at a general election. The temper of the House seems to be anything but good, and unless we are very soon cheered and encouraged by much better accounts from the Crimea, this Government will not fare much better than the last. The "Times" is going into furious opposition, and Palmerston will soon find the whole press against him except his own paper, the "Morning Post," and the "Morning Chronicle," neither of which have any circulation or any influence in the country. The whole conduct of the "Times" is a source of great vexation to me, for I am to the last degree shocked and disgusted at its conduct and the enormous mischief that it is endeavoring to do ; and I have for many years had intimate personal relations with its editor, which I do not well know how to let drop, and I am at the same time not satisfied that their unbroken maintenance is inconsistent with the feelings I entertain, and which ought to be entertained, toward the paper.

February 19th.—The Government have determined to knock under about Roebuck's Committee, and they would have done much better to have done so at first. What they are now doing will not strengthen them or avert future attacks ; but the state of the House of Commons is such that nothing but some very unexpected turn can enable them to go on long. Palmerston has no authority there, the House is in complete confusion and disorganization, and, except the Derbyites, who are still numerous and act together in opposition, in hopes of getting into power, nobody owns any allegiance or even any party ties, or seems to care for any person or any thing.   There seems a general feeling of distrust and dissatisfaction, and, except the scattered Radicals and Revolutionists, who wish to upset everything, nobody seems to know what he would be at, or what object he wishes to attain.   For the first time·in my life I am really and seriously alarmed at the aspect of affairs, and think we are approaching a period of real difficulty and danger.   The press, with the "Times" at its head, is striving to throw everything into confusion, and running a muck against the aristocratic element of society and of the Constitution.   The intolerable nonsense and the abominable falsehoods it flings out day after day are none the less dangerous because they are nonsense and falsehoods, and, backed up as they are by all the regular Radical press, they diffuse through the country a mass of inflammatory matter, the effect of which may be more serious and arrive more quickly than anybody imagines.   Nothing short of some loud explosion will make the mass of people believe that any serious danger can threaten a Constitution like ours, which has passed through so many trials and given so many proofs of strength and cohesion. But we have never seen such symptoms as are now visible, such a thorough confusion and political chaos, or the public mind so completely disturbed and dissatisfied and so puzzled how to arrive at any just conclusions as to the past, the present, or the future.   People are furious at the untoward events in the Crimea, and cannot make out the real causes thereof, nor who is to blame, and they are provoked that they cannot find victims to wreak their resentment on.   The dismissal of Aberdeen and Newcastle seems an inadequate expiation, and they want more vengeance yet, hence the cry for Roebuck's absurd Committee.   Then, after clamoring for Palmerston from a vague idea of his vigor, and that he would do some wonderful things, which was founded on nothing but the recollection of his former bullying despatches and blustering speeches, they are beginning to suspect him ; and the whole press, as well as the malignants in the House of Commons, tell them that they have gained very little, if anything, by the change, and they are told that it is not this or that Minister who can restore our affairs, but a change in the whole system of government, and the substitution of plebeians and new men for the leaders of parties and members of aristocratic families, of whom all Governments have been for the most part composed.   What effect these revolutionary doctrines may have on the opinions of the people at large remains to be seen ; but it is evident that the " Times," their great propagator, thinks them popular and generally acceptable, or they would not have plunged into that course.

I sat next to Charles Wood·at dinner yesterday and had much talk with him on the state of affairs, and found that he takes just the same view that I do, and for the first time he is alarmed also, and so, he told me, is Sir George Grey. He talked much about Raglan, and said that the Government had been placed in the most unfair position possible, it being impossible to throw the blame of anything that had occurred on him, or even to tell the truth, which was that, so far from his making any exertions to repair the evils so loudly complained of, and sending away inefficient men, he never admitted there were any evils at all, or that any of his people were inefficient, or anything but perfect ; and he said that Raglan had never asked for anything the want of which had not been anticipated by the Government here, and in no instance was anything required by him which had not been supplied a month or more before the requisition came. Palmerston, too, said to me that nothing could exceed the hopelessness of the military authorities there ; that they seemed unable to devise anything for their own assistance, and they exhibited the most striking contrast to the navy, who, on all emergencies, set to work and managed to find resources of all sorts to supply their necessities or extricate themselves from danger.

February 20th.—Nothing certainly could be more mortifying than the reception Palmerston met from the House of Commons on the first night when he presented himself as Minister, nothing more ungracious or more disheartening. His entreaty to *postpone* the Committee was received with a sort of scorn and manifestation of hostility and distrust. His position was at once rendered to the last degree painful and difficult.   He cannot avert the Committee, he cannot submit to it without deep humiliation ; many of his colleagues are supposed to shrink from the disgrace of such a submission and to prefer any alternative to it.   Already there is a general impression that this Government cannot last long ; nobody thinks they would gain anything by a dissolution, the result of one would be uncertain ; but the probability seems to be that the Conservatives would gain and the Radicals likewise, while the Whigs would lose, and the Peelites and Moderates would be scattered to the winds. We should most likely see a Parliament still more ungovernable than this, unless a widespread alarm in the country should rally the whole Conservative and anti-revolutionary element to Derby and his party, which would bring them all into office for a time. Palmerston spoke much better last night than the first night, and with a good deal of spirit and force ; but he has a very uphill game to play, and must already be aware how fleeting his popularity was, and on what weak foundations it was built.

February 23d.—Graham, Gladstone, and Sidney Herbert have resigned, greatly to the disgust and indignation of their colleagues, to the surprise of the world at large, and the uproarious delight of the Whigs and Brooks's Club, to whom the Peelites have always been odious. These stupid Whigs were very sorry Palmerston did not leave them out when he formed his Government, and take whomever he could get instead of them ; and they are entirely indifferent to the consideration that the greater part of the brains of the Cabinet is gone out with these three, that it is exceedingly difficult to fill their places, and that we exhibit a sad spectacle to all Europe, with our Ministerial dissensions and difficulties and the apparent impossibility of forming anything like a stable Government. The first thing done was to send off for John Russell at Paris, and ask him if he would come back and join the Government. Cardwell was offered the Chancellorship of the Exchequer, which he refused. It is much to be regretted that these Peelites do not now dissolve themselves as *a party* and make up their minds to act independently and according to their several opinions and circumstances. Aberdeen much disapproves of the exodus of the three, and was very anxious Cardwell should accept ; but he does not choose to separate himself from the rest.

February 24th.—Never was I more surprised than when I heard that John Russell had accepted the Colonial Office and joins the Government, still continuing in the House of Commons, and of course acting under Palmerston. When we think of all he has been doing for the last two years, his discontent at being in a subordinate capacity though still leader of the House of Commons, and the various pranks he has played in consequence thereof, it is inconceivable that he should consent not only to take office under Palmerston, but to serve under him in the House of Commons.   But it is impossible not to give him credit for patriotic motives in making such a sacrifice of personal pride and vanity.   What his conduct may be if the Government lasts long enough to allow him to come home and take his place in it, may be considered doubtful.   Last night the retiring Ministers gave their explanations—Graham in a very good speech ; Gladstone was too diffuse, and Sidney Herbert feeble, but coming after Graham they had nothing new to say.   There is much to be said for and much against their conduct.   If they had accepted office under Palmerston with the condition that he should try and get rid of the Committee and that they should retire in case he failed, there would have been nothing to say, because without doubt they ought not to hold high offices while a Committee of the House of·Commons is sitting in judgment on their conduct ; but the whole course of proceeding is so anomalous, and the exigencies of the time are so great and peculiar, that on the whole I think they ought to have stayed in.   Palmerston speaks almost every night, and his speeches do not read amiss ; but everybody says they are feeble and flat, and nothing at present indicates anything like stability or a long existence to the present Government.   The tone of the House of Commons last night was on the whole rather pacific than not.   Bright made an admirable speech, the peroration of which was very eloquent.

February 25th.—This morning George Lewis came to me very early and told me Palmerston had proposed to him to be Chancellor of the Exchequer ; he set forth very fairly all the reasons for and against accepting.   We discussed the whole subject, and I asked him whether he felt sufficient confidence in himself to undertake an office of such vast importance, whether he had sufficiently turned his attention to financial matters and had mastered the principles and details of finance.   He said he thought he was sufficiently versed therein to undertake it, having given much attention to taxation and its principles, and to political economy generally, though he did not know much about the Funds, but supposed sufficient knowledge about them was easily attainable. Finally I advised him to accept, and he said he should make up his mind to do so.   So the Admiralty, Colonial Office, and Exchequer are settled.   There is much difficulty and much discussion and difference of opinion about some of the other places. They are very wisely going to take in Laing, but very unwisely will not give a place to Lowe, who, if left out, will contrive to do them some damage. Granville has moved Heaven and earth to get Lowe an office, but Palmerston and others set their faces against him. Lansdowne has most unreasonably and unwisely insisted on Vernon Smith being taken in, and it is at present intended to make him President of the Board of Control. He is very unpopular and totally useless, and just the man they ought not to take in ; while Lowe is just the man they ought, to meet the prevailing sentiment about old connections and new men.

March 2d.—News just arrived that the Emperor of Russia is dead. John Russell had telegraphed from Berlin that he was given over. This great and unexpected event must have the most important consequences whether for peace or for war. A disputed succession is not impossible, as it has long been reported that the Grand Duke Constantine was disposed to contest the succession with the Cesarewich, but this will probably turn out to be a fable. It is supposed that the new Emperor has been all along inclined to peace, and that he was in disgrace with his father on that account. If this be true, it renders it still more probable that he will be anxious to put an end to this destructive and dangerous war, and the Allied Powers may be less exacting with him than they were disposed to be with the late Emperor. On the other hand, should the war unhappily continue, the death of Nicholas is likely to damp the ardor of the Russians and to relax their exertions, so that we can hardly fail to profit by it. Clarendon is gone over to Boulogue to confer with the Emperor Napoleon.

There seems something like a lull here for the moment, and less of excitement and violence than there was. Palmerston has not been in office a fortnight, and already he is enormously *baissé;* his speeches night after night are miserable. The truth is, he never had any power as a debater, and he is out of his element as leader in the House of Commons, where he has to answer everybody, to speak on every subject, and to be continually debating more or less. He has made a few great speeches, prepared, and on his own subject of foreign affairs, and every now and then a smart chaffing retort which excited the hilarity of the House, and that has been all he could do.   Then he seems supine and undecided; he does not fill up the vacant places or seemingly endeavor to do so, and he does not put good men in the places he does fill up, all of which does him harm in general estimation.   Clarendon has told Lady Palmerston very frankly that he will soon ruin himself in public opinion if he goes on in this way.   Few things are more extraordinary than the notion that was abroad of Palmerston's fitness and efficacy.   Never was there a greater delusion, and never one that is so rapidly being dissipated.

March 10*th*.—It is remarkable that, though seven days have elapsed since the news of the death of the Emperor of Russia reached us, and that we heard of it by electric telegraph the very day it happened, we are still without authentic and detailed information of what has since occurred at St. Petersburg; and of the manifesto of the new Emperor, which is looked for with so much curiosity, we have only a partial extract or imperfect summary, so that we have still no means of judging whether the chances of peace are improved by the accession of Alexander II.

Palmerston's Government does not seem to take root or gain much strength; every day seems to prove the more clearly that he is unfit for the task he has taken on himself. He inspires neither respect nor confidence, and is totally unable to manage the House of Commons; his speeches are feeble and bad, and he is not always prudent and conciliatory, but, on the contrary, pettish and almost offensive. He finds great difficulty in filling the vacant offices, and he evinces much want of tact and good management in his endeavors to do so, offering and retracting his offers in a very loose way.   For example, he offered Sir Robert Peel the Clerkship of the Ordnance, which he accepted; and then he found Monsell did not mean to resign it, so he had to withdraw the offer.   Then he told him he should be Colonial Under-Secretary if John Russell would consent.   John Russell would not consent, and then he offered him a seat at the Admiralty.   Sir Robert in some dudgeon demurred, and Palmerston, inferring from his ill humor that he would not take this place, offered it to Henry Brand, who accepted, desired his writ might be moved for, and went to the railway station to go down to the place he represented.   Just as he was starting, a messenger arrived with a letter from Palmerston saying Sir Robert Peel had taken the Admiralty, so he could not have it, and the gentleman had to return home without any office at all. This is a sad way of doing business, and will not make him more popular. Grenville Berkeley (whipper-in) told me he thought Palmerston was doing rather better latterly and that there was a better disposition in the House of Commons; but Jonathan Peel, who is a shrewd, dispassionate observer, and tolerably impartial, though with no good will to the present Government, told me a different story. He says the Government is as weak as possible, Palmerston wretched, and the House of Commons ill disposed and unruly, and he thinks it absolutely impossible that this concern can last many weeks. The Derbyites are quite confident of forcing their way to office, and quite determined to do so; but it is their game to damage the present Government as much as possible, and they will do everything in opposition but what may recoil upon themselves after they have got into office, and no other consideration will restrain them. I regard with the utmost dislike the prospect of their return, because I think their conduct so monstrously unprincipled. I hear Gladstone is very much out of humor, and expect soon to see him and his small band in overt opposition to the Government. Many fancy that it will end in his joining Derby, but so do not I. I am not sure that he would be indisposed if a proper occasion presented itself, but I do not believe any consideration or any circumstances whatever would induce the Derbyites to admit him again into their party. Their indignation—that is, of a great many of them—was unbounded at Derby having offered him office the other day, and at the great meeting at Eglinton's such manifestations of resentment were made on that account as to make it nearly impossible (for in these days nothing is quite impossible) for any future attempt at reconciliation and reunion to be made.

March 11*th.*—A fresh shuffling of the cards is being arranged by which Frederick Peel is to go to the Treasury, *vice* Wilson, Vice President of the Board of Trade; Sir Robert to the War Department, *vice* his brother; and Henry Brand to the Admiralty. Palmerston seemed to consider all the blunders he made about these officers rather a good joke than a mischievous *gaucherie.* " Ha, ha!" he said, "a Comedy of Errors." George Lewis told me this morning he thinks the temper of the House of Commons more favorable, and, if he can succeed in producing a palateable Budget, that

10

they may get on; he told me the revenue was extremely flourishing and the country very rich, but the expenses are enormous. He means to meet them by a loan, but the question is of what amount, and how much of the additional expense shall be provided by it. He will want ninety millions to cover the whole.

Clarendon was much pleased with his visit to the Emperor, who talked to him very frankly and unreservedly about everything. They lit their cigars and sat and talked with the greatest ease. He said the Emperor spoke to him about the English press, and all he said was sensible and true; that he was aware that a free press was a necessity in England, and as indispensable as the Constitution itself, and that he had hitherto believed that the editors of the principal newspapers had the good of their country at heart, and always acted from conscientious motives; but that he could no longer entertain that opinion. The press during the past months, and the "Times" particularly, had done an incalculable amount of mischief to England and to the alliance between us. The effect produced by their language in Germany was most injurious, and of service only to Russia. When the English papers talked of their own country in the way they did, of its degradation and disgrace, its maladministration, the ruin of its military power, and the loss of all that makes a nation great and powerful, though he (the Emperor) knew what all this meant, and how much or how little of truth there was in such exaggerated statements, yet in France they were generally believed, and it became very difficult for him to reconcile the nation to an alliance for which he was reproached with making sacrifices and shaping his policy in accordance with ours, when it was evident from our own showing that our alliance was not worth having, and our impotence was so exposed that, whenever peace should put an end to the necessity of the alliance, we should be entirely at their mercy; and while such was the feeling in France, in Germany it was still stronger, and there the "Times" had succeeded in creating a universal conviction that we are in the lowest condition of weakness and inefficiency: at all of which he expressed the greatest regret. I was surprised to hear Clarendon say that he did not believe the resources of Russia to carry on the contest to be in any sensible degree exhausted, that her commerce had not suffered at all, and as to her finances she could go on for a good while with her paper money and the gold which, in a certain quantity, she drew from the Ural Mountains.[1]

---◆◆◆---

CHAPTER IX.

The Vienna Conference—Literary Occupations—A Roman Catholic Privy Councillor—Negotiations at Vienna—The Emperor Napoleon in London—The Emperor's brilliant Reception—Russia refuses the Terms offered—The Sebastopol Committee—Debate on the War—Visit to Paris—Resignation of M. Drouyn de Lhuys—The Emperor's Journey to the Crimea—The Repulse at the Redan—Visit to Thiers—A Dinner at the Tuileries—Conversation with the Emperor—M. Guizot on the War—Death of Lord Raglan—A Dinner at Princess Lieven's—The Palace of Versailles—Revelations of Lord John Russell's Mission—Dinner with the Emperor at Villeneuve l'Etang—Lord John Russell's Conduct at Vienna—Excitement in London—Lord John's Resignation—Lord John's Conduct explained—" Whom shall we Hang?"—Prorogation of Parliament.

March 31st, 1855.—Three weeks have passed away and I have had nothing to say; nor indeed have I anything now of the least importance, and can only glance at the general aspect of affairs. The Government, on the whole, seems in a somewhat better condition. They say Palmerston speaks better than he did, and his good humor and civility please. At last the offices, except the Under-Secretaryship to the Colonies, are filled up. Lord Elgin and Lord Seymour successively refused the Duchy of Lancaster, and after going a begging for many weeks Lord Harrowby has taken it. Laing and Wilson, and I think somebody else, declined the Vice Presidency of the Board of Trade, and they have got Bouverie.

Within these few days the hopes of peace have waxed faint. The fatal third point is an insurmountable obstacle, and it seems likely that we shall be condemned to fight it out more fiercely than ever, and without Austria, who, as I all along expected, will not join us in forcing hard conditions on Russia. It remains to be seen whether we or Austria are

---

[1] [In justice to the conductors of the " Times " it must be said that although the language of the paper was violent and extremely annoying to the Government and its Allies, yet it was by the power and enterprise of the press that the deplorable state of the army was brought to the knowledge of the public and even of Ministers themselves; and it was by the " Times " that the first steps were taken to supply the deficiencies of the Administration. The fund raised by voluntary contributions for this purpose amounted to £25,000, and competent persons were sent out to apply it to the most pressing wants of the army.]

in fault, assuming the rupture of the negotiations to be inevitable. If Austria recedes from what she had already agreed to, she is; if we require anything more, we are. Drouyn de Lhuys has been here for twenty-four hours, and goes on to Vienna directly to bring things to a conclusion one way or another. Clarendon is pleased with him. The Emperor is to be here in three weeks.

Having no public events nor any secret information to record, I must put down my own private concerns, uninteresting as they are. I am busy on the task of editing a volume of Moore's correspondence left to me by John Russell, and finishing the second article upon King Joseph's Memoirs.[1] These small literary occupations interest and amuse me, and being quite out of the way of politics, and seeing nobody, except Clarendon at rare intervals, who can or will tell me anything, it is well I can amuse myself with them; and now that I am growing old (for I shall be sixty-one the day after to-morrow) it is my aim to cultivate these pleasures more and more, and make them my refuge against the infirmities which beset me, and the loss of youth. My great fear is lest my eyesight should fail, and I earnestly hope I may die before such a calamity should befall me.

The war goes languidly on, and I hear Raglan and Canrobert are squabbling instead of acting, and that it seems to be more the fault of Canrobert; but the melancholy truth is that there are two incompetent generals in command, who have no skill or enterprise, and are letting the opportunity for attacking the enemy slip away. A divided command and two independent armies are in themselves an immense drawback, but when they begin to disagree it becomes fatal. We have now an enormous force there, and yet they seem incapable of doing anything and of striking any great and serious blow.

April 1st.—I went to a Council yesterday and got into a difficulty. Without any previous notice, Mr. Monsell, a Roman Catholic, came to be made a Privy Councillor. I had never sworn a Roman Catholic and did not know what to do, so I proposed to Monsell to put it off till another day, and meanwhile I would ascertain how he was to be sworn. The difficulty was told to the Queen, and the Prince set about finding what was to be done. He looked out the 10th

---

[1] [Mr. Greville wrote the review of the Memoirs of King Joseph Bonaparte which appeared in two successive articles of the *Edinburgh Review*.]

George IV. (Emancipation Act), and, just as we were summoned into the Queen's presence, Granville brought the volume, put it into my hands, and told me I must administer to Monsell the oath set forth there, in lieu of the oaths of abjuration and supremacy. I was sure it was a mistake; but there was no time to remonstrate, and I was compelled to bring him in and administer the oath. As soon as I got back to my office and looked into the matter I found it was all wrong, and that he had not, in fact, been sworn at all. What he ought to have done was to take this oath in one of the Law Courts, and then to have the Privy Councillor's oath administered to him, and so I sent him word.

Afterward I met Sidney Herbert, and he told me what he believed to be the cause of Drouyn de Lhuys' coming here, and the actual state of affairs at Vienna. We have proposed the reduction of the fleet; the Russians refuse. The Emperor Napoleon would like, if possible, to obtain some great success in the Crimea, and is not indisposed to continue the war if he can see a reasonable hope of such an achievement; but when he despairs of this his mind inclines to the other alternative, to make peace (which would be popular in France), and he does not care very much about the terms, and is not averse to waive the condition as to the fleet. But our Government want to insist on it, or go on with the war, and Sidney Herbert believes they have succeeded in talking over Drouyn de Lhuys and persuading him to join us in this determination, and to carry it off to Vienna. However, he is very likely to be talked over again there, and it remains to be seen whether the Emperor, if he really wishes for peace, will not join with Austria in opposing us, and accepting some other conditions. I always fancied that we had come to a regular unmistakeable agreement with Austria what we should ask of Russia, and that she had bound herself to join in the war if the terms agreed in were refused, but, according to Sidney Herbert, this has never been done. Clarendon did, indeed, *at last* state distinctly to Austria the terms on which France and England meant to insist, and Austria expressed her concurrence in them as a matter of opinion, and her desire to obtain them, consenting also to unite her efforts to theirs in attempting to obtain them; but she never consented to go to war if they were not conceded, therefore we have no reason to complain of her if the negotiations break off on these grounds, and she refuses to depart from her neutrality. She has all along said, she wished with all her heart we could succeed in taking Sebastopol, but as we had not succeeded, and apparently could not, it was impossible to press very stringent terms on Russia; and she has never held out any expectation to us of joining in the war against Russia, unless Russia refuses such reasonable and not humiliating terms of peace as she herself thinks indispensable for the objects to the attainment of which she has all along been a party. The best chance of peace now is that the Emperor Napoleon may think he is not likely to do any great things in the Crimea and that peace is his best policy, and he is the real arbiter of peace and war. If he prefers following in the wake of England, and to defer to our war policy, peace will ascend to Heaven, and the odious war will be resumed with more fury than ever, and no one can guess how long it will last, nor what will be the end of it.

April 17th.—Yesterday I went out " with all the gazing town " to see not the least curious of the many curious events I have lived to witness, the entry of the Emperor and Empress of the French into London. The day was magnificent, the crowd prodigious, the reception not very clamorous, but cordial and respectful. A fine sight for them to see such vast multitudes, so orderly and so prosperous, and without a single soldier except their own escort. The Queen received them with the utmost cordiality, and omitted none of the usual forms practised between Sovereigns. She met the Imperial pair at the entrance to the Castle, embraced the Emperor and then the Empress when she was presented to her.

April 20th.—The visit of the Emperor has been one continued ovation, and the success of it complete. None of the Sovereigns who have been here before have ever been received with such magnificence by the Court or by such curiosity and delight by the people. Wherever and whenever they have appeared, they have been greeted by enormous multitudes and prodigious acclamations. The Queen is exceedingly pleased with both of them; she thinks the Empress very natural, graceful, and attractive, and the Emperor frank, cordial, and true. He has done his best to please her, talked to her a great deal, amused her, and has completely succeeded. Everybody is struck with his mean and diminutive figure and vulgar appearance, but his manners are good and not undignified. He talked a very long time to Lord Derby on Tuesday at Windsor, and to Lord Aberdeen on Wednesday.   This last was very proper, because he had a great prejudice against Aberdeen, and fancied he was his enemy, which Aberdeen knew.   When he was invested with the Garter, he took all sorts of oaths—old feudal oaths—of fidelity and knightly service to the Queen, and he then made her a short speech to the following effect: "I have sworn to be faithful to Your Majesty and to serve you to the best of my ability, and my whole future life shall be spent in proving the sincerity with which I have thus sworn, and my resolution to devote myself to your service."   The fineness of the weather brought out the whole population of London, as usual kept in excellent order by a few policemen, and in perfect good humor.   It was a beautiful sight last night when the Royal and Imperial party went to the Opera in state ; the streets lit by gas and the houses illuminated and light as day, particularly opposite the Travellers' Club, where I was.   I am glad the success of the visit has been so great, and the contentment of all the parties concerned so complete, but it is well that all will be over to-morrow, for such excitement and enthusiasm could not last much longer, and the inconvenience of being beset by crowds, and the streets obstructed, is getting tiresome.

I saw Cowley for a moment yesterday.   He told me the Russians refused any conditions which imposed loss of territory or limitation of naval forces, and they declined to offer any counter project, though they are ready to discuss anything we propose.   He therefore considers the continuance of the war unavoidable, and does not believe Austria will join in it, though Drouyn de Lhuys still writes his own expectation that she will.   He said they had never said or done anything which bound them to join, and that their diplomacy had been much more adroit and successful than our's, but that this was principally the fault of the French, who never would consent to take a peremptory course so as to compel them to be explicit.   The consequence of this is, that it will be impossible to produce the diplomatic correspondence, and its retention will put Parliament and the press in a fury, and expose the Government to attacks which they will find it very difficult to repel or to silence.   They cannot give the reason why, and their enemies and detractors will believe, or at least insist, that they do not

dare disclose their own share in the transaction. I asked
Clarendon how it was that the French Government in their
last paper in the "Moniteur" said so positively that they
had secured the co-operation of Austria if the last conditions
were refused by Russia ; he replied that he supposed they
said so in order to make it the ground of an accusation
against Austria when the Conference broke up and she refuses to declare war. Clarendon thinks we shall get the
better of Russia, but that it will be by blockading her ports
and ruining her commerce, and not by military operations,
and that this may take two or three years or more, but is
certain in the end.[1]

May 24th.—The Sebastopol Committee is finished, and
the result proves that it is a very good thing to have had it,
for no ill consequences have come of it, and the evidence
has benefited instead of injuring both the Government and
those who were most bitterly abused, especially Hardinge
and Newcastle, about the latter of whom there has been a
considerable reaction of opinion. In Parliament nothing has
taken place of much consequence. Ellenborough gave battle in the Lords and was signally defeated. Layard had announced a hostile motion in the House of Commons, which
he has since given up to Disraeli, who brings forward a regular want of confidence motion to-night, which will decide
the fate of the Government. Sir Francis Baring has moved
an amendment which the Peelites will not vote for, because
it pledges the House to support the war, they having now
become furiously pacific ; as if they were not unpopular
enough already, they are now doing all they can to mar
their own efficacy by giving their enemies a plausible case
for attacking and abusing them, and by breasting the tide of
warlike zeal and passion, which, though very absurd and very
mischievous, is too strong and too general to be openly and
directly resisted at present. It is quite fit and becoming to
reason with it, and to endeavor to bring the public to a more
reasonable frame of mind, but great tact, caution, and good
management are required in doing this. It is very difficult
to make out what Gladstone and his friends (for it would be
ridiculous to call them a party) are at, and what they expect
or desire in reference to their political future. Palmerston

---

[1] [The failure or suspension of the negotiations for peace at Vienna was
formally announced to Parliament on May 21, and the protocols of the Conference laid upon the table.]

is said to have done better in the House of Commons lately
than he did at first, but it is curious to see how completely
his popularity has evaporated.   All the foolish people whose
pet he was, and who clamored for him with the notion that
he was to do every sort of impossible thing, now that they
find he can do no more than other men, and that there never
was any real difference between him and his colleagues, are
furious with him because they so deceived themselves, and
want to break the idol they set up.

May 30th.—The division last Friday night gave Government a larger majority than anybody expected,[1] and if it did
not give them permanent strength it averted immediate danger.   Gladstone made a fine speech, but gave great offence
to all who are not for peace, and exposed himself to much
unpopularity.   The discussion is only suspended till Parliament meets again, when the amendments will be debated,
and there will be no more divisions ; but in the meantime the
news which has arrived of the successes in the Crimea, and
the fair prospect there appears of still greater advantages,
must serve to silence the advocates of peace and encourage
those who are all for war, and to render a contest popular
which is likely to be crowned with brilliant results, and, as
many imagine, to give us the means of dictating peace on
our own terms.   I believe in the prospect of success, but not
that it will reduce the Russians to make peace on our terms,
particularly as the conditions will infallibly be harder than
before.   But I do marvel that they did not make peace at
Vienna on the terms which were there offered them, when
they must have known that all the chances of war were
against them.   The Emperor of Russia might have taken
warning from the history and fate of Napoleon, who constantly refused the terms he could have obtained, and continually insisted on something more than his enemies would
give him, and by this obstinacy lost his crown.   The most
interesting incident which occurred last week was the scene
at the end of the debate between Graham and John Russell,
who had a fight of considerable asperity ; and according to
all appearances the Peelites and the Whigs are completely
two.   When Graham was reconciled to Lord John two or
three years ago, he vowed that nothing should separate them

---

[1] [Mr. Disraeli's Motion condemning the Government for their misconduct
of the war was rejected by 319 to 219.   Lord John Russell made a warlike
speech in the course of this debate.]

again, but " quam parum stabiles sunt hominum amicitiæ,"
and now they appear to be as antagonistic as ever.   But, to
be sure, Graham could not contemplate or foresee all the
tricks which Lord John played during the whole time he was
a member of Aberdeen's Government.

Notwithstanding the success of Government in the House
of Commons and of the armies in the Crimea, things are in
a very unsatisfactory and uncomfortable state here, and nobody knows what will happen.   There is no confidence in
any party or any men, and everybody has a vague apprehension of coming but undefined evil and danger.   The world
seems out of joint.

Paris, June 17th.—Having resolved to go to Vichy for
my health, here I am on the road ; I crossed over yesterday
morning, a very disagreeable but short passage from Folkestone, good journey by rail, and got here at nine o'clock, being lodged very hospitably at the Embassy.   French carriages
on the railway are much better than ours, particularly the
second class ; the country between Boulogne and Paris looks
well and thriving.   I had some talk with Cowley last night
before we went to bed, when he gave me an account of the
circumstances of Drouyn de Lhuys' resignation.[1]   He also
descanted on the difficulties of the Government here and of
the maintenance of the alliance, which he attributes up to
this time entirely to the good faith and fairness of the Emperor himself, and his determination that nothing shall interrupt the good understanding between the two countries,
on which he is above all things bent.   The Emperor says it
is a great misfortune that there are no men of capacity or
character whose services he can command, nor in fact any
men, if he could command their services, in whom the public would be disposed to place confidence.   Cowley had no
very good opinion of Drouyn de Lhuys, and said no reliance
could be placed in him ; but in some respects he is a loss, because he has a certain capacity and clean hands, he is enormously rich, and guiltless of any peculation or jobbery.   When
Drouyn announced that he meant to go to Vienna, Lord Cowley urged him to go to England first and come to an under-

---

[1] [At the Conference at Vienna M. Drouyn de Lhuys departed from the
conditions of peace agreed to between the French and British Governments,
and was disposed to accept the more favorable terms which were supported by
Austria.   This led to his disavowal and resignation on his return to Paris.   It
turned out that Lord John Russell, the British envoy to the Conference, had
taken a similar course.]

standing with the Cabinet there as to the terms which should be proposed at the Conference. He consented and went, and Cowley urged Clarendon to have the agreement put down in writing that there might be no mistake about it. This was done, and Drouyn went to Vienna. When he took upon himself to make the proposition he did, it was in direct opposition to his agreement with us, but he thought he should bring the Emperor to concur with him and to sanction it. The Emperor seemed at first disposed to do so, and when he saw Cowley intimated as much to him. Cowley submitted that it was quite contrary to the understanding with us, and objected on every ground to the proposal. The Emperor said he really got quite confused in the intricacies and details of this affair, but he would see Drouyn again and speak to him upon it. Cowley requested (a very strange request as he owned) that he might be present at the interview. The Emperor seemed somewhat surprised, but acquiesced. When Cowley came he found Drouyn had been there an hour, and that Marshal Vaillant was also present. They went over the ground again and Drouyn said what he had to say. when Cowley merely said he would not go into the general question and would only ask whether M. Drouyn's proposal was in conformity with what had been settled in London, and he appealed to Marshal Vaillant whether the termination of the war on such terms would be advisable. It was impossible to maintain that the terms were consistent with the joint agreement, and Vaillant declared that if the French army was brought away, and a peace made on conditions which would appear to tarnish the honor of their arms, he would not answer for the consequences. This put an end to the discussion. Drouyn de Lhuys retired, and as soon as he got home sent his resignation to the Emperor, who wrote him back a very good-humored answer advising him to recall it, and expressing a wish that he would come and talk the matter over with him, when he had no doubt they should come to a satisfactory understanding. Drouyn persisted, and then the Emperor accepted his resignation and sent for Walewski. I asked Cowley how Walewski was likely to do, and he said wretchedly, and that he was not of a calibre to fill such a post.

He told me all about the intended journey of the Emperor to the Crimea and why it was given up. The Emperor was bent on it, while all the Ministers deprecated it and did all they could to prevent it. They suggested that, if any misfortune occurred while he was there, he could not quit the army ; if any success, he would infallibly stay to pursue it, so that his speedy return could not be counted on. This failed to move him. The intention was that Jérome should be, not Regent, but Chief of the Council of Ministers, and they advised Jérome only to consent to take this office on condition that he was invested with the same despotic power as the Emperor himself. This His Majesty would not consent to, as the Ministers foresaw, and this was the reason why the expedition was given up.

Paris, June 23d.—I came here to pass through to Vichy, and accordingly on Tuesday last to Vichy I went. I arrived there in the evening, found a detestable apartment without a fireplace ; the weather was intolerable, it never ceased raining, and the cold was intense. Finding that it was useless to take the waters or baths in such weather, and being disgusted with the whole thing, I resolved to return to Paris, which I did on Friday, and here I am comfortably established in the Embassy again.

On my arrival I was greeted with the painful intelligence of the repulse sustained by the French and English on the 18th in the attack on the Mamelon and Redan batteries, and of the great losses which both armies had suffered. This failure has cast a great gloom over Paris and London and the disappointment is greater because we had become so accustomed to success that everybody regarded failure in anything as impossible. Cowley told me that the Emperor was excessively annoyed, and the more because they entirely disapprove of Pélissier's proceedings. Without tying him down or attempting from hence to direct the operations of the campaign, they had given Pélissier the strongest recommendations to abstain from assaults which they had reason to believe would not be decisive and would cost a vast number of lives, and they were very anxious the operations against the Russians in the field should be pressed instead. There had been some half angry communications between the Government and Pélissier, who had talked of resigning the command. The opinions of the Government had been principally formed from those of General Niel, who had constantly reported his conviction to the above mentioned effect, and had earnestly deprecated these assaults. Then there is reason to apprehend that such unsuccessful attempts may produce bad blood and mutual accusations between the allied forces. Already Pélissier and Raglan have begun to cast the blame of the failure on each other, though apparently the difference has not yet swelled to any serious amount. I have always thought that it would have been better to have no divided command, but to place an English corps under a French commander-in-chief, and a French squadron under an English admiral. This was what the Emperor proposed, and he wrote a letter himself on the subject, which Cowley promised to show me. We have had much conversation about the Emperor, his character and his capacity, and I am puzzled how to understand and to do justice to the latter. Being such as he is represented to be, and having the defects he has, it is difficult to comprehend his having accomplished the great things he has, and raised himself to such a situation and such a height of personal power.

June 24th.—Last night I went to Thiers', where I found Mignet, Roger du Nord, and others of his adherents, none of whom I recollected, nor they me. This morning I called on Achille Fould, who told me the Emperor knew I was here and would like me to be presented to him, and it was settled that this should be done. I am nothing loath, for I have a curiosity to see this remarkable man and to converse with with him. Madame de Lieven told me this morning that not long before the Revolution of '48, Jérome Bonaparte had entreated her to exert her influence to get him made a peer.

June 26th.—Yesterday morning arrived an invitation to dine at the Tuileries the same evening. I went there, was ushered into a room with eight or ten men in it, none of whom I knew except Count Bacciochi, whom I had met at Fould's the day before—three in uniform, the rest in plain clothes. A man, whom I suppose to be the *aide de camp de service*, came forward to receive me and invited me to sit down. Presently the same or another man came and said "Milord" (they all milorded me), "vous vous mettrez à table, s'il vous plaît, à côté de l'Empereur à sa droite." I was then taken into the next room, which adjoins the cabinet of the Emperor. In a few minutes His Majesty made his appearance; he immediately came up to me, bowed very civilly, and asked me the usual questions of when I came to Paris, etc. In a minute dinner was announced, and we went in. As we walked in he said to me, "L'Impératrice sera bien fâchée de ne vous avoir pas vu." At dinner, which did not last above twenty-five minutes, he talked (a sort of dropping conversation) on different subjects, and I found him so easy to get on with that I ventured to start topics myself. After dinner we returned to the room we had left, and after coffee, seeing me staring about at the portraits, he said all his family were there, and he told me who they all were and the history of these portraits, which, he said, had made the tour of the world.

After this he asked me to sit down, which I did at a round table by his side, and M. Visconti on the other side of me, and then we had a conversation which lasted at least an hour and a half on every imaginable subject. It was impossible not to be struck with his simplicity, his being so natural and totally without any air or assumption of greatness, though not undignified, but perfectly *comme il faut,* with excellent manners, and easy, pleasant, fluent conversation. I was struck with his air of truth and frankness, and though of course I could not expect in my position and at this first interview with him that he should be particularly expansive, yet he gave me the idea of being not only not reserved but as if, when intimate, he would have a great deal of *abandon.* It was difficult to bring away all the subjects he discussed, and I do not know that he said anything wonderfully striking, but he made a very favorable impression on me, and made me wish to know more of him, which I am never likely to do.

He talked of the war and its conduct, of the faults committed, and of the characters and talents of the generals engaged, comparing them, much to their disadvantage, with the generals of the Empire. I asked him which were the best, and he said all the African generals were much of the same calibre : Changarnier, Lamoricière, St. Arnaud, Canrobert, Pélissier—very little difference between them. The war they waged in Africa was of a peculiar character, and did not render them more capable of conducting great strategical operations in Europe. He talked of Thiers and Odilon Barrot, and described scenes with the latter in Council when Barrot was his Minister; of the "Times" and its influence; of Spain; in short, of a vast variety of subjects; of the Exhibition here, and with some appearance of disappointment that the people will not go to it. His simplicity

and absence of all *faste* were remarkable ; thus, I asked him
what he thought of the Hango affair, when he said it was
not so bad as had been reported.   "I have had an account
of it from Admiral Penaud to-day ; should you like to see
it ?"   I said "Yes," when he got up, went into his cabinet,
and came back with the letter in his hand ; and a little
while after, when we were talking of the siege of Sebastopol,
he asked if I had ever seen a very good engineer's map of
the whole thing; and when I said I had not, he said, "Then
I will show you one ; " and he again went into his cabinet
and brought it out.   After this long palaver he took leave of
me, shaking hands with much apparent cordiality.

June 27th.—Bosquet has written to the Emperor that
these assaults on the Russian works are only a useless waste
of time.   Marshal Vaillant has told Cowley that they ag ee
in this, but they must either recall their general or let him
go on in his own way, and if they interfere, the blame of any
disaster will inevitably fall on them, no matter what might
be the cause.   I dined with Flahaut yesterday ; in the morning rode round all the boulevards, a grand promenade by
which Paris is well seen ; and I met Guizot at Madame de
Lieven's, who talked of the war and asked how it was ever to
end.   "People go to war," he said, "to make conquests or to
make peace ; you profess not to intend the first, how do you
propose to effect the second ?   By reducing Russia to accept
your terms—can you do so ? will she yield ?   If not, what
then ?—you may wound her, but you can't strike her in a
vital part ; and the more barbarous she is, the more she will
consent to suffer and the less she will be disposed to yield."
He gave me an account (in short) of the bother about the
Academy and the Emperor's interference.   They do not
mean to give way, but they think he will ; if he does not, he
will have to dissolve them.

Paris, July 5th.—One of my attacks of gout came on
this day week and disabled me from going anywhere, doing
anything, and still more from writing anything.   In the
meanwhile we received the news of Lord Raglan's death.[1]
Though they do not care about it here, there has been a very
decent display of sympathy and regret, and the Emperor
wrote to Cowley with his own hand a very proper letter.
There is good reason to believe that the fatal termination of

---

[1] [Lord Raglan died in the Crimea on June 28.]

Lord Raglan's illness was in some (perhaps in great) measure produced by vexation and disappointment at the failure of the 18th, and annoyance at the many embarrassments of his position.   It is certain that for a considerable time great disunion and poignant differences existed between him and the French generals.   Canrobert wrote home a very unhandsome letter, in which he gave as one of his reasons for resigning the impossibility of going on with Raglan.   I believe Raglan complained of Canrobert with much better reason. On the 18th Pélissier changed the plan of attack that had been agreed on between them ; and, besides all the mistakes that occurred in the French operations, there seems to have been a want of continual and active concert between the two commanders-in-chief during the operations.   Raglan proposed a general attack on the town when the assaults failed, which Pélissier refused to agree to.   There is a fair probability this would have succeeded, as an English force did get into a part of the town, stayed there some time, and got away unobserved.   There is now a bad feeling, a disposition to recrimination, between the two armies, which may have very bad effects, and it is awful to think our army is under an untried man of whom nothing is known, and who is not likely to have more weight with, and receive more consideration from, the French generals than his predecessor.   However desirable unity of command may be, in the present temper of the troops, and after all that has occurred, it would be impossible.   General Torrens, who is here, speaks in high terms of Raglan, especially of his magnanimity in bearing all the blame which has been thrown upon him and never saying one word in his own vindication, which might have entirely exonerated him, but have done some injury to the cause. Torrens thinks that in all or almost all in which he has appeared most obnoxious to censure he could have triumphantly excused himself, and have proved that the causes were attributable to others and not to himself.   His must have been a painful as it was an ungrateful service, and it was a melancholy and untimely end.

Paris, July 6th.—I went yesterday to the Exhibition in the morning ; then to Notre Dame and the Luxembourg Gardens, and drove about Paris ; dined *en trio* with Madame de Lieven and Guizot, when there was of course nothing but political talk.   Guizot thinks there has been not only a series of diplomatic blunders, but a wonderful want of *invention*, not to strike out some means of adjusting this quarrel, in which I agree with him. This morning Labouchere and I went to Versailles. Fould had given me a letter to the Director of the Museum there, M. Soulié, whom we found very intelligent, well informed, and obliging. We told him our object was to avoid the *giro regolare* of the endless rooms fitted up with bad pictures by Louis Philippe, and to see the apartments full of historical associations from the time of Louis XIV. down to the Revolution. We were completely gratified, and he took us over everything we wished to see, being admirably qualified as a cicerone by his familiarity with the localities and the history belonging to them. We saw all the apartments in which Louis XIV. lived, and what remains of those of Madame de Maintenon. The Palace has been so tumbled about at different times, and such alterations made in it, that it is not always easy to ascertain correctly where the rooms of certain personages were, but our guide proved to our complete satisfaction that certain rooms he showed us were those which really did belong to Madame de Maintenon. We saw too in minute detail the apartments of Louis XVI. and Marie Antoinette, and the passages through which she fled to escape from the irruption of the mob on the 5th of October. The whole thing was as interesting as possible.

Paris, July 9th.—I meant to have left Paris last night, but, an invitation arriving to dine with the Emperor at St. Cloud to-day, I put off going till to-morrow. I went yesterday to Versailles to see the *grandes eaux* and was disappointed, and dined there with the Ashburtons. This morning telegraphic news came of a Russian sortie last night; no details of course. Yesterday we were thrown into consternation by the intelligence from London of the revelations of John Russell in the House of Commons and the discussion thereupon. Le Marchant wrote to Labouchere and told him the effect was as bad as possible, and the whole case very deplorable. My own opinion is that nobody could have acted more indiscreetly and unjustifiably than John Russell has done, and he has sacrificed his character and authority in a way which he will find it difficult to get over. But I am disposed to agree with him that the terms proposed by Austria, if they could have been brought to maturity and carried out, were quite sufficient to make peace upon, and that the negotiations ought to have continued in order to endeavor to bring about this result. The effect of this

public announcement to the whole world, that the English
Minister at the Congress as well as the French one was
willing to accept the terms proposed by Austria, will not fail
to make a great sensation, and produce a considerable effect
both in Germany and in France. In England it is doubtful
whether it will have any other result than to damage John
Russell himself, and increase the vulgar prejudice against
public men. My own idea is that it will render the war
still more unpopular in France, and the English alliance
likewise, because it will encourage the prevailing notion
that the war is carried on for English interests and in
deference to the wishes of England. Though John Russell
declared that the resolution of the Emperor to part with
Drouyn de Lhuys and reject the Austrian proposal had been
made before the intention of the English Cabinet was known,
this will not be believed, or at all events everybody will be
convinced that he knew what the sentiments of England
were, and that he really acted in conformity with them, as
was beyond all doubt the case.

July 10th.—I dined at Villeneuve l'Étang. We went to
the Palace of St. Cloud in Cowley's carriage, where we found
an equerry and one of the Emperor's carriages, which took us
to Villeneuve. A small house, pretty and comfortable enough,
and a small party, all English—Duke and Duchess of Hamilton, Lord Hertford, Lord and Lady Ashburton, General
Torrens and his *aide de camp*, Cowley and myself, the Duc
de Bassano, Comte de Montebello, the *aide de camp de service*,
and M. Valabrègue, *écuyer*, that was the whole party. The
Emperor sat between the two ladies, taking the Duchess in
to dinner. It lasted about three quarters of an hour, and as
soon as it was over His Majesty took us all out to walk about
the place, see the dairy and a beautiful Bretonne cow he ordered to be brought out, and then to scull on the lake, or
étang, which give its name to the place. There were a number of little boats for one person to scull and one to sit, and
one larger for two each ; the Emperor got into one with the
Duchess, and all the rest of the people as they liked, and we
passed about half an hour on the water. On landing, ices,
etc., were brought, and the carriages came to the door at nine
o'clock, a *char à banc* with four *percherons* and postillions
exactly like the old French postboy, and several other open
carriages and pair. The two ladies got into the center of
the *char à banc*, Cowley, Hertford, and I were invited to get

up before, and the Emperor himself got up behind with
somebody else, I did not see who. We then set off and
drove for some time through the woods and drives of Villeneuve and St. Cloud, and at last, at about ten o'clock, we
were set down at the Palace. There we all alighted, and,
after walking about a little, the Emperor showing us the part
which Marie Antoinette had built and telling some anecdotes
connected with Louis XVIII. and Louis Philippe, and the
Château, he shook hands with all of us very cordially, and
dismissed us. His Majesty got into the *char à banc* and returned to Villeneuve, and we drove back to Paris. When
we were walking about the court of the Château (it was quite
dark) the sentinel challenged us—"Qui va là?" when the
Emperor called out in a loud voice—"L'Empereur."

Of course, in this company there was nothing but general
conversation, and I had no opportunity of having any with
His Majesty; but he was extremely civil, offering me his
cigars, which I declined, and expressing anxiety that I
should not catch cold. He made the same impression on
me as before as to his extreme simplicity and the easiness of
his intercourse; but I was struck with his appearance being
so very *mesquin*, more than I thought at first.

Lady Ashburton told me she had received a letter from
Ellice, telling her that the affair in the House of Commons
had produced the most serious effect, and that it would
probably end in the retirement of John Russell, and eventually to a change of Government. He had got a story, which
I utterly disbelieve, that Milner Gibson had been instigated
by John Russell himself to give him this opportunity of saying what he did, which was certainly more than he need
have said.[1] Lord John seems for some time past to have
been bereft of his senses, and to commit nothing but blun-

---

[1] [On July 6, Lord John Russell declared in the House of Commons, in
answer to a question put by Mr. Milner Gibson, that he was personally convinced that the terms proposed at Vienna by the Austrian Government gave a
fair prospect of the termination of hostilities, but that on his return to England
the Government declined to accept them. M. Drouyn de Lhuys, the French
envoy, had also been in favor of these terms. This declaration appeared to be
wholly inconsistent with the warlike speech which Lord John had made, on
his return, on May 24. Sir E. B. Lytton then gave notice of a motion condemning the conduct of the Ministers charged with negotiating at Vienna; but
Lord John Russell anticipated the inevitable vote of censure by resigning office,
and he was succeeded in the Colonial Department by Sir William Molesworth.
This transaction was held to reflect deep discredit on Lord John Russell's conduct, and justifies the severe language applied to him in the text, but this was
somewhat mitigated by Mr. Greville in a subsequent passage.]

ders one after another. What has been passing in his mind, and what his real objects are or have been, it would puzzle anybody to say. If he had personal views and wanted to regain the station and power which he had lost, never did any man take such false steps and pursue so erroneous a course to obtain his ends. He had in some measure retrieved the character and consideration which he forfeited by his conduct at the beginning of this year ; but I do not see how he is ever to get over this, nor how his followers can any longer have any confidence in him, and I do not believe the country at large ever will. As to his opinion on the terms of peace, I agree with it, and think it would have been wiser to close with Buol's proposal, and to continue to negotiate ; but this makes no difference as to his conduct in the affair, for which there is no excuse. He never ought to have committed himself at Vienna ; his instructions were clear and precise and quite inconsistent with Buol's proposition. He might have engaged to bring it before his Government, but should, especially as he was a Cabinet Minister, have abstained from expressing any opinion of his own upon it. He appears at Vienna to have been easily talked over, and to have been exceedingly wanting in diplomatic finesse and penetration ; but all I have picked up here in conversation proves to me that there have been errors innumerable and the greatest mistakes in the conduct of these affairs throughout, and the exigencies of the alliance and the necessity of concerting everything to the most minute particular with both Cabinets have produced results not less unfortunate in diplomacy than in war. The affair before Sebastopol the night before last turns out to have been of no importance, only a demonstration against the English lines.

London, July 13th.—I left Paris on Tuesday night at 7.30, got to Calais at three ; low water and steamer three miles out at sea ; went out in a boat in a torrent of rain which had lasted the whole journey and all day. Train was just gone when we got to Dover, but we arrived in town about eleven. I found a precious state of affairs, all confusion and consternation, Bulwer having given notice of a motion of want of confidence on account of John Russell, whose affair has brought himself and the Government to the very brink and almost to the certainty of ruin. There is as much excitement against Palmerston's Government, all on account of Lord John, as there was a few months ago against

Aberdeen. I found Brooks's in a state of insurrection, and
even the Attorney-General (Cockburn) told me that the Liberal party were resolved to go no further with John Russell,
and that nothing but his resignation could save the Government, even if that could ; that they might be reconciled to
him hereafter, but as long as the war lasted they repudiated
him. Meanwhile he has not resigned. There was a long
Cabinet the day before yesterday in which they discussed the
state of affairs, and what measures could be taken. Lord
John offered to resign, but they would not hear of it, and
came to a resolution to stand or fall together. I saw Clarendon yesterday, who was fully aware of the imminence of
the danger, and of the probability of their being out on Monday ; he said Lord John's whole conduct was inconceivable,
and he knew not to what to attribute his strange speech, in
which he had made for himself a much worse case than the
circumstances really warrant, and given to the world impressions which are not correct ; for in point of fact he did not
urge Buol's proposal upon the Cabinet, but when he laid it
before them and found it not acceptable, he at once yielded
to all the arguments against it, and instead of making any
attempt to get peace made on those terms, he joined with all
his colleagues in their conviction of the necessity of carrying
on the war vigorously ; and this conviction induced him to
make the warlike speech with which he is now reproached
as being inconsistent with the opinions he was entertaining (as it is said) at the time he made it. Yesterday he attempted to make something of an explanation, but he
only floundered further into the mire, and was laughed at.
Everybody thinks he made his case worse rather than better,
but he really seems to have lost his head. His whole conduct at Vienna and here has exhibited nothing but a series
of blunders and faults, and he has so contrived it that no
explanations he can possibly make will extenuate them, or
place him in a tolerable light in the eyes of the public. In
the morning yesterday I had occasion to call on Disraeli
about some business, when he talked over the state of affairs
very freely, and gave me to understand that he intended
and expected to turn out the Government and to come
in with his party, but he owned that their materials for
forming a tolerable Government were very scanty, that he
would not attempt their old Government over again, but,
except Lytton Bulwer, of whom he spoke in terms of high

praise, he knew not where to find any fresh men worth anything.

Bath, July 19th.—I came here on Saturday night.   In the course of Friday morning I met Drumlanrig, who told me the subordinate place men had caused John Russell to be informed that if he did not resign they should, and vote for Bulwer's motion on Monday.   This produced his resignation, but under circumstances as mortifying as possibly could be, and which must have made him deeply regret that he did not resign at first, although he is not to be blamed for having yielded to the wishes of his colleagues, and I am satisfied he did so from the best motives.   It was no sooner known that he had resigned than the excitement began to subside, and everybody thought that Bulwer would withdraw his motion, and at all events nobody doubted that it would come to nothing.   The motion was withdrawn but the debate took place, and such a debate !—it was impossible to read it without indignation and disgust.   Bulwer's speech was a tissue of foul abuse with the grossest and most wilful misrepresentations and endeavors to draw inferences he knew to be false and fallacious, with the hope and purpose of damaging the characters of the Ministers.   In these times, when the great evil is the bad opinion which the public has been led to entertain of public men, Bulwer endeavors, for a mere party purpose, to aggravate that hostile feeling and to make the world believe that, in a great party and a Cabinet composed of men whose characters have never been impugned, there is neither truth, sincerity, nor good faith, and by producing such an impression to bring the aristocracy into greater disrepute.   Disraeli, of course, spoke in the same tone, Palmerston was very bad, and his speech was quite unbecoming his position.   John Russell's defence was not calculated to relieve him from the weight of obloquy and unpopularity he had brought on himself, and the whole thing was unsatisfactory, except that it denoted the end of the contest and the disappointment of the Opposition, whose hopes had been so highly raised.

After much consideration of John Russell's conduct, I think it is not obnoxious to the severe censure with which it has been visited, and though he has committed errors, they are venial ones and admit of a fair explanation.   Had not Buol's publication revealed to the world what had passed between them confidentially, nothing of it would have been known, and he would have been left to the enjoyment of the popularity he had gained by his anti-Russian speech. The statement about him in Buol's Circular naturally led to questions, and then it was necessary to tell everything and lay bare the arcana of Cabinets and Conferences; and when he endeavored to explain his own conduct it became, amid all the complexities of the case itself, its endless variety of details and confusion of dates, next to impossible to unravel it satisfactorily, and quite impossible to protect himself from the imputations which an unscrupulous and malignant assailant could easily contrive to bring against him; and in this great difficulty he displayed no tact and ingenuity in extricating himself from the dilemma in which he was placed; on the contrary, he went blundering on, exposing himself to many charges, all plausible and some true, of inconsistency, inaccuracy, and insincerity, and he made in his speeches a case against himself which left very little for his enemies to do. It might be strange in any other man, but is perhaps only consistent in him, that he is now more indignant with the friends who refused to follow and support him on this occasion than either ashamed or angry with himself for having blundered into such a scrape. He writes, meanwhile, to his brother, who has sent me his letter, in these terms:— "I have endeavored to stand by and support Palmerston, too much so, I fear, for my own credit, but had I resigned on my return from Vienna, I should have been abused as wishing to trip him up and get his place : in short, the situation was one of those where only errors were possible. I have acted according to my own conscience; let that suffice." False reasoning and wounded pride are both apparent in this letter, but he is quite right when he says that "only errors had become possible." There is no course he could have taken that would not have exposed him to bitter attacks and reproaches, and these unavoidable errors were not confined to himself.

The first thing that strikes me is that the Cabinet ought to have accepted his resignation when he first tendered it ; but there were no doubt difficulties and objections to that course, and their reluctance to let him throw himself overboard was not unnatural and was generous. The defence which his conduct really admits of may be (to state it very briefly) thus set forth. I put it loosely, and as it strikes me, taking a general view of the case ; to make it more accurate and complete, the dates and the documents should be before me, which they are not. He went to Paris with instructions precisely corresponding with what was verbally arranged in London between Drouyn de Lhuys and the Cabinet, and they were conjointly to propose the conditions which the two Governments had agreed to require from Russia; but still they were not the bearers of an Ultimatum, they did not go to give law to Russia, or as judges to pronounce sentence upon her. They went to confer and to negotiate, to endeavor to obtain the precise terms which would be entirely satisfactory to their two Governments, and failing in this to see what they could obtain. If they were instructed to insist on the limitation, just as they proposed it at the Conference, and to accept nothing else, nothing either short of it or varying from it, then the very idea of a Conference and a negotiation was a mockery and a delusion. It was a mockery to invite the Russian plenipotentiary to make proposals, and the conduct of the Allies was disingenuous and deceitful. Certainly Austria never contemplated, still less would she have been a party to, such a course of proceeding; and her notion was, and, of course, that of Russia also, that there should be a *bonâ fide* negotiation, and an attempt to bring about an understanding by the only way in which an understanding ever can be brought about —mutual concessions. We proposed the limitation scheme, and Austria backed us up in it cordially, sincerely, and forcibly, at least to all appearance. Russia rejected it on the ground of its incompatibility with her honor and dignity. Then Russia made proposals, which the Allies, Austria included, rejected as insufficient. John Russell and Drouyn de Lhuys appear to have fought vigorously in the spirit of their instructions, but when they found there was no chance of the Russians consenting to the limitation, they both became anxious to try some other plan, by which peace might possibly be obtained, and they each suggested something. At last, when the Conference was virtually at an end, as a last hope and chance Buol produced his scheme. John Russell had already committed himself to an approval of the principle of it, by the plan he had himself suggested, and, when he found that both his French and Turkish colleagues were willing to accept it, it is not surprising that he should have told Buol privately and confidentially that he acquiesced in it, and would urge it on his Government. As it has turned out, this was a great indiscretion for which he has been severely punished. As he had every reason to believe that Buol's plan would not be acceptable to his own Government, what he ought to have done was to give notice to Clarendon that such a proposal had been made, and to beg it might be considered before any final resolution was taken, and to tell Buol that he had done so ; to promise that he would submit to the Cabinet all the arguments that had been used in its favor, but to abstain from any expression of his own opinion, and shelter himself from the necessity of giving any by the tenor of his own instructions. When he found the French Minister for Foreign Affairs consenting, he might very well suppose that the French Government would not reject the proposal, and that he should not be justified in putting a peremptory veto on what France was disposed to accept as sufficient. Besides, although he has never put forward such an argument in any of his speeches, he may have thought, as I do, that "counterpoise" and "limitation" were the same thing in principle, and the only difference between them one of mode and degree. Buol's counterpoise involved limitation, our limitation was to establish a counterpoise ; therefore, even in the spirit of the instructions and arguments of the French and English Governments, their plan of limitation having failed, Buol's plan of counterpoise was entitled to consideration,[1] and the only question ought to have been whether it would have been effectual for the purpose common to all, and whether it would be an honorable mode of terminating the war.

John Russell's fault was committing himself to Buol as approving his plan before he knew how it would be viewed at home ; but I see neither impossibility nor inconsistency in his having regarded it favorably at Vienna, and being biassed by all the arguments in its favor which there beset him on all sides, and when he returned to England and found the opinions of all his colleagues adverse to it, and heard their reasons for being so, that he should have been convinced by them, have subscribed to the general decision, and joined cordially with them in the vigorous prosecution of the war. Having come finally to this conclusion, his warlike speech

---

[1] [The proposal submitted to the Conference by Count Buol was that each of the Powers should have the right to maintain a limited naval power in the Black Sea. The whole discussion turned upon suppression of the naval supremacy of Russia in the Black Sea and the manner in which it was to be effected.]

11

was not unnatural, and he made it probably very much to
prove to his own colleagues that he was in earnest with them.
There was no necessity for his proclaiming what had passed
at Vienna, as nothing had happened in consequence, and
the question was not what impression had been made on his
mind there in the course of the negotiations, but what was
the opinion, and what the resolution at which he finally
arrived when all was over.   But he has repeatedly in the
course of his career contrived to do a vast deal of mischief
by a very few words, and so it was in this instance.   When
he was driven to *confess* that he had endorsed Buol's proposal, and said that he was still of the same opinion, his
opponents were able with every appearance of truth to say
that he had intended to conceal what he had done at Vienna,
and to deceive the country, both as to his past conduct and
his present opinions ; and as it was obvious from his own
avowal that he still was of the same opinion as at Vienna,
his war speech was hypocritical and insincere, and he was
unfit to be in a Cabinet pledged to carry on the war earnestly
and vigorously.   Against such an attack it was very difficult to make a good defence, and I doubt whether the most
lucid and circumstantial statement and the most natural
explanation of his own motives and sentiments at different
periods of the transaction would have received a patient
hearing and dispassionate consideration.   The House of
Commons and the public were in that frame of mind that
will not listen, and cannot be fair and just, and he became,
and could hardly avoid becoming, the victim of his own
want of caution and prudent reserve and the excessive com-
plication of the circumstances and details of the case.

London, July 28th.—I returned from Bath yesterday ;
went to Newmarket in the evening and returned this morning.   There is nothing new at home and abroad ; to all outward appearance the siege standing still, but they say it is
going on in a safe and judicious manner calculated to bring
about success.   General Simpson wants to resign, but no man
fit to succeed him can be found.[1]   I have read the pamphlet
" Whom shall we Hang ? " and think it makes a very good
case for the late Government, especially Newcastle, but it is

---

[1] [Upon the death of Lord Raglan General Simpson, an officer of whom little
was known, succeeded, as senior in rank. to the command of the army.   He
retained the command but a short time, General Codrington having been appointed by the Government to succeed him.]

so long that few people will read it ; and though it may convince and satisfy some one here and there, it will not suffice
to stem the torrent which is so swollen by ignorance and
malice.   At Brooks's this afternoon I met Fitzroy, who said
a great deal to me about the condition of the Government, '
of the state and disposition of the House of Commons, and
Palmerston's management there, and his conduct as a leader.

London, August 14th.—Since my last date I have been to
Goodwood, and since then here, having had nothing to note
beyond what has appeared in all the newspapers.   Parliament
was prorogued yesterday, after a session of average duration,
but marked by a great many incidents of a disagreeable character, and exhibiting a downward tendency as regards the
future tranquillity and prosperity of the country.   The last
few days were marked by an angry contest provoked by Lord
Grey in the Lords, not altogether without cause : the Limited
Liability Bill came up so late that, according to the Standing
Order, it could not be considered.   Government moved the
suspension of the Order, which was carried, but there was no
time to discuss properly the provisions of the bill, and it was
hurried through the House by force, probably in an incom-
plete form.   Grey was very angry, and fought it tooth and
nail, declaring his opposition to a Government which had,
he insisted, behaved so ill.   Mr. Monsell was made a Privy
Councillor, the oath having been altered to meet his scruples,
in spite of all the remonstrances I could offer against such
an unworthy compliance as this appears to me.

CHAPTER X.

London, August 21st.—The Queen as usual has had magnificent weather for her Paris visit, and all has gone well there except that unluckily she arrived after her time at Boulogne and still more at Paris, consequently the Emperor was kept waiting at Boulogne, and the whole population of Paris, which turned out and waited for hours under a broiling sun, was disappointed, for they arrived when it was growing dark. However, in spite of this, the scene appears to have been very fine and animated. Clarendon, who is not apt to be enthusiastic, writes so to Palmerston, and tells him that Marshal Magnan said he had known Paris for fifty years, and had never seen such a scene as this, nor even when Napoleon returned from Austerlitz.

George Lewis called on me yesterday. I have hardly seen him during the session, and, having advised him to take his present office, I was glad to be able to congratulate him on his success. He was very natural about it, and owned that he had every reason to be satisfied with his reception both by the House of Commons and the City. I found that his sentiments about war and peace were identical with my own. He had been all along against the war, and thought it ought to have been prevented, and might have been in the outset, and that peace ought to have been made the other day; but, as he was in no way responsible for the war, he had nothing to do but to submit to the *fait accompli* and to do his best to raise the necessary supplies in the most advantageous manner. It is evident that, if there could have been a potential peace party in the Cabinet, he would have been one of them, but as it is he kept his real sentiments to himself and subscribed to the decision of the majority. We talked of the cession and its incidents. He said history recorded nothing like the profusion with which the present House of Commons was inclined to spend money. It was impossible to ask for too much ; their only fear seemed to be lest the war should not be conducted with sufficient vigor, and to accomplish this they were ready to vote any amount of money. Lewis thinks the rage for war as violent as ever, and the zeal of the country not at all diminished, he sees no symptoms of it. The wealth and resources which the crisis has developed are most curious ; thus, he reduced the interest on Exchequer Bills not long ago—an operation he believes never before attempted in time of war. War has had little or no effect on trade, which is steady and flourishing ; but he thinks, unless some great successes infuse fresh animation into the public mind, that before long they will begin to tire of the contest, and to reflect that it is being carried on at an enormous cost for no rational object whatever, and merely from motives of pride and vanity and a false notion of honor. Charles Villiers thinks differently, and that there is already a manifest change of opinion, and that opposition to the war has already begun. I wish I could see some symptoms of it, but, though there may be some, I think they are slight. Lewis thinks John Russell has completely done for himself by his last speech. He was recovering from the effects of his first ; there was a reaction in his favor ; his friends were anxious to be reconciled to him and to renew their support and confidence, when he played into the hands of his enemies and made his own position worse than it was before.

Lewis told me that he was much struck with the mediocrity of Panmure, who was one of the dullest men he ever knew, and that he was by far the least able man in the Cabinet, and as bad as possible as Minister of War—prejudiced, slow, and *routinier*. It is evident that Newcastle was a much abler man, and if he had happened to have come after Panmure, he would have been as much belauded as he has been abused.

September 5th.—A complete stagnation in every way ; no news whatever since the battle of the Tchernaya,[1] and nobody has the least idea, Ministers included, of the state and progress of the war. I asked Granville, who is just come

---

[1] [The battle of the Tchernaya was fought on the 16th of August, when General Liprandi attacked the French and Sardinian armies in their lines, with a large force, but was repulsed with great loss.]

from Paris, if he knew anything, and he said he did not, and that the Emperor, whom he had seen a day or two ago, complained of being equally in the dark. His Majesty, Granville said, was very low about the war, and complained that none of the expeditions and diversions had been undertaken which might have advanced the cause more rapidly. Pélissier seems to be very much *déconsidéré* and thought worth very little as a general.

I saw Clarendon one day last week for a short time, but had no opportunity of hearing the details of his sojourn at Paris. He said the Queen was delighted with everything and especially with the Emperor himself, who, with perfect knowledge of women, had taken the surest way to ingratiate himself with her. This it seems he began when he was in England, and followed it up at Paris. After his visit the Queen talked it all over with Clarendon, and said, "It is very odd; but the Emperor knows everything I have done and where I have been ever since I was twelve years old; he even recollects how I was dressed, and a thousand little details it is extraordinary he should be acquainted with." She has never before been on such a social footing with anybody, and he has approached her with the familiarity of their equal positions, and with all the experience and knowledge of womankind he has acquired during his long life, passed in the world and in mixing with every sort of society. She seemed to have played her part throughout with great propriety and success. Old Jérome did not choose to make his appearance till just at the last moment, because he insisted on being treated as a king, and having the title of *Majesté* given him—a pretension Clarendon would not hear of her yielding to.

September 7th.—I had a long visit from the Duke of Bedford this morning, who came to talk to me about his brother John, his position and prospects. He has seen John and heard from him in great detail all his case, and he has likewise seen Clarendon and heard his and the Government's case. He tells me that he has never in his life suffered more pain than at hearing these cases and witnessing the bitter feelings which exist and the charges which are mutually made, especially between Clarendon and Lord John. The latter thinks he has been very ill-used by most of his former colleagues, but especially by Clarendon, whose conduct he thinks both unjust and ungrateful. Clarendon wrote to him while he was at Vienna in such a tone and language that Lord John had determined to resign his embassy and return home, and had actually written a letter to Clarendon for the purpose, but he gave up doing so partly because he felt that it would make a prodigious noise all over Europe and partly because, having consulted his brother-in-law, George Elliot, he prudently advised him against such a step; but he felt deeply, and resented what he thought bad conduct toward himself.   I read to the Duke all that I had written about John in the preceding pages, against which he had nothing to say.   He asked his brother how he came to speak so ill *for himself* in the House of Commons, and he replied that he was embarrassed by the impossibility of saying everything that he knew, especially the fact, which I have mentioned, of the way in which the Emperor Napoleon determined to throw over Drouyn de Lhuys and to reject the Vienna proposals.   This was told to John by Baudin; and one of the things he complains of is that the Cabinet never was informed of what had passed, and its members were allowed to suppose, like the public, that the Emperor's rejection had been spontaneous, instead of having been suggested and urged upon him by us.   John bitterly feels his own position, his estrangement from his old friends, and, above all, the unkindness and ingratitude he thinks they have been guilty of toward him.   He is now intent upon his own vindication, and is preparing to compose it with a view of giving it to the world, though he does not know, and it is difficult to determine, in what shape.   He seems less dissatisfied with his old enemy Palmerston than with any of the others, and says he thinks Palmerston is the best man there is at present to be Prime Minister.   After Clarendon he most reproaches Charles Wood.

September 17*th.*—Went to The Grove with Clarendon last Saturday sennight; on Monday to Doncaster, where I had no time to write anything but bets in my betting-book, all of which I lost.   On the Saturday we heard from General Simpson by telegraph that the assault was to take place that day.   We were kept in suspense all Sunday, but on Monday morning read in the "Times" that the Malakoff was taken, but we had no idea then that the city with all its vast defences would fall immediately after, but I heard it the same night at the Huntingdon station.[1]

[1] [The final bombardment of Sebastopol commenced on the morning of Sep-

I heard a great deal from Clarendon about the royal visit to Paris, and details connected with it, and we talked over the quarrel with John Russell, at which he expressed great regret, though not without bitterness.   Clarendon said nothing could exceed the delight of the Queen at her visit to Paris, at her reception, at all she saw ; and that she was charmed with the Emperor.   They became so intimate, and she on such friendly terms with him, that she talked to him with the utmost frankness, and even discussed with him the most delicate of all subjects, the confiscation of the Orleans' property, telling him her opinion upon it.   He did not avoid the subject, and gave her the reasons why he thought himself obliged to take that course ; that he knew all this wealth was employed in fomenting intrigues against his Government, which was so new that it was necessary to take all precautions to avert such dangers.   She replied that, even if this were so, he might have contented himself with sequestrating the property and restoring it when he was satisfied that all danger on that score was at an end.   I asked Clarendon what he thought of the Emperor himself, and he said that he liked him, and he was very pleasing, but he was struck with his being so indolent and so excessively ignorant. The Prince of Wales was put by the Queen under Clarendon's charge, who was desired to tell him what to do in public, when to bow to the people, and whom to speak to.   He said that the Princess Royal was charming, with excellent manners, and full of intelligence.   Both the children were delighted with their *séjour,* and very sorry to come away. When the visit was drawing to a close, the Prince said to the Empress that he and his sister were both very reluctant to leave Paris, and asked her if she could not get leave for them to stay there a little longer.   The Empress said she was afraid this would not be possible, as the Queen and the Prince would not be able to do without them ; to which the boy replied, "Not do without us ! don't fancy that, for there are six more of us at home, and they don't want us."   The Emperor himself proposed to the Queen to go to the Chapel consecrated to the memory of the Duke of Orleans upon the spot where he met with his fatal accident and expired.   It

tember 5th, and continued without intermission until the 8th, when the Russians blew up their magazines and in the night evacuated the southern portion of the city.   The intelligence of the fall of Sebastopol reached England on the afternoon of Monday, September 10, and was received with great enthusiasm throughout the country.]

is creditable to her that she talks without *gêne* or scruple
to the Emperor about the Orleans family, making no secret of her continued intimacy with them, and with equal
frankness to them of her relations with him.   She
wrote to the Queen Marie Amélie an account of her going
to the Chapel and of the Emperor taking her there, and
received a very amiable reply.   The first thing she did on
her return was to receive the Duc and Duchesse de Montpensier.

Clarendon told me a few things besides of no great importance, and which I am not sure that I recollect : about
Spain, he said that matters were going on better there and
the Government had contrived to get money—the Spaniards
were very anxious to take part in the war, but he had dis-
couraged it entirely.   As to Naples, that we were calling the
Neapolitan Government to account for their recent impertinence to us, but that Palmerston and he had disagreed as to
what should be done, Palmerston, according to his old habit,
wanting to send ships of war to Naples and to proceed to
violence, while he was opposed to having another Pacifico
affair on our hands, and proposed to proceed with caution
and quietly.

While they were in the yacht, crossing over, Prince Albert
had told him that there was not a word of truth in the prevailing report and belief that the young Prince of Prussia
and the Princess Royal were *fiancés*, that nothing had ever
passed between the parents on the subject, and that the
union never would take place unless the children should
become attached to each other.   There would be no mere
political marriage.   The Prince showed Clarendon all the
correspondence which had taken place between the Emperor
of Russia and the Prince Regent about the Holy Alliance,
which he said was very curious, and George IV.'s letter declining to be a party to it very good indeed.   These documents were left in Lord Liverpool's papers, and fell into the
hands of Harcourt, who married his daughter.   Harcourt
lent them to the Prince to read, but exacting a promise that
he would not take a copy of them, and he had since repeatedly pressed the Prince to return them.   I told Clarendon
they ought not to be returned, or at least that Harcourt
ought to be desired to give them to be preserved in the Government Archives, for they can in no way be considered as
private property.   Lord Liverpool's papers were for the most

part destroyed, but these were preserved. This is all I can recollect of what he told me.

September 23d.—At The Grove from Saturday to Monday; nobody there but Reeve; nothing very particular. Clarendon said Prussia was very anxious to interpose to renew negotiations, but they would not hear of her interference, and if anything was done it could only be by Austria. He showed me a paper sent by Hudson with an account, very brief, of the state of Italy, which is in fermentation though not in open disturbance. The Sicilian malcontents sent to the King of Sardinia an offer of their crown for one of his sons. He replied, "You have need of a man, and a boy will be of no use to you." This they took for a refusal, and they are now thinking of a Coburg; in no case will they have a Murat. I forget what the Neapolitan Liberals want, but I doubt if the country will have either the courage or the power to emancipate itself.

September 28th.—No fresh news, but a letter from Charles Windham (the hero of the Redan), in which he gives an account of that affair which corresponds very closely with the report of Russell, the "Times" Commissioner. He gives a poor character of the generals in the Crimea, and says the troops, except some of the old soldiers, behaved by no means well. The whole thing seems to have been grievously mismanaged on our part.[1]

I have had much correspondence with the Duke of Bedford about Lord John and his case, which the Duke says, now that he has heard it all and seen the correspondence, he thinks much better than he had supposed, and that John was meditating the publication of a defence of himself, but could not determine in what shape it should be. I earnestly advised him to dissuade his brother from publishing anything, as he could not make an effectual defence of his conduct without making revelations that would be held unjustifiable and cause all sorts of ill humor and recriminations, and render his position, both personal and political, worse than it now is. Some communications in a friendly spirit have taken place between Lord John and Clarendon, but

[1] [The British attack on the Redan failed, while the French attack on the Malakoff succeeded, to the extreme annoyance of the British army and public but in his assault Colonel Charles Windham (as he then was) displayed the most signal bravery, which in some measure redeemed the credit of the British forces. This circumstance gave him an amount of popularity and distinction which his rank in the army and his previous services did not altogether justify.]

I can see that there is still existing a great deal of soreness and a not very cordial feeling between them. I have been reading Lord Grey's speech on the war, which he has published in a pamphlet, and I think it excellent and unanswerable. I long to write something on the subject and to add to Grey's argument on other parts of the case. I do not care about the unpopularity of doing so, and am only deterred from taking so much trouble by feeling that it would be unavailing, and that to attempt to make the public listen to reason and take a dispassionate view of the various questions connected with the war on which they have been so completely bamboozled and misled, would be like Mrs. Partington and her mop.

October 2d.—I have been in correspondence for a long time with Charles Windham, and had a letter from him written a few days after his great exploit at the Redan. I showed his letter to Granville, and he to Palmerston and Clarendon. I was glad to find every disposition to reward his bravery and conduct, and Henry Grenfell told me they had made him a general and were going to give him a division, as Markham and Bentinck are both coming home. This was no more than was reasonable to expect; but great was my astonishment when I was told yesterday morning that they were thinking of making Windham *Commander-in-Chief*, and I was asked to give any of his letters to me, from which extracts might be made to show to the Cabinet to enable them to judge of his character and talents. I offered to get his journal and letters, from his wife and others, which I did; but at the same time I said I thought it a hazardous speculation to raise him *per saltum* from being a colonel and brigadier to the command of a great army. B—— said this was true, but the matter pressed and they did not know where to find a man. This morning I gave him some papers, and he then told me Simpson had resigned, and it was necessary to come to some immediate decision. Codrington would have been undoubtedly chosen if he had not apparently (for as yet we know very little) failed in what he had to do on the 8th. With regard to Windham what the Cabinet will do I know not, I suggested that it would be better to try him first in his command of a division and go on if possible for some time longer, but Simpson's resignation compels them to come to some immediate decision, and they do not like to appoint another man *pro tempore*.

I still incline to the opinion that Windham's extraordinary promotion from so low to so high a rank, and his passing over the heads of such multitudes of officers, will occasion great jealousy, envy, heart-burning, and resentment, besides casting a slur on the whole service in the eyes of the world; for when every general in the service is passed over, and a colonel appointed who has never done any but subordinate work, and shown extraordinary bravery and coolness, but no aptitude for command, because he has had no opportunity of so doing, every general and superior colonel now on service will feel himself insulted and a stigma cast upon him. I am not at all sure Windham may do better than any other man would do, but to justify such an appointment he ought to do far better; and though he is a sharp fellow enough, I have never seen anything in him which indicates real genius or a superior intellect.

October 7th.—At Woburn, where the Duke and I had much conversation about Lord John and his position, and he showed me a great many of John's letters to him about his quarrel with the Government and the conduct of Clarendon to him, which he cannot forgive, though they are again corresponding with ostensible amity. The Duke owns that he does not see how John can take any prominent part in public life, at least for the present, and indeed considers it probable that his career as a statesman is closed; and, what is more, John seems to consider it so himself and to acquiesce in his position, though what his secret aspirations may be none can tell. He has, however, determined to give up his house in town, which looks like retirement. I strongly advised that John should go to the House of Lords, where he might still act a dignified and useful part; his position in the House of Commons would be very anomalous and disagreeable, and it is not at all certain that he would not lose his seat in the event of an election—very doubtful whether he would be returned again for the City; and the thing most to be deprecated is that he should stand and be defeated for that or any other place. The Duke neither agreed nor dissented, but he owned what I said of John's position was true, though he still thought he would be very reluctant to quit the House of Commons for ever, and retire to the Lords.

On Tuesday last, after a few days' illness, Sir Robert Adair died at the age of 93, having preserved his faculties,

and especially his remarkable memory, quite to the last. He
was the last survivor of the intimate friends of Fox and of
the political characters of his times. He had entertained a
warm affection for Fox, and he preserved a boundless veneration for his memory; and the greatest pleasure he had
was in talking of Fox and his contemporaries, and pouring
forth to willing circles of auditors anecdotes and reminiscences of the political events with which he had been mixed
up, or of which he had been cognizant in the course of his
long life. This he did in a manner quite remarkable at so
advanced an age, and he never had any difficulty in finding
listeners to his old stories, which were always full of interesting matter, and related to the most conspicuous characters
who flourished during the reigns of George III. and George IV.

October 29th.—All last week at Newmarket, and probably very nearly for the last time as an owner of racehorses,
for I have now got rid of them all, and am almost off the
turf, after being on it more or less for about forty years. I
am sorry that I have never kept any memoranda of my turf
life, which might have been curious and amusing; for I
have known many odd characters, and lived with men of
whom it would have been interesting to preserve some record. Perhaps I may one day rake together my old recollections and trace the changes that have taken place in this
racing life since I first knew it and entered into it, but I
cannot do so now.

Since I last wrote, the war has proceeded without any
great events, but with the same progress and success on the
side of the Allies which have marked the contest throughout
and have excited my wonder. The most important of these
successes has been the defeat of Mouravieff at Kars by the
Turks under English officers, which, after what Clarendon
told me, was the very last thing I expected. The death of
Molesworth has made a difficulty for Palmerston; I knew
so little of him that I cannot pretend to say anything about
him. That of Lord Wharncliffe touches me more nearly;
but this is more matter of private regret than of public concern, as the part he played in life was never important,
though very honorable. The appointment of Codrington
seems to be well taken, more perhaps because nobody can
suggest a better choice than from any peculiar merits of the
new Commander-in-Chief.[1]

[1] [The Right Hon. Sir William Molesworth, Secretary of State for the Colo-

London, November 7th.—The event of the last few days has been the offer of the Colonial Office to Lord Stanley and his refusal to take it. When Palmerston proposed it to him he said that he could not give an answer without consulting his father, which *implied* that he would accept if his father gave his consent. He posted down to Knowsley, from whence he had just come, and entered the room where Derby was playing at billiards, and much to his astonishment saw his son suddenly return. "What on earth," he cried out, "has brought you back so soon? Are you going to be married, or what has happened to you?" Stanley said he wanted to speak to him, and carried him off. What passed is not known, but of course he advised his son to refuse office. He wrote to Palmerston in very becoming terms, and, I hear, a very good letter. He had, if not consulted, certainly imparted to Disraeli what passed, for Disraeli told me so. I think he judged wisely in declining, for it would have been an awkward thing to pass at once from the Opposition side of the House to the Treasury Bench, and take high office in a Cabinet without having any political or personal connection with a single member of it, and to which he has hitherto been opposed generally, although upon many subjects his opinions have much more coincided with theirs than with those of the party to which he still nominally belongs. He is young and can afford to wait, and his position and abilities are certain before long to make him conspicuous and to enable him to play a very considerable part. He is exceedingly ambitious, of an independent turn of mind, very industrious, and has acquired a vast amount of information. Not long ago, Disraeli gave me an account of him and of his curious opinions—exceedingly curious in a man in his condition of life and with his prospects. Last night Lord Strangford (George Smythe) talked to me about him, expressed the highest opinion of his capacity and acquirements, and confirmed what Disraeli had told me of his notions and views even more, for he says that he is a real and sincere democrat, and that he would like if he could to prove his sincerity by divesting himself of his aristocratic character and even of the wealth he is heir to. How far this may be true I know not: if it be true, it may possibly

nial Department, died on October 22, 1855, aged 45. John, 2d Baron Wharncliffe, also died on the 22d. General Sir William Codrington had been appointed to the command of the British forces in the Crimea, on the resignation of General Simpson.]

be ascribed in some degree to his own consciousness that the realization of his ideology is impossible, and at all events time will show whether these extreme theories will not be modified by circumstances and reflections. Nothing appears to me certain but that he will play a considerable part for good or for evil, but I cannot pretend to guess what it will be. At present he seems to be more allied with Bright than with any other public man ; and, as his disposition about the war and its continuance is very much that of Bright, it would have been difficult for him to take office with Palmerston, whose whole political existence, or at least his power, rests on the cry for war and its active and energetic prosecution.

London, November 12th.—I saw John Russell on Saturday morning to have a talk with him about the state of affairs and the questions of peace and war. There still exists a great deal of bitterness between him and Clarendon, he thinking that he has been very ill used by Clarendon and others of his former colleagues. He is particularly sore about their allowing so many things to be said to his disadvantage concerning the Vienna negotiations which they know to be untrue, without saying a word to contradict them and cause justice to be done to him, particularly in reference to the matter of Austria having engaged to join if Russia refused her last proposals. George Grey denied that Austria had so engaged, and none of the others ever admitted it, whereas it was perfectly true. Lord John and I do not agree as to the earlier part of the question, because he was originally a party to the war while I was always against it. He was, however, rather against it quite at first, being, as he told me, with Aberdeen, and against Clarendon and Palmerston, who were all along inclined to go to war. He had been at the Mansion House dinner the night before, where he was very ill received, though he would not allow it ; he prefers to flatter himself that the signs of his unpopularity were not so strong and marked as everybody else who was present thought them.

I likewise saw Disraeli and had some talk with him. He told me that he had now nothing whatever to do with the "Press," and that the series of articles in that paper on the war and in favor of peace were all written by Stanley. He said he had received a letter from Stanley to this effect: "My dear Disraeli,—I write to you in confidence to tell you that I have been offered and have refused the Colonial Office.

As it is due to Lord Palmerston to keep his offer secret, I have told nobody of it but yourself and my father, and I beg you not to mention it to anybody." On receiving this he said he began to concoct an answer in his mind of rather a sentimental kind, and conveying his approbation of the course he had taken, but before he put pen to paper he got the "Times" with Stanley's letter to Sir——, which was tantamount to a disclosure of the whole thing, on which he wrote instead, "Dear Stanley,—I thank you for your letter, but I had already received your confidential communication through your letter to Sir——."

I have occasion to see Disraeli very often about ——'s affairs, about which he has been wonderfully kind and serviceable, and on these occasions he always enters on some political talk, and in this way we have got into a sort of intimacy such as I never thought could have taken place between us.

London, November 24th.—After his failure with Stanley, Palmerston applied to Sidney Herbert, who went to Broadlands, but, finding that he and Palmerston could not agree upon the subject of war and peace (the details of their disagreement I do not know), he declined the offer of the Colonial Office. Palmerston then sent for Labouchere, who accepted.[1] He called on me the day after and told me he had been to Broadlands, that Palmerston had told him everything about the state of affairs and his own views and opinions, and, as he could find nothing therein to object to, he had accepted the office. As Labouchere is certainly moderate, this would indicate more moderation on the part of Palmerston than Sidney Herbert found in him, unless Labouchere and Sidney Herbert take totally dissimilar views of affairs.

After this, a few days ago, I had a long conversation with George Lewis, who told me that France and Austria were endeavoring to bring about peace, and that communications were going on between France and our Government on the subject, and he said, moreover, that Palmerston was by no means so stiff and so bent on continuing the war as was generally supposed. This intelligence appeared to me to explain

---

[1] [The Right Hon. Henry Labouchere, born in 1798, a highly respected member of the Whig party, who filled many offices in Liberal Governments. He was created Baron Taunton on his retirement from office in 1859, and died in July, 1869.]

what I could not understand in his communications with Sidney Herbert and Labouchere ; for, if the Emperor has really intimated to our Government his determination to try and make peace, Palmerston must needs come down from his very high horse and evince a disposition to go along with our Imperial ally, who has got the whole game in his own hands, and whom we must perforce follow when he is determined to take his own course.   Then our warlike propensities may be probably restrained by the alarming prospect of financial difficulties which Lewis sees looming in the distance.   He said to me, "I am sure I do not know how I shall provide ways and means next year, for the enormously high prices will be a great blow to consumption, and the money market is in a very ticklish state." I said, "You will have to trust to a great loan, and ten per cent. income tax ;" to which he assented. They have now patched up the Government, by getting Baines to take the Duchy of Lancaster with a seat in the Cabinet— a very respectable man, who cannot speak, and who will be of no use to them.   Neither he nor Labouchere will add much to their strength, but they are both very unexceptionable appointments.   I think that, in spite of the undiminished violence of the press, the prevailing opinion is that there is the beginning of a change in the public mind, and an incipient desire for peace ; and I agree with Disraeli, who thinks that, when once the current has fairly turned, it will run with great rapidity the other way.

November 27th.—At length there really does appear to be a prospect of putting an end to this odious war, and my conjectures of a few days ago are assuming the shape of realities.   Yesterday morning I met George Lewis in the Park and turned back and walked with him to the door of his office, when he told me the exact state of affairs.   I had received a letter from the Duke of Bedford in the morning, who said that Charles Wood, who was at Woburn, had told him the statement in the " Press " a week ago was so substantially accurate that they must, he thought, have received their information from some French official source.   This was in itself confirmatory of all I had already inferred and believed.   Lewis's story was this : The Austrians have framed a proposal for peace which they offer to send to Russia, and, if she refuses it, Austria engages to join the Allies and to declare war.   The Emperor Napoleon agrees with Austria, and is resolved not to go on with the war if peace can be

arranged on the Austrian terms. This resolution he has
communicated to us, and invited us to accede thereto ; Walewski's letters are not merely pressing, but even peremptory. It is in fact a second edition of the Vienna Conference
and proposals, with this difference, that, while on the last
occasion the Emperor knocked under to us and reluctantly
agreed to go on with the war, he is now determined to go
on with it no longer, and requires that we should defer to
his wishes. Our Government are aware that they have no
alternative, and that nothing is left for them but to acquiesce
with a good grace and make the best case they can for themselves here, the case being that the Emperor is determined
to make peace, and that we cannot carry on the war alone.
This was the amount of Lewis' information, to which he
added the expression of his disgust at the pitiful figure we
cut in the affair, being obliged to obey the commands of
Louis Napoleon, and, after our insolence, swagger, and bravado, to submit to terms of peace which we have already
scornfully rejected ; all which humiliation, he justly said, was
the consequence of our plunging into war without any reason
and in defiance of all prudence and sound policy. Afterward
I saw Charles Villiers and had a talk with him. He told me
Clarendon had been sent for on Sunday to Windsor in a great
hurry to meet Palmerston there. The Queen had received a
letter from the Emperor, brought by the Duke of Cambridge,
which no doubt contained in a private and friendly shape to
her the communications which Walewski had already made
officially to the Government and she wanted to know what
answer she should send to it. Charles Villiers told me that
Palmerston had already thrown out a feeler to the Cabinet
to ascertain if they would be willing to carry on the war
without France, but this was unanimously declined. I can
hardly imagine that even Palmerston really contemplated
such a desperate course.

November 29th.—I met Sidney Herbert last night. He
seems to know what is going on and thinks we shall have
peace ; he only doubts whether the terms will be such as
Russia will accept, for he is not convinced, as I am, that
Austria has already settled that with Russia. He told me
that, when Palmerston offered him office, he had not received
the French communication, and was ignorant that it was
coming.

December 4th.—At The Grange the last four days, where

I found everybody in total ignorance of what is passing about peace, except Sidney Herbert, who told me that the plan is *neutralisation*.   On coming back yesterday I met Lord Malmesbury just come from Paris ; he is supposed to be the person who supplied all its information to the "Press" paper, and I believe it was he. He confirmed the Emperor's desire for peace, but thought it very doubtful whether Russia would accept the terms of the Allies. He told me likewise that Pélissier has sent word he is in a fix, as he cannot advance or expel the Russians from their positions ; and James Macdonald told me the Duke of Cambridge is going again to Paris to represent us at a grand council of war to be held there, to decide on future operations. If it were not that the Allies seem infallible and invincible, and the Russians unable to accomplish anything, offensive or defensive, I should augur very ill from this council of war, for nothing can be worse than to have a set of men at Paris forming plans to be executed by another set in the Crimea who have had no share in the deliberations.

This morning the Duke of Bedford writes me word that Westmorland tells him he has heard from Clarendon the state of affairs, and the answer we have sent to France, and he augurs ill of peace, as he thinks there can be no agreement with Russia on such terms ; and the "Morning Post," which has long been quite silent about war or peace, has this morning an article which is evidently a regular Palmerstonian manifesto, decidedly adverse to any hope of peace, for it is certain that Russia will continue the war, *coûte que coûte*, rather than submit to such conditions as the "Morning Post" says we are to impose on her.   I am persuaded Palmerston and Clarendon will do all they can to prevent peace being made on any moderate terms, and the only hope is that the Emperor Napoleon may take the matter into his own hands and employ a *douce violence* to compel us to give way.

December 5th.—I met Charles Villiers last night, who told me a good deal of what is going on, and cleared up some matters.   The Austrian proposal transmitted here by the Emperor Napoleon was considered by the Cabinet and sent back with amendments—that is, it was made more stringent.   The Emperor consented to send it so amended to Vienna, and it remains to be seen what course Austria will take—whether she will send it in its present shape to Russia

or adhere to her own edition, and whether, if she does send
it, she will (supposing it to be rejected) join the Allies and
declare war. The latter, I think, she will not do, nor be
bound to do. Next is the question what the Emperor Napoleon will do if Austria declines to adopt the amended version, or if Russia should reply she would take the original
proposal, but not our amendments. The Emperor is certainly very anxious to make peace, and when he is bent upon
a thing he generally does it, and my own opinion and hope
is that he will refuse to give way to us *now* as he did last
May. It is universally admitted that every man in France
desires peace ardently. There is, Charles Villiers tells me,
great uneasiness among Palmerston's adherents, and some
idea that, if peace cannot be had on the terms he has insisted
on, he will be no party to making it, and if the majority of
the Cabinet are for taking the original terms proposed, supposing the Emperor Napoleon again to press their acceptance,
that he will resign. throw himself on the popular enthusiasm
for the war, and leave his colleagues to make an unpopular
peace. If Palmerston was forty instead of seventy he would
probably do this; but he has not time to wait for fresh combinations and to speculate on distant chances, so he will
probably consent to make peace if he is obliged by France to
do so, and trust to fortune to enable him to reconcile Parliament and the country to it. This is rendered more likely by
Disraeli having made a communication to the Government
that he and Stanley will be ready to support any peace they
may now make.

December 6th.—I saw George Lewis yesterday. who told
me the state of affairs so far as he recollects it; but it is evident that he takes but a secondary interest in the details
of diplomacy, however anxious he may be about the results,
and what passed shows the extreme difficulty of keeping
clear of mistakes, even when one's information is derived
from the best sources. He said he did not think Russia
would accept the offered terms, and Clarendon thought not
also. The terms which it will be most difficult for her to
swallow are the neutralization of the Black Sea, which as
worked out is evidently worse than limitation, for she is to
have no fortress and no arsenal there, so that she will, in
fact, be quite defenceless, while the other Powers can at any
time collect fleets in the Bosphorus and attack her coasts
when they please. Then she is to cede half Bessarabia to

the Turks, including the fortress of Ismail, the famous conquest of Souvaroff when he wrote to the Empress Catherine, "L'orgueilleuse Ismailoff est à vos pieds;" and they are not to repair Bomarsund, or erect any fortress on the Aland Isles. The alterations we made in the scheme sent to us were not important, and what surprised me much was, the terms, instead of being tendered by Austria, were concocted at Paris by Walewski and the Emperor—at least so Walewski asserts, but there must I think be some incorrectness in this, for it is impossible to doubt that the Emperor and Austria really concerted them between themselves, though Walewski may have had a hand in the matter in some way. However, the terms are gone or going directly to St. Petersburg. I earnestly hope they may be accepted, be they what they may. Russia is to be asked whether she will take them Yes or No, and, upon the preliminaries being signed, hostilities will cease. I asked if Russia might not accept as a basis, and negotiate as to modification and details, but Lewis professed not to understand how this is, or whether her acceptance generally would or not bind her to *all* the conditions precisely as they are set forth. He knows nothing in fact of diplomacy and its niceties and operations.

Lord John Russell met Clarendon at Windsor Castle,[1] but refused to hear what Clarendon offered to tell him of the state of the negotiation; he thought he should compromise his own independent action if he did. He says, "Were peace to be made on the four points newly explained and enlarged, I would do nothing but applaud and support." The only men Lord John communicated with at Windsor were Cavour and Azeglio. He writes: "I asked Cavour what was the language of the Emperor of the French; he said it was to this effect: France had made great efforts and sacrifices, she would not continue them for the sake of conquering the Crimea; the alternative was such a peace as can now be had by means of Austria, or an extension of the war for Poland," etc. The Sardinians, Ministers and King, are openly and warmly for the latter course. I suspect Palmerston would wish the war to glide imperceptibly into a war of nationalities, as it is called, but would not like to profess it openly now. I am convinced such a war might suit Na-

[1] [The King of Sardinia, Victor Emmanuel, arrived in England on the 30th November, accompanied by his Minister, M. de Cavour. Lord Clarendon and Lord John Russell were invited to Windsor to meet the King.]

poleon and the King of Sardinia, but would be very dangerous for us in many ways.   Cavour says if peace is made without anything being done for Italy, there willbe a revolution
there.   Clarendon is incredulous.

London, December 11th.—I met Clarendon at the Travellers' on Friday evening, and had a talk with him.   He did
not seem inclined to enter much into the question of peace
and war, but he told me that Buol declared most solemnly
that he had had no communication with Russia about *the
terms*, and that he had only slight hopes that peace might
be made.   Of the terms themselves Clarendon did not say a
word.   He talked a great deal about the King of Sardinia,
and gave me an account of his conversations both with the
King and Cavour.   He thinks well of the King, and that he
is intelligent, and he has a very high opinion indeed of
Cavour, and was especially struck with his knowledge of
England, and our Constitution and constitutional history.   I
was much amused, after all the praises that have been
lavished on Sardinia for the noble part she has played and
for taking up arms to vindicate a great principle in so *unselfish* a manner, that she has after all a keen view to her
own interest, and wants some solid pudding as well as so
much empty praise.   The King asked Clarendon what the
Allies meant to do for him, and whether he might not expect
some territorial advantage in return for his services.   Clarendon told him this was out of the question, and that, in the
state of their relations with Austria, they could hold out no
such expectation ; and he put it to the King, supposing
negotiations for peace were to take place, and he wished his
pretensions to be put forward by us; what he would himself
suggest that a British Minister could say for him ; and the
King had the candor to say he did not know what answer
to give.   Cavour urged the same thing, and said the war had
already cost them forty millions of francs, instead of twenty-
five which they had borrowed for it and was the original
estimate, and they could only go on with it by another loan
and fresh taxes, and he did not know how he should propose
these to the chambers without having something advantageous to offer to his own country, some Italian acquisition.
They would ask for what object of their's the war was carried
on, and what they had to gain for all their sacrifices and
exertions.   Clarendon said they must be satisfied with the
glory they had acquired and the high honor their conduct

had conferred on them ; but Cavour, while he said he did
not repent the part they had taken, thought his countrymen
would be very little satisfied to have spent so much money
and to continue to spend more without gaining some Italian
object.   They complained that Austria had, without any
right, for a long time occupied a part of the Papal territory,
and suggested she should be compelled to retire from it ; but
Clarendon reminded him that France had done the same,
and that this was a very ticklish question to stir.

The King and his people are far better satisfied with their
reception here than in France, where, under much external
civility, there was very little cordiality, the Emperor's intimate relations with Austria rendering him little inclined
toward the Piedmontese.   Here the Queen was wonderfully
cordial and attentive ; she got up at four in the morning to
see him depart.   His Majesty appears to be frightful in person, but a great, strong, burly, athletic man, brusque in his
manners, unrefined in his conversation, very loose in his
conduct, and very eccentric in his habits.   When he was at
Paris his talk in society amused or terrified everybody, but
here he seems to have been more guarded.   It was amusing
to see all the religious societies hastening with their addresses to him, totally forgetting that he is the most debauched and dissolute fellow in the world ; but the fact of
his being excommunicated by the Pope, and his waging war
with the ecclesiastical power in his own country, covers every
sin against morality, and he is a great hero with the Low
Church people and Exeter Hall.   My brother-in-law said
that he looked at Windsor more like a chief of the Heruli or
Longobardi than a modern Italian prince, and the Duchess
of Sutherland declared that, of all the Knights of the Garter
she had seen, he was the only one who seemed as if he would
have the best of it with the Dragon.

My hopes of peace wax fainter.   Everybody seems to
think there is no chance of Russia accepting our terms, or of
her proposing any that the Allies would accept.   Lewis told
me yesterday evening that he expected nothing, and that
Russia had now made known (but in what way he did not
say) that she was disposed to treat.   Meanwhile Palmerston
continues to put articles in the " Morning Post" full of arrogance and *jactance,* and calculated to raise obstacles to
peace.   I told Lewis so, and he said it was very foolish, and
that he held very different language in the Cabinet, but this

is only like what he did in '41, when he used to agree to
certain things with his colleagues and then put violent articles in the " Morning Chronicle," totally at variance with
the views and resolutions of the Cabinet. Labouchere told
me that he thought the condition of the cession of Ismail
ought never to have entered into the terms proposed to
Russia.

December 14*th.*—My hopes of peace, never very sanguine,
are now completely dashed, for Lewis told me last night that
he thought the terms were at last pretty well agreed upon
between England, France, and Austria. I was greatly surprised, for I thought they had been agreed upon long ago,
and must be by this time on their way to St. Petersburg. I
said so ; and he replied, " Oh no, they are only just on the
point of being settled." It was quite extraordinary, he said,
how eager Palmerston was for pursuing the war. I gathered
from him that our Government has been vehemently urging
that of France, through Cowley, to be firm in pressing the
most stringent terms on Russia, and particularly not to
consent to any negotiation, and to compel her to accept or
refuse. I said this was not reasonable, and that we had no
right to propose the terms as an ultimatum. That, he
replied, was exactly what we were doing, that Cowley was
very urgent with the Emperor, who appeared to be intimidated by him, and that he was evidently very much in awe
of England, and afraid of having any difference with us. I
said I could not believe that the Emperor would not leave
himself a loophole, and if, as was most probable, Russia declined the terms, but offered to negotiate, that he would
agree to that course, which, however, Lewis clearly thought
he would not do against our inclination. I was greatly surprised to hear this, because I had a strong impression that
the Emperor, when he really desired anything very much (as
I believe that he did this piece), would obstinately persevere
in it ; and it seems so obviously his interest to gratify his
own people rather than to be led by this country, that I was
persuaded he never would consent to this proposal being *un
dernier mot*, and thus to ensure the failure of the attempt.
Palmerston, who is the most obstinate man alive in pressing
any object he has once set his mind upon, was sure to press
the French Government with the utmost vehemence and
pertinacity as soon as he found there was a chance of making
them yield to his will.

December 17*th*.—This morning the two new volumes of
Macaulay's History came forth.   The circumstances of this
publication are, I believe, unprecedented in literary history;
25,000 copies are given out, and the weight of the books is
fifty-six tons.   The interest and curiosity which it excites
are prodigious, and they afford the most complete testimony
to his immense popularity and the opinion entertained by
the world of his works already published.   His profits will
be very great, and he will receive them in various shapes.
But there is too much reason to apprehend that these may
be the last volumes of his history that the world will see,
still more that they are the last that will be read by me and
people of my standing.   Six years have elapsed since the
appearance of the first volumes, and these two only advance
about ten years.   He announced at the outset that he meant
to bring down the history of England to a period within the
memory of persons still living, but his work has already so
much expanded, and of course will do so still more from the
accumulation of materials as he advances, that at his present
rate of progress he must live much beyond the ordinary duration of human life, and retain all his faculties as long, to
have any chance of accomplishing his original design ; and
he is now in such a precarious state of health that in all
human probability he will not live many years.   It is melancholy to think that so gifted an intellect should be arrested
by premature decay, and such a magnificent undertaking
should be overthrown by physical infirmities, and be limited
to the proportions of a splendid fragment.   He is going
to quit Parliament and to reside in the neighborhood of
London.

This morning the " Morning Post " has published the
terms which are offered by the Allies and are now on their
way from Vienna to St. Petersburg.   They were already
pretty well known, but it is the first time that Palmerston
(for the article is evidently his own) has announced them so
openly and distinctly, and they state *totidem verbis* that it
is an Ultimatum which is sent to St. Petersburg.   I believe
this course to be unprecedented, and it is certainly unfair.
If Russia had applied to the Allies and expressed a desire
for peace, if she had asked them on what terms they would
consent to terminate the war, it would have been quite fair
and reasonable that they should have stated the precise conditions, adding if they pleased that they would consent to

12

no others and to no change whatever in them, though it may be doubted if it would be wise to be thus peremptory. But to send to Russia and propose to her to make peace, and accompany the proposal with an Ultimatum and an announcement that they would listen to no remonstrances or suggestions, much less any alterations, and that she must say Yes or No at once, is a stretch of arrogance and dictation not justified by the events of the war and the relative conditions of the belligerents, or by any usage or precedent that I ever heard of.

Reports are very rife of the distressed state of Russia and of her inability to make head any longer against the Allies, but very little is really known of the condition of the country, of its remaining resources, and of the disposition of the people. Nobody can doubt that the terms are deeply humiliating to the pride of such a Power, which has been long accustomed to stand in so high a position and hold such lofty language ; and if she consents to accept the offered terms, it must be that her enormous losses have really incapacited her for going on with the war, and that her Government is conscious that the next campaign will be still more disastrous to her than the two preceding ones have been. I have very little doubt that Palmerston has hastened to publish these terms in hopes that they may find acceptance with a considerable part of the public here, and that they may the more tightly bind the Emperor Napoleon, and, in the event of Russia sending any conditional acceptance and proposing to treat, that he may be unable to enter into any negotiation whatever. It has surprised me that he should have so completely given way to Palmerston as he has done.

December 21st.—The poet Rogers died two days ago at the age of 93. I have known him all my life, and at times lived in a good deal of intimacy with him, but for some years past he had so great an aversion to me that I kept away from him and never saw anything of him.[1] He was an old man when I first made his acquaintance between thirty and forty years ago, or probably more. He was then very agreeable, though peculiar and eccentric ; he was devoured by a morbid vanity, and could not endure any appearance of indifference or

---

[1] [Samuel Rogers, the author of the *Pleasures of Memory* (which was published in 1792), was born at Stoke Newington in 1762. His father was a banker, and he remained a partner in the bank all his life. He died on December 18, 1855.]

slight in society. He was extremely touchy, and always wanted to be flattered, but above all to be listened to, very angry and mortified when he was not the principal object in society, and provoked to death when the uproarious merriment of Sydney Smith or the voluminous talk of Macaulay overwhelmed him and engrossed the company; he had a great friendship nevertheless for Sydney Smith, but he never liked Macaulay. I never pretended, or could pretend, to be a rival to him, but I was not a patient and attentive listener to him, and that was what affronted him and caused his dislike to me as well as to any one else of whom he had the same reason to complain. His voice was feeble, and it has been said that his bitterness and caustic remarks arose from the necessity of his attracting attention by the pungency of his conversation. He was undoubtedly a very clever and accomplished man, with a great deal of taste and knowledge of the world, in the best of which he had passed his life. He was hospitable, generous, and charitable, with some weaknesses, many merits, and large abilities, and he was the last survivor of the generation to which he belonged.

The Grove, December 23d.—Came here for Christmas. No other guests but the family. We have had some talk about the peace propositions and other odds and ends. Clarendon told me that Walewski and Persigny are bitter enemies, and their estrangement the greater because Walewski is a corrupt jobber and speculator, and Persigny an honest man. When Drouyn de Lhuys resigned the Foreign Office, much to the Emperor's annoyance and regret, he did not know where to find a man, and he determined to appoint Walewski because he knew not whom else to take. Not choosing to send the offer to him through Drouyn, he employed Cowley, and requested him to telegraph in cypher to Clarendon a request that Cowley would send for Walewski and communicate to him the Emperor's intentions. A curious shift to be reduced to, but throughout the Eastern Question Cowley has acted the part of Foreign Minister to the Emperor almost as much as that of Ambassador.

Lewis this morning recapitulated to me the exact circumstances of the overtures from France about peace. It arrived here on a Saturday; was submitted to the Queen on Sunday, who approved of it; on Monday (or Tuesday) it was read to the Cabinet, when no discussion took place, but Palmerston shortly said, without giving any reasons, that he thought we must agree to the proposal, which was generally concurred in.   The next day there was another Cabinet, when they examined in detail all the articles and discussed them.   A few alterations were made, none of which were of any importance except the Bomarsund question.   The cession of Bessarabia and the neutralization of the Black Sea both formed part of the original proposal, and the latter was particularly insisted upon, and reasoned out at considerable length by France, for it turns out that the Emperor has never had so much in view the object of *making peace* (not expecting, nor ever having expected, that these proposals would be accepted) as the object of securing the active co-operation of Austria, which he expects to do.   Austria engages, if Russia refuses the conditions, to put an end to diplomatic relations between the two Empires, and Napoleon thinks this cannot fail to end in hostilities, and to this extension of the alliance he looks for bringing the war to a conclusion.   He thinks, moreover, that, when Austria has declared war, Russia will attack her defenceless frontier, and that as any attack upon Austria will compel the whole of Germany to assist her and to take part in the war against Russia, this offer will lead to Prussia and the whole of the German States being engaged on the side of the Allies, and that such a confederacy cannot fail to bring the war to a successful issue, because Russia would be absolutely incapable of offering any resistance to it.   This is a new view of the policy and motives of France, but I very much doubt if the whole of the Emperor's scheme will be realized.   Even though Austria may take up arms, it is probable that Russia will act strictly on the defensive, and will avoid giving any cause to the German States to depart from their neutrality. We both agreed that the conduct of Austria is quite inexplicable, and that Russia will never forgive her for the part she has acted and is acting now.

The Grove, December 24th.—George Lewis and I have been walking and talking together all the morning.   He is fully as pacific as I am, and entertains exactly the same thoughts that I do, of the egregious folly of the war, of the delusion under which the English nation is laboring, and of the wickedness of the press in practising upon the popular credulity in the way it has done.   He seems to like to talk to me on this subject, because he can talk freely to me, which he could hardly do with any of his own colleagues, still less in any other society. This morning he again recurred to the circumstances of the negotiations now going on, and he gave me an account of the transaction which puts the whole thing in a very ridiculous light, which would be very comical if it were not so very tragical. "Think," he said, "that this is a war carried on for the independence of Turkey, and we, the Allies, are bound to Turkey by mutual obligations not to make peace but by common consent and concurrence. Well, we have sent an offer of peace to Russia of which the following are among the terms : We propose that Turkey, who possesses one half of the Black Sea coast, shall have no ships, no ports, and no arsenals in that sea ; and then there are conditions about the Christians who are subjects of Turkey, and others about the mouths of the Danube, to which part of the Turkish dominions are contiguous. Now in all these stipulations so intimately concerning Turkey, for whose independence we are fighting, Turkey is not allowed to have any voice whatever, nor has she ever been allowed to be made acquainted with what is going on, except through the newspapers, where the Turkish Ministers may have read what is passing, like other people. When the French and Austrian terms were discussed in the Cabinet, at the end of the discussion some one modestly asked whether it would not be proper to communicate to Musurus (the Turkish Ambassador in London) what was in agitation and what had been agreed upon, to which Clarendon said he saw no necessity for it whatever ; and indeed that Musurus had recently called upon him, when he had abstained from giving him any information whatever of what was going on. Another time, somebody suggesting in the Cabinet that we were bound to Turkey by treaty not to make peace without her consent, Palmerston, who is a great stickler for Turkey, said very quietly that there would be no difficulty on that score ; in point of fact, the Turk evidently

'Stands like a cypher in the great account.' "

The Grove, December 26th.—Since I have been here Clarendon has resumed all his old habits of communication and confidence with me, has told me everything and shown me everything that is interesting and curious. I wish I could remember it all. Such fragments as have remained in my memory I will jot down here as they recur to me. Here are letters from Seymour at Vienna describing his good re-

ception there, gracious from the Court, and cordially civil
from the great society, especially from Metternich who seems
to have given the *mot d'ordre.* Metternich talked much to
Seymour of his past life and recollections, complimented him
for his reports of conversations with the Emperor Nicholas,
and said that many years ago the Emperor had talked to him
(Metternich) about Turkey in the same strain, and used the
same expression about "le malade" and "l'homme malade,"
when Metternich asked him " Est-ce que Votre Majesté en
parle comme son médecin ou comme son héritier ? " Also
letters from Bloomfield (Berlin) and from Buchanan (Copen-
hagen) with different opinions as to the probability of Russia
accepting or refusing—the former for, the second against ;
some curious letters from Cowley, full of his indignation
against Walewski ; the quarrels of Persigny and Walewski ;
the perplexity of the Emperor, his desire for peace, his hopes
that Russia may lend a favorable ear to the proposals ;
Cowley's suspicions of Walewski, and in a smaller degree of
the Emperor himself, especially of His Majesty's communications with Seebach, the Saxon Minister, and not impossibly
through him with St. Petersburg.

A curious anecdote showing the strange terms the parties
concerned are on : One day Cowley was with Walewski (at
the time the question of terms was going on between France
and Austria) and the courier from Vienna was announced.
Walewski begged Cowley, who took up his hat, not to go
away, and said he should see what the courier brought. He
opened the despatches and gave them to Cowley to read,
begging him not to tell the Emperor he had seen them. In
the afternoon Cowley saw the Emperor, who had then got
the despatches ; the Emperor also gave them to Cowley to
read, desiring him not to let Walewski know he had shown
them to him !

There has been a dreadful *rixe* between Walewski and
Persigny. I have forgotten exactly the particular causes,
but the other day Persigny went over to Paris partly to
complain of Walewski to the Emperor. He would not go
near Walewski, and told the Emperor he should not ; the
Emperor, however, made them both meet in his Cabinet the
next day, when a violent scene took place between them,
and Persigny said to Walewski before his face all that he
had before said behind his back ; and he had afterward a
very long conversation with the Emperor, in which he told

him plainly what danger he was in from the corruption and
bad character of his *entourage*, that he had never had anything about him but adventurers who were bent on making
their own fortunes by every sort of infamous *agiotage* and
speculation, by which the Imperial Crown was placed in
imminent danger. "I myself," Persigny said, "am nothing
but an adventurer, who have passed through every sort of
vicissitude; but at all events people have discovered that I
have clean hands and do not bring disgrace on your Government, like so many others, by my profligate dishonesty."
"Well," said the Emperor, "but what am I to do? What
remedy is there for such a state of things?" Persigny replied that he had got the remedy in his head, but that the
time was not come yet for revealing his ideas on the subject.

As we went to town, we talked over the terms proposed
to Russia. Clarendon said he could not understand the
policy of Austria nor what she was driving at. She had
entered very heartily into plans of a compulsory and hostile
character against Russia, who would never forgive her, especially for proposing the cession of Bessarabia. I said I
thought the most objectionable item of their propositions
(and I believed the most unprecedented) was the starting by
making it an Ultimatum. He replied that it was Austria
who tendered the Ultimatum, and that it was not exactly so,
the sharp edge having been rounded off by the mode to be
adopted, which was as follows: Esterhazy was to communicate the project to the Cabinet of St. Petersburg, and say he
had reason to believe that the Allies would be willing to
make peace on those terms; he was then to wait nine days.
If in that time the Russian Government replied by a positive
negative, he was, as soon as he got this notification, to quit
St. Petersburg with all his embassy; if no answer was returned at the end of nine days, he was to signify that his
orders were to ask for an answer in ten days, and if at the
end thereof the answer was in the negative, or there was no
answer, he was to come away, so that there was to be no
Ultimatum in the first instance. "But," I said, "what if
Russia proposed some middle course and offered to negotiate?" "His instructions were not to agree to this."
"Well," said I, "but when you abstain from calling this an
Ultimatum, it is next to impossible that Russia should not
propose to negotiate, and if she does beg that her proposal
may be conveyed to the Allies before everything is closed, it

will be very difficult to refuse this ; and is it not probable that France and Austria will both vote for entering into *pourparlers ;* and, if they do, can you refuse ? He seemed struck with this, and owned that it was very likely to occur, and that, if it did, we should be obliged to enter into negotiation.   So probable does this contingency appear, that there has already been much discussion as to who shall go from hence to the Congress, if there is one.   I said he had much better go himself.   He expressed great dislike to the idea, but said the Queen and Prince wished him to go, and that Cowley urged him also, and was desirous of going with him.   I see he has made up his mind to prevent any negotiation if he can, and, if it is unavoidable, to take it in hand.

This afternoon Persigny arrived from Paris and came directly to the Foreign Office.   The Emperor had given him an account of his interview with M. de Seebach,[1] who had gone off directly afterward *via* Berlin to St. Petersburg. The Emperor told him to do all he could to induce the Russian Government to consent to the terms, and to assure them that, if they did not, it would be long enough before they would have any other chance of making peace ; that he wished for peace, but that above everything else he was desirous of maintaining unimpaired his alliance and friendship with England ; that England had most fairly and in a very friendly spirit entered into his difficulties and his wishes ; that she was a constitutional country with a Government responsible to Parliament, and that he was bound in honor to enter in like manner into the obligations and necessities of this Government.   They had had some differences of opinion which were entirely reconciled ; they were now agreed as one man, and no power on earth should induce him to separate himself from England or to take any other line than that to which he had bound himself in conjunction with her.   This announcement, which the Emperor made with great energy, carried consternation to the mind of Seebach, and he resolved to lose no time in getting to St. Petersburg to make known the Emperor's intentions.

It is thus evident that the Emperor's mind is divided between his anxiety to make peace and his determination to have no difference with England ; but his desire for peace

---

[1] [M. de Seebach was the Saxon Minister in Paris, through whom many of these communications passed.]

must be great when, as Clarendon assures me, it was not without difficulty that he was deterred from ordering his army away from the Crimea.   The feeling here toward the Emperor seems to be one of liking and reliance, not unaccompanied with doubt and suspicion.   He is not exempt from the influence of his *entourage,* though he is well aware how corrupt that is, and he listens willingly to Cowley and to whatever the English Government and the Queen say to him, but his own people eternally din into his ears that we are urging him on to take a part injurious to his own and to French interests for our own purposes, and because our Government is itself under the influence of a profligate press and a deluded people ; and although he knows that those who tell him this are themselves working for their own private interests, he knows also that there is a great deal of truth in what they say.   His own position is very strange, insisting upon being his own Minister and directing everything, and at the same time from indolence and ignorance incapable of directing affairs himself, yet having no confidence in those he employs.   The consequence is that a great deal is ill done, much not done at all, and a good deal done that he knows nothing about, and he is surrounded with quarrels, jealousies, and struggles for influence and power both between his own Ministers and between them and the foreign diplomatists at his Court.

We have had a good deal of talk about Palmerston. Clarendon says nothing can go on better than he and Palmerston do together.   They seldom meet except in the Cabinet, and their communications go on by notes between Downing Street and Piccadilly.   Palmerston, much more moderate and reasonable than he used to be, sometimes suggests things or expressions in despatches, which Clarendon always adopts or declines according to his own ideas, and Palmerston never insists.   Palmerston is now on very good terms with the Queen, which is, though he does not know it, greatly attributable to Clarendon's constant endeavors to reconcile her to him, always telling her everything likely to ingratiate Palmerston with her, and showing her any letters or notes of his calculated to please her ; but he says it is impossible to conceive the hatred with which he is regarded on the Continent, particularly all over Germany.   An agent of his (Clarendon's) who, he says, has supplied him with much useful information, has reported to him that he finds the old feeling of antipathy to Palmer-

ston as strong and as general as ever, and that it is as much
on the part of the people as of the Governments, both thinking they have been deceived and thrown over by him.

CHAPTER XI.

France and Prussia—The Emperor's Speech—Faint Hopes of Peace—Favorable View of
the Policy of Russia—Progress of the Negotiations—Russia accepts the Terms of
Peace –The Acceptance explained—Popular Feeling in Favor of the War—Lord Stratford and General Williams—Mr. Disraeli s Prospects—Meeting of Parliament—Baron
Parke's Life Peerage—The Debate on the Address—Debate on Life Peerages—Report
on the Sufferings of the Army—Strained Relations with France—Lord Clarendon goes
to the Congress at Paris—Opening of the Conference—Sabbatarianism--Progress of
the Negotiations—Kars—Nicolaieff—The Life Peerage Question—Blunders and Weakness of the Government—A Visit to Paris—Count Orloff's View of the War—Lord
Cowley on the Negotiations—Princess Lieven on the War—An Evening at the Tuileries—Opening of the Legislative Chamber—Lord Cowley's Desponding Views—The
Austrian Proposals—Bitterness in French Society—Necessity of Peace to France—Conversation with M. Thiers—A Stag Hunt at St. Germains—The Emperor yields to the
Russians—Birth of the Prince Imperial.

January 1st, 1856.—Intelligence arrived yesterday that
Esterhazy had presented the Austrian proposal to Nesselrode
on the 28th, who had received it *in profound silence*.   Yesterday morning the " Morning Post," in communicating this
fact, put forth an article indecently violent and menacing
against Prussia ; and as it contained a statement of what the
Emperor Napoleon had said to Baron Seebach, which was
exactly what Persigny had told Clarendon, this alone would
prove, if any proof were required, that the article was inserted either by Palmerston or by Persigny.   The " Morning
Post " derives its only importance from being the Gazette of
Palmerston and of the French Government, and it is not
very easy to determine which of the two is guilty of this
article.   These are the sort of manifestoes which make us so
odious all over the world.

Hatchford, January 2d.—The speech which Louis Napoleon addressed to the Imperial Guard the day before yesterday when they marched into Paris in triumph, gives reason
for suspecting that the manifesto against Prussia in the
" Morning Post " was French, for there is no small correspondence between the speech and the article.   In the article Prussia is openly threatened and told, if she will not join
the allies in making war on Russia, the allies will make war
upon her ; in the speech the Guards are told to hold them-

selves in readiness and that a great French army will be
wanted.   Nothing is more within the bounds of probability
than that the Emperor may determine, if he is obliged to
make war, to make it for a French object, and on some
enemy from whom a good spoil may be taken, a war which
will gratify French vanity and cupidity, and which will
therefore not be unpopular.   He may think, and most probably not erroneously, that in the present temper of this country the people would be quite willing to let him do what he
pleases with Prussia, Belgium, or any other part of the continent, if he will only concur with us in making fierce war
against Russia.   But though this I believe to be the feeling
of the masses, and that their resentment against Prussia is
so strong that they would rejoice at seeing another Jena followed by similar results, the minority who are elevated
enough in life to reason and reflect will by no means like to
see France beginning to run riot again, and while we have
been making such an uproar about the temporary occupation
of the Principalities and the crossing of the Pruth by Russia,
that we should quietly consent to, nay, become accomplices
in the passage of the Rhine and an aggression on Germany
by France.   The very possibility of this shows the necessity
of putting an end to a war which cannot continue without
so many and such perilous contingencies.   Nothing in fact
can exceed the complications in which we can hardly help
being plunged, and the various antagonistic interests which
will be brought into collision, creating perplexities and difficulties which it would require the genius of a Richelieu to
unravel and compose.   The earth under our feet may be
mined with plots ; we know not what any of the Great Powers are really designing ; the only certainty for us is that we
are going on blindly and obstinately spending our wealth and
our blood in a war in which we have no interest, and in keeping Europe in a state of ferment and uncertainty the ultimate consequences of which it is appalling to contemplate.
Clarendon showed me a letter from Francis Baring from
Paris the other day, which told him that the Emperor
wished to make peace, because he knew that France, with
all her outward signs of prosperity, was unable to go on with
the war without extreme danger, that she is in fact "using
herself up," has been going on at a rate she cannot afford.

Hatchford, January 4th.—I was in London, yesterday,
where I saw George Lewis, who was very low, sees no chance

of peace, and everybody thinks it hopeless since the Russian
Circular has appeared.   It is difficult to understand the
motive of the Russians in publishing such a proposal, when
they must know it would not and could not be accepted, and
were also aware of the terms the Western Powers were going
to offer to her.   Lewis says our financial prospect is very
bad, a declining revenue, rising prices, a large loan wanted
which will be got on bad terms, and more money to be lent
to Sardinia and Turkey.   He thinks, if the Russians propose
to negotiate, that Palmerston will never consent ; but though
he will no doubt resist, if France presses it I have no doubt
he will give way and that the majority of the Cabinet will be
for doing so.   Everything looks as black as possible, and the
Emperor Napoleon's speech to the Imperial Guard following
Persigny's article in the "Morning Post" wears a very
menacing aspect.   It is possible indeed that he may have
held this language in order to frighten us into a more pacific disposition, but so far from being alarming or unpalatable to the majority here, they will hail with satisfaction
any intimation of his resolution to make war on Prussia ;
and if Louis Napoleon will only go on fighting against Russia, they will be quite willing that he should take whatever
he pleases from any other power which will not join us in
our present crusade.   I often wonder what the Duke of
Wellington would have said and thought if he could have
lived to see this day, and the madness of this nation.

London, January 9th.—I came to town on Monday and
found when I arrived that there was a fresh glimmering of
peace.   Austria had sent word she was inclined to believe
that Russia intended to accept the terms.   I went to Lewis,
who told me this was true, but he did not know on what
ground their opinion rested more than that ten days had
elapsed during which no symptoms of a flat refusal had
appeared, and Lewis himself thought there was no doubt they
were considering whether they should accept or what reply
they should make.   Colloredo called on Clarendon the other
day, and, after some unimportant talk, asked him if he had
ever heard, or had reason to believe, that Russia had made a
communication to France to the effect that if France had a
mind to take the Rhenish Provinces and make peace with
her, she should not oppose such a design.   Clarendon replied that he knew nothing of it, but thought it not at all
improbable.

Bernstorff had a conversation with Reeve the other day in which he told him that he was much put out at the isolated condition of Prussia, and gave him to understand that he should like the King to join the alliance, but he did not think anything would induce him to do so. It might perhaps be prudent, but it would be enormously base if Prussia were to come *au secours des vainqueurs*, and, now that Russia is in exceeding distress, to join England and France, to whom she certainly is under no obligations, in crushing her. But then it would only be prudent for the moment and to remove an immediate and impending danger, for in the more comprehensive view of the balance of power and with reference to general policy, it would be far wiser to leave the power of Russia undiminished. Germany has nothing to fear from Russia, for the notion of her being eternally animated with designs of conquest in every direction is a mere chimæra which the people who propagate it do not themselves believe. The part she has played for many years past has been that of a pacificator, and her only intervention has been to appease quarrels, and resist the progress of democracy and revolution. In 1848 it was the authority of the Emperor Nicholas which prevented a great war between Austria and Prussia which would have made all Germany a scene of havoc and bloodshed. Our Government now evidently expect a proposal from Russia to negotiate, and are living in hopes that it may be rejected *in limine* by Esterhazy, and that they shall be able to prevail on the Emperor Napoleon not to consent to any overture that may be made to him through any other channel.

January 15th.—I came to town yesterday morning and found on my arrival the Russian answer, which was pretty much what I expected. I suspect our Government will have been disappointed that so much was conceded as to make a peremptory rejection so monstrous as to be hardly safe. However, Esterhazy has been ordered to withdraw on the 18th, unless everything else is conceded. Granville fancies they are not unlikely to do this, but I am persuaded they will not. It remains to be seen what the French will do, for all depends on them. I asked Granville what he thought would be the end of it; he said *on the whole* he was rather disposed to expect it would lead to peace; he said Austria did not mean to go to war with Russia in any case, he thought she had played her cards with considerable dexterity, and made herself a sort of arbitress, and, what she most desired, had got a decided lead of Prussia, the object of her hatred.   I asked him if Prussia was terrified at the menaces contained in the Emperor's speech and other things against her, and he said he thought she was irritated but not frightened, and he inveighed against the folly of such speeches, and especially such articles as Persigny, if it was he, had put into the "Morning Post."

January 16*th.*—So far as I can as yet discover of public opinion, it is in favor of accepting, or at all events of negotiating on, the Russian proposals.   The "Times" has an ambiguous article on the subject.   Nobody will approve of the continuation of the war merely to obtain an Austrian object, which the cession of Bessarabia is, and the article about Bomarsund, which has nothing to do with the avowed object of the war.   I have not the least doubt one half of the Cabinet, at least, are in their hearts of this opinion, but I am afraid they will not have the courage to stand forth, avow, and act upon it.

January 17*th.*—I saw Lewis yesterday and for the first time saw something approaching to *a certainty* of peace. His information was curious : the "Morning Post," in the statement inserted by Persigny, said that the Russians had rejected the conditions about Bessarabia, and about Bomarsund, and had accepted the rest.   In the counter proposition of Russia there was no mention of Bomarsund, and for this very good reason, that no such proposal was made to them.   When the terms of Austria and France were sent here our Government objected to that article which said the allies reserved to themselves to make *other* conditions, or some such words.   They said it was not fair, and that they should at once say what they wanted, and *all* they wanted, and the additions they proposed were that Bomarsund should not be restored, that Consuls should be admitted to the Black Sea ports, and that "something" should be done about Georgia and Circassia.   This was their answer, and our allies agreed to these additions, but for what reason has not as yet appeared.   They sent the terms to St. Petersburg in their original shape and without our articles, so that in fact no condition about Bomarsund was made to them.   The Cabinet met yesterday to determine what answer should be sent to Paris, the French having notified that they would make no reply to the counter proposal till they were apprised of our sentiments thereupon.   Lewis said he had no doubt that both governments would be willing to enter upon negotiation on these terms, France and Austria being anxious for peace and our Government not averse, for they begin to perceive that there is a rapidly increasing disposition to put an end to the war, and particularly that nobody will desire to continue it merely to obtain an exclusively Austrian object, which the cession of part of Bessarabia would be, especially as Austria has no thought of going to war.   The Russian Government have written in a very conciliatory tone to Paris, which is known, though the letter has not yet arrived.   The King of Prussia had written a private, but very pressing letter to the Emperor of Russia entreating him to make peace.   Though very private, the French Government contrived to get a copy of it, and Cowley sent this copy home. It is said to be a very able letter written in a most confidential style.   Such being the state of affairs and all parties apparently being agreed in a disposition to put an end to the war, it seemed to me quite certain that the negotiations would be established, and that they would lead to peace.   In the evening I asked Granville if he did not think we should now certainly have peace, and he said "I think so, but there are still a great many complications," and he said Cowley and Walewski were on such bad terms that they hardly spoke. The fact is that Cowley is a gentleman and a man of honor and veracity, but he is sensitive and prone to take offence ; the other is an adventurer, a needy speculator, without honor, conscience, or truth, and utterly unfit both as to his character and his capacity for such an office as he holds. Then it must be owned that it must be intolerably provoking to Walewski or any man in his situation to see Cowley established in such strange relations with the Emperor, being at least for certain purposes more his Minister for Foreign Affairs than Walewski himself.

12 *o'clock.*—Payne has just rushed in here, to say that a telegraphic message, dated Vienna, ten o'clock last night, announces that "Russia accepts *unconditionally* the proposals of the allies."   The consequence of this astounding intelligence was such a state of confusion and excitement on the Stock Exchange as was hardly ever seen before.   The newspapers had one and all gone on predicting that the negotiations would lead to nothing, and that the war would go

on, so that innumerable people continued to be "bears," and they were all rushing to get out as fast as they could. It remains yet to be seen whether it is really true ; if it is, the Russians will be prodigiously provoked when they find that this concession was superfluous, and that the allies would have accepted *their* terms.

January 18*th*.—Though the account in the "Times" was not exactly correct, it proved substantially so. The right message came from Seymour soon after. There was such a scene in the Stock Exchange as was hardly ever witnessed ; the funds rose three per cent., making five in the last two days. The Rothschilds, and all the French who were in the secret with Walewski, must have made untold sums. I have been endeavoring to account for what appears the extraordinary conduct of Russia in accepting the Austrian terms purely and simply, and this strikes me to be the solution of it, and if my idea is correct it will account for the exceedingly bad terms which Cowley and Walewski are on. The conditions offered to Russia contained none of the points insisted on by our Government. I believe that the French and Austrians believed, very likely were certain, that if they had been sent Russia would have refused them, and, being bent on peace, they resolved to leave them out, and excuse themselves to England as they best could ; they therefore simply presented their proposal as it originally stood. . Russia replied with a qualified acceptance, and then Esterhazy was obliged by the compact to say that he could only take yes or no ; then, finding them not inclined to give any other answer, that he or somebody else told them the true state of the case, viz., that he had kept back the conditions *we* had demanded, and that unless they accepted his proposition, it must of necessity fall to the ground, and that nothing would then prevent the English points being brought forward and made absolute conditions of any fresh preliminaries. This was very likely to determine them to accept the proposals as put before them, for although by so doing they accepted the fifth condition, which exposes them to further and not specified demands, the especial points on which we insist can only be brought forward as points for negotiation, and will not form part of those conditions to which by their acceptance they stand completely and irrevocably pledged.

London, January 22*d*.—I went to Trentham on Friday, and returned yesterday. Granville is very confident of peace,

fancying that Russia will make no difficulties, and will agree
to our additional demands, which may be so, but seems to
me far from certain. The intelligence of peace being at
hand, or probable, gives no satisfaction here, and the whole
press is violent against it, and thunders away against Russia
and Austria, warns the people not to expect peace, and in-
cites them to go on with the war. There seems little occasion for this, for the press has succeeded in inoculating the
public with such an eager desire for war that there appears a
general regret at the notion of making peace. When I was
at Trentham, I asked Mr. Fleming, the gardener, a very intelligent man, what the general feeling was in that part of
the world, and he said the general inclination was to go on
with the war till we had made Russia, besides other concessions, pay all its expenses. It appears to me impossible the
entente cordiale with France can go on long if the war goes
on, when the people here are passionate for war, and in
France they are equally passionate for peace. If the Emperor goes on with the war he will be very popular here,
which does not signify much to him, but give deep offence
to his own countrymen, which will be of vital importance to
him, and no wonder, for their disgust will be intense at
being compelled to carry on a war at a ruinous expense,
merely because it is the pleasure of the English to do so.
This seems so obvious that I do not believe, after having gone
so far, and excited such strong hopes of peace, that he will
dare to disappoint the expectations of the country. What
the people of England would really like would be to engage
France to continue, and to issue a joint declaration of war
against Austria and Prussia.

January 23d.—Telegraphic news yesterday that Austria
positively refuses to send our supplementary conditions to
St. Petersburg. France backed us up, or at least pretended
to do so, for it is quite impossible to know what she really
does. Baudin is come over here, supposed to be for the purpose of explaining and apologizing for Walewski's not having
sent the conditions originally. I do not know what excuse
he makes. Lewis thinks as I do, that the real reason was
his fear lest they should endanger the acceptance by Russia
of the conditions. Our Government believe, or at least pretend to do so, that the Emperor was innocent of this *ruse*
and that Walewski is alone guilty ; but I doubt it, for I cannot believe Walewski would dare to do such a thing without

his master's knowledge and consent, and should not be surprised if the whole thing was the Emperor's doing.

There is a tremendous clamor got up by the press against Lord Stratford on account of his neglect of General Williams at Kars and leaving his appeals for aid unattended to. Stratford has sent home a defence of himself, and, I hear, a skilful one. I do not think they will remove him, because they say he is now acting *bond fide* according to his instructions, and exerting all his influence to smooth any difficulties that may arise at Constantinople in adjusting the terms of peace. But it is likely that the Turks are now very anxious for peace, as they are exceedingly sick of their protectors, by whom their dignity and independence are quite as much compromised as by their enemies, while the process of exhaustion is going on at a constantly increasing ratio.

January 26th.—Yesterday morning Disraeli called on me, and after we had discussed some private affairs, he began talking politics. He is very triumphant at his pacific views and expectations having turned out so true, and at the "Press" newspaper having proved to be right. He said, he had never stood so well with the *best* men of his party as he did now, that he is to have forty-five men, the cream of the Conservatives, to dine with him on Wednesday next. He then talked of Derby and the blunders he had made in spite of all the advice he had given and the remonstrances he had made to him, that he had written to him and told him what he knew from undoubted authority must and would happen about peace, and implored him not to commit himself to the continuance of the war, but that Derby with all his great talents had no discretion, and suffered himself to be led and influenced by some of the weakest and least capable men of his party. So instead of listening to what Disraeli said to him, he writes a long, reasoned reply to his arguments in the same way he would have replied to a speech in the House of Lords, and when he went to Scotland he had the folly to go to some meeting got up for the purpose, and then to make a violent war speech. I asked him how Derby and Stanley got on together, and he said that they were so much attached to each other, and Stanley had so profound a filial veneration for his father, that personal feelings silenced all political differences, and nothing would induce Stanley to take any public part adverse to his father's policy and opinions. It was evident that there is little political cordiality between Derby and Disraeli, and a considerable split in the party. If Disraeli is to be believed, the best of the Conservatives are disposed to go with him rather than with Derby, but I own I much doubt this. However, it will soon be seen what the state of that party is.

No further advance has been made toward the arrangements, but it is clear peace will be made. George Grey told me so yesterday, and intimated as much as that small difficulties must and would be got over. France, Austria, and Russia are resolved on peace, and England cannot alone make herself an obstacle. I suppose it will end in some compromise upon the points remaining in dispute.

Macaulay has retired from Parliament, where he had done nothing since his last election ; he hardly ever attended and never spoke, or certainly not more than once. It is to be hoped his life will be spared to bring down his history to the end of Queen Anne's reign, which is all that can possibly be expected.

January 31*st.*—Parliament meets to-day. Who would have thought a few weeks ago that the Queen's Speech would announce the preliminaries of peace ? Who would ever have thought that tidings of peace would produce a general sentiment of disappointment and dissatisfaction in this nation ? There are, however, sundry symptoms of an approaching change in the public mind. The press is much perplexed ; the newspapers do not know what to say. They confidently predicted that there would be no peace, and urged the people to go on clamoring for war as long as they could ; but since they have seen that their noise is ineffectual, and that peace is inevitable, they have nearly left off inveighing against it, because doing so without any result only exhibits their own impotence, which is just what they most wish to avoid. They therefore now confine themselves to a sort of undergrowl, muttering abuse against Russia and Austria, calling out for more stringent terms, and still indulging in a desperate hope that some unexpected difficulty may occur to break off the negotiations and plunge us into war again. The Opposition are as much perplexed as the press, and do not know what course to take, or what is the most vulnerable part of the Government, and they are not agreed among themselves.

So in the meantime they seem disposed to vent themselves in a fierce attack on Baron Parke's Life Peerage.

This peerage has excited great wrath even in many who are friendly to the Government, and probably in all who are unfriendly. Among those who most vehemently resent it are Lord Campbell, Lord Lyndhurst, and, as I am told, Brougham. There is much to be said about it either way, and it will probably give rise to some good debates and not uninteresting.

As one of many other proofs of the difficulty of getting at truth, and therefore of having history correctly written, I must record a fact not very important in itself. Lewis distinctly told me that it was *France* (i.e. Walewski) who kept back our conditions when the Austrian propositions were returned to Vienna ; now Granville tells me it was not France, but Austria, who is responsible for their not having been sent to St. Petersburg, and that Walewski did send them to Vienna. The truth probably is that he gave notice to Buol that we wanted these things, but did not incorporate them with the propositions, and that Buol, though apprised of them, did not choose to insert what France had not chosen to insert herself. It is quite impossible to believe that they can make any serious difficulty ; it is time to make peace with Russia when our relations with America are assuming a very unpleasant aspect.

February 3d.—Parliament opened very quietly, and there was no disposition evinced to find fault with the Government, or to throw obstacles in the way of making peace. A great change has certainly come over the country within the last fortnight or three weeks, not that people are not still sorry to see the end of the war, and rather inclined to view the peace with suspicion as well as dislike, but they have no grounds for complaint, they see that it is inevitable, and they are disposed to acquiesce.

Derby came down full of opposition but rather puzzled how to vent it, so he criticised the Speech, which was a very poor and bald composition, made a great stir about Kars, and announced a fierce attack on Baron Parke's Life Peerage.

In the House of Commons everything was very *piano*, and Disraeli quite moderate. The Government are much puzzled about this unlucky Life Peerage. The thing is done, and now they find themselves condemned by a large majority which includes all the Law Peers. If any vote can be taken on it in the House of Lords, they will be beaten.

The Conferences will begin in about three weeks, and

probably be very soon over, for it is the object of all parties to put an end to the enormous expense which, every day that the war lasts, is increased, and no doubt is entertained by the well-informed that Russia is in earnest, and will go through with it firmly and sincerely. The most unpleasant incident is the difference with America, which has a bad aspect, but when they learn· that we are going to make peace with Russia we flatter ourselves the Americans will become reasonable.[1] If a war should ensue it would be still more insane than the Russian war, for we should be fighting absolutely for no object whatever, and merely from the collision of the proud and angry feelings of the two nations. Neither would gain anything if the other were to give way and concede all that is in dispute as to the Central American question.

February 7th.—Nothing can be more extraordinary than the lull here, after so much sound and fury, while the negotiations and question of peace or war are pending. There is evidently a complete acquiescence in the coming peace, though if the terms are not as stringent as people expect, there will be a great deal of grumbling and abuse of the Government.

The case with America looks bad, but nobody can seriously believe that war between the two countries can possibly arise out of such questions as those now pending. It will probably end in the return of Crampton, and the return of Buchanan, suspension of diplomatic relations for a time, then fresh negotiations and a reconciliation, but no war.

February 9th.—The debate in the House of Lords on the Wensleydale Peerage was interesting but inconclusive. Lyndhurst made, as usual, a wonderful speech for his age. He contrived with much dexterity to avoid the question of legality, which he evidently thought he could not disprove; Campbell and St. Leonards boldly pronounced it illegal; Brougham admitted the legality; all the lawyers but the Chancellor are dead against the Life Peerage. Out of the House, Lushington is clear for it; Pemberton Leigh against; both of them have been offered and have refused peerages. The result appears to be that the patent is not illegal, but that there was no sufficient cause, and therefore that it was a great folly to deviate from the usual course in Parke's case.

---

[1] [Differences had arisen between the British and the American Government in consequence of the enlistment of American citizens in the British army during the war, and also with reference to the British possessions in Central America.]

It is awkward, and both the Opposition and the Government seem very much puzzled what to do. The best course on the whole seems to be (and it probably will so end) to confer on the Baron an hereditary peerage, and let the question of life peers stand over for the present, to be better considered and discussed hereafter when circumstances may require such a measure.

Palmerston made a very good speech last night on the American questions, judicious and becoming, and it was very well received. According to present appearances the Government is in no danger of being turned out, and if they make a peace which satisfies, and bring in and pass some good measures, they may actually become strong,

February 15th.—While the world is waiting with tolerable patience for the opening of the negotiations, it has got two subjects to occupy and interest it, and to give rise to plenty of discussion and dispute. The first is the Life Peerage question, which is become very embarrassing to its opponents and its advocates. There is a great majority of the lawyers against it, but more on the score of its being improper and inexpedient, *perhaps* unconstitutional, than that it is absolutely illegal. The highest authority in favor of it seems to be Dr. Lushington, who refused to be made a peer when a peerage was pressed upon him. The Government are determined to fight it out, and on no account to give way. Nobody knows with whom the project originated, but there is a very general idea that it was with the Prince. General Grey, however, told his brother, the Earl, that the Prince had nothing to do with it, and that his Royal Highness knew nothing of the matter till after it had been settled. I cannot see how it can be *illegal*, and neither the danger nor the inexpediency of making Life Peers is quite apparent to me ; but I think it has been a blunder, and that so great a novelty ought not to have been suddenly sprung upon the world without any attempt to ascertain how it would be regarded, and Derby's argument it is very difficult to meet. He says that when a certain prerogative has not been exercised for 400 years, such long disuse of it, if it does not amount to an abrogation of it, at all events throws such a doubt upon it as to make the exercise of it now exceedingly questionable, and it appears by the precedents that in every case of a Life Peerage it was done *consensu procerum,* or *consensu procerum et communitatis*—that is, by consent of the Lords, or by Act of Parliament. The whole question is so obscure and uncertain, that it is impossible to come to any satisfactory conclusion drawn from precedents and usage. In spite of the resolution of the Government, I doubt whether they will not be compelled to give way in some manner, for the Opposition appear to be equally resolved not to let Baron Parke take his seat.

The other subject is Sir John McNeill's report,[1] which has already elicited violent articles in the papers, and will occasion hot debates in the House of Commons, perhaps in both Houses. The report furnishes a strong *primâ facie* case against Airey and Gordon, Q. M. and A. Q. M. Generals, and *par ricochet* against Hardinge himself, also against Luean and Cardigan. The accused parties vehemently complain, and insist upon being allowed to vindicate themselves. Probably in the course of the discussions a good deal of the truth, but not all, will come out. It may be doubted whether there is any part of our military administration, as well as of our military operations during this war, on which it is possible to reveal and explain everything without showing up the French, and this has been the reason why all investigations and explanations have had such imperfect and unsatisfactory results. If the charges of McNeill are true, it seems to me that the man most to blame was Raglan, who was supreme, omnipotent, and responsible, and who ought not to have allowed the evils, which were notorious, to go on accumulating, without applying those effectual remedies which, according to the report, were abundantly at his disposal; but of course everybody will shrink from casting the blame posthumously upon him. The "Times" has now found that the losses and sufferings of the army were erroneously and wrongfully attributed to the Government at home. McNeill has brought back with him notes of conversations with Raglan, in which Raglan told him that most if not all of the things he had been so bitterly reproached for were all owing to the opposition and contradiction he met with from the French, Canrobert especially.

Cowley, who called on me the day before yesterday, said he should be very glad to have peace concluded, in order that our intimate connection and dependence on each other might be at an end, for the difficulties arising therefrom, and the

[1] [Sir John McNeill had been sent to the Crimea and Constantinople to investigate the causes of the sufferings of the troops in the winter 1854–'55.]

impossibility of placing any reliance on the French Ministers, were a perpetual source of annoyance. He thinks the
Emperor honest and true, but that he is surrounded by a
parcel of men every one of whom is dishonest and false.
The Emperor knows this, and knows what is thought of his
ministers, but he says, " What am I to do? and where can I
find better men who will enter my service?"

Clarendon came here to-day to take leave of me on going
to the Conference in Paris.   He talks despondingly, but
less about making peace than about making one that will
be acceptable here.   He augurs well from the choice of
Russian Plenipotentairies who are both personally agreeable
to him, for he knows Orloff very intimately.   When he took
leave of Brunnow three years ago he said to him, " If ever
you see a good chance of peace, let me know," and now
Brunnow has sent him a message reminding him of what
he had said, and telling him he now saw it. It was Clarendon
who fixed on Paris for the Conference, everybody else being
against it, especially the Emperor Napoleon and Palmerston,
but Clarendon thought the advantage of having personal
communication with the Emperor himself outweighed every
other consideration, and he is right.   Louis Napoleon will
be the arbiter, and the struggle will be between England
and Russia to get possession of him.   Brunnow arrived at
Paris to-day, the first arrival of the Plenipotentiaries, and
he was received with great acclamations and manifestations
of joy.   Clarendon is dissatisfied at Brunnow's having got
there first as if to steal a march on him, but this is unreasonable, as no particular day was fixed for their coming
at once, and Clarendon might have been the first if he had
chosen it, and Cavour is to be there to-day or to-morrow.

February 21*st*.—A week has passed since most of the
Plenipotentiaries arrived at Paris, and we hear nothing of
what has been going on amongst them; at least I hear
nothing except that Clarendon writes word he is quite
satisfied with the Emperor—the Hollands, that all sorts of
intrigues are rife, Brunnow, Morny, and Madame de Lieven
closeted together for hours, and Madame de Lieven writes
to me in melancholy mood, saying she anticipates many difficulties, and complaining of the *exigeances* which she hears of
as probable, and how ungenerous as well as impolitic it is to
make no allowance for the difficulty of the Emperor's position
vis à vis of his own people, and to bear so hard upon him.

From all this I infer that the Russians have been informed that the Emperor Napoleon has engaged to back us up in our *exigeances*, the principal of which is probably the dismantling of Nicolaieff; this may be inferred from what has appeared in the French press. The "Journal des Débats" published an article saying we had no right to demand this, to which the "Siècle" replied asserting we had a right, and the article in the "Siècle" was copied into the "Moniteur," which was tantamount to a recognition and approval of it. There are rumors afloat here that matters are not going on satisfactorily at Paris, and, taking all these things together, it looks as if the horizon was a little overcast, but as Orloff was only to arrive at Paris last night nothing essential can as yet have passed. Meanwhile this country remains in the same passive and expectant state, so far behaving very well that there is not the least stir or any attempt to make peace more difficult, not a word said in Parliament, no meetings or petitions, the "Times" nearly silent, and only an undergrowl from time to time from the Radical or malignant journals. But all who have had any opportunity of testing the state of public feeling agree that the peace, be it what it may, will be taken with regret, and that if Clarendon were to return having broken off the negotiations, and to announce that the war would go on, he would be hailed with the greatest enthusiasm, and the ardor for war would break out with redoubled force.

While this lull has been going on upon the great question, the world has been less passionately moved and interested by the affairs of the Wensleydale Peerage, and nobody has talked of anything else for the last ten days but this and the Crimean Report. The general feeling among the lawyers and in society is against the Life Peerage, but the Government are very reluctant to give way and to own themselves beaten upon it. To-night is the great, and, it may be hoped, final struggle in the House of Lords upon it, when nobody doubts that the Government will be beaten.

Last night the Evangelical and Sabbatarian interest had a great victory in the House of Commons, routing those who endeavored to effect the opening of the National Gallery and British Museum on Sunday. The only man of importance who sustained this unequal and imprudent contest was Lord Stanley. At this moment cant and Puritanism are in the ascendant, and so far from effecting any anti-sabbatarian

13

reform, it will be very well if we escape some of the more stringent measures against Sunday occupations and amusements with which Exeter Hall and the prevailing spirit threaten us.

February 24th.—A letter from Lady Clarendon, who says "the report about things going ill is false, and as yet things have hardly begun. The Emperor in feelings and opinions is everything that Clarendon could desire." Madame de Lieven received Clarendon *à bras ouverts*, but said very little to him. This morning I called on George Lewis, and had a long talk about the prospects of peace. He said Palmerston, according to his ancient custom, was doing all he could to extort as much as possible from Russia, writing to Clarendon in this strain constantly and urging him to insist on more and more concessions ; but Lewis thinks notwithstanding this that Palmerston has quite made up his mind for peace, and that he makes demands very often with the expectation of being refused, and the intention of not insisting on them if he finds a very determined resistance. One point of difference is Kars ; the Russians not unfairly wish to have some equivalent for surrendering it, and Palmerston insists that they are not entitled to any. In the preliminaries it was settled that we were to restore all our conquests, and they were in return to give up part of Bessarabia. At that time Kars was not taken, and now they say the relative positions of the parties are altered, and "if we are to restore Kars, that ought to be set against the restoration of Kinburn, the part of the Crimea you occupy, &c., and having got an equivalent in Kars, you ought to relax your demand for Bessarabia." To this Palmerston replies that the Russians are to guarantee the integrity of the Turkish dominions, of which Kars is a part, and therefore their restoration of it is a matter of course for which no equivalent is necessary. This argument is not logical, and no arbitrator would admit it. It is a good point to wrangle upon, and if the Russians knock under it will be because they are resolved to submit to any terms rather than not have peace.

It is much the same thing about Nicolaieff, as to which the Emperor appears at present disposed to back us up. Lewis disapproves of our *exigeances* and Palmerston's tone. He thinks on both points the Russians have good cases, and that Palmerston and Clarendon are only fighting for them in order to have a more plausible and showy peace to set

before the country.   He says we never thought of demanding the destruction of the docks of Nicolaieff *at first*, and
that our demanding it now is a mere afterthought, and in
pursuance of the plan of starting as many demands as we
can to take the chance of what we can get.   Lewis disapproves of this course, and urged me to encourage Clarendon
not to lend himself to exigencies unjust in themselves, but
to do what he really thinks right and necessary without fear
of the consequences.

When we had done talking of this matter he said he
wanted to speak to me about the Peerage question, which had
assumed a shape which he thought menaced great embarrassment, if not danger.   The government, he said, would not
give way, and he was himself opposed to their doing so ; but
what was to be done ?   I said I did not see what the Government could do, nor why they should not give way when
they had resolved to fight and had been fairly beaten ; but
he thought they should stultify themselves by acknowledging they had been wrong, and that such a course would
oblige the Chancellor to resign.   I controverted these propositions and said they would stultify themselves much more,
if from motives of vanity and pride they chose to let the
House of Lords remain without that assistance to obtain
which was the pretext for Parke's creation.   On the whole,
Lewis seemed to think the least objectionable course would
be to pass a bill enabling the Crown to make a certain number of Life Peers, but he overlooked the fact that this would
be as much a confession of error, and an acknowledgement
that the Queen had no such prerogative, as to make Lord
Wensleydale an hereditary Peer.   My advice was to make
him an hereditary Viscount.   I was obliged to go away and
had not time to talk it out.   In the afternoon, I spoke to
Campbell and Lyndhurst about it, and asked what they proposed, and how the difficulty was to be got over.   They
naturally want the Government to knock under and give up
the hereditary peerage ; they both scouted the idea of Parke
coming down to the House of Lords and insisting on being
admitted and making a scene.   Lyndhurst to-night is to
give notice of motion for a Committee to consider the Appellate Jurisdiction.

February 27th.—The debate in the Lords on Monday
night affords a prospect of an amicable termination of the
Peerage case, but the Government still have a lingering hope

that by some management and contrivance they may avoid
the necessity of submitting to their defeat and acting accordingly.   There is to be a Committee on the Appellate Jurisdiction, and they think they may obtain some report which
may enable them to get out of their scrape, but the only way
I can make out by which they think of doing this is to lay
the foundation of a bill to enable the Crown to make a
limited number of Life Peers.   This would, however, be a
more formal acknowledgement of error, and that the Queen
does not possess the prerogative, than any other course.   I
expect they will at last be driven to adopt the course I recommended, that of making Park a Viscount, hereditary of
course.

Last night, Disraeli made a bitter attack on the Government, to which Labouchere replied with a spirit for which
nobody gave him credit.   The Opposition displayed great
warmth, and a disposition to show serious fight on any occasion they could find.   Certainly the Government cuts a very
poor figure, and it is difficult not to think that as soon as
the all absorbing question of peace or war is decided, they
will be much put to it to defend themselves, unless they conduct affairs much better for the future than they have done
up to the present time.   Hitherto they have presented a
series of blunders, failures, and exposures.   First of all the
Peerage question ; then, much worse, in the House of Commons, Lowe's Bill on Shipping Dues, which Palmerston was
obliged to withdraw last night, not at all creditably, and the
failure of which was in a great measure attributable to
Lowe's very injudicious speech, which, as he is the organ of
the Board of Trade in the House of Commons, was in itself
a great evil and misfortune.   George Grey's Bill on County
Police meets with such opposition that though it is a very
good measure he will probably not be able to carry it.   But
still worse than these are the case of the Crimean Report
with all its incidents, one blunder after another, and the
wretched exhibition of Monsell in moving the Ordnance Estimates, amounting to a complete break-down.   All these
things, one after another, place the Government in a very
weak and contemptible position, and show that in spite of
Palmerston's having recovered a good deal of his personal
popularity in the House of Commons, his Government has
no strength, and his being able to go on at all is only owing
to the peculiar circumstances in which the country is placed,

and the extreme difficulty of any other Government being formed which would be palateable to the country, more effi-cient, and therefore stronger and more durable than the present.

To-morrow I purpose going to Paris to see and hear what is going on at this interesting moment.

Paris, March 1st, 1856.—I left London on Thursday with M. de Flahault and my brother. We slept at Boulogne, and after a prosperous journey in all its stages, found myself in my old quarters at the Embassy yesterday evening at seven o'clock. I had hardly arrived before a card came from Morny, who gave a great evening party with two *petites pièces* and music. I went there with Lady Cowley. The crowd was so great that I saw nothing whatever of the spectacle, but was pretty well amused, for I met some old acquaintance, made some new ones, and was presented to some of the celebrities of the day. I was much struck with the ugliness of the women, and the extreme *recherche* of their costumes. Na-ture has done nothing for them, their *modistes* all that is pos-sible. The old friends I met were La Marre and Bourqueney, whom I have not seen since he was Secretary of Embassy to Guizot, when we had so much to do together about the affairs of the East. I made acquaintance with Fleury, the Em-press's Grand Écuyer, renewed it with Bacciochi, and I was presented to Cavour and the Grand Vizier, as little like the *beau idéal* of a Grand Vizier as can well be imagined, but by all accounts a Turk *comme il y en a peu.* He is a very lit-tle, dark, spare, mild-looking man, speaks French perfectly, and exceedingly clever, well-informed, enlightened, and hon-orable. He was Grand Vizier once before, and owes his pres-ent elevation to his great personal merit. He accepted the post with reluctance, feeling sure Stratford would torment him to death and get him turned out again, but it seems as if his high qualities, and the general respect with which he is regarded, would enable him to maintain himself against all intrigues, and even against Stratford's predominance. I met Clarendon, but had hardly any opportunity of talking to him, as he was every moment interrupted by people come up to do civilities to him. He had just time to tell me that matters are going on very slowly, and that he sees no reason why he should not be kept here for the next six months. Orloff had met him *à bras ouverts* and renewed their old Petersburg friendship. Brunnow he is disgusted with, and

says he has made a bad-impression here.   He told me he had
said to Brunnow · "You were in England long enough to
know what a special pleader is ; well, if all other trades
should fail you, take to that."

Orloff spoke very frankly about the war, and the conduct
of the late Emperor, which he had always regarded as insane
in sending Menschikoff to Constantinople.   If he had sent
him, Orloff, instead, he would answer for it, there would
have been no war.   Then marching into the Principalities,
and finally not accepting the modifications of the Vienna
Note.   After this, Orloff said, he had declined to have anything more to do with those affairs, and had retired in disgust.   He thought Nicholas's mind had undergone a change
after he had reached sixty years of age.

Clarendon said he was delighted with the Emperor and
liked him better and better every time he saw him.   I met
Walewski, who said he wanted to talk to me, when he expressed great anxiety to know the state of opinion in England, and talked of the chances of peace, and particularly
wished to know if I thought Palmerston really and sincerely
desired peace.   I told him the exact truth as to opinion in
England, and said I believed Palmerston was now sincere in
wishing to make peace, but that it was in his nature to be
exigeant, and he thought it necessary to be so now because
it was of great moment to him to present to the country a
peace with as many concessions as possible from Russia.   I
said it depended on France after all, and then I found that
while they thought Bomarsund ought to be an indispensable
condition, Nicolaieff ought not ; and so we parted, and I
promised to dine with him on Monday.

This morning after breakfast I had a long conversation
with Cowley.   He did not speak despondingly of the peace,
but he dilated on the difficulty of coming to satisfactory
terms, and such as Clarendon could consent to, which he
attributes principally to the French, who, having gained all
the glory they want for the satisfaction of their national vanity, have no longer any desire to go on with the war, and we
are placed by them in a fix.   "If," he said, " our army was
in Asia Minor he should not care, because then we might say
to them, Do just what you please, make peace if it suits you,
we shall not resent it or have any quarrel with you, but we
will carry on the war on our own account.   As it is, if we
insist on renewing the war, the French *cannot*, and would

not abandon us, and leave us to be attacked by superior
Russian armies; they would therefore very reluctantly go
on with the war, but it would be well known that we were
dragging them on with us, and the exasperation against
us would be great and general, and, say what we might,
a quarrel between France and England would infallibly ensue." He said all the objections he had entertained against
Paris being the place of conference had been more than
realised, and that the thing to have done would have been
to have it in some dull German town, where there would
have been no amusements and occupations, and no intrigues,
and where they would have applied themselves vigorously to
their work in order to get it done as quickly as possible. I
have not, however, as yet made out what intrigues there
are, but there is of course a vast deal of *commérage* going on.

The conferences take place every other day, beginning at
one, and they generally last about four hours. Walewski
presides, and, they say, does it pretty well; M. Benedetti,
the Chef de Département in the Foreign Office, is the Proto-
collist and Rédacteur; the manner of it is conversational
but they occasionally make speeches, Walewski told me.
I asked Clarendon in the evening how they were going on
and he said he thought they were making a little progress,
but that the French did all they could to render it impossible.

I called on Madame de Lieven in the morning, who did
not seem to know much beyond what lies on the surface.
She is craving for news and eager for peace. Orloff has kept
aloof from her, to her great mortification, and rather to the
malicious satisfaction of her enemies, but he went to see her
at last the day before yesterday, and, I suppose, accounted
for the delay, for she spoke of him as if they were friends,
though of course she would take care not to say a word of
complaint or to have it supposed, if she could help it, that
he had neglected her. She complained that in our *exigeance*
we did not make allowance enough for the difficulties of
the Emperor of Russia's position, for, however necessary
peace might be to Russia, there is a very great party there
who from pride and obstinacy would carry on the war at
all risks and hazards. She talked much of the enormous
faults that had been committed throughout the whole of the
Eastern Question, and of the severe retribution the pride
of the late Emperor had drawn down on his country, and
remarked, which is quite true, that this would be the first

time in the history of Russia in which she had made a disadvantageous peace ; for even in her wars against Napoleon, when she had suffered defeat after defeat, she had still concluded peace with a gain of territory.   I saw the Hollands, Guizot at Madame de Lieven's door, called on Lady Clarendon, and then went to ride with Lady Cowley in the Bois, and so the evening and the morning were the first day.   The weather is cold and gloomy, and I don't think I shall stay here long.

March 3d.—Went about visiting yesterday, and at night to the Tuileries, an evening party and play, two small pieces ; the Emperor was very civil to me as usual, came up to me and shook hands ; he talked to Orloff and to Clarendon, then the Grande Maitresse told him the Empress was ready, when he went out and came back with her on his arm, Mathilde, Princess Murat, and Plon Plon following.   As the Emperor passed before me, he stopped and presented me to the Empress.   I was introduced to Orloff, and in the course of the evening had a long talk with Brunnow, who said *they* had made all the advances and concessions they could, and it was for us to move toward peace, and not to advance one step and then retreat two.

This morning I went to see the opening of the legislative bodies, and hear the Emperor's Speech.   It was a gay and pretty sight, so full of splendor and various colors, but rather theatrical.   He read his speech very well and the substance of it gave satisfaction ; it was not easy to compose it, but he did it exceedingly well, and steered clear of the ticklish points with great adroitness and tact.   It sounded odd to English ears to hear a Royal Speech applauded at the end of each paragraph, and the shouts of " Vive l'Empereur " from the Senators and Deputies.

After Cowley came home he began talking over the state of affairs, and the peace we are going to make, about which his grief and disappointment are overflowing.   He says the Emperor had the best intentions, but has been beset with men who were determined on peace for their own ends, and whom he could not resist.   What he blames him for is not having at once said that he would go so far with us and no further, and not have allowed us to delude ourselves with expectations of support from him that were not to be realised.   He says it is now all over, the matter decided, it will proceed rapidly, and all be finished by Easter

At night.—I have been dining with Walewski, a very handsome dinner to the Sardinians, and a party afterward. Knowing none of the people, it was a bore; I found nobody to converse with but Cavour and Flahault; talked over the state of affairs with the latter and our discontents. He said the Emperor could not refuse, and when Clarendon came over and found His Majesty's conversation so satisfactory, he was misled by it and fancied he should obtain his support to all our demands; he owned that it would have been better if the Emperor had been more explicit. When I got home I found Cowley, who was engaged in drawing up a statement of the comparative state of Russia, as to her aggressive power against Turkey before the war and now, after peace has been made. He is doing this for Clarendon and to assist him in making his case good in Parliament when the peace is attacked, as he says it is quite certain it will be. I asked him what were the points on which the Russians made the most difficulty. He said on *all* except Bomarsund. He is quite convinced that Walewski has played false, and that he has made known to Orloff exactly what he must give up, and when he may be stout.

March 5th.—Little to record; Cowley continues talking to me of the state of affairs as it is and as it might have been, and is excessively dejected and disgusted at the idea of the peace he is about to sign; he thinks it neither creditable nor likely to be durable, but we start from such different points of view that it is impossible for us to agree. He harps upon the evil done by having the Conference here, and certainly the advantage Clarendon promised himself from having it here has proved null, for the Emperor does not send for him, having no mind to talk to him, and he will not ask an audience of the Emperor, though Cowley urges him very much to do it. He acknowledges, however, that it would be now too late, and that nothing more can be done; he thinks Clarendon will bring himself with great reluctance to sign such a Treaty; but he must swallow the pill, however bitter. The bitterness proceeds from having had such vast pretensions and having encouraged, if not held, such lofty language.

It is no wonder that this Government want to get their army home when typhus is raging there, and they have by their own account 22,000 men in hospital, while ours is quite healthy. We took all sorts of precautions, and strongly advised the French to do the same, and to adopt a sanitary plan we imparted to them ; they held it cheap, did nothing, and here are the consequences. It is said that while those who have been in the Crimea and have distinguished themselves are eager for peace, those who have not yet earned medals are averse to peace, and that there will be a good deal of jealousy between the regiments.

March 6th.—We talked yesterday morning about the origin of the Austrian proposals, and Čowley said he had never been able exactly to make out whether the scheme had originated at Vienna or here, but he was inclined to believe that the first hint was given by Austria, and that Walewski then put the thing on paper, which was sent to Vienna and returned thence in the shape of a proposal. Bourqueney first brought it from Vienna, Buol having obtained his Emperor's consent to it. Cowley told me Buol had been all along willing to join us in the war, but the Emperor never would consent to it. Cowley's notions are that we never ought to have listened to any intervention, nor to any proposals for peace but from Russia herself, that we should have made her sue for peace. He would have had our demands from the first stated distinctly, and have allowed of nothing but acceptance or refusal ; he would never have agreed to the article for the cession of Bessarabia, nor have asked for territory at all. If it could have been managed he would have preferred giving the Principalities to Austria, who should for them give up Lombardy to Sardinia. Not a bad idea. By the by, it is much noticed that in the Emperor's Speech he calls the King of Sardinia the King of Piedmont, probably without any particular meaning or intention, but they say he never does anything without a meaning. I rode to the new racecourse yesterday, near the Bois de Boulogne, and went to the Opera last night to see a beautiful new ballet, "Le Corsaire." Went to Passy to see the Delesserts, who were out.

In this head quarter of gossip every trifle makes a noise, a little scene in society excites interest and shows the continued violence of party feeling. A party dined at Lord Holland's and more came in the evening, mostly, as it happened, Orleanists, for the Hollands live with all parties indiscriminately. There were Mesdames de Rémusat, d'Haussonville, and several others of that color, when the door opened and MM. de Flahault and Morny were announced, on which the women all jumped up like a covey of partridges and walked out .of the room, without taking any notice of the men.   It is said that the Orleanist party entertain a peculiar rancor against M. de Flahault for having seen behind a door or a curtain the arrest of General Changarnier on the 2d of December, which he afterward had the folly to avow.

At night.—Just before dinner came an invitation to go to the Tuileries to-night, which with much reluctance I was forced to do.   Two *petites pièces* as on Sunday.   I did not attempt to get into the gallery, and sat in the next room, first with Brunnow, then with the Grand Vizier, who is become a great friend of mine.   The Emperor did nothing but take off one Plenipotentiary after another : first Clarendon, next Buol, then Orloff, and lastly Walewski, and probably more was done there than at the Conference in the morning. Brunnow and Walewski both told me the affair was progressing, and Cowley seemed very low coming home.   His dejcction is extreme, and he said this morning that he could not recover from his extreme disappointment at the conduct of the Emperor, that he had always had a bad opinion of Walewski, and no reliance on him or any of the ministers, but he would have staked his life on the Emperor's remaining true to us, that he had always assured our Government that they might depend implicitly on him, and it was a bitter mortification to him to have been deceived himself and to deceive them.   I asked him how Clarendon felt all this, and he said Clarendon had never spoken to him about it, and preserved a calmness which astonished him.   "What," I asked, "did the Cabinet at home say ?"   He said, "They seemed to place entire confidence in Clarendon, and to leave all power and responsibility to him."

March 8th.—Called on M. de Greffuhle yesterday, whom I had not seen for years.   He is eighty, enormously rich, full of activity and intelligence, Orleanist by social habits, but well affected toward this Government and not hostile to the Emperor, though despising his Government.   He said that he was *compelled* to make peace, and that it would cost him his Crown if he did not ; that *something* would happen and then he would be upset, so great would be the consequences of his running counter to the universal desire for peace here ; that the finances are in a very difficult state and there must be another loan, but it would not be contracted like the last, which was a piece of absurd *charlatanerie.*

I went in the afternoon to see the Imperial stables, a
wonderful establishment ; and then the stallions, near Passy.
In the evening to Madame Baudon's, where I was presented
to General Cavaignac, but had no conversation with him.
He is a tall, gentlemanlike man, with a very military air. I
was surprised to see him there in the midst of the Legiti-
mists, he, a republican, but it seems he was once near marrying Madame Baudon, who was sous-gouvernante des En-
fants de France when Madame de Gontaut was Gouvernante.

March 9th.—Went about visiting as usual. Called on
Achille Fould, who introduced me to Magne, Minister of
Finance, said to be a great rogue. Everything here is intrigue and jobbery, and I am told there is a sort of gang,
of which Morny is the chief, who all combine for their own
purpose and advantage : Morny, Fould, Magne, and Rouber,
Minister of Commerce. They now want to get out Billault,
Minister of the Interior, whom they cannot entirely manage,
and that ministry is necessary to them on account of the
railroads, which are under his management. Fould was full
of civilities and offers of services, and he told me the Emperor has a mind to talk to me ; whether anything will come
of it I know not. I went thence to Madame de Galliera's,
where I met Thiers and made a *rendezvous* with him for to-
day ; then to Madame de Lieven, who had had Orloff with
her ; lastly to Madame de Girardin and renewed our old
acquaintance, dined with Delmar, and came home to a great
party here.

March 10th.—I called on Thiers yesterday, and had a
long talk with him ; he declared he was happier unemployed
and quite free than he had ever been ; he had been all for
the war, and was now as much for peace—like every other
Frenchman he considered it a necessity ; anxious as ever for
the English alliance, and ridiculed the idea that we had not
accomplished everything that our honor and glory required ;
bitter against this Government, and maintained that the
Emperor might very safely relax the severity of it without
giving up anything ; indignant with the peculation and corruption that prevailed, and the abominable acts of injustice
committed, one of which he mentioned towards his own
family. Very pleasant as usual.

The news of the day was the dangerous illness of King
Jerome, whose life hangs on a thread. This morning I went
to St. Germains to see a stag hunt in the forest—a curious

sight, with the old-fashioned *meute;* the officers, and those
privileged to wear the uniform, in embroidered coats, jack-
boots, and cocked hats ; piqueurs on horseback and foot with
vast horns wound round their bodies ; the costume and the
sport exactly as in the time of Louis XIV., rather tiresome
after a time.   The old château is a melancholy *délabré* build-
ing, sad as the finishing career of its last Royal inhabitant.
These recollections come thick upon one—Anne of Austria
and the Fronde, Louis XIV. and Mademoiselle de la Vallière
—for here their lives began.   When the Queen was here she
insisted on being taken up to see Mademoiselle de la Vallière's
apartment, to mark which some slight ornaments remain.
Here too James II. held his dismal Court and came to his
unhappy and bigoted end.   After it ceased to be a palace, it
became successively a prison, a school, and a barrack, and
now the Emperor has a fancy to restore it.   I went at night
to a great concert at Walewski's, where I fell in with Clarendon, and found he was quite prepared to make peace even
on such terms as he can get, in which I encouraged him,
and to my surprise he said he did not think it would be a
bad peace, though it was not so good as we might have got
if the generals had done all they might, or if we had had
another campaign.   He asked me how I thought people
would look on it in England, and I told him from all I
heard I thought *now* the wish was for peace, and that the
peace would be well enough taken.   This he now thinks
himself, and he said peace would certainly be concluded before the end of the month.

March 15th.—From Cowley's account the Conferences
appear to be drawing to an end, as a committee has been
formed to draw up the Treaty.   It consists of Cowley, Bourqueney, Brunnow, Cavour, Buol, and the Grand Vizier.
Cowley is still bemoaning the insufficiency of the terms, and
while he admits the necessity of peace here, maintains that if
the Emperor would only have joined us in insisting upon the
terms we wished to impose, it is certain the Russians would
have consented to everything, for he says they now know
from unquestionable information that the Russians expected
much harder terms.   The Emperor was, however, so beset by
his *entourage,* and so afraid of running the slightest risk of
the Russians breaking off the negotiations, that he would
not insist on anything which he was not certain the Russians
would agree to, and Cowley says he thinks Clarendon was

not so firm as he might have been, and if he had pressed the
Emperor more strongly, that the latter would have yielded
and told Orloff that, though anxious to make peace, he was
still more anxious to continue on good terms with us, and
that if the Russian Government wanted peace, they would
only have it on such and such terms.   All this may be true,
and I am myself inclined to think the Russians would have
agreed to our terms, if those terms had been heartily backed
up by the Emperor ; but except to give something more of
a triumph to the English public, I am not of opinion that
the difference between what we required and what we shall
get is worth much.   When the *dénouement* is before the
world, it will appear how insane it was to plunge into such
a war, and that the confusion and unsettled state of affairs
which will be the result of it are more dangerous to the stability of the Turkish Empire than the ambitious designs of
Russia ever were.   Whether the Emperor Nicholas was premature or not in his idea of "the sick man," it will soon
appear how sick the man will be left by the doctors who
have stepped in to save him, and I believe the *bouleversement*
of the old Turkish dominion will have been greatly accelerated by the war and the consequences which will flow from
the successes of the allies.

What Cowley particularly laments over is having failed
to dismantle Nicolaieff and to stop the outlet from the Bug
to the Black Sea, and having got no satisfactory arrangement with regard to the Circassian coast and the contiguous
provinces which were ceded to Russia by the Treaty of
Adrianople.   We wanted that Russia should acknowledge
the independence of these provinces or of some part of them ;
but I cannot see of what use this would have been, and it
would have been a matter of the greatest difficulty how to
secure their independence and under what Government.
There is a sort of sympathy with the Circassians in England,
which would have made some stipulations with regard to
them popular ; but the independence would be illusory, Russia would soon reassert her authority, and our stipulations
would become a dead letter, or we should be involved in endless disputes without any satisfactory results.   As to forming another coalition for the sake of semi-barbarous nationalities on the coasts of the Caspian, nothing would be more
impossible.   England herself, who will soon recover from her
madness, would not hear of it, and France still less.   The

war was founded in delusion and error, and carried on by a factitious and ignorant enthusiasm, and we richly deserve to reap nothing but mortification and disappointment in return for all the blood and treasure we have spent.

March 16th.—We passed the day in momentary expectation of hearing of the Empress's confinement. No news arrived, but at six in the morning we were awakened from our beds by the sound of the cannon of the Invalides, which gave notice of a son. Will his fortune be more prosperous than that of the other Royal and Imperial heirs to the throne whom similar salvos have proclaimed? It is a remarkable coincidence that the confinement was as difficult and dangerous as that of Marie Louise, with the same symptoms and circumstances, and that the doctor accoucheur (Dubois) in this instance was the son of the Dubois who attended the other Empress. From all I hear the event was received here with good will, but without the least enthusiasm, though with some curiosity, and the Tuileries Gardens were crowded. People were invited by the police to illuminate.

CHAPTER XII.

Lord Clarendon's favorable View of the Peace—General Evans' Proposal to embark after the Battle of Inkerman—Sir E Lyons defends Lord Raglan—Peace concluded—Sir J. Graham's gloomy View of Affairs—Edward Ellice's Plan—Favorable Reception of the Peace—A Lull in Politics—A Sabbatarian Question—The Trial of Palmer for Murder—Defeat of the Opposition—Danger of War with the United States—Ristori as an Actress—Defeat of the Appellate Jurisdiction Bill—Return of the Guards—Baron Parke on the Life Peerage—Close of the Session—O'Donnell and Espartero in Spain—Chances of War—Coronation of the Czar—Apathy of the Nation—Expense of the Coronation at Moscow—Interference at Naples—Foreign Relations—Progress of Democracy in England—Russia, France, England, and Naples—Russian Intrigues with France The Bolgrad Question—The Quarrel with Naples—The Formation of Lord Palmerston's Government in 1855—Death of Sir John Jervis—Sir Alexander Cockburn's Appointment—James Wortley Solicitor-General—Conference on the Treaty of Paris—Low Church Bishops—Leadership of the Opposition—Coolness in Paris—Dictatorial Policy to Brazil.

London, March 21st, Good Friday.—I left Paris on Wednesday morning with Mr. and Mrs. Reeve, dined at Boulogne, crossed over in the evening, and arrived in London yesterday morning at eleven o'clock. When near Folkestone we were caught in a fog, lost our way, and were very near having to anchor and pass the night at sea. After a vast deal of whistling and bellowing, stopping and going on, the fog

cleared a little, lights became visible, and we entered the
harbor with no other inconvenience than having made
a long *détour*, and being an hour later than our proper
time.   I regretted leaving Paris, where I was treated with
so much affection and hospitality, and on the whole very
well amused.   On Monday, I dined with the Duchesse de
Mouchy ; on Tuesday night Clarendon came after dinner
to see me before my departure, and we had some talk about
the peace and the terms.   He spoke very cheerfully about
it, and seems not at all dissatisfied, nor to feel any alarm
about its reception.   As it is, without at all acknowledging
that he has made any sacrifices, he considers that the influence he has acquired for England, particularly with
Austria and Turkey, is far more valuable than any items of
concession from Russia would have been.   Buol told him
that he was now quite convinced that England was the
Power to which Austria must really look with confidence and
reliance on her honor and friendship, and the Turk was still
more warm and vehement in assurances of the same kind,
This was elicited from the Austrians by the fact of England
having supported the condition of the Bessarabian cession,
while France took part with Russia and threw Austria over.
Moreover, Clarendon does not, like Cowley, complain of the
Emperor Napoleon, but speaks with great satisfaction of His
Majesty's conduct to him, and the renewed cordiality with
which he has recently expressed himself toward England,
and for the maintenance of his alliance with us.   In short,
he evidently thinks, and not without reason, that he will
return, having obtained a sufficiently good peace, and having
placed England in a very fine position.   He said that he had
been able to accomplish his task by being ready to incur
responsibility at home, and by being able to act unfettered,
and taking on himself to disregard any instructions or recommendations from home that he did not approve of.   Yesterday I saw George Lewis and had a talk with him and his
wife about Clarendon and the peace.   He said he thought the
peace quite sufficient, and he did not understand what it was
Cowley found fault with, nor why he is dissatisfied.   He
denies that we have given up anything that it would have
been just and reasonable to stand out upon, and will not
hear of taking an apologetic tone, but that Clarendon should
defend the peace on its own merits.   He thinks it will be
well enough received in the House of Commons and by the

country, and he is in good spirits about the Government.
He says Palmerston has been moderate and reasonable, and
that he is not aware of Clarendon's having been harassed
with any instructions, but left entirely to his own discretion.
They all think he has done exceedingly well.

March 29th.—I went to Hatchford on Saturday last ; on
Wednesday to Althorp. I met Sir Edmund Lyons at Hatchford, who talked incessantly about the incidents of the war
and the conduct of the people concerned in it, and very interesting his talk was, for besides having been one of the
most conspicuous and important actors in it, he was completely in the confidence of the Commanders-in-Chief, and
consulted by them on every occasion and with regàrd to all
operations.   He told us what had passed between Evans and
Raglan and between Evans and himself on a most important
occasion, to this effect : Evans went to Raglan immediately
after the battle of Inkerman, and proposed to him to embark the army immediately, leaving their guns, and (Lyons
says he is almost certain) their sick and wounded to the enemy.   Raglan said, "But you forget the French : would you
have us abandon them to their fate?"   He replied, "You
are Commander-in-Chief of the *English* army, and it is your
business to provide for *its* safety. . . ."   Raglan would not
hear of the proposal.   Almost immediately after Evans met
Sir Edmund Lyons and told him what had passed with
Raglan, and urged him to suggest the same course.   Lyons
made the same observation about the French that Raglan
had done, and said one of two things would happen : either
the French would take Sebastopol alone, when we should be
covered with shame and dishonor, or they would fail and
probably suffer some great disaster.   The expression of
"perfide Albion" had long been current in France, and then
indeed it would be well deserved and would become a perpetual term of reproach against us.   These rebuffs did not
prevent Evans going on board ship and there giving out that
the army would in a few days be obliged to embark, and
Captain Dacres came to Lyons and told him he heard this
was going to happen.   Lyons asked him where he had heard
this, and he said Evans had announced it, and talked of it
unreservedly as certain to happen. Lyons said, "It is false ;
the army will not go away, and Sebastopol will be taken.   It
is very mischievous that such reports should circulate, and I
order you not to allow such a thing to be said by anybody on

board your ship, and to contradict it in the most positive manner."

Everything that Lyons said, and it may be added all one hears in every way, tends to the honor and the credit of Raglan, and I am glad to record this because I have always had an impression that much of the difficulty and distress of the army in 1854 was owing to his want of energy and management. He was not a Wellington certainly, and probably he might have done more and better than he did, but he was unquestionably, on the whole, the first man in the army, and if he had not been continually thwarted by the French, would have done more. While many here were crying out for placing our army under the command of French generals, and recalling Raglan (and I must confess I had myself a considerable leaning that way), he was struggling against the shortcomings or the inactivity of Canrobert and Pélissier. Canrobert acknowledged that he had not nerves sufficient for the duties of his station, and he never could be got to agree to adopt the bold offensive movements which Raglan was continually urging upon him, especially after the battle of Inkerman, when Raglan entreated him to follow up the discomfited Russians, his whole army being ready and not above 1,500 of them having been engaged. With Pélissier, Raglan had very little to do, for his death occurred soon after Pélissier took the command.

Lyons gave us an interesting account of Raglan's last illness. He seemed to have no idea that he was in serious danger, nor had the people about him. At last, when he was so rapidly sinking that the doctors saw his end was approaching, and it was deemed necessary to apprise him thereof, he would not believe it, and he insisted to his aide-de-camp who told him of his state that he was better, and he fell into a state of insensibility without ever having been conscious of his dying condition. One of the best authenticated charges against Raglan was that of his not showing himself to his soldiers, and it was said many believed that he had quitted the camp : at last this idea became so prevalent that his own staff felt the necessity of something being said to him about it, but none dared, for it seems they were all exceedingly afraid of him. At last they asked Lyons if he would speak to him and tell him what was said. Lyons said he had no scruple or difficulty in so doing, and told him plainly the truth. Raglan not only took it in good part, but thanked him very much, and said his reason for not riding round all the divisions was that he could not prevent the soldiers turning out to salute him, and he could not bear to see this ceremony done by the men who had been all night in the trenches or otherwise exposed to fatigue, and that this was the sole reason why he had abstained, but henceforward he would make a point of riding round every day, and so he ever after did ; so that the main fact as reported by " correspondents " was not devoid of truth. I wish I could recollect all the various anecdotes Lyons told us, but I neglected to put them down at the time, and now they have faded from my memory. He discussed the qualities of the English generals with reference to the command of the army after Raglan's death. He never had well understood why it was that 'Colin Campbell was always considered out of the question, and his own opinion seemed to be that he was the fittest man. The French thought so, and one of the alleged reasons against him, viz., that he could not speak French, was certainly not true. Simpson was very reluctant to take the command at first, and wrote home to say so, but after he had received certain flattering encouragements his opposition waxed fainter, and by the time it was taken from him he became anxious to retain it. Raglan was not at all annoyed at Simpson's being sent there, and did what he pleased with him. Simpson never attempted to interfere with him or to control him in any way, but on the contrary was entirely subservient to Raglan.

April 1st.—News of peace reached London on Sunday evening, and was received joyfully by the populace, not from any desire to see an end of the war, but merely because it is a great event to make a noise about. The newspapers have been reasonable enough, except the " Sun," which appeared in deep mourning and with a violent tirade against peace.

April 3d.—Yesterday I met Graham at the Council Office, where he had come to attend a committee. Since the formation of Aberdeen's Government three years ago I have hardly ever seen him, and have never had any conversation with him. Yesterday he sat down and began talking over the state of affairs generally, and the prospects of the country, which he considers very gloomy and full of danger, more particularly from the outrageous license of the press, which has now arrived at a pitch perfectly intolerable, but which it is impossible to check or control. Then the total

destruction of parties and of party ties and connexions, to
say nothing of the antipathies and disagreements of such
public men as these are. He says there is not one man in
the House of Commons who has ten followers, neither Gladstone, nor Disraeli, nor Palmerston. The Government goes
on because there is no organized opposition prepared and able·
to take its place, and the Government receives a sufficiency
of independent support, because all feel that the business of
the country must be carried on, and hitherto Palmerston
has been supported as a War Minister, and the best man to
carry on the war ; but Graham is very doubtful what will
happen when the discussions on the peace and all matters
relating to the war are over, and other questions (principally
of domestic policy) come into play. Palmerston, always sanguine, fancies he can stand, but it is very doubtful, for he is
not backed by a party constituting a majority ; the Treasury
Bench is very weak, and Palmerston himself a poor and
inefficient conductor of the Government in the House. John
Russell has taken up the question of education, which he
hopes to render popular, and through it means again to
recover his former influence and authority. He said that
John Russell is (in spite of all that happened last year)
more looked up to by the Whig party than Palmerston,
and that they would rather have him for their leader, as,
notwithstanding the faults he has committed, he is by
far the ablest man, has a much greater grasp of intellect,
more foresight, and is much more of a statesman, and has
more fixed principles. Palmerston (Graham thinks) has a
passionate love of office and power, and will cling to it with
tenacity to the last, and never resign it but on compulsion,
not caring with whom he acts, nor on what principles. This,
I think, is partly true and partly false. I do not think he
cares whom he acts with, but I do not believe he is quite indifferent as to the principles. He says Lewis has done well,
and is liked in the House of Commons, and Gladstone likes
him and gives him a cordial support ; that Baines is a good
man, and those two are the most respected and considered
of all the men on the Treasury Bench, the House accepting
their sterling qualities in place of greater brilliancy such as
Gladstone can command ; that Gladstone is certainly the
ablest man there, though it is still doubtful whether his
talents are equal to such an emergency as the present to
master public opinion, enlist it on his side, and to adminis-

ter the Government on certain principles of administrative reform, which Graham himself considers necessary. His religious opinions, in which he is zealous and sincere, enter so largely into his political conduct as to form a very serious obstacle to his success, for they are abhorrent to the majority of this Protestant country, and (I was rather surprised to hear him say) Graham thinks approach very nearly to Rome. Gladstone would have nothing to do with any Government unless he were leader in the House of Commons, and when that Government is formed, there should be previously a clear and distinct understanding on what principles it was founded and what their course of action should be. His tone is now that of disclaiming party connections, and being ready to join with any men who are able and willing to combine in carrying out such measures as are indispensably necessary for the good government of the country, such a system as he briefly shadowed out in his speech at the Mansion House the other day. Graham's idea is, that in the event of this Government breaking down, the best chance of another being formed would be by Clarendon undertaking it, whom on the whole he regards as the man best fitted by his experience and ability to be at the head of affairs ; that he and Gladstone might be brought together, but would Lord John consent to go to the Lords, and to serve under Clarendon as President of the Council and Head of the Education Department ? This opens questions full of doubt and difficulty. Derby, he thinks, has no desire to form another Government, and would prefer to go on as he is now, leader of a large party of Peers who are willing to follow him and to make the House of Lords one of the scenes and instruments of his amusements as usual, provided it supplies him with occupation and excitement, indifferent to the consequences and to the mischief he may do. Disraeli appears to be endeavoring to approach Gladstone, and a confederacy between those two and young Stanley is by no means an improbability. What Stanley is disposed to do and capable of doing is still an enigma, and although his speeches are not devoid of matter, they are without a particle of the spirit and stirring eloquence of his father.

The change which has taken place in the country presents to Graham a most alarming prospect. Hitherto it has been governed by parties, and patronage has been the great instrument of keeping parties together ; whereas Sir Robert

Peel has destroyed party, which had now entirely ceased to
exist ; and between the press, the public opinion which the
press had made, and the views of certain people in Parliament, of whom Gladstone is the most eminent and strenuous, patronage was either destroyed or going rapidly to
destruction. The only hope of escaping from great perils
was in that broad stratum of good sense and firmness which
still existed in the country, and of which manifestations had
been recently given. He admires the resolute and unflinch-
ing spirit with which the war had been entered into, carried
on, and the country was quite willing to persist in ; and not
less the sensible and reasonable manner in which the peace,
by which they were mortified and disappointed, had been
acquiesced in, for he says that it is beyond all question that
there is throughout the country a strong feeling of mortification and regret that we have not played a more brilliant
part, and that our share of glory has been less than that of
our ally, and there would have been a general feeling of exultation and satisfaction if we had fought another campaign
in order to end the war with greater *éclat*. But this sentiment has been sufficiently mastered by prudent considerations and a just appreciation of the circumstances of Europe
generally, and of our relations with other Powers, to check
all ebullitions of mortified pride, and to induce a prudent
reserve and acquiesce in the management of the Government,
and in a spirit like this there appears some hope for the
future. We had a very long talk about these and other
matters, the substance of which I record as it recurs to my
mind.

A day or two before I met Ellice at Hillingdon, where
we interchanged our thoughts, and a good deal that he said
was much in Graham's sense : that this Government could
not stand but by being remodelled, and his notion is that
half of it should be got rid of, the Peelites taken in, and Lord
John to go to the House of Lords as President of the Council, Granville taking Cowley's place as ambassador at Paris,
and Cowley replacing Stratford Canning at Constantinople.
A propos of Stratford Canning, Graham thinks the Opposition will attack the Government and not the ambassador on
the case of Kars, and that it is not impossible they may
carry a vote of censure against them, which I told him I did
not believe was possible, or that they could be able to carry
any resolution affecting the Government so much as to com-

pel their resignation, and I suggested to him how fatal this would be to his scheme of reorganizing a Government under Clarendon, as such censure would more especially touch him, and this would make it impossible for the Queen to entrust the formation of another Government to his hands.

April 7th.—Since my conversation with Graham, I have learned from the Duke of Bedford that Lord John is not very much disinclined to go to the House of Lords, particularly as his position in reference to his seat for the City is so embarrassing. The Dissenters, always unreasonable and ungrateful, will not forgive his speech upon Church Rates the other night, and his general popularity is gone. Then it is probably a consideration with him to secure to his family the settlement his brother will make on him if he takes the peerage.

London, May 4th.—For nearly a month I have let this journal fall into arrear, during which period the most interesting occurrences have been the return of Clarendon, the publication of the conditions of peace with the accompanying protocols, and the debate upon Kars. With regard to the peace, Clarendon comes very well out of his mission, and no fault is found with the peace. The Kars debate was a great error on the part of the Opposition, and ended with a great triumph for the Government. Just before it, Palmerston called a meeting of his supporters, where he harangued them with great success, and managed to rally them round him with more of zeal and cordiality than they have hitherto shown. His position is certainly improved, and according to present appearances he will get through the session without much difficulty. All agree that he has been doing well in the House of Commons; his assiduity, his punctual attendance, and his popular manners make him agreeable to the House, and he has exhibited greater facility and resource in dealing with all sorts of miscellaneous subjects than anybody gave him credit for. There is not the smallest danger of the peace proving dangerous to him, and it is evident that the House of Commons, however independent and undisciplined it may be, will not allow him to be placed in any danger, and is determined not to have any change of Government at present. The Peelites and John Russell supported him and had nothing else to do, for they are neither of them in a condition to attempt to play a game of their own.

May 14th.—Every day my disinclination to continue this work (which is neither a journal nor anything else) increases, but I have at the same time a reluctance to discontinue entirely an occupation which has engaged me for forty years, and in which I may still find from time to time something to record which may hereafter be deemed worth reading, and so at long intervals, and for short periods, I resume my reluctant pen.

We are now in the Whitsuntide holidays, in a profound political and parliamentary calm, the Government perfectly secure, Palmerston very popular, the Opposition disheartened and disunited, and having managed their matters as awkwardly and stupidly as possible, attacking the Government on questions and points on which the assailants were sure to be beaten, and strengthening instead of weakening it by their abortive attempts.   There was great difference of opinion among them about fighting battles, on Kars, and on the peace ; Lyndhurst and Derby were against, Disraeli was for. Roebuck, whom I fell in with on Sunday in a railway train, told me that if they had laid hold of the one point of the protocol in the Belgian press, and worked this well, they might have put the Government in a minority, but they missed this obvious opportunity.[1]   I called on Lyndhurst yesterday, who said they had unaccountably overlooked this plausible topic.   He is going to make a speech on Italy when Parliament meets, and we agreed entirely that either too much or too little was done at Paris on this question, and that either it ought not to have been entertained and discussed at all, or some more decided measures ought to have been adopted with regard to it.   To stir up such delicate questions, and leave them in their present unhappy condition, is an egregious error.

The questions of war and of peace having now ceased to interest and excite the public mind, a religious question has sprung up to take their place for the moment, which though not at present of much importance, will in all probability lead to more serious consequences hereafter.   Sir Benjamin Hall having bethought himself of providing innocent amusement for the Londoners on Sunday, established a Sunday

---

[1] [An attempt had been made at the Congress of Paris by Count Walewski to bring forward some measure or resolution reflecting on the independence of the press in Belgium. It led to nothing, but Lord Clarendon was accused of not having protested against it with sufficient energy.]

playing of military bands in Kensington Gardens and in the other parks and gardens about the metropolis, which has been carried on, with the sanction of the Government, with great success for several Sundays. Some murmurs were heard from the puritanical and sabbatarian party, but Palmerston having declared himself favorable to the practice in the House of Commons, the opposition appeared to cease. The puritans, however, continued to agitate against it in meetings and in the press, though the best part of the latter was favorable to the bands, and at last, when a motion in Parliament was threatened to insist on the discontinuance of the music, the Cabinet thought it necessary to reconsider the subject. They were informed that if the Government resisted the motion they would be beaten, and moreover that no man could support them in opposition to it without great danger of losing his seat at the next election. It is stated that the sabbatarians are so united and numerous, and their organization so complete, that all over the country they would be able to influence and probably carry any election, and that this influence would be brought to bear against every man who maintained by his vote this "desecration of the Sabbath." Accordingly it was resolved by the Cabinet to give way, and the only question was how to do so with anything like consistency and dignity. The Archbishop of Canterbury was made the "Deus ex machinâ" to effect this object. He was made to write a letter to the Premier representing the feelings of the people and begging the bands might be silenced. To this Palmerston wrote a reply in which he repeated his own opinion in favor of the music, but that in deference to the public sentiment he would put an end to their playing. All this has excited a good deal of interest and discussion. For the present, the only question is whether the angry public will not vent its indignation and resentment to-morrow in acts of uproar and violence; but though these acts will not be serious or lasting if they do take place, it may be expected that the sabbatarians will not rest satisfied with their triumph, but will endeavor to make fresh encroachments on our free will and our habits and pursuits, and that fresh and more serious contests will arise out of this beginning.

May 28th (day of the Derby).—Yesterday on Epsom racecourse arrived the news of Palmer's being found guilty of the murder of Cook. This case and the trial have excited

14

an interest almost unprecedented, unlike anything since the case of Thurtell about twenty years ago or more. People who never heard of either of the men took the deepest interest in it, the women particularly, though there was nothing peculiar in it or of a nature to excite them particularly. The trial lasted a fortnight, all the details of it were read with the greatest avidity, half the town went one day or other to hear it, and the anxiety that the man should be convicted was passionate. Cockburn gained great applause by the manner in which he conducted the prosecution.

This trial has proved more attractive and interesting than anything in the political world, though there has been a pitched battle in the Lords on the question of Maritime Law and Right of Search given up in the recent Treaty. Derby made a violent onslaught on the Government, and was at first very confident of a majority. He soon found these hopes were fallacious, when he got angry and was more violent than he has ever been before this session. The Government got a majority of above fifty, which puts an end to any further contest there. The Government have now nothing to fear, the Opposition are routed and dispirited, and one can see nothing to alter the present state of affairs. The minor questions which have occupied attention are settling quietly. The Chelsea Commission is over, and the result will be harmless, on the whole rather good than bad, because it will prove that the violent attacks on the military authorities during the war have been exaggerated and in many cases unfounded. A sort of compromise has been made about the Wensleydale peerage, not a very happy one, and it remains to be seen whether the House of Commons is sufficiently acquiescent as to sanction it by agreeing to the 12,000l. a year to be paid to two new judges and peers for life. The Government have virtually abandoned the principle they contended for, and have yielded to the adverse vote and Committee. When they appeal to Parliament and limit the number of life peerages, they abandon the prerogative of the Crown.

June 1st.—The state of affairs with America becomes more and more alarming.[1] Grey told me the other night

---

[1] [In consequence of the dispute with the American Government on the subject of Foreign Enlistment, Mr. Crampton, the British Minister, was ordered to leave Washington on May 28th. He arrived in England on June 15th: but Lord Palmerston stated in the House of Commons that the dismissal of Mr. Crampton did not break off diplomatic relations with the United States, as Mr.

that he had had a long conversation with Dallas, whose tone was anything but reassuring as to the prospect of peace ; and yesterday I met Thackeray, who is just returned from the United States.   He thinks there is every probability of the quarrel leading to war, for there is a very hostile spirit, constantly increasing, throughout the States, and an evident desire to quarrel with us. He says he has never met with a single man who is not persuaded that they are entirely in the right and we in the wrong, and they are equally persuaded if war ensues that they will give us a great thrashing ; they don't care for the consequences, their riches are immense, and 200,000 men would appear in arms at a moment's notice. Here, however, though there is a great deal of anxiety, there is still a very general belief that war cannot take place on grounds so trifling between two countries which have so great and so equal an interest in remaining at peace with each other.   But in a country where the statesmen, if there are any, have so little influence, and where the national policy is subject to the passions and caprices of an ignorant and unreasoning mob, there is no security that good sense and moderation will prevail.   Many imagine that matters will proceed to the length of a diplomatic rupture, that Crampton will be sent away and Dallas retire in consequence, and that then by degrees the present heat will cool down, and matters be amicably arranged without a shot being fired.   I feel no such confidence, for if diplomatic intercourse ceases numerous causes of complaint will arise, and as there will be no means left for mutual and friendly explanation and adjustment, such causes will be constantly exaggerated and inflamed into an irreconcilable quarrel.   Matters cannot long go on as they now are without the public here becoming excited and angry, and the press on both sides insolent, violent, and provoking, and at last, going on from one step to another, we shall find ourselves drifted into this odious and on both parts suicidal contest, for there is not a blow we can strike at America and her interests that will not recoil on us and our own.   It has often been remarked that civil wars are of all wars the most furious, and a war between America and England would have all the characteristics of a civil and an international contest ; nor, though I have no doubt that

Dallas remained in this country.   It is remarkable that within a few months or even weeks two British Ministers received their passports from foreign governments and were sent away—a very uncommon occurrence !]

America is in the wrong, can I persuade myself that we are entirely in the right on either of the principal points in dispute. We have reason to congratulate ourselves that the Russian war is over, for if it had gone on and all our ships had been in the Baltic, and all our soldiers in the Crimea, nothing would have prevented the Americans from seizing the opportunity of our hands being full to bring their dispute with us to a crisis.

June 7th.—1 went last night to see the celebrated Ristori in a very bad play called "Medea," being a translation into Italian from a French tragedy by a M. Legouvé. This play was written for Madame Rachel, who refused to act the part, which refusal led to a lawsuit, in which the actress was (I think) defeated. Ristori is certainly a fine actress, but she did not appear to me equal to Pasta in the same part, or to other great actresses I have seen. However, my inability to hear well and want of familiarity with Italian acting and imperfect knowledge of the language disqualify me from being a competent judge.

The American horizon is rather less dark. Nothing is yet known as to Crampton's dismissal, and Dallas does not believe it. The Danish Minister at Washington writes over here that he thinks that the clouds will disperse and there will be no serious quarrel.

London, July 12th.—After the lapse of a month or more, during which I could not bring myself to record anything, or to comment upon passing events, I am at last roused from my apathy, and am induced to take up my pen and say a word upon the defeat of the Appellate Jurisdiction Bill in the House of Commons the other night, which gave me the greatest satisfaction, because I regard it as a just punishment for the stupid obstinacy with which the Government have blundered on from one fault to another throughout this whole business. It has been a complete comedy of errors, and every one who has taken a part in it has been in the wrong. I told Granville how it would be in the first instance, and urged him, after the House of Lords had refused to let in Parke as a life peer, to accept the defeat quietly by making him an hereditary peer and thus give the go-by to the main question. This nothing would induce them to do, and they fancied that they could avoid the mortification of appearing to knock under, and save their own consistency, by the contrivance of this bill. Every mischief that it was possible to do they have managed to accomplish, and the leaders of the opposite parties, who all felt themselves in a scrape, came to a sort of compromise in the Lords' Committee, the result of which was this unpopular bill. Among them they have assailed the prerogative of the Crown, they have damaged the judicial authority of the House of Lords, they have deeply offended many of their own friends by tendering to them such a measure, and they have behaved most unkindly and unhandsomely to Baron Parke, who thinks he has great reason to complain.

I have been at Knowsley for the last three days, and so missed the march of the Guards into London on Wednesday. Lord Hardinge was struck down by paralysis as he was speaking to the Queen at Aldershot on Tuesday last. It is supposed that the Duke of Cambridge will succeed him, and that Jim Macdonald will be his Military Secretary. The American question is still undecided, but everybody appears to be very easy about it.

July 20th.—I met Baron Parke the other day, who talked over his affair, complained of the treatment he had received from the Government, but said he gathered from what the Chancellor had said to him that they meant now to make him an hereditary peer, declared there was not a shadow of doubt about the legality, and that Campbell had as little doubt as he himself had, but finding the measure was unpopular with certain lawyers, he had suddenly turned against his own recorded opinion and opposed it. The Baron said the Government were greatly to blame for not having ventilated the question, and ascertained whether they could carry it or not, and if he had had an idea of all the bother it had made, he never would have had anything to do with it. George Lewis told me that the life peerage had never been brought before the Cabinet, and he knew nothing of it till he saw it in the Gazette, nor did Clarendon ; in fact it was confined to the Chancellor, Granville, and Palmerston. They none of them, however, know with whom it originated. Now that the measure turns out to be so unpopular and is so scouted, and the transaction has been attended with so many blunders and defeats, no one is willing to accept the responsibility of it, or to acknowledge having had anything to do with it. It is strange that Palmerston should ever have consented to it, but he knew nothing and cared nothing about it ; he was probably assured it would go down without

any difficulty, and in this *poco curante* way he suffered himself to be committed to it, not seeing the storm it would
cause.   He allowed Granville to manage it all his own way,
and at last he had the good luck to be beaten upon it in the
House of Commons, for the scrape would have been more
serious if he had carried it there.   These last days of the
session have been as usual marked by the withdrawal and
abandonment of various bills that were for the most part introduced at the beginning of it, and which were found to be
quite worthless, especially the Law Reform Bill.

   London, July 27th.—Parliament has finished its debates,
and will be prorogued on Tuesday.   Dizzy wound up by a
" review of the session," a species of entertainment which
used to be given annually some years ago by Lord Lyndhurst
with great skill and effect, but which on the present occasion, and in Disraeli's hands, was singularly inopportune and
ineffective.   Lord Wensleydale has at last taken his seat as
an hereditary peer ; the Government, after various abortive
attempts to wriggle out of their absurd position, having done
at last what they ought to have done at first—knocked under
and endured what could not be cured.   The Government go
into summer and winter quarters in a very healthy and prosperous state, with nothing apparently to apprehend, and
with every probability of meeting Parliament next year in
the same condition, and, barring accidents, going through
next session as successfully as they have gone through this.

   August 4th.—I was at Goodwood all last week ; the
Prince of Prussia came there.   Not a word of news ; the
Queen still engaged in reviewing the troops, and complimentary fêtes are still going on to Sir W. Williams of Kars,
and Charles Wyndham " the hero of the Redan."   The disturbances in Spain seem to be over, and O'Donnell remains
victorious.   My first impression was (the common one) that
Espartero had been ousted by an intrigue, and that it was a re-
actionary *coup d'état*, but I now hear that it is no such thing,
and that we ought to desire the success of the present Government.   Espartero and O'Donnell could not agree, as was
not unlikely in a coalition Government the two chiefs of
which were men of such different opinions and antecedents.
After many abortive attempts to reconcile their differences,
it was agreed that a council of Ministers should be held
which the Queen herself should preside over, and when a
final attempt should be made.   A long discussion took place,

and the queen did all she could to reconcile the two generals, and to enable the Government to go on unchanged. Finding it impossible to effect this, she ended by saying, "Well, gentlemen, since I cannot prevail on you to go on together, I must needs choose between you, and as I think Marshal O'Donnell will be the best able to carry on the Government, I appoint him." Then the National Guards began an insurrection which was put down, but no violent measures seem to have been adopted, and O'Donnell has declared that Spain can only be successfully governed on constitutional principles, and that he means to retain the Cortes in its integrity. How far his acts will correspond with his professions remains to be seen. Narvaez was recommended to go to France, and Queen Christina appears not to have been allowed to return to Spain, which are good signs. It is a good thing for Spain that Espartero should have retired, for though probably the honestest Spaniard, he is at the same time the weakest and the most wanting in moral courage and decision.

History is full of examples of the slight and accidental causes on which the greatest events turn, and of such examples the last war seems very full. Charles Wyndham told me that nothing but a very thick fog which happened on the morning of Inkerman prevented the English army being swept from their position and totally discomfited. The Russians could see nothing, lost their own way, and mistook the position of the British troops. Had the weather been clear so that they had been able to execute their plans, we could not have resisted them ; a defeat instead of the victory we gained would have changed the destiny of the world, and have produced effects which it is impossible to contemplate or calculate.

On the other hand, nothing but miscalculation and bad management prevented the capture of Sebastopol immediately after Alma. My nephew is just returned from a voyage with Lord Lyons to the Crimea, where he went all over the scenes of the late contest, all the positions, and the ruins of Sebastopol as well as the northern forts. He was well treated by the Russians, who showed him everything, and talked over the events of the war with great frankness. They told him that if the allies had marched at once after the battle on the north side, no resistance could have been made, and the other side must have fallen. We had long known that the north side would have fallen if we had attacked it at once.   Frank asked the Russian officer whether there was any bad feeling on the part of the Russian army toward the French or English, and he said none whatever, but a great deal toward the Austrians, and that they desired nothing more than an opportunity of fighting them.   He also said that they had been misled by our newspapers, from which they obtained all their information, and thinking that the announcements there of an intended invasion of the Crimea were made for the purpose of deceiving them, they had withdrawn a great many troops from the Crimea, so that while Sebastopol had been emptied of the garrison to increase the army of Menschikoff, the Russians had not more than 30,000 or 35,000 men at the Alma.

Hillingdon, August 17th.—It is impossible to find anything of the least interest to write about, and my journal is in danger of dying of starvation or of atrophy.   The causes of discontent we have had with Russia are disappearing, and the Emperor's coronation will not be clouded by fresh *doléances* on our part.   Bulwer is just gone to the Principalities, where the commissioners are to endeavor to ascertain what are the wishes of the people as to the union. France and England are in favor of it, Turkey and Austria against it, while Russia professes to be indifferent and neutral.   Spain is settling down into submission to the Government of O'Donnell.   Naples is relieved from her fears of English intervention, and there seems some chance that she may relax the rigor of her Government now that she may do so *salvo honore* and not under compulsion.   This country is profoundly tranquil and generally prosperous ; everybody seems satisfied with Palmerston and his administration.   I myself, who for so many years regarded him politically with the greatest aversion and distrust, have come to think him the best minister we can have, and to wish him well.

September 15th.—Another month has passed away, and still I have had nothing to record.   The coronation at Moscow appears to have gone off with great *éclat*, and to have been a spectacle of extraordinary magnificence, the prodigious cost of which betrays no sign of exhaustion or impoverishment by the late war.[1]   We were probably mistaken,

---

[1] [The Emperor Alexander II. of Russia was crowned with great pomp in Moscow on September 7 ; the ceremony was attended by special ambassadors from all the great Powers ; Lord Granville, accompanied by Lady Granville and a brilliant suite, was the representative of Great Britain on this occasion.]

as we were in so many other things, in fancying that the power and resources of Russia were very greatly impaired, but during the war, whatever we wished we were ready to believe.

The state of affairs at home and abroad is curious : abroad there is uneasiness and uncertainty as to the future, the elements of future disturbances being in a sort of abeyance ; at home the fever and excitement which prevailed during the war having been succeeded by a torpor and an apathy such as I never remember to have seen before. All party politics seem to be extinct, the country cares about nobody, desires no changes, and only wishes to go on and prosper. There is not a public man to whom public opinion turns, and no great questions are afloat to agitate and divide the country, or around the standards of which different opinions, principles, or passions can flock. Palmerston may remain Minister as long as he lives, if he does not commit any gross faults either of commission or of omission. or unless something may occur, which nobody can foresee or imagine, to rouse the nation from its apathy.

September 21*st*.—The old Crimean correspondent of the "Times" has despatched a very interesting and graphic account of the coronation at Moscow, and Granville writes word that whereas he had estimated the cost of it at a million sterling, he was now led to believe it would be not much less than three. The coronation of George IV. cost 240,000*l.*, which was considered an enormous sum and a monstrous extravagance. Our last two coronations cost from 30,000*l.* to 50,000*l.*

The quarrel with the King of Naples appears to be coming to a crisis, and though it will not produce any serious consequences now, the precedent of interference we are establishing may have very important ones at some future time, and though philanthropy may make us rejoice at some coercion being applied to put an end to such a cruel and oppressive government as that of King Bomba (as they call Ferdinand), it may be doubted whether it would not be sounder policy to abstain from interference with what only indirectly and remotely concerns us, and from enforcing a better and more humane system of government in a country where the people do not seem to care much about its tyranny and inhumanity. And then there is the great objection of dictating to and interfering with weak governments while we do not venture to deal in the same way with the equally flagrant abominations of stronger ones, to say nothing of a host of difficulties and objections which suggest themselves as possible, if not probable, results of our interference. It will afford to other Powers an excuse if not a right to interfere in like manner, whenever they require a pretext, and they consider it their interest to do so ; and if such cases occur, the peace of the world will be largely endangered. As it is, I strongly suspect (for I know nothing) that the agreement on the Neapolitan question between France and ourselves is by no means cordial and complete. Mrs. Craven writes me word she has been in a house in the country with Walewski, who talked very openly (and no doubt imprudently) to her, telling her that Palmerston was very difficult to go on with. I know not what Palmerston has been doing, nor what his present policy may be, but I thought he had either abandoned or greatly modified that old policy of meddling and bullying to which he used to be so addicted, and at all events that while the foreign policy of England is directed by Clarendon, we should abstain from anything very arbitrary and violent. It is, however, whispered that Walewski is no longer in the good graces of the Emperor, and what I heard long ago about Her Majesty's opinion of him renders it not unlikely.

September 23d.—All the little I hear tends to confirm the notion that there is an antagonism growing up between French and English policy, and that France and Russia are becoming more and more intimate every day. The points of the Treaty on which there are still some differences, and on which we appear to be making a great fuss, the French seem to care very little about, perhaps being rather disposed to side with Russia. These differences are very inconsiderable in themselves, but if they lead to coolness and estrangement between us and the French, and to an alliance between France and Russia, they may hereafter be very important. Nothing can be more perplexed and unintelligible (at least to those who are not behind the curtain) than the international relations of the Great Powers and of their dispositions toward the smaller ones, and in such a chaos no little tact, discretion, and firmness are required to shape our foreign policy.

September 25th.—The void which the march of events fails to fill up cannot be better occupied than by the follow-

ing extract from Guizot's notice on Sir Robert Peel in the
" Revue des Deux-Mondes" (1856).   He is speaking of democracy in England   M. de Talleyrand disait dans la
Chambre des Pairs, il y a quelqu'un qui a plus d'esprit que
Napoléon ou que Voltaire, c'est tout le monde.   On peut
dire aujourd'hui même à propos de l'Angleterre il y a quelqu'un qui a plus de pouvoir que la couronne, plus de pouvoir
que l'aristocratie, c'est tout le monde, et tout le monde c'est
la démocratie.   Où commence-t-elle ? où finitelle ? à quels
signes visibles se distingue-t-elle des autres éléments de la
société ?   Personne ne pourrait le dire, mais peu importe :
pour être difficile à définir, le fait n'en est ni moins certain,
ni moins puissant, les éléments les plus divers entrent dans
la composition de la démocratie moderne, des classes riches
et des classes pauvres, des classes savantes et des classes
ignorantes, des maitres et des ouvriers, des conservateurs et
des novateurs, des amis du pouvoir et des enthousiastes de
liberté, bien des aristocrates mêmes, détachés de leur origine
par leurs mœurs, par leur aversion des gênes et des devoirs
que l'aristocratie impose.   Et la position de la démocratie
anglaise n'est pas moins changée que sa composition ; elle
ne se borne pas comme jadis à défendre au besoin ses liber-
tés, elle regarde les affaires publiques comme les siennes,
surveille assidûment ceux qui les font, et si elle ne gouverne
pas l'état, elle domine le gouvernement."   All this seems
to me perfectly true, and the best definition of the English
democracy, its nature, and its position that could possibly
be given, and that the nature of things admits of.   Guizot
evidently saw clearly a truth which might be elaborated into
a very interesting essay, and which has often suggested itself to me, namely, that without any violence or ostensible
disturbances or any change in external forms, this country
has undergone as great a revolution as France itself, or any
of the continental nations which have been torn to pieces by
civil discords and contests.   If we compare the condition
of England at any two not very distant periods, and the
manner in which power and influence have been distributed
at one and at the other, this will be very apparent, and
nobody can doubt that this process is still going on.   We
are, as Guizot says, "dans une époque de transition . . .
sous l'empire des principes et des sentiments encore confus,
perplexes et obscurs, mais essentiellement démocratiques,
qui fermentent en Europe depuis quinze siècles et y rem-

portent de nos jours des victoires dont personne ne saurait
dire encore quel sera le vrai et dernier résultat."

October 3d.—There appears to be a general feeling of
uneasiness, almost of alarm, as if something was impending
to disturb the peace of the world and interrupt the prosperity
of nations, though nobody can very well tell what it is they
dread. The apprehension is vague, but it is general. The
only political question of any consequence in which we are
concerned is that of Naples, and some fancy that the Russian
manifesto prognosticates a renewal of the contest with that
Empire. I have no such idea, but I am quite unable to comprehend what it is the different Powers are about; there is a
general impression, probably not unfounded, that France
and Russia are meditating a close alliance, and if this be the
truth, it is not likely that Russia should have put forth a
State paper offensive to France. It is by no means impossible
that Gortschakoff may have ascertained that the declaration of his Emperor's opinion would not be distasteful to
the Emperor Napoleon, who probably does not enter *con
amore* into this contest with Naples and merely does it to
please us.[1]

When Baudin took leave of him at Paris the other day
on his going to Russia, he said to him, " Is it your Majesty's
wish that I should cultivate the most friendly relations with
the English Ministers at Moscow and St. Petersburg ?" to
which the Emperor replied " Certainly," and " L'Angleterre
avant tout." In this there can be little doubt of his personal
sincerity, but probably his personal disposition and the policy
of his Government and the sentiments of the French people
do not altogether coincide, and this places him in a somewhat false position, and will most likely lead to apparent
vacillation and inconsistency in his conduct.

Madame de Lieven writes to me that the Neapolitan
Minister at Paris affirms that his King will not give way at
the dictation of the allied Powers. We do not, however, as
yet know what it is that is required of him. If it be true

---

[1] [The British and French Governments had on more than one occasion remonstrated with the King of Naples on the cruel and arbitrary policy of his Government, which led eventually to his own destruction ; but the King received
these remonstrances very ill, and on October 28 the differences between these
Courts had become so serious that the British and French Ministers were withdrawn from Naples, and a naval squadron appeared off the city. The Russian
Government at this time issued a circular despatch complaining of these proceedings of the Western Powers, and denying their right to interfere for the
purpose of extorting concessions from the King of Naples to his own subjects.]

that he should govern his people more mildly and liberally,
nothing can be more vague, and our greatest difficulties
would begin when we had extorted from him promises and
engagements to act according to *our* notions of justice and
humanity.   He would be more than mortal if he was disposed
honestly to act up to engagements and promises extorted
from him by fear, and it would be impossible for us to super-
intend and secure their due performance without taking
upon ourselves virtually the government of his kingdom and
superseding the King's authority.   We never should get
France to concur in this, and on the whole it appears more
probable that differences will arise in the course of this joint
action between us and France than that we should succeed
in ameliorating the condition of Naples.   I fear that the rage
for interfering in the internal affairs of other countries will
never be extinguished here.   I see in the papers to-day an
address to Clarendon from the Protestant Society, requesting he will interpose with the Spanish Government in favor
of some Spanish subject who has got into trouble in consequence of having turned Protestant, and being engaged in
diffusing the Scriptures, and trying to convert others to
Protestantism, which is an offence against the laws of Spain.

October 7th.—I have seen Clarendon and asked him about
the affair of Naples.   He was not very communicative, and I
suspect he is not very easy about the course we are pursuing
and the part he has to play.   He first said that it was impossible for us to tolerate the conduct of the King to us, and
the impertinence of his note.   I asked what it was he said :
Clarendon replied it amounted to this, "Mind your own
business."   Then he alluded to the atrocities of the Government, which ought not to be endured ; that no man was safe
for a minute, or could tell when he went to bed at night
that he might not be arrested in the morning, all which
was done by the King's personal orders ; that there was continual danger of an outbreak or insurrection, particularly
of a Muratist revolution.   I told him my opinion of the
very questionable policy of interference, either as a matter
of right or of expediency, and nothing could be more lame
than the case he made out.   He said the ships were not to
act any hostile part, or to coerce the King, which makes the
case worse in my opinion.   It is doing neither one thing nor
the other, violating a sound principle, and incurring great
future risks without any present object, or effecting any

good, or benefiting the people in whom we take an interest.
He says the Emperor Napoleon has a great horror of a Muratist movement, the Prince Murat, his cousin, being a most
worthless blackguard ; but his son, who married Berthier's
granddaughter and heiress, is a young man full of merit of
every sort.

London, October 10th.—I met Clarendon again at the
Travellers', and had some conversation with him, but was interrupted by Azeglio, or I might probably have learned more
about the present state of affairs. He told me that we had
been squabbling with the French Government, and that the
persevering attempts of Russia to disturb the harmony between us and them had not been unsuccessful. Nothing in
the way of cajolery had been omitted at Moscow to captivate
the French, while on one occasion the Emperor had been so
uncivil that Granville felt himself obliged to go to Gortschakoff and make a formal complaint, which was met by all
sorts of assurances and protestations in order to mollify him,
and after this everything went on smoothly. It is a curious
state of things, for as far as I can make it out, the policy of
the French Government appears to be to become intimate
with Russia and to be cool with us ; but all the time the
Emperor (who is the Government) shrinks from anything
like a breach with England, and clings to the intimacy established between the two Courts, and has a profound respect
for the Queen and value for her good opinion. I asked him
how he reconciled the offensive Circular of Gortschakoff with
the anxiety of Russia to please France, when he said that he
had no doubt they had told the French that it was aimed
exclusively at *us*, and had come to an understanding with
Morny about it, so that France was not to take offence at it.
We are now, he said, on the best terms with Austria, and
Austria on the worst with Russia. Russia knows that the
article of the treaty compelling her to surrender a part of
Bessarabia was the work of Austria, and this was an injury
and an insult (for she had never before disgorged territory)
which she never would forgive. The Russian Circular would
have the effect of complicating the Neapolitan question, as it
made the King more resolved not to yield to the demands of
the two Powers. He told me that Palmerston had resolved
to take up in earnest the question of Law Reform next year,
and that he (Clarendon) had strongly urged him to do so as
the best way of procuring both strength and credit for his

Government; that Palmerston had readily come into it, and was resolved to carry out those measures which have so long been under discussion, and which for various reasons have hitherto failed of their accomplishment.

November 10*th.*—I went to The Grove on Saturday and had a good deal of comfortable talk with Clarendon about foreign affairs, especially the Bolgrad question and Naples. He described the former very clearly, and satisfied me that we are entirely in the right. It was settled, he said, at Paris mainly between him and Orloff. He drew the line on the map as the boundary had been agreed upon, and as he was doing so, Orloff said, "I wish you would draw it a little more to the south; it.will make no sort of difference to you, and by this means it includes within our line a strip of territory which the Emperor wishes to retain because it forms a part of a military colony which he is anxious to keep intact;" and Clarendon agreed to draw the line accordingly and to accomplish the Emperor's wishes. They have since attempted to quibble about another Bolgrad which was not even marked at all on their map; and it turns out that the story of the military colony was a mere pretence, as they have themselves given that up without making any difficulty. The state of the case and the difference which has since arisen with Russia and with France is this: the Emperor Napoleon, who is very indolent and abhors the trouble of examining details, and consequently remains often ignorant of what it behoves him to know, suffered himself to be bamboozled by Brunnow and misled by Walewski into giving his assent to the Russian interpretation of the boundary line, and to giving a promise of his support in the controversy. Recently at Compiègne Cowley, in a long audience, went through the whole question with him and minutely explained the case against Russia. The Emperor said he had never really understood it before, acknowledged that our case was good, regretted that he had committed himself, but said that having pledged his word he did not know how to break that pledge and to withdraw the support he had promised to give to Russia in the dispute, and this is the fix in which the question now is. While the foolish and ignorant newspapers here (except the "Times") are endeavoring to separate the Emperor from his ministers, and to make out that he is one with our Government, and that the difficulties and obstructions proceed from other parties, the truth is that they now

proceed entirely from himself, worked upon and deceived
certainly by Russian agents and pro-Russian ministers ; but
if he really was in the disposition which our press attributes
to him, he might break through such obligations as he suffered himself to be entangled in and settle the question at
once ; nor is it very easy to see why he does not, for there is
good reason to believe he is sincerely desirous of remaining
on good terms with us.   I asked Clarendon why the question
could not be again referred to a Conference of the Powers
parties to the Treaty, and he said we could not consent to
this, because we should be in a minority, for Sardinia, partly
cajoled by Russia and partly from antipathy to Austria,
would go against us.

I asked him about Naples, of which affair he could give
but a very unsatisfactory account and a lame story. He said
France had acted with us very steadily, but that it was she
who had started this hare, and he had engaged in it in the
belief that the Emperor would never have mooted the question unless he had been assured that the King of Naples
would yield to the remonstrances of the two Courts, and but
for that conviction he would never have meddled in it, which
he now very much regretted. He had given Carini notice to
quit, and at their parting interview he had entreated him to
persuade the King if possible to change his system, and,
now that he was relieved from all interference, menace, or
coercion, and his dignity could not suffer, to give satisfaction to all Europe by putting an end to the inhuman and
impolitic system, which had occasioned our interference
and had drawn upon him remonstrances and advice from
every Sovereign in Europe. Very good advice, and I hope
it may be followed, but it is a lame and impotent conclusion
to the menacing demonstrations with which we began to
quarrel. Clarendon talked of the various atrocities of the
King of Naples, but with an evident consciousness that the
fact, even if it be true, and not, as is probable, exaggerated,
affords no excuse for our policy in the matter. As the subject could not be agreeable I did not press it, and abstained
from telling him how general the opinion is that he has committed a great blunder. He will probably hear enough of
it before the chapter is closed ; even Granville, who never
says much, said to me yesterday that " it was a very foolish
affair."

Clarendon talked to me of Palmerston, and told me (what

I think I had heard, and have very likely noted before) that on Aberdeen's fall Palmerston was quite ready to join Derby when Derby tried to form a Government, and that it was Clarendon's refusal which frustrated that attempt. Palmerston endeavored to persuade Clarendon to join, but when Clarendon put to him all the reasons why the had both of them better refuse, Palmerston saw them all very clearly, and rather imprudently said on leaving him, " We are *both* agreed that it will not do to have anything to do with Derby and his Government." When Clarendon went to the Queen and explained his own conduct to her, and she expressed to him the embarrassment which she felt, and asked him what she could do, he at once said, "Send for Lord Palmerston, who is the only man, in the present temper of the people and tate of affairs, who can form a Government that has a chance of standing. Send for him at once, place yourself entirely in his hands, give him your entire confidence, and I will answer for his conduct being all that you can desire." The Queen took the advice, and has had no reason to repent of it, and Clarendon told me he had done everything in his power, and seized every available opportunity to reconcile them to each other, to promote a good feeling and understanding, and to soften any little asperities which might have made their intercourse less smooth, and the consequence is that Palmerston gets on with her very well, and his good sense as well as Clarendon's exhortations make him see of what importance it is to him for the easy working of his Government and his own ease to be on good and cordial terms with the Queen. It is therefore really to Clarendon that Palmerston is indebted in great measure, if not entirely, for being in his present position, but Clarendon has too much tact ever to remind him of it, or of what he was himself inclined to do in 1855.

November 19th.—The death of Jervis made the office of Chief Justice of Common Pleas vacant.[1] According to established (but as I think bad) usage, the Attorney-General, Cockburn, had a right to take the place, and for the last fortnight nothing occupied public attention more than the question whether he would take it or not. He was much averse to take it, but everybody pressed him to accept it, and after much hesitation and consultation he agreed to be Chief

[1] [Right Hon. Sir John Jervis, Chief Justice of the Common Pleas, died on November 1, 1856, at the age of fifty-four.]

Justice, and now it is said he regrets his determination and thinks he has made a mistake. He gives up Parliament, for which he is well adapted, where he acts a conspicuous part, being a capital speaker, and which he likes, and feels that it is his element. He gives up the highest place at the bar, where he is a successful advocate, and makes 15,000*l.* or 16,000*l.* a year, and he sees that he shall be obliged to give up in great measure his loose habits and assume more decorous behavior, which will be a great sacrifice to him, and he becomes a judge with 6,000*l.* a year for life, not being a good lawyer, and conscious that he will be inferior to his colleagues and to the Puisne Judge in his own court. As soon as he had consented to the promotion a fresh difficulty presented itself as to the office of Solicitor-General, for such is the penury of legal ability at this time that Westminster Hall cannot furnish any men of unquestionable fitness for the office, and the difficulty is increased by the choice being necessarily restricted to men holding the opinions of the present Government, and being able to command a seat in Parliament. They have offered the place to the Recorder, James Wortley, but up to this moment I know not if it has been accepted.[1]

November 23d.—After long delay and apparently much hesitation James Wortley has accepted the Solicitor-Generalship. He consulted Gladstone and Sidney Herbert, neither of them very eligible advisers on such a question. Gladstone is said to have replied that he would run a great risk as to his pecuniary interests, but if he could support the foreign policy of the Government, there was no reason why he should not accept. He retains his rank of Privy Councillor, of which I doubt the fitness, as it places him at all events in a very anomalous position, for the law officers are the official advisers of the Privy Council and are often called upon to sit there as assessors. However, the Judges are said to have pronounced an opinion that there is no reason why he should not plead in any of the courts. It is said, and I believe truly, that now Cockburn has taken the irretrievable step he is very sorry for it, and is more struck by the necessary consequences of his promotion than he was at first. He has all his life been a very debauched fellow, but he is clever,

---

[1] [Right Hon. James Stuart Wortley, a younger son of Lord Wharncliffe, who then filled the office of Recorder of London, which he surrendered for that of Solicitor-General.]

good-natured, and of a liberal disposition and much liked by his friends. A story is told of him that he was in the habit of going down on Sundays to Richmond or elsewhere with a woman, and generally with a different one, and the landlady of the inn he went to remembered that Sir A. Cockburn always brought Lady Cockburn with him, but that she never saw any woman who looked so different on different days, and this gave rise to another story. When Lord Campbell went to some such place with Lady Stratheden (who had been raised to the peerage before her husband), the mistress of the house said that Sir A. Cockburn always brought *Lady Cockburn* with him, but that the Chief Justice brought another lady and not *Lady Campbell.*

While we have meetings perpetually held and innumerable writings put forth to promote education and raise the moral standard of the people, we are horrified and alarmed day after day by accounts of the most frightful murders, colossal frauds, and crimes of every description. War has ceased, though the Temple of Janus seems only to be ajar; but the world is still in commotion, in alarm, and visited by every sort of calamity, moral and material, in the midst of which it is difficult to discover any signs of the improvement of the human race, even of those portions of it which are supposed to be the most civilised and the most progressive.

December 7th.—At Wrotham and at Ossington last week. The news of the day is that we are to have another "Conference" at Paris, to settle the Bolgrad affair, our Government having given way to what Clarendon told me he certainly would not consent; but we had managed to get matters into such a fix, and it was so necessary to extricate all the several parties from the embarrassed positions in which they were placed by their own or by each other's faults, that no alternative remained. This arrangement, which is not very consistent with Palmerston's recent declarations at Manchester and in London, is proclaimed by the Government papers, and generally understood to be a means of enabling Russia to concede our demands with as little loss of dignity and credit as possible, and to terminate the difference between us and France by our making an apparent concession to France, while she makes a real one to us. Everything has evidently been carefully arranged for the playing out of this diplomatic farce, and Cowley, who is to be our sole representative, is to be accommodating and not quarrelsome; but *reste à savoir* whether the manœuvres of some of the others may not provoke his temper and bring about angry collisions. Between this matter and the *bévue* we have made of our Neapolitan interference, never was there such a deplorable exhibition as our foreign policy displays ; but nobody seems to care much about it, and though there will in all probability be a good deal of sparring, and taunts and sneers in Parliament, Palmerston's Government will incur no danger of any adverse vote, for everybody is conscious that in the actual state of parties and the dearth of parliamentary leaders, every man of sufficient ability being disqualified for one reason or another, no man but Palmerston can conduct a Government or command a majority in Parliament ; nor does there appear in the distance any man likely to be able to fill his place in the event of his death or his breaking down, events which must be contemplated as not very remote when he is seventy-three years old, although his wonderful constitution and superhuman vigor of mind and body make everybody forget his age and regard the possibility of his demise with the sort of incredulity which made the courtier of Louis XIV. exclaim on the death of that monarch, "Après la mort du Roi on peut tout croire."

Great astonishment has been excited by the appointment of a Mr. Bickersteth as Bishop of Ripon, against whom nothing can be said, nor anything for him, except that he is a very Low Churchman. All the vacant sees have now been filled with clergymen of this color, which is not very fair or prudent, as it will exasperate the moderate High Churchmen and set them strongly against a Government which appears determined to shut the door of ecclesiastical preferment against all but the Lowest Churchmen, and such a policy will most likely have the effect of encouraging the advocates of those extreme measures of an anti-Catholic or a puritanical character which always give so much trouble and embarrassment when they are brought forward in Parliament.

December 12th.—The Conference to which Clarendon told me he would not agree is going to take place after all, but everybody is ridiculing what is notoriously a got-up comedy with a foregone conclusion, devised to solve the difficulty into which all the great actors had got themselves, but it is not yet quite clear what the *modus operandi* is to be. From what I have picked up here and there I gather that Sardinia is to be induced to give a casting vote against Russia, leaving

France still at liberty to fulfil her original engagement and vote with her, while we obtain the object for which we have stood out, and by such a *dodge* to bring the dispute to an end. When Parliament meets there will be plenty to be said about this affair and about Naples, and no doubt the Opposition or the malcontents will be able to bombard the Government and vent their spleen, but that will be all, for Palmerston is perfectly invulnerable and may commit any blunders with impunity.

A report has been lately current that Gladstone will become the leader of the Opposition *vice* Disraeli, a report I thought quite wild and improbable, but I heard the other day something which looks as if it was not so much out of the question as I had imagined. George Byng told me he had met Sir William Jolliffe, who is the Derbyite whipper-in, at Wrotham, and having asked him whether there was any foundation for the above report, he replied that it certainly was not true at present, that he could not say what might or what might not happen hereafter, but that he could not at once be accepted as *leader*, and must in any case first serve in the ranks. I do not know what may be the value of Jolliffe's opinions, or what he knows of the intentions of his chief, but he may probably be more or less acquainted with the sentiments of his party, and may be aware that their necessities have modified their extreme repugnance to Gladstone, and that they may now be willing to accept him as leader (eventually), though two years ago they so peremptorily insisted on his entire exclusion from their political society. Meanwhile there is no combination among them. Derby is at Knowsley amusing himself, and Disraeli at Paris, doing nobody knows what.

There is talk of Lord Granville resigning the lead and his office and going to Ireland instead of Carlisle, or to Paris instead of Cowley, but he has never intimated the least intention of doing either. Ireland he certainly will not go to; Paris is not so impossible. There seems some doubt whether his health will admit of his going on in the House of Lords, and if they knew how to get Cowley away from Paris without doing him an injustice or an unkindness, I think they would not be sorry, for his position there is unsatisfactory. It is a serious inconvenience to be on such terms with Walewski that they never converse at all except when business obliges them to meet, and the consequence

of their relations is that all affairs between the two countries
are carried on between Clarendon and Persigny in London,
and as little as possible at Paris, because the Emperor now
fights rather shy of Cowley, and is by no means on the same
terms with him as heretofore, though always very civil and
cordial enough when they meet; and His Majesty will not
part with Walewski, who, although of a moderate capacity,
is clever enough to know how to deal with his master, and
make himself agreeable to him, and the Emperor knows
that if he were to change his Minister for Foreign Affairs, it
would be attributed to the influence of England and be
on that account unpopular.   The English press has rendered Walewski the incalculable service of making him
popular in France, and rendering it impossible for the Emperor to dismiss him, even if he had a mind to do so, which
he has not.

December 17*th*.—There was an article in the "Times"
the day before yesterday commenting in severe terms upon a
transaction of our Foreign Office, as set forth in a Blue
Book, in relation to Brazil.   It was the old subject of the
slave trade, and the old method of arrogant overbearing
meddling and dictation, a case as odious and unjust as any
one of those by which Palmerston's foreign administration
has ever been disgraced.   I really no longer recognize my
old friend Clarendon, in whose good sense and moderation
I used to place implicit confidence, and believed that he
would inaugurate a system at the Foreign Office very different from that of Palmerston, and which would tend to relieve us from the excessive odium and universal unpopularity
which Palmerston had drawn upon us.   It appears that I
was mistaken.   I told Granville yesterday morning what I
thought of this case, and asked him if it was correctly
stated.   He said he regarded it just as I did, and that it was
quite true, every word of it.   I then expressed my astonishment that Clarendon should have acted in this way, and he
replied. "The fault of Clarendon is that he is always thinking of the effect to be produced by Blue Books, and he looks
after popularity, and is influenced by those he acts with.
Under Aberdeen he was very moderate, but he saw that the
moderation of Aberdeen made him unpopular, while Palmerston's popularity in great measure arose from his very different manner toward other Powers, so when Palmerston became Prime Minister instead of Aberdeen, he fell readily

into the Palmerstonian method." I dare say this is the truth, and besides the contagion of Palmerston himself, he is surrounded by men at the Foreign Office who are prodigious admirers of Palmerston and of his slashing ways, and who no doubt constantly urge Clarendon to adopt a similar style. All this is to me matter of great regret personally, and it is revolting as to good taste, and, as I believe, to our national interests. It is, however, a consolation to see that the most powerful and influential of our journals has the courage, independence, and good sense to protest publicly against such violent and unjustifiable proceedings.

❖

CHAPTER XIII.

January 9th, 1857.—The old year ended and the new year began strangely. After three years of expensive war the balance-sheet exhibited such a state of wealth and prosperity as may well make us "the envy of surrounding nations;" but while we have recovered the great blessing of peace, we have to look back upon a year stained beyond all precedent with frightful crimes of every sort and kind: horrible murders, enormous frauds, and scandalous robberies and defalcations. The whole attention of the country is now drawn to the social questions which press upon us with appalling urgency, and the next session of Parliament, which is rapidly advancing, must be principally engaged in the endeavor to find remedies for the evils and dangers incident to our corrupted population, and our erroneous and inadequate penal system, the evils and dangers of which threaten to become greater and more difficult to remedy every day. From this question it is impossible to dissever that of education, for at least we ought to make the experiment whether the

diffusion of education will or will not be conducive to the
diminution of crime, and we shall see whether the sectarian
prejudices, the strength and obstinacy of which have hitherto
erected impassable barriers to the progress of educating the
people, will retain all their obstinacy in the face of the existing evil, or whether the bodily fear and the universal persuasion of the magnitude and imminence of the danger will
not operate upon bigotry itself and render the masses more
reasonable.   Besides these important questions the new year
opens with a most unpleasant prospect abroad, where everything seems to go wrong and our foreign relations, be the
cause what, or the fault whose it may, to be in a very unhappy state.

The quarrel between Prussia and Switzerland [1] is one in
which we appear to have no immediate interest, except that
it is always our interest to prevent any infraction of the general peace, but of course we could not think of not interfering in some way or other in the matter.   The King of Prussia
has behaved as ill and as foolishly as possible, and our Government entirely disapprove of his conduct and have given
the Swiss to understand that all our sympathies are with
them, and that we think they have right on their side.   If
France and England were now on really good terms, and
would act together with cordiality and authority, nothing
would be so easy as to put a prompt extinguisher on the
Swiss affair ; but as we cannot agree upon a common course
of action, there is danger of the dispute drifting into a war,
though it is evidently so much the interest and the desire of
the Emperor Napoleon to allow no shots to be fired, that I
still expect, even at this almost the eleventh hour, to be in a
complete fix.   The Swiss will not release the prisoners unless
the King will at the same time abandon his claims on Neufchâtel, or unless England and France will guarantee that he
will do so.   The King will do nothing and agree to nothing
unless the Swiss will previously and unconditionally release
the prisoners, and moreover he repudiates our intervention,
as he thinks us unfairly disposed to himself.   The simplest

---

[1] [The Prussian Crown retained, by the Treaty of Vienna, rights of sovereignty over the Swiss Canton of Neufchâtel, and appointed a Governor there.
In other respects the Neufchâtelese enjoyed all the rights and liberties of Swiss
citizens.   This anomalous state of things naturally gave rise to friction.   The
King of Prussia derived no sort of advantage from his nominal sovereignty ;
but as a matter of dignity he declined to renounce it, and even threatened a
military occupation of the Canton, which the Swiss Confederation would have
resisted.]

course would be for England and France to declare that a
Prussian invasion of Switzerland should be a *casus belli*, and
I think we should have no objection to this, but France
won't go along with us.   Then if the Swiss should deliver
over the prisoners to France, and she would accept the dépôt,
all might be settled.   As it is, we have backed up Switzerland to resist, and if war ensues we shall leave her to her fate
—a very inglorious course to pursue ; and although I have a
horror of war, and am alive to the policy of keeping well
with France, I am inclined to think that having encouraged
the Swiss to a certain point it would better become us to take
our own independent line and to threaten Prussia with war
if she does not leave Switzerland alone, than to sit tamely by
and see her, unimpeded, execute her threats.   The Government are evidently much embarrassed by this question, which
is still further complicated by the matrimonial engagement
between the two Royal families.

January 13th.—The Swiss affair seems settled, so far at
least that there will be no war.   The prisoners will be re-
leased, but I dare say the King of Prussia will *chicaner* about
the abdication of his rights over Neufchâtel.   All the world
is occupied with Sir Robert Peel's speech, or lecture as he
terms it, at Birmingham, where he gave an account, meant
to be witty, of his *séjour* in Russia and its incidents.   It was
received with shouts of applause by a congenial Brummagem
audience, and by deep disapprobation in every decent society
and by all reasonable people.

January 14th.—I met Clarendon last night, who told me
the Swiss question was still in doubt, for the King was
shuffling and would probably play them a trick, and though
he knew the prisoners were going to be liberated, he would
not engage positively to give up his claim.   The Emperor
Napoleon has behaved very ill and ungratefully to the Swiss,
who in consequence were more irritated against him than
against the King of Prussia himself.   Nothing could equal
the fawning flattery and servility of the King to the Emperor, who was at the same time tickled by it and disgusted.

January 20th.—At Woburn for two days.   I found the
Duke entirely occupied with a question (on which he had of
course a various correspondence), whether when Aberdeen's
Government was formed, Aberdeen had *at the time* imparted
to John Russell his wish and intention to retire as soon as
possible, so that John might take his place as Premier.   To

15

ascertain this fact, he had applied to Lord John and Aberdeen, to Lansdowne and to Clarendon, all of whom he invited to send him their recollections and impressions, which they did.   The matter now is not of much importance, but is worth noticing from the evidence it affords of the difficulty of arriving at truth, and therefore of the fallibility of all history.   Though this circumstance is so recent, and at the time was so important, not one of the parties, neither Lord John nor Aberdeen nor the other two, can recollect what did pass, but as they all concur in their impressions that no such engagement was given when the Government was formed, it may safely be concluded that this is the truth.   I know I heard all that passed, and certainly I never heard of any such intention, though I did hear some time afterward that such had been Aberdeen's expressed wish and Lord John's expectation.   I read Aberdeen's letters, in which he entered into other matters connected with his Government, and I must say more creditable, gentlemanlike, and amiable letters I never read.

January 28th.—At Stoke from Saturday to Monday. On returning to town, we heard that the Persian war was over, Palmerston's usual luck bringing a settlement of the only question that could be embarrassing on the eve of the meeting of Parliament.   But the news only comes telegraphically, so unless confirmed must be doubtful, and cannot be named in the Speech.[1]

Two remarkable deaths have occurred, one of which touches me nearly, that of Madame de Lieven ; the other is that of the Duke of Rutland.   Madame de Lieven died, after a short illness, of a severe attack of bronchitis, the Duke having lingered for many months.   Very different characters. Madame de Lieven came to this country at the end of 1812 or beginning of 1813 on the war breaking out between Russia and France.   Pozzo di Borgo had preceded the Lievens to renew

---

[1] [Differences had arisen in the spring of 1856 between Great Britain and the Court of Persia, in consequence of which the British Minister was withdrawn from Teheran. In October, 1856, Herat was attacked and taken by the Persians, which led to war. A detachment of British troops under General Outram landed at Bushire on January 27, 1857, and the Persians were defeated at Kooshab on February 8. Peace was signed in Paris between Her Majesty and the Shah on March 4, the Persians engaging to abstain from all interference in the internal affairs of Afghanistan, and to respect the independence of Herat. If these dates are correct, as given in Irving's *Annals of our Time,* the intelligence of the peace cannot have reached London so soon as Mr. Greville supposed, and rumor anticipated the event.]

diplomatic relations and make arrangements with us.   She
was at that time young, at least in the prime of life, and
though without any pretensions to beauty, and indeed with
some personal defects, she had so fine an air and manner,
and a countenance so pretty and so full of intelligence, as to
be on the whole a very striking and attractive person, quite
enough so to have lovers, several of whom she engaged in
succession without seriously attaching herself to any.   Those
who were most notoriously her slaves at different times were
the present Lord Willoughby, the Duke of Sutherland (then
Lord Gower), the Duke of Cannizzaro (then Count St.
Antonio), and the Duke of Palmella, who was particularly
clever and agreeable.   Madame de Lieven was a *très grande
dame*, with abilities of a very fine order, great tact and *finesse*,
and taking a boundless pleasure in the society of the great
world and in political affairs of every sort.   People here were
not slow to acknowledge her merits and social excellence,
and she almost immediately took her place in the cream of
the cream of English society, forming close intimacies with
the most conspicuous women in it, and assiduously cultivating relations with the most remarkable men of all parties.
These personal *liaisons* sometimes led her into political partisanship not always prudent and rather inconsistent with
her position, character, and functions here.   But I do not
believe she was ever mixed up in any intrigues, nor even, at a
later period, that she was justly obnoxious to the charge of
caballing and mischief-making which has been so lavishly
cast upon her.   She had an insatiable curiosity for political
information, and a not unnatural desire to make herself
useful and agreeable to her own Court by imparting to her
Imperial masters and mistresses all the information she
acquired and the anecdotes she picked up.   Accordingly
while she was in England, which was from 1812 to 1834, she
devoted herself to society, not without selection, but without
exclusion, except that she sought and habitually confined
herself to the highest and best.   The Regent, afterward
George IV., delighted in her company, and she was a frequent guest at the Pavilion, and on very intimate terms
with Lady Conyngham, for although Madame de Lieven was
not very tolerant of mediocrity, and social and colloquial
superiority was necessary to her existence, she always made
great allowances for Royalty and those immediately connected with it.   She used to be a great deal at Oatlands, and

was one of the few intimate friends of the Duchess of York, herself very intelligent, and who therefore had in the eyes of Madame de Lieven the double charm of her position and her agreeableness.   It was her duty as well as her inclination to cultivate the members of all the successive Cabinets which passed before her, and she became the friend of Lord Castlereagh, of Canning, the Duke of Wellington, Lord Grey, Lord Palmerston, John Russell, Aberdeen, and many others of inferior note, and she was likewise one of the *habitués* of Holland House, which was always more or less neutral ground, even when Lord Holland was himself a member of the government.   When Talleyrand came over here as Ambassador, there was for some time a sort of antagonism between the two embassies, and particularly between the ladies of each, but Madame de Dino (now Duchesse of Sagan) was so clever, and old Talleyrand himself so remarkable and so agreeable, that Madame de Lieven was irresistibly drawn toward them, and for the last year or two of their being in England they became extremely intimate ; but her greatest friend in England was Lady Cowper, afterward Lady Palmerston, and through her she was also the friend of Palmerston, who was also well affected toward Russia, till his jealous and suspicious mind was inflamed by his absurd notion of her intention to attack us in India, a crotchet which led us into the folly and disaster of the Afghan war. In 1834 the Lievens were recalled, and she was established at St. Petersburg in high favor about the Empress, but her *séjour* there was odious to her, and she was inconsolable at leaving England, where after a residence of above twenty years she had become rooted in habits and affections, although she never really and completely understood the country. She remained at St. Petersburg for several months, until her two youngest children were taken ill, and died almost at the same time.   This dreadful blow, and the danger of the severe climate to her own health, gave her a valid excuse for desiring leave of absence, and she left Russia never to return.   She went to Italy, where M. de Lieven died about the year 1836 or 1837, after which she established herself in Paris, where her salon became the rendezvous of the best society, and particularly the neutral ground on which eminent men and politicians of all colors could meet, and where her tact and adroitness made them congregate in a sort of social truce.

I do not know at what exact period it was that she made the acquaintance of M. Guizot, but their intimacy no doubt was established after he had begun to play a great political part, for his literary and philosophical celebrity would not alone have had much charm for her. They were, however, already great friends at the time of his embassy to England, and she took that opportunity of coming here to pay a visit to her old friends. The fall of Thiers' Government and Guizot's becoming Minister for Foreign Affairs of course drew Madame de Lieven still more closely to him, and during the whole of his administration their alliance continued to be of the closest and most intimate character. It was an immense object to her to possess the entire confidence of the French Minister for Foreign Affairs, who kept her *au courant* of all that was going on in the political world, while it is not surprising that he should be irresistibly attracted by a woman immensely superior to any other of his acquaintance, who was fully able to comprehend and willing to interest herself about all the grand and important subjects which he had to handle and manage, and who associated herself with a complete sympathy in all his political interests. Their *liaison*, which some people consider mysterious, but which I believe to have been entirely social and political, grew constantly more close, and every moment that Guizot could snatch from the Foreign Office and the Chamber he devoted to Madame de Lieven. He used to go there regularly three times a day on his way to and his way from the Chamber, when it was sitting, and in the evening ; but while he was by far her first object, she cultivated the society of all the most conspicuous and remarkable people whom she could collect about her, and she was at one time very intimate with Thiers, though his rivalry with Guizot and their intense hatred of each other eventually produced a complete estrangement between her and Thiers.

The revolution of 1848 dispersed her friends, broke up her salon, and terrified her into making a rather ludicrous, but as it turned out wholly unnecessary, escape. She came to England, where she remained till affairs appeared to be settled in France and all danger of disturbance at an end. She then returned to Paris, where she remained, not without fear and trembling, during the period of peril and vicissitude which at length ended, much to her satisfaction, with the *coup d'état* and the Empire.   Guizot had returned to Paris, but constantly refused to take any part in political affairs, either under the Republic or with the new government of Louis Napoleon.   This, however, did not prevent Madame de Lieven (though their friendship continued the same) from showing her sympathy and goodwill to the Imperial *régime*, and her salon, which had been decimated by previous events, was soon replenished by some of the ministers or adherents of the Empire, who, though they did not amalgamate very well with her old *habitués*, supplied her with interesting information, and subsequently, when the war broke out, rendered her very essential service.   When the rupture took place all the Russian subjects were ordered to quit Paris. She was advised by some of her friends to disobey the order, for as she was equally precluded from going to England, the circumstances in which this order placed her were indescribably painful and even dangerous, but she said that however great the sacrifice, and though she was entirely independent, she was under so many obligations and felt so much attachment to the Imperial family that, cost her what it might, she would obey the order, and accordingly she repaired to Brussels, where for a year and a half or two years she took up her melancholy and uncomfortable abode.   At last this banishment from her home and her friends, with all the privations it entailed, became insupportable, and she endeavored, through the intervention of some of her Imperialist friends, to obtain leave of the French Government to return to Paris, either with or without (for it is not clear which) the consent of her own Court.   The Emperor Napoleon seems to have been easily moved to compassion, and signified his consent to her return.   No sooner did this become known to Cowley and the English Government than they resolved to interpose for the purpose of preventing her return to Paris, and Cowley went to Walewski and insisted that the Emperor's permission should be revoked.   The *entente cordiale* was then in full force, nothing could be refused to the English Ambassador, and Madame de Lieven was informed that she must not come back to Paris.   She bore this sad disappointment with resignation, made no complaints, and resolved to bide her time.   Some months later she caused a representation to be made to the French Government that the state of her health made it impossible for her to pass another winter at Brussels, and that she was going to Nice, but as it was of vital importance to her to consult her medical adviser at Paris, she craved permission to proceed to Nice *viâ* Paris, where she would only stay long enough for that purpose. The permission was granted. She wrote me word that she was going to Paris to remain there a few days. I replied that I was much mistaken in her if once there she ever quitted it again. She arrived and was told by her doctor that it would be dangerous in her state to continue her journey. She never did proceed further, and never did quit Paris again. The Government winked at her stay, and never molested or interfered with her. She resumed her social habits, but with great caution and reserve, and did all she could to avoid giving umbrage or exciting suspicion. It was a proof of the greatness of her mind, as well as of her prudence and good temper, that she not only testified no resentment at the conduct of Cowley toward her, but did all she could to renew amicable relations with him, and few things annoyed her more than his perseverance in keeping aloof from her. From the time of her last departure from England up to the death of Frederic Lamb (Lord Beauvale and Melbourne) she maintained a constant correspondence with him. After his death she proposed to me to succeed him as her correspondent, and for the last two or three years our epistolary commerce was intimate and unbroken. She knew a vast deal of the world and its history during the half century she had lived and played a part in it, but she was not a woman of much reading, and probably at no time had been very highly or extremely educated, but her excessive cleverness and her *finesse d'esprit* supplied the want of education, and there was one book with which her mind was perpetually nourished by reading it over and over again. This was the "Letters of Madame de Sévigné," and to the constant study of those unrivalled letters she was no doubt considerably indebted for her own epistolary eminence, and for her admirable style of writing, not, however, that her style and Madame de Sévigné's were at all alike. She had not (in her letters at least) the variety, the abundance, or the *abandon* of the great Frenchwoman, but she was more terse and epigrammatic, and she had the same graphic power and faculty of conveying much matter in few words.

Nothing could exceed the charm of her conversation or her grace, ease, and tact in society. She had a nice and accurate judgment, and an exquisite taste in the choice of her associates and friends; but though taking an ardent pleasure in agreeableness, and peculiarly susceptible of being bored, she was not fastidious, full of politeness and good breeding, and possessed the faculty of turning every one to account, and eliciting something either of entertainment or information from the least important of her acquaintance. It has been the fashion here, and the habit of the vulgar and ignorant press, to stigmatise Madame de Lieven as a mischievous intriguer, who was constantly occupied in schemes and designs hostile to the interests of our country. I firmly believe such charges to be utterly unfounded. She had resided for above twenty years, the happiest of her life, in England, and had imbibed a deep attachment to the country, where she had formed many more intimacies and friendships than she possessed anywhere else, and to the last day of her life she continued to cherish the remembrance of her past connection, to cultivate the society of English people, and to evince without disguise her predilection for their country. She had never lived much in Russia, her connection with it had been completely dissolved, and all she retained of it was a respectful attachment to the Imperial family, together with certain sympathies and feelings of loyalty for her native country and her Sovereign which it would have been unnatural and discreditable to disavow. Her well-known correspondence with the Imperial Court was only caused by the natural anxiety of those great persons to be kept *au courant* of social and political affairs by such an accomplished correspondent, but I do not believe she was ever employed by them in any business or any political design; on the contrary, she was rather distrusted and out of favor with them, on account of her being so denaturalized and for her ardent affection for England and the English. Russia was the country of her birth, France the country of her adopted abode, but England was the country of her predilection. With this cosmopolite character she dreaded everything which might produce hostile collision between any two of these countries. She was greatly annoyed when the question of the Spanish marriages embittered the relations between France and England, but infinitely more so at the Turkish quarrel, and the war which it produced. Those who fulminated against her intrigues were, as I believe, provoked at the efforts she made, so far as she had any power or influence, to bring about the restoration of peace, an unpardonable offence in the eyes of all who were bent on the continuation of the war. She lived to see peace restored, and closed her eyes almost at the moment that the last seal was put to it by the Conference of Paris. Her last illness was sudden and short. Her health had always been delicate, and she was very nervous about herself; an attack of bronchitis brought on fever, which rapidly consumed her strength, and brought her, fully conscious, within sight of death; that consummation, which at a distance she had always dreaded, she saw arrive with perfect calmness and resignation, and all the virtues and qualities for which the smallest credit was given her seem to have shone forth with unexpected lustre on her deathbed. Her faculties were bright and unclouded to the last, her courage and presence of mind were unshaken, she evinced a tender consideration for the feelings of those who were lamenting around her bed, and she complied with the religious obligations prescribed by the Church of which she was a member with a devotion the sincerity of which we have no right to question. She made her son Paul and Guizot leave her room a few hours before she died, that they might be spared the agony of witnessing her actual dissolution, and only three or four hours before the supreme moment, she mustered strength to write a note in pencil to Guizot with these words: "Merci pour vingt années d'amitié et de bonheur. Ne m'oubliez pas, adieu, adieu!" It was given to him after her death.

February 8th.—I am just come from hearing the celebrated Mr. Spurgeon preach in the Music Hall of the Surrey Gardens. It was quite full; he told us from the pulpit that 9,000 people were present. The service was like the Presbyterian: Psalms, prayers, expounding a Psalm, and a sermon. He is certainly very remarkable, and undeniably a very fine character; not remarkable in person, in face rather resembling a smaller Macaulay, a very clear and powerful voice, which was heard through the whole hall; a manner natural, impassioned, and without affectation or extravagance; wonderful fluency and command of language, abounding in illustration, and very often of a very familiar kind, but without anything either ridiculous or irreverent. He gave me an impression of his earnestness and his sincerity; speaking without book or notes, yet his discourse was evidently very carefully prepared. The text was "Cleanse me

from my secret sins," and he divided it into heads, the
misery, the folly, the danger (and a fourth which I have forgotten) of secret sins, on all of which he was very eloquent
and impressive.   He preached for about three-quarters of an
hour, and to judge of the handkerchiefs and the audible
sobs, with great effect.

We have had a week of Parliament, and though nothing
important has occurred, the discussions do not seem to have
raised the reputation of the Government or to promise them
an easy session, though nobody seems to expect that their
stability is likely to be shaken.   Disraeli and Gladstone
seem verging toward each other in opposition, but there is
no appearance of a coalition between them ; the only striking
fact is that the Opposition, of whose disunion we have heard
so much, and of the internal repulsion supposed to prevail
among them, seems to be as united as ever it has been, and
the usual people appeared at Derby's and Disraeli's gather-
ings.   I take it that any appearance of vulnerability of the
Government silences all manifestations of their mutual antipathies, and puts them on the *qui vive* to turn out their
opponents.

Gladstone seems bent on leading Sir George Lewis a weary
life, but Lewis is just the man to encounter and baffle such
an opponent, for he is cold-blooded as a fish, totally devoid
of sensibility or nervousness, of an imperturbable temper,
calm and resolute, laborious and indefatigable, and exceedingly popular in the House of Commons from his general
good humor and civility, and the credit given him for honor,
sincerity, plain dealing, and good intentions.

February 11*th.*—The Duke of Bedford told me yesterday
that Clarendon had complained to him bitterly of John Russell's speech the first night of the session, of the hostility
it manifested, and particularly of what he said about Naples.
On looking at the report of the speech, the Neapolitan part
was certainly strong, but it was not stronger than was warranted by the circumstances of the case, and there seems
no reason why Lord John should abstain from speaking out
his opinions fairly on any important point of foreign policy.
His speech, on the whole, was not regarded as hostile or
acrimonious.   Disraeli has got into a scrape by blurting out
an accusation which he has entirely failed in making good,
and he has afforded Palmerston an occasion for a triumph
over him not a little damaging.   I am told the effect in the

House was very bad for Disraeli.   Palmerston is said to be beginning to show some symptoms of physical weakness, which if it be so, is very serious at the beginning of a long and arduous session.   He is rising seventy-three, and at that age, and loaded with the weight of public affairs, it is not wonderful if the beginning of the end should be discernible.

February 14th.—The defeat which Disraeli sustained the other night was turned the night before last into something like a triumph, and Palmerston found himself in a disagreeable position.   Disraeli had asserted that a Treaty had been concluded between France and Austria for certain ends and at a certain time.   Palmerston flatly contradicted him, and with great insolence of manner, especially insisting that it was nothing but a Convention, and that conditional, which *never had been signed.*   Two nights after Palmerston came down to the House, and in a very jaunty way said he must correct his former statement, and inform the House he had just discovered that the Convention *had been signed.*   Great triumph naturally on the part of Disraeli, who poured forth a rather violent invective.   Then Palmerston lost his temper and retorted that Disraeli was trying to cover an ignominious retreat by vaporing.   This language, under the circumstances of the case, was very imprudent and very improper, and (unlike what he had ever experienced before) he sat down without a single cheer, his own people even not venturing to challenge the approbation of the House in a matter in which, though Disraeli was not right, Palmerston was so clearly wrong.   What business had he to make such a mistake ? for he ought to have· been perfectly and accurately informed of every detail connected with foreign affairs.   He certainly is not *qualis erat*, and I am disposed to believe that he is about to begin breaking, and that he will not be able to go through a long and arduous session with the same vigor and success which he has hitherto manifested.   Every sign and symptom of weakness and failing strength which he may show will raise the hopes and stimulate the exertions of the Opposition, and we may expect to see not a coalition, but such a concurrence between Gladstone, Disraeli, and Lord Stanley as will prevent the possibility of an alternative Government.   Gladstone and Disraeli are already on friendly terms, and Gladstone and Stanley seem to be still more intimate.   The present Government only exists by Palmer-

ston's personal popularity, and it would not require much to
pull that down.

February 17th.—I called on Lyndhurst on Sunday.   He
was in high force, with the Blue Book before him, getting
up the China case, on which he means to have a day in the
House of Lords.   He told me that Gladstone says the Budget
is the worst that was ever produced, and he stakes his credit
on proving that it is full of errors from beginning to end,
that, instead of a present surplus of nearly a million, there
is a present deficit of four millions, and that there will be
one of nine millions in 1860.   I don't believe he will make
his words good.

I saw Clarendon yesterday morning, and found him low,
worn, and out of sorts ; said he wished to Heaven he could
be delivered from office ; everything went wrong, the labor,
anxiety, and responsibility were overwhelming, and the difficult state of our relations with France more than could be
endured.   He could not depend on the French Government,
and never knew from one day to another what the consequences of their conduct might be.   He believed the Emperor
sincerely desired to keep well with us, but his Government
were constantly doing things which rendered our acting together and cordially almost impossible ; that his excessive
levity and carelessness perpetually made him the dupe of other
people, and led him into saying things and committing himself, and then he did not know how to get out of the engagements to which he stood committed.   Clarendon added that
it was impossible such a state of things should not produce
first coolness and then quarrels, and then God knows what
consequences, and he was obliged to pick his way through
the embarrassments that spring up around him with the utmost care and circumspection.   Palmerston, who never saw
difficulties, took it with his usual easy way, and said we were
not tied to France like Siamese Twins, and why should we
care so much what she did, and why might she not take her
way, and we ours ; but Clarendon feels that it is impossible
for him, on whom the responsibility is more immediately
thrown, to take a matter fraught with such consequences in
so easy a style ; that if any serious dispute arose, France and
Russia would probably become allied against us, and that
America would join them.   Russia pays the most unceasing
and the most abject court to Louis Napoleon, and not without success.   He (Clarendon) said nothing could be worse

than the conduct of the French Government about the affair
of the Principalities, which was of vital importance to Austria, who threatened (though she would not keep her resolution) to make it a *casus belli* if it is insisted on.   He said
Austria had behaved very well about the amnesty in Italy,
and was going to do the same thing in Hungary.   We were
interrupted as usual in our conversation, and I had not time
to ask him about many things I wanted to hear of.   I told
him I thought the China case was a very bad one.

John Russell seems to me to be drifting into hostility to
the Government more and more.   He made a strong, but
very just, speech on Naples the first night, which irritated
Clarendon very much.   A few nights ago he said something
in the House about China, and backed up the Government
against Roebuck, at which Clarendon expressed great satisfaction, and evinced a disposition to seize that pretext to
put himself on good terms with Lord John, but Lord John
showed no readiness to meet the overture, and when the
Duke of Bedford wrote to him what Clarendon had said, he
replied that Clarendon owed him nothing, for he had said
what he thought right and not what he thought would be
agreeable to him, and that it was very probable he should
say something he would not at all like before long.

Yesterday morning the Judicial Committee finished the
case of Liddell and Westerton, after eight days of elaborate
argument, and a powerful case was made in appeal against
Lushington's judgment, which I expect to see reversed, and
I hope it will, for I detest the proceedings of the people who
back up Mr. Westerton, who would drag down the Church
to a puritanical level, and strip it of its splendor.

February 19th.—Yesterday morning, at half-past twelve
o'clock, my brother-in-law Lord Ellesmere, expired at Bridgewater House, after an illness of three months.   He was surrounded by all his family, and died most peacefully, and
without any suffering, and in possession of his mental powers
till within a few hours of his death.   Few men have quitted this
world more beloved, respected, and lamented than this excellent person.   He had just completed the fifty-seventh year of
his age, so might naturally have been expected to live many
years, and till he was taken ill, little more than three months
ago, he appeared to be in his usual state of health and likely to
have a long and enjoyable existence before him.   It is no exaggeration to say that he was most estimable in every relation

of life, and as such he enjoyed universal respect and regard.
He never at any time played a conspicuous part in politics,
for which he had neither ambition nor the necessary qualifi
cations, but in such part as he was occasionally called upon
to take, he acted with propriety and general approbation.
But he had no taste for the turmoil of political life, and his
temper was too serene and his love of repose too great to
allow him to plunge deeply in political warfare. His abilities were not of a very high order, but he had a good understanding, a cultivated mind, and an inquisitive disposition,
and, though not profound in any branch of literature or
science, he loved to wander over the vast fields of knowledge,
so that he was stored with much superficial information on
a great variety of subjects. His taste was good both in literature and art ; he was an elegant poet, and a fair writer of
his own tongue ; he was naturally kind-hearted and charitable, more particularly to meritorious artists who stood in
need of assistance, by whom his loss will be severely felt. All
his tastes and pursuits were of the most refined character,
and he delighted in the society of all who were remarkable
for ability in any walk of life, and from whom he could derive information of any description. In political opinions
he was the very type and model of a Liberal Conservative,
and the statesman to whom he gave all his allegiance, together with a boundless admiration, was the Duke of Wellington. But he was always much more of a patriot than a
political partisan, and he was oftener to be found giving an
independent support to different Governments than fighting
in the ranks of Opposition. He will, I have no doubt, be
regarded as a loss to the country, even a greater loss than if
he had been more actively and conspicuously engaged in
politics, for he stood nearly alone in the station he occupied,
with vast wealth, unblemished character, esteemed by people
of all parties, without an enemy in the world, and having no
personal objects to pursue ; and, though never thrusting
himself forward, alike fitted for either active or contempla-
tive life, he was at all times ready to exert his best energies
in the public service or to promote the benefit and happiness
of his fellow-creatures. He was sincerely religious, without
intolerance and austerity, or the slightest particle of osten-
tatious or spiritual pride. It was not, however, in the annals of political history or in the modest and unambitious
incidents of his public career that his best panegyric is to be

found, but in the more placid walk of private life, in the strict and conscientious discharge of his domestic and social duties, which was at the same time congenial to his sense of moral obligation, and to the benevolent impulses of his heart.

Lord Francis Leveson Gower, upon the death of his father, the late Duke of Sutherland, succeeded to the immense fortune entailed upon him by his great-uncle, the Duke of Bridgewater, in the shape of the Bridgewater Canal, and found himself the possessor of vast wealth, and surrounded by a population sunk in ignorance and vice. From the first moment of his succession he considered himself in the light of a trustee for working out the moral and spiritual improvement of the people who were in a great measure committed to his charge. He accepted the obligation in a spirit of cheerfulness and resolution, and the due discharge of it continued to be the principal object of his interest and care for the remainder of his life. He employed his wealth liberally in promoting the material comfort and raising the moral condition of those by whose labor that wealth was produced. Churches, schools, and reading-rooms rose around Worsley Hall. His benevolent efforts were crowned with success, and he reaped his reward in the blessings of the surrounding multitudes and in the contemplation of their enjoyment of all the good which his active bounty had bestowed upon them. Such qualities as were here displayed, and a life thus devoted to works of duty and beneficence, made Lord Ellesmere an object of general veneration and attachment; but those alone who belonged to his family, or who had familiar access to the sanctuary of his domestic life, could appreciate fully the excellence and the charm of his character, and comprehend the immensity of the loss which those who were nearest and dearest to him have sustained by his death. He regarded with indifference the ordinary objects of worldly ambition; he lived in and for his family, and he was their joy, their delight, and their pride, fulfilling in the most exemplary manner all the duties of his station, political, social, literary, and artistic; unsurpassed as a husband, father, brother, or friend. He cultivated unremittingly the society of the best and wisest of his fellow-creatures, and it may be as truly said of him as it was of certain sages of antiquity, that "his excellent understanding was adorned by study, . . . and his days were spent in the pursuit of truth and the practice of

virtue." The length of these precious days was not permitted
by the Divine Will to be extended to the ordinary duration
of human life. In the three last months, while death was
gradually but surely, and with his full consciousness, advancing, his courage was never shaken and the serenity of
his temper was never disturbed ; he always seemed to have
more consideration for others than himself ; and he met
his approaching end with the firmness of a philosopher and
the resignation of a Christian. To witness such an end free
from bodily pain, with the mental faculties remaining unclouded till the last, full of peace and charity and love, was
the best consolation that was possible to the family which
surrounded his deathbed ; to them he has left a memory
which will be long reverenced by all who honor virtue and
patriotism, and which they will cherish with never-ending
sentiments of duty and affection. He has left them an example how to live and how to die, and the world in which
he had no enemy will ungrudgingly acknowledge

> That to the realms of bliss was ne'er conveyed
> A purer spirit or more welcome shade.

February 27th.—The political war is raging furiously,
and personal animosities are becoming bitterer than ever.
Confusion, disorder, and doubt rage in both the great camps.
Derby made a grand onslaught in the beginning of last
week on the China question, and there was (an unusual
thing in the Lords) an adjourned debate. Granville was
very apprehensive of being beaten, but Bessborough, his able
whipper-in, made such exertions that they ended by getting
a very good majority. All the speaking was on the side
of the Opposition, but it is quite curious how afraid people
are of seriously shaking the Government. The day the debate in the Lords ended, that in the Commons began on
the same question, *duce* Cobden.[1] The great event of the
first night was John Russell's speech and powerful attack
on the Government. It was one of his very best efforts
and extremely successful with the House, but it was exceedingly bitter and displayed without stint or reason his

[1] [A motion was made by Mr. Cobden condemning the violent measures re-
sorted to by the British authorities in the Canton river in consequence of the
seizure of the lorcha " Arrow " by the Chinese when she had hoisted the British
flag. The debate was carried on with great acrimony, and ended by the adoption
of Mr. Cobden's motion by 263 to 247, a majority of 16 against the Government.]

hostile *animus*.   It did all the mischief he wished to do, and everybody admits that if a division had then taken place Government would have been beaten by a great majority ; but they have since adjourned twice, and the debate stands over till Monday, and the aspect of affairs appears to be very much altered.   Whether it be that the effect of Lord John's speech has evaporated, that a rally has taken place among the Liberals, or that the aversion of the stiff Tories to the union between Gladstone and their leaders, the approaching consummation of which seems not to be denied, the general opinion has veered round, and now it is expected that Government will have a majority.   Here again, as in the Lords, the speaking was all with the Opposition.   Palmerston's speech is looked for with interest and curiosity.   The remarkable incidents connected with these transactions have been the Parliamentary conduct of Gladstone and John Russell and their respective positions.   Gladstone seems to have been so inflamed by spite and ill-humor that all prudence and discretion forsook him ; he appears ready to say and do anything and to act with everybody if he can only contribute to upset the Government, though it is not easy to discover the cause of his bitterness, or what scheme of future conduct he has devised for himself.   Lord John came over in a state of ill-humor which at first he appears to have kept under to a certain degree, and to have wished to have the appearance of acting with perfect independence, but still fairly and impartially speaking out what he thought the truth without caring whom he offended or whom he pleased by so doing.   Thus he shocked Clarendon by what he said on the affair of Naples, and then pleased him very much by his next speech on foreign affairs.   Then on the Budget he came to the aid of Lewis with great effect and bowled over Gladstone and Disraeli, yet even then evincing a certain spirit of hostility about the tea duties ; but on the China question he gave way to all the bitter feeling that is in him, and cast all moderation to the winds.   It is impossible to conjecture what he promises to himself, and what purpose he has in view by this conduct, for it is quite extraordinary to what absolute nothingness his political power has fallen. Here is a man who has been leader with occasional intervals of Whig Governments and of the Whig party since 1834, and with great and admitted abilities, and yet he is so entirely without following in the House of Commons that three insignificant votes are the most he can command. His speech the other night was very well received because it was a very good one, and because he spoke the opinions of the greater number of his hearers.

There is, in fact, a strong feeling, both in Parliament and the country, against all that has been done at Canton, and this is the more remarkable because the press has upon the whole, taken the opposite side. I never could understand why Palmerston and Clarendon were in such a hurry to identify themselves with Bowring's proceedings, and to send out without delay a full approbation of all he had done, till Granville told me that both of them had been under the extraordinary delusion that the Canton affair had been very well done and would be received with great applause and satisfaction here; in point of fact, that it was a great *hit*, from which the Government would derive considerable advantage, he (Granville) himself showing his good sense by taking exactly the opposite view. He tells me that George Lewis does so likewise, and I dare say, if the truth were known, that the majority of the Cabinet coincide with them. It is remarkable that the defence of the Government in the Lords should have fallen on a man who was speaking all the time against his own opinion, and I should think Labouchere, who took up the defence in the House of Commons, was the most unlikely man in the world to approve of such proceedings. Political necessities which compel men to act thus insincerely, and to strive to make the worse appear the better cause, with the full consciousness that they are fighting against truth, appear to me frightfully demoralizing, a sad searing of the political conscience, the spectacle of which is enough to scare honorable minds from entering into an arena where the contest is to be carried on in such a manner.

If the Government should be beaten on the pending question, they will dissolve, at least if the state of their financial affairs will allow them; but at all events they will not resign without an appeal to the country, and this appeal they will make not on this or that question, but on the great one of all, whether the country desires that Palmerston should continue to be its minister, and on this it is impossible to doubt what will be the reply. His popularity is a fact beyond all doubt or cavil, and it is the more decisive, because not only is there no rival popularity, but every one of the other public men who have been, are, or might be his rivals

are absolutely unpopular.   Nobody cares any longer for
John Russell ; everybody detests Gladstone   Disraeli has no
influence in the country, and a very doubtful position with
his own party.   He and Derby have made up their minds to
coalesce with Gladstone on the first good opportunity, but it
seems not unlikely that they will make such a split among
their own followers by so doing as to lose more than they
will gain by the junction.   Palmerston's popularity does not
extend to his colleagues, for not one of whom does anybody
care a straw.   It is purely personal, and I do not think he
would strengthen himself by any other alliance he could
form.   This fact of his popularity just at the end of his
strange and chequered career is most remarkable and not a
little unaccountable ; but innumerable circumstances prove
this to be the undoubted truth, and that it is manifested more
decidedly out of the House than in it, for in the House of
Commons it does not amount to a certainty of his having
always a majority.   It is curious that a session which not
long ago looked like being a very quiet one, in which there
would be ample leisure for consideration of legal and other
practical reforms, should in the first weeks be a scene of
tremendous conflict, in which the very existence of the
Government is trembling in the balance.

March 2*d.*—Derby has announced to his assembled party
that he is ready to join with Gladstone, though he has not
done so yet, and that as they are a minority in the House of
Commons, they ought to form any junction that would
make them strong enough to oust the present Government
and form a Conservative one.   He finds it, however, a difficult matter to reconcile them all to any alliance with the
detested Gladstone.   Great exertions have been made to
secure a majority to the Government, and John Russell's
friends (the Duke of Bedford especially) are bestirring themselves to take away some of the odium that attaches to
Lord John by securing his two or three followers for the
division.

March 3*d.*—Nothing can equal the excitement and curiosity here about the division.   All sorts of efforts have been
made all ways to influence votes.   George Byng and others
who meant to vote with John Russell have been obliged to
promise to vote with the Government.   Palmerston has had
a meeting and harangued them cheerily, but in spite of
everything Hayter does not think he will have a majority,

but everybody expects it to be so near that there are as many opinions as men.   Much is expected to depend on Palmerston's speech, and unluckily for him he is ill with both gout and cold.   If they are beaten they will dissolve as speedily as possibly.

March 4th.—A majority of 16 against the Government, more than any of them expected.   A magnificent speech of Gladstone ; Palmerston's speech is said to have been very dull in the first part, and very bow-wow in the second ; not very judicious, on the whole bad, and it certainly failed to decide any doubtful votes in his favor.   I rejoice that the House of Commons has condemned this iniquitous case for the honor of the country.   I do not believe it will make any difference as to the Government.   When Palmerston appeals to the country it will not be on the merits of the Canton case, but on his own political existence, whether they will have him for Minister or no.   It is not, however, yet by any means clear what the real opinion of the country is upon the question itself, and whether they will be for the right or for the expedient, or that which the Government thinks to be the expedient.

Hatchford, March 10th.—The intention of Government to dissolve Parliament was announced on Friday last, and as far as one can judge at present, Palmerston seems likely to have it all his own way.   The press generally espouses his cause, and the "Times" particularly takes up the cudgels for him vehemently, and cries out "Coalition," and abuses the majority and all who voted in it.   At present, public opinion seems to be running in his favor, and there is every appearance of his having a triumphant election.   But the cry of "coalition and faction" is perfectly absurd, and nothing more than the mere jargon which all parties employ as their battle cry.   There has been no coalition whatever, and that those who clamor against it very well know.   The only coalition of which there has been any question has been one between Gladstone (with or without the other Peelites) and Disraeli and Derby, but that has hitherto been *in posse* rather than *in esse*, and it would have been much more plausible to raise the cry on the Budget than on the Canton question. Nobody can read the list of the division without seeing that the majority comprised the names of people who have never dreamt of any coalition with anybody, and who voted entirely with reference to the merits of the particular case, and though some (including Disraeli and Gladstone) wished to damage the Government, many others were either friendly to them generally, or at least neutral. To say that the majority was made up of a factious coalition of men who sought to turn the Government out and to take their places, is a wilful and deliberate lie, but it suits the Government to raise the cry, and they find plenty of people to re-echo and to believe it. As to the question itself, I am sure that some of the Cabinet, and probably more than I know of, were in their hearts and consciences as much against the question as any of their opponents. Palmerston's popularity, and the manner in which he is encouraged and supported by the country, and the sympathy he finds are really most extraordinary. It provokes me, because I think his great success unmerited, but I have no wish to see him defeated at the election, because I see no prospect of any better Government being formed. The pretension of the Government and of their noisy supporters to find fault with the House of Commons for expressing its independent opinion upon the conduct of the officials in China is most preposterous and arrogant. Everybody admits that the Government was not morally responsible for what was done, but because they chose, without any necessity, to approve those acts and to accept the political responsibility of them, it is pretended that the House of Commons ought not to have taken the liberty to express any adverse opinion on the matter, and that it was factious to do so. The scrape, if it was one, the Government got themselves into by their precipitate approval of Bowring, and there was nothing in the resolution and the vote which ought to have been considered as implying any general want of confidence on the part of the House of Commons, more particularly when the Government has just before carried their Budget by large majorities, and had not met with any difficulty or rebuff on any point. If, indeed, matters are come to such a pass, and such divinity hedges in the Palmerston Government that the House of Commons is to be precluded from censuring any transaction, wherever and by whomsoever done, which the Government thinks fit to sanction and approve of, and if the fact of many men of very different opinions and opposite parties concurring in such a vote is to expose the majority by which the vote is carried to a charge of faction, coalition, and all sorts of base motives, then indeed, instead of asking the Duke of Wellingtons's celebrated question, "How is the King's Government to be carried on ?" it will be time to ask whether the Queen's Government is to be considered despotic and infallible, and the functions of the House of Commons reduced to the very humble ones of registering their acts and re-echoing their approbation.

It seems to be entirely forgotten that in times when the Royal and ministerial authority were much stronger than they are supposed to be now, and before the Reform Bill had effected a sort of revolution in favor of the democratic principle, all governments, however powerful or popular, sustained occasional defeats and were obliged to submit to them, it being of course perfectly understood that defeats which conveyed want of confidence and the withdrawal of the general support of the House of Commons were to be deemed fatal and conclusive. Every case of this kind must be determined according to the especial circumstances of it, but it is a mere pretence to treat the Canton question as one of this description, and the truth is that it is a dodge on their part, and a pretext for going to the country and obtaining a majority, as they think they have an opportunity of doing, on false pretences and by means of a vast deal of humbug. The worst is, that after the immediate purpose has been answered, there is certain to be some dangerous reaction, and as the cry of "Palmerston" will be the only one got up for the occasion, and everybody will be acceptable who will declare for him, whatever crotchets or cries he may join to his partisanship, we shall probably have a House of Commons full of all sorts of mischievous people stirring every variety of mischievous question.

March 14th.—I returned yesterday from Hatchford and find the current still running strong, but some think a reaction in favor of John Russell has already begun. He stands for the City and is in very good spirits, though his chances of success do not look bright ; but he is a gallant little fellow, likes to face danger, and comes out well in times of difficulty.

March 24th.—The dissolution took place on Saturday, and all the world is busy about the elections ; many places are without candidates, or with very bad ones, and unable to find good ones. The dinner at the Mansion House the other day to the Ministers was a sort of triumph to Palmerston, who was rapturously received and cheered. He made a very bad speech, but which did very well for such an audience. It was full of claptraps and reiterations of the exploded charges of coalition, etc., which he is not ashamed to harp upon, and in his address to Tiverton he talks of the "combination only formed last session" to turn him out. I find myself, *malgré moi*, thrown back into my old state of antagonism toward Palmerston, and what is very paradoxical, I am so without any hostility to his Government or any desire for its being overthrown, for I cannot descry any chance of a better, or, indeed, any possibility of forming another able to carry on affairs at all; but I am inexpressibly disgusted at the egregious folly of the country at his being made such an idol in this ridiculous way, and at the false and hypocritical pretences upon which this dissolution has been founded, and the enormous and shameful lying with which the country is deluged. I long to write, print, and publish the truth, and to expose this miserable delusion; but I repress the desire, because I cannot do so without exciting bitter personal animosities, probably quarrels, and I can see no reasonable hope of producing any effects which would sufficiently repay me for such consequences.

The day before yesterday Pemberton Leigh gave judgment in the Privy Council in the case of Liddell and Westerton; the Judicial Committee reversed in great measure the judgments in the Courts below of Dr. Lushington and Sir John Dodson, but not entirely. It was a very able judgment, and prepared with great care and research, and so moderately and fairly framed that it was accepted unanimously by the Committee, and even by the Bishops of Canterbury and London, both Low Churchmen. It was drawn up by Pemberton Leigh himself, and its publication will give the world in general some idea of his great ability, with the extent of which few are acquainted. It is a very singular thing that in such times as these, and when there is such a dearth of able men and so great a demand for them, that he should voluntarily condemn himself to a state of comparative obscurity, and refuse to take the station in public life which it would be difficult to find any other man so well qualified to fill.

March 28th.—At Althorp the last two days. Palmerston's address to Tiverton, following his speech at the Mansion House, has excited great indignation in all who are not thorough Palmerstonians. Both were full of deception and falsehood. John Russell is particularly incensed, and said these two productions were unworthy of a gentleman, and so they were. Malmesbury has addresssed to Palmerston a letter in the newspapers on the subject, which though not well written is true, and fully justified by what Palmerston said ; but all this signifies very little, the current is too strong to be opposed, and it is provoking to see the Conservatives endeavoring to bolster up their pretensions by saying they would have supported Palmerston on the China question, if they had been in Parliament, or promising to support him if they are elected. Yesterday, which was the first day of returns, does not give much difference ; to-day is the polling for the City, and nobody has an idea how the election will go, whether Lord John will come in, and if he does which of the four will go to the wall. He was enthusiastically received yesterday, and the show of hands was unanimous in his favor, but this proves very little, and his organization is miserably defective ; had it been better and begun earlier, it is probable that his success would have been certain ; he is the favorite as it is. Palmerston's speech at Tiverton yesterday was less objectionable than his address and speech at the Mansion House, and he left himself entirely unfettered on the subject of Reform, and rightly. The Parliament promises to be a Radical one, and I fully expect that the result of all this great commotion will be to give a stimulus to organize Reform ; nor will it surprise me if Palmerston should find it conducive to his interest as minister to appear in the character of a Reformer, if he were to fling overboard all his old opinions, and to pay this price for a renewed lease of his own power. Wilkes used to say he had never been a *Wilkite*, but Palmerston has never been anything but a Palmerstonian, and I firmly believe that at seventy-three years of age his single thought is how to secure for himself power for his life, and that he will not scruple to accept measures which, so far as he thinks about it, he believes to be constitutionally dangerous and mischievous if by so doing he can maintain himself on the Treasury Bench.

March 29th.—Great excitement yesterday in the town, particularly at Brooks's. The most interesting event was the City election, and the return, which under the circumstances may be called triumphant, of John Russell, which was made more agreeable to himself and his friends by the defeat of Raikes Currie, who came from Northampton on purpose to turn him out. Up to the last hour John Russell continued to lead at the head of the poll, after which he fell off and only ended third, but still he had 7,000 votes after having been assured by his old adherents (J. Abel Smith in particular) that his success was hopeless, that he would be beaten "disgracefully," and probably would have hardly any votes at all.

After this the most interesting events were the defeats of the Manchester men, and generally, though not universally, of the voters for Cobden's motion, Bright and Milner Gibson, Cobden, Ricardo, Layard, all defeated. It seems that Manchester and the other great towns had got tired of their leaders, who had made themselves unpopular by their opposition to the war. I am sorry for the loss of Bright and Cobden, because such able men ought not to be ousted and replaced by mediocrities.

Palmerston's speech at Tiverton was in the same style, but far less offensive and objectionable than his address and his Mansion House harrangue. The most remarkable part of it was the total silence which he observed as to his intention upon reforms and domestic questions generally, or rather his positive refusal to say a word on the subject or to pledge himself in any way; he evidently means to meet his Parliament free to take any course his interests may dictate. There was one remarkable speech yesterday, considering what the man is who uttered it. Vernon Smith at Northampton spoke as follows: "Mr. Disraeli said Lord Palmerston was the Tory chief of a Radical Cabinet. I do not admit the description as regards Lord Palmerston, but I accept the designation as to the Cabinet of which I am a member. A great statesman once said that parties were like fishes (it was snakes, I believe), and their heads were propelled by their tails, and it will very likely be found that the head of the Government will in like manner be propelled by his tail." The words are not exact, but the meaning is, and it must be owned a remarkable declaration for a Cabinet Minister to make as to his chief, and such a chief. I believe that it will turn out to be the truth. The returns so far as they have gone are frightful, and a deluge of Radicalism and violence will burst out in the House of Commons. There will be a Radical majority prepared to support Lord Palmerston and to keep him in power, but on the condition of his doing their bidding, and consenting to their demands, nor will he be able to help himself. He will no doubt try to do as little as possible, but there will be no strong Conservative party to which he can appeal from and against his own Radical supporters; the Conservatives will be too weak to help him, and probably will not be inclined to help him out of his difficulty if they could. At his age his only object will be to grasp power while he lives. *Après moi le déluge* will be his motto, and my expectation is that he will never consent to sacrifice power from scruples or upon principles, and will consent to anything that may be necessary rather than allow himself to be outbid and to see power torn from his hands. The prospect seems to me tremendous. The cry of Palmerston, and nothing but Palmerston, has done very well to go to the hustings on, but having accomplished its purpose, other cries much more serious will soon take its place, and we shall see, as the Prince said, Constitutional Government on its trial with a vengeance.

March 31st.—The elections continue to be unfavorable to the Conservatives, but the people at Brooks's, and the Government generally, are too sanguine when they call everything gain to them where a Conservative is replaced by a Liberal, for in many cases the so-called Liberal is a violent Radical, very likely to give much more trouble to the Government than the Conservative who was turned out. The gains to Government up to this time (and the borough elections are all over) are calculated at 20, making a difference of 40 votes; but the Conservatives do not admit this, and will make other calculations with different results.

There is no denying the fact, however, that a strong sense has been evinced of partiality for Palmerston and resentment against the China vote. The news of the Emperor of China having ordered Yeo to make peace on any terms comes very opportunely, but nothing can be so absurd as the pretence that by so doing the Emperor himself condemns his Viceroy and justifies our conduct at Canton. It only proves that His Majesty is very much alarmed, and wishes to heal the breach as quickly as possible, and on any terms he can. I am bound to say that many people, not extravagant either, maintain that this promises to be a very good Parliament, and by no means so dangerous as my fears have pictured it to myself; still I cannot look upon it as a safe and innocent Parliament. Cardwell's defeat at Oxford proves how low the Peelites are. Frederick Peel's loss of his seat is a great inconvenience to the Government, and one does not see how it is to be repaired, for it is almost impossible in these days to treat any place (if one can be found) as a nomination borough, turn the sitting member out, and put him in instead.   The serious part of it is that he has to move the Army Estimates, and nobody else can do it now.

Old Lady Keith is dead, at some prodigious age.   She was the "Queeny" of Dr. Johnson, Mrs. Hale's daughter, and was the last surviving link between those times and our own, and probably the only person surviving who could remember Johnson himself and his remarkable contemporaries, or who had lived in intimacy with them.

———— •◆• ————

.

CHAPTER XIV.

Results of the Elections—Defeat of Cobden and Bright—The War with China—Death of Lady Ashburton—Lord Palmerston's Success—The Handel Concerts—M. Fould in London—The Queen and Lord Palmerston—The Indian Mutiny—The Prince Consort —Death of General Anson—The State of India—Royal Guests—The Government of India—Temper of the House of Commons—Debates on India—Royal Visits—The Divorce Bill—The Divorce Bill in the House of Lords—Close of the Session—A Dukedom offered to Lord Lansdowne—Death of Mr. Croker—History of the Life Peerages —The Indian Mutiny and the Russian War—The Struggle in India—Reinforcements for India—The Queen's Attention to Public Business—Attacks on Lord Canning—Big Ships and Big Bells—Lord Canning defended—Courteous Behavior of Foreign Nations —The Capture of Delhi and Lucknow—Difficulties in India—Depression in the City— Speculations on the Contingency of a Change of Government—The East India Company and the Government—Exaggerated Reports from India—A Queen's Speech— The Bank Charter Act.

April 4th, 1857.—The elections are drawing to a close. It is strange that what ought to be a matter of fact is made matter of opinion, for while the Whigs of Brooks's and the Liberals generally claim an immense gain, the Conservatives and the Carlton Club and their organs only admit an inconsiderable loss.   There can be no doubt, however, that a great many Conservatives have lost their seats, and a great many Radicals and Palmerstonians have been elected.   At Brooks's they insist that it will be a very good Parliament, and they are throwing their caps up at the Government successes ; but it seems to me that they are reckoning somewhat rashly, and counting as gains to the Government many men who will be found more troublesome and unmanageable than the moderate men over whose defeats they are exulting.

But as to gains and losses, and all calculations, I agree with the late Speaker, Lord Eversley, who said to me the other day that nothing could be so fallacious as all such calculations, and that it is impossible to know the result till Parliament meets, and it is seen how the new members group themselves. The most striking and remarkable feature of this election is the complete rout of the Peelites and of the Manchester men, the Old Leaguers. For a long time past it has been absurd to talk of the Peelites as a Party. There were not a dozen men in the House of Commons who could by any possibility be so designated, and in fact only a few formerly members of Sir Robert Peel's Government or of Lord Aberdeen's, who still kept together, and were called Peelites, because they would not be either Whigs or Tories or Radicals. Now the designation must fall to the ground. Half these men have lost their seats; of the rest, some repudiate the association and announce their independence; some join, or ready to join, Derby and the Tories; others openly declare their adhesion to Palmerston; and thus in one way or another there are no *Peelites* left.

The fate of Bright, Cobden, and Co. exhibits a curious example of the fleeting and worthless nature of popular favor. They who were once the idols of millions, and not without cause, have not only lost all their popularity, but are objects of execration, and can nowhere find a parliamentary resting place. No constituency will hear of them. The great towns of Lancashire prefer any mediocrities to Bright and Cobden. It seems that they had already ceased to be popular, when they made themselves enormously unpopular, and excited great resentment, by their opposition to the Russian War, the rage for which was not less intense in Manchester and all the manufacturing district than in the rest of the kingdom. This great crime, as it appeared in the eyes of their constituents, was never pardoned, and their punishment was probably determined while the war was still going on. As the favor of Cobden fell, so that of Palmerston rose, and his visit to Manchester a few months ago raised the favor to a pitch of enthusiasm. When Cobden therefore originated the China motion, he no doubt gave great offence, and he sealed his own condemnation. Bright has been long abroad, and has done nothing lately that any one could take umbrage at, but his opposition to the war has not been forgotten or forgiven, and when Cobden appeared at Manchester as his representative, and made a very able speech in his behalf, it is highly probable that his advocacy was in itself fatal to his re-election. It seems quite clear that another man, Sir Elkanah Armytage, lost his election at Salford solely because he was strongly supported and recommended by Cobden.

May 1st.—Parliament met yesterday, the last (Irish) election having ended only a few days before. Denison's election as Speaker went off very quietly. The prevailing opinion now seems to be that this will prove a good Parliament, on the whole safe and moderate, and an improvement on the last. All the news we get from China, or in reference to Chinese affairs, only proves the more strongly how foolish and mischievous the conduct of Bowring was, and what a sound and correct judgment the vote of the House of Commons expressed upon it. It is impossible to conjecture what the result of the war now begun will be, but is quite certain that we shall have to wade to our ends through all sorts of horrors and atrocities, which it does not become us to inflict, though the Chinese are a savage, stupid, and uninteresting people, who in some degree deserve the sufferings that will be inflicted on them, though perhaps not at our hands.

George Anson [1] writes to me from India that there is a strange feeling of discontent pervading the Indian Army from religious causes, and a suspicion that we are going to employ our irresistible power in forcing Christianity upon them. It is not true, but the natives will never be quite convinced that it is not, as long as Exeter Hall and the missionaries are permitted to have *carte blanche* and work their will as they please in those regions.

May 10th.—I passed the last week at Wynnstay for Chester races; a very fine place. The events that have occurred in the course of the last ten days are the opening of the Manchester Exhibition, very successfully; the first proceedings of the new Parliament, which promise a quiet session and a peaceful reign to Palmerston, who has put the House in good humor by promising a Reform Bill next year; the death of the Duchess of Gloster, and, what inter-

---

[1] [General Anson was at this time Commander-in-Chief in India. He died there shortly after the outbreak of the great military revolt, of which the letter mentioned in the text was the first premonitory indication.]

ests the world still more, the death of Lady Ashburton.[1]
Milnes has written a short, but very fair and appropriate
notice of her for the "Times" newspaper, which of course
was intended as a eulogy, and not as a *character*, with the
bad as well as the good that could be said of her.   Lady
Ashburton was perhaps, on the whole, the most conspicuous
woman in the society of the present day.   She was undoubtedly very intelligent, with much quickness and vivacity
in conversation, and by dint of a good deal of desultory
reading and social intercourse with men more or less distinguished, she had improved her mind, and made herself a
very agreeable woman, and had acquired no small reputation for ability and wit.   It is never difficult for a woman in
a great position and with some talent for conversation to
attract a large society around her, and to have a number of
admirers and devoted *habitués*.   Lady Ashburton laid herself
out for this, and while she exercised hospitality on a great
scale; she was more of a *précieuse* than any woman I have
known.   She was, or affected to be, extremely intimate with
many men whose literary celebrity or talents constituted
their only attraction, and while they were gratified by the
attentions of the great lady, her vanity was flattered by the
homage of such men, of whom Carlyle was the principal.   It
is only justice to her to say that she treated her literary
friends with constant kindness and the most unselfish attentions.   They, their wives and children (when they had any),
were received at her house in the country, and entertained
there for weeks without any airs of patronage, and with a
spirit of genuine benevolence as well as hospitality.   She
was in her youth tall and commanding in person, but
without any pretension to good looks ; still she was not
altogether destitute of sentiment and coquetry, or incapable
of both feeling and inspiring a certain amount of passion.
The only man with whom she was ever what could be called
in love was Clarendon, and that feeling was never entirely
extinct, and the recollection of it kept up a sort of undefined relation between them to the end of her life.   Two

---

[1] [Harriet Mary, eldest daughter of the sixth Earl of Sandwich, was married
in 1823 to William Bingham Baring, afterward second Baron Ashburton.   One
son, the only issue of this marriage, died in infancy.   Lady Ashburton was distinguished for her wit, her social qualities, and her hospitality, which made Bath
House and the Grange the centres of a brilliant literary society, well known by
the records of it in the Life of Mr. Carlyle and the Autobiography of Sir Henry
Taylor.]

men were certainly in love with her, both distinguished in different ways. One was John Mill, who was sentimentally attached to her, and for a long time was devoted to her society. She was pleased and flattered by his devotion, but as she did not in the slightest degree return his passion, though she admired his abilities, he at last came to resent her indifference, and ended by estranging himself from her entirely, and proved the strength of his feeling by his obstinate refusal to continue even his acquaintance with her. Her other admirer was Charles Buller, with whom she was extremely intimate, but without ever reciprocating his love. Curiously enough, they were very like each other in person, as well as in their mental accomplishments. They had both the same spirits and cleverness in conversation, and the same quickness and drollery in repartee. I remember Allen well describing them, when he said that their talk was like that in the polite conversation between Never Out and Miss Notable. Her faults appeared to be caprice and a disposition to quarrels and *tracasseries* about nothing, which, however common among ordinary women, were unworthy of her superior understanding. But during her last illness all that was bad and hard in her nature seemed to be improved and softened, and she became full of charity, good-will, and the milk of human kindness. Her brother and her sister-in-law, who, forgetting former estrangements, hastened to her sickbed, were received by her with overflowing tenderness, and all selfish and unamiable feelings seemed to be entirely subdued within her. Had she recovered she would probably have lived a better and a happier woman, and as it is she has died in charity with all the world, and has left behind her corresponding sentiments of affection and regret for her memory. I was once very intimate with her, but for a long time past our intimacy had dwindled into ordinary acquaintance.

June 3d.—There is really nothing to write about, but it is evident that the session is going to pass away in the most quiet and uneventful manner. Never had Minister such a peaceful and undisturbed reign as Palmerston's. There is something almost alarming in his prodigious felicity and success. Everything prospers with him. In the House of Commons there is scarcely a semblance of opposition to anything he proposes; a speech or two here and there from Roebuck, or some stray Radical, against some part of the

Princess Royal's dowry, but hardly any attempt at divisions ; and when there have been any, the minorities have been so ridiculously small as to show the hopelessness of opposition. The only men who might be formidable or troublesome seem to have adopted the prudent course of not kicking against the pricks. John Russell evinces no hostility, and accepts Hayter's letters. Gladstone hardly ever goes near the House of Commons, and never opens his lips. There seems to be a disposition in both Houses to work and bring legislative reforms to a conclusion. The House of Lords has been very busy with the Divorce Bill, and there has been a good deal of vigorous debating, particularly among Lyndhurst, the Bishops of Oxford and London, and Campbell and Wensleydale, who hate each other, and have interchanged blows.

June 20th.—All this past week the world has been occupied with the Handel Concerts at the Crystal Palace, which went off with the greatest success and *éclat.* I went to the first (" Messiah "), and the last ("Israel in Egypt"); they were amazingly grand, and the beauty of the *locale,* with the vast crowds assembled in it, made an imposing spectacle. The arrangements were perfect, and nothing could be easier than the access and egress, or more comfortable than the accommodation. But the wonderful assembly of 2,000 vocal and 500 instrumental performers did not produce musical effect so agreeable and so perfect as the smaller number in the smaller space of Exeter Hall. The volume of sound was dispersed and lost in the prodigious space, and fine as it undoubtedly was, I much prefer the concerts of the Harmonic Society.

Fould [1] came over from Paris the other day for the purpose of going to see the Manchester Exhibition. He was received with great distinction. The Queen invited him to Windsor for Ascot, and Granville gave him a breakfast here to meet the financial notabilities whom he wanted to talk to. We had the Chancellor of the Exchequer and an ex-Chancellor (C. Wood), the Governor of the bank, and the ex-Govcruor of the Bank, *cum multis aliis.* He said that their financial affairs in France were in a very healthy state, which is contrary to the general impression here.

[1] [M. Achille Fould, who had made a large fortune as a banker in Paris, was one of the ablest and most honorable of the Ministers of Napoleon III. He was much attached to this country, where he had many friends, and he encouraged the Emperor in that Free Trade policy which led to the Commercial Treaty of 1860, and strengthened the ties between England and France.]

I met Clarendon in the Park a day or two ago, and had
some talk with him in the friendly and intimate tone of
former times, which rejoiced my heart, because it proved that
though circumstances and accidental habits had impeded our
intercourse, there exist still the same feelings of regard
toward me in his mind, and if our intercourse was restored again, he would probably fall into the same habit of
confidence and communication which formerly existed, but
which has lately been completely interrupted. He talked
of Palmerston, his position and his health, and his *rapports*
with the Queen, who is now entirely reconciled to him. She
treats him with unreserved confidence, and he treats her
with a deference and attention which have produced a very
favorable change in her sentiments toward him. Clarendon
told me that Palmerston had lately been ailing in a way
to cause some uneasiness. He had had a bad leg with a
sore that it had been found difficult to heal, but he appears
to have got over it. This might have been very serious.
Clarendon talked one day to the Queen about Palmerston's
health, concerning which she expressed her anxiety, when
Clarendon said she might indeed be anxious, for it was of
the greatest importance to her, and if anything happened to
him he did not know where she could look for a successor to
to him, that she had often expressed her great desire to have
a *strong* Government, and that she had now got one, Palmerston being a really strong Minister. She admitted the truth
of it. Clarendon said he was always very earnest with her
to bestow her whole confidence on Palmerston, and not even
to talk to others on any subjects which properly belonged
to him, and he had more than once (when according to her
custom, she began to talk to him on certain things) said to
her, "Madam, that concerns Lord Palmerston, and I think
your Majesty had better reserve it for your communications
with him." He referred to the wonderful change in his own
relations with Palmerston, that seven or eight years ago
Palmerston was full of hatred and suspicion of him, and now
they were the best of friends, with mutual confidence and
good will, and lately when he was talking to Palmerston of
the satisfactory state of his relations with the Queen and of
the utility it was to his Government that it should be so, Palmerston said, "And it is likewise a very good thing that she
has such boundless confidence in her Secretary for Foreign Affairs, when after all there is nothing she cares about so much."

June 28th.—I went last Saturday week to Strawberry Hill.[1] A large party of people, the Persignys, the Speaker and Lady Charlotte, etc. ; it is an enjoyable villa, with its vast expanse of grass, profusion of flowers, and fine trees affording ample shade. Horace Walpole's ridiculous house is unaltered, but furbished up and made comfortable. I regret to hear that Denison does not make a very good Speaker, and that the Government think they made a mistake in putting him into the Chair. It was Palmerston's doing, who would hear of nobody else. There are several men among the Opposition who would probably have been fitter, but with the great majority the Government have they were in a manner compelled to take a man from their own party. Denison says it is owing to the laxity of Palmerston himself if things do not go on so well as they might in the House of Commons.

At Hatchford the past week, and when I got to town I was apprised of the disastrous news from India,[2] the most serious occurrence that has ever been in that quarter, not only from the magnitude of the events themselves as the telegraph conveys them, but because it is quite impossible to estimate the gravity of the ease, nor what the extent of it may be. Till we receive the details it is idle to speculate upon it.

The Queen has made Prince Albert " Prince Consort " by a patent ordered in Council, but as this act confers on him neither title, dignity, nor privileges, I cannot see the use of it. He was already as high in England as he can be, assuming the Crown Matrimonial to be out of the question, and it will give him no higher rank abroad, where our acts have no validity.

July 15th.—For the last three weeks or more all public interest and curiosity have been absorbed in the affairs of India and the great Mutiny that has broken out there, and which has now assumed such an alarming character. I had intended to take some notice of this, and of other matters

---

[1] [Strawberry Hill was the residence of the Countess of Waldegrave, to whom it had passed on the death of her second husband, the Earl of Waldegrave. It was then, and continued to be until her death in 1879, the most hospitable villa in the neighborhood, and the constant resort of all that was distinguished in politics and in letters.]

[2] [The Indian mutiny broke out at Meerut on Sunday, 10th May, but the details were not known in England till nearly six weeks later. General Anson died at Kurnaul on the 27th May.]

which time and the hour have brought forth ; but, according to my bad custom, I kept putting it off, till at last all other things were driven out of my mind by the news which so unexpectedly reached us on Saturday last of the death of George Anson from a sudden attack of cholera. He was the oldest and most intimate friend I had, and almost the last surviving associate of my youth. I reserve for another moment to say a word or two of a man who, without great abilities or a great career, was too conspicuous a member of society to be passed over without some notice.

The alarm created here by the Indian news is very great, and Ellenborough (reckoned a great authority on Indian matters) does his best to increase it. The serious part of it is that no one can tell or venture to predict what the extent of the calamity may be, and what proportions the mischief may possibly assume. It is certain that hitherto the Government and the East India Company have been in what is called a fool's paradise on the subject. They have been so long accustomed to consider our Empire there as established on so solid a foundation, and so entirely out of the reach of danger, that they never have paid any attention to those who hinted at possible perils, and I don't think anybody ever foresaw anything like what has occurred, and they were disinclined to adopt any of the precautionary recommendations which would have been attended with expense, and the Press, and the public who are always led by the Press, took the same easy view of the subject. While the Russian War was going on a clamor was raised against Government for not calling away *all* the British troops in India and sending them to the Crimea, and those who went mad about the Crimean War would willing having left India without a single European regiment, and have entrusted all our interests to the fidelity and attachment of the Native army. Though our Government was willing enough to enter into anything that the passion of the multitude suggested, they were not so insane as all that ; but as it is, we may consider it most providential that the mutiny did not show itself during the Russian, or indeed during the Persian war. If it had happened while we were still fighting in the Crimea, we could not have sent out the force that would have been indispensable to save India. At the present moment the interest of the public is not greater than its apprehensions and alarm. Rumors of every sort are rife, generally of the most

disastrous kind, and though the mails only come at a fortnight's interval, and it is physically impossible that any intelligence should reach us during those intervals, the public
curiosity is fed and excited by continual rumors, which generally circulate stories of fresh disasters and dangers.   There
is a disposition in some quarters to make if possible poor Anson the scapegoat, and, now that he is dead and cannot defend himself, to attribute to him and to his misconduct or
laches the misfortunes that have befallen us.   I know not
what he may have written home to the civil and military
authorities ; but, if I may judge by the tenor of his correspondence with me, I should infer that he has warned the
Government against leaving India without adequate protection, and constantly urged the expediency of sending out
fresh troops.   I have long expected that the day would come
when we should find reason for regretting our expansive
policy and our going on with continual conquests and annexations,

We are overrun with Royalties present and prospective.
Besides our Princess Royal's bridegroom, there are here the
King of the Belgians' son and daughter, Prince Napoleon,
the Queen of the Netherlands, and the Montpensiers *as
Spanish Princes*, in which capacity Persigny has had to pay
his court to them, and they have had to receive the Ambassador of Louis Napoleon.

July 19th.—Although it is impossible that any fresh accounts should have come from India, reports are rife of fresh
insurrections and of all sorts of evils.   Amid all the bad news
from India the good fortune is that so many of the Native
troops, and not only the military, but the whole population
of the Punjaub, have shown so much fidelity and attachment
to the British Government.   It is the strongest testimony to
the wisdom and justice of our rule, and of the capacity of
the natives to appreciate the benefits they derive from it,
for beyond all question the introduction of European civilization into the East, and the substitution of such a government
as that of England for the cruel, rapacious, and capricious
dominion of Oriental chiefs and dynasties, is the greatest
boon that the people could have had conferred upon them.
Our administration may not have been faultless, and in some
instances it may have been oppressive, and it may have often
offended against the habits and prejudices of the natives, but
it is certainly very superior in every respect, and infinitely

more beneficent than any rule, either of Hindoos or Mahometans, that has ever been known in India. However, people much more civilized and more sagacious than the Indians do not always know what is best for them, or most likely to promote their happiness, so it will not be surprising if these disorders should continue to increase, supposing the means of immediately and effectually suppressing them should be found wanting.'

For the last week the House of Commons has presented a more animated appearance than during the preceding months of this dull and passive session. Gladstone has reappeared and proved that his oratorical powers have not been rusted by his retirement, and John Russell has come forth showing his teeth, but not yet attempting to bite the Government. Palmerston, evidently nettled by these two, as well as by Roebuck and Disraeli, has spoken with considerable asperity, and with an insolent air of superiority and defiance, which has hitherto not been usual to him, and which has given no little offence. There are evident symptoms of an approaching cessation of that humble and deferential submission to his will which has hitherto distinguished his servile majority, and though it is not clear in what way they will assert their independence, those who watch the symptoms think that he will not find the same passive disposition in the next session, and if anything should go seriously wrong there would be open and general rebellion. Up to the present time, however, there is nothing to be seen but a certain amount of restlessness and a disposition to find fault, and the Government seem still to command the same enormous majorities, and Palmerston to be as powerful as ever, if he is not quite so popular. A violent effort is made by a number of Liberals in the House of Commons to renew the contest with the House of Lords for the admission of the Jews (the newspapers contain all the details of this attempt), which cannot be pursued without mischievous results, and will fail in its objcet.

August 2d.—The Civil War in India, for such it may be called, supersedes every other object of interest, and the successive mails are looked for with the utmost impatience. The Government, though anxious and nervous, are not disheartened, and as far as we can judge the authorities in India have not been deficient in the emergency. Canning writes in good spirits, and all accounts agree in reporting that he has done his work hitherto very well.   The discussions in Parliament have been on the whole creditable.   Disraeli came down to the House of Commons with a long set oration, in which he entered at great length into the causes of the present confusion, and the misgovernment and bad policy which had engendered it, and although his speech was able, and probably contained a great deal that was true, it was deemed (as it was) mischievous and ill-timed, and very ill received by the House.   He was rebuked with some asperity by Tom Baring, his own political adherent, and by Lord John Russell, who declared it to be the duty of the House to give every support to the Government in such a crisis.   In the House of Lords Ellenborough was as mischievous and ill-disposed as Disraeli in the Commons, and was no better received.   Granville administered to him a severe lecture, by no means ill done, and the House of Lords went with Granville.

Last week was passed at Goodwood, with fine weather, and the usual fête with the unusual accompaniment of foreign Royalties.   First the Comte de Paris for a night, and then the Queen of the Netherlands for two.   The young French Prince is good-humored and unpretending, the Queen is very gay, natural, and pleasing.   I renewed an acquaintance I had made with her at Ems many years ago.   It is a new feature in the present day the flitting about of Royal personages.   Besides these I have named, the Prince Napoleon has been finishing a tour through England and part of Ireland by a visit to Osborne, and the Emperor and Empress are coming to Osborne for a week.   Prince Albert has been to Brussels for the marriage of the Princess Charlotte, where he seems to have made his first experiment of the effect to be obtained from his newly-acquired title of " Prince Consort of England," as I see that he signed the marriage contract immediately after the Queen Marie Amélie, and before an Austrian Archduke who was present.

August 12*th.*—I was at Stoke on Saturday and Sunday, and went over to see Bulstrode ; surprised to find the place less *délabré*, and more capable of being restored than I expected.   I passed the first fifteen years of my life there, and don't know whether the place or myself is the most changed. To feed our curiosity during the intervals between the Indian mails, the newspapers, the " Times " especially, collect all the letters they can obtain, and publish them day by day.   We have had a success in China, but I always tremble for the consequences of our successes there, lest we should be seduced or compelled into making permanent settlements and further extensions of our Empire in the East. Parliament is approaching its close, and the Government ends the session with unimpaired strength, but depending entirely on Palmerston's life, for there is nobody else capable of leading the House of Commons. There are growing symptoms of independence on the part of the House in the shape of adverse votes every now and then, principally on matters of estimates.

August 20th.—I have read over the few preceding pages, and am disgusted to find how barren they are of interest and how little worth preserving. They show how entirely my social relations have ceased with all those friends and acquaintances from whom I have been in the habit of drawing the information which the earlier parts of this journal contain, and consequently my total ignorance of all political subjects. There was a time when I should have had a great deal to say upon passing events of interest or importance, but all that is gone by.

The visit of the Emperor Napoleon at Osborne seems to have been spent in discussing the affairs of the Principalities and patching up the quarrels of the Ambassadors at Constantinople. As far as outward appearances go we do not appear to have played a very brilliant part, and the Opposition papers think they have got a good case on which to twit Palmerston, but as I do not know what has really taken place, I abstain from expressing any opinion upon the conduct of our Government.

The session of Parliament has been prolonged beyond all expectation by the vehement and acrimonious debates upon the Divorce Bill in the House of Commons, which has been very ably and vigorously fought by Bethell on one side *cum quibusdam aliis*, and Gladstone, Walpole, and Heathcote on the other. The Opposition hoped by constant obstructions to wear out the patience of Palmerston and to get the Bill put off till next session. Palmerston, however, was firmly resolved not to submit to this, and when they found that he was so determined, they contented themselves with insisting upon certain amendments, which Palmerston thought it prudent to consent to, and the spirit of compromise and concession which the Government have lately evinced has softened in some degree the asperity of the debates, and at last enabled the Government to carry the Bill. Bethell, who has fought

the battle with great ability, is not a little disgusted at the
concessions to which he has been forced to consent, and has
done so with a solemn protest and warning with regard to
the exemption clause for the clergy, which the Government
have very reluctantly consented to, but on which Granville
assures me they had no option, and that if they had refused
to give way they would have infallibly been beaten upon it.
I dined at Richmond with Lord Lansdowne yesterday, to
meet the Duchess of Orleans and the Comte de Paris   I had
never seen her before.   She is plain, but pleasing, and with
very good manners.

August 21st.—The Divorce Bill having passed the House
of Commons, went up to the House of Lords yesterday, when
Lord Redesdale attempted to strangle it by a dodge, which
he was obliged to give up in consequence of the vigorous
attacks made upon him by the Ministerial side, who were
supported even by St. Leonards, and particularly by an indignant and effective speech made by Lord Lansdowne,
who, in spite of weakness and gout, from which he was
actually suffering, spoke with extraordinary spirit.   If Redesdale had persisted, and gone to a division, the Government
would probably have been beaten, and the labor of half the
session would have been thrown away.   As it is, there is to
be a fight on Monday next, the result of which depends on
which side can get the greatest number to come up from the
country to vote.

September 6th.—Went to Worsley on Thursday last, in
order to go from thence to see the Manchester Exhibition,
which is very pretty, but appears diminutive after the London and Sydenham Exhibitions.   Its principal attraction is
in the excellent collection of pictures ; it will be a failure in
a pecuniary point of view, but there are plenty of rich people
in Manchester able and willing to bear the expenses.   The
session closed very quietly, though not without some grumbling.   Some complained that Parliament should not continue to sit while the Indian troubles are going on with
undiminished force, others that the Queen should go to
Scotland ; but the Government have brought their labors
to a close very prosperously, and Palmerston continues as
powerful and as secure as ever.   There is no longer the
same enthusiasm there was for him, but there is a universal
impression that he is indispensable, and on the whole a
feeling of satisfaction and confidence in his administration.

Even I myself am compelled in candor to acknowledge that he does at least as well as anybody else would be likely to do, and no complaints can justly be made against the Government of any supineness in sending out adequate reinforcements to India. Lewis told me, just as Parliament was prorogued, that they were thoroughly impressed with the gravity of the case, and conscious of the danger, and that they were going to send out every man they could muster here or in the Colonies, and they have already despatched troops in great numbers with remarkable celerity.

They have made some Peers, of whom the most conspicuous is Macaulay, and I have not seen or heard any complaints of his elevation. Lord Lansdowne has declined the offered Dukedom, which I rather regret, for such a public recognition of his character and services during a long life would have been graceful and becoming, and the report of it elicited from all quarters expressions of satisfaction at such an honor having been so worthily conferred.

While Macaulay is thus ascending to the House of Peers, his old enemy and rival Croker has descended to the grave, very noiselessly and almost without observation, for he had been for some time so withdrawn from the world that he was nearly forgotten. He had lived to see all his predictions of ruin and disaster to the country completely falsified. He continued till the last year or two to exhale his bitterness and spite in the columns of the "Quarterly Review," but at last the Editor (who had long been sick of his contributions) contrived to get rid of him. I never lived in any intimacy with him, and seldom met him in society, but he certainly occupied a high place among the second-rate men of his time ; he had very considerable talents, great industry, with much information and a retentive memory. He spoke in Parliament with considerable force, and in society his long acquaintance with the world and with public affairs, and his stores of general knowledge made him entertaining, though he was too overbearing to be agreeable. He was particularly disliked by Macaulay, who never lost an opportunity of venting his antipathy by attacks upon him.

Holwood, September 10th.—I came here on Tuesday on a visit to the Chancellor.[1] This beautiful place formerly belonged to Mr. Pitt, and abounds in local recollections of

---

[1] [Lord Cranworth at this time occupied Holwood as a summer residence.]

the great Minister in the shape of "Pitt's Oak," "Pitt's Well," &c.   It is close to Hayes, where his father, the great Lord Chatham, lived and died.   Nobody is here but Pemberton Leigh.

I asked the Chancellor what was the real history of the Life Peerage last year, and he told me that it originated in his finding great inconvenience from himself and Lord St. Leonards frequently sitting together in the House of Lords without any third, and as St. Leonards invariably opposed his view of every case great injustice was often done to suitors, and he urged on Palmerston the expediency of giving them some assistance.   Palmerston said it would be a good opportunity for making some Life Peers.   Wensleydale was willing to retire from the Bench and to accept a Life Peerage, so it was determined to create him a Peer for life only, and they did this without the slightest idea that any objection would be made in any quarter.   He owned that he regretted this design had not been abandoned at once when the storm of opposition began.   I told him that I had no doubt there would have been no opposition if he had imparted the intentions of Government to some of the Law Lords, and obtained their acquiescence, for Lyndhurst would certainly not have objected, having himself told me that he meant to comply with Parke's request to him to introduce him to the House of Lords.   The Chancellor said this was very likely true, but that he had never liked the attempt to force it through the House of Lords.   He thought the opposition had originated with Campbell, who had probably forgotten that he had recorded his own opinion, in his "Lives of the Chancellors," that Life Peerages would be advisable in certain cases.

September 22*d*. — I am just returned from Doncaster, Bretby, and Wilby.   The Indian mail arrived on Monday last, just as I was starting for Doncaster.   The news it brought at first appeared rather good, but when it all came out it seemed so checkered with good and evil that it produced great despondency.   Still it is a curious circumstance (which I have heard no one else remark) that, with all the deep interest universally felt on account of this Sepoy war, not only as it regards our national interests, but out of feeling and sympathy for the vast numbers of our countrymen and women exposed to its horrors and dangers, it does not produce the same degree of enthusiasm as the Crimean War did, in which we had no real interest concerned, and which was only a gigantic folly on our part. People are very anxious about this war, and earnestly desire that the mutiny may be put down and punished, but they regard the war itself with aversion and horror, whereas they positively took pleasure in the war against Russia, and were ready to spend their last guinea in carrying it on. A subscription has been set on foot, but although there never was an occasion on which it might have been expected that vast sums would be subscribed, the contributions have been comparatively small in amount, and it seems probable that a much less sum will be produced for the relief of the Indian sufferers than the Patriotic Fund or any of the various subscriptions made for purposes connected with the Crimean War. I was so struck with the backwardness of the Government in rewarding General Havelock for his brilliant exploits, that I wrote to George Lewis and urged him to press his colleagues to confer some honor upon him and promote him.

I am on the point of starting for Balmoral, summoned for a Council to order *a day of humiliation.*

Gordon Castle, September 27th.—I left town on Tuesday afternoon, and slept that night at York, on Wednesday at Perth, and on Thursday posted to Balmoral, where I arrived between two and three o'clock. Granville, Panmure, and Ben Stanley formed the Council. Granville told me the Queen wished that the day appointed should be a Sunday, but Palmerston said it must be on a weekday, and very reluctantly she gave way. What made the whole thing more ridiculous was, that she gave a ball (to the gillies and tenants) the night before this Council. The outside of the new house at Balmoral, in the Scotch and French style, is pretty enough, but the inside has but few rooms, and those very small not uncomfortable, and very simply decorated ; the place and environs are pretty. In the afternoon I drove over to Invercauld with Phipps. On Friday morning came on here, by post, by rail, and by mail. Without any beauty, this is rather a fine place, and the house very comfortable.

September 28th.—Went to Elgin to see the fine old ruin of the Cathedral, which is very grand, and must have been magnificent. It was built in the beginning of the thirteenth century, burnt down, and rebuilt in the fourteenth. I see they have done all I wanted to have done for General Havelock.   He has got a good service pension, is made Major-General and K. C. B.

Dunrobin Castle, October 2d.—I came here from Gordon Castle on Wednesday, by sea from Burghead to the Little Ferry, a very tiresome way of travelling, the delays being detestable.   Have long been most desirous of seeing this place, which has quite equalled my expectations, for it is a most princely possession, and the Castle exceedingly beautiful and moreover very comfortable.   I start for London tomorrow morning with a long journey before me.

The Indian news of this week as bad and promises as ill as well can be, and I expect worse each mail that comes.   We are justly punished for our ambition and encroaching spirit, but it must be owned we struggle gallantly for what we have perhaps unjustly acquired.   Europe behaves well to us, for though we have made ourselves universally odious by our insolence and our domination, and our long habit of bullying all the world, nobody triumphs over us in the hour of our distress, and even Russia, who has no cause to feel anything but ill will toward us, evinces her regret and sympathy in courteous terms.   Whatever the result of this contest may be, it will certainly absorb all our efforts and occupy our full strength and power, so that we shall not be able to take any active or influential part in European affairs for some time to come.   The rest of the Great Powers will have it in their power to settle everything as seems meet to them, without troubling themselves about us and our opinions.   For the present we are reduced to the condition of an insignificant Power.   It is certain that if this mutiny had taken place two years earlier, we could not have engaged at all in the Russian War.

London, October 6th.—I left Dunrobin after breakfast on Saturday morning, 3d inst., and arrived in London on Monday (yesterday) at 11 A. M.   My journey was after this wise : We (i. e., Mr. Marshall of the Life Guards, an aide-de-camp of Lord Carlisle's, who travelled from Dunrobin with me) got into the mail at Golspie and took our places to Inverness.   At Tain, the first stage, we walked on, leaving the coach to overtake us.   After walking three miles, and no coach coming, we got alarmed, and, on enquiry of the first man we fell in with, found we had come the wrong way, and that the mail had gone on.   We started on our return to Tain, and falling in with a good Samaritan in the shape of a banker in that place, who was driving in the opposite direction, he took us up in his gig, and drove us back to the inn, where we took post, and followed the mail to Inverness, where we arrived an hour after it.   There we slept, and at five minutes before five on Sunday morning we were in the mail again, and arrived at Perth at six o'clock, making 117 miles in thirteen hours.   In twenty minutes more we were in the mail train, and reached Euston Square safe and sound at eleven o'clock, doing the distance between Perth and London in seventeen and a half hours.   I have seen a vast deal of very beautiful scenery of all sorts, but the most beautiful of all (and I never saw anything more lovely anywhere) is the road from Blair Athol to Dunkeld, which includes the pass of Killiecrankie.

I fell in with Granville and Clarendon at Watford, and got into their carriage.   Of course my first enquiries were about India, when they told me that the general impression was not quite so unfavorable as that produced by the first telegraphic intelligence.   Clarendon said that if it was possible for Havelock to maintain himself a short time longer, and that reinforcements arrived in time to save the beleaguered places, the tide would turn and Delhi would fall; but, if he should be crushed, Agra, Lucknow, and other threatened places would fall, with renewals of the Cawnpore horrors, and in that case the unlimited spread of the mutiny would be irrepressible, Madras and Bombay would revolt, all the scattered powers would rise up everywhere, and all would be lost.   We both agreed that the next would probably be decisive accounts for weal or for woe.   I told Granville afterward that I was glad to see they had called out more militia, but regretted they had not done more, when he said that he was inclined to take the same view, from which it was evident to me that there has been difference of opinion in the Cabinet as to the extent to which the calling out of the militia should be carried.   I urged him to press on his colleagues a more extensive measure.   It is evident that public opinion will back them up in gathering together as great a force as possible in this emergency, regardless of expense, and at all events the course of this Government is not embarrassed and annoyed as that of another Government was three years ago in reference to the Crimean War.   As a very true article in a very sensible paper set forth, the difference between then and now is, that the Government of

Palmerston has fair play, while that of Lord Aberdeen never had it.   The Press, and public opinion goaded and inflamed by the Press, treated the latter with the most flagrant injustice, while Palmerston and the whole Government, out of regard for him, are treated with every sort of consideration and confidence.

London, October 19th.—I spent last week at Newmarket; the details of the last Indian news which arrived there put people in better spirits, but they were too much occupied with the business of the place to think much about India. Returned to town on Friday, and went to The Grove yesterday; had some talk with Clarendon, who said Palmerston was very off-hand in his views of Indian affairs, and had jumped to the conclusion that the Company must be extinguished.   At the Cabinet on Friday last he said, "They need not meet again for some time, but they must begin to think of how to deal with India when the revolt was put down.   Of course everybody must see that the India Company must be got rid of, and Vernon Smith would draw up a scheme in reference thereto."   This brief announcement did not meet with any response, and there was no disposition to come to such rapid and peremptory conclusions, but it seemed not worth while to raise any discussion about it then.

Clarendon then talked of the Court, and confirmed what I had heard before, going into more detail.   He said that the manner in which the Queen in her own name, but with the assistance of the Prince, exercised her functions, was exceedingly good, and well became her position and was eminently useful.   She held each Minister to the discharge of his duty and his responsibility to her, and constantly desired to be furnished with accurate and detailed information about all important matters, keeping a record of all the reports that were made to her, and constantly recurring to them, e.g. she would desire to know what the state of the Navy was, and what ships were in readiness for active service, and generally the state of each, ordering returns to be submitted to her from all the arsenals and dockyards, and again weeks or months afterward referring to these returns, and desiring to have everything relating to them explained and accounted for, and so throughout every department.   In this practice Clarendon told me he had encouraged her strenuously.   This is what none of her predecessors ever did, and it is in fact the act of Prince Albert, who is to all intents and purposes King, only acting entirely in her name. All his views and notions are those of a Constitutional Sovereign, and he fulfils the duties of one, and at the same time makes the Crown an entity, and discharges the functions which properly belong to the Sovereign. I told Clarendon that I had been told the Prince had upon many occasions rendered the most important services to the Government, and had repeatedly prevented their getting into scrapes of various sorts. He said it was perfectly true, and that he had written some of the ablest papers he had ever read.

Clarendon said he had recently been very much pleased with the Duke of Cambridge, who had shown a great deal of sense and discretion, and a very accurate knowledge of the details of his office, and that he was a much better Commander-in-Chief than Hardinge. He had been lately summoned to the Cabinet on many occasions, and had given great satisfaction there. Clarendon talked of Vernon Smith, of whom he has no elevated opinion, but still thinks him not without merit, and that at this moment it would not be easy to replace him by some one clearly better fitted. He takes pains, is rather clever, and did better in the House of Commons than anybody gave him credit for last session ; he makes himself well informed upon everything about his office, and is never at a loss to answer any questions that are put to him, and to answer them satisfactorily.

November 2d.—Gout in my hand has prevented my writing anything, and adding some trifling particulars to what I have written above. In the meantime has arrived the news of the capture of Delhi, but though we have received it now a week ago we are still unacquainted with the particulars. All the advantages of the electric telegraph are dearly paid for by the agonies of suspense which are caused by the long intervals between the arrival of general facts and of their particular details. It still remains to be seen whether the results of this success turn out on the whole to be as advantageous as it appears to be brilliant. The Press goes on attacking Canning with great asperity and injustice, and nobody here defends him. Though I am not a very intimate or particular friend of his, I think him so unfairly and ungenerously treated that I mean to make an effort to get him such

redress as the case admits of, and the only thing which oc-
curs to me is that Palmerston, as head of the Government,
should take the opportunity of the Lord Mayor's dinner to
vindicate him, and assume the responsibility of his acts.   His
"Clemency" proclamation, as it is stupidly and falsely called,
was, I believe, not only proper and expedient, but necessary,
and I expect he will be able to vindicate himself completely
from all the charges which the newspapers have brought
against him, but in the meantime they will have done him
all the mischief they can.   Among other things Clarendon
told me at The Grove, he said, in reference to Canning's war
against the press, that the license of the Indian press was
intolerable, not of the native press only, but the English in
Bengal.   Certain papers are conducted there by low, dis-
affected people, who publish the most gross, false, and malignant attacks on the Government, which are translated into
the native languages, and read extensively in the native regiments, and among the natives generally, and that to put
down this pest was an absolute necessity.

November 4th.—I have been speaking to Granville about
Canning, and urged him to move Palmerston to stand forth
in his defence at the Lord Mayor's dinner on the 9th.   This
morning he received a very strong and pressing letter from
Clanricarde, in the same sense in which I had been urging
him, and a very good letter, and this he is going to send to
Palmerston.   Clanricarde is struck, as I am, with the fact
that nobody and no newspaper has said a word in Canning's
favor, and he sees as I have done all the damage which has
already been done to him by the long and uncontradicted
course of abuse and reproach with which the press has
teemed.

Hatchford, November 8th.—Granville made a speech in
defence of Canning, at a dinner given at the Mansion House
to the Duke of Cambridge.   He writes me word it was
"rather uphill work," and I was told it was not very well
received, but nevertheless it produced an effect, and it acted
as a check upon the "Times," which without retracting
(which it never does) has considerably mitigated its violence.
It was the first word that has been said for Canning in public, and it has evidently been of great use to him.

The most interesting event during the last few days is
the failure of the attempted launch of the big ship (now called
"Leviathan"), and it is not a little remarkable that all the

great experiments recently made have proved failures. Besides this one of the ship, there was a few weeks ago the cracking of the bell (Big Ben) for the Houses of Parliament, and not long before that the failure of the submarine telegraph in the attempt to lay it down in the sea. The bell will probably be replaced without much difficulty, but it is at present doubtful whether it will be found possible to launch the ship at all, and whether the telegraphic cable can ever be completed.

November 10*th*.—Palmerston pronounced a glowing eulogium on Canning last night at the Lord Mayor's dinner, which will infallibly stop the current of abuse against him. It has already turned the "Times." He seems to have been induced to do this by the great pressure brought to bear on him, for otherwise he had no desire to stand forth and oppose public opinion and the press; but Clarendon, Lansdowne, and others all urged him strenuously to support Canning, and he did it handsomely enough. His speech in other respects was an injudicious one, full of jactance and bow-wow, but well enough calculated to draw cheers from a miscellaneous audience.

November 11*th*.—I was told yesterday that Palmerston's swaggering speech would produce a bad effect in France, and those whom I have spoken to agree in thinking it very ill-timed and in very bad taste. It is the more objectionable because he might have said something very different that would have been very becoming and true. He might have observed upon the remarkable good taste and forbearance which had been so conspicuous in all foreign nations toward us, even those who may be supposed to be least friendly to us, or those whom we have most outraged by our violent and insulting language or conduct. It is at once creditable to other countries and honorable to us that no disposition has been shown in any quarter to act differently toward us, or to avail themselves of what they may suppose to be our weakness and difficulty; but, on the contrary, the same consideration and deference has been shown to us as if there had been no Indian outbreak to absorb our resources. Our position in Europe is not only as high as ever, but no one shows any disposition to degrade or diminish it; and while this is a gratifying homage to us and a flattering recognition of our power, it is, or at least ought to be, calculated to inspire us with amicable sentiments, and to be an inducement

17

to us to depart from the insolent and offensive tone which
has so long prevailed here, and which has made England
universally an object of aversion. It was of course impossible that some expressions should not be given here and
there and now and then to such feelings, but on the whole
we have no reason to complain, but much the contrary ; not
even in Russia, whose power and pride we have so deeply
wounded, and whom we have so outraged by every topic and
expression of insult and injury which the bitterest hatred
could suggest, has there been anything like asperity, or any
rejoicing over our misfortunes.

Frognal, November 14*th.*—The news of the capture of
Delhi and the relief of Lucknow excited a transport of delight
and triumph, and everybody jumped to the conclusion that
the Indian contest was virtually at an end. Granville told
me he thought there would be no more fighting, and that
the work was done. I was not so sanguine, and though I
thought the result of the contest was now secure, I thought
we should still have a great deal on our hands and much
more fighting to hear of before the curtain could drop. But
I was not prepared to hear the dismal news which arrived
to-day, and which has so cruelly damped the public joy and
exultation. It appears that Havelock is in great danger and
the long suffering garrison of Lucknow not yet out of their
peril, for the victory of Havelock had not been complete, the
natives were gathering round the small British force in vast
numbers, and unless considerable reinforcements could be
speedily brought up, the condition of the British, both
military and civilians, of men, women, and children, would
soon again be one of excessive danger.

The Grove, November 15*th.*—I talked with Clarendon about
the Government letter to the Bank [1] and the state of financial
affairs. It is evident that Clarendon knows very little about
these questions, and takes very little part in them, but he

---

[1] [On the 12th of November a letter was addressed to the Governors of the
Bank of England by Lord Palmerston and Sir George Cornewall Lewis, the
Chancellor of the Exchequer, empowering the Bank to exceed the limits prescribed by the Bank Act of 1844 (if necessary) to meet the demands for discount
and advances on approved security. This measure was rendered necessary by
the extensive failures which had recently taken place, and the severe pressure
on the money market. On the 4th November discount had advanced to 9 per
cent. The Issue Department made over to the Banking Department two millions in excess of the statutable amount, of which about one million was advanced to the public. On the 1st December the whole amount was repaid.
Parliament was summoned to pass a Bill of Indemnity, and public confidence
was restored.]

told me one curious fact. A letter which appeared about a week ago, addressed by the Emperor of the French to his Finance Minister, made a great sensation here. In it the Emperor deprecated all empirical measures for the purpose of meeting the prevailing difficulties, financial and commercial, at Paris. About a week before this Clarendon received a letter from Cowley, who said that he had been conversing with the Emperor and with Walewski on these matters, and Walewski had begged him (by the desire of the Emperor) to write to Clarendon and request the advice of the English Government as to the course he should adopt. Clarendon said that George Lewis was out of town, but as there could be no delay, he sent his private secretary to the Governor and Deputy Governor of the Bank, and requested their advice and opinion. They said it was so important they would go down to the Foreign Office, which they did, when they told Clarendon that their advice was that the Emperor should insist on the Bank of France following as nearly as possible the example of the Bank of England, to keep their rates of discount high, and to avoid all rash experiments of any kind. He wrote to Cowley accordingly, who communicated the answer, and judging from the dates it would appear that the Emperor's letter was the consequence of the advice so tendered. But Clarendon seemed to think that the appearance of the Government letter was rather awkward, and would appear to the French Government very inconsistent with our communication to them. However, it will probably be easy to afford satisfactory explanations on this head. The measure itself here has apparently had the desired success, and they hope the panic and distress will gradually subside, without any more mischief happening. Lewis thinks that the best mode of dealing with Peel's Act will be to retain it, but to give a power to the Queen in Council to relax it in the same manner as has been now twice done by the interposition of Government, whenever an urgent necessity should arise, and I suppose this is the course that will be adopted, though not without a great deal of discussion and diversity of opinion. I have hitherto said nothing about the very curious and important state of affairs in America and in this country, because I am too ignorant of financial questions to talk about them, and I have not been apprised of any facts beyond what all the world knows that it was worth while to record, but this anecdote of the French

Government and our own appears sufficiently curious to have a place in this book.

November 17th.—A council was held yesterday at Windsor to summon Parliament, where I found the ministers much dejected at the news from India. There was a letter from Colin Campbell, expressing great alarm at the position of Outram and Havelock, whom he thought to be in a great scrape, though without any fault of theirs, and there was also a report from Sir John Lawrence that affairs were in a ticklish state in the Punjaub, and expressing a great anxiety for reinforcements, which he had very little prospect of getting; in short the apparently bright sky in which we were rejoicing only a few days ago seems to be obscured by black clouds, and the great result to be as uncertain as ever.

I met Clarendon at dinner this evening, when he told me that affairs were in a bad state in the City, and that Lewis had received very unsatisfactory accounts, so that it is not clear that the Government letter is producing the good which at first seemed to be following from it. There is a good deal of uneasiness in the financial and commercial world and no confidence. The very prudence of the trading community in arresting the course of production is becoming a source of distress, for already vast numbers of people are out of employment, or working short time with reduced wages. The prices of everything are falling, consumption will be diminished, and the revenue must be diminished likewise, while our expenses cannot but be increased by the war. A general cry is getting up for making India pay for the expense of this Indian war, which, even supposing it to be just and reasonable, will make the ultimate settlement of the Indian question more difficult, and a measure little calculated to reconcile the native population to our rule. Then, as if we had not embarrassments enough on our hands, America is going to add to them, for President Buchanan, who hates England with a mortal antipathy, threatens to repudiate the Clayton-Bulwer Treaty, upon the pretence that we have not abided by its conditions, and if he proposes to the Senate to declare it null and void, the Senate will do so at his bidding. This would be a flagrant violation of good faith, and of the obligations by which all civilized nations consider themselves bound. If this event happens, it will place us in a very perplexing dilemma, especially after Palmerston's absurd bravado and confident boastings of our

power, for we are not in a condition to enable us to take a
high line corresponding with that lofty language, and we shall
have to eat humble pie and submit to the affront.   Hitherto
all other nations and governments have behaved to us as well
and as respectfully as we could desire, and far more than we
deserve ; but if America bullies us in one instance, and we
are found pocketing the affront, it is by no means improbable that other governments will begin to take advantage of
our weakness, and adopt toward us a conduct injurious to
our interests or a tone galling to our pride.[1]

November 25th.—Last week I went to Ampthill from
Wednesday till Saturday ; on Saturday to The Grove, with
the Duke of Bedford, the Lewises, Charles Villiers, and Ben
Stanley.   The Duke of Bedford told me he was very uneasy
about his brother John, who seemed in an irritable frame of
mind, and disposed to wage war against the Government
when Parliament meets.[2]   He told Sir George Grey the other
day that they would not find him friendly.   Clarendon told
me of a conversation he had recently had with the Queen
à propos of Palmerston's health, concerning which Her Majesty was very uneasy, and what could be done in the not impossible contingency of his breaking down.   It is a curious
change from what we saw a few years ago, that she is
become almost affectionately anxious about the health of
Palmerston, whose death might then have been an event to
be hailed with satisfaction.   Clarendon said she might well
be solicitous about it, for if anything happened to Palmerston she would be placed in the greatest difficulty.   She said
that in such a case she should look to *him,* and expect him
to replace Palmerston, on which Clarendon said he was glad
she had broached the subject, as it gave him an opportunity
of saying what he was very anxious to impress upon her
mind, and that was the absolute impossibility of his undertaking such an office, against which he enumerated various
objections.   He told her that Derby could not form a
Government, and if she had the misfortune to lose Palmer-

---

[1] [These apprehensions were unfounded. Mr. Buchanan did not seek to
abrogate the Clayton-Bulwer Treaty with reference to the eventual construction
of a passage through the Isthmus of Central America, and the neutral character
of that undertaking, which is now said to be in progress by the Canal of Panama,
has remained unchanged to the present time.]

[2] [Lord John Russell had taken office in Lord Palmerston's first Administration as Colonial Secretary, but he resigned on June 13, 1855, and remained out
of office.]

ston, nothing remained for her to do but to send for John Russell and put him at the head of the Government. She expressed her great repugnance to this, and especially to make him Prime Minister. Clarendon then entreated her to conquer her repugnance, and to be persuaded that it would never do to offer him anything else, which he neither would nor could accept; that the necessity was to have a man who could lead the House of Commons, and there was no other but him ; that Lord John had consented to take a subordinate office under Lord Aberdeen, who was his senior in age, and occupied a high position, but he would never consent to take office under him (Clarendon), and the proposal he would consider as an insult. For every reason, therefore, he urged her, if driven to apply to him at all, to do it handsomely, to place the whole thing in his hands, and to give him her full confidence and support. He appears to have convinced her that this is the proper course, and he gave me to understand that if Lord John acts with prudence and moderation all the present Government would accept him for their head, and Clarendon is so anxious that this should be the turn affairs should take, that he urged me to talk to the Duke of Bedford about it, and to get him to exert all his influence with Lord John to conduct himself in such a manner as shall conduce to his restoration to office at a future time. I had only time to exchange a few words with the Duke before we parted the next morning, and we agreed that I should write him a letter on the subject which he may show to Lord John if he sees fit to do so. I went to Wrotham on Monday, and yesterday penned an epistle to be shown to Lord John, in which I set forth his position, and dilated on the great importance to himself and to the country of his conducting himself with patience and forbearance, and of his abstaining from any such vexatious opposition to the Government as might render his future union with them impossible. It remains to be seen whether my remonstrance (which I tried to couch in terms that would not be disagreeable to Lord John) will produce any effect.[1]

[1] [These speculations are curious, but happily the apprehensions caused by the supposed state of Lord Palmerston's health were unfounded, for with the short interval of the second Derby Government in 1858 and 1859, he continued to hold office and to discharge the duties of Prime Minister with his accustomed vigor and success until his death in October, 1865, when he was succeeded by Lord Russell. At this particular moment (1857) the latent danger of the Government lay, not in the failing health of Lord Palmerston, but in an unforseen

Hitchinbrook, November 28*th.*—I came here to-day from Riddlesworth, where I have now been for the first time for twenty years. I received there two letters from the Duke of Bedford, the first telling me he should show, and the second that he had shown, my letter to Lord John. He received it graciously, saying he agreed with almost all I said, but that it was easier to give than it was to take such advice, and that he had been blamed by certain persons for not having given more opposition to the Government last year on some questions than he had done, especially to the Persian War; but I rather infer on the whole that my letter made some impression on him, though it remains to be seen how much.

The last news from India is as good as could be expected, and the current there has evidently turned. I met Martin Smith (Indian Director) at Riddlesworth, and had much talk with him about Indian affairs. It is clear that the Company do not mean to submit to be summarily extinguished without a struggle. He told me that with regard to the great subject, the sending out troops by sailing vessels instead of by steamers, which is made matter of bitter reproach against the Directors, the fault lay entirely with the Government. The Directors wanted to send 10,000 men across Egypt, and the Government would not do it. They proposed it formally to the Board of Control, who referred it to the Foreign Office, and Clarendon said it could not be done on account of certain political considerations which rendered it inexpedient, so that if the Directors could have had their own way the thing would have been done. There may have been good grounds for the refusal of the Government, but in this instance the double Government was productive only of a sacrifice of Indian to Imperial interests, and it will not be easy to draw from this transaction any argument in favor of abolishing the East India Company and the Leadenhall Street Administration.

London, December 2*d.*—Yesterday morning Lord Sydney received a letter from Lady Canning, who said that although undoubtedly many horrible things had happened in India, the exaggeration of them had been very great, and that she had read for the first time in the English newspapers stories of atrocities of which she had never heard at Calcutta, and

occurrence which caused the unexpected defeat of Lord Palmerston's Ministry within four months of this date, and the accession of Lord Derby and his friends to office.]

that statements made in India had turned out to be pure inventions and falsehoods.   Yet our papers publish everything
that is sent to them without caring whether it may be true
or false, and the credulous public swallow it all without the
slightest hesitation and doubt.   Shaftesbury too, who is a
prodigious authority with the public, and who has all the
religious and pseudo-religious people at his back, does his
utmost to make the case out to be as bad as possible and to
excite the rage and indignation of the masses to the highest
pitch.   He is not satisfied with the revolting details with
which the Press has been teeming, but complains that more
of them have not been detailed and described, and that the
particulars of mutilation and violation have not been more
copiously and circumstantially given to the world.   I have
never been able to comprehend what his motives are for talking in this strange and extravagant strain, but it is no doubt
something connected with the grand plan of Christianizing
India, in the furtherance of which the High Church and the
Low Church appear to be bidding against each other ; and
as their united force will in all probability be irresistible, so
they will succeed in making any Government in India impossible.

B—— showed me the Draft of the Queen's Speech this
evening after dinner.   Cobbett in his Grammar produces
examples of bad English taken from Kings' Speeches, which
he says might be expected to be the best written, but generally are the worst written documents in the world.   It would
be difficult to produce any former Speech more deplorably
composed than this one.   Long sentences, full of confusion,
and of which the meaning is not always clear, and some
faults of grammar for which a schoolboy would be whipped.
B—— was so struck by one I pointed out that he said he
would beg Palmerston to alter it.   If this Speech escapes
severe criticism and ridicule I shall be much surprised, as I
am already that George Lewis, who has so lately been a literary critic, and is a correct writer himself, should have allowed it to pass in its present shape, and indeed the sentence
he himself put in about his own business is as bad as any
other part of it.

I have no idea what they mean to propose about the Bank
Charter Act, but if it be what Lewis told me some time ago,
to give the Queen the power of suspending the Act by Order
in Council, I much doubt if they will carry such a proposal,

and it appears to me on reflection thoroughly unconstitutional, and as such I expect it will be vehemently attacked by all the opponents and the quasi-opponents of Government, and indeed by all except those who are prepared to follow Palmerston with blind submission, and to vote for anything rather than allow him to be put in jeopardy. John Russell, for instance, would hardly be able to resist the temptation of falling foul of such a proposal, though he would approve of their having followed a precedent which he had himself set in a case somewhat similar, though in some respects less urgent.

CHAPTER XV.

London, December 4th, 1857.—Parliament opened yesterday, very quietly, and at present a quiet session seems probable, but such appearances are often fallacious. The most alarming consideration is the probability of a very hard and hungry winter for the working classes, vast numbers of people being already out of employment. I met Sir James Shuttleworth yesterday, who knows a great deal about Lancashire, where he lives, and he told me that though the distress was considerable and threatening to increase, the conduct of the people was admirable. There was no disaffection or bad feeling toward the upper classes and employers; they semed to have greatly improved in good sense and reflection, and were satisfied of the sympathy felt for them, and the disposition entertained by the rich to do all in their power to alleviate the distress of the poor. And he stated (what seemed to me a curious fact) that they preferred that the

time of working should be shortened, or even mills closed,
rather than a general reduction in the rate of wages. This
moral condition of the laboring classes is a most satisfactory
sign of the times.

The Duke of Bedford has just been here, and tells me
Lord John is in a better frame of mind, and has already done
two sensible things. He has given notice to some of his
supporters that he will have nothing to do with the organisation of any party, and he has responded to an invitation of
Vernon Smith's by a promise to impart to him his opinion
and advice upon Indian affairs, and the best mode of providing for the future government of that country.

December 6th.—John Russell has begun well in the House
of Commons and *si sic omnia* he will put himself in a good
position, but it is impossible to rely upon him. At present
his disposition to the Government appears friendly. I had
a conversation about him and his future relations with
the Government last night with B——. I infer from what
dropped from him that he thinks the probability of Palmerston's breaking down is not a remote and unlikely one. I
do not think he considers him broken in health, but that he
thinks the strength of his intellect is impaired, and that he
begins to show signs of decay to those who have the means of
observing them. He particularly noticed the failure of his
memory, and he said, what I have no doubt is true, that he
will never be himself conscious, still less acknowledge, that
his faculties are less vigorous and active than they were.
What the nature and amount of the decay in him is I know
not, and they will not say, but from the uneasy feeling, and
these speculations as to future contingencies among his colleagues, I am sure they are prepared for something. B——
said if the case occurred there were only two men who could
be Minister, Derby or Clarendon, and he fancies that John
Russell might be induced to take office under Clarendon, and
he does not believe that Clarendon really means what he says
when he expresses his extreme reluctance to take the post,
or that he would not in reality prefer it even to the Foreign
Office. He treats his scruples as a sort of *nolo episcopari*, in
which I think he is partially, but not entirely, right. There
can be no doubt that in the present state of affairs it is much
to be desired that Palmerston should be able to go on. I
was amused by a trifling incident, so very Palmerstonian,
told me the other day. I have already alluded to the bad

writing in the Queen's Speech, and it seems one phrase was criticised and altered in the Cabinet, but when he got back to his office he altered the alteration, and made it as it was before. I am not sure that the alteration was not the one suggested by B—— upon the strength of my criticism, and that Palmerston declined to alter the passage.

December 7th.—I called on Lord Grey in the morning and dined with Lyndhurst in the evening, and had much talk with both of them about the pending questions, Reform, India, Bank Act. Lord Grey is bringing out a book upon Reform. Lyndhurst is decidedly against any strong and subversive measure about India, and is for improving and not upsetting the present system. Public opinion, led by the Press, has hitherto leant to the dissolution of the Company and the Directorial Government ; but as time advances and the extreme difficulty of concocting another system becomes apparent, people begin to dread the idea of destroying an ancient system without any certainty of a better one replacing it, and I think there is a general feeling of alarm at the notion of the Indian Empire being placed under the direction of such a man as Vernon Smith ; more, indeed, than is quite just and called for, as his talents, though of a second-rate calibre, are not so low as is supposed, and he is not the cipher in his office he is thought to be, but is well enough acquainted with all its details, and always able to explain everything to the Cabinet clearly and correctly. But these merits, which are those of a diligent clerk, are far from being sufficient to qualify him for having the direction of an office which circumstances have rendered by far the most important and difficult in the whole Government. Till recently the Board of Control has been looked upon as a very subordinate department, and one of mere routine, which anybody might fill. I remember when John Russell offered it to Graham some years ago, he treated the proposal as an insult.

December 8th.—I went to the House of Lords last night and heard for the first time Ellenborough speak—an admirable style of speaking. It was a good night for Canning. The "Times" has turned right round ,and defends him, finding the Government are in earnest in doing so. The account of Lucknow just come by telegram is very alarming, and keeps one in a state of nervous excitement, difficult to describe.

London, December 17*th.*—Though the last advices from
India were satisfactory as far as they went, it is generally
understood that the next mail must bring the account of a
bloody battle at or near Lucknow, in which, though no one
doubts that the British will be victorious, it is certain that
there will be great loss of life.   Sanguine people and the
Press with hardly any exception, imagine that this anticipated victory will terminate the contest and leave only some
straggling conflicts to go on for a short time longer, ending
by a speedy suppression of the rebellion.   In this expectation
I do not share, but, on the contrary, believe it will be a pro-
tracted affair, not indeed doubtful in its ultimate result, but
which will cost us much time and money and many men, for
all who know anything of the matter tell us that the wear
and tear in India is enormous, and that a continual stream
of reinforcements must be poured into the country to keep
the army in a state of efficiency.   Captain Lowe, lately aide-
de-camp to poor George Anson, and who was in the storm
of Delhi, an intelligent officer, confirms all these notions,
and he says that nothing can be more inexpedient than the
scheme propounded here with great confidence, of forming
the native force, on which we are hereafter to rely, of Sikhs
instead of Hindoos.   He says that inasmuch as they are very
brave and excellent soldiers, it would only be to place ourselves in a state of far greater danger and uncertainty, for
though the Sikhs have proved very faithful to us, and rendered excellent service, it is impossible to predict how long
this humor may last, and whether circumstances may not
arise to induce them to throw off our yoke and assert their
own independence.   It is marvellous and providential that
on this occasion the Sikhs were disposed to side with us instead of against us, for if they had taken the latter course, it
would have been all up and nothing could have saved us.
A propos of this consideration he told me a curious anecdote.
A Sikh was talking to a British officer in a very friendly way,
and he said, "Don't you think it very strange that we, who
were so recently fighting against you, should be now fighting
with you?   And should you be very much surprised if a
year or two hence you should see us fighting against you
again?"
    Disraeli called on me a day or two ago, when we had a
political chat.   He talked with much contempt of the present
Government, except of George Lewis, of whom he spoke in

the highest terms.   He said Palmerston's popularity was of
a negative character, and, rather more from the unpopularity
of every other public man than from any peculiar attachment to him ; he talked bitterly of Derby's having declined
to take the Government in 1855, which he seemed to consider as an irreparable blow to his party.   He is evidently
not without hopes that the Government may find themselves
in some inextricable difficulty about their Reform Bill, and
thinks they will be incapable of concocting an India Bill
which will go down with the country.   He does not appear
to have made up his mind what course to take on the Indian
question, and it is evident that at present the Tory party
have decided on nothing.   The Cabinet has committed the
scheme of Reform to a select number of its members, as was
done in 1830, but what they are doing about India I do not
know.   There is certainly a difference of opinion amongst
them, as there no doubt is about Reform, but as little doubt
that they are all agreed upon not letting their conflicting
opinions break up the Government.

December 21st.—I called on George Lewis the day before
yesterday and had a long talk with him.   He told me that
Palmerston had given notice to the Chairs that the Government had come to the resolution of bringing in a Bill to put
an end to their dominion, and that the plan was to have an
Indian Secretary of State with a Council, and the Council to
have the distribution of the patronage.   I was surprised to
hear him say that he saw no difficulty in the settlement of
the Indian question, either in passing it through Parliament
or in producing a good measure which would work better
than the present system, and he said he wished the other
great question they had upon their hands, that of Reform,
was as easy, but that the more they went into it, the more
difficult it appeared.   I need not enter into the details
which we discussed, as the Bill is not yet settled, and in a
few weeks more it will come forth.   He said that the great
misfortune was their having thrown out Locke King's motion
this year, for if they had done what they had originally
intended with regard to it, they should in all probability
have laid the question at rest for ten years longer at least,
and he then told me a curious anecdote on this matter,
giving an example of strange levity and incapacity on the part
of the Government.   When Locke King brought forward
his motion, it was considered in the Cabinet, and they came

to a unanimous resolution to let his bill be read a second
time, but to oppose the amount of his franchise in Committee
and raise it from 10l. to 20l., which they had no doubt they
should carry.   On the very night on which the question was
to be moved Lewis went down to the House of Commons
with this understanding, never dreaming that any alteration
was contemplated, when George Grey said to him, "You
know Palmerston is going to oppose Locke King's motion"
(for leave to bring in his Bill).   Lewis expressed his surprise, and asked what had happened to set aside the unanimous agreement come to in the Cabinet.   Grey said there
had been a dinner at Charles Wood's, at which certain
Ministers were present (whom he named, but I forget if
Palmerston was one), when the question had been discussed,
and the result had been to make a change in their opinions,
and Palmerston had agreed that Locke King should be
opposed *in limine*.   This Lewis told me he regarded as a
fatal error, to which they owed the dilemma in which they
found themselves placed.   But what struck me most was the
mode of doing business of such importance, and that there
should not be found a single individual to protest against
it, and to resign his office rather than to submit to be so
dragged through the mire ; but the present doctrine seems
to be that *Palmerston's* Government must be held together at
any price, and this is the more curious when it is obvious to
me that his colleagues, while conscious of the difficulty of
doing without him, have an exceedingly mean opinion of his
intrinsic value.   I told Lewis all that Disraeli had said to
me about him as well as about Palmerston, when he expressed his surprise at the manner in which Disraeli had
spoken of *him*, for which he was not at all prepared, but said
he estimated Palmerston at his real worth.   He told me of
Harrowby's resignation on account of his health, and that
his place had been offered to Clanricarde, and wanted to
know if I thought Clanricarde would be objected to.[1]   We
talked of the stories which John Russell had heard of, about
our being on bad terms with France, and the Emperor
Napoleon out of humor with us, and of Palmerston's meditating hostile designs against Russia, all of which he said
were pure fabrications, as we were on the best terms with

[1] [The Earl of Harrowby held the office of Lord Privy Seal. He was succeeded by the Marquis of Clanricarde, which proved a very unpopular appointment.]

France, and Palmerston entertained no hostile designs against Russia or any other Power. We both agreed that our hands were too full to think of any fresh quarrels or aggressions, and I found him of the same opinion as myself about our arbitrary and dictatorial system, and of the mischief it had done, and as much with reference to the slave trade as any other question.

I told him of the slave case just decided in the Judicial Committee of the Privy Council, and of the sum of money it would cost our Government, to say nothing of the mortification. He said no doubt Palmerston would proclaim it to be a wrong decision, and would defend the Foreign Office and all the agents who had been concerned in the outrage.[1]

Hatchford, December 26th.—Christmas Day, usually coming in frost and snow, was yesterday like a fine day in May, the glorious weather being in unison with the general gladness at the good news from India and the tidings that Lucknow, with its wounded and its long suffering band of women and children, had been relieved at last, and for good and all. This news arrived on Christmas Eve, to make the day itself as merry as it is proverbially said to be.

Brougham has taken Normanby's book, "A Year of Revolution," under his protection, for what reason nobody can divine. He wrote to Mrs. Austin, begging she would exert her influence with her nephew Reeve to get it noticed favorably in the "Edinburgh Review," that it was a good book, had the merit of being true, and that it was much approved by Louis Napoleon, who had encouraged its being translated. I had imagined Brougham was improved, but it is evident from his conduct on this occasion that he is the same man he ever was. The book contains page after page of matter the most offensive to Guizot and to Louis Philippe and his family, with which everybody is revolted, and its malice is not redeemed by literary merit or attractiveness in any shape.

---

[1] [This refers to the case of the "Newport," a vessel which had been condemned by the Vice-Admiralty Court at St. Helena for alleged trading in slaves, together with penalties to the amount of 13,000*l.* on the shippers and owners of the cargo. The Lords of the Judicial Committee reversed this sentence with costs and damages, and declared that the owners of the ship must look to the Government for their indemnity. They added that "merchants who, having engaged only in a lawful adventure, have been subjected to an unjust and illegal sentence, are entitled to be indemnified against its consequences, and against the costs which they have incurred in obtaining its reversal, in relieving themselves from the heavy pecuniary loss which it inflicted, and from the deep stain which it cast upon their characters, and that the national honor must be vindicated at the national expense."]

That Brougham should take up such a production is as
unaccountable as it is indecent, for he affected to be exceedingly attached to the Orleans royalties, to be on very
intimate terms with the King, and he treated Guizot with a
familiarity quite at variance with good taste and propriety,
and which had excited the astonishment, with no small
disgust, of Guizot himself. It might have been expected that
he would have resented such a production as Normanby's,
instead of patronizing it. He told Mrs. Austin he could not
himself speak to Reeve about it, since he had made the
"Edinburgh Review" the vehicle of a personal attack upon
himself. What he alluded to was, that when Lord Cockburn's life was published an article (anonymous of course)
appeared in the "Law Magazine" in which Lord Cockburn
was very ill-used, and another in reply to this, and in vindication of Lord Cockburn, but without a word against Brougham, appeared in the "Edinburgh." This was what he called
a personal attack upon himself. He was the author of the
paper in the "Law Magazine," but the writer in the "Edinburgh" had no right to assume this, or to know anything
about it, though as a matter of fact he did know, or at least
had good reason to suspect, that it was penned by Brougham.
It had already been settled that the "Edinburgh Review"
should take no notice whatever of "The Year of Revolution," and Mrs. Austin having sent Brougham's letter to
Reeve, Reeve answered it himself, utterly denying that he
had made or intended to make any attack upon him, and
telling him in plain terms what the general opinion is of
Normanby's book.

Meanwhile Guizot writes to Reeve that the book is full of
lies, and not worth notice; that he will take none of what
concerns himself alone, but cannot leave uncontradicted
such parts of it as relate to the King, and give utterly false
statements of the relations between the King and himself.
He then refers to various passages which he says are all false,
and desires Reeve to show his letter to Lord Lansdowne,
Granville, and me, and to anybody else he thinks fit. All
this will contribute to bring Normanby into a very unpleasant dilemma about this ill-advised book, and it must be said
that it is all Clarendon's fault for his weakness and good
nature in abstaining from renewing his prohibition, and when
Normanby was here giving a sort of tacit consent to its appearance, although that was accompanied with a strong ex-

pression of opinion that it ought to be suppressed. And now a report has got about that before the book came out Clarendon read and approved of it, which I requested Mrs. Austin to deny in the most peremptory manner, for it was to her that this assertion had been made.[1]

December 29th.—The long-pending dispute about the Crown jewels claimed by the King of Hanover was settled the other day. The history of it is this. The late King of Hanover on the death of William IV. claimed these jewels upon the ground that they were partly belonging to the Crown of Hanover and partly had been bequeathed to him by Queen Charlotte. Our Government, on behalf of the Queen, naturally resisted the claim. After a good deal of wrangling they were at last prevailed on to name a commission to investigate the question, and Lord Lyndhurst, Lord Langdale, and Chief Justice Tindal were appointed accordingly. After a considerable delay and a troublesome inquiry, they arrived at a conclusion, but when they were just about to give their award Chief Justice Tindal died. Lyndhurst and Langdale were divided in opinion, so no award could be given. The Chancellor, Lord Cottenham, refused to renew the Commission, and the matter has stood over ever since. In the present year, however, the Government thought the matter ought to be decided one way or another, and they issued a fresh Commission, consisting of Lord Wensleydale, Vice-Chancellor Page Wood, and Sir Lawrence Peel (ex-Indian judge), and they have given judgment unanimously in favor of the King of Hanover, i. e., with regard to the bulk of the jewels, some few seem to have been allotted to the Queen. Lord Wensleydale came into my room at the Council Office just after they had finished their award, and told me about it. I asked him if they had decided it on *evidence* or only by a sort of rough estimate, but he said they had ample evidence, and they were all quite satisfied upon the point. Last night I asked

---

[1] [Lord Normanby had written this narrative of the events of 1847 to 1848 while he was Ambassador in Paris, and he proposed to publish it at an earlier period when he was still in office. But upon this coming to the knowledge of the Foreign Office, Lord Clarendon (without having read the work) intimated to Lord Normanby that he could not allow a diplomatic servant of the Crown of the first rank to publish a polemical narrative of transactions in which he had been engaged, at any rate while he held office. The book therefore was suppressed for some years. But when Lord Normanby had quitted office, he felt at liberty to disregard Lord Clarendon's injunction, and the book was published, to the great detriment of his own reputation.]

Lord Lyndhurst about his share in the question, when he told me their difficulty had been to make out whether the jewels which Queen Charlotte had disposed of by her will had really been hers to leave, or whether she had only had the use of them, but that this had been decided by the discovery of George III.'s will, in which he expressly left them to her. Tindal entirely agreed with Lyndhurst, and if he had lived a little longer, judgment would have been given then in favor of Hanover. Lyndhurst said the Court was very anxious about it, for Prince Albert had told him the pearls were the finest in Europe. The value of them has been enormously exaggerated, but is still considerable. Lord Lyndhurst said they were worth about £150,000, and Kielmansegge told me the same thing.

By the Indian papers just arrived it appears that the relief of the Residency of Lucknow and the deliverance of all who were confined in it was complete, but there was no great battle (which everybody expected), though much severe fighting, and Lucknow itself was still untaken. The mutineers, though always worsted, seem to fight better than they were thought capable of doing, and everything tends to show that the suppression of the Mutiny is still far from being accomplished.

December 31st.—I met Clarendon last night, who talked about the Hanoverian jewel question ; he said the Queen was very anxious to know Lord Lyndhurst's opinion upon the award, so last night I went to his house and asked him, telling him the reason why. He said he had no doubt the award was correct ; that in their case the jewels were divided into two categories : first, those which came from George II. and were undoubtedly Hanoverian ; and secondly, those which George III. had given Queen Charlotte. They had heard counsel on both sides, but neither side chose to produce the will of George III., which they never had before them, so they were in a difficulty about these latter stones. Tindal died the day they were to have met to draw up an award. He and Lyndhurst were agreed, Langdale doubted. Lyndhurst said he had no doubt if they had had King George III.'s will, which Wensleydale and his colleagues had before them, they should all three have agreed, and to the same award.

Clarendon complained of the recent pro-slavery articles in the "Times," and told Delane they were calculated to encourage the French in holding to their African operations. The French Government had told us that they must have labor, but they did not care if it was black or brown, and if we would undertake to find coolies for them in the same way as Mauritius is supplied, they would give up their scheme. Clarendon said this was fair enough, but it did not get rid of the difficulty, because it was impossible to get the coolies in sufficient numbers, and that our own Colonies, which were perishing for want of labor, would complain loudly, and not unjustly, if we brought the French into competition with them, thus enhancing the difficulty and the cost of supply to themselves. The probability then is that the French will go on, and that all other nations who have the same wants will follow their example, and we shall be reinvolved in endless remonstrances and squabbles under very disadvantageous circumstances.

January 1st, 1858.—It is worth noticing that after a year of fine weather, of which nobody can recollect the like, this first day of the New Year has opened like one of a genial spring. This nearly unbroken course of wonderful weather for about nine or ten months gives rise to many speculations as to its cause, and no doubt there is some physical cause, although it has not yet been ascertained.

January 5th.—To-day the winter seems to have set in in earnest.

January 7th.—Not many days ago the "Times" concluded an article on the Indian war in these words (it was after describing the relief of the Residence at Lucknow by Sir Colin Campbell): "thus ends the Indian Mutiny of 1857;" and to-day we have the news of Wyndham having been defeated by the Gwalior Force; of Sir Colin having been obliged to quit Lucknow, *without having captured it,* in order to repair this check (which he seems to have done very effectually) and deplorable event; of the death of Havelock, the hero of this war, who, after escaping unhurt through battle after battle, has succumbed to disease, not having lived long enough to know all that is said of him and all that has been done for him here. It is impossible not to feel the loss of this man as if he belonged to one individually, so deep is the interest which his gallantry and his brilliant career have excited in every heart.

Every account we receive only confirms the impression that this war will be a long and difficult affair, and if we are

able by our military successes to put down all opposition and
suppress the mutiny thoroughly, we shall have a still more
difficult task to re-establish order and a quiet and regular
government in the country, and this difficulty promises to
be enormously increased by all that is passing here on the
subject.   Shaftesbury is stirring up all the fanaticism of the
country, and clamoring for what he calls the *emancipation*
of Christianity in India, and even the "Times," once celebrated for its strong sound sense and its fearless independence, is afraid to rebuke this nonsense, and endorses it by
saying "we have committed great errors," but without explaining what it means, or giving any exemplification of the
assertion.   The real meaning, however, of the Exeter Hall
clamor is, that we should commence as soon as we can a
crusade against the religions of the natives of India, and attempt to force Christianity upon them.   I begin to have
the most dismal forebodings upon this Indian question.   I
continue indeed to believe that by dint of·enormous exertions, by a vast expenditure of money, and sending out every
man we can raise and make a soldier of, we shall sooner or
later conquer the mutineers and suppress the rebellion, but
I expect we shall lose our Indian Empire.   I may possibly
not live to see the catastrophe, but those who are twenty or
may be ten years younger than I am in all probability will.
All our legislation is conducting us to this end.   We are
taking this moment of war and confusion to revolutionize
our Indian Empire and government, to root up all that the
natives have been accustomed to regard with veneration,
and to pronounce sentence of condemnation upon the only
authority of which they know anything, and which has been
the object of their fears and hopes, and sometimes of their
attachment.   The Government is about to hurry into this
measure as if the existing system had been the cause of the
present rebellion and conflict, and that the one they propose
to substitute would be so much better and capable of repairing the mischief which the government of the Company has
caused by its alleged mismanagement.   I have no prejudice
or partiality for the Company, but I believe any great
change at this moment to be fraught with danger, and that
the notion of improving the state of affairs by the abolition
of what is called the double government is a mere delusion.[1]

[1] [The experience of nearly thirty years has proved that these gloomy forebodings were unfounded. The Government and the condition of the Indian

January 16*th.*—I went to The Grange on Tuesday and returned yesterday morning, when I was met by the news of an attempted assassination of the Emperor Napoleon, whose escape seems to have been providential.

It is since I last wrote anything here that we have received the news from India of Wyndham's defeat at Cawnpore, and of Sir Colin's subsequent victory, but we are not yet informed of the details so as to be able to pass a judgment on these events, and upon Wyndham's conduct. It may be doubted, however, whether the small defeat in the one case is not more prejudicial than the considerable victory in the other is advantageous; and the inference to be derived from the whole is to my mind of a gloomy character, for I think unless we can manage to pour into India an unceasing stream of fresh troops for an indefinite period, we shall succumb in the contest by the mere weight of numbers, and the question is, whether we shall be able to do this, which seems to me exceedingly doubtful. The Government appear never to have been sufficiently alive to the danger and the difficulties of this warfare, and have contented themselves with going on leisurely and lazily, preparing reinforcements to be sent out from time to time, but have never thought it incumbent on them to make the extraordinary efforts that the case imperatively demands.

When Parliament meets I shall be surprised if there is not before long a great storm in both Houses, and if Palmerston means to rest upon his popularity, and to endeavor to conjure it by his habitual offhand manner and assurances that they have done all they could, expecting that such assurances will be accepted as a matter of course, I think he will be greatly mistaken. In spite of all that has been said to John Russell, and his not unfriendly disposition during the short autumnal session, his patience and prudence are evidently well-nigh exhausted, and we may soon expect to see him in vehement opposition. He writes to his brother that "he is appalled at the part he may be obliged to take in the coming session," and he seems to be under the in-

Empire have undergone enormous changes in that interval of time, but upon the whole the suppression of the military revolt of 1857 has placed British authority in India upon a more secure basis, the loyalty of the native princes to the Crown has increased, the native population is more enlightened and more prosperous, and the dangers which may still threaten the British Empire in India are not those which struck the mind of Mr. Greville in 1858. He himself, however, soon changed his opinion. See entry of the 12th March, *infra.*]

fluence of a fresh feeling of antipathy to Palmerston.   It is
not unlikely that he thinks it not worth his while to wait
for the chance of Palmerston's being withdrawn from the
field, and that he may as well gratify his inclination by
going into Opposition, and it is likely enough that he fancies
he has more influence in the House of Commons and the
country than he really possesses, and may collect a party of
his own, instead of being grudgingly accepted by the present
Government as a matter of necessity, rather than one of
choice.   If this is his view, I believe he is egregiously
mistaken.   Lowe, whom I met at The Grange, and who
knows something of both Parliamentary and public opinion,
told me that John Russell would find no support in the
House of Commons where his influence was extinct, and that
so far from forming a party of his own, he did not believe if
Palmerston were to die to-morrow, and Lord John take his
place at the head of the Government, that the Government
itself would stand.

Woburn Abbey, January 19th.—Yesterday morning we
were astounded by the receipt of a telegraphic message
informing Granville that the Duke of Devonshire had been
found dead in his bed.[1]   Nothing could be more sudden and
unexpected, and the immediate cause of his death is not
known.   At different periods of my life I have lived in great
intimacy with him, but he was capricious, so the intervals
were long and frequent during which we were almost
strangers to each other.   Spoiled by his mother as a boy,
and becoming Duke of Devonshire with a colossal fortune
at twenty-one years old, and besides afflicted with incurable
deafness, his existence was *manqué,* and he was a disappointed and unhappy man.   His abilities were of a very high
order, and if he had not been relieved by his position and
wealth from the necessity of exertion and disqualified by his
infirmities from taking an active part in public life, he might
have been a considerable and important as well as a far happier man ; but as he had unfortunately no positive tastes or
active pursuits, no domestic ties to engage his affections, and
no public duties to occupy his mind, he was reduced to fill
up the vacuum of his existence by capricious *engouements*

[1] [William Spencer, sixth Duke of Devonshire, born May 21, 1790, died January 17, 1858.   He was Mr. Greville's second cousin, the Duchess of Portland,
mother of Lady Charlotte Greville, having been the daughter of the fourth Duke
of Devonshire.]

and frivolous society. He was very clever and very comical, with a keen sense of humor, frequently very droll with his intimate friends, and his letters were always very amusing. The Duke lived very much like a grand seigneur, hospitable and magnificent ; he was very fond of his family, and very kind to them, as he was also to those of his friends whom he took into favor, many of the poorer of whom will have great reason to regret the loss of a benefactor. There was for a long time a vague notion that some mystery attached to his birth, and that he was not really the son, or at all events not the legitimate son, of his reputed father. The idea was that Lady Elizabeth Foster (whom the Duke afterward married as his second wife) and the Duchesse had been con- fined at the same time at Paris, and that the latter having a girl and the former a boy, the children had been changed, the Duke being the father of both children. I always treated the story as a myth, and this opinion has been con- firmed by the deposition of the woman who had received the child in her arms upon his birth, which was conclusive evidence of his legitimacy. It is remarkable that the whole of the vast property of the late Duke was in his own power. The entail was cut off upon his majority, and his father died before the estates were resettled.

January 20th.—The more I hear from India and about Indian affairs, and the more I read and reflect upon the sub- ject, the more desponding I become as to our future pros- pects there ; first, as to our means of bringing the war to a successful issue, and secondly, as to our power to govern the country and keep it quiet and contented when the first ob- ject has been accomplished.

January 23d.—On arriving in town yesterday, I received a visit from Disraeli, who said he had come to consult me *in confidence,* and to ask my opinion, by which his own course would be very much influenced. I was not a little surprised at this exordium, but told him I should be glad to hear what his object was, and that he was welcome to any opinion he wished for from me. He then began a rather hazy discourse, from which I gathered, or at least thought I gathered, that he thinks the present state of affairs very serious, and the position of the Government very precarious ; that he is meditating on the possible chances there may be for him and his party in the event of Palmerston's fall, and knowing that some sort of coalition with some other party would be indispensable to form any other Government, an idea had crossed his mind that this might be practicable with some of the most moderate of the Whigs, especially with the younger ones, such as Granville and Argyll, and he wished to know if I thought this would be possible, and whether I could be in any way instrumental in promoting it, and if I did not think so what my ideas were as to the most advisable course in order to avert the threatened Reform, and to give the country a better Government than this. This, with a great deal of verbiage and mixed with digressions about the leading men of the present day, seemed to me to be the substance and object of his talk. He professed to speak to me of his own sentiments without disguise, and with entire confidence about everything, but I cannot call to mind that he imparted to me anything of the slightest interest or importance. It would be difficult and not very interesting to write down our somewhat vague and *décousu* conversation, but I told him that I knew very little of the dispositions of any of the men he alluded to, but I did not believe they any of them would be parties to any such combination as he looked to, or separate from their present colleagues.

January 25th.—We are still without any advices from India. The petition to Parliament of the East India Company, which is very able, and was written by John Mill, has produced a considerable effect in the world, and doubts are expressed in all quarters whether Government will be able to carry their Bill.

January 26th.—The Princess Royal's wedding went off yesterday with amazing *éclat,* and it is rather ludicrous to contrast the vehement articles with which the Press teemed (the "Times" in particular) against the alliance two years ago with the popularity of it and the enthusiasm displayed now. The whole thing seems to have been very successful. At the breakfast after the wedding, to which none but the Royalties were invited, the French Princes were present, which was amiable and becoming on the part of the Queen.

January 28th.—As the day approaches for the re-assembling of Parliament there is an increasing impression that this Government is very likely not to get through the session, and the "Times," which is always ready to assist in the discomfiture of a losing party, is now showing unmistakeable symptoms of its own doubts whether the Government is any longer worth supporting, and Delane told me yesterday he thought they would not remain long in office, and that it is time they should go, and he ridiculed the idea of its not being practicable to form another Government.   It is absurd, but nevertheless true, that nothing has damaged Palmerston so much as his making Clanricarde Privy Seal.   It was an unwise appointment, but the fault of it is grossly exaggerated. I Everybody agrees that from one end of the country to another there is a feeling of universal indignation against it.   Then there is a great turn in the public mind in favor of the East India Company, or rather against the Government measure, of which nothing is known, but that the result of it will be to place the Indian Empire in the hands of Vernon Smith.

February 2d.—The Indian question has for the moment been superseded by the French question as it may be called, that is by the storm which is raging in France against this country, its institutions and laws, in reference to the assassination plot of January 14.[1]   It was well known that the French Government had been urging our Ministers to adopt measures or to pass laws against the refugees and their machinations in this country ; but while this question was under discussion, we were astounded by a speech made by Persigny in reply to an address from the City, and still more by the publication in the "Moniteur" of certain addresses from corps or regiments of the French army to the Emperor, full of insult and menace to this country.   These offensive manifestations naturally excited great indignation here, and the Press did not fail to hurl back these insults, and to retort with interest upon the persons from whom they had proceeded or who had permitted their appearance.   On Sunday I spoke to Clarendon on the subject.   He was very much annoyed and embarrassed by this posture of affairs as might be expected, but more than this he is very much alarmed, more

---

[1] [It was known in France that the explosive bombs with which Orsini had attempted the life of the Emperor Napoleon were manufactured in England, and that some of the accomplices of that conspirator were still in this country, where the law could not reach them for a crime committed abroad.   These facts called forth a strong hostile feeling, and England was accused of harboring assassins. On January 20 Count Walewski addressed a remonstrance to the British Government, which remained unanswered, and on January 23 Count Persigny spoke in strong language to a deputation from the City of London.   Military addresses of a violent character from several French regiments to the Emperor were published in the *Moniteur*.   On February 9 Lord Palmerston introduced a bill, called The Conspiracy to Murder Bill, making conspiracy to murder a felony.   The opposition to this bill gave rise to the ensuing events and overthrew the Ministry.]

18

than I think he need be. I said it seemed to be that the Emperor had forgotten his usual good sense, and that he who knows this country ought to have felt that if he wishes to have anything done here, he is taking the most effectual means to prevent it by permitting the military addresses to appear in the "Moniteur," since in the present state of the Press this is tantamount to their being published by the Government itself. I said I could not believe that these hot and enthusiastic expressions were to be taken entirely as proofs of a passionate attachment to the Emperor's person, but that these were outbreaks of that hatred of England which sometimes slumbered, but never died. He said the Emperor felt that his alliance with this country was indispensable to him, and regretted sincerely the displays of feeling in France, but that he did not dare to repress the sentiments evinced by the army, though he kept them in check as well as he could, and the truth was, as I have said above, that it was the undying animosity to us which had found a vent upon this occasion. He added that he had not blamed Morny, who could not say less than he did without being denounced by the Chamber as an inadequate exponent of its sentiments. The French, seeing how all our force is absorbed in our Indian war, think they may treat us as they please, and Clarendon fancies that if any accident were to befall the Emperor, any Government that might be able to establish itself would go to war with us as the best means of ingratiating itself with the nation and of being able to establish itself. He says they can march 50,000 men at a moment's notice to Cherbourg, where there is an abundance of war steamers ready to transport them across the Channel, while we have no soldiers and no ships to defend us in case of such a storm suddenly bursting. George Lewis says that Clarendon is haunted with this apprehension, which he does not share in the slighest degree.

Though there is some truth in this account of the Emperor's position, I cannot believe that he might not have kept matters more quiet in France than he has done, if he had exerted his influence and power for that end. There can be no doubt that our international relations are upon a very unpleasant and perilous footing, and that the evil is not corrected by the fact of the two Courts being on friendly terms, by mutual interchanges of soft sawder and proofs of friendship in the shape of handsome bridal gifts from the

Emperor and Empress to the Princess Royal. We are going
to do something to soothe the French ; but as it will, I believe, be no more than to make that a felony which is now
only a misdemeanor, it may be doubted if this will satisfy or
appease them ; but it would be impossible to do more even
if it were desirable, which I think it is not, and I doubt if
even this slight concession will be obtained from Parliament
without some strong and indignant remarks upon the tone
which has been adopted toward England.

February 3d.—The Directors have got Tom Baring and
Lord Grey to present their petition in the two Houses, and
they mean to adopt the moderate and judicious course of not
agitating any further, but trust to the course of events, which
is now turning in their favor, and to ask for delay and a
Committee. Graham, acting, I believe, independently, means
to move for a Committee. John Russell intimated to him
that he did not think he should support such a motion, but
he has not finally determined what to do, and I rather expect he will end in voting for it. Palmerston's friends still
tell him that his name is all powerful, and that he is sure of
carrying through the House of Commons whatever he proposes, if the House thinks there is any possibility of a defeat
leading to his resignation, and such is evidently his own
opinion. In a Committee on Indian affairs and the intended
bill, at which Bethell was present, on some objection or possible objection being suggested by one of the members, Palmerston said, in his usual jaunty way, "Oh, they will fall in
love with our bill when they see it ;" when Bethell, in his
niminy-piminy manner and simper, said, "Oh, my dear
Lord!" Granville, who told me, says it was very funny.
They all seemed conscious of the diminution of Palmerston's
energy and power. He is always asleep, both in the Cabinet
and in the House of Commons, where he endeavors to conceal it by wearing his hat over his eyes. Clarendon made
me laugh heartily the other day at his account of the Cabinet, where one half of them seem to be almost always asleep,
the first to be off being Lansdowne, closely followed by
Palmerston and Charles Wood. I remember his giving me
a very droll account of Melbourne's Cabinet, and of the
drowsiness which used to reign there, more particularly with
Melbourne himself.

February 11th.—I never remember Parliament meeting
with much greater curiosity and excitement. The situation

of the Government is generally regarded as so precarious, and the revolution in Palmerston's popularity and therefore his power is so extraordinary, that everybody is expecting some great events will occur, and the hopes of all who wish for a change and who expect to profit by it are reviving. The bill brought in by Palmerston on Tuesday for the purpose of punishing conspirators and with a view to satisfy the exigency of the French Government made a great stir. The leave to bring it in was carried by a large majority, thanks to the Conservatives, but its success was principally owing to the Emperor's apology arriving just before the debate began. This pacified most of those who were enraged at the publications in the "Moniteur," and disposed to oppose the measure on account of the conduct of the French Government. I have no sympathy with such a feeling, but it is well calculated to go down with the public, and to afford a plausible pretext to the Ultra-Liberals and the crotchety politicians. The greatest objection to this bill is that it will probably be quite useless for its alleged object, and though perhaps something more stringent might be useful, the Government do not dare propose anything beyond the present measure.

Perhaps the most serious reflection to which this matter gives rise is the suspicion that the conduct of the Emperor Napoleon betrays either some strange infirmity in his faculties, or something so unsound and dangerous in the state of France, as to be pregnant with possible consequences it is frightful to contemplate. All that he has been doing, or has allowed to be done of late, is indicative of a change; for the moderation and prudence, together with firmness and decision, which have hitherto formed his best claim to the admiration and approbation of this country seem to have completely deserted him. The penal laws enacted or to be enacted in France are considered as the inauguration of a reign of terror, and there is rapidly growing up the same sort of feeling about the French Empire that there is here about the Palmerston Government. Nobody pretends to foresee what will happen, but every one thinks that the state of France is rendered more combustible, and that any spark may produce an explosion. Those who are most attached or most favorable to the Imperial Government are the most alarmed, and, when they dare speak out, express the greatest regret and alarm at all that is passing in France.

To turn to the Government here, their two great rocks ahead are the India Bill and the Reform Bill, but with regard to these there seems no knowledge how parties will act, and how leading individuals will vote. Most people, however, are impressed with the idea that neither measure will be carried, and that the Government will in all probability not get through the session. It will be too absurd if Palmerston, after being the idol of the public, in spite of or in consequence of all his foolish speeches and his outrageous acts, should find himself deserted and his power shaken because he made Clanricarde Privy Seal ; but there can be no doubt that this appointment has had more effect than any other cause in the change of public opinion about him.

February 14th.—Last week saw the debates in the House of Commons about the Conspiracy Bill, and the first act of the India Bill. The first is very unpopular, but it will be carried nevertheless. John Russell has taken it up with extraordinary vehemence and anger. His opposition to it is furious, on high constitutional grounds, which appear to me absurd and uncalled for. If I were in Parliament I should be puzzled how to vote, for there is much to be said against the Bill, and much against voting against it, particularly against leave to bring it in. Almost all the Tories voted with Government, and John Russell carried very few with him, and neither of his own nephews. He is more than ever exasperated against Palmerston for bringing it in. The apology tendered by the Emperor, which was read to the House, reconciled a great many to the bill, but I have no notion that it will do any good, or that the French Government will be satisfied with it. After such a bill, which will certainly be carried, the British Lion must put his tail between his legs, and " Civis Romanus " give up swaggering so loftily. If Aberdeen had attempted such a measure when Louis Philippe was King and Guizot minister, what would Palmerston have said, and what would not have been the indignant outcry throughout the country ? The balance of opinion now seems to be that Government will carry their India Bill, and the report is that they are willing, if the second reading is carried, to consent to any alterations that may be pressed upon them in Committee. Lewis seems to have made a good speech on Friday, though rather of a didactic character.

February 20*th.*[1]—Unless I were to write down day by day the events and the *impressions* of each day I should fail in giving anything like a picture of the time, and I regret that my indolence or other occupations have prevented my doing this. I have each day promised myself I would not neglect it, and then, failing to keep that promise (to myself), I have found some fresh occurrence sweeping away the interest, and generally the accurate recollection, of what the preceding days have produced. The varieties of the aspects of public affairs have been like the figures in a kaleidoscope, and one ought to catch each fleeting symmetrical arrangement before it is changed into some other equally fleeting in order to comprehend the rapidity and importance of the changes which are going on. Not long ago (that is, not many weeks) a vague idea began to circulate that the Government would have difficulty in getting successfully through this session, and that their power had suffered some diminution. It was thought that the India Bill and the Reform Bill would be too much for them, and when a little later the events in France induced them to bring in the Conspiracy Bill, the excessive unpopularity of this last measure strengthened the impression of their instability. Everybody out of the pale of the Government itself admitted that Palmerston was not the man he was, and the diminution of his popularity was visible universally. This was attributed to several smaller causes, but the great one was the appointment of Clanricarde, which beyond all doubt has been regarded with a disgust and indignation to the last degree exaggerated and uncalled for. Such was the state of public feeling and opinion when the Parliamentary campaign opened with the discussions first of the Conspiracy Bill, and secondly of the Reform Bill. After a few days, however, a great change seemed to have taken place, though the country and the Press watched with great jealousy the progress of the Conspiracy Bill, keeping up a very loud growl of dislike to the Bill, and resentment against the French Government. In the division on the question of leave to bring in the bill the majority of the Conservatives came over to the Govern-

[1] [On February 19 the Government were defeated on the Conspiracy Bill, in the House of Commons, by a majority of 234 to 215, Mr. Milner Gibson's amendment having been carried against them. The majority consisted of 146 Conservatives, 84 Liberals. Mr. Gladstone, Lord John Russell, Sir James Graham, Mr. Cardwell, and Mr. Sidney Herbert voted against the bill. Lord Palmerston immediately resigned.]

ment, and they got a majority of the Conservatives of three to one. A few days after Palmerston brought in the India Bill, about which for a moment it was thought Baring with his amendment might run him hard, but after a very poor debate, in which the Chancellor of the Exchequer made a very good speech, and the President of the Board of Control made no speech at all, the Government got a majority of near 150. These two victories, though the first was obtained by the aid of opponents, raised the spirits of the Ministerialists, and were generally taken as indicative of more strength than they had been supposed to have, and as pretty clear proofs that Palmerston would at all events get unscathed through this session with not much diminished authority and influence.

- But while they were triumphing in the fancied security which these divisions seemed to promise them, a storm was gathering, for the bursting of which they were far from being prepared, nor did they estimate its importance. The public feeling had become more and more exasperated at the Conspiracy Bill, and at the conduct of France. The first reading of the bill would not have been carried as it was, perhaps not at all, but for the *apology*, as it was called, of the Emperor, and the soothing effect of Walewski's despatch carrying expressions of his master's regret and a sort of half disclaimer of the military addresses. But this soothing effect was very transitory. It was remarked that while the "Moniteur" continued to insert fresh addresses of an offensive character, the apologetic despatch did not appear at all, and the original despatch of Walewski (January 20), which had excited so much indignation here, and which was not denied to have been the origin of the Conspiracy Bill, lay upon the table of the House of Commons unanswered by our Government. On this point a good deal of surprise and anger had been evinced in the Press and in society, and the discontent against the Government generally, and Palmerston in particular, was still spreading, when Milner Gibson took advantage of the prevailing temper, and moved a resolution in the shape of an amendment to the second reading of the bill, very skilfully concocted, but which was a direct vote of censure upon the Government (particularly of course directed against Palmerston and Clarendon) for not having answered that despatch.

Palmerston, I have been assured, when he saw the terms

of this amendment, perceived that it might be dangerous, and that it was well calculated to get votes; but it is certain that the Government generally were in no apprehension, and that nobody of any party (I believe literally nobody) had the least idea that any vote of censure, which of course involved the existence of the Government, had the slightest chance of being carried. I met Sir Edward Lytton at the Athenæum on Friday, just as he was going to the House, and had some conversation with him. He treated Palmerston's position as impregnable, and said he would have a very large majority that evening. So confident were the Government whippers-in that they made no exertions, and Hayter actually allowed some of his people to go away unpaired, telling them that they were quite safe, and their presence not necessary. I went to the House of Lords that evening to hear Macaulay, who was to have spoken but did not speak, and afterward went home, hearing nothing more that night. Great was my astonishment when I read in the "Times" this morning that Government had been beaten on Milner Gibson's motion by 19, and a few minutes after Granville came in and said that this defeat must be conclusive and nothing left for them but to resign. A Cabinet was held in the afternoon, at which it was decided that Palmerston should repair to Buckingham Palace with the resignations of himself and his colleagues.

February 21st.—Nothing more was known last night, but it was evident that Derby had been sent for in preference to Lord John, whom I met at Brooks's in the morning, and who did not expect the Queen to send for him. He told me Gladstone, he believed, and Graham, he knew, would not join Derby, and he thought neither Sidney Herbert nor Cardwell would either. As to the future, there really are *quot homines tot sententiæ.* Some think Derby cannot form a Government, some that he will not try. The sanguine Palmerstonians think all other attempts will fail and Palmerston remain in power, as Lord Grey did in 1831, and some fancy he will endeavor to propitiate the House of Commons and public opinion by throwing overboard Clanricarde, to whose appointment the mischief is in great measure attributed. Such is at this moment the state of doubt and confusion which generally prevail.

February 23d.—Nothing is y   known of Derby's progress except that he tried the Peelites, not one of whom would join. He sent for Newcastle from Clumber, who came up, saw him, and declined. It is evident that they mean to act in concert, except probably Graham, who has espoused John Russell, and who will not separate himself from Lord John's fortunes. There was a prevailing expectation yesterday that Derby would abandon his attempt, and that Palmerston would come back, but Derby seems quite determined to go on. The Palmerstonians certainly expect their exclusion to be of short duration, and nobody thinks that any Government Derby can possibly make will last long.

Never was there a great catastrophe so totally unexpected. Within an hour of the beginning of the debate no one doubted that the Government would have a majority, but Milner Gibson's speech was not concluded before it was evident that his amendment would be carried, and Palmerston's conduct was very unaccountable. It was clear from the tone of his speech, which was as bad as possible, feeble and intemperate, that he was aware of what was going to happen, and yet when the true state of the case was urged upon him, and he was pressed to adjourn the debate till Monday, which could easily have been done, he obstinately refused. If he had done this, there is little doubt that he would have whipped up a majority by Monday. Certainly no people ever so mismanaged their affairs. There is no excuse for their having put on the table of the House of Commons such a despatch as Walewski's, without any reply being made to it. It required no great sagacity to anticipate that such a course of proceeding could not fail to throw the House of Commons into a flame, and exasperate the country, already much excited, and all the excuses they made only made their case worse, and were generally inconsistent with each other. George Grey's was the most pitiful, when he said that after the second reading an answer should be sent. Then they made shuffling statements : at one time that they had sent no answer, and that to have answered it as alone it could be answered must have increased the irritation. Then, that they had given a verbal answer, and at last it transpired that an answer had been sent in the shape of a *private* letter from Clarendon to Cowley.

There were two courses open to the Government, either of which might have been very naturally and not improperly taken. Palmerston might have announced that it was not his intention to produce any of the correspondence between the two Governments, and asked the House of Commons to place confidence in him, and allow him to take the steps he deemed best to satisfy the French Government, and at the same time vindicate the honor and dignity of this country, and if he had stated that he thought it would be injurious to the interests of peace and amity to produce any papers, it is perfectly certain he would have met with unanimous acquiescence. The only objection I have heard to this is that the French Government published the despatch in the "Moniteur;" but, if Palmerston had resolved upon silence here, he could have informed Cowley of his resolution, and instructed him to come to a common agreement with Walewski that they should publish nothing in the "Moniteur," and we should keep the correspondence from Parliament here. Not acting in this way, he ought to have sent an answer, and who can suppose that such men as Palmerston and Clarendon, whose lives have been passed in writing despatches, and who are both so remarkably expert at that work, should be unable to concoct a reply to Walewski which should be conciliatory in tone and matter, and at once suffice for the fears and exigencies of France and for the national pride and honor of England? Clarendon's private letter is said to have been excellent, and of course it must have been well adapted for its purposes. What difficulty could there have been, therefore, in converting the private into a public letter, which, if it had accompanied the French letter, would have pacified both the House of Commons and the country, for the Government ought not to have forgotten, as it seems they did, that the English and French Governments were not the only parties in this transaction, but there were the English Government and the House of Commons and the country, between whom accounts had to be settled. (There are people who fancy that Palmerston was not sorry to be beaten on Milner Gibson's motion, thinking it better to go out upon that than upon the motion against Clanricarde on March 4 (the abolition of the Privy Seal), on which they think they certainly would have been defeated, and on which they must have resigned ; but I don't think their defeat on the latter was so certain, and they might have been saved by Clanricarde's resignation before the debate came on. The conduct of those who brought forward and those who supported the vote of censure, and that of the Government in

going out upon it, admits of much diversity of opinion.
The friends of the Government, and those who were averse
to a change, maintain that the amendment was inexcusable,
and that the House of Commons had no business to meddle
with the functions of the Executive, or to express any opinion as to the propriety of answering or not a despatch which
ought to have been left to the discretion of the Minister, and
the ex-Ministers say that the vote made it impossible for
them to do anything but resign, and that their opponents
must have been fully aware that this would be the couse-
quence of their victory.

Their conduct is inexplicable to me, for I believe they
were very sorry to go out, and yet if they had wished it they
might have very well stayed in.   According to ancient practice any vote of censure produced resignation as a matter of
course, no matter what the subject of it, but it did so because a vote of censure, and indeed any adverse vote on any
important measure, implied that the House of Commons had
withdrawn its confidence from the Government, the fact of
which rendered it impossible for them to carry on the affairs
of the country, and obliged them to resign.   But it is impossible to pretend that the late vote indicated the withdrawal of the confidence of the House of Commons generally.
They had had two immense majorities a few days before,
and they would have had another as large a few days after if
they had gone on with the bill.   If I had been able to advise
the Queen, I would have recommended her to refuse Lord
Palmerston's resignation, and have insisted on his testing the
question of confidence on the Conspiracy Bill, or on some
question in which the national passions were not concerned,
and he could not have refused to take this course.   Even
after she had sent for Derby he gave her the opportunity
(though not I suppose the advice to do so), for he said she
had better take another day for consideration, and then if
she decided on wishing him to form a Government, he would
undertake it.

February 26th. — I met George Lewis yesterday, and
talked over with him the whole affair.   He thinks that it
has all been fearfully mismanaged, and that the catastrophe
might have been avoided in many different ways : first, by
answering the despatch ; secondly, by doing what I have
suggested, producing no papers and asking for confidence ;
then by the Speaker's declining to allow the amendment to

be put, as be well might have done, and as a *strong* Speaker would have done. Lord Eversley advised him to do this, and gave his strong opinion that the amendment was inadmissible. It is curious that Palmerston's overthrow should be the work of a Parliament elected expressly to support him, and immediately caused by the act of a Speaker whom he insisted upon putting in the chair, contrary to the advice of many others who thought he would prove inefficient.

I told Lewis I thought their resignation was not called for, and what I would have advised the Queen. He said the whole question was well and most calmly and dispassionately considered, and they were unanimous as to the necessity of resignation, with the sole exception of Vernon Smith, and that was without any *arrière pensée* of returning on an anticipated failure of Derby ; that the Queen had begged Palmerston not to resign upon this vote, and he had returned to the Cabinet, and reported what she said, but they were all without exception for adhering to their resignation. Derby, too, had evidently wished to afford Palmerston an opportunity of recalling it, for he had begged the Queen to take twenty-four hours to consider of it ; but it is probable that Her Majesty, having failed to persuade Palmerston in the first instance, had thought it useless to make any further attempts.

Lewis gave me such strong reasons for their determination, that I confess they materially shook my opinion. He said there was no possibility of mistaking the feeling there was against Palmerston, which if I had been present and seen what passed in the House that night, I could not have doubted ; that the only way in which they could have stayed in was by getting somebody to move a vote of confidence, which was too dangerous an experiment, as in the present state of the House of Commons it was at least an even chance that such a vote would not have been carried, and certain that they would have had all the great guns of all sides thundering against them. He thought Palmerston's speech had been very ill advised, and had done much harm, and that it was a mistake not to have adjourned the debate, when it was very probable that they might have had an opportunity of changing the fortune of it.

CHAPTER XVI.

The Second Derby Administration—Lord Derby's first Speech—Lord Clanricarde defends himself—The New Ministry—Coincidences—Lord Derby's favorable Position—Opinion of the Speaker—Lord Derby's Liberal Declarations—Dinner to Mr. Buckle—Instability of the Government—Mr. Disraeli's sanguine Views—India—Prospects of the new Government—A Visit to the Duc d'Aumale—Delicate Relations with France—Lord John Russell and Lord Palmerston—Irritation of the Whigs—Marshal Pélissier Ambassador in London—The Peelites and the Whigs—Failure of the India Bill—An Overture from Lord John Russell—Dissensions of the Whigs—Lord Derby resolves to remain in Office—Lord John Russell proposes to deal with the India Bill by Resolutions—Mistake of the Whigs in resigning on the Conspiracy Bill—Withdrawal of the India Bill—Policy of the Whigs in Opposition—Lord Cowley on the Relations of France and England—Strong Opposition to the Government—Lord Derby on the State of Affairs—Disunion of the Whigs—Lord Canning's Proclamation—Littlecote House—Vehemence of the Opposition—Lord Lyndhurst displeased—Debates on the Indian Proclamation—Collapse of the Debates—Triumph of the Ministry—Disraeli's violent Speech at Slough—Lord Palmerston's Discomfiture—Prospects of a Fusion—Success of the Government—Concessions to the Radicals—The Queen's Visit to Birmingham Progress of the India Bill—The Jew Bill—The Jew Bill passed—Disturbed State of India—Baron Brunnow on the Russian War.

London, 27th February, 1858.—All yesterday lists of the new appointments were put forth from hour to hour, unlike each other, and proving what changes had been made during the last hours. Nobody was prepared for Bulwer Lytton having no place, and still less for Lord Stanley taking office in this Government, which must have been settled at the eleventh hour. On the whole it presents a more decent-looking affair than anybody expected, but the general impression is that it cannot last, and must be overthrown by the mere weight of numbers, whenever the different sections of the House should unite on any question whatever. Their staff is not so despicable, but their rank and file are sadly inadequate if they are attacked in earnest.[1]

[1] [The second Administration of the Earl of Derby was composed as follows:

First Lord of the Treasury	Earl of Derby.
Lord Chancellor	Lord Chelmsford.
Lord President	Marquis of Salisbury.
Lord Privy Seal	Earl of Hardwicke.
Chancellor of the Exchequer	Mr. Disraeli.
Home Secretary	Mr. Walpole.
Foreign Secretary	Earl of Malmesbury.
Colonial Secretary	Lord Stanley.
War Secretary	Colonel Peel.
Board of Control	Earl of Ellenborough.
Board of Trade	Mr. Henley.
Duchy of Lancaster	Duke of Montrose.
Admiralty	Sir John Pakington.
Lord-Lieutenant of Ireland	Earl of Eglinton.
Chief Secretary	Lord Naas.
Woods and Forests	Lord John Manners.]

March 2d.—Last night Derby made his statement. He was very nervous and unlike himself, scarcely audible at first, much less fluent than usual, and he spoke from notes, which I never saw him do before. It was, however, a very judicious and becoming speech. Granville and Clarendon both spoke very well, and the whole affair was very creditable and satisfactory, civil, courteous, and good-humored on all sides. Clarendon made a very plausible defence of his own conduct in not answering Walewski's despatch, which was so good that Hardwicke crossed the House to compliment him, and said if that speech had been made in the House of Commons there would have been no division. The impression left on me is that though it was a pretty good defence, he would have exercised a sounder discretion if he had sent an answer, and that there was no difficulty in doing so. Clanricarde has given notice of what the "Times" calls favoring the House with some leaves of his autobiography. He has been advised to take this course by some of his friends and colleagues, particularly Lord Lansdowne ; but in spite of such respectable authority, I think it an ill-advised step, from which he is likely to derive little if any benefit. He is going to defend himself against something intangible, for no accuser will appear, and there is no charge which he is called upon to rebut. No doubt his appointment has been the real cause of the downfall of the Government. It is this which ruined the popularity of Palmerston. It is only fair to admit that they could not have been expected to anticipate all the hubbub it made, nor anything like it.

People are now wondering that Palmerston's fall has made so little sensation and the event fallen so flat, considering what his popularity was only a few months ago, but this proves what an unsubstantial and factitious popularity it was. Derby has done better than his predecessor in one way, for he has brought forward some new men who have a good reputation, and may distinguish themselves in Parliament, and show us that we have something to look to beyond the old worn out materials of which everybody is tired. The first class of this Government is not worse than that of the last, and the second class is a great deal better. There are some rather curious coincidences noticeable in this smash. The majority by which the Whigs fell was nineteen. It was the same on the China question last year, and nineteen turned out Derby in 1858. Derby has been three times

called on to form a Government, and each time on the 21st
of February.   At the present moment there appears to be a
disposition to give him what is called a fair trial, but it is
difficult to say how long this will last.   The Whigs are in
great perplexity.   Some talk of Palmerston coming back
again, others want to bring about a reunion between him
and Lord John, and others still talk of setting them both
aside and electing a new leader of the party.

March 3d.—The discussion, for there was no debate, on
Monday has produced a very favorable effect.   Derby's speech
is much admired for its calm and dignified tone, and the
matter of it considered judicious and satisfactory.   As an
exhibition the whole proceeding is thought eminently creditable to the country, and such as must strike foreigners particularly.   This is unquestionably true, and it has been a
very good start for Derby.   As far as one can judge in so
short a time, there is a growing opinion that he ought to
have fair play and no vexatious opposition, and Granville
this morning told me he thought he would get on very well.
Palmerston has begged Cowley not to resign, which is very
honorable and becoming.   There are symptoms of a disposition on the part of the "Times" to support the new Government, and I have little doubt that they can secure this
great advantage if they manage their affairs with common
prudence, and set to work diligently to frame such measures
of improvement and utility as will satisfy public opinion.   I
entreated Jonathan Peel to lose no time in dealing with the
matter of the health of the soldiers and the mortality amongst
them brought to light by Sidney Herbert's Committee.   This
alone, well and quickly done, would be of prodigious service
to the new Government. ·

March 6th.—I gather from what I hear that Lord Palmerston is preparing to buckle on his armor, and to wage
war against the new Government with the hope and expectation of forcing himself back into office speedily, and that
the new Opposition mean to attack the new Government as
quickly and as vehemently as they can.   John Russell says
they "ought not to be recklessly or prematurely opposed."
Guizot, it seems, has written to Aberdeen about the "union
of all shades of Liberals" as a desideratum, to which Lord
John says "whether it be possible he knows not, but that he
is an obstacle to it on our side, and Palmerston on the other."
The Speaker, with whom I had a long talk yesterday,

thinks this Government never can stand, and he says, truly enough, that though Derby and Co. did not *make* the situation which compelled the resignation of the last, they *accepted* it with full knowledge of the consequences of their vote, and are therefore responsible.   He considers that what has happened and is likely to happen is all to the benefit of the Radicals, who well know this, and rejoice at it accordingly, and he thinks Milner Gibson framed his amendment with the design of its leading to the defeat of Palmerston, · and the advent of Derby to a power which he never desired to be of long duration.   All this I could not gainsay, and it is certainly true that this change has only produced a fresh set of difficulties and dangers, the result of which who can foresee ?

Derby's liberal declaration in his programme last Monday has been taken up and extended by his followers, but it is very improbable that the enunciation of such principles and intentions will carry with it the assent of the old and genuine Tories, many of whom will most likely ere long declare their adhesion to their old creed, and their abhorrence of the new-born liberalism of their chief, and Derby may one day find himself in a lesser degree in something like the position of Peel when he gave notice of his intention to propose the repeal of the Corn Laws.   Derby's declaration now affords a practical justification of Peel's course then, for Peel was never so much opposed to Free Trade as Derby and all his followers to Reform, and his excuse is based on similar grounds, namely, the progress and irresistible force of public opinion.

March 10*th.*—I dined with Grote yesterday to meet Mr. Buckle, the literary lion of the day.   He is not prepossessing in appearance, but he talks very well and makes a great display of knowledge and extensive reading, though without pedantry or dogmatism.   There was a small party of literary men to meet him, and Lady William Russell and I acted the part of gallery.   The guests were Count Platen the Swedish Minister, the Master of the Rolls, Dr. William Smith, young Bunbury (Sir Henry's son), and Lowe.   It was pleasant enough.

There is a prevailing and an increasing impression that this Government will not last long, and I think its days are numbered.   The old Government are evidently impatient to resume their places, and within the last two or three days there is an evident change in their spirits and their expectations. Whether it is desirable or not that Derby should be permitted to go on for some time I know not, but I doubt if it is possible. John Russell might perhaps prefer keeping Derby in place for a time, in order to prevent Palmerston's coming back, but I do not think he will be able to do so if he wishes it, and even those Liberals who are not very fond of Palmerston seem to be indignant at a Tory party holding office with an immense majority against them in the House of Commons. It is certainly a question whether any set of men have a right under any circumstances to accept office with full knowledge that there is a majority of at least two to one against them, and if one set of ministers are bound to resign, not merely on finding the majority against them, but upon a single adverse vote, *à fortiori* must another set be precluded from taking office without the power of commanding the assent and support of Parliament upon any question whatever. Sir Francis Baring writes to John Russell, "that the *existence* of the present Ministry is contrary to Parliamentary Government," and this seems to be the general sentiment of the Liberal party, of course loudly insisted on by those who expect to profit by ousting them.

March 11*th.*—My mind fluctuates back to a notion that the Government will be able to maintain themselves for some time. Ellice said yesterday that he for one would not join in any attempt to oust them till he saw his way to the formation of a better Government, and thinks time ought to be afforded for a reunion of the Liberal party. In the afternoon I called on Disraeli, and found him rather sanguine about their prospects. He said they should settle, in fact had settled, the French question "with flying colors." He sees no difficulty about finance, as there can be no quarrels on the score of principles, and he will only have to provide for the expenses either by some increased taxation, or if that is opposed, by a loan, and he does not think the Palmerstonians will venture to refuse the supplies, or that they would succeed in such an attempt. His Indian Bill he thinks will be a better and more popular measure, and he knows of nothing else but the chapter of accidents on which they will have any serious difficulty.

Afterward I fell in with Charles Villiers, and talked over the fall of the Government, which be attributed, as I do, to the enormous and inconceivable blunders which his friends

committed.   He is always sensible, unprejudiced, and the
most satisfactory person to talk to I am acquainted with.
John Russell is in great indignation at Disraeli's speech at
his election, and his attributing all sorts of bad motives to
the Whigs in their Reform of 1831, which was certainly very
imprudent to say the least of it, for in his condition it was
most desirable for him to avoid giving offence to any of the
influential people, whose hostility may be very dangerous to
him.   I had not read his speech when I saw him, or I should
have told him so.

March 12*th*.—It is remarkable how completely the affairs
at home have superseded the interest belonging to those of
India.   Nobody seems to think about what so recently absorbed everyone's thoughts and feelings.   This is, however,
in great measure owing to the general belief that the great
question of suppressing the rebellion and re-establishing our
rule is virtually settled, and though we may yet have a great
deal of trouble and even difficulty, all serious danger is at an
end, and that we are as secure of possessing India as of any
of our colonies.   The apprehensions I had on the subject,
and which I have expressed, have been very far from realized,
and those who took more sanguine and confident views of
the issue of the contest have been justified by the event.

March 17*th*.—The new Government is looking up.   On
Monday evening Bernal Osborne attacked Disraeli in his
usual style, and gave him an opportunity of making a speech
in reply, which everybody acknowledges to have been most
able and successful.   Bernal was very bad, Palmerston spoke
feebly, professed moderate intentions toward the new Government, but clearly indicated that he meant to take office
again if he could.   His speech was tamely received, and furnished a fresh proof of the loss of his popularity and influence.   Last night again, in a little skirmish between Disraeli
and George Lewis, the former had the best of it.   Clanricarde having had the egregious folly to announce to the
House of Lords his intention to make "a personal statement," in which he was unaccountably supported by such
men as George Lewis and Lansdowne among others, found
out that everybody thought he was making a great fool of
himself and withdrew it, but his colleagues are annoyed at
his putting himself forward to ask questions of Derby.   He
sits on the front Opposition bench in the midst of his late
colleagues, who would be glad to be rid of him, particularly

as they know that in the event of their return to office he would be left out.

March 20th.—I went on Friday with M. de Jarnac to Orleans House to pay a visit to the Duc d'Aumale and see his interesting collection of books and pictures. He is very courteous, obliging, and intelligent, and the Duchess very civil and pleasing. His house was formerly occupied by his father, Louis Philippe, improved and enlarged by Lord Kilmorey, who lived there with Miss Hoste, and bought from him by the Duke, who has filled it full of objects of historical or artistic interest, especially of memorials of the great Condé. The family portraits, of which there is a vast collection, are particulary curious. He has two sons, who bear the fine titles of Prince de Condé and Duc de Guise, but it is melancholy to contemplate the *avenir* of these boys, whose high birth is their misfortune, and to whom no profession or occupation seems open. They have lost their own country by no fault of their own, and are so situated that they cannot or will not get adopted in any other.[1] It is a false position if ever there was one. The family appear to have been alarmed by the recent events in France, and the indirect effect which those events might have upon them, for they have reason to believe that they are exposed to a constant system of *espionnage* by the French Government, who wish very much to implicate them if possible in some of the plots that they believe to be constantly going on here, and great vigilance on their part is necessary not to commit themselves in any way to unknown Frenchmen who approach under pretences of attachment to their family or to make appeals to their charity.

The other day I got a note from Lord Derby about a Council, at the end of which he earnestly begged me if I had any influence with the "Times" to get them to abstain from writing any more irritating articles about France, for that these articles provoked the French to madness, and, as matters are, that nothing but the utmost care and moderation on both sides enabled the two Governments to go on in harmony. I accordingly sent his note to Delane, who promised to attend to it, though it was hard to leave the French press without replies. It is curious that I should be

---

[1] [Alas! both these interesting and promising young Princes were cut off in early life, the Prince de Condé dying in New South Wales, at the outset of a journey on which he had started under the most auspicious circumstances. The Duc de Guise, then the sole surviving child and heir of the Duc d'Aumale also died soon after the return of the Royal Family to France in 1871.]

found acting a friendly part toward Derby's Government, he being of all men the one to whom I have felt the greatest political repugnance ; but I am now so free from all political predilections, and regard constant changes as so objectionable, that I wish this Government to be fairly tried, especially as it appears to me quite as good as any other we are likely to have ; disposed to work hard and promote good measures, and to be unable, even if they were disposed, to do any harm.

I find a disposition to carp at the settlement of the French quarrel, though without any good reason. Lord Malmesbury's letter might have been better composed, and more showy, but the object was to close the quarrel in a manner that would satisfy the pride and allay the irritation of this country, without being so exacting toward France as to pique her into fresh ebullitions offensive to us, and this has been done, though it cannot be said with truth that they had settled the dispute "with flying colors." The French Government have had the last word, and exhibited some spleen, which is not very unnatural considering the part they have had to play, eating humble pie and retracting almost everything they said.

The Duke of Bedford is in town, having been urgently pressed to come up and see what he could do to effect a political reconciliation between Lord John and Palmerston, which he has certainly not effected, and probably will fail in effecting. Lord John said some months ago that he never would take office again but as Premier, but what the Whigs want is that he should join them, consent to co-operate in ousting Derby, and then to take office under Palmerston ; but if he would not do this before the present session began, much less would he be inclined to do so now. He knows very well that they are only trying to make it up with him, because they feel that they cannot do without him, and as they still prefer Palmerston, and mean to stick to him, and to come back with him as their chief, there is very little chance of any negotiation being brought to a successful issue. The best chance of the Whigs being reunited is, that the present Government should take sufficient root, and stay in office long enough to show that nothing but a complete reconciliation of the Liberals of all shades and opinions can drive them out, and for this time is required. The notion the late Government cherished of being able to turn out their opponents in a very brief space is already gone, and they find that the majority of the House of Commons will be no party to such an overthrow.

March 21st.—The Duke of Bedford has just been here; he has been occupied with vain attempts to bring about the reconciliation so much desired by his political friends, but without success or any hope of it; he finds the estrangement between Palmerston and Lord John great as ever, and even between Lord John and Clarendon, the latter complaining bitterly that Lord John " went out of his way to insult him," which meant that in his speech the other day he spoke civilly of Malmesbury, saying he had no doubt he would uphold the honor and dignity of the country. All this shows the excessive soreness and ill-humor of the outgoing party, and though Clarendon expresses the most unalloyed satisfaction at being out of office, it proves there is the *amari aliquid* to detract from his pleasure at being free; and it is not unnatural that the great part he has himself had in bringing about the catastrophe should make him very sore and uneasy, and a blow has been given to his reputation the effects of which may be hereafter serious.

March 25th.—Marshal Pélissier is going to replace Persigny here as Ambassador, a strange choice. He is a military ruffian, who knows no more of diplomacy than he does of astronomy. Persigny goes because he cannot agree with Walewski; I don't know the details of his dissatisfaction. His departure is regretted, as he is believed to be honest and true, and sincerely anxious to promote a good understanding between the two countries.

The Duke of Bedford has just been here; he came from Lord Aberdeen, who tells him the Peelites are all verging toward a union with Lord John, some more, some less; Graham is devoted to him, Sidney Herbert and Cardwell perfectly well disposed, the Duke of Newcastle gradually becoming so, and Gladstone at present the least friendly, but Aberdeen thinks is getting more friendly, and will eventually join his standard, and Aberdeen himself is doing all he can to bring about this union. He is going to speak to the Queen about it, with a view of reconciling her to Lord John without knowing how necessary it is. The Duke said he rather doubted the expediency of Aberdeen's speaking to Her Majesty, but I told him it was better he should, and very necessary to take all means to remove her feeling against Lord John. I also told him what had passed between the Queen and Clarendon, and how he had endeavored to persuade Her Majesty that it would be impossible for himself to be Prime Minister, and that if Palmerston failed from any cause, her only course would be to send for Lord John, and to do so frankly and graciously. I begged him to let Lord John know this, as it was so desirable to bring about a reconciliation between them, which this fact would be calculated to promote. The Duke owned it was very handsome conduct on the part of Clarendon, as it is indeed on the part of Aberdeen, after all that Lord John did in breaking up his Government; but Aberdeen is a gentleman and a patriot, sincerely attached to the Queen, and to the best interests of the country, and while he has retired altogether from public life and the turmoil of politics, he is anxious still to exercise the great moral influence which he possesses to advance the public interests according to the dictates of his judgment and his conscience.

Hatchford, March 30th.—On Friday last Disraeli brought on the Government India Bill, which Ellenborough told some of his friends would be "a great success," and which everybody expected would be an improvement on Palmerston's. Never was there a greater failure; the bill was received with general aversion and contempt. The Radicals, who want to keep the Government in for the present, could not stomach it, Roebuck pronounced it a sham, and Bright, who detests Palmerston, said he preferred his bill of the two. It is evidently impossible that this bill can pass, and everybody sees what a fix it places public affairs in, and what difficulties and uncertainties present themselves on all sides. The only people who are pleased are the Palmerstonians. They think that when this bill has been rejected or withdrawn theirs will pass, and this will, *ex necessitate*, compel Derby to retire and open the way to Palmerston's return to office. They are therefore chuckling over the dilemma, but it may be without its leading to the realization of their hopes. There are a great many men in the House of Commons, Peelites or Radicals principally, but also some others, who cannot endure the notion of Palmerston's coming back, and who will oppose his bill, after the other has been swept away, merely to prevent his return. What the Radicals would like is that both bills should be referred to a Select Committee, and a third bill be concocted out of the two ; but this scheme would not be likely to meet with general approbation, for it would be in fact a delegation of the proper functions of government to the House of Commons. It appears not unlikely that both bills will fail and that no measure at all will pass this year. The Government people are extremely dejected at the state of affairs, but it is said they do not mean to resign upon the defeat of their bill.

Meanwhile John Russell has made a sort of overture to Granville, i. e., he sent George Byng to him on Sunday to invite him to say what he thought would be the most eligible course to adopt in the present state of affairs, and with reference to the Government bill. This was not very judicious on his part, and Granville was an odd man to select, being in a different House of Parliament, and so bound to Palmerston that he could not avoid communicating to him the overture and his reply to it. George Byng says Granville appeared a good deal surprised, but he thought rather pleased. Granville said he could give no immediate answer, but would write to him, which he did the next day, and told him George Lewis would go down to Pembroke Lodge to see Lord John. I have no idea that anything will come of this, for none of the late Cabinet can or will transfer their allegiance from Palmerston to Lord John, unless the former consents to it, and abdicates his position of chief of the Whig party, which he seems to have no thoughts of doing, and it is impossible to conciliate their rival claims and pretensions.

April 2d.—A letter from the Duke of Bedford this morning says that Lord John is inclined to throw out the India Bill, as it is too bad to admit of any improvement, and that he thinks if he does this Palmerston will support him ; but the Duke adds that it is rumored that the Government will not go out if their bill is defeated. It is easy to understand that Palmerston can desire nothing so much as that Lord John should take the lead in opposing the India Bill, and that he should support him, because in that case, and the defeat of the bill by a large majority, which probably would happen, and the Government going out, he would infallibly be sent for again, and in reforming his Government he would no doubt invite Lord John to join it, but this would only lead to a fresh series of difficulties, and most likely to a long course of abortive negotiations. How the junction between the two leaders is to be effected it is difficult to conceive, although there are several ways in which it might be brought about, if they were disposed to make mutual concessions. The starting point might be the complete union of the whole Whig and Liberal party, which all profess to desire most anxiously, and which the mutual antipathies and disagreements of the two leaders at present prevent. If Palmerston would consent to go to the House of Lords as Premier, and to leave Lord John with a high office (India, for example) as leader in the House of Commons, something might be done. Lord John might possibly be induced to cede his claim to the highest place on this condition, but it is not unlikely that he would require more than that : first, that Clarendon should not be at the Foreign Office, which Palmerston would no doubt not agree to ; and secondly, certain places and seats in the Cabinet for the Peelites, who have recently consented to follow his standard and cast their own lots with his. Then various complications present themselves connected with these questions.

April 4th.—The Duke of Bedford has written to Lady Derby that her lord must make up his mind to be beaten on his India Bill, but that he hopes he will not think it necessary to resign upon it when he is.   Brougham writes from Paris that the feeling against us there has been greatly exaggerated, that the Emperor *alone* is friendly to us, but that though the general sentiment is unfriendly, nobody dreams of going to war with us, nor indeed with any other Power.

April 8th.—Derby made a striking speech at the Mansion House the other night, which has been severely ridiculed by the "Times," but which nevertheless contained a good deal of truth.   He said that there were very few questions nowadays in which different Governments *could* act differently, and he invited not only every sort of criticism, but of suggestion, as to the Indian Bills and measures now before Parliament.   The inference deducible from his speech (and in which I have since been confirmed) is that, happen what may, he does not mean to resign, and that the Government will not go out, unless they are positively turned out. They say this unlucky India Bill was the sole work of Ellenborough, and that the democratic clauses are the result of an old fancy of his, but nobody can be desirous of admitting the paternity of such a measure.

April 16th.—I have been confined to the house for several days, and unable to mix in the world and hear

what is going on, but have seen enough to know that there
is nothing but confusion, perplexity, and irritation in the
political world.   During the brief recess everybody was
speculating about what would be done when Parliament met
again, what was to be the fate of the rival India Bills, and
how far the Government would be affected by the result of
contests concerning them.   The Government hangers-on
affected to be very well satisfied with the state of affairs, and
proclaimed their intention not to go out whatever might
happen with regard to their bills.   The Palmerstonians evidently expected that such storms would arise as the Government would not be able to weather, and that something
would turn up advantageous to them.   John Russell, who
must be doing something, said that the Government bill
was so bad that no alterations could make it tolerable, and
that he was disposed to move some Resolutions, which
might be the foundation of a really good measure.   He concocted these Resolutions, and wrote word to the Duke that
" he had written to George Lewis and to Macaulay, who
both approved of his scheme."   Accordingly, as soon as
Parliament met he announced that Resolutions ought to be
drawn up, and that he was ready to draw them up.   This
produced great excitement.   The Government saw in this
move a plank of safety for themselves, and Disraeli said he
was ready to receive Lord John's Resolutions, or to draw up
Resolutions of his own ; many people said that if Resolutions
were to be drawn up at all, it ought to be by Government,
and not by any independent member, and it was eventually
settled that Disraeli was to do it.   Everybody saw that this,
as far as it went, was advantageous to the Government; it
gave them certainly a reprieve, and possibly an opportunity
of ridding themselves of the Indian difficulty altogether for
this year, and the consequence was a burst of indignation
and resentment against Lord John for thus coming to their
aid as it was called, and concerting such a measure (as he
was accused of doing) with Disraeli himself.   The "Times"
attacked him with the utmost bitterness, and there is a general clamor against him on the part of the late Government
and their friends.   It is not very easy to divine his true motives in this matter.   To judge by the asperity with which
he has spoken of the Government bill, one should not suppose he could be moved by any auxiliary purpose to them,
and I do not believe there has been any concert, direct or

19

indirect, between them; but as all parties agree that the Government have derived advantage from his move, the rage he has excited is not unreasonable, and the breach between him and the Palmerstonian Whigs is much widened, and become more difficult to heal. Granville, who I suppose speaks the sentiments of his colleagues, says that it is evident they could not return to office with the *same* Government exactly as before, and that it is not desirable to turn the Government out at present, even if they could, and he thinks it would not be wise to attempt to carry Palmerston's India Bill, in which it is not sure they should succeed. He thinks there *was* concert between Lord John and Disraeli, not direct, but through Horsman, and he says that George Lewis, so far from approving his Resolutions, strongly protested against them; but it is not impossible to reconcile two statements which seem at first sight to be directly opposed to each other. Lord John says he imparted to George Lewis and Macaulay his *scheme* (i. e. of drawing up Resolutions), not the Resolutions themselves, while George Lewis seems to deny approval of the Resolutions; but this is only a possible solution of the apparent contradictions.

I told Granville that all that was now happening only served to confirm my original opinion, that they were wrong in resigning, and that there was no occasion for their doing so, and they now saw how difficult it was, when they had let this Government in, to get them out again, and he not only had not a word to say in reply, but all he did was rather indicative of concurrence in my opinion. In the most palmy days of party government, and when the old traditions with regard to the relations of Government with the House of Commons were in full force, it was not considered as an invariable and unavoidable necessity that a Government when beaten on an important question must go out. I recollect the Government of the day in 1815 being beaten on the Income Tax, without therefore resigning, and it is so obvious that the vote on the French despatch did not imply any general withdrawal of confidence and support, that I never shall believe they would have resigned as they did unless they had thought they should gain more strength and power by doing so without losing their places, and consequently that they were caught in a trap of their own setting.

April 24th.—The events of the past week have been Disraeli's Budget, which has been received with favor and

excited no opposition in any quarter, and the withdrawal of
the Government India Bill, which was done by Disraeli,
rather unwillingly ; but their maxim seems to be "anything
for a quiet life," and they agree to whatever is proposed or
opposed in any influential quarter. The general notion is
that they are safe for this session, but it is a very inglorious
safety. It now appears as if they would scramble and hobble
on until the whole Liberal party is reunited, and a reconciliation effected between Palmerston and John Russell, to
bring about which it is clear that much exertion is being
made.

While I was at Newmarket this week I had several
letters from the Duke of Bedford, all bearing upon this
matter. He writes on the 16th : " I hear that the feeling
against John has been very strong and that lies have been
told as usual. It is said that he has been in communication
with Derby indirectly, through Lady Derby, and that he
wrote to Disraeli. If he did, it was only on a matter of
ordinary courtesy, to ask him to postpone the second reading of the India Bill, to give time for a different course
which he intended to suggest and did the first day the
House met. John has been left by circumstances or by his
old colleagues to pursue his own independent course, and
ought not to be found fault with, if he pursued that course,
as he did in this instance, after conferring with the friends
I named to you, and receiving their approval. No doubt his
move was very successful to the Government, and helped
them out of an enormous difficulty, but I can see no harm in
that." There was a great deal more about the communications between Lord John and George Lewis, which now only
signifies as demonstrating the extreme difficulty of getting
at the truth. It is evident that there is a great desire on
the part of the Whigs to bring about a reunion with Lord
John and those who follow him, in order to get the Government out, for which the rank and file are getting more and
more impatient. Lewis told me last night that *they* are
holding constant Cabinets, which always ended with the
same resolution, not to do anything, or to make any serious
attack ; and they have made up their minds to acquiesce in
Derby's going on through this session ; but nothing can exceed the contempt and aversion with which Lewis speaks of
the Government and of all their proceedings, certainly not
without reason, for there is no example of any Government

consenting to hold office on terms so humiliating, and to such a powerless existence. They dare not originate anything, and they submit to everything that anybody proposes or suggests, having seemingly no object but that of currying favor, and avoiding to give offence. The way in which Disraeli withdrew his India Bill upon a few words spoken by John Russell is a curious exemplification of their forlorn state.

Lord Cowley, whom I saw yesterday, is desirous, like everybody else, to see the end of this feeble rule ; but he thinks Palmerston's disposition is very unbending, and doubts his and Lord John's being brought together, notwithstanding that Lady Palmerston tells the Duke of Bedford that Palmerston "has a great affection for John." Cowley talked a great deal about French affairs and the state of things between the two countries, and he expressed great apprehensions lest Malmesbury should make to many concessions to the French Government,[1] which, however, he meant to prevent if he could. He mentioned one or two odd things. First of all he told me that he had foreseen all the effects produced by the Waleswski letter, and had done all he could to prevent its being sent, and he was amazed at Clarendon having taken it so quietly, and that he should have seen no impropriety or danger in it, but on the contrary thought it would do good. Then with regard to Walewski's other letter in reply to Malmesbury, which, objectionable as it was, had been greatly softened from the original draft, had it been despatched as at first composed by Walewski, he said it would have raised an inextinguishable flame here. Cowley said that the Emperor's nerves were shaken to pieces by the *attentat,* and he was greatly changed.

April 29th.—Every day the position of the Government gets worse and worse. The disposition there was to give them a fair opportunity of carrying on public affairs as well as they could has given way to disgust and contempt at their blundering and stupidity, and those who have all along resented their attempt to hold office at all are becoming more impatient and more anxious to turn them out. There

---

[1] [The publication of Lord Malmesbury's autobiography has proved that he was not at all disposed to make any undue concessions to the French Government, and that he acted as long as this Administration lasted in strict union with Lord Cowley. The Emperor Napoleon complained that his old friend assumed too stern an attitude toward France in the course of the events which followed in the next few months and led to the Italian War.]

is a very temperate, but very just, article in the "Times" to-day, which contains all that is to be said on the subject, stated without bitterness or exaggeration. The Whigs, how-ever, seem aware that it is not expedient to push matters to extremity, and to force their resignation, until the quarrels of the Liberal party are made up, and till Palmerston and John Russell are brought together and prepared to join in taking office, and to effect this object the most strenuous efforts are making. What the pacificators aim at is, that Palmerston should go as Premier to the House of Lords, and leave Lord John to lead the House of Commons. This is the most reasonable compromise, ànd one which ought to be satisfactory to both; but even if this leading condition were agreed to, it is not certain that there might not be others presenting great obstacles to the union, such as whether Lord John would agree to join without bringing a certain number of men with him, and whether Palmerston would consent to exclude so many of his former Cabinet to make room for them. Graham, Lord John would, I sup-pose, certainly insist upon; Gladstone would probably be no party to any arrangement, and he has recently evinced his extreme antipathy to Palmerston by a bitter though able review in the "Quarterly" on France and the late Ministry, in which he attacks Palmerston with extraordinary asperity.

Ever since he resigned Palmerston has been very active in the House of Commons, and kept himself constantly be-fore the public, evidently with the object of recovering his former popularity as much as possible, and he made a very clever and lively speech two nights ago, which his friends praise up to the skies.

I met Derby in the Park yesterday, and soon after the Chancellor in Piccadilly, and had some talk with both of them. They were neither of them in a very sanguine mood, and apparently well aware of the precariousness of their position. Derby attributed the state of affairs, which he owned was very bad, to the caprice and perverseness of the House of Commons, which he said was unmanageable. I did not, as I might have done, tell him that he had no right to complain of this House, and that it was the mismanage-ment of his own colleagues which was the cause of the evil. Lyndhurst made an extraordinary speech on the Jew Bill on Tuesday night.

May 1*st.*—Ellice flattered himself that he could get up a party in the House of Commons which would have power enough to stop the progress of the Indian measure, and to lead to a better measure next year, as well as to the formation of a Government ; and in pursuance of this scheme it was arranged that Lord Harry Vane should move the postponement of Indian legislation, and Ellice told me they should be supported by 150, and many men of note. All this went off in smoke last night. After a short debate the motion was rejected by an immense majority, and Ellice could only muster 55 people.

The hopes of those who are trying to bring Lord John and Palmerston together are damped by a letter I have received (and shown to George Byng) from the Duke of Bedford, who says : " I saw much of Palmerston and Lady Palmerston last week, but could see no disposition to reunion, although we came to that point more than once. I suggested to Lady Palmerston the wish of many that Palmerston should go to the House of Lords. She said that Palmerston had always entertained a great dislike to it, and hinted, or more than hinted, that he would place no confidence in John as leader of the House of Commons." I went to hear Professor Owen lecture yesterday. His style of lecturing is very good, but the subject (vertebrated animals) was too scientific for my ignorance.

Savernake, May 11th.—I have been out of town all the last week, at Chester, and came here on Saturday. While I was at Chester the Duke of Bedford sent me a note he had received from Lord John, which looked like the beginning of a *rapprochement* between him and Palmerston, though it did not amount to a great deal, and may lead to nothing. I was obliged to return it, and was too much occupied to copy the contents of it here. I refer so often to this subject, because it appears to be the one upon which the existence of the present Government depends, for as soon as the Liberals can come to an understanding and act in concert, the doom of the Ministry will be sealed. Without their committing any great faults they seem to be falling into greater contempt every day.

The only point of attack the Opposition have found has been the affair of Canning's recent proclamation.[1] Canning

---

[1] [The Proclamation of March 3, addressed to the chiefs and people of Oude, is here referred to. It was strongly opposed and attacked as a wholesale measure of confiscation, before the motives and policy of the act were understood ;

has not been lucky in his Proclamations, the first having been severely criticised for its clemency, and the second for its severity. The complaint against the Government is for having made public their disapproval of it and their censure of his acts. I think their disapprobation quite right, and that they were right in conveying it to Canning, but they might have refused to express any opinion or to publish or half publish any of the correspondence that passed, though it cannot be doubted that such refusal would have drawn upon them all sorts of attacks and reproaches, but it would have been the proper course for them to adopt. It is, however, certainly premature to express any definite opinion upon an act of which we are not yet furnished with an explanation.

I went yesterday to see Littlecote House, Mr. Popham's, a very curious, interesting old house, and the scene of the Wild Dayrell story and murder, the tradition of which has been often narrated, but the truth never ascertained. I saw all the rooms, including the one in which the murder is supposed to have been committed; but they have been much altered. There is a fine old hall, hung round with the armor and buff coats of Colonel Popham's troopers, and it is a remarkable fact that they are all so small that no man of ordinary size could wear them, a clear proof that the present generation are much bigger than our ancestors of two centuries ago. King William III. slept at Littlecote for two or three nights in 1689 (while King James was at Salisbury), and he seems to have left behind him a good many papers, which have ever since been preserved in the house. There is also a large collection of miscellaneous letters of the time of the Civil War, more or less curious, which were preserved by a lucky accident. Popham told me that his father told him there was a mass of papers in an old box under the roof of the house which had better be destroyed. His son went up for the purpose, and discovered the contents of the box, saved the papers, and had them arranged in a book. I urged him to publish them, and I hope he will. I had only time to look over a few of them; as autographs alone they are valuable.[1]

but Lord Canning's object was to reinstate the talookdars in their possessions by a tenure under the British Crown, and subsequent events have shown that the resettlement of the conquered province was accomplished without violence or injustice.]

[1] [Among these Littlecote papers was found the correspondence of Queen

London, May 13th.—Nothing ever was like the state of
confusion and excitement which has prevailed here during
the last fortnight, while I have been out of town, particularly
on the resignation of Ellenborough, which took everybody by
surprise.   Before I went away the impression had become
general that this Government neither could nor ought to be
endured much longer, and that their repeated and enormous
blunders made them a nuisance which must be abated.   All
the Liberals (except some of the extreme Radicals who
wished them to stay on some time longer), however they differed on other questions, were agreed on this.   Numerous
meetings took place, and there was a prodigious activity of
negotiation, communication, and going backward and forward, with a view to some general organization and combination of attack on the unfortunate Ministry.   The Duke
of Bedford was brought up to see what he could do to bring
Lord John and Palmerston together.   Lord John joined
heartily in the plan of turning the Government out, and said
that *anything* was preferable to leaving them any longer in
office.   Clarendon, who had been informed of Lord John's
peculiar grudge against him, expressed a wish to have an interview with him, which the Duke brought about.   Lord
John called on Clarendon, and they had a frank communication, so far as Lord John telling him all that he thought
about foreign affairs, and in what he disagreed with the late
Government on various questions; but he did not allude to
Vienna, which is the real gist of his grievance and the source
of his hostile feeling, so that with that reticence it is not
strange that they should have parted much as they met.
Then Palmerston expressed a wish to have a *tête-à-tête* conversation with Lord John, which the latter assented to,
but Palmerston seems to have changed his mind, and to
have shrunk from it when the opportunity presented itself.
Charles Wood is the man who has been constantly communicating with Lord John in behalf of the Whig Cabinet, and
one day Palmerston came into Charles Wood's while Lord
John was there.   It rained, and Palmerston offered to take
Lord John home, which he accepted, but nothing passed on
the way, nor did Palmerston propose to get out and enter
the house when he might have had the conversation he had
expressed a wish for, and so it ended.   The plans imagined

Henrietta Maria with Charles I. when she went to Holland to raise money for
carrying on the Civil War.   I am not aware that they have been published.]

by mutual friends for effecting a political reconciliation have vanished into air.   Palmerston is resolved not to go to the House of Lords, and Lord John is equally determined not to take office under him.   Palmerston says he cannot trust Lord John to lead the House of Commons.   Personally, meanwhile, they are ostensibly friends, and Lord John dines at Cambridge House to-morrow.   Charles Wood asked the Duke of Bedford, supposing the Government resigned, and Palmerston was again sent for, what he thought Palmerston ought to do, to which he replied that he ought to accept the task, send to Lord John, and on his refusal to join (as he probably would), to do the best he could with the materials he could command.   This advice would, I conceive, be very palateable to Palmerston, and it is what he would naturally do without any advice.

I called on Lyndhurst the night I came to town, and found him very dissatisfied with the Government, both on account of their management and errors, and because they have treated him with personal neglect; he had begged Derby and Disraeli to do something for his son-in-law, but both put him off with excuses, and would do nothing.   He is particularly disgusted with the state of the Jew question and with the foolish and obstinate conduct of the Government in the House of Lords about it, on which he was very eloquent, particularly for their having made a great whip, and getting up every man they could lay hands on to come and vote, instead of leaving it to take its chance, and at least making an open question of it.

May 16*th*.—The first great battle took place in the House of Lords the night before last, at which I was present.[1] It was a very spirited fight, and I never recollect seeing the House of Lords so crowded both with ladies and lords. Pretty good speaking; Lord Grey's was about the best speech and the one I most agreed with.   I cannot see the matter of Canning's Proclamation and Ellenborough's despatch in the light that either side does, and think there is much to be said both ways.   In the Commons the fight began on Friday

---

[1] [On May 14, Mr. Cardwell moved a resolution condemning the despatch which Lord Ellenborough had written and published, censuring the Proclamation of the Governor-General of India.   A similar resolution was moved by Lord Shaftesbury in the House of Lords, where it was defeated by a majority of nine.   The debate in the House of Commons lasted four nights, and in the interval Lord Ellenborough resigned.   Mr. Cardwell then withdrew his motion, and the attack on the Government suddenly collapsed.]

also, and the most remarkable speech in it was that of Cairns, the new Solicitor-General, which was very clever and effective. John Russell also spoke very well and vigorously, quite in his old style. There is much difference of opinion as to the amount of majority, though it is generally expected there will be one against Government, and I now hear that they have determined positively to dissolve if they are beaten, though with little or no chance of their bettering themselves by a dissolution.

May 23d.—The excitement of Epsom during the whole of last week was not greater than that which prevailed in London during the great debates in the House of Commons, the result of which, on Thursday night, produced such unusual surprise, with so much triumph on one side and such mortification and disappointment on the other. In my long experience I do not recollect to have seen so much political bitterness and violence (except perhaps during the great contests of the Catholic question and Reform), and certainly there never was a great Parliamentary battle distinguished by so much uncertainty and so many vicissitudes, and in which the end corresponded so little with the beginning and with the general expectation. For a considerable time not only all the late Cabinet and their supporters, but the whole body of Whigs, both Palmerstonians and Russellites, had been growing more and more impatient of the Derby Government, and they were considering how they could make a final and irresistible attack upon them, and for the last three weeks there had been nothing but negotiations and *pourparlers* to effect a coalition between the rival leaders and their friends for the purpose of their at least uniting in one great hostile vote, which should drive the Derbyites to resignation or dissolution, hoping and expecting that their majority would be so large as to put the latter out of the question. The occasion seemed to present itself upon Ellenborough's letter to Canning censuring his Proclamation. A meeting took place at Cambridge House, when the whole plan was matured, and though John Russell did not attend it, he agreed to be a party to the Motion of Censure. Shaftesbury was put forward in the Lords, and Cardwell was induced to take the initiative in the House of Commons. Nobody doubted of success, and the only question was (much debated and betted upon) by how many the Government would be beaten. Meanwhile Ellenborough resigned, which gave a new aspect to the affair, and the Government got a small majority in the Lords. It was evident that no popularity attached to the motion, and many of the Liberals were of opinion that upon Ellenborough's resignation the affair ought to drop and the motion be withdrawn. But the die was cast, the Palmerstonians were quite confident and eager for the fray, and would not hear of stopping in their career. The debate began, the speaking being all along better on the Government side, and every day their prospects as to the division appeared to be mending and public opinion more and more inclining against the Opposition and the Proclamation, though still blaming Ellenborough's letter. If the debate had ended on Tuesday as was expected, Government would probably have been beaten, but Sir Charles Napier had got Tuesday, and would not give it up, so that the decision was of necessity adjourned : the delay was all in favor of the Government, and on Thursday night arrived the Indian despatches with Canning's explanations and the Outram correspondence, which was immediately published, and although Palmerston and his friends and newspapers pretended that they considered these documents favorable to their cause, the general impression was rather the other way. All this time the Government people found their cause improving, and their chances in the division mending, and though their enemies still pretended to be certain of success, and I was told on Thursday night that I might safely lay any odds on their having a majority, the best informed of them in the House of Commons began to see danger, and at last they confessed only to expect a bare majority, and the Speaker told somebody it was very likely he should have to give a casting vote. The Radicals, or those of them who professed to be adherents of the Whig Cabinet, strongly urged the withdrawal of Cardwell's motion, and at last on the Thursday seem to have made up their minds that defeat in some shape was inevitable, and that the best thing left for them to do was to get rid of the debate in any way they could. Henry Lennox called on me yesterday morning to tell me what had passed, to this effect : that on Friday Disraeli had received a letter from Cardwell, in which he asked if Disraeli would allow him to withdraw his motion, and subsequently Palmerston desired to confer with him, when he put the same question to him, to which (according to Henry Lennox's statement) Disraeli replied, in a very lofty tone, that he would hear of nothing which could possibly be construed into any admission on their part of their meriting any part of the censure which the Opposition had been laboring to cast upon them. The Government had by this time ascertained that the Opposition had made their minds up to back out of the motion as best they might, and their retreat was not very cleverly done, beginning with Cardwell's refusal to withdraw, and ending with Palmerston's recommendation to him to yield, which was a got up thing. The scene in the House was most extraordinary, and particularly mortifying to Palmerston, who saw himself involved in inevitable defeat, and without the power of rallying again for some time. If anybody could be excused for the impatience which brought him and his party into this dilemma, it was Palmerston, who in his seventy fourth year, and resolved to die in harness if he could, had no time to lose. This affair has been the battle of Marengo of political warfare. The Whigs appeared to be victorious, and carrying everything before them up to the eleventh hour, and then came a sudden turn of affairs, and the promise of victory was turned into rout and disaster. The campaign is lost, and for the rest of this session the Government have it all their own way. The Whigs are in the condition of a defeated army, who require to be completely reorganized and re-formed before they can take the field again. The general resentment and mortification are extreme. They have naturally lost all confidence in their leaders, and they are now all ready to complain of the tactics of which they entirely approved till they found that defeat had been the consequence of their adoption. It is not probable that Palmerston and his late Cabinet will attempt anything more during this session, and everything is in such a state of confusion and uncertainty that the best thing they can do is to remain quiet, merely in a state of watchfulness, and to see what the *volvenda dies* may bring about in the course of the next six months, leaving the Derbyites unmolested during that time. Derby will get Gladstone if possible to take the India Board, and this will be the best thing that can happen. His natural course is to be at the head of a Conservative Government, and he may, if he acts with prudence, be the means of raising that party to something like dignity and authority, and emancipating it from its dependence on the discreditable and insincere support of the Radicals.

June 7th.—At Cleveden, at Ascot, and at Hatchford all the past week, during which I heard little or nothing about politics.   The matter which made the most stir was Disraeli's impudent and mendacious speech at Slough, in which he bitterly ˙attacked the last Ministry and glorified his own. The Whigs were stung to madness, and two or three nights were occupied in both Houses, principally by Palmerston and Clarendon, in answering this speech, and demonstrating its falsehood.   The proceeding was not very dignified, and they might just as well have left it alone, particularly as nobody cared much about what Disraeli said ; but there was so little sympathy for the ex-Ministers, that no indignation was excited by it, except among themselves and their immediate friends.   There seems little chance now of anything but a desultory warfare going on in the House of Commons, without any serious attack on the Government, who seem safe for this session at least.   The most interesting event last week was the virtual settlement of the eternal Jew Question, which the House of Lords sulkily acquiesced in. It was very desirable for many reasons to put an end to it.

Norman Court, June 16th.—Every day it appears more and more evident that Palmerston's political career is drawing to a close, and he alone seems blind to the signs which denote it.   Few things are stranger than the violent reaction which has deprived him of his popularity, and made him an object of bitter aversion to a considerable part of the Liberals, not only to such men as Graham and Bright, but even to many of his former followers and adherents.   I cannot say I am sorry for it, but I do in fairness think that this reaction is overdone and exaggerated, and the hostility to Palmerston greater than there is any reason for.   I do not wish to see him again at the head of affairs, but I should be sorry to see a man so distingushed, who has been exalted so high, and who has many good qualities, end his life, or at least his political career. under circumstances of mortification and humiliation.   If this happens it will be owing principally to his obstinacy in persisting in leading a party who have no longer any mind to be led by him, and the insatiable ambition which cannot brook the notion of retirement at any time of life.   If he was wise, and was not blinded by vanity and the flattery of his hangers-on, he would take a juster and clearer view of his position, and supposing him still intent on playing the political game, he would endeavor to act a part as

nearly like that which Peel acted in his last years as the difference of circumstances would admit.

But the determination to have no more to do with Palmerston has not made the Whigs and Liberals more disposed
to throw themselves into the arms of Lord John, and as yet,
so far from any appearance of a reorganization of the Liberal party, they seem more disunited and scattered than
ever.   Even Lord John and Graham, who seemed to be most
closely allied, are now continually voting different ways ; and
as to the other leading men, it is impossible to predict how
they will vote on any subject that comes before Parliament.
In this state of confusion many Liberal-Conservatives are
beginning to wish for the consolidation of the Government,
and are inclining to support it, if the Government itself will
give them an opportunity of doing so, by asserting their own
independence as a *Conservative* Government, and will leave
off truckling to the Radicals, by accepting measures which
everyone knows to be repugnant to their feelings and opinions, and inconsistent with the principles they have always
professed.   Men who supported Palmerston's Government
because they considered it to be a Conservative one, foresee
that before long parties must assume the character of Radical and Conservative, the Whigs being merged in the former,
and that the party of the present Government forms the only
force capable of resisting the Whig and Radical union when
it takes place, and that their best course will be to join the
Conservative camp, if the presnt Government do not, by unprincipled and inconsistent concessions for the sake of an
easy official existence, render it impossible for them to do so.
I do not know to what extent this feeling prevails, but I believe it is extending, and Lord St. Germans, who is a very
staunch friend to the late Government, and latterly belonged
to them, told me the other day that Granville had great
difficulty in keeping his people together.   Ashburton is very
warm and eager in this sense, and though neither of these
men have much weight, I have no doubt they are exponents
of the sentiments of a much larger number.   I called on
Lyndhurst on Monday Evening, and talked this question
over with him, and entreated him to speak to Derby upon it.
We were very well agreed, and he said he would endeavor to
talk to Derby, but he is rather embarrassed, because he does
not know what Derby is going to do about the Jew Bill,
there being some strange signs of an intention on the part

of Derby to throw it over after all, though this would be so extremely foolish, as well as so false and dishonorable, that I cannot believe it is in his contemplation.

June 22d.—During the week I passed at Norman Court the Government here were gaining ground. They had two good divisions in the House of Commons, sufficient to prove that if they cannot command a majority here, they have at least as much influence and power and are as well supported as any other leader or party. Then the publication of the Cagliari papers, and the way in which that question was settled, was a real triumph to the Foreign Office, and acknowledged to be so by the whole Press of every shade, and by everybody in Parliament, not excepting the ex-Ministers themselves. They are undoubtedly gaining strength, while the chances of another Palmerston Government became more and more faint and remote. All information coincides in representing Palmerston's unpopularity as great and general, certainly the most extraordinary change that ever took place in so short a time. The Duke of Bedford writes to me from Endsleigh : "I hear of only one general feeling against Palmerston in the West. What a change since this time last year !"

I had a long talk with Tom Baring at Norman Court about the Government, their proceedings and their prospects, and we agreed entirely on the subject. I wanted him to speak to some of his friends the ministers, and to endeavor to get them to act a bolder and more consistent part as a Conservative Government, and he urged me to speak to Disraeli, which I told him I would do, and only refrained from doubting if I could do any real good with him. The Government are certainly placed in a difficult position. The Government and party whom they replaced were determined to thrust them out again as soon as possible, and their weakness and danger drove them into a quasi-alliance with the Radicals, or at least into so much deference and so many concessions to Radicals and Ultra-Liberals, that the Whigs, who were baffled and kept out by this policy, held them up to bitter scorn and reproach for acting in this manner, and now, when they agree to any measure with regard to which concession is reasonable and prudent, they are always assailed with the same reproaches instead of getting credit for so doing. To be sure they often contrive to make their concessions in such a way as to deprive them of all grace and merit. This has been pre-eminently the case with the Jew Bill.

Among the events of last week one of the most interesting was the Queen's visit to Birmingham, where she was received by the whole of that enormous population with an enthusiasm which is said to have exceeded all that was ever displayed in her former receptions at Manchester or elsewhere. It is impossible not to regard such manifestations as both significant and important. They evince a disposition in those masses of the population in which, if anywhere, the seeds of Radicalism are supposed to lurk, most favorable to the Conservative cause, by which I mean not to this or that party, but to the Monarchy and the Constitution under which we are living and flourishing, and which we may believe to be still dear to the hearts of the people of this country. This great fact lends some force to the notion entertained by many political thinkers, that there is more danger in conferring political power on the middle classes than in extending it far beneath them, and in point of fact that there is so little to be apprehended from the extension of the suffrage, that universal suffrage itself would be innocuous. Among the concessions of last week was the passing of Locke King's Bill for abolishing a property qualification, which was done with hardly any opposition. There can be no doubt that the practice was a mere sham, and that a property qualification was very often a fiction or a fraud, and such being the case, that it was useless to keep up the distinction; but it struck me, though I do not find that it occurred to anybody else, that the abolition might sooner or later have an indirect influence upon the question of the suffrage, for it may be urged, not without plausibility, that if it be held no longer necessary that a representative should have any property whatever, there is great inconsistency in requiring that the elector should have a certain amount of property to entitle him to vote.

June 26th.—The India Bill appears now likely to pass rather rapidly and in the shape presented by the Government. Everybody is tired to death of the subject and anxious to have it over, and the general impatience is increased by alarm at the foul state of the Thames, which (long discussed in a negligent way, and without much public attention or care) has suddenly assumed vast proportions, and is become an object of general interest and apprehension.

This makes the House of Commons eager to finish its business as expeditiously as it can, and members impatient to betake themselves to a purer and safer atmosphere. The Government continues to maintain its ascendency there, and last night Palmerston was beaten by considerable majorities on two amendments he moved to the India Bill.

The Chancellor has drawn down great obloquy on himself by a speech which he made at the Mansion House a night or two ago. Derby's illness having prevented his going to the dinner (given to the Ministers), Thesiger had to speak for him, and he made the very worst, most injudicious, and unbecoming speech which was ever delivered on such an occasion. No rule is more established than that politics are not to be introduced at these dinners, and yet his speech was nothing but a political song of triumph and glorification of his own Government and colleagues, as somebody said, a counterpart (though less offensive one) of Disraeli's Slough speech. All their heads are turned, and the Chancellor's as much or more than any.

Then there is a grand mess about the Jew question, which is hung up in a sort of abeyance in consequence of Derby's not being able to come down to the House of Lords. From the moment that Derby took upon himself to announce his abandonment of the contest, which he did not frankly and fully, but sulkily and reluctantly, he seems to have half repented of what he did, and to have, if not made, permitted and connived at, all sorts of difficulties and obstacles, while his subordinates and some of his colleagues have interposed to prevent or delay the final settlement. It is difficult to believe that he himself ever cared a straw about the Jew question, or that his opposition had any motive except that of pleasing the bigoted and narrow-minded of his party. His good sense saw that the moment was come when surrender was the best policy if not an absolute necessity, and having given utterance to this conviction, no doubt to the enormous disgust of many of his followers, it was his interest to get rid of the question as quickly as possible, and dismiss what as long as it remained on the *tapis* in any shape was a source of disagreement and ill-humor between him and his party. It is marvellous, therefore, that so clever a man should have acted so foolish a part as he has done. Having disgusted his own party by his concession, he is now disgusting everybody else and all other parties by his hesitation and pusillanimity in carrying it out, and, with an absence of dignity and firmness which is utterly unworthy of the high position he holds, he has permitted his Chancellor and some half-dozen subordinate members of his Government to do all they can to thwart the settlement of the question, and prolong the exclusion of the Jews. Instead of taking the matter into his own hands, and dealing with it according to the plain suggestions of common sense and sound policy, he has permitted a sort of little conspiracy to go on, which is exceedingly likely to bring about a collision between the two Houses, and to raise a flame in the House of Commons the consequences of which may be more serious to the Government than any one contemplates. Lyndhurst, whose wise head is provoked and disgusted to the last degree at all these proceedings, has bitterly complained of them, and at the way in which they have treated him, and the bill he drew up for the express purpose of putting an end to the dilemma.

July 9th.—After all Derby ran true to the Jew Bill, and if he did it in an awkward way, allowances must be made for him and for his difficulties with his party, who are full of chagrin at being compelled to swallow this obnoxious measure. It is on the whole better that the bulk of them should have voted in conformity with their notorious opinions, as it made no difference as to the result, and has a better appearance than if they had whisked round at Derby's bidding. The India Bill has passed the House of Commons pretty harmoniously, and people seem to think it has been licked into a very decent shape.

The most interesting event of the present day is the marriage of Lord Overstone's daughter to a Major Lindsay,[1] who has got the greatest heiress who ever existed, that is, supposing she inherits her father's prodigious wealth, which since old Jones Loyd's death is reckoned to amount to six or seven millions.

July 13th.—After an ineffectual attempt on the part of the Opposition to get rid of the "reasons" of the Lords, the Jew Bill has passed, Granville and Lansdowne protesting against the absurdity of the conduct of Derby with re-

---

1 [Afterward Sir Robert Loyd Lindsay, V. C., raised to the Peerage in 1885 by the title of Lord Wantage. The property of Lord Overstone, as disposed of by his will, amounted to about three millions, and would pass in reversion to the Loyd family on the failure of issue by his daughter.]

gard to it. It is remarkable that though Lord Lansdowne has for some time appeared much *baissé*, his speech was as good and sensible a speech as he ever made in his life. As to Derby, as it is impossible that so clever a man as he is could willingly act so foolish and even ridiculous a part as he has done on this occasion, I conclude that he felt obliged to do what he has done in order to avoid quarrelling with his own friends, who without doubt are intensely disgusted at the bitter pill he has obliged them to swallow, and as he knows best what he can venture with them and what not, it is more reasonable to accept the measure on his own terms than to be angry with him for the way in which he has contrived it.

The last accounts from India are far from satisfactory, and the apprehensions which I long ago felt and expressed, but which I had begun to think unfounded, seem not unlikely to be realised. It is clear that the contest is neither over nor drawing to a close. Our danger consists in the swarms of armed and hostile natives, and in the climate. The rebels we always beat when we can grapple with them, but we cannot crush and subdue them. They gather together and assail our people when a good opportunity presents itself, and when they are repulsed (as is always the case) their masses are dissolved and scattered abroad, without any material diminution of their numbers, and ready to assemble and attack any other vulnerable point, while the British troops are harassed to death by unceasing pursuits of foes so much more nimble and able to endure the climate than themselves. This species of warfare must be disheartening and disgusting, and it involves a consumption of life requiring more reinforcements than we can supply. All the accounts we receive concur in the insufficiency of the European force, and the necessity of fresh supplies. One letter I saw yesterday talks of 40,000 men being requisite.

Petworth, July 31st.—I came here from Goodwood, not having been here for twenty years, and am rather glad to see once more a place where I passed so much of my time in my younger days. I think it is the finest house I have ever seen, and its collection of pictures is unrivalled for number, beauty, and interest. Parliament is to be up on Monday, and the Council for the prorogation is to take place to-day at Osborne.

I met Brunnow at Goodwood, who talked over the political events of the Russian war, and assured me that the part he had played in it had been much misrepresented, that he had never been misled by Aberdeen, nor had he ever misled the Emperor Nicholas, but on the contrary had told him, without any disguise, the real state of affairs, and the almost certainty that war would ensue, that he was well aware himself, and had impressed on his master, that although Aberdeen was most anxious to avoid war, he had no power to do so, and that though he was nominally Prime Minister, he was destitute of the authority of one. He said the Emperor was quite sincere in all he had said to Hamilton Seymour, and if we had had at Petersburg a minister with more tact and judgment, war would not have taken place. He (Brunnow) had urged Aberdeen to send Granville there for the purpose, who, he thinks, would have done very well, and of whom he has a high opinion.

London, August 15th.—I returned to town from Petworth last Monday week, and on Tuesday a fit of gout came on, which has laid me up ever since, leaving me no energy to do anything, and least of all to execute the purpose I entertained of sketching the past session of Parliament, and the curious events which it evolved; the decline and fall of Palmerston and his Government, the advent of Derby, and the vicissitudes of his career, deserve a narrative which might, if well handled by some well-informed writer, be made very interesting : but I am conscious of my own unfitness and dare not attempt it. It is in truth time for me to leave off keeping a journal, for by degrees I have lost the habit of communicating with all the people from whom I have been in the habit of obtaining political information, and I know nothing worth recording.

CHAPTER XVII.

Hinchinbrook, September 5th.—At The Grove last week, and on Friday to Osborne for a Council. At the Grove I met Charles Villiers and the Duke of Bedford, and had much talk with both of them about affairs in general, particularly with the Duke about Lord John. He is busily employed in concocting a Reform Bill, which he had probably better leave alone. He seems to have shown his project to several people, and recently to Aberdeen, who wrote him word that he must take care not to make it too mild, so much so as to be inconsistent with what he has before proposed. It seems it is very mild, for it embraces no Schedule A, no disqualification, though a good deal of addition to the constituency. Lord John has recently struck up a great intimacy with Lord Stanley, and has had him repeatedly down to Pembroke Lodge. They take very kindly to each other, and Lord John is evidently anxious to cultivate him, for he asked the Duke to invite Stanley to go to Woburn, where Lord John and all his family are gone to stay. He has been talking a great deal to Stanley on past politics, but not on present, which would have been rather awkward in their relative positions, but he has told Stanley a great deal about the political affairs in which he has been engaged, especially with respect to the great Reform Bill, its history and incidents, which details no doubt were very interesting and useful to him, and I am not surprised at Stanley's being much pleased with Lord John's society and conversation, for Lord John is very agreeable and full of that sort of political information in which Stanley takes the greatest delight and interest.

Although Lord John has abstained from making any attempt to establish political relations between them, it is highly probable that he should look forward to the possibility of some such relations being hereafter established, for in the present state of parties a fresh organization and combination is almost inevitable, and he may very naturally look forward to a combination into which they may both enter, and with this view he may be very glad to cultivate a personal and social intimacy, and the Duke thinks he has some such view in his mind.

The Duke told me that he was at Lord Broughton's the other day, when Broughton said he had been applied to by some of Palmerston's former followers to make a representation to Palmerston of the present state of affairs and of the Liberal party, and to suggest to him the expediency of his abdication of the lead of it, and the impossibility of that party regaining its ascendency as long as he insisted on continuing its chief and retaining his pretensions of returning to office. To this request he sent a refusal. He said he entirely agreed with the people making it, but that it would have no effect whatever except that of making a personal quarrel between himself and the Palmerstons, with whom he had always been on very good terms. I did not learn the names of these Whig malcontents. Charles Villiers takes a similar view, but does not think that anything would induce Palmerston to retire, or that his former colleagues and immediate adherents would transfer their support to any one else as long as he continues to claim it from them. He thinks, moreover, and he has very good means of judging, that his position and that of John Russell and the impossibility of their reunion will effectually paralyze the Liberal party and secure the possession of office to the present Government, and that there is on the whole rather a preference for the continuation of the present state of things than any desire for a change which would bring the Whigs back again. He had recently been with George Lewis, and found him at length rather disposed to come into my view of the matter of their resignation, and to regret it. It is entirely the opinion of Charles Villiers himself, and he said there would have been no difficulty in obtaining from the House of Commons a vote of confidence, for there was no wish to turn them out, and having administered the rebuke which the Government so well merited, the majority would have seized with alacrity an occasion to make it up with them, and to show that they had no desire to quarrel with them outright.

The Opposition now found all their hopes on the dissensions which they expect to arise in the Tory Government and camp, which is a very uncertain prospect, and as to which they are very likely to be disappointed. The day I went to Osborne I had some conversation with Disraeli, who gave me to understand that he was well aware the Opposition relied on this contingency, but that it was not likely to happen. He was aware of Lord Stanley's *liaison* with Lord John, and it was evident that the former had made no secret of it, and had told Disraeli that there was (at present) nothing political in it. Lord John had not said a word about his Reform Bill to Stanley, and Disraeli knew that he had not. All this looks like union and confidence between them.

As far as outward appearances go, the Queen is on very good terms with them, for she gave audiences to several of them, and long ones. Her conduct at the time of the breakup was certainly curious and justifies them in saying that it was by her express desire that Derby undertook the formation of the Government. If Palmerston and his Cabinet were actuated by the motives and expectations which I ascribe to them, Her Majesty certainly did not play into their hands in that game. When Derby sat before her all the difficulties of his situation, and entreated her again to reflect upon it, a word from her would have induced him (without having anything to complain of) to throw it back into Palmerston's hands. But the word she did speak was decisive as to his going on, and there is no reason to believe that she was playing a deep game and calculating on his failure. Nor do I believe that she would herself have liked to see Palmerston made all powerful. She can hardly have forgotten how inclined he has always been to abuse his power, and how much she has suffered from his exercise of it, even when he was to a certain degree under control, and although she seemed to be quite reconciled to him, and to be anxious for the stability of his Government, it is difficult to know what her real feelings (or rather those of the Prince) were, and it is more than probable that her anxiety for the success of Palmerston's Government was more on account of the members of it whom she personally likes, and whom she was very reluctant to lose, than out of partiality for the Premier himself. To Clarendon she is really attached, and Granville

she likes very much ; most of the rest she regarded with
indifference.

London, November 4th.—Two months have elapsed during which I have felt no inclination to note down anything
in this book, but now that the Newmarket meetings are at an
end, and I must needs think of other things, I shall jot down
the very few things that have come across me in the interval. When I was at Hillingdon a few weeks ago, I was
surprised to hear from Charles Mills a glowing panegyric on
Lord Stanley, who has gained golden opinions and great popularity at the India House.[1] I was prepared to hear of his
ability, his indefatigable industry, and his businesslike qualities ; but I was surprised to hear so much of his courtesy,
affability, patience, and candor, that he is neither dictatorial
nor conceited, always ready to listen to other people's
opinions and advice, and never fancying that he knows
better than anybody else. I afterward told Jonathan Peel
what I had heard, and he confirmed the truth of this report,
and said he was the same in the Cabinet ; but he made me
comprehend his popularity with the Council by telling me
that he espoused all their views and interests, and co-operated
with them in endeavoring to retain certain powers which belonged to the extinct Court of Directors, but which ought,
as a consequence of the change, to pass into other hands,
particularly military appointments and matters of military
control. This received confirmation not long ago from the
Duke of Cambridge, whom I met at Cheveley, and who gave
me an account of some matter in which he had received and
executed certain orders from the Secretary of War, and soon
after received a very sharp letter from Stanley calling him
to account for having interfered in what, he said, belonged
to the Indian Secretary. The Duke referred him to the War
Office, so that there seems already a conflict of jurisdiction
between the two offices. From all this it is apparent that
we shall have fresh Indian discussions when Parliament
meets, and there will be a necessity for fresh arrangements
for the transaction of business. This may seem to be a very
trifling matter, and not worth noticing, but Lord Stanley is
so completely *the man* of the present day, and in all human
probability is destined to play so important and conspicuous

---

[1] [Lord Stanley, the present Earl of Derby, had succeeded to the Presidency
of the Board of Control upon the resignation of Lord Ellenborough, and was the
first Secretary of State for India upon the abolition of the former office.]

a part in political life, that the time may come when any details, however minute, of his early career will be deemed worthy of recollection.

I hear the Queen has written a letter to the Prince of Wales announcing to him his emancipation from parental authority and control, and that it is one of the most admirable letters that ever were penned. She tells him that he may have thought the rule they adopted for his education a severe one, but that his welfare was their only object, and well knowing to what seductions of flattery he would eventually be exposed, they wished to prepare and strengthen his mind against them, that he was now to consider himself his own master, and that they should never intrude any advice upon him, although always ready to give it him whenever he thought fit to seek it. It was a very long letter, all in that tone, and it seems to have made a profound impression on the Prince, and to have touched his feelings to the quick. He brought it to Gerald Wellesley in floods of tears, and the effect it produced is a proof of the wisdom which dictated its composition.

November 17th.—The principal topics of interest for the last fortnight have been Bright's speeches, the visit of Palmerston and Clarendon to Compiègne, the Portuguese and French quarrel, and the pamphlet and approaching trial of Montalembert, on all of which there is plenty to say. Bright's speeches have evidently been a failure, and if they produce any effect, it will probably be one rather useful to the Government ; but the very failure only proves more strongly the bad policy of Derby in bringing forward a Reform measure, and how much more safe he would have been if he had let it alone. There is a considerable though not universal impression that by some means and through the operation of the chapter of accidents this Reform Bill will prove fatal to him. Mr. Elwin, the editor of the "Quarterly Review," told the Duke of Bedford he thought so, and that he had been told by a Cabinet Minister that there had been such serious differences of opinion among them on this subject that if the session had been prolonged the Government would probably have gone to pieces at that time, and Lord John told the Duke that Walpole had intimated to him something of the same kind. Lord John is expecting, and Palmerston is hoping, that the Government will fall, and the latter is still confident that his day will

20

come again, a confidence which no one else seems to partake
of.   Clarendon, who is the staunchest of Palmerston's allies
and colleagues, has been endeavoring to dissipate this illu-
sion and to bring him to take a more accurate view of his
own position, but without success.   "He cannot see why
John Russell should not again take office under him," and
it is in vain that Clarendon assures him that nothing on
earth will induce Lord John to do so.   Lord John seems
disposed to bide his time, and evidently cherishes a hope and
expectation that the Whig party will return to their allegiance to him and enable him to form another Government.
He seem to have a liking for Bright, though he does not
agree with all his views of Reform.   At this moment my
own belief is that the present Government have the best
chance in this race for power from the mere fact of their
being in possession, and from the hopeless disunion and confusion in which the Whigs and Liberals are plunged.

Montalembert's paper is admirable, and I agree with almost every part of it, especially about the Indian debate
and Indian policy, and the causes of Palmerston's extraordinary fall and the loss of his popularity.   His prosecution
by the Imperial Government is either an enormous mistake
and political error, or a stroke of policy so deep and refined
as to be beyond my comprehension.   Here everybody regards it as a great imprudence.

December 2d.—I returned to town yesterday, having been
to Badger Hall, thence to Grimstone, then to Ossington, and
yesterday from Hinchinbrook.   If I have written nothing it
is not from want of interesting events worth notice, but
because I have known and heard nothing more than all the
world learnt from the newspapers.   The chief topics of
interest have been the pamphlet and the trial of Montalembert and the visit of Palmerston and Clarendon to
Compiègne.   The first seems to have excited more interest
here than in Paris, where the tyrannical proceeding was
taken very quietly, and little sympathy felt for a man who
wrote so enthusiastically about England, and rebuked his
own countrymen, and particularly his co-religionaries, for
their unworthy conduct and language toward us.   There
appears to have been a general feeling of regret or disapproval of the visit to Paris, even on the part of those who
are most friendly to the two Lords.   I think it is a pity
they should have gone just at this moment, when the

Montalembert affair and the Portuguese quarrel have made
the Emperor Napoleon very unpopular here; but it does
not seem to me to be a matter of much consequence, or to
be worth the indignation which in some quarters it has
elicited.

Hillingdon, December 12th.—I went to The Grove on
Wednesday last and came back on Friday. There I had
long talks with Clarendon for the first time for many a day,
when he told me a great deal that was interesting, just as he
used to do formerly, first about his visit to Compiègne and
his conversations with the Emperor. The Emperor told
him that his motive for prosecuting Montalembert was that
he was aware that there was a conspiracy of literary men,
enemies of his Government, to write it down in a very in-
sidious manner, not by any direct attacks, but, under the
pretence of discussing subjects either not political or not
French, to introduce matter most hostile and most mischievous to him, and that it was necessary to, put down such a
conspiracy, and he thought the best course was to proceed at
once against a man so conspicuous as Montalembert, and to
make an example of him, by which others would be deterred.
This was his excuse, whatever its value. It appears to me a
very bad one, and I doubt if the fact itself is true, though
Clarendon seemed to think it was. They had a great deal
of conversation about Italy and the anti-Austrian projects
attributed to France, touching which the Emperor's ideas
were most strange and extravagant. He said there had been
two questions in which France was interested : one the regeneration of Poland, the other the regeneration of Italy ;
that in the pursuit of the first France naturally became the
ally of Austria against Russia, in the pursuit of the other
she became the ally of Russia and Sardinia against Austria ;
that the peace with Russia had put an end to anything being
done about the first, and the second alone became possible.
Clarendon then pointed out to him all the difficulties of involving himself in such a contest as this scheme supposed,
that Austria would sacrifice her last florin and her last man
in defence of her Italian provinces, that to go to war with
her would almost inevitably sooner or later plunge all Europe
into war, and that the object to be gained by it, even by
France herself, would be wholly incommensurate with the
cost and the danger that would be incurred. The Emperor
appeared to have no reply to make to Clarendon's remon-

strances, nor did I gather that His Majesty had any *casus belli* against Austria, nor even any just cause of complaint to urge against her, from which I draw the inference not only that his policy is of a very wild and chimerical character, but that at any moment when he might see, or think he saw, any advantage in attacking another Power, no considcration of justice and good faith, still less of moderation and care for the happiness and peace of the world, would restrain him, and from such a contingency England would be no more exempt than any other country.[1]

December 12*th.*—Another day the Emperor asked Clarendon to come into his room, when he told him that he wanted his advice, that he was in a great dilemma and embarrassment in regard to his Roman occupation, and in a false position, from which he did not know how to extricate himself. He was dying to recall the French troops, and yet unable to do it. He had always hoped to be able to get the policy laid down in the Edgar Ney letter carried out, but as soon as the Pope and his ecclesiastical councillors returned to Rome they refused to do anything, and whenever he held out any threat of withdrawing his troops they always said he might do so whenever he pleased, for they knew very well the reasons which prevented his doing it : the moment the French troops marched out there would be an uprising in Rome and in the Papal States. The religious party in France would deeply resent his exposing the Pope to any such danger, and as soon as the French went away the Austrians would march in and be masters of the whole country. Clarendon acknowledged the gravity of the situation and the difficulty, but could suggest no solution of it. They discussed the possibility of indncing the Pope to relinquish his temporal sovereignty, and to accept a great revenue instead, but neither of them seems to have thought this plan feasible.

January 14*th*, 1859.—I purposed at the close of the last year to say a few words about a year which might well be called *annus mirabilis* and *annus mœstissimus* besides, for I do not remember any year marked by a greater number and

---

[1] [It is remarkable that this conversation of the Emperor with Lord Clarendon at Compiègne took place within a month of the speech to Baron Hübner on New Year's Day, which was the signal of war between France and Austria, and at a time when the secret alliance between the Emperor and M. de Cavour had been already concluded. The Emperor's object was evidently to delude his English guests, and Lord Clarendon was partially deceived by him, although he clearly perceived that there was danger of war ahead.]

variety of remarkable events and occurrences, and certainly none which has been so fatal to the happiness of so many of our friends.   One calamity has succeeded another with frightful rapidity, till it is difficult to point to any one who has not sustained some terrible bereavement in the persons of near and dear relations or intimate friends.   A severe fit of gout which attacked me on Christmas Day, and has kept hold of me ever since, prevented my executing my purpose, and now I have forgotten all I intended to say, and can only take up the present condition of affairs as they present themselves at the beginning of this year, and this is dark and unpromising enough.   All Europe has been thrown into alarm by the speech which the Emperor Napoleon made to the Austrian Ambassador Hübner on New Year's Day, and by the announcement which followed it that Prince Napoleon was going to Turin to marry the King of Sardinia's daughter. The language of the King of Sardinia in his speech to his Parliament shortly afterward confirmed the general apprehensions.   The menacing manifestations having produced their effect, the Emperor seems to have thought it advisable to draw in his horns, and to try and calm the effervescence he had produced.   This, however, was not so easy, and in spite of certain tranquillizing articles which the French Press was instructed to put forth, the impression that mischief is brewing cannot be effaced, and though many think that there will be no immediate outbreak, and the money dealers and speculators comfort themselves with thinking that want of money will prevent the great military Powers from going to war, the best informed persons, and those who are most accustomed to watch the signs of the times, are convinced that the time is near at hand when the peace of the world will be broken, that the Emperor is determined upon an aggression on Austria, and that he is only undecided as to the time when the operation shall be begun.   It is now evident that when our Ex-Ministers were at Compiègne, and when the Emperor pretended that he wanted to consult Clarendon confidentially, he only made a half-confidence of his views and his position, and that he concealed from Clarendon the important fact of the marriage of Prince Napoleon, which was arranged at the time.

The Grove, January 25th.—I have passed three days here very agreeably ; a large party on Saturday and Sunday, after which Clarendon, George Lewis, and I, talking over every-

thing interesting at home and abroad. There has been a
good deal of correspondence between Clarendon and John
Russell in a very friendly spirit, quite different from the
terms they have been on till lately, and indicating the possibility of their coming together again in Opposition and in
office. I saw also some letters of Palmerston's upon foreign
affairs, exceedingly sound and judicious. I am bound to say
that all I hear and see of Palmerston's views, opinions, and
conduct is highly creditable to him, and very different from
what I expected. He evinces no impatience to return to
office, and no misconception of his own position. All he
writes on foreign affairs, on France and Austria and Italy,
is marked by great wisdom and moderation. He is taking
his proper place as head of the Liberal and Whig party, prepared to go to Parliament and wait for the development of
the policy and measures of the Government, before forming
any plan of a political campaign. Reading at the same time
the letters of Lord John and those of Palmerston on the same
subject, that of foreign policy, I am struck with the great
superiority of the latter.

Bretby, January 27th.—I left The Grove yesterday morning, and came here to-day. At breakfast yesterday Clarendon handed over to me a letter from Reeve, enclosing one
from Guizot upon the aspect of affairs in Europe and the
chances of war and peace ; an admirable letter, as all his
are. Reeve said that he had been told that Palmerston was
likely to give utterance to some sentiments very anti-Austrian, and in favor of Italian nationality, than which nothing could be more mischievous or more conducive to the
objects of Louis Napoleon. This seemed to me so inconsistent with the spirit of moderation and good sense which I
had remarked in the letters I had already seen of Palmerston's, that I said I could not think it possible that he was
meditating anything of the sort, and I was greatly surprised
when Clarendon replied, and George Lewis agreed with him,
that nothing was more possible, and that he should not be
at all surprised if he expressed sentiments which were very
much those which he had always entertained. Of course
they both deprecated any such language in the strongest
manner. When I got to town I told Reeve what had passed,
and he then told me his authority for what he had written,
and that his informant had gathered it from conversations
with Palmerston himself. It was at all events satisfactory

to find that the language of the "Times" had undergone no alteration, and that they adhered to the same judicious course and vigorous argumentation which they have all along adopted. Clarendon and George Lewis are equally afraid of what John Russell may say, but they are aware that though he may do considerable mischief, his dicta are infinitely less important than Palmerston's. Granville arrived last night from Paris and Rome, and I saw him for a few minutes as I was starting to come here. I had just time to ascertain that his views are identical with those of Clarendon and George Lewis, and that his efforts will be joined to theirs in attempting to persuade both Palmerston and John Russell to refrain from saying anything which may serve as an encouragement to the Emperor, and George Lewis said that on Palmerston's language in the House of Commons the peace of the world might possibly depend. There seems no reason to doubt that one of the things which keeps the Emperor's mind in suspense and uncertainty is his desire to hear what passes in our Parliament, and to ascertain what amount of sympathy and support the Italian cause and a war against Austria are likely to find in this country. Palmerston must have already taken such a measure of the public feeling here as to know that any appeal to anti-Austrian and pro-Italian sympathies would meet with no respouse either in or out of Parliament. The most, therefore, that he will probably venture to do will be strenuously to recommend a complete neutrality, and that this country should determine to keep aloof from any contest that may ensue. This would be playing the Emperor's game, and might perhaps be more useful to him than any other course we could take, for it would find pretty general concurrence, and most likely elicit many expressions of opinions which the Emperor would be able with some plausibility to construe in the manner most favorable to his own pretensions and designs.

January 31st.—Dined with Lord Salisbury on Saturday at the Sheriffs' dinner, when I met all the Cabinet, except Malmesbury, Hardwicke, and John Manners. Derby told me a curious thing. An experiment was made of the possible speed by which a telegraphic message could be sent and an answer got. They fixed on Corfu, made every preparation, and sent *one word*. The message and return were effected in six seconds. I would not have believed this on any other authority.

Granville is just come from Paris, where he spent a week; he saw and conversed with everybody, beginning with the Emperor and ending with Thiers. All the Ministers he talked to, Walewski, Fould, and Rouher, are dead against war, Morny the same, Baroche said to be for it, and Fleury, who wants to distinguish himself in the field. The Emperor talked over the whole question and assured him he had not committed himself to the King of Sardinia, but on the contrary had told him he would not support him if he committed any imprudence toward Austria. Granville's impression is that the question is adjourned for the present, owing to the clear manifestation in France, but much more to the unanimous tone of the German and English Press. He is, however, waiting in great anxiety for the debates in our Parliament, and still hopes for some anti-Austrian expression which may favor his own views. He has such a contempt for his own nation and for the opinions of the French people that these last do not weigh much with him, and he fancies that they may be at any moment changed and run in a warlike current. Granville thinks our Government have acted properly throughout these transactions, so far as he can judge.

February 5th.—Parliament opened on Thursday with, as everybody owned, a very good speech, and the discussions in both Houses were in a very good tone, and all that could be desired as to foreign policy. It will be impossible for the Emperor to derive from what passed a single word from any quarter favorable to his projects. The disappointment of his expectations in this respect may be very annoying to him, and possibly induce him still to defer his final resolution, but it is too much to hope that the language of our Parliament will turn him altogether from his design. Indeed it has now become equally difficult for him to advance without danger or to retreat without discredit, and in his position discredit is in itself fraught with danger.

February 12th.—The Emperor Napoleon's speech, looked for with so much anxiety here, arrived a few hours after its delivery on Monday last, and was on the whole regarded as rather pacific than the contrary, but still so reserved and ambiguous that it might mean anything or lead to anything or nothing. The general opinion seems to be that nothing will take place *for the present.* The Government have begun their campaign so quietly, and with so little disturbance or threatening of any, that if such calm appearances were not often fallacious, one should predict their passing smoothly through the session ; but when one thinks of this time last year, of the apparent strength and security of Palmerston's Government, and of the suddenness of his fall, it is impossible to rely upon the continuance of this unclouded sky.

February 19*th*.—The general complaint is that nothing is done in Parliament, and that there is a general apathy, under the continuance of which the Government gets on without hindrance, while their faults or blunders pass unchecked. The Chancellor incurred a momentary odium by his attempt at perpetuating a very shameless job, by making his son-in-law a Judge in Lunacy without having any qualifications for such an office ; but after a little spurt in the House of Commons, the result of which was the appointment being rescinded, the matter quietly dropped. Gladstone's extravagant proceedings at Corfu [1] have elicited something like an attack led on by Lord Grey, but although this subject will probably be more seriously and warmly discussed after he comes home, it does not seem likely to lead to much at present, and Derby will probably parry Grey's attack on Monday next.

February 27*th*.—Derby prevailed on Grey to defer his Ionian motion till Gladstone's return, which he said would be in a fortnight at least. Palmerston had given notice of his intention to call the attention of the House of Commons to the present state of Europe, and to ask if the Government could give the country any information on the subject. The Government tried to persuade him to defer his intention, but without effect, and he persisted in his course. In the meanwhile Cowley suddenly arrived in England, sent for by the Government, as it was said, for the purpose of receiving instructions in respect to the conferences expected at Paris on the Danubian affairs. On Thursday morning the world was electrified at reading an article in the " Times " stating that Cowley was going on a special mission to Vienna for the purpose of making matters up, if possible, between France and Austria. The day before I had been apprised of the fact by Granville, who had heard it from Clarendon, to

---

[1] [Mr. Gladstone had accepted, temporarily, the office of Lord High Commissioner of the Ionian Islands, under Lord Derby's Government. His proceedings there excited great surprise in England. The eventual result of his mission was the surrender of the Protectorate of the Ionian Islands to the Kingdom of Greece.]

whom Cowley had imparted the secret of his mission. The mission was in fact rather one from the Emperor than from our Government, who had really done nothing whatever, but were too happy to allow Cowley to go and try his hand in patching matters up. He has done it all off his own bat. Seeing how day after day war appeared to be becoming more imminent, he resolved to see if he could not do something to arrest the evil; he found the French Ministers quite agreed with him, and the Emperor in a state of mingled rage, disappointment, and perplexity, clinging with his characteristic tenacity to the designs on which his mind has been so long fixed, and to which he probably stands committed more than we are aware of, by his own professions, and by his cousin, who no doubt gave Cavour to understand he might certainly count upon the Emperor's aid. This course also he is the more reluctant to abandon, as he has certainly persuaded himself, or has been persuaded by others, that in no other way can he secure himself from the attempts of Italian conspirators and assassins, so that it is personal fear which is the real ground of what is called his policy. On the other hand, he is intensely disgusted and enraged at finding the whole feeling and opinion of England so decidedly pronounced against him, and that in no quarter whatever, neither in Parliament nor the Press, which represents the mind of the whole country, nor in any public men, can he find the slightest sympathy or encouragement, or anything but the most indignant disapprobation.[1]

The sentiment of England is if possible still stronger in

---

[1] [The war of 1859 is now judged of more favorably than it was at the time of its inception, and the result obtained—the independence and unification of Italy—has led men to condone the tortuous and deceitful policy by which it was arrived at. The object of M. de Cavour was a noble one, although the means he employed were unscrupulous. The chief motive of the Emperor Napoleon was the fear of his old allies the Carbonari. Orsini's attempt on his life had powerfully affected him.

To English statesmen of all parties (with one or two exceptions) it was apparent that the declaration of war by France on Austria was the destruction of the great compact of 1815, which (whatever may have been its defects) had given forty-four years of peace to the Continent of Europe, and which had survived the Revolution of 1848 and the Crimean contest of 1854. It was the first outbreak of the military power of the French Empire and it was likely to lead to future wars, as the result has proved. The defeat of Austria and the dissolution of the Germanic Confederation in 1866 was the result of the combined action of Prussia and Italy, north and south of the Alps; and the Franco-German war of 1870 was the result of the military ascendency Prussia had thus acquired in Europe. The policy of England was simply based on the principle that the duration of peace depended on the maintenance of the existing territorial arrangements of Europe.]

the same sense in Germany, and it is universal in France, where it is only prevented from manifesting itself with as much force and vivacity as in Germany and here by the fettered and subservient condition of the Press.   In addition to this I am informed that the project of war is not popular with the army itself ; and as it is not morally certain that by plunging into war the Emperor will be secure from the danger of assassination, and there is at least as good a chance of war bringing with it perils of another sort quite as formidable, so his very selfishness makes him doubt and waver, and inclines him to listen to the remonstrances which are addressed to him.   Upon this uncertain and varying state of mind Cowley has been endeavoring to work, and he has so far succeeded as to have been entrusted by the Emperor with a commission to go to Vienna and negotiate with the Austrian Government a settlement of their differences, or rather, as there are in fact no differences to settle, to obtain from the Austrian Government some concessions by virtue of which he may be enabled to withdraw from his present false position without discredit, by which means he may give satisfaction to France and Europe, though at the risk of disappointing Sardinia and exasperating the Italian Carbonari.

When Palmerston's discussion came on upon Friday last, it was already known (through the "Times") that Cowley was going to Vienna, though he himself had told nobody of this expedition (except Clarendon), and he evidently did not mean it should have been proclaimed.   On Friday, Disraeli and Malmesbury said nothing of Cowley's mission, but they both announced that the Papal territories would be evacuated by the French and Austrian troops, and the public inferred that this evacuation was going to take place by a mutual agreement, and everybody asked, "Why then is Cowley going to Vienna?" but the truth was that the Pope had requested the two Governments to withdraw their troops, and one of Cowley's objects is to procure the assent of Austria to that withdrawal, France having no doubt agreed to it on certain conditions, of which I do not know the details, but which are committed to the management of Cowley.   Clarendon seemed to think that there was no more danger *now* of the pacific purpose of Cowley being obstructed at Vienna than at Paris, for he said that the Austrians are so proud, and moreover so greatly incensed at the conduct of France, that it is very doubtful whether they will be induced to make any

concessions at all, and whether the Emperor of Austria will
not prefer to encounter all the danger of war, prepared as he
is, than consent to anything which should have the appearance of humbling himself before the outrageous pretences
and intolerable insolence of the Emperor of the French.

In the midst of the absorbing interest of this great question, the Government Reform Bill is coming on.   They appear to have thought it advisable to bespeak the good word
of the "Times," and accordingly they sent Delane a copy of
their Bill.   This morning the heads of it appear in the
"Times" with an approving article.   Mild as it appears to
be, it is too strong for Walpole and Henley, who have resigned, but why they did not resign before it is difficult to
understand.   At Kent House yesterday afternoon there was
a little gathering of Clarendon, Charles Wood, and George
Lewis, when they all agreed that if the Government measure
was such a one as they could possibly support, their proper
policy would be to assist the Government in carrying it.

March 1st.—According to all political calculations Cowley's mission ought to succeed, but I feel no confidence in
his success, and rather believe that the Emperor Napoleon
is acting with his usual duplicity and treachery, and duping
Cowley to gain time, which is necessary to his plans.[1]   It is
revolting to see that the peace of the world and so much of
the happiness or misery of mankind depend upon the caprice
and will and the selfish objects and motives of a worthless
upstart and adventurer, who is destitute of every principle
of honor, good faith, or humanity, but who is unfortunately
invested with an enormous power for good or evil.   And this
is the end of fifty years of incessant movement, of the progress of society, of the activity and development of the
human intellect in the country which is eternally mouthing
about its superior civilization and its mission to extend the
benefits of that civilization over the whole world.

Disraeli brought forward his Reform Bill last night in a
well-set speech, only too elaborate.   It was coolly received,
except by its most angry opponents, who lost no time in denouncing it.

---

[1] [This was the fact.   It was not known until long afterward that positive
engagements had been entered into at Plombières between the Emperor and M.
de Cavour in the preceding autumn, including the marriage of Prince Napoleon
to the daughter of the King of Sardinia, and the cession of Savoy and Nice as a
compensation for the conquest of Northern Italy.   Cavour had the Emperor in
his power, and threatened, if he drew back, to publish the correspondence.]

March 3d.—It would be difficult to say what the feeling
of the House of Commons really is on the subject of the
Government Reform Bill. The night it came out everybody
who spoke spoke against it. The Ultra-Reformers, from
Bright down to John Russell, naturally express nothing
but abhorrence and contempt for such a measure; half-
and-half Reformers, who consider Reform a necessity, and
who would be glad to have the question settled for the
present on such easy terms, do not venture to say much in
its favor; and the Whigs generally, particularly at their
head-quarters, Brooks's, discuss with much variety of opinion
whether the second reading ought to be resisted or not,
the prevailing opinion being that the principle of the Bill
(which is the equalisation of town and county franchise) is
so inadmissible that it ought to be rejected, and they come
to that conclusion the more readily because they think its
rejection in that stage would put an end to the Government.
On the other hand, Derby brought together two hundred of
his supporters the day after the Bill appeared, and obtained
their assent to it, and an engagement to support it. The
resignations of Henley and Walpole have been prejudicial to
the Government. Their explanations, which were full of
half-suppressed bitterness toward their colleagues, were considered damaging, and to have revealed trickery on the part
of Derby, though they seem to me to have rather exhibited
weakness on the part of the retiring Ministers. But what
they have clearly shown is the extreme penury of the party
in point of intellectual resources, when they can find no man
of any weight or reputation to fill up the vacancies. But if
the Government is weak, and their position very precarious,
the state of the Opposition is at least as deplorable, for there
is no union or agreement amongst them, and Granville acknowledged to me last night that if Derby should fall on the
second reading, and Palmerston be sent for, as it may be expected he would be, by the Queen, that it is impossible to
see how another Government could be formed. This state
of affairs and the magnitude of the embarrassment will probably at last make some of those who so obstinately insisted
upon their being right in resigning last year after the Vote
of Censure, begin to think that they would have done better
to accept the rebuke and stay in. All that is now occurring
serves to confirm my own opinion upon that point.

Since Cowley's arrival at Vienna nothing has been heard

of his mission, but there is nothing apparent tending to lead to the conclusion that he has been able to do any good, and the general impression is that the Emperor Napoleon is only endeavoring to gain time, and making a tool of Cowley in hopes of thereby committing this country in some degree to his ulterior designs, and there are not wanting persons who believe that it will after all be against this country that his arms will be turned, and not against Austria.

March 8th.—On Saturday morning the "Times" published the article in the "Moniteur" (evidently the Emperor's composition), in which a formal denial was given to the imputed warlike intentions of France. The general impression produced by this manifesto was that the Emperor had at last been diverted from his purpose by the various manifestations which he had seen at home as well as abroad, and that he had resolved to abandon it altogether. Many, however, refused to believe in this happy result, and thought that he was only trying to throw dust in the eyes of the world, and endeavoring to gain time. All things considered, I incline to believe that he has resolved to postpone his warlike designs *sine die,* though retaining his wish to employ the vast means on which he has expended so much money, and looking forward to some pretext which the chapter of accidents may afford him to execute his purpose.

Strenuous efforts are making to bring about an understanding and agreement between the Whig leaders as to opposing the Government Bill, in which nobody is so active as George Lewis, who being very intimate with John Russell, and much in his confidence, and at the same time still on a footing of an adherent of Palmerston, is better qualified than any one to form a link between the two and to produce a mutual accord. John Russell has drawn up certain Resolutions which he intends to move on the second reading. These Resolutions have been shown to George Grey and to Palmerston, who have agreed to support them, and it may be presumed that if all the Whig leaders, or even most of them, take this course, they will be followed by the majority of the rank and file. The Government and their friends are considerably alarmed at this hostile demonstration, and the more disappointed because they had been led to believe that Palmerston intended to support the second reading, and they knew that many moderate Whigs were inclined to take the same course. Some may do so still, but if the rival leaders can agree upon an attack on the Bill, though they may be agreed on nothing else, it is certainly probable that the Government will be beaten.   Then will come the question of dissolution or resignation.   This will probably depend on the amount and composition of the majority, and it will be a knotty point for Derby to decide upon.

Savernake, March 9th.—I met George Lewis at the Athenæum yesterday, and had a talk about the state of affairs here.   He told me that the whole Liberal party, he believed, would support John Russell's Resolutions.   There had been considerable doubt at first whether the second reading of the Bill should be opposed or not, but upon a close examination of the Bill they found that it was such a dishonest measure that it could not be allowed to pass, and therefore it was better to throw it out at once.   Palmerston and Lord John are now on very good terms.   Lord John had sent his Resolutions to Palmerston, and Palmerston had sent him word he would support whatever he proposed.   Lewis thinks, though there is no agreement between them further than this with regard to the Reform Bill, that if this Government falls, and the Whigs return to power, means will be found of adjusting the rival pretensions of the two leaders, and getting them to act together.   To effect this, his reliance is mainly on the Queen, who he thinks may and will exert her influence and authority for this end.   There is, however, a notion abroad that if John Russell persists in his Resolutions, the Government will withdraw the first clause, which is tantamount to withdrawing the Bill itself. Lewis believes in this intention, and that if they do it they will become so unpopular, and incur so much discredit, that it will be impossible for them to go on or to attempt a dissolution.   Another notion is that they will withdraw the Bill, and endeavor to go on without any Bill at all, trusting to the Opposition not daring to propose a vote of want of confidence, which it is very doubtful if they could carry.   The only thing clear is that they are very anxious to turn the Government out, and to take their chance of the consequences.   Their success seems not at all unlikely, but when they have accomplished their object their embarrassments will begin.   First there will be Lord John and Palmerston, then *l'embarras des richesses* of the numerous candidates for office, and settling who is to come in and who are to be thrown overboard.

March 15th.—Cowley arrived from Vienna on **Saturday**, I have not yet seen him, but Clarendon told me **yesterday** that he brings back the most satisfactory assurances on the part of Austria, who is ready to give every pledge of her pacific intentions, and to come to any agreement with France upon the withdrawal of both their forces from the Papal States, but that she will make no concessions inconsistent with her rights and her dignity, or which could seem to damp the enthusiasm now prevailing in Germany in her favor ; in fact, that she has no concessions to make. Within the last few days the symptoms from France have been more menacing. At Paris the conviction is general that war is meant, and I am obliged to believe it likewise. The resignation of Prince Napoleon seems to have been a mere sham, and his intimacy with the Emperor as close as ever. There is no reason to believe that the military preparations in France are suspended, and in Piedmont they are certainly going on actively.

The other great topic of interest, viz. the Reform Bill and John Russell's Resolutions, does not look in a more satisfactory state. While many sensible people deprecate this move of John Russell's, and lament that Palmerston should have consented to support it, the probability seems that it will be carried, but the greatest uncertainty prevails as to the course which the Government will adopt, and whether they will try to go on, dropping their Bill altogether, or continue the fight with its remaining clauses, or whether they will take the chance of a dissolution. It is now clear enough that Derby made a great blunder in undertaking to deal with the question of Reform at all, and that a consistent Conservative course would have been the most honorable and the wisest, and have afforded him the best chance of staying in office. By bringing forward a measure to the principle of which it is well known that he and his whole Government and party are in their hearts adverse, and then trying to vitiate the principle by certain contrivances in the details, by which the scruples of his own party may be obviated, he exposes himself to the charge of producing a dishonest measure, and this is what the Whigs urge as their ground for attacking it in front and at once. This is what Lewis said to me, "We are bound to defeat a measure which is so dishonest that it is not susceptible of such improvement in Committee as would warrant our passing it."

The conduct of the Whigs, however, is not a whit more honest.   Their allegation is a mere pretext, and their real motive is that they think they see their way back to office through an attack upon the Government Bill ; they are indifferent to the consequences, and all they want is to get the coast clear for themselves, and take the chance of settling the difficult questions which will arise as to the formation of a Government and the conditions on which it can be formed.   All this appears to me quite as dishonest as anything the Government have done or are doing.   Palmerston never was a Reformer.   He was opposed as much as he dared and could be even to the great measure of 1832, which all the world was for.   When he brought forward a measure of his own two or three years ago, he did it without sincerity or conviction, and merely for a party object, and now he is uniting with John Russell without any real agreement with him in opinion, and with full knowledge that if they succeed and climb into office on the ruins of the Government Bill he will be obliged to propose a measure much stronger than he believes to be either necessary or safe.   Believing that Palmerston and John Russell were agreed no further than upon the Resolutions on Monday next, I thought that a difference must arise between them (in the event of their coming into office) on the Reform Bill they should produce, but I was told just now that upon this point they are already nearly if not completely agreed.   They are, however, not yet agreed upon the great question of the Premiership, or which of them shall go to the House of Lords.   The impatience and confidence of Lord John seems to be unbounded, and in spite of his being the younger by seven years, his eagerness to be in office again much more intense than that of Palmerston.   Although this is such a miserable Government, both discreditable and incompetent, and it is a misfortune to have the country ruled by such men, I cannot desire the success of such selfish and unpatriotic manœuvres as those by which the Whigs are endeavoring to supplant them, and consequently I regard the whole state of affairs with indescribable disgust and no small apprehension.   I believe the country to be in nearly equal danger from Louis Napoleon abroad and Mr. Bright at home, and I fear that there is no capacity in the Government to cope with the one, and no such amount of wisdom and patriotism among the chief men of all parties as is requisite to defeat the designs of the other.

March 16*th.*—Cowley called on me yesterday at the
Council Office. He said that he had never believed there
would be war, and he did not expect it now; that all the
agitation and turmoil .that had been vexing Europe for the
last three months were to be attributed to the conduct of
Cavour and his attempts to drag France into assisting
Piedmont in her aggressive policy, and to misunderstand-
ings which had been produced by the strange conduct of the
French Government, the imprudent speech of the Emperor
to Hübner on January 1st, and the ambiguous manifestations which had followed it. To comprehend all these things
it was necessary to be acquainted with the whole course of
Cavour's policy and his dealings with France, and to understand the peculiar character of the Emperor and the motives
and impulses by which he is actuated. When Austria refused to join England and France in the Russian War,
Cavour thought that an opportunity presented itself of
which he might take advantage, and which would lead to a
realisation of his views for the aggrandisement of Piedmont,
and he offered to join the alliance and send an army to the
Crimea. This offer (as Cowley thinks very imprudently and
unfortunately) was accepted. He thinks it was unwise, because the assistance of Piedmont was not required, and could
not have any material effect on the result of the contest,
while it was sure to excite hopes and expectations, and to
give rise to demands which would be afterward found very
inconvenient and embarrassing. Accordingly Cavour took
the earliest opportunity of expressing his hopes that when
peace should return Sardinia and her services would not be
overlooked. General expressions of goodwill were given,
but Cowley cannot answer for what more the Emperor may
have said.

His account of his mission does not quite correspond
with what I had before heard of it, and is an additional proof
of the difficulty of arriving at truth. He told me that he
had written to Malmesbury and told him he thought it very
expedient to send somebody to Vienna to talk to Buol and
the Emperor, and to try and mediate between Austria and
France, to which Malmesbury had replied he had better go
himself, as nobody else would be so likely to effect the object.
The consent of Buol having been previously obtained, he
proposed it at Paris, where his services were gladly accepted.
He had already spoken very openly to the Emperor, and

told him very plain truths as to his position and his conduct, and when he went he told his Majesty without disguise what his intentions were and his wishes, and what he desired that Austria should do.   The Emperor was very frank, totally disdained any wish to make war, but said he should like Austria to do certain things, which amounted to full security for Piedmont and renunciation of any unfair and unjustifiable predominance in Italy.   He found them at Vienna more angry than alarmed ; suspicious, but not unreasonable ; their military condition so good and powerful that, believing France really bent on attacking them, there was a very general feeling that it was better war should come at once than have it indefinitely hanging over them, and at first it seemed unlikely that they would return any conciliatory assurances which he might carry back to France. At last, however, he got them to say what he thought was as much as could be expected from them, and what ought to satisfy the French Government.   Since he left Paris (now three weeks ago or more) he has not had a line from thence, and he is wholly ignorant of the march of affairs during his absence ; but he hopes and expects to find a pacific disposition, and his object is to prevail on the Emperor to put an end to the general state of uncertainty and alarm by announcing to Sardinia that she is in no danger from Austria, and that therefore no assistance from France will be necessary, and she may safely desist from her warlike preparations.   This is in fact the only way by which the crisis can be put an end to, and if the Emperor really has been sincere in his professions and means to make his acts correspond with them, he will forthwith put forward some clear and unambiguous declaration, and some definite communication to Piedmont which will leave no room for doubt or suspicion, and restore confidence and tranquillity to Europe again.

March 22d.—Yesterday the "Times" announced that a Congress had been agreed upon, which was believed, so the funds rose and there was a general belief that a solution was at hand, but it turns out not to be true.   The Emperor wishes for one as a means by which he may back out of his scrape, which Cowley writes is now his object, but it is impossible to believe that Austria will listen to it, and Clarendon thinks that she would do wrong to consent to it, and that we should get into a scrape by being a party to it, as no **reliance** whatever can be placed on the good faith or honesty of France, who would deceive us and Austria, as she has often done before.

Yesterday the Neapolitan exiles arrived at an hotel in Dover Street in several hack cabs, decorated with laurels, and preceded by a band of music. I did not see the men, but saw the empty cabs ; there was no crowd.

Nothing could be more uninteresting than the first evening of the debate on John Russell's Resolutions last night. Lord March told me in the morning that the Government would certainly dissolve as soon as the Resolutions were carried. Every day makes the folly of Derby more apparent in bringing in any Reform Bill at all.

March 24th.—When I think of the Reform Bill of 1832, and compare the state of affairs at that time with that of the present time, nothing can be more extraordinary. Then the interest was intense, the whole country in a fever of excitement, the Press rabid, the clamor for Reform all but universal, party running tremendously high, no doubt or hesitation about individual wishes and opinions, and each camp perfectly united in itself, and full of energy and zeal. In this condition of the public mind and of politics the debates began and continued. This debate has begun and seems likely to continue, how differently ! There are neither zeal nor union on one side or the other, everybody is dissatisfied with the state of affairs, and nobody can see a satisfactory issue from the general embarrassment. There have been two nights of debate, and as yet all the speaking has been one way, all on the anti-Reform side. John Russell was flat, and Stanley, who replied to him, actually read his speech, which, though it was much complimented by his own friends, seems to have been far from effective. Horsman made a very good speech the first night, and Bulwer Lytton spoke with great eloquence and effect on Tuesday, far better than anybody thought he could speak, and the Solicitor-General made a magnificent speech, in which he attacked John Russell with great vigor and complete success. The only tolerable speech on the Opposition side was Sidney Herbert's. Nobody has the least idea what course the Government will take of the three open to them, whether they will resign, dissolve, or go on with the second reading. The inference from Stanley's speech was that they will dissolve, but Lytton and Cairns seemed anxious to do away with the impression that speech had made, and one is led to infer from

what they said that the Government will most likely proceed
to the second reading, which would probably be their wisest
and certainly their most popular course. The majority of
those who are going to vote for the Resolutions do so unwillingly, and would have preferred going into Committee,
or to have fought the battle on the second reading. As it is,
if Government do not throw up their cards, the second reading is in my opinion sure to pass, and not improbably the
Bill itself with great alterations.

The state of foreign affairs is as uncertain as ever. So
incurable is the distrust of the Emperor Napoleon that the
greatest doubts prevail whether he means peace or war, and
whether even this Congress which he is trying to bring about
is not a mere dodge for the purpose of gaining time, and in
order to extract out of it a plausible case for a complete
breach with Austria.

Gladstone is come back from Italy completely duped by
Cavour, who has persuaded him that Piedmont has no ambition or aggressive objects, and that Austria alone is guilty
of all the trouble in which the world has been plunged. He
told this to Aberdeen, who treated his delusions and his credulity with the utmost scorn and contempt, but he is said to
have found John Russell more credulous, and ready to accept
Gladstone's convictions.

March 26th.—The debate goes on, to the intense disgust
of everybody, though enlivened by a few clever and telling
speeches. But everybody is disgusted with the whole affair,
from which all see that no good can come, and probably
much mischief will ensue. The Government side continues
to have the best of the debate, Horsman, who spoke for them,
and Lytton and Cairns having been very superior to all the
speakers on the other side. On Friday Palmerston spoke,
with great vigor, but not much effect. His speech was very
jaunty, but very insincere. When he said that he cordially
supported the Resolutions of his noble friend, everybody knew
that it was not true, that he really disapproved of them, and
that he only consented to go with Lord John in order to
evince his willingness to make up their political difference,
and to lend himself to the reunion of all the Whig party; but
in his speech he said enough to show that there is not likely
to be an entire or lasting agreement between them, and that
the two Kings of Brentford will not long continue to smell at
the same nosegay. The Opposition have been all along quite

confident of victory on the Resolutions, and it has been impossible to make sure of the intentions of the Government in the event of their being beaten, as they have severally held such very different language on the point.

But an incident has occurred which is very likely to extricate the Government from their difficulty, and of which I presume they will avail themselves. Owen Stanley (brother of Stanley of Alderley) the other night blurted out, without previous concert with anybody, a notice of a motion of want of confidence in the event of the second reading not passing. The Opposition are unanimously disgusted at this piece of folly and meddling, while the Government are of course delighted at such a plank of safety being held out to them, and if they use it dexterously, they may completely defeat Lord John and Palmerston, and prolong their own tenure of office for some time at least.

April 1st.—The great debate came to an end last night. The majority was greater than either side expected, and the Government and their friends were sanguine to the last that they should win by a few votes.[1] Although there was a great deal of tedious speaking, it was on the whole a very able and creditable debate, and there were several very powerful speeches, but principally on the side of the minority. Gladstone's was particularly good, and Dizzy's reply, with a very effective philippic against John Russell, was exceedingly clever, and delivered with much dignity and in very good taste. Although the question of Reform was regarded with so much indifference, as the debate proceeded and party spirit and emulation waxed hot, the interest and curiosity became intense. They have become still more intense to-day, and the town is in a state of feverish anxiety to know what is going to happen, and, as usual on such occasions, there are a thousand reports, speculations, and guesses afloat, This morning the prevalent idea was that they would resign, but this evening, and since Derby's brief notice in the House of Lords, it is rather that they will dissolve. Certainly the Queen might very well refuse her consent to a dissolution if proposed to her, and this would of course compel the Government to resign ; but nobody knows whether she wishes Derby to stay in, or would prefer to take the chance of forming another Ministry. I have no idea that happen what may she

---

[1] [The numbers were: For the second reading of the Bill 291, for Lord John Russell's Resolutions 330 ; majority against the Government 89.]

will send for Lord John Russell; but no doubt she knows all
that has recently passed between him and Palmerston, and
about the formation of another Government, and it is not
impossible that she may shrink from being plunged into the
difficulties which would attend the attempts to form a Government in which they were to divide the power and authority between them.

April 4th.—The report yesterday was that Derby does
not mean to resign or dissolve, or to go on with the present
Bill, but perhaps bring in a fresh one.   As we shall hear it
all this evening, it is useless to speculate on the subject.
The Opposition are evidently puzzled what to do.   I went to
Kent House, where Lewis said the Government were much
mistaken if they imagined they should be left alone; he did
not know what would be done, but certainly they must look
to be attacked in some shape or other.   Granville in the
evening took the opposite line, and said the best party game
would be to let them alone.   Nothing, however, will ever induce John Russell to keep quiet.

Clarendon came in, and we talked of foreign affairs.   He
thinks war inevitable, and that the French are only gaining time to complete their preparations.   I said I thought
Cowley had been duped by the Emperor, but he thought not.
Cowley had all along seen all the objections to the proposed
Congress and suspected the *arrière pensée* of it, but said it
was impossible when proposed to object to it, as the Emperor
would put forward such a refusal as a pretext, and say that it
would have prevented war.   Two years ago he had a reliance
upon the Emperor which he had no longer; that he was
completely changed now from what he was, and it was difficult to know what he really meant, and when he was sincere or the reverse.   Clarendon told us he had lately seen
Marliani, an old acquaintance of his, a Spanish Liberal and
friend of Cavour's.   Marliani said that the Italian question
was ill understood in England, and he had come over for the
express purpose of seeing Clarendon and talking it over with
him, and putting before him a paper he had written upon it.
The conversation was curious.   Clarendon told him he was
quite mistaken if he thought the Government or any other
Government could take any part at variance with the existing treaties, or that the country would allow them to do so,
even if inclined.   He then asked him what his friend Cavour
meant to do in the dilemma in which he had got himself

and his country, and expressed very strong opinions on his conduct. Marliani replied that it was not quite just to censure Cavour with such severity, and without considering his position, that during his whole life his most ardent desire and fixed idea was that of purging Italy of the Austrians and aggrandising his own country, and now when he saw before him the probable realisation of his fond hopes, that he was backed up and encouraged by the master of 300,000 men in the game he was playing, and taught to rely upon that aid, could it be wondered at that he should yield to the seduction ? Clarendon asked what would happen if the Emperor proved faithless to him, as he had done to others, and in what position Cavour would find himself. Marliani replied that he had no hesitation in telling him what he thought need not be a secret, at least to him, as he was sure Cavour would tell Clarendon himself if he saw him, and that Cavour had fully made up his mind what to do. If the Emperor ended by throwing over the Italian cause and refused to go to war, Cavour would resign, the King would abdicate, and the whole correspondence with all the Emperor's letters (of which they had an immense number) would be published and circulated over all Europe to show the baseness and perfidy of the man in whom they had trusted, and to force him to hide his head from the indignation and contempt of the world. Everything indicates that, whether from fear of this vindictive explosion or because he thinks it his policy, he is hastening his preparations, has renewed his engagements to Cavour, and that he means to go to war as soon as he can.

CHAPTER XVIII.

April 7th, 1859.—The determination of the Government,
announced in both Houses on Monday evening, took the
world by surprise.   Nobody thought there would be a dissolution.   Derby's speech was very bad, much below his usual
level.   The attack on John Russell which formed a chief
part of it was merely a *réchauffé* of that of Disraeli, but
very inferior to it in every respect.   Disraeli in the
other House spoke much better, and with more taste and
temper.   The Opposition leaders are evidently much taken
aback ; the Derbyites assert that they have reason to expect
a gain of forty votes, but nobody believes it.   Many think
a much more Radical and an angry Parliament will be
returned, but ;there is no excitement, and it seems to me
more probable that those are right who think the relative
proportions will not be materially altered.   The Whig chiefs
are very angry with John Russell for committing himself as
he did on Monday night by his speech and announcement of
his own plan of Reform.   Great attempts were made to
dissuade him from doing this, but he would not listen to
reason.   Palmerston made a speech clearly indicative of
disagreement with Lord John, though with a semblance of
union.   The Resolutions on one side and the Dissolution on
the other have both been great faults, of which the mischievous consequences may be very serious, but which cannot
be made manifest till we see the result of the election.   .

April 15th.—I have been reading over to George Lewis
my account of what took place about the Reform Bill of

21

1832, to assist him in reviewing that period of history, and in so doing it is impossible not to be struck with the contrast between the public excitement which prevailed then and the apathy and absence of interest which we witness now. At every general election there is a great deal of bustle, activity, party zeal, and contention, but there are not more of these now than on ordinary occasions, if anything less. Both parties are confident that they shall gain, and the Derbyites are making great efforts, and have collected a very large sum of money. Derby has given 20,000*l.* to the fund, but candidates are slack in coming forward with the prospect of the new Parliament not lasting many months. The question of peace or war is still in abeyance, but inclines rather toward war ; the public securities oscillate like a barometer, and people are puzzled and unable to form any opinion.

April 20th.—The long promised statements were made in both Houses on Monday night, but they told us nothing that was not already known, and merely expressed hopes that war might still be averted. Disraeli in the Commons was more sanguine than Malmesbury and Derby in the Lords. Clarendon and Derby both made excellent speeches, the former particularly ; all he said was sound and true. The most striking thing in both Houses was the extreme caution and reserve of the speakers on both sides, and particularly their reticence and forbearance about France. Not one word of blame of the Emperor of the French ; no more about him, his sayings and doings, than about the Emperor of Russia, or than if he had had nothing whatever to do with the present state of things. This was probably politic, but it was lamentable and disgraceful that we should be obliged, or think ourselves obliged, to abstain from speaking the truth, for fear of offending this rascally adventurer, who by the egregious folly and cowardice of the French nation has been invested with such an awful power of mischief, and whom neither fear nor shame deters from pursuing his own wicked ends at the expense of any amount of misery and desolation which he may inflict upon mankind. One cannot help contrasting the extreme delicacy and forbearance exhibited toward him with the violence and abuse which were directed against the Emperor Nicholas in 1854.

I met Disraeli yesterday afternoon, when he told me they had got such satisfactory news from the Continent that he considered the affair as virtually settled and the danger at

an end.   God grant it may be so, but I am far from being
satisfied that the danger is over.   On the eve of great
resolutions, and as the moment of taking an irrevocable step
draws near, the actors in great events have generally some
misgivings, and pause upon the brink, and so probably will
these quasi-belligerents do now ; but I believe the concessions which France expresses herself willing to make to our
entreaties to be a part of her game.   Clarendon or Derby
said that if Cowley had been allowed to work out his purpose
of mediation, probably all would have been settled, and
that the proposition of Russia for a Congress had been mischievous, and only involved the question in fresh doubt and
delay.   But it appears evident that this was a French trick,
and that Russia proposed the Congress at the instigation of
France, who sought it for the purpose of delay, and most
likely in order to extract from it a plausible cause of quarrel.
Derby in his speech attributed a great deal to the menacing
and disturbing speech of the King of Sardinia in opening his
Chambers, but nobody said a word of Napoleon's sortie to
the Austrian Minister on the 1st January, nor was any allu-
sions made to various important facts which were well known
to many people in both Houses.   No reproaches were cast
upon Sardinia, but a good many upon Austria ; no comment
made upon the flagrant breach by Sardinia of the treaties existing between her and Austria, and of the forbearance of the
latter in not making that breach a *casus belli*, as she might
well have done.

I went to a Council on Monday for the prorogation, when
I had some conversation with Disraeli, and asked him what
his real belief was as to their prospects in the election.   He
said there was so much luck in these matters that it was
difficult to speak positively, but that he had endeavored to
ascertain the true probabilities of the result, and his conclusion was that *if they had luck* they should gain sixty votes ;
and what, I asked, if there was no luck on one side or the
other ?   Then, he said, they should gain forty.   I told him
the Opposition calculators did not believe the Government
would gain at all, or at most not above eight or ten, if so
many, and asked if he was confident they should gain from
twenty to thirty anyhow.   He said from the day of their
taking office they had looked forward to a dissolution, that
their organization was excellent, they had plenty of candidates and of money, and he was quite confident they should

gain that number and more ; he added that there was in no
part of the country the slightest desire for Reform, and he
had altered the address he had first intended to put forth, in
consequence of finding what the prevailing sentiment was on
that question.   I suppose they hold this language to justify
their dissolution, for it is difficult to believe they can really
expect such results, or that their opponents, who tell such a
different story, can be so completely mistaken.

April 24th, Newmarket.—Disraeli's information on Tuesday last, when I met him at Lady Jersey's, might well have
warranted me in believing that no war would take place, but
I have never been able to persuade myself that this calamity
would be averted, and it appears that my apprehensions
were well founded, for now the die seems to be really cast,
and at the moment when I am writing it is probably actually declared and begun.   Though Austria is perfectly justified in declining to wait any longer while France is maturing
her preparations, and cannot justly be blamed for bringing
the affair to a crisis, she is certain to be exposed to every
sort of obloquy and misrepresentations even in this country,
and of course much more in France.

April 27th.—On Monday we heard that the Austrians
had sent their ultimatum to Sardinia, and there was a complete panic in the City.   Yesterday we were informed that
she had given fourteen days' grace to Sardinia, and everything was up again.   But this morning we were undeceived,
and found this latter report had no foundation.   Meanwhile
the clamor against Austria has been senseless and disgraceful ; nothing could be more unworthy than Derby's allusion
to her in his speech at the Mansion House dinner on Monday.   It was a claptrap, and meant to obtain popularity and
assist the Ministerial interest at the election.   Nothing has
ever disgusted me more than to see the readiness with which
everybody finds fault with Austria, and the care with which
they avoid any notice of France, not, however, that this can
or will last.   What sort of relations we shall continue to
have with France I cannot imagine.   We have been treated
in a manner which puts an end to the possibility of any
amicable feelings between the two countries.   We can never
trust the Emperor again, and must take measures for our
own security as best we may ; but unhappily the Indian war
has so materially diminished our power and absorbed our
resources, and France has so enormously gained upon us in

point of naval strength, that we are not in a condition to hold the language and play the part that befit the dignity and the honor of the country. We can revile Austria with impunity, for we know that we are in no danger of an attack from her, but, on the contrary, that she has so much need of our good will that she will endure our taunts and reproaches, and not quarrel with us even in words. It was a prophetic saying of Mackintosh forty years ago at Roehampton that it remained to be proved whether the acquisition of our Indian Empire was in reality a gain to us, and we must hope that the remark will not be illustrated in our days by seeing England herself placed in danger by her exertions to retain or reconquer India, whose value is so problematical and of which nothing is certain but the immense labor and cost of her retention.

May 14*th.*—Another severe fit of the gout, principally in the right hand, has prevented my writing a line for the last fortnight, during which war has broken out, and the general election has been begun and ended, and, what is most important to myself, I have resigned my office. Hitherto the war and the election have equally disappointed the expectations they gave rise to. The Austrians committed a blunder in plunging into the war, and have not taken the only advantage such a measure seemed to promise, viz. that of overpowering the Sardinians before the French could join them, and now nobody can make out what their tactics are or when and where the contest will begin in earnest. Meanwhile *we* are taking an imposing attitude of armed and prepared neutrality. Disraeli's anticipated sixty votes have dwindled down to a gain of twenty, but Malmesbury told Cowley that they should have force sufficient to maintain their ground, which I see their opponents do not believe.

May 17*th.*—The elections are nearly if not quite over, and, as well as can be collected from the conflicting calculations of the rival parties, they present a gain of nearly thirty for the Government. With this they evidently hope and their opponents fear they will be able to go on at least to the end of the session, and I incline to think so likewise. Their Government is miserably weak and incapable, their numbers respectable, but their staff deplorable. It is expected they will propose to Lord Elgin to take Lytton's place. The general election has been eminently satisfactory in this, that it has elicited the completely Conservative spirit of the country. Palmerston, who predicted that the consequence would be a large increase of Radical strength, has been altogether mistaken. It may be added (whether this is a good or an evil) that it has also manifested the indifference of the country to all parties and to all political ties and connexions. In the last general election the cry was all for Palmerston, in this there has been no cry for anybody, neither for Palmerston nor Derby, and less than all for John Russell or Bright. And yet John Russell is flattering himself he shall have an opportunity of forming a Government, and talks of his regret at being obliged to leave out so many of his friends. It is remarkable that the Catholics have supported the Government, and that they have done so under orders from Rome. Archbishop Cullen is there, and has signified to the priests the pleasure of the Pope that the Derby Government should be supported. Clarendon told me this yesterday, and that the reason is because they think this Government more favorably inclined to Austria than any other, especially than either Palmerston or John Russell would be. The Papal Government have never forgiven the Whigs for the Ecclesiastical Titles Bill, and this accounts for the otherwise strange support given by the Catholics to those who have always been their bitterest enemies.

The war still languishes, and nobody can make out what the Austrian plans are. A great sensation has been made by the retirement of Buol and the appointment of Rechberg. The first report was that it was a sacrifice made to appease the resentment of Russia, but Clarendon told me yesterday he did not believe this, but that it was rather to satisfy some of the German Powers whom Buol had deeply offended. Nothing could have exceeded the stupid blundering and misconduct of the Austrian Government during the last few critical weeks, and their want of tact toward Prussia and the German Powers. The Archduke Albrecht was sent to Germany for the purpose of stirring up the German Powers, and professedly to procure such a demonstration as should be the means of preventing war, and then, while the Archduke was still at Berlin, they blurted out their ultimatum (which was a declaration of war) without letting Prussia know what they were about. The Archduke was obliged to declare his own ignorance of the intentions of his Government, and Prussia consequently to announce her disapprobation of the measure and to signify the same to France, which was just what suited the Emperor Louis Napoleon. I hear also that his departure from Paris was accelerated by the necessity of repairing as speedily as possible to the seat of war, in order to quiet the dissensions and quarrels which were already raging between the French generals. Not a very promising beginning of the campaign. This used to be the case formerly in the great Napoleon's time wherever he was not present. His presence silenced these quarrels, but it remains to be seen whether this man will have equal authority over unruly subordinates, who cannot possibly regard him with the same deference with which the old marshals looked up to their mighty master.

May 24th.—The elections are all over, and the Opposition leaders are already busy in devising the means of attacking the Government. On Friday Palmerston went to Pembroke Lodge, and had a long conference with John Russell. On Sunday there was a gathering there, attended by Granville, George Lewis, Charles Wood, and probably others. The question immediately to be decided is whether an Amendment shall or not be moved to the Address. A very nice point of political strategy. The Whig leaders are impatient to drive the Government to resignation, without, as I believe, knowing how they are to form a Government likely to be durable and strong. As matters stand, the Government appear to be too strong to be driven out, and not strong enough to count upon staying in. A greater fix can hardly be seen.

May 26th.—Palmerston and John Russell have now made up all their differences, and have come to a complete understanding and agreement on all points, so that the schism may be considered at an end. Upon Reform, upon foreign policy, upon the mode of opposition, they are fully agreed, and even upon their respective personal pretentions. Both are resolved not to quit the House of Commons, and Lord John himself says that the question of the Primacy must be determined by the Queen herself, and that whomever she may send for and charge with the formation of a Government must necessarily be Premier. There is not much doubt that this will be Palmerston, but what post Lord John would require for himself I have not heard. It may possibly be the Foreign Office, which Palmerston could hardly refuse to him, particularly as they are agreed on foreign policy, and Clarendon is not inclined to share their opinion. This

reconciliation will be very favorable to Granville's pretensions, and secure to him the lead of the House of Lords, and
not improbably, at some not very distant day, lead to his
being Prime Minister. In this age of political Methuselahs
it is an enormous advantage to be little more than forty
years old. This state of affairs I heard at Brooks's from
the Duke of Bedford. It was Lord John who took the initiative in their approaches to each other. He wrote to
Palmerston, on which Palmerston repaired to Pembroke
Lodge, where they had a long conversation, with the result
aforesaid. Soon afterward I met Disraeli in the street.
He did not appear to me to be in very high spirits, and
talked of the position and chances of his Government without any expressions of confidence, though without despond-
enee. He said he hoped that they would move an Amendment to the Address, as it was better to fight it out at once
and bring the question of strength to a crisis.

May 29th.—It seems not unlikely that the Government
may be after all relieved from the immediate danger of an
Amendment by the divisions amongst the Opposition, or
rather between the rival leaders. After all I was told of the
meeting between Palmerston and Lord John, and the agreement they had come to on all the important points, I was
astonished at hearing on Friday evening that everything
was again thrown into uncertainty because Lord John would
not say what he intended to do. On the important question
of who should be Premier he would make no frank statement. He had, indeed, before said that the Queen must
decide it, and the man she sent for would naturally be at
the head of the Government ; but he refused to say whether,
supposing Palmerston to be sent for, he would take office with
and under him, or even whether he would sit in the House
of Commons on or behind the Treasury Bench—in short he
would give no clear and positive assurance of his intentions.
This is naturally very disgusting to the Whigs, and throws
everything into doubt and confusion. The Duke of Bedford
is to go down to him and tell him the plain truth, which no
one else would venture to do, pointing out to him the effect
of his conduct on the sentiments of the Liberal party and on
his own position, with regard to which his conduct is inde-
fensible and suicidal. It remains to be seen whether any
effect will be produced on his mind, but in any case nothing
can look more hopeless than it does, or promise worse for the

future. Even though Lord John should consent to act under Palmerston (and nobody expects that it is Lord John for whom the Queen would send), there seems little hope of any cordial or lasting union between them, or of his being satisfied with any position in which he might consent to place himself, for his mind is evidently in a sour and jaundiced state. The majority of the Whig and Liberal party who are come up full of resentment from the elections are certainly desirous of attacking the Government, but there is a considerable number of them who are averse to joining in any vote of want of confidence, or any other move which may turn the Government out without first being assured that another Government can be formed, and that the union is sufficiently complete to promise that such new Government would be strong enough to maintain itself when formed.

June 6th.—As I was at Epsom every day this week, I have heard nothing of what has been going on, except the fact that there is to be a great meeting of the Liberals at Willis's Rooms this afternoon, called by a list of people which includes Palmerston and Lord John and Milner Gibson, whose signature betokens the assent of the Radicals to the object of it, which I conclude to be an agreement as to the attack to be made on the Government to-morrow, and certain explanations as to the intentions and sentiments of the Whig leaders. I see that there are many dissentients from the course that is going to be adopted, many who think this attempt to oust the Government at once neither patriotic nor politic. Without any very decided opinion, or the means of forming one, I am rather inclined to think that it would be better to leave them alone, and to trust to their furnishing good cause for turning them out, as they probably will do. The Government does not appear to be obnoxious to any serious reproach and objection, except about their mismanagement of foreign affairs. But it is very questionable whether another Government might not give us a policy equally or still more mischievous.

June 7th.—The meeting of the Opposition yesterday at Willis's Rooms went off as well as they could expect or desire. The two leaders gave the required assurances that each would serve under the other, in the event of either being sent for. There was a general concurrence in the plan of attacking the Government at once, in which even Bright and Ellice joined, the former disclaiming any desire for office in his own person, but claiming it for his friends.   The result promised is that with very few exceptions all the opponents or quasi-opponents of the Government will unite in support-ing the vote of want of confidence, and they are very confi-dent of success.   On the other hand, the Derbyites do not despair of having a majority, and they comfort themselves with the certainty that the division must be so close, that the successful Whigs will be able to form no Government which will have a certain working majority, and, not im-possibly, that the majority itself may be turned into a mi-nority by the events of the re-elections.   This is not very probable, and it is rather more likely that if Palmerston forms a Government, he will have the support of a good many of those who will vote with the Government, as long as they remain in.   There were, however, some rather ominous manifestations made at this meeting.   It seemed to be agreed that the new Government should embrace not only Whigs and Peelites, but "Advanced Liberals," *i. e.*, the fol-lowers of Bright, and this, besides introducing the seeds of disunion, will probably frighten away the Liberal Conserva-tives, who would like to support Palmerston, inasmuch as a Government so formed would afford little security for the maintenance of Conservative measures.   Then Palmerston in no ambiguous terms announced his pro-Gallican sym-pathics, and the neutrality he declared for in every possible case which he could contemplate, together with his desire for a cordial union with France, can mean nothing but that under his rule England should look quietly on while France crushes Austria, and accomplishes all her ambitious and revo-lutionary objects.   That this policy will be hateful to many who will be his colleagues cannot be doubted, but what is doubtful is whether those who will object to it will have virtue and firmness enough to decline office rather than be parties to such a policy.

June 9th.—There is great excitement about this debate and the probable division, and equal confidence on both sides of a majority.   The Opposition is the favorite, but their friends will not lay any odds.   Everybody says it must be very close, and on either side the majority will not ex-ceed ten.   On the first night Disraeli made a capital speech, and nobody else on their side would speak at all.   This was a sort of manœuvre and attempt to bring about a division that night, for they found out that seventeen of the Opposition had not taken their seats, which would have secured a majority to the Government. The Whigs therefore refused to divide, and put up one man after another to keep the debate open, and eventually obtained an adjournment. Palmerston's speech was in accordance with his declaration at Willis's, and with his ancient practice; it was violently pro-French and anti-Austrian, and it was full of gross falsehoods and misrepresentations, which he well knew to be such. In his seventy-fifth year, and playing the last act of his political life, he is just what he always was.

June 12th.—After a not very remarkable debate, the division yesterday n orning gave a majority of thirteen to the Opposition, which was more than either side expected.[1] Derby resigned at eleven o'clock, and the Queen immediately after marked her sense of his conduct by sending him an extra Garter in an autograph letter. Much to his own surprise she sent for Granville (and for nobody else) and charged him with the formation of a Government. What passed between Her Majesty and him I know not, but he accepted the commission and has been busy about it ever since. How he is to deal with Palmerston and Lord John, and to make such a project palatable to them I cannot imagine. What the Queen has done is a very significant notice to them of her great reluctance to have either of them at the head of affairs, and it cannot but be very mortifying to them to be invited to accept office under a man they have raised from the ranks, and who is young enough to be son to either, and almost to be grandson of the elder of the two. Nor will the mortification be less, after they have both so publicly avowed their expectations that one or other of them must be sent for, and their having, in what they consider a spirit of self-sacrifice, consented to serve under each other, but without ever saying or dreaming that it could be necessary to say they would take office under any third party. Nobody, indeed, has ever thought of the possibility of any but one of them being called upon by Her Majesty, and the only question has been which it would be.

June 13th.—Lord Granville told me yesterday evening what had passed, and that his mission was at an end, and Palmerston engaged in forming a Government. The account

---

[1] [The Amendment to the Address, implying a want of confidence in Ministers, was moved by the Marquis of Hartington. The votes on the division were: For the amendment 323, against it 310.]

of it all appears in the "Times" this morning quite correctly. Granville was rather disappointed, but took it gayly enough, and I think he must have been aware from the first of the extreme difficulty of his forming a Government which was to include these two old rival statesman. Palmerston had the wisdom to accede at once to Granville's proposal, probably foreseeing that nothing would come of Granville's attempt, and that he would have all the credit of his complaisance and obtain the prize after all. The transaction has been a very advantageous one for Granville, and will inevitably lead sooner or later to his gaining the eminence which he has only just missed now, which would have been full of difficulties and future embarrassments at the present time, but will be comparatively easy hereafter. Lord John's conduct will not serve to ingratiate him with the Queen, nor increase his popularity with the country.[1]

June 26th.—All the time that the formation of the new Government was going on I was at a cottage near Windsor for the Ascot races, and consequently I heard nothing of the secret proceedings connected with the selection of those who come in, and the exclusion of those who belonged to Palmerston's last Government, nor have I as yet heard what passed on the subject.[2] The most remarkable of the exclusions is Clarendon's, who I was sure when the Foreign Office was siezed by John Russell, would take nothing else ; and of the

---

[1] [It was the refusal of Lord John Russell to serve under Lord Granville which rendered the formation of a Cabinet by that statesman impossible. At the same time Lord John Russell expressed his willingness to serve under Lord Palmerston on condition of his taking the department of Foreign Affairs.]

[2] [Lord Palmerston's second Administration consisted of the following members :

First Lord of the Treasury	Viscount Palmerston.
Lord Chancellor	Lord Campbell.
Lord President	Earl Granville.
Lord Privy Seal	Duke of Argyll.
Chancellor of the Exchequer	Mr. Gladstone.
Home Secretary	Sir George C. Lewis.
Foreign Secretary	Lord John Russell.
Colonial Secretary	Duke of Newcastle.
War Secretary	Mr. Sidney Herbert.
Indian Secretary	Sir Charles Wood.
Duchy of Lancaster	Sir George Grey.
Postmaster General	Earl of Elgin.
Admiralty	Duke of Somerset.
Board of Trade	Mr. Milner Gibson.
Lord-Lieutenant of Ireland	Earl of Carlisle.
Irish Secretary	Mr. Cardwell.

This Administration lasted until the death of Lord Palmerston on October 18, 1865.]

admissions, Gladstone's, who has never shown any good will toward Palmerston, and voted with Derby in the last division. This Government in its composition is curiously, and may prove fatally, like that which Aberdeen formed in 1852, of a very Peelite complexion, and only with a larger proportion of Radicals, though not enough, it is said, to satisfy their organs, and Bright is displeased that he has not been more consulted, and probably at office not having been more pressed upon him. It is still very doubtful whether Cobden will accept the place offered to him.

The Tories are full of rancor, and express great confidence that this Government will not last, and that they shall all be recalled to power before the end of the year. Derby had a large gathering at Salisbury's house, when he made them a speech recommending union and moderation, the first of which recommendations they seem more likely to adopt than the second. The affair of his Garter was in this wise. On resigning he wrote to the Queen and besought her to bestow Red Ribbons on Malmesbury and Pakington. She wrote him an answer acceding to his request, and adding that she could not allow him to retire a second time from her service without conferring upon him a mark of her sense of his services, and she therefore desired him to accept the Garter, though none was vacant. He told me this, and said it was the only way in which he could have taken it, as he never should have given it to himself, and I believe if a vacancy had occurred he meant to have given it to the Duke of Hamilton.

While we have been settling our Government for good or for evil, the war has continued to pursue its course of uninterrupted success of the Allies, and unless something almost miraculous should occur, the Austrian dominion in Italy may be considered as at an end. The sentiments of people here are of a very mixed and almost contradictory character, for they are on the whole anti-Austrian, anti-French, and though more indulgent than they deserve to the Sardinians, not favorable to them. The most earnest and general desire is that we should keep out of the *mêlée*, and any termination of the war would be hailed with gladness, because we should thereby be relieved from our apprehensions of being involved in it. We should not be sorry to see the Austrians driven out of Italy for good and all, though most people would regret that the Emperor Louis Napoleon should be triumphant, and that such a course of perfidy, falsehood, and selfish ambition should be crowned with success. The Austrians deserve their fate, for nothing can exceed the folly of their conduct, first in rushing into the war, and thereby playing the whole game of their adversaries, and secondly in placing in command men evidently incapable, and who have committed nothing but blunders since the first day of the campaign.

June 27th.—Yesterday I went to Kent House, where I found Clarendon and his sister alone, and we had a long talk, in the course of which he told me all that had passed (especially with regard to himself) about the formation of the Government. Although he spoke very good-naturedly about Granville and his abortive attempt, I saw clearly that he thought Granville had been in the wrong to undertake it, and that he ought at once to have told the Queen it was impossible, and have declined it. Though Palmerston had given a qualified consent to act with him, it was with evident reluctance, and he had guarded it by saying it must be subject to his approbation of the way in which the Government was composed. Lord John's consent was still more qualified, and he annexed to it a condition which at once put an end to the attempt. This was, as I had suspected, that he should be leader of the House of Commons. To this Palmerston refused to agree, and so the whole thing fell to the ground. Granville, by Clarendon's advice, at once reported his failure to the Queen, gave her no advice as to whom she should send for, and of her own accord she sent for Palmerston.

Previously to this, and I think before the vote, Palmerston and Clarendon had discussed the probability of Palmerston's forming a Government, when Palmerston told him he should expect him to return to the Foreign Office. As soon as Palmerston had been with Her Majesty, he went off to Pembroke Lodge, and saw Lord John; told him all that had happened, and that he would of course take any office he pleased. Lord John said, "I take the Foreign Office." Palmerston said he had contemplated putting Clarendon there again, enumerating his reasons and Clarendon's claims, but that if he insisted on the Foreign Office as a right, he must have it. Lord John said, "I do insist on it," and so it was settled.

I ought to have inserted that when Palmerston and Clar-

endon talked the matter over at first, Clarendon begged him
not to think of him, and that if, as was probable, John Russell desired the Foreign Office, he *must* give it him, for if
he did not, or even made any difficulty, an immediate breach
would be the consequence, and John Russell would get up a
case against Palmerston which would be very embarrassing.
Palmerston at first said he should certainly insist on Clarendon's not being put aside to please Lord John, but in the
end Clarendon persuaded him not to adhere to that resolution. After all was settled there was a small gathering at
Cambridge House, when Palmerston told Clarendon that he
might have the choice of any other office, but Clarendon
replied that he was not conversant with Colonial, Indian, or
War affairs, and he would not take an office for which there
would be many candidates, while he much preferred being
out, and Palmerston would not have half offices enough to
satisfy the demands for them. Palmerston said he would
not take this as his last word, and the next day the Queen
sent for Clarendon, by Palmerston's own desire, to try and
persuade him to take office. He went to Buckingham Palace and had an audience, or rather interview, of three hours
with Her Majesty and the Prince, in which she treated him
with the most touching kindness and confidence, and exhausted all her powers of persuasion to induce him to join
the Government, but he was firm and would not. She then
said, in the event of a vacancy of the Foreign Office, "You
must promise me you will take it," to which he replied,
"Your Majesty knows I would do anything in the world for
your service ; but you must allow me, in any case which may
occur, to exercise my own discretion under the circumstances, and to rest assured that I shall in every case be actuated solely by a desire to do what is best for your Majesty,
and most conducive to your pleasure and interest." The
Queen talked to Clarendon of the publication in the "Times"
with much indignation, and said, "Whom am I to trust?
These were my own very words." Clarendon, however, endeavored to convince her that the article had in fact (however indecorous it might appear) been eminently serviceable
to her, inasmuch as it negatived any suspicion of intrigue or
underhand dealing in any quarter, and represented her own
conduct in a manner to excite universal approbation. He
dilated on this in a way which made great impression both
on the Prince and on her, and ultimately satisfied her that

all had been for the best, thereby acting a very good-natured part and a very wise one.

July 4th.—Cobden has declined to take office, though he was advised by his friends to accept, and he approves of Milner Gibson and Charles Villiers having joined the Government. The reasons he gives are that he has always been a strenuous opponent of Palmerston, and that his conduct will be liable to reproach in taking office under him, that he has been the advocate of economy and low establishments, and would find himself obliged to act very inconsistently, or to oppose his colleagues in a policy respecting which popular opinion would be against him ; but he expresses great satisfaction with Palmerston, who he says is a much better fellow than he was aware of, and he means to give the Government all the support in his power. These reasons do not seem sufficient for his not joining, which he had better have done. Granville laments Clarendon's having declined to take office as a Secretary of State, and that he will not be in the Cabinet to throw into the scale of foreign policy his political weight. I said I knew nothing of his motives, but assuming that he did not see foreign affairs in the same light as Palmerston and John Russell, he would be placed in an awkward position before long. Granville said this might be true, but he thought before very long he would be at the Foreign Office again. What he meant by that I do not know.

July 12th.—On Friday morning the world was electrified by reading in the "Times" that an armistice had been agreed upon between the belligerent Emperors in Italy, and the subsequent announcement that they were to have a personal meeting yesterday morning, and the armistice to last for five weeks (till August 15th), led to a pretty general conclusion that peace would be the result.[1] The Stock Exchange take the same view, for everywhere and in all securities there has been a great rise. I saw George Lewis on Sunday and asked him if the Government had any intelligence, when he told me that the only thing, besides what had appeared in the papers, was that France had proposed to us to interpose our mediation on the basis of Austria giving up everything, and Prussia had made the same proposal on the basis of Austria giving up nothing, both which proposals we had very naturally declined.

---

[1] [The battle of Solferino was fought on June 24, and an armistice between the Emperors of France and Austria was signed at Villafranca on July 7.]

July 13*th.*—We had scarcely had time to begin discussing and speculating on the probable results of the armistice, before the news of peace being actually concluded burst upon us. As yet we have only the great fact itself and the skeleton of the arrangement, and we shall probably be for some time without materials for judging as to the merits of the Treaty of Peace and its probable consequences, but the first impressions and the first ideas that present themselves may be worth recording. There is no denying that the Emperor Napoleon has played a magnificent part, and whatever we may think of his conduct, and the springs of his actions, he appears before the world as a very great character.[1] Though he can lay no claim to the genius and intellectual powers of the first Napoleon, he is a wiser and a soberer man, with a command over himself and a power of self-restraint, and consequently of moderation in pursuit .of objects, which the other did not possess, and therefore while the towering genius of the uncle led him on through magnificent achievements and stupendous vicissitudes to his ruin, it appears highly probable that the better regulated mind and the habitual prudence of the nephew will preserve him from the commission of similar errors, and render his career somewhat less splendid, but more durable and infinitely more beneficial to his country.

With regard to the present affair, the first thing we must be struck with is the way in which the King of Sardinia has been treated. Napoleon, indeed, tosses him a large share of the spoils, but not only was he not admitted to the Conference which led to peace, but he does not appear to have been consulted upon it any more than any of the French generals ; the only notice that was taken of the King (so far as we know) being that he was ordered, upon the conclu-

---

[1] [The conclusion of the peace after the battle of Solferino was creditable to the Emperor Napoleon, but was no indication of a great character. His motives were that he had not the means of undertaking a siege of the great fortresses of the Quadrilateral, and that if the war had been prolonged it was not improbable that the forces of the Germanic Confederation, including Prussia, would have taken the field against France. He therefore acted wisely in terminating the war, and if the Austrians had withdrawn within the Quadrilateral and refused to treat, the Emperor Napoleon might have been placed in great difficulties. As it was, he broke his engagement to Cavour to liberate Italy from the Alps to the sea, and to Kossuth to support a Hungarian insurrection. Italy eventually owed the liberation of Venice, not to France, but to Prussia, as the reward for her combined action with that Power in the war of 1866.

Cf. the account of the manner in which the peace was concluded in Lord Malmesbury's " Autobiography," vol. ii. p. 200.]

sion of the armistice, to desist from the siege of Peschiera.
I had heard before that the Emperor was extremely disgusted with his ally and Cavour, and at all that the latter
had said and done, at the proclamations and other documents he had put forth, and at the audacious manner in
which that Government had annexed every serap of territory they could lay their hands on, and assumed the government of every State that they could manage to revolutionize, and all without the sanction and concurrence of the
Emperor.   Nothing is more likely than that the Italian
War will not be closed without much bickering and heart-
burning between the two allies, and that the King and his
Cavour will find, in spite of all they are to obtain, that they
will have no bed of roses to repose upon after their fatigues
and labors.[1]

Then, so far as we can judge of the settlement, it seems
one that is likely to give more offence and disappointment
than satisfaction to the bulk of the Italian people, and to
imagine that affairs will relapse or resolve themselves into
a peaceable and quiescent state is a mere delusion.   What
passed between the two Emperors we may perhaps never
know, though the effects of their interview may one day
becomes dangerously apparent ; but it is not unreasonable to
conjecture that Napoleon exerted all his arts and blandish-
ments to make a friend of Francis Joseph, and to persuade
him that a cordial alliance with France would be more advantageous to him than one with England, and he might
with every appearance and much of the reality of truth
tell him that England had done nothing for him ; that
neither the Government nor the nation had any sympathies
with Austria, whom, so far from assisting, they had gladly
seen defeated in Italy ; and that the forbearance of the
Emperor in leaving Austria in possession of any part of Italy
would be unpalateable to Palmerston and John Russell, and
generally unpopular.   One cannot but suspect that an alliance was at least projected, if not formed, between the three
great despotic Powers, France, Austria, and Russia, for the
purpose of domineering over Europe, and dealing with the
several States according to their pleasure, or the pleasure of
France, and with the ultimate object of attacking, weakening, and humbling England.

[1] [M. de Cavour bitterly resented the prompt conclusion of peace, and for a
time quitted the Ministry of which he was the head.]

Of all the provisions of this treaty that which regards the sovereignty of the Pope is the most curious and seems the most difficult to carry out; it is indicative of the necessity under which the Emperor thinks he is placed of disarming the hostility and consulting the prejudices of the Catholic party and the Church in France. Whether the Pope will accept the temporal office assigned to him may be doubted, but it can hardly be doubted that his supremacy will not be willingly accepted and acknowledged by the Italians generally, to whom the Papal rule is already odious.[1] One cannot but feel glad at the deep mortification and disappointment which will overtake the Republicans and Socialists, the Mazzinis, Garibaldis, Kossuths, *et hoc genus omne*, at a pacification so ruinous to all their hopes and designs. Clarendon told me he believed the account in the "Times" of the compact between the Emperor and Kossuth, and nothing is more likely than that at the beginning of the contest he employed Kossuth in the way stated, and gave him all sorts of promises, and when he found he could do everything *sine tali auxilio*, and that he had a stronger interest in making friends with Austria, he threw Kossuth over without scruple or hesitation. This is exactly the course he would be likely to follow.[2]

July 15th.—The news of the peace took everybody so much by surprise, that people had no time to arrange their thoughts upon it ; but, in the midst of the general satisfaction that the war is over, it is already apparent that there is an explosion of disappointment and resentment to come. All the Italian sympathisers here are in despair, Palmerston is much dissatisfied, and the anti-Austrian Press is indignant. The King of Sardinia has not openly testified any ill-humor, and has published an Address to his new Lombard subjects in a joyful style, but it is impossible he should not deeply feel and resent the contemptuous way in which he has been treated by his Imperial ally, and the resignation of Cavour is a clear manifestation of *his* feelings on the subject.

When it was announced that an interview was to take place between the two Emperors, everybody predicted that the elder of the two would have as much success in diplo-

---

[1] [It was proposed by the Sovereigns to place the Pope at the head of an Italian Confederation—a wild scheme, which entirely failed.]

[2] [This was so. The details of Kossuth's negotiations with the Emperor have been published by Kossuth himself in his memoirs.]

macy over his rival as he had already obtained in arms, but
the result does not appear to bear out that expectation,
though we do not yet know what the real motives of the
Emperor Napoleon were in concluding such an extraordinary
peace.   Granville told me that at this interview the Austrian
Emperor had taken a very high line, and shown little disposition to concession.   He said to Napoleon, " You have
conquered Lombardy, and I do not contemplate making any
attempt to recover it.   I am therefore quite ready to cede it
to *you*, and *you* will deal with it as you please.   I have
nothing to say to the King of Sardinia, and make no concessions to him.   With regard to Venetia, and the country of
which I remain in possession, I have nothing to concede or
to offer, *all that* I mean to retain, but I have no objection to
my Venetian dominions forming part of the Italian Confederation."   They appear to have had a vast deal of conversation
and discussion, for they are said to have been together for
above twelve hours.   What they talked about it would be
interesting to know, but which they will neither of them tell
us.   The field for speculation is as wide as can well be.   How
the settlement of Italy is to be accomplished, how the Italians
are to be contented, and how peace in that country is to be
permanently secured, are questions enough to puzzle the
acutest politicians.

We congratulate ourselves at having kept entirely clear
both of the war and the peace, but no doubt Palmerston is
mortified, and I think England generally will be provoked
that changes of such importance should have been made
without any consultation or even communication with us.

The friends of the Emperor Napoleon say that they believe his motive for making peace on any terms he could get
to have been principally that he was so shocked and disgusted at the fearful scenes of pain and misery that he had to
behold after the battle of Solferino, in addition to the other
battle-fields, and at the spectacle of thousands of killed and
wounded presented to his eyes, that his nerves could not bear
it.   Lady Cowley told me that he was so tender-hearted that
he could not bear the sight of pain, much less being the cause
of inflicting it, and she had seen him quite upset after visiting hospitals at the sufferings he had witnessed there, which
of course are not to be compared with the horrible scene of
a battle-field.   It is impossible to say that this may not be
true, wholly or in part ; it is impossible to account for human

idiosyncrasies ; but it is quite certain that the man who is said to shrink with horror from the sight of suffering does not scruple to inflict it in quite as bad a form when he does not himself witness the infliction. He has hundreds and thousands of people torn from their families, and without form of trial or the commission of any crime sends them to linger or perish in pestilential climates, when he fancies it his interest to do so, and for *their* sufferings he evinces no pity or any nervous sensations.

August 7th.—I have found it impossible to collect anything to record in this book for the last month almost. The session is drawing to a close, having glided on without difficulty for the Government, and almost without opposition. The Election Committees have made great havoc in Palmerston's small majority, having unseated no less than seven Liberal members. I am told, perhaps on no good authority, that Palmerston, John Russell, and Gladstone are anxious to join in a Congress to mix themselves up in the settlement of Italian affairs, but that they cannot have their way, the majority of the Cabinet being opposed to it, and the House of Commons and the country (as represented by the Press) being decidedly against any such reference.[1]

I met Edward Mildmay the other day, who gave me some account of his own personal experiences during the last Italian campaign, when he was attached to the Austrian Army. He confirmed all previous accounts of the excellence of that army and the incompetency of its chiefs ; that nothing could have saved the French Army at Magenta if the Austrians had been tolerably commanded ; that Giulai, who had never seen any service, had been allowed to retain the command by the influence of General Grünne, whose friend he is, and that the indignation and disgust of the army at having been thus sacrificed to Court favor and partiality had been extreme. He told me that at Solferino the Austrian loss was (within a fraction of) 20,000, the French 19,000, and the Sardinians 9,000 men ; Benedek is the ablest of the Austrian generals, and if he had had the command probably

---

[1] [I think it was at this time that Lord Palmerston and Lord John Russell proposed to the Cabinet that England should enter into a Treaty of Alliance with France and Sardinia, but the proposal was negatived by their colleagues. The feelings of these Ministers, however, speedily changed when the cession of Savoy and Nice, and the manner in which it was brought about, were known, and their language became so hostile that it gave great offence to the Emperor Napoleon. See Lord Malmesbury, "Autobiography," vol. ii. p. 225.]

affairs would have taken a very different turn.   Mildmay has
no doubt that peace was much more necessary to the French
than to the Austrians, and he still believes that if the war
had continued the tide of victory would have been rolled
back, as the latter had 90,000 fresh troops coming into line.
It is probably better as it is than if the Austrians had recovered all their losses : the Emperor Napoleon seems likely
to be satisfied with his military exploits, and to be really
intending to revert to his peaceful policy.   He is certainly
doing all he can to persuade the world that such is his intention, and there seems a disposition here to take him at
his word.

Viceregal Lodge, Phœnix Park, August 22d.—I have at
last accomplished the object I have desired for so many years,
and find myself in Ireland.   I have seized the first opportunity of being my own master to come here.   I left London the week before last, and went to Nun Appleton, thence
to Grimstone, and on Saturday I came here, railing through
York and Manchester to Holyhead ; crossed over on a beautiful evening, with sea as smooth as glass, but it was too
dark to see the Bay of Dublin.   Most hospitably received by
Lord Carlisle, and very comfortably lodged.   Passed the day
in Dublin yesterday ; twice at church, in the morning at
Christ Church, afternoon St. Patrick's, attracted by the
celebrity of the choir and the performance of the cathedral
service, which was finely done, though the best voices (three
brothers Robinson) were absent.   I am greatly struck by the
fineness of the town of Dublin, and of the public buildings
especially.

Dublin, August 23d.—On Monday morning the Lord-
Lieutenant went to pay his first visit since his return to
the National School and took me with him.   I was much
gratified at the sight, with the appearance of the children and their intelligence.   There was a grand gathering of Commissioners and others to meet Carlisle, but no
Catholics except Lord Bellew and Dean ——, who alone of
all the Catholic ecclesiastics has had courage and resolution
to adhere to the system.   Not one Catholic Bishop now remains ou the board.   Bishop Denver was the last to resign,
which it is believed he did reluctantly, but it seems that the
rule of their Synod is, that when a majority has decided,
those who are in the minority give in their adhesions, and
produce unanimity.   The National System is apparently in

he crisis of its fate, and a desperate struggle is being made
y the Popish clergy to destroy it, while the ultra-Protes-
ants will join them (for different reasons and with different
bjects) for the same end.　I earnestly hope these factions
ill fail.　The most encouraging circumstance is found in
the return which was given me of the "Central Model
Schools," in which the number of pupils seeking admission
is 1,179, an evident proof of the popularity of the system,
and that up to this time the priests have not been able to
deter their flocks from giving their children its benefits.
This return is sufficiently interesting to be copied into this
journal :—

	Males	Females	Infants
Number of pupils on roll	564	447	375
Pupils in attendance .	436	348	311
Seeking admission	203	866	110

Carlisle was received with great enthusiasm by both
pupils and teachers.　After this we went to the Hill of
Killinie, whence there is a grand panoramic view of the
Bay of Dublin and the surrounding country, and then to
my old friend Lady Campbell [1] (Pamela Fitz-Gerald), whose
beautiful daughters are as well worth seeing as anything in
Ireland.

Dublin, August 24th.—Yesterday in the morning a review in the Phœnix Park, after which Bagot took me to
Howth Castle, which I was curious to see, but it is not very
remarkable, though very ancient.　It has a modernized appearance, and is a comfortable house, said to be the oldest
inhabited house in Ireland, and one of the towers of fabulous
antiquity.　I remarked that the hall door was left open, according to the traditional obligation.　One of the Ladies St.
Lawrence told me the story as follows : An old woman, "the
Granawhile," came to the castle and asked for hospitality or
alms, and was refused and driven away.　She was the wife
of a pirate.　On the seaside she found the young heir with
his nurse, whom she seized and carried off.　Afterward she
brought the boy back, and consented to restore him on condition that henceforward no beggar should be refused admit-
tance, that the hall door should be kept continually open,
and that at dinner a place should be kept and a plate laid
for any stranger who might appear.　The beggars are kept

---

[1] [Lady Campbell was the daughter of Pamela and Lord Edward Fitz-
Gerald.]

away by not being admitted through the lodge gates; the hall door is open, but there is another door behind it, and the vacant place has by degrees fallen into disuse. I know not how old the story is, but there is enough to show that it had a foundation of some sort, and that it retains a relic in the customs of the family. On returning to Dublin I went to see Trinity College, and the beautiful museum erected a few years ago. Dublin is, for its size, a finer town than London, and I think they beat us hollow in their public buildings. We have no such squares as Merrion Square, nor such a street as Sackville Street.

Bessborough, August 26th.—I came here on Wednesday viâ Kilkenny. A very nice place, comfortable, and in as good order as any place in England. People apparently well off, and cottages clean and not uncomfortable.

August 28th.—Went yesterday to Waterford; pretty good town, but looking very foreign. They showed me a hill, to which it is said Cromwell advanced, but found the town too strong to be attacked; hence Waterford has been called the *Urbs invicta.* I doubt the story, for he would have stormed Waterford easily enough if he had chosen. Saw the National School; a very good establishment, boys absent on holidays, but a very civil intelligent master, a Roman Catholic. The clergy of neither persuasion will come near the school, except the Dean of Waterford, who still supports it. Went on to Curraghmore, a vast and magnificent park, but a mean house.

August 31st.—Went on Tuesday to Woodstock; very pretty place, and in admirable trim. Weather changing, and I fear I shall see Killarney in rain and cold.

Viceregal Lodge, September 6th.—Went to Muckrosson Thursday last; passed three days there in exquisite enjoyment of the beautiful scenery of Killarney; weather was perfect, and I went over and round all the lakes; returned here on Monday, and went yesterday to the Curragh.

Jervaulx Abbey, Sunday, September 11th.—Crossed over from Kingstown to Holyhead on Thursday last; beautiful passage. Passed the last day, Wednesday, in Dublin with William Fitzgerald seeing the town. He took me over the old Leinster House, now the Royal Institution, and then to the Bank to see the Old House of Lords; a fine room, exactly as it was, and what was the House of Commons, now completely altered and not retaining a vestige of the famous

locality where Flood and Grattan and Plunkett once shook
the walls with their eloquence. I left Ireland with regret,
for I spent several very happy days there, interested and
amused even more than I expected, and treated with great
kindness and hospitality. Went from Holyhead to Manchester, and on to Worsely to sleep ; came here on Friday.
The old Abbey is very picturesque, and very perfect as a
ruin. It reminds me, place and all, of Bolton Abbey.

London, September 26th.—I stayed three days at Jervaulx,
then to Doncaster, Bretby, and to town. All the Ministers
in London, having passed their lives during the last fortnight
in the railway or in Cabinets, which have been very numerous,
as well they may, for they have plenty to occupy them in the
Italian, Chinese, and American questions, all, in their several
ways and degrees, extremely embarrassing. I have not the
slightest conception what our Government are doing about
the Italian question, but I suppose trying to keep well with
Napoleon III., and to obtain good terms for the Italian
Duchies. At present it looks as if a Congress would be got
together to untie this complicated knot, but I fear we are
not likely to play in it a part which will be consistent with
our principles, or creditable to our national character, and I
wish we could abstain from having anything to do with it.
The incident about the American Boundary is awkward, but
I feel confident it will be amicably settled.

The Chinese affair is the most serious, and one can see
no solution of it that is not full of objections and embarrassments.[1] In the first place it looks at present very much as
if our case was a bad one. We had no business to go with
an armament and force our way up the river, and even if we
were upon any ground justified in such an extreme measure,
it was to the last degree impolitic and unwise to exercise
such a right. The object for which Bruce was sent to China
was to conclude a peace, and to establish amicable relations
with the Chinese Government, and it might have occurred
to him that the employment of force, even if it was ever so
successful, must infallibly defeat his object. It required no

---

[1] [Mr. Bruce having been detained in his mission to Pekin, which was of a
pacific character, Admiral Hope made an attempt to force the passage by reducing the forts at the mouth of the Peiho. The attack failed, with a loss of
nearly 400 men killed and wounded in the storming party and the gunboats.
The " Plover " and " Lee " gunboats grounded, and the " Cormorant " was so
damaged by the enemy's fire that she sank soon afterward. The whole proceeding was injudicious and disastrous.]

great sagacity to perceive that the arrival at Pekin of a victorious Ambassador, who had forced his way to the capital at the head of an imposing force, would not serve to make his reception a friendly one, or to establish permanent harmonious relations between the English and the Chinese Governments. As long as there was a possibility of procuring access to Pekin by peaceful means and by negotiation, it would have been better to be patient and to wait any time than to employ force; and besides the political objections that seem conclusive against the adoption of such a course, it seems highly probable that no such force as that which we employed on this occasion could have been pushed on into the heart of the country without imminent danger of its being cut off and eventually destroyed. The mere fact of destroying again the Peiho forts would be deemed by the Chinese as the renewal of the war, and the perpetrator of the outrage would not have been received in the sacred character of an Ambassador, but would have been looked on as an invader, and treated accordingly. This is the first view of the question which presents itself. Then comes that of vindicating our honor, and retrieving the disaster we have suffered, which involves the necessity of rushing into war again and scattering havoc and desolation through the country, massacring thousands of people who can make no effectual resistance to our power, and making territorial conquests, which will only embarrass us, and which we shall have more difficulty in getting rid of than we shall have in making their acquisition. In short, we are going to be engaged in a contest in which failure will be disgraceful, and success will be inconvenient, and to place additional obstacles in the way of that good understanding which it is so much our interest to establish with China. Nor are our difficulties diminished by the fact of being connected with, and therefore more or less dependent on the French, and in a less degree with the Russians and the Americans in this unfortunate contest. This local and accidental alliance impairs our freedom of action, and of necessity introduces delays and complications of all sorts into the affair.

October 19*th.*—Nearly a month and nothing to record, besides the events of the day, of which I know nothing more than the newspapers report. I only take up my pen now because Clarendon called on me, and it is worth while to recollect the little he told me during a very short visit. I had not seen him since his visit to Osborne in the summer, and he began by giving me an account of it. The Queen was delighted to have him with her again and to have a good long confidential talk with him, for it seems she finds less satisfaction in her intercourse with either Palmerston or Lord John. The relations of these two are now most intimate and complete, and Palmerston has obtained an entire influence and authority over Lord John, who only sees with his eyes and without any contest submits to be entirely guided and controlled by Palmerston. The *jeu* of the thing is rather amusing. Palmerston, who is thoroughly versed in foreign affairs (while Lord John knows very little about them), in every important case suggests to Lord John what to do. Lord John brings it before the Cabinet as his own idea, and then Palmerston supports him, as if the case was new to him.

But to return to the Queen and Clarendon. He was unfortunately attacked by gout and confined to his room. He was sitting there with Lady Clarendon, when Lady Gainsborough came in and told him that she was desired by the Queen to beg he would if possible move into the next room (the Lady-in-waiting's room) and establish himself there; that the Queen would come in, when all the ladies present were to go away and leave her *téte-à-téte* with him. All this was done, and she remained there an hour and a half, talking over everything, pouring all her confidences into his ears, and asking for his advice about everything. He said he had endeavored to do as much good as he could by smoothing down her irritation about things she did not like. As an example, he mentioned that while the Prince was with him a box was brought in with a despatch from Lord John, which the Prince was to read. He did so with strong marks of displeasure, and then read it to Clarendon, saying they could not approve it, and must return it to Lord John. Clarendon begged him not to do this, that it was not the way to deal with him, and it would be better to see what it contained that really was good and proper, and to suggest emendations as to the rest. He persuaded the Prince to do this, advised him what to say, and in the end Lord John adopted all the suggestions they had made to him. On another occasion the Queen had received a very touching letter from the Duchess of Parma imploring her protection and good offices, which she sent to Lord John desiring he would

write an answer for her to make to it. He sent a very
short, cold answer, which the Queen would not send. She
asked Clarendon to write a suitable one for her, which he
did, but insisted that she should send it to Lord John as her
own. She did so, Lord John approved, and so this matter
was settled.

Newmarket, October 21st.—Clarendon told me, and has
since written to me, that Government regard in a very serious light the approaching war between Spain and Morocco,
which they think will have the effect of putting Gibraltar in
peril;[1] that Spain is playing the part of catspaw to France,
who wants to get possession of Morocco, giving Tangier to
Spain, which would give her, and France through her, the
command of both sides the Straits, and as we depend upon
Tangier for supplies to Gibraltar, it would be difficult for us
to hold the place when this scheme is accomplished. He
writes to-day : " No news to-day except that things look very
fishy with Spain and Morocco, and I suspect we are going to
be vigorous, which, though it may be expedient, may also be
productive of much trouble."

He was lately at Broadlands, and had much talk with
Palmerston, who was very friendly and confidential, told him
everything, and appeared very anxious to have his opinions
and advice. He says that Palmerston's hatred of Austria
amounted to a monomania, and this of course produces a
divergence between the present policy of France and ours.
He talked about America. When Clarendon was lately at
Clumber he discussed that affair with the Duke of Newcastle
and offered to write to Buchanan, with whom it seems he
is in correspondence, and say to him what it is desirable
should be said, unofficially; and he suggested that he should
hold out to Buchanan the prospect of a visit from the Prince
of Wales, who it seems is going to Canada some time or other.
This the Duke mentioned at the Cabinet, where the proposal
was highly approved, but when it was broached to the Queen,
Her Majesty objected to anything being said about the Prince
of Wales going to the United States, so it fell to the ground.[2]

[1] [On October 22, Spain declared war on Morocco, on the ground that further
territory was required for the protection of her settlements on the North African
coast. Tetuan was captured by the Spaniards on February 4, 1860, and peace
was signed on April 27, the Emperor of Morocco paying an indemnity of twenty
million piastres. Marshal O'Donnell, who had commanded the expedition, was
created Duke of Tetuan.]

. [2] [Whatever may have been the objection to the mention of the Prince of

London, October 30*th.*—Clarendon came to town yesterday morning on his way to Windsor and called here. He told me that we were going to send a representative to the Congress, and I was not a little surprised to perceive that he would not be at all disinclined to go there himself. He did not indeed say so, but unless I am greatly deceived this is in his mind, though not without feeling the difficulty of his acting with John Russell. Clarendon says that the preparations going on in France are on the most enormous scale, and can have no object but one hostile to this country, and that the feeling against England is fomented by the Government and extending all over France. He is persuaded that the fixed purpose of Louis Napoleon is to humble this country, and deprive her of the great influence and authority she has hitherto exercised over the affairs of Europe. He is bent upon getting us to take part in the Congress, and that in order to persuade us he will pretend to be entirely agreed with us in opinion, and only wishing to concert the most proper means of carrying out our common objects, and when he has thus cajoled us into a participation he will throw us over, and place us under the necessity of agreeing to what we disapprove, or of putting ourselves *en désaccord* with all Europe. He told me that John Russell is supposed on the Continent to be the implacable enemy of the Catholic religion, and this will be a great disqualification for his acting at a Congress mainly composed of Catholic Powers ; that this opinion, which is rife in Ireland, is propagated all over the world, and that the recollections of the Durham Letter and the Ecclesiastical Titles Bill are still as strong as ever.[1]

November 18*th.*—Last week at the Grove to meet the Duc d'Aumale, who is one of the most enlightened and agreeable Princes I ever met, very simple and natural, and full of information and knowledge of all sorts.

Wales's visit to the United States at this moment, the project did not fall to the ground, for on July 9 in the following year (1860) the Prince started on a visit to Canada and the United States, accompanied by the Duke of Newcastle, where he was entertained by President Buchanan on October 25.]

[1] [The Congress which it was proposed to hold had reference to the affairs of Italy, which were extremely perplexing to the Emperor Napoleon himself. But Lord Clarendon's apprehensions were certainly unfounded, for it deserves to be remarked that about this time negotiations were opened between the Emperor and Mr. Cobden for a commercial treaty, which was intended to strengthen, and did strengthen, the amiable and pacific relations of France and England.]

I.do not remember to have gathered anything partien-
larly interesting from Clarendon in our various conversations,
except that in the event of our consenting to join the Congress he would not be unwilling to'go to it, and that he
thinks he might be able to effect an arrangement.　This
confidence has in great measure been produced by a letter
from Cowley which he showed me, containing an accour.t
of his visit to Biarritz and his communications with the
Emperor.　He said he had resolved not to say a word to
His Majesty of Italian affairs, thinking the Emperor would
abstain from talking of them to him, but as soon as they
met he began to talk, and went at length into the whole
subject.　The upshot was that he found the Emperor in
such a state of perplexity and embarrassment, and so fully
conscious of the scrape into which he had got himself, that
he did not know what to do or which way to turn ; his
object evidently is to get us to help him out of his difficulty,
and Clarendon thinks that he should be able to draw him
into such measures as we could support if the matter was
well managed.

A day or two ago the Duke of Bedford, whom I have not
seen or communicated with for a long time, called on me.
He told me one curious anecdote, which he had heard from
his brother.　Persigny called on Lord John one day, and
told him he was come in strict confidence to show him the
letter which the Emperor had written to the King of Sardinia,
but which he must not mention even to his own colleagues,
except of course to Palmerston.　Lord John promised he
would not, and a day or two after he read the letter in the
"Times."　He sent for Persigny and asked for an explanation.　Persigny said he could not explain it, but would write
to Walewski.　John Russell also wrote to Cowley, who spoke
to Walewski about it. . Walewski declared he could not
account for it, and that it must have been sent from Turin,
and he would write to that Court to complain of the indiscretion and would also speak to the Emperor.　He went to the
Emperor, told him what had passed, and showed him what
he proposed to write to Turin, when the Emperor said : " No,
don't write at all, take no notice of the publication.　The
fact is, I sent the letter myself to the 'Times' Correspondent."　It was Mocquard who took it to him.　A most extraordinary proceeding, and showing the extreme difficulty of
all diplomatic dealing between the two Governments.　The

Emperor is by way of being indignant with the "Times," and never fails to pour forth complaints and abuse of the paper to whomever he converses with. He did so, for instance, to Cobden, to whom he gave an audience at Paris. But who can tell whether this is not a pretence and a deceit, and whether he may not all the time have a secret understanding with the "Times"? Such a supposition would seem to be inconsistent with their articles and his conduct, and the comments of the former upon the latter; but how difficult it is to form any certain judgment upon a policy so tortuous as his, and upon designs so close and councils so crooked!

CHAPTER XIX.

London, December 25th, 1859.—The Government are getting ready for the session which is near at hand, Palmerston with his usual confidence, but Granville, who is not naturally desponding, and who I dare say represents the feeling of his colleagues, is conscious of the want of that strength and security which a commanding majority alone can give, and, without thinking the danger great or imminent, anticipates the possibility of their being defeated on some vital question. The Opposition, conscious of their numerical force, but anything but united, profess the most moderate views and in-

tentions.   Derby professed at Liverpool to have no wish
to turn out the Government or to come into office himself.
Disraeli himself told me that he and all his party desired
the Reform question to be settled quietly, and that if the
Government only offered them such a Bill as they could possibly accept, they should be ready to give them every assistance in carrying it through.   Since this, Walpole has made
a formal communication to Granville (through Henry Lennox) of his and Henley's disposition to the above mentioned
end.   We are told, moreover, that a great number of the
Conservative party will not only support a fair and moderate
Reform Bill, but support the Government generally, not so
much, however, from wishing well to the Government as
from their antipathy to Disraeli and their reluctance to see
him in power again.   That they will join in carrying through
a safe and moderate Reform Bill is no doubt true, but it is
not probable that the division among them and the hostility
to Disraeli will last long, or continue a moment after the
appearance of any prospect of the return of the Conservative party to power.

Disraeli raised himself immensely last year, more, perhaps, with his opponents and the House of Commons generally than with his own party, but it is universally acknowledged that he led the House with a tact, judgment, and
ability of which he was not before thought capable.   While
he has thus risen, no rival has sprung up to dispute his pre-
eminence.   Walpole and Henley are null, and it is evident
that the party cannot do without Disraeli, and whenever Parliament meets he will find means of reconciling them to a
necessity of which none of them can be unconscious, and I
have no doubt that whenever any good opportunities for
showing fight may occur the whole party will be found united
under Disraeli's orders.

With regard to the Reform Bill, it is being proposed by a
large committee of the Cabinet, but George Lewis has the
chief management of it.   The state of public opinion admits,
indeed compels, the utmost moderation, but hitherto the
anticipated difficulty has been the sort of pledge which John
Russell foolishly gave last year with reference to the franchise, to which it has been supposed he must consider himself
bound.   But there is reason to believe that he is not taking
any active part in the concoction of this Bill, probably on
account of his being so absorbed in foreign affairs, and under

these circumstances we may not unreasonably expect that a fair Bill will be produced, and the question eventually settled.

The question of still greater and more pressing interest is that of the Congress. The nomination of Hudson met with such opposition in the Cabinet that it was not pressed, and Lord Wodehouse was named instead. He is a clever man, well informed, speaks French fluently, and has plenty of courage and *aplomb ;* his opinions are liberal, but not extravagant. Clarendon, who had him down at The Grove, was pleased and satisfied with him. Granville is much *contrarié* that Clarendon himself has not been asked to go, thinking justly that he would have much more weight than any other man, and would be far more likely to conduct our affairs in the Congress with credit and success ; but Clarendon now tells me he certainly would not have gone if it had been proposed to him. My own conviction *was* that he would have accepted a proposal, and though for many reasons he would not have liked such a mission, I think he is somewhat mortified that it was not offered to him.

The recent appearance of the pamphlet of " Le Pape et le Congrès," [1] which has produced such a sensation and so much astonishment, has no doubt been a great thing for us, and rendered our diplomatic course much more easy and promising. Clarendon writes to me : " This last pamphlet of the Emperor's is important and I am sure authentic, as it is simply a development of what I have heard twenty times from his own lips. It ought of course to have been reserved for the Congress, but as far as we are concerned it is well timed." It was a bold but a clever stroke of policy to give notice to the whole world of the sentiments and intentions with which the Emperor enters the Congress, and it renders a good understanding and joint action between France and England feasible and perhaps easy, unless Palmerston spoils everything by some obstinate and extravagant pretensions

---

[1] [The object of the Congress proposed by the Emperor Napoleon was to extricate himself from the embarrassments in which he was placed by the terms of the Peace of Villafranca with reference to the affairs of Italy. The proposal to establish a Confederation of the Italian States was found to be impracticable, and the unification of Italy was a more difficult problem than the conquest and cession to Piedmont of the Milanese territory. M. de Cavour was the only statesman who contemplated the entire realisation of this vast scheme, which was at last accomplished by revolutionary means, without the concurrence of France. His views were shared and supported by Lord Palmerston, Lord John Russell, and Mr. Gladstone.]

which he may insist on his plenipotentiaries bringing forward.   But if he should be so ill advised, I believe that he would meet with an insuperable resistance in his own Cabinet and at Court, and that Cowley certainly, perhaps Wodehouse also, would decline being made the instruments of such a vicious and mischievous policy.

January 2d, 1860.—The death of Macaulay is the extinction of a great light, and although every expectation of the completion of his great work had long ago vanished, the sudden close of his career, and the certainty that we shall have no more of his History, or at most only the remaining portion of King William's reign (which it is understood he had nearly prepared for publication), is a serious disappointment to the world. His health was so broken that his death can hardly create any surprise, but there had been no reason lately to apprehend that the end was so near. I have mentioned the circumstance of my first meeting him, after which we became rather intimate in a general way, and he used frequently to invite me to those breakfasts in the Albany at which he used to collect small miscellaneous parties, generally including some remarkable people, and at which he loved to pour forth all those stores of his mind and accumulations of his memory to which his humbler guests, like myself, used to listen with delighted admiration, and enjoy as the choicest of intellectual feasts. I don't think he was ever so entirely agreeable as at his own breakfast table, though I shall remember as long as I live the pleasant days I have spent in his society at Bowood, Holland House, and elsewhere.   Nothing was more remarkable in Macaulay than the natural way in which he talked, never for the sake of display or to manifest his superior powers and knowledge.   On the contrary, he was free from any assumption of superiority over others, and seemed to be impressed with the notion that those he conversed with knew as much as himself, and he was always quite as ready to listen as to talk. "Don't you remember?" he was in the habit of saying, when he quoted some book or alluded to some fact to listeners who could not remember, because in nineteen cases out of twenty they had never known or heard of whatever it was he alluded to. I do not believe anybody ever left his society with any feeling of mortification, except that which an involuntary comparison between his knowledge and their own ignorance could not fail to engender. For some years past I had seen little or nothing of Macaulay. His own health compelled him to abstain in great measure from going into the world. He bought a house at Campden Hill, from which he rarely stirred, and to which he never invited me, nor did I ever call upon him there. I have often regretted the total cessation of our intercourse, but what else could be expected from the difference of our habits, pursuits, and characters? I have only recently read over again the whole of his "History of England" with undiminished pleasure and admiration, though with a confirmed opinion that his style is not the very best, and that he is not the writer whom I should be most desirous to imitate : but what appears to me most admirable and most worthy of imitation in Macaulay is the sound moral constitution of his mind, and his fearless independence of thought, never sacrificing truth to any prejudice, interest, or preconceived opinion whatever.   Above all he was no hero worshipper, who felt it incumbent on him to minister to vulgar prejudices or predilections, to exalt the merits and palliate the defects of great reputations, and to consider the commission of great crimes, or the detection of mean and base motives, as atoned for and neutralised by the possession of shining abilities and the performance of great actions.   Macaulay excited much indignation in some quarters by the severity with which he criticised the conduct and character of the Duke of Marlborough, and the Quakers bitterly resented his attacks upon Penn.   He was seldom disposed to admit that he had been mistaken or misinformed, and I thought he was to blame in clinging so tenaciously to his severe estimate of Penn's conduct after the vindication of it which was brought forward, and the production of evidence in Penn's favor, which might have satisfied him that he had been in error, and which probably would have done so in any case in which his judgment had been really unbiassed.   I always regretted, not for the sake of Penn's memory, but for the honor of Macaulay himself, that he would not admit the value and force of the exculpatory evidence, and acknowledge, as he very gracefully might, the probability at least of his having been in error.   But the case of the Duke of Marlborough is very different, and reflects the highest honor on his literary integrity and independence.   Undazzled by the splendor of that great man's career and the halo of admiration which had long

surrounded his name, he demonstrated to the whole world
of what base clay the idol was made and how he had abused
for unworthy ends the choice gifts which Nature had
bestowed upon him. Macaulay no doubt held that in proportion to the excellence of his natural endowments was his
moral responsibility for the use or abuse of them, and he
would not allow Blenheim and Ramillies to be taken as a set-
off against his hypocrisy, perfidy, and treason. Macaulay's
History is the best ethical study for forming the mind and
character of a young man, for it is replete with maxims
of the highest practical value. It holds up in every page
to hatred and scorn all the vices which can stain, and to
admiration and emulation all the virtues which can adorn, a
public career. It is impossible for any one to study that
great work without sentiments of profound admiration for
the lessons it inculcates, and they who become thoroughly
imbued with its spirit, no matter whether they coincide or
not with his opinions, will be strengthened in a profound
veneration for truth and justice, for public and private
integrity and honor, and in a genuine patriotism and desire
for the freedom, prosperity, and glory of their country.

January 7th.—In a letter from Clarendon yesterday from
The Grove he says : " Cowley came over here last night. I
had a long talk with him ; he is low and unhappy, and does
not see his way out of the labyrinth ; he is not for the Congress meeting *now,* but still does not think we should abandon the Emperor altogether in his Italian policy. The fact
is, we are in a great difficulty. If we had from the first
taken the wise part of saying that as we had had nothing to
do with the war or the peace, and should therefore not interfere with the arrangements the Emperor thought proper
to make, we should now be on velvet ; but from the moment
we knew of the Villafranca arrangement we have been
thwarting the Emperor, and goading him on further than he
wished to go, and encouraging the Italians to persist in their
own ideas, till at last when he does what we want, and is
prepared to throw over the Pope and asks to be backed by
us, it is rather awkward to break away and declare we only
wanted the credit of recommending a fine liberal policy, but
that we don't mean to be at any trouble or expense about
it." All this is undoubtedly true, but it is the old inveterate
habit of Palmerston's policy. united with John Russell's
crotchets, which has brought it to this pass. Palmerston has

always been Conservative at home and Revolutionary abroad, and the gratification of a silly spite against Austria has always been paramount to any other consideration and object. While the enemies of the late Government accused them, very unjustly as the documentary evidence has shown, of having unduly favored Austria during the recent conflict, and therefore having been neutral only in name, it is true that the present Government, *i. e.*, Palmerston and John Russell, have gone out of their way to interfere in an underhand manner, and have been constantly patting on the back the insurgent Italians, and, as Clarendon says, urging the Emperor to go further than he wishes, or than he can do consistently with the engagement he has entered into. When Cowley was here some months ago, I remember his telling me that one day when he met Cavour, either at Compiègne or Paris, I forget which, when it was the question of the Congress before the war, Cavour said to him, "So you are going to have a Congress." "Yes," said Cowley, "thanks to you and all you have been doing in Italy." "Thanks to *me!*" cried Cavour, "I like that; why don't you say thanks to your own Minister at Turin, to Sir James Hudson, who has done ten times more than ever I did?"

Hatchford, January 12th.—Clarendon writes to me (on the 10th): "Cowley dined here on Saturday and did the same at Pembroke Lodge on Sunday. He is on very good terms with John Russell, but hardly understands what he would be at, and for the good reason probably that Johnny does not know himself. There is a Ministerial crisis going on at this moment about Italy, the three confederates wanting of course to dò more than the sober-minded majority can agree to. I suppose it will be decided at the Cabinet to-day, and that some middle course will be discovered, as I shall not believe, till it is a *fait accompli*, that Palmerston will allow the Government to break up on a question which will not carry the country with him. The people dislike Austria and wish well to the Italians, but they want not to interfere in the affairs of either, and I doubt if they would give a man or a shilling to help Palmerston in blotting Austria out of the map of Europe and giving Sardinia a much larger slice of the map. That twofold object amounts to monomania now with Palmerston, and I believe he would sacrifice office to attain it, which is the highest test of his sincerity. The three confederates are Palmerston, John Russell, and Gladstone.

London, January 22d.—For the last three weeks the sayings and doings of the Emperor Napoleon have occupied all thoughts in every part of Europe, and he has wellnigh recovered in this country the confidence and popularity which had been exchanged for distrust, suspicion, and alarm. It would really look as if the sole or at least the main object of his policy was to conciliate English opinion and to ingratiate himself with the present Government ; and he certainly has exhibited great courage and above all a boundless confidence in his own power and authority in his own country. There was a time when he paid great court to the Catholic clergy in France, and it was supposed that his motive in retaining the French troops in Rome (which it was known he very much disliked) was his apprehension lest their withdrawal should expose the Pope's person or Government to danger, which the clergy in France would not readily forgive him for doing. When he made peace with Austria he still evinced a desire to uphold the dignity and authority of the Pope, and therefore nobody was the least prepared for the pamphlet of "The Pope and the Congress." It fell like a thunderbolt, striking terror into the minds of all the Papal supporters and adherents, and filling with joy all revolted Italy, and with a more sober satisfaction all the Liberals and ultra-Protestants here.

We had hardly recovered from our amazement at this great change in the foreign policy of France, when we were still more astonished and pleased by the publication of the Emperor's letter to Fould, in which he announced his intention to change the whole commercial policy of France, and to make her a country of Free Trade. In thus confronting at once the Clerical body and the Protectionist interest in France, he has certainly acted with enormous boldness and reliance on his own interest and power, and it will be very interesting to see whether the success of his policy corresponds with its audacity. The Commercial Treaty has been in great measure the work of Cobden, who went over to Paris under the wing of Michel Chevalier and with letters to Cowley, who introduced him to everybody who could be of use to him in his endeavors to forward a Free-Trade policy. The scheme seems to have been arranged between the Emperor and Fould without the knowledge or participation of any of the other Ministers. Cobden had no mission, but he reported his progress home, and as an acknowledgement of his exertions he is to be made joint Plenipotentiary with Cowley in signing the Commercial Treaty.

The return of Cavour to power looks as if there was a secret understanding between France and England that the King of Sardinia should be permitted to consummate the annexation of all the revolted provinces to his dominions ; for this object, which Palmerston has so much at heart, he would gladly consent to the transference of Savoy to France, which most people think will take place ; but everything is still and must be for some time in the greatest uncertainty in North Italy, the only thing *apparently* certain being that the Dukes will not recover their Duchies, and still less the Pope his Romagna.

January 24th.—To-day Parliament opens, and everything promises a prosperous session for the Government. So little spirit is there in the Opposition, that very few of them are expected to make their appearance, and Disraeli, under the pretext of a family affliction, gives no dinner ; but the probable cause of this is not the death of his sister, which happened two months ago, but his own uncertainty as to whom he should invite, and who would be disposed to own political allegiance by accepting his invitation. Such is the disorganized state of that party.

Clarendon called on me yesterday, and told me various things more or less interesting about passing events, about Cobden and the Commercial Treaty. Cobden went over to Paris with letters from Palmerston to Cowley, begging Cowley would give him all the aid he could in carrying out his object of persuading the leading people there to adopt Free Trade principles, saying he went without any mission and as " a free lance." Cowley did what he could for him, and he went about his object with great zeal, meanwhile putting himself in correspondence with Gladstone, who eagerly backed him up, but all this time nothing was said to the Cabinet on the subject. At length one day Walewski sent for Cowley, and asked him whether he was to understand that Cobden was an agent of the British Government, and authorized by it to say all he was saying in various quarters. Cowley denied all knowledge of Cobden's proceedings, but wrote a despatch to John Russell stating what had occurred, and at the same time a private letter, saying he did not know whether he would wish such a despatch to be recorded, and therefore to number it and place it in the Foreign Office, or put it in the fire as he thought fit.   John Russell accepted the despatch, and at the same time told him he might endorse whatever Cobden did in the matter of commercial engagements.

Clarendon said that when he was at Paris four years ago for the Congress, the Emperor one day said to him, "I know you are a great Free Trader, and I suppose you mean to take this opportunity of advancing Free Trade principles here as far as you can." Clarendon said certainly such was his intention, when the Emperor said he was happy to be able to take the initiative with him on this subject, and that he would tell him that it had just been settled in the Council of State that a great change in their commercial and prohibitive system should be proposed to the Chambers, which it was his intention to carry out as as soon as possible. But not long after the Emperor renewed the subject, and told him he found the opposition so strong to his contemplated measures and the difficulties so great, that he had been obliged to abandon them for the present, and as there is no reason to doubt that the elements of opposition will be found as strong now as they were then, it is by no means certain that His Majesty will be able now to do all he wishes and has announced. It has already been stated in the French papers that something is to be done to meet the objection or allay the apprehensions of the French Protectionists, and Clarendon thinks it very doubtful whether the Commercial Treaty, which will confer advantages on France immediately without any reciprocal ones to us for eighteen months to come, will be received with much favor here, especially as the loss to our revénue will require the imposition of fresh taxes to a considerable amount.

We discussed the Italian question, and he said the Emperor is in a constant state of doubt and perplexity, one while inclining to the Congress, and another to leaving affairs to be settled without one. Granville told me last night there appears a chance of the Pope's consenting to enter the Congress with the expectation of being supported there by a majority of the Powers, and deriving considerable benefit from such support. The Emperor Napoleon, too, now shows some signs of drawing closer to Austria again, while Austria is quite determined never to consent to any of the schemes of revolution and annexation which France and England are intent upon carrying out. Apponyi told Clarendon, with tears in his eyes, that they were ruined, and quite unable to take any active part, but that in the way of *passive* resistance they might still do a great deal, and that they should not only refuse with the greatest perseverance to set their hands to any paper acknowledging the new state of things, but that they should solemnly protest against it on every occasion and in every way in their power. Austria therefore never will consent to the annexation of Central Italy to Piedmont, and if it takes place in spite of her remonstrances and in direct violation of the conditions of Villafranca and Zurich, she will not only *refuse* her recognition, but proclaim her intention of biding her time, with a view to avail herself of future possible contingencies to redress the wrongs of which she may justly complain. I asked Clarendon if he did not think it possible a *mezzo termine* might be effected by which France and Austria might again be put *d'accord*, France saying, " I would carry out the stipulations of Zurich if I could, but you see it is impossible. Still I will not consent to arrangements obnoxious to you and in direct violation of them, such as the annexations to Piedmont ; let us recur to the formation of a Central Italian independent State." Clarendon said this had been his own idea, and he still thought it was not impossible that such a compromise should be effected. It is hardly possible to doubt that if Cavour succeeds in annexing to Piedmont all the Central Italian States, a very short time will elapse before war will break out again between Sardinia and Austria, and that Austria will have to relinquish her Venetian possessions or fight for their retention.

January 27th.—The session opened with great appearance of quiet and prosperity for the Ministers, which nothing that passed the first night in either House threatened to disturb. Derby made a very good and moderate speech. When he left office the Queen entreated him not to use the power he seemed to have from the nearly balanced state of parties to upset this Government, urging the great objections there were to eternal changes, and she repeated the same thing to him when he was at Windsor on a visit not long ago. Derby expressed his entire concurrence with her, and he promised to act in conformity with her wishes, and he has entirely done so. Nothing could be more temperate and harmless than the few remarks he made on Tuesday night, but leaving himself quite unfettered on every point.

In the meantime there is apparently a strong feeling of doubt and quasi-hostility getting up against the Commercial Treaty, and it looks as if the English and French Governments would both have great difficulties in the matter. Public opinion here remains suspended till the Treaty is produced, and till we are informed what the immediate sacrifices may be that we shall have to make for it, and what are the prospective advantages we obtain in return. The French Protectionists are more impatient and have begun to pour out their complaints and indignation without waiting to see the obnoxious Convention. Thiers is said to be furious. So far from any Commercial Treaty like this cementing the alliance, and rendering war between the two countries more difficult, it is much more likely to inflame the popular antipathy in France, to make the alliance itself odious, and render the chances of war between the two countries more probable. In maturing his scheme Louis Napoleon has given it all the appearance of a conspiracy, which is in accordance with his character and his tastes. The whole thing was carried on with the most profound secrecy, and the secret was confined to a very few people, viz. the Emperor himself, Fould, Rouher (Minister of Commerce), Michel Chevalier, and Cobden. All the documents were copied by Madame Rouher, and Rouher was so afraid that some guesses might be made if he was known to be consulting books and returns that were preserved in the Library of the Council of State, that he never would look at any of them, and made Chevalier borrow all that he had occasion to refer to. Now the Emperor springs this Treaty upon his reluctant Chambers and the indignant Protectionist interest. His manner of doing the thing, which he thinks is the only way by which it can be done at all, naturally adds to the resentment the measure excites. They feel themselves in a manner taken in. The objections here are of a different kind and on other grounds, but Gladstone kept his design nearly as close as the Emperor did, never having imparted it to the Cabinet till the last moment before Parliament met. I do not know how the Cabinet looked at it, only that they were not unanimous.

While, however, it seems at least doubtful how the Government will fare when they produce this Treaty, it appears certain that they will get into a scrape with their Reform Bill. I had imagined from all I heard that the

Government were certain to bring forward a measure so moderate as to insure the support or at least prevent the opposition of the Conservatives, or certainly of a large proportion of them. Everything rendered this probable. The assurances conveyed to the Government by Walpole, the professions of Disraeli, the apathy of the country, and the total failure of Bright's attempts to get up the steam, all encouraged them to take this course, and the Duke of Bedford told me Lord John was not so tied and bound by his declarations last year that he would not concur in any moderate measure that the Cabinet might frame. A few days ago, however, I asked Clarendon what the Bill would be, and he alarmed me by his reply that "it would be as bad as possible," John Russell having insisted upon the franchise being in accordance with his pledges, and upon his consistency being entirely preserved. This meant of course a 6*l.* franchise, which everybody denounces as full of mischief and danger.

Just now Henry Lennox came to me and told me that all the dissensions and jealousies of the Conservative party and the Carlton Club had been suddenly appeased, and that from being split into little sections and coteries, squabbling among themselves and forming plots to oust Disraeli, and elevate one man or another in his place, they were suddenly reunited as one man in opposition to the Bill that they hear is to be offered to them, and that Disraeli will be higher than ever in their confidence and support. The Government estimate their majority at four, leaving out of calculation the Irish Catholics, who will probably all vote against them on every question, and the Conservatives boast of having 320 men who will cling together with immoveable constancy in opposition to the 6*l.* clause. That they will be able to carry it under these circumstances seems impossible. Lord John is himself to bring on the Reform Bill. The best thing that could happen (unless they are warned in time and alter their measure) would be that he should be beaten on the 6*l.* franchise, go out upon it and the rest stay in; but whether they would think themselves bound to stand or fall with him and break up the Government for his sake, I have at present no idea. The Queen would no doubt do all in her power to induce Palmerston to let him go, replace him, and carry on the Government without him. His loss would be a gain in every possible way, and the Government would be strengthened instead of being weakened by his absence, even though he should throw himself into the arms of Bright and join him in a Radical opposition to his former colleagues.

Bath, February 15th.—When I left London a fortnight ago the world was anxiously expecting Gladstone's speech in which he was to put the Commercial Treaty and the Budget before the world. His own confidence and that of most of his colleagues in his success was unbounded, but many inveighed bitterly against the Treaty, and looked forward with great alarm and aversion to the Budget. Clarenden shook his head, Overstone pronounced against the Treaty, the "Times" thundered against it, and there is little doubt that it was unpopular, and becoming more so every day. Then came Gladstone's unlucky illness, which compelled him to put off his *exposé*, and made it doubtful whether he would not be physically disabled from doing justice to the subject. His doctor says he ought to have taken two months' rest instead of two days'. However, at the end of his two days' delay he came forth, and *consensu omnium* achieved one of the greatest triumphs that the House of Commons ever witnessed. Everybody I have heard from admits that it was a magnificent display, not to be surpassed in ability of execution, and that he carried the House of Commons completely with him. I can well believe it, for when I read the report of it the next day (a report I take to have given the speech verbatim) it carried me along with it likewise. For the moment opposition and criticism were silenced, and nothing was heard but the sound of praise and admiration. In a day or two, however, men began to disengage their minds from the bewitching influence of this great oratorical power, to examine calmly the different parts of the wonderful piece of machinery which Gladstone had constructed, and to detect and expose the weak points and objectionable provisions which it contained. I say *it*, for, as the Speaker writes to me, it must be taken as a whole or rejected as a whole, and he adds the first will be its fate.

Clarendon, who has all along disapproved of the Treaty, wrote to me that Gladstone's success was complete, and public opinion in his favor. He says, "I expect that the London feeling will be reflected from the country, so that there will be no danger of rejection, though I think that the more the whole thing is considered, the less popular it will become. The no-provision for the enormous deficit that will exist next year will strike people, as well as the fact that the Budget is made up of expedients for the present year. The non-payment of the Exchequer bonds is to all intents and purposes a loan; the war tax on tea and sugar, the windfall of the Spanish payment, the making the maltsters and hop-growers pay in advance, &c., are all stopgaps. If anybody proposes it, I shall not be surprised if an additional 1*d.* Income Tax in place of the war duties was accepted by Gladstone. He has a fervent imagination, which furnishes facts and arguments in support of them; he is an audacious innovator, because he has an insatiable desire for popularity, and in his notions of government he is a far more sincere Republican than Bright, for his ungratified personal vanity makes him wish to subvert the institutions and the classes that stand in the way of his ambition. The two are converging from different points to the same end, and if Gladstone remains in office long enough and is not more opposed by his colleagues than he has been hitherto, we shall see him propose a graduated Income Tax." These are only objections to the Budget, and speculations (curious ones) as to the character and futurity of Gladstone.

In another letter he says: "Gladstone made a fair defence of the Treaty, though there are things in it which deserve the severest criticism and will get it, such as tying ourselves down about the exportation of coal (which is a munition of war), letting in French silks free while ours are to pay thirty per cent., and establishing a differential duty of nearly fifty per cent. in favor of light French wines against the stronger wines of Spain and Portugal, for that will be the operation of the Treaty." Since all this was written there has been a meeting of the Conservative party, and I hear this morning that Derby has decided to take the field with all his forces with a Resolution against the condition about the exportation of coal, and confining himself to that, which will very likely be carried. On the other hand, the publicans and licensed victuallers appear to be in arms against that part of the Budget which more immediately interests them, and are waging a fierce war in the Press by their paper, the "Morning Advertiser," so that in spite of his great triumph and all the admiration his eloquence and skill elicited, it is not all sunshine and plain sailing with his measures. Delane writes to me that Gladstone will find it hard work to get his Budget through, that Peel when he brought forward his Budget had a majority of ninety, all of which he required to do it, whereas Palmerston cannot command a majority of nine.

London, February 22d.—I returned to town on Monday. The same night a battle took place in the House of Commons, in which Gladstone signally defeated Disraeli, and Government got so good a majority that it looks like the harbinger of complete success for their Treaty and their Budget. Everybody agrees that nothing could be more brilliant and complete than Gladstone's triumph, which did not seem to be matter of much grief to many of the Conservative party, for I hear that however they may still act together on a great field-day, the hatred and distrust of Disraeli is greater than ever in the Conservative ranks, and Derby himself, when. he heard how his colleague had been demolished, did not seem to care much about it. They say that he betrays in the House of Commons a sort of consciousness of his inferiority to Gladstone, and of fear of encountering him in debate.

February 26th.—On Friday night Gladstone had another great triumph. He made a splendid speech, and obtained a majority of 116, which puts an end to the contest. He is now *the* great man of the day, but these recent proceedings have strikingly displayed the disorganized condition of the Conservative party and their undisguised dislike of their leader. A great many of them voted with Government on Friday night, and more expressed satisfaction at the result being a defeat of Disraeli. The Treaty and Budget, though many parts of both are obnoxious to criticism more or less well founded, seem on the whole not unpopular, and since their first introduction to have undoubtedly gained in public favor. This fact and the state of the Opposition prove the impossibility of any change of Government. Gladstone, too, as he is strong, seems disposed to be merciful, and has expressed his intention of taking fairly into consideration the various objections that may be brought forward, and to consent to reasonable alterations when good cases are made out for them. There seems no doubt that his great measures were not approved by the majority of the Cabinet, but the malcontents do not seem to have been disposed to fight much of a battle against the minority, which included both Palmerston and Lord John.

It is curious how this great question has thrown into the

background all the questions about Italy and foreign policy, in regard to which public interest seems to be for the moment suspended, while Italian affairs are at a dead lock. It would be very inconsistent with the Emperor's character if he had given up his design of appropriating Savoy, but he has certainly postponed it, and will probably employ his versatile imagination in weaving some fresh web by means of which he may get it into his power. I have been reading the Italian Blue Book, which is a creditable compilation. John Russell's positions are not unsound, but he is too controversial in his tone, and though he treats Austria with a decent consideration, and in no unfriendly spirit, he might as well have avoided arguing with Count Rechberg upon points and principles on which it was impossible they should ever agree. Throughout this compilation the embarrassment and perplexity of the Emperor Napoleon are conspicuous, and the difficulties into which he got himself by his vacillations and incompatible objects and obligations. His desire to adhere to the engagements he contracted at Villafranca is obvious throughout, and the advice he gave the Pope seems to have been the best possible, and given in all sincerity.[1]

February 27th.—Gladstone is said to have become subject to much excitement, and more bitter in controversy in the House of Commons than was his wont. The severe working of his brain and the wonderful success he has obtained may account for this, and having had his own way and triumphed over all opposition in the Cabinet, it is not strange that he should brook none anywhere else. He has not failed to show a little of the cloven foot, and to alarm people as to his future designs. Clarendon, who watches him, and has means of knowing his disposition, thinks that he is moving toward a Democratic union with Bright, the effect of which will be increased Income Tax and lowering the estimates by giving up the defences of the country, to which Sidney Herbert will never consent, and already these old friends and colleagues appear to be fast getting into a state of antagonism. Aberdeen told Clarendon that they would never go on together, and he thought Sidney Herbert would retire from the Cabinet

---

[1] [The Emperor told Metternich the other day that he had made one great mistake, which he had never ceased to regret, that immediately after Villafranca he ought to have marched 100,000 men into Tuscany on the plea of embarking them at Leghorn, and continued to occupy the country till the restoration of the Grand Duke was accomplished, but that he had never contemplated the invincible resistance of the whole population.—C. C. G.]

before the end of the session. This of course implies that Gladstone's policy is to be in the ascendant, and that he is to override the Cabinet.

There has been a dispute about the introduction of the Reform Bill. Lord John's colleagues wished him to defer bringing it on, till more progress had been made in the fiscal and commercial measures, and represented the inconvenience of having the two discussions going on at the same time, but nothing would induce him to postpone it, and for the absurd reason that he wanted to bring in this Bill on the *same day* on which he had introduced the great Reform Bill in 1831, and to this fanciful object he insisted on sacrificing all others.

Hatchford, March 7th.—Lord John Russell brought in his Reform Bill last week without exciting the smallest interest, or even curiosity, amid profound indifference in the House and in the country. His measure was very moderate, and his speech temperate. It produces no enthusiasm, or satisfaction, or alarm. It will probably pass without any violent debates, and perhaps with very slight alterations. If the opponents should succeed in making some, Lord John is not prepared to adhere obstinately to his measure, but will come to terms. It was settled that no discussion should take place at the time, and nobody was inclined for any. It hardly delayed the progress of Gladstone's measures, so we heard no more complaints of Lord John's pertinacity in bringing it on upon March 1st.

The Treaty, the Budget, and the Reform Bill had thrown foreign affairs into the background, but the interest in them was suddenly aroused, and speedily absorbed every other, by the Emperor's speech and M. Thouvenel's despatches all so mortifying and provoking to us. Up to this moment Palmerston had been highly elated, and he and Lord John had been exulting in the fancied glory of being the Liberators of Italy, and of having procured the complete success of their own objects. As Clarendon wrote to me, "The Emperor must greatly enjoy the helplessness of Europe, and in feeling that he may do just what he likes with perfect impunity. Russia is crippled, Austria rotten, Germany disunited, and England, though growling, occupied in gnawing the Treaty bone he has tossed to her. All must submit to the laws made known to them through the 'Moniteur.'" If it were not so melancholy to see the miserable figure which

England cuts in all this, it would be amusing to see it happen *regnante* Palmerston, and after all his incurable meddling and blustering to see him obliged to eat so much dirt. He may (though probably he does not) think he has lived too long to be reserved at the last period of his political career for such mortification. The Emperor said to somebody, "L'Europe boudera, nais ne fera rien," and he is quite right. We seem to have arrived at the last act of the Italian drama, but it is still very uncertain how the *dénouement* will be worked out and what the Emperor's final will and pleasure will be. The Romagna seems to present the greatest difficulty; all the rest will find a tolerably easy solution. France will take what she wants of Savoy and give the rest to Switzerland, who upon those conditions is desirous of annexation, and Piedmont does not seem to care much about it. In this way the question of Savoy will be settled, if not by general consent, at least with general acquiescence and without any opposition.

March 9th.—After all it is not improbable that Palmerston will have the gratification of seeing Tuscany annexed to Sardinia. Cavour has taken the line which Clarendon and I agreed that he would very likely do, and sets France and Austria at defiance. We have seen France and Sardinia joined in making war upon Austria, and now we have France and Austria joined in diplomacy against Sardinia. Nothing can be more curious than to see the unravelling of this web. Next week the Italian States will severally vote their annexation to Sardinia, or their separate existence. If, as is almost certain, the former is their decision, the King will accept their resolution, and Piedmontese troops will march into Tuscany. Then we shall see what the Emperor Napoleon will do, and what he will permit Austria to do.

Savernake, March 18th.—The affair of Savoy has been summarily settled by the will of the Emperor and the connivance of Cavour. The whole affair now appears to have been a concerted villainy between these worthies, which as the plot has been developed excites here the most intense disgust and indignation. The feeling is the stronger because we have no choice but that of sulky and grumbling acquiescence. The one redeeming point in the French act of violence *was* the apparent respect paid to Treaties and to the claims of Switzerland, Thouvenel having only the other day said that Faucigny and Chablais should be ceded at once

23

to Switzerland ; and now we hear that nothing of the kind
is to be done, and that France seizes everything.[1] It is in
vain that the Houses of Parliament are advised to cease bark-
ing, as they certainly do not mean to bite, and that the
"Times" recommends silence and moderation ; such enor-
mities as are unblushingly exhibited to the world excite an
indignation which breaks through every restraint, and people
will not hold their peace, happen what may. The Opposition
have turned the current of their wrath upon our Government, and have proved clearly enough that they had ample
and timely notice of the Emperor's intentions, and that
nevertheless they continued to urge with all their might that
policy which was certain to lead to the annexation of Savoy.
That the Emperor and Cavour have been plotting together
seems now quite certain, but we are still ignorant, and may
perhaps ever remain so, of the details of their delusive
operations.

The three great subjects which have occupied public
attention all this year have been the Italian and its branches,
Gladstone's Treaty and Budget, and the Reform Bill. Up
to the present time the two first have absorbed all interest,
and the new Reform Bill has been received with almost complete apathy, nobody appearing to know or care what its
effects would be, and most people misled by an apparent
show of moderation and harmlessness in its details. But in
the course of the last week the "Times" set to work, in a
series of very able articles, to show the mischievous and dangerous effects that the proposed franchise will produce, and
these warnings, supported by ample statistical details, have
begun to arouse people from their indifference and to create
some apprehensions. I am informed that John Russell
framed his Bill in utter ignorance of these important details,
and, with the mixture of levity and obstinacy which has
always distinguished him, has plunged the country into this
dilemma for the sake of his own selfish and ambitious objects.
But what is incomprehensible is that in such a numerous

---

[1] [It is within my own knowledge than M. Thouvenel expressed at that time
the desire of the Emperor to do anything he could *to help Lord Palmerston*, and
accordingly he proposed, unofficially, to surrender and annex a considerable
portion of the Faucigny district, down to the Fort de l'Ecluse, in the Jura, to
the Canton of Geneva, provided the British Government would assent to the
acquisition by France of the rest of Savoy. Lord Palmerston rejected the proposal, saying to the person who conveyed it to him, " We shall shame them out
of it."—H. R.]

Cabinet as the present, and containing many men who certainly once had strong Conservative opinions, he should not have met with a more strenuous opposition, and have been forced to alter his most obnoxious propositions, and I think those who were better informed than Lord John, and saw whither his plan of Reform was leading them, are more to blame than himself. It is impossible to meet with any man who approves of this Bill, and who does not abhor the idea of any Reform whatever. All say that if the members voted by ballot there would be almost unanimity against it, and yet such is the disorganized state of the Conservative party, and such the want of moral courage and independence generally, that this Bill will most likely pass unaltered.

The prevailing hope is that the House of Lords will amend it, but Derby told somebody (I think it was Clarendon) that if those who dreaded the mischief of the measure in the House of Commons had not the courage and honesty to oppose it there and correct it, the House of Lords should not, so far as his influence went, incur the odium of doing the work which the House of Commons ought itself to do. Lyndhurst told me the other day that Derby had told Lady Lyndhurst he was so disgusted with the state of affairs at home and abroad, that he had serious thoughts of withdrawing from public life, and Clarendon told me that an eminent Conservative, who had begged not to be quoted, had said that he knew Derby was violently discontented with Disraeli, and prepared to dissolve their political connection.

Wells, March 21st.—I came here from Savernake on Monday. On Friday last in the House of Lords the Commercial Treaty and Budget, but the latter especially, were powerfully assailed by Grey, Overstone, and Derby, and very considerably damaged *in argument,* but probably in nothing else. The Government are as weak in the Lords as the Opposition are in the Commons, where, however, Disraeli seems to have made a very good speech against the Reform Bill on Monday night.

Torquay, March 28th.—The past week has been remarkable for the speech in which John Russell denounced in strong language the conduct of France, declared that we could no longer trust her, and that we must renew our intimacies with the other Powers. Whether all this was sincere and meant all it seems to do is yet to be discovered. The week was near being still more remarkable, for the Reform Bill was within an ace of falling to the ground by the House being counted out in the midst of a debate.   This would have been very ridiculous, but would have been hailed with delight by the House of Commons, and without dissatisfaction by the country.   Clarendon writes to me in a strain of bitter hostility to the Bill and disgust at everything, complains of the general apathy and the impossibility of rousing any spirit of opposition to what all abhor.   Derby told him that if twenty-five or even twenty Liberals would *take the lead* in opposing this Bill, the whole Conservative party would support them.   Clarendon wrote to me when I was at Bath that the time would probably come when Gladstone would propose a graduated Income Tax, and lo! it has nearly come, for Gladstone gave notice the other night to people to be prepared for it.   The Triumvirate of Palmerston, John Russell, and Gladstone, who have it all their own way, dragging after them the Cabinet, the House of Commons, and the country, will probably be the ruin of this country.   They are playing into the Emperor Napoleon's hands, who has only to be patient and bide his time, and he will be able to treat all Europe, England included, in any way he pleases.   Nothing but some speedy change of Government and of system can avert the impending ruin.

London, April 2d.—One day last week (as mentioned above), on one of the numerous discussions of the Savoy question in the House of Commons, John Russell electrified the House and rather astonished the country by delivering a very spirited speech, denouncing in strong terms the conduct of the Emperor Napoleon, and declaring the necessity of cultivating relations with the other Great Powers for the purpose of putting an effectual check upon the projects of French aggrandizement and annexation.   I must own that my first impression was that this speech was made merely to deceive the House and the country, and was only a part of the collusive system between our Government and the French, by virtue of which Louis Napoleon has been enabled to work out all his objects and designs ; but though it is impossible to doubt that John Russell and Palmerston have all along been aware of the Emperor's intentions with regard to Savoy, and that they have been more intent upon procuring advantages for Sardinia and provoking Austria than upon thwarting the projects of France, I am inclined to see Lord John's speech in another light from what I hear since I came to town.   He made it without any previous consultation with his colleagues, it having been one of those impromptus which he is so apt to indulge in, and Palmerston, seeing the way in which it was received in the House and by the Press, approved of its tone and expressed a full concurrence with it.   Flahault, who went to Paris a few days ago, called on Palmerston before he went and asked if he wished him to say or do anything there.   Palmerston said he might inform the Government that Lord John's speech expressed the unanimous opinion of the Cabinet here.   In my opinion his speech was a great imprudence, and will probably involve the necessity of our eating a great deal of humble pie.   We have long ago declared that though we disapprove very much of the annexation of Savoy, we should take no steps to prevent it; but Lord John made a great distinction between the question of Savoy and Nice and that of Faucigny and Chablais, and though he did not commit himself to any positive course, he gave it to be inferred that something more would be required from us, in the way of opposition to the seizure of the latter, than there was any necessity for our making to that of the former.   But the Emperor makes no such distinctions, and if, as is most probable, he does not admit our right to draw them, we shall be in an unpleasant fix, and have to back out of the position we have assumed in a way neither dignified nor creditable.

The accounts from Paris are that this speech has made the French very insolent, and the Emperor more popular than he has been for a long time, as even his enemies say that they will rally round him to chastise English impertinence.   Then as to forming alliances with the other Powers, which of course will be taken (as was intended) as a menace to France, nothing could be more ill-advised than such an announcement, for the other Great Powers have neither the ability nor the inclination to join us in any coalition, present or prospective, against France.   Russia and Austria hate us, as well they may, for we have done them both all the injury in our power, besides heaping every sort of insult upon them. Austria is totally ruined, hopelessly bankrupt and torn to pieces with internal disaffection and discontent.   Russia is hampered with her great serf question, and overwhelmed with financial embarrassments, which she owes in great measure to the Crimean War, and the unfortunate dissension and estrangement between her and Austria are at-

tributable to the same cause and to our policy. Prussia, the
only one of the three that is able to make any efforts, and
that has no cause of enmity against us, is always selfish
and timorous, and is more occupied in trying to supplant
Austria in Germany than in taking defensive measures
against French ambition ; nor is there in Germany any such
strong sentiment of national independence as might induce
the various States to sink their minor jealousies and partisan-
ships in a general union, to meet any aggression that may
proceed from France. Among the many schemes which the
Imperial brain is supposed to be continually engendering, it
is far from impossible that one may be the reconstruction
of the kingdom of Westphalia, or at least of some Rhenish
kingdom with the concurrence of Prussia, by concluding a
bargain of partition with her. He might then replace old
Jérome on the throne, and so get rid of his obnoxious son, of
course taking as much of such acquired territory as he wanted
for himself. All this is mere vague conjectural speculation,
but it is *on the cards*, and it is at least as probable as that we
should be able to form another coalition, like that which
overthrew the first Napoleon, strong enough to cope with
the present Napoleon. People are beginning at last to doubt
whether the war we waged against Russia four years ago was
really a wise and politic measure ; but the whole country
went mad upon that subject, I never could understand why.
Palmerston took it up to make political capital out of it, and
made himself popular by falling in with the public humor,
and making the country believe that he was the only man
really determined to make war on Russia, and able to bring
the war to a successful end. Aberdeen, who was wise enough
to see the folly of quarrelling with Russia and sacrificing all
our old alliances to a new and deceitful one with France, was
unable to stem the torrent, and fell under its violence. His
fault was his not resigning office when he found it impossible to carry out his policy and maintain peace.

A propos of the Russian War, I heard lately an anecdote for the first time that surprised me. Everybody knows
that we beat up for allies and even mercenary aid against
Russia in every direction, but it is not known that our
Government earnestly pressed the Portuguese Government
to join in the war, and to send a contingent to the Crimea,
and that on the refusal of the latter to do so, the Ministers
made the Queen appeal personally to Lavradio and urge him

to persuade his Government to comply with our wishes; but Lavradio represented to Her Majesty, as he had done to her Ministers, that Portugal had no quarrel with Russia, and no interest in joining in the war; on the contrary, Portugal was under obligations to the Emperor of Russia, and she therefore would have nothing to do with the contest. This was a most extraordinary proceeding, and it was contrary to all usage as well as all propriety to make the Queen interpose in person on such an occasion.

April 4th.—Clarendon has just been here talking over the state of affairs, in the course of which he alluded to what had passed in the autumn of '58 between the Emperor and him, and between His Majesty and Palmerston. In September he had a long conversation with the Emperor, in the course of which he asked Clarendon, "Supposing I find myself compelled to go to war with Austria, what part would England take in the contest?" Clarendon replied that it would depend upon the circumstances of the case and the cause that would be shown for such a war, and that he must not be misled by the language of the English Press and the prejudice which no doubt existed in England against Austria and her system of government, which would not be sufficient to make us take any part against her. On comparing notes with Palmerston afterward, Clarendon found that Louis Napoleon had put the same question to Palmerston, who had given him the same answer. When they went to Compiègue in November of the same year, they both had conversations separately of the same character, and when they afterward compared notes and Clarendon asked Palmerston what impression the Emperor's words had left on his mind, Palmerston replied he thought either that the Emperor had abandoned the design he had certainly been meditating to go to war, or he had resolved upon it, but did not choose to acknowledge his intentions to them, and this Clarendon said was exactly the same opinion as he had formed. This, however, was not above six weeks before his famous speech to the Austrian Ambassador (which was a declaration of war), and therefore the latter conjecture was the correct one. We talked over Lord John's speech and his letter in answer to Thouvenel. Clarendon said that this dispatch was entirely written by Palmerston himself, that anybody as well acquainted with their styles as he was must be quite certain of this, but that *he* knew it to be the case. He had a conversation with Palmerston the other day, who praised Lord John's speech and said it would do good, and he thought *the question of Savoy was in a very satisfactory state.*

Palmerston, he told me, had said more to Flahault[1] than I had been apprised of. Flahault went to him, and found him just going to the House of Commons. Flahault asked him to let him get into his carriage, which he did, and when Flahault asked what he should say to the Emperor, and Palmerston told him to say that the Emperor had better read Lord John's speech, and understand that he (Palmerston) agreed in every word of it, Flahault said, "Then you mean that you have no longer any confidence in the Emperor, or place any reliance upon his word." Palmerston replied, "I do mean this. After having been repeatedly deceived and misled by his professions and assurances, it is impossible that I can place any further confidence in him." Then said Flahault, "There will be war," to which Palmerston rejoined that he hoped not, that nobody could be more anxious to avoid war than he was.

This was very spirited and becoming, and Clarendon said he highly approved of such a tone. I said that I had all along suspected that there was a secret understanding and collusion between Palmerston and the Emperor, and that Palmerston had given His Majesty to understand that if he would set Italy free, he might do what he pleased with regard to Savoy, but that what had recently passed seemed to negative that idea. Clarendon replied he had no doubt Palmerston had very often said to Persigny what, if repeated by Persigny to the Emperor with some exaggerations and suppressions, would convey as much to His Majesty, for Palmerston had a dozen times said to him (Clarendon) that the liberation and settlement of Italy was of far greater consequence than the preservation of Savoy to Piedmont.

April 8th.—To The Grove on Thursday afternoon, and returned yesterday. On Good Friday morning George Lewis and I were left alone, when we talked over the questions of the day, and he quite amazed me by the way in which he spoke of his principal colleagues. I asked him if John Russell was not exceedingly mortified at the ill-success of his Reform Bill and its reception in the House of Commons and in the country. George Lewis said he did not think he

---

[1] [Count de Flahault was at this time French Ambassador in London.]

felt this, that at present his mind was entirely occupied with foreign politics, and he was rejoicing in the idea of having been largely instrumental to the liberation of Italy ; and as to Reform, that he was satisfied with having redeemed the pledge he gave to Bright to propose a 6*l.* franchise, and having done this he did not care about the result, as he had never pledged himself to carry it.   The most strange thing to me is, that George Lewis seemed not to be alive to the culpable levity of such conduct, or to the censure to which his own conduct is obnoxious in consenting to act with such a man, and to be a party to such a measure.

With regard to Palmerston, he said that Palmerston thought of nothing but his pro-Sardinian and anti-Austrian schemes, and he was gratified by seeing everything in that quarter turning out according to his wishes, that in the Cabinet he took very little part and rarely spoke.   Gladstone George Lewis evidently distrusts, and his financial schemes and arrangements are as distasteful to him as possible.   He is provoked at Gladstone's being able to bear down all opposition, and carry all before him by the force of his eloquence and power of words, and what I have said of his conduct in supporting John Russell is still more applicable to it in reference to Gladstone and his measures, which he thinks more dangerous by far than he does Lord John's Reform Bill and 6*l.* clause.   I asked him what was to be the end of this Bill, and he said he did not expect it to pass, that probably the debates on it would be so spun out and so many delays interposed that either it would fail in the House of Commons itself, or even if it passed, the House of Lords would say it came up too late for them to examine and consider it, and it would be thrown out there.   I gathered in the course of conversation that Palmerston (whose whole antecedents and recorded opinions forbid the idea of his approving such a measure) would be glad to see the franchise raised, and that 8*l.* and 15*l.* would in his view improve the Bill.

May 6th.—Since I wrote the above, nearly a month ago, I have been out of the way of hearing anything on public affairs, till a day or two ago when I called on Clarendon, when he told me some things not without interest, partly about domestic and partly about foreign affairs.   The latter of course related to the inexhaustible subject of the Emperor Napoleon's projects and machinations.   His Majesty, it seems, has recently had a conversation with M. de Moustier, French Minister at Vienna, in the course of which he told him that it was an absolute necessity to France to carry her frontier to the Rhine. About the same time Cavour had signified (I forget whether it was to the same de Moustier or to some other person) that Sardinia must obtain possession of Venetia. These necessities, it can hardly be doubted, are expressed and resolved upon by a common accord. Austria has been already completely crippled by the late war; if threatened in Italy she will employ all her resources in defence of her Italian territory, and she will be quite unable, even if she were willing, to join in any measures of resistance to the attempts of France upon Germany. Prussia has had the egregious folly to renew her feud with Denmark upon the affair of Schleswig-Holstein, and is about to provoke a fresh war on that question. Denmark thus threatened appeals to France for aid, which France is too happy to afford, as she will thereby in all probability find a good pretext for inter-ference, and for the furtherance of all her designs. There seems no doubt that a Treaty of some sort has been con-cluded between France and Denmark. In this difficult and menacing posture of affairs, England will sooner or later have to play a part of some sort, and it is disquieting enough to reflect upon our diplomacy being under the charge of John Russell and of Palmerston.

After lingering on for several weeks with unprecedented tardiness and delay, and a languid, uninteresting discussion —debate it cannot be called—the second reading of the Re-form Bill has at last passed without opposition. The last nights have been remarkable for the speeches hostile to the Bill of several Liberal members, and the increasing proofs of its prodigious unpopularity. Everybody is sick of the sub-ject, and those who desire that some modified and amended measure may pass, only do so because they have a horror of seeing another Bill brought in next year, and they hope that they may now purge this Bill of its worst and most danger-ous defects, and close the subject for several years to come. Some think that it is impossible to devise any means by which this Bill can be made anything like safe and expedient, and would therefore prefer to throw it out and run all chances for the future. At least one half of the Government, with Palmerston himself at the head of the dissentients, re-gard this Bill with alarm and aversion, and now that the difficulty, if not impossibility, of passing it is obvious, they are prepared to make every sort of sacrifice, even of its most vital provisions. Palmerston told George Lewis so, and that John Russell himself would submit to an alteration of the franchise to the amount of £15 for the counties and £8 for the towns. They know that no question of resignation is involved in this discussion, and that whatever may be the fate of their Bill, they will still keep their places, which no concession will endanger, and accordingly they are ready to agree to any compromise which will secure the Bill's passing through Parliament in any shape or way; but, notwithstanding this pliant disposition, it is very doubtful whether the Bill can pass. It will not commence its career in Committee till the first week in June, and it is hardly possible it can reach the House of Lords before the middle or end of July, and the Lords may very well decline to enter on its consideration at that late period.

May 9th.—A correspondence appears in the newspapers between Lord Grey and John Russell, couched in terms of no small bitterness. Such a correspondence between men of such eminence and of the same political color shows up to the world the insincerity with which, for political motives at the time urgent, they have spoken in their places in Parliament. It is no new thing that members of the same Cabinet should often differ, and that vehemently on particular questions, and yet when these questions come under Parliamentary discussion, that they should exhibit to the world the semblance of an agreement and concurrence which is remote from the truth. But though this is well understood to be of not unfrequent occurrence, and sooner or later the details of the truth often leak out, it is much to be regretted that men should exhibit themselves and each other in the way which this correspondence does, for such exhibitions cannot fail to excite suspicions of the sincerity, conscientiousness, and truth of public men. When Governments are entirely of one party color, either wholly Whig or wholly Tory, and when they are presided over by some man of supereminent authority, such differences and consequent difficulties are not likely to happen often; but as of late years parties have been broken up, and composite Governments have been formed, combining men of the most opposite original principles, and imbued with very different and incompatible opinions on various subjects, it must be continually happening that candid discussions and disputes in the Cabinet should be followed by insincere and untruthful declarations and argumentations in public. The understood practice from time immemorial has been, that a dissentient from the general opinion of his colleagues upon any *important* question must either consent to merge his own opinion in theirs, or retire from office ; and then the conduct of the dissentient was regulated by his view of the *importance* of the matter at issue. Of course if a man were to break off from his colleagues upon every matter of difference, however small, no Government could possibly go on for many months or perhaps weeks, but it is impossible in these days not to be struck with the fact that so many men are indisposed to consider anything of sufficient importance to resign their offices rather than sacrifice their enlightened consciences and mature judgments.

May 12th.—Not more than three months ago Gladstone was triumphant and jubilant ; he had taken the House of Commons and the country captive by his eloquence, and nothing was heard everywhere but songs of praise and admiration at his marvellous success and prodigious gcuius. There never was a greater reaction in a shorter time. Everybody's voice is now against him, and his famous Treaty and his Budget are pronounced enormous and dangerous blunders. Those who were most captivated now seem to be most vexed and ashamed of their former fascination. They are provoked with themselves for having been so duped, and a feeling of resentment and bitterness against him has become widely diffused in and out of the House of Commons, on his own side as well as on the other. It was the operation of this feeling which caused the narrow majority on the Paper Duties the other night, when it seems as if a little more management and activity might have put him in a minority, and it is the same thing which is now encouraging the House of Lords, urged on by Derby, to throw out the Resolution when it comes before them. Derby has announced that he shall exert himself to the utmost to procure the rejection of the Bill in the House of Lords, and if he perseveres he will probably obtain a very unwise and perilous success, which he will before long have to regret.

May 17th.—Clarendon dined with Derby about a week ago, when Derby explained to him all his reasons for persisting in his opposition to the Paper Duties Bill. · Clarendon said he did not talk rashly and in Rupert vein, but gave a well-considered and well-argued statement of the grounds on which he purposed to proceed. Clarendon evidently sympathized with him, but not without much apprehension and doubt as to the expediency of his course. Derby appears to have taken and to be taking prodigious pains with his case, and he said that his object was to have a great financial debate in the Lords on the Treaty and the Budget. Granville tells me they shall be beaten by a large majority, and he owns that the debate will be almost all one way. There is nothing on the Treasury Bench or behind it able to grapple with Derby, Monteagle, Overstone, and Grey on such a question, though Granville expects Argyll to get up the question and to speak well on it, and he expects something from Newcastle and Ripon, but Clarendon told me (which of course he had from Lewis) the curious fact that Palmerston himself views with pleasure the prospect of the rejection of the Bill. A queer state of things indeed when the Prime Minister himself secretly desires to see the defeat of a measure so precious to his own Chancellor of the Exchequer.

Frederick Cadogan came over from Paris the other day, and told Clarendon that Cowley was in very bad spirits about the aspect of foreign affairs, that all intimacy and confidence between the Emperor and him was at an end, and that it was more and more evident that His Majesty meant to follow his own devices, whatever they might be, without reference to anybody, or caring for the opposition or the assent of any other Powers.

The Garibaldi expedition is supposed to have given great umbrage to France, but not without some suspicions that secretly she is not sorry for it, and thinks in its complications she may find matter to turn to her own account. Everybody believes that Cavour has covertly connived at it, though he pretends to oppose it. Certainly no resolute attempts were made to obstruct the expedition by the Sardinian Government, and none whatever by France, who, if she really cared to stop it, might easily have done so by sending ships from Toulon for the purpose.

Talking of Neapolitan affairs, Pahlen told me yesterday an almost incredible anecdote, but of which he said there was no doubt of the truth. There is just arrived a new Neapolitan Minister, Count Ludolph, grandson of the Ludolph who was formerly here. He has replaced the former Minister, who by his own desire was recently recalled, and he had begged for his recall because he had been grossly insulted by Palmerston at the Queen's Drawing Room, his story being that in that room, in the Queen's presence (who was of course out of hearing), Palmerston had attacked him on the proceedings of his Government and the conduct of the King, telling him that a revolution would probably be the consequence thereof, which would be nothing more than they deserved, and which would be seen in this country with universal satisfaction. The man was so flabbergasted by this unexpected and monstrous sortie that he had not presence of mind to make a suitable answer, and to *riposter* with the spirit which the occasion required of him. I must endeavor to find out if this is true. Palmerston has always been noted for the vivacity and often acerbity of his language in despatches, but in oral communications and in speeches he has never been reproached with intemperance or incivility, but, on the contrary, has always evinced self-control and gentlemanlike and polite behavior and language.

May 28th.—Epsom engaged all my attention last week, and I could not find time to notice the debate in the Lords on the Paper Duties, and the extraordinary majority, so much greater than anybody expected. Lyndhurst undertook to speak on the constitutional part of the question, and got leave to speak early (between Granville and Monteagle) that he might go home to celebrate his birthday, which fell on that day, when he completed his eighty-eighth year. He made a very good speech, and met with an enthusiastic reception. Lady Palmerston was in the gallery, openly expressing her wishes that the Bill might be rejected by a large majority. Her language on this and other occasions so shocked some of the more zealous Whigs, that the Duke of Bedford was asked by one or more of them to remonstrate with her on the way she talked, but she knows very well that Palmerston is of the same mind, though he cannot avow his real sentiments in the way she does. Palmerston said to Gladstone, "Of course you are mortified and disappointed, but your disappointment is nothing to mine, who had a horse with whom I hoped to win the Derby, and he went amiss at the last moment." The affair has gone off very quietly, the House of Commons not being the least disposed to quarrel with the Lords about it. Even John Russell; who had talked very absurdly, held moderate and prudent language in the House.[1]

June 15th.—At Ascot last week. Palmerston was there, and went up to town on Thursday (going reluctantly) to assist at the withdrawal by John Russell of the Reform Bill. There was a Cabinet the preceding day, at which Palmerston said, "We must now settle what is to be done about the Reform Bill." John Russell said, "I know what my opinion is, and if anybody wishes to hear it I am ready to give it." They all said they did wish it, when he announced that he thought it ought to be withdrawn. Everybody agreed except Gladstone, who made a long speech in favor of going on with it, which nobody replied to, and there it ended. A discussion took place as to what should be said, and strong opinions expressed that nothing but moderate language should be employed, which John Russell agreed to, and he acted up to it by making a very becoming speech, which would have been faultless if he had not announced another Reform Bill on the earliest possible occasion. This, too, he did entirely off his own bat, and without any consultation or agreement with his colleagues. · Fortunately these announcements are no longer so important or so binding as heretofore, and I think it probable, unless there is some great change in public opinion (which is not likely), that when the time draws near Palmerston and a majority of the Cabinet will not consent to a fresh attempt.

July 8th.—I have been so ill till within the last few days that I have not had energy enough to do anything. I have known but little, and that little I could not bring myself to write down here. In fact, it is high time that I should close these records once for all, which I am morally and physically incapable of continuing with any probability of making them interesting. It is not very consistent with this opinion to fill a page or two with the recent transaction in the House of Commons, with reference to the duty on paper. Everybody allows that Palmerston got out of his difficulty with consummate tact and discretion, and that Gladstone's conduct was inexcusable. The Resolutions concocted by Palmerston had been fully discussed and agreed to in the Cabinet

[1] [A Bill for abolishing the duty on paper was carried in the House of Commons on March 12 by a majority of 245 to 192. It was rejected on May 21 by the House of Lords by a majority of 193 to 104. The dispute was eventually settled by a resolution for removing so much of the duty on paper as exceeded the Excise duty at home.]

(reluctantly of course by Gladstone), and Palmerston's speech
was received with general approbation in the House. It was
excellent, fair and moderate, the argument logically consistent with the Resolutions, but displeasing to Gladstone and
the highflyers because it made a sort of excuse for the Lords,
or rather it set forth the grounds on which the Lords might
think themselves justified in acting as they did, without
having any of the motives and designs which the Gladstones
and Brights attributed to them.   All this elicited great applause from the Opposition side of the House, and their
cheers were very offensive to and grated on the ears of the
ultra-Liberals.   Everything would have ended quietly, and
the Resolutions would have passed without a debate, but
Gladstone could not stand it, and, urged by spite and mortification, he must needs get up and make a most violent
speech, really, though not avowedly, in opposition to Palmerston, and with the object of provoking a long and acrimonious debate. In this he only partially succeeded, and not for
long.   The debate lasted one night more, but nothing could
be made of the Amendments.   Palmerston kept his temper
and displayed great firmness and resolution.   The House
was with him.   Bright, partly from being very unwell, and
probably partly from some discretion, made a moderate
speech ; everybody seemed determined to bring the matter
to an end, and the Resolutions were very triumphantly carried. Granville told me yesterday morning that it was a
toss up whether Gladstone resigned or not, and that if he
did, it would break up the Liberal party, to which I replied
that I was confident he would not resign, and if he did, it
would have no effect on the bulk of the Liberal party.

July 17th.—I met Charles Villiers at dinner at the
Travellers' last night and had some talk with him, particularly about Gladstone.   He thinks it far better that he
should not resign, as he could, and probably would, be very
mischievous out of office.   He says people do not know the
House of Commons, and are little aware that there is an obscure but important element in it of a Radical complexion,
and that there are sixty or seventy people who would consti-
tute themselves followers of Gladstone, and urge him on to
every sort of mischief.   They are already doing all they can
to flatter and cajole him, and once out of office, his great
talents and oratorical powers would make him courted by all
parties, even the Tories, who would each and all be very glad

to enlist him in their service. It is impossible to calculate on the course of a man so variable and impulsive, but at present it looks as if he had made up his mind to swallow his mortifications and disappointments and to go on with his present colleagues, though Charles Villiers says he is very dejected and uneasy in his mind, and very gloomy in the Cabinet.

I asked him if he had seen Senior's last Journals, relating his visit to Paris, which he had not. I told him they were very interesting, and that all his interlocutors, however varying in opinions upon other subjects, were agreed as to the certainty of the Emperor's meditating fresh wars and aggressions, and sooner or later a war with us. He said he thought it probable that any attempt on Belgium would be deferred till after King Leopold's death (who is seventy-five years old), at which time in all probability the annexation would be attempted, and with very reasonable prospects of being assented to by the Belgians themselves, an idea which had not struck me, but which I think exceedingly likely.

Buxton, August 11th.—I came here for my health and to try and patch myself up a fortnight ago, since which I have heard and learnt nothing of what is passing in the world but what I read in the newspapers. The session of Parliament was drawing to a close, and it was understood that there was to be one more fight in the House of Commons (on the removal of the Customs duties on paper), and then the remaining business was to be hurried through as quickly as possible. The Opposition made strenuous efforts to obtain a majority, and were sanguine of success. The Speaker wrote me an account of what passed, and I shall copy out the greatest part of his letter. "The division of thirty-three on the Paper Duties was a surprise to all on the spot. As late as eleven that evening Sir George Grey told us the division seemed very doubtful. The Irishmen held off indignant at Palmerston's having mentioned with approval the landing of Garibaldi on the mainland. This was held to be an insult to the Pope, so More O'Farrell, Monsell, Sir John Acton, and eight or ten more would not vote at all. It seemed doubtful to the last. It is a great thing for the Government in many ways, not the least in having won the battle without the Pope and his men. It puts the Government in so much better and stronger a position with that party. The great result is to give some life to half-dead, broken-down, tempest-tossed Gladstone. When after the division he rose to propose the second Resolution, he was cheered by the Free-traders as he had not been cheered since the Budget Speech. Colonel Taylor tells me they had been led to success by promises from two quarters. First the paper-makers and the 'Times' engaged to bring fifty men to the post, and only brought five. The Irishmen promised to be twenty-five, but were only eleven, the others standing off and not voting. I have a long letter from Cobden, angry about fortifications and Volunteers." This morning I received another letter from the Speaker, enclosing Cobden's, which he has sent me to read. He says, " It is written in rather a spirit of exaggeration, but it is the fault of Cobden's mind to see one object so strongly, that his view cannot embrace another at the same time." Cobden's is well written, and contains much that is true, but he has evidently been so cajoled and flattered at Paris that he is now completely bamboozled, and so credulous that he takes for gospel all the Emperor says, and complains bitterly of "all that is going on at home" and especially of the tone of Palmerston's and Sidney Herbert's speeches. "Believing," he says, "that the new French tariff will realize a complete revolution in the commercial relations of the two countries, and having taken pains to impress this opinion on the Government, I am amazed at the course they are taking. The language of Palmerston and Sidney Herbert, coupled with the fortification scheme (he says), cuts the ground, on which I urged the Emperor to enter on the Free Trade policy, from under my feet. Nine tenths of his motives for making the plunge into that policy now were political rather than politico-economical ; he aimed at conciliating the English people, and I did not hesitate to assure him that if he entered without reserve on the Free Trade path it would be taken as a proof of his pacific intentions by the British public."

· *London, November 13th.*—At the end of three months since I last wrote anything in this book, I take my pen in hand to record my determination to bring this journal (which is no journal at all) to an end. I have long seen that it is useless to attempt to carry it on, for I am entirely out of the way of hearing anything of the slightest interest beyond what is known to all the world. I therefore close this record without any intention or expectation of renewing it, with a full consciousness of the smallness of its value or interest, and with great regret that I did not make better use of the opportunities I have had of recording something more worth reading.

INDEX.

THE END.

BIOGRAPHY.

THE HUNDRED GREATEST MEN. PORTRAITS OF THE ONE HUNDRED GREATEST MEN OF HISTORY. Reproduced from Fine and Rare Steel Engravings, with Biographies. 8vo. Cloth, $6.00.

A General Introduction to the Work was written by RALPH WALDO EMERSON; Introduction to Section I by MATTHEW ARNOLD; Section II by H. TAINE; Section III by MAX MÜLLER and R. RENAN; Section IV by NOAH PORTER; Section V by A. P. STANLEY; Section VI by H. HELMHOLTZ; Section VII by J. A. FROUDE; Section VIII by Professor JOHN FISKE.

HOURS WITH GREEK AND LATIN AUTHORS. From Various English Translations. With Biographical Notices. By G. H. JENNINGS and W. S. JOHNSTONE. 12mo. Cloth, $2.00.

LIFE OF HIS ROYAL HIGHNESS THE PRINCE CONSORT. By Sir THEODORE MARTIN. With Portraits and Views. Complete in 5 vols. 12mo. Cloth, $10.00.

"The literature of England is richer by a book which will be read with profit by succeeding generations of her sons and daughters."—*Blackwood.*

BEACONSFIELD. A SKETCH OF THE LITERARY AND POLITICAL CAREER OF BENJAMIN DISRAELI (Earl of Beaconsfield). With Two Portraits. By GEORGE M. TOWLE. 18mo. Paper, 25 cents; cloth, 60 cents.

LIFE OF CHARLOTTE BRONTE. By E. C. GASKELL. With Engravings. Two volumes in one. 12mo. Cloth, $1.50.

Charlotte Brontë was one of the most extraordinary female characters of modern times. From perfect obscurity, and notwithstanding a most unpropitious training, she sprang at one bound to the height of popularity, founded an entirely new school of novel-writing, and, after a life of severe trial and suffering, died when she was just beginning to be happy.

LIFE AND WRITINGS OF THOMAS HENRY BUCKLE. By ALFRED HENRY HUTH. 12mo. Cloth, $2.00.

"The book deals with Mr. Buckle less as a philosopher than as a man. . . . Mr. Huth has done his part well and thoroughly."—*Saturday Review.*

THOMAS CARLYLE: HIS LIFE—HIS BOOKS—HIS THEORIES. By ALFRED H. GUERNSEY. 18mo. Paper, 30 cents; Cloth, 60 cents.

New York: D. APPLETON & CO., 1, 3, & 5 Bond Street.

BIOGRAPHY.

ERASMUS DARWIN. By ERNST KRAUS. Translated from the German by W. S. DALLAS. With a Preliminary Notice by CHARLES DARWIN. With Portraits and Woodcuts. 12mo. Cloth, $1.25.

CHARLES DARWIN. By GRANT ALLEN. (English Worthies Series.) 16mo. Cloth, 75 cents.

LIFE OF CHARLES DICKENS. By JOHN FORSTER. The concluding volume of Chapman & Hall's Household Edition of the Works of Charles Dickens. With 40 Illustrations. Square 8vo. Paper, $1.25; cloth, $1.75.

SHORT LIFE OF CHARLES DICKENS. With Selections from his Letters. By CHARLES H. JONES. 18mo. Paper, 35 cents; cloth, 60 cents.

FARADAY AS A DISCOVERER. A Memoir. By Professor JOHN TYNDALL. 12mo. Cloth, $1.00.

"It has been thought desirable to give you and the world some image of Michael Faraday as a scientific investigator and discoverer. . . . I have returned from my task with such results as I could gather, and also with the wish that these results were more worthy than they are of the greatness of my theme."— *The Author.*

SHORT LIFE OF GLADSTONE. By C. H. JONES. 18mo. Paper, 35 cents; cloth, 60 cents.

"In two hundred and fifty pages, the author has succeeded in giving a clear impression of Gladstone's career, and, what is better still, of his personality. Extracts from his speeches and estimates of his literary work are given, and an excellent feature of the book is its short but significant citations from the press, which help the reader to see the great statesman through the eyes of his contemporaries, both friend and foe."—*Boston Courier.*

A JOURNAL OF THE REIGNS OF KING GEORGE IV AND KING WILLIAM IV. By the late CHARLES C. F. GREVILLE, Esq., Clerk of the Council to those Sovereigns. Edited by HENRY REEVE, Registrar of the Privy Council. 2 vols. 12mo. Cloth, $4.00.

"Since the publication of Horace Walpole's Letters, no book of greater historical interest has seen the light than the Greville Memoirs. It throws a curious, and, we may almost say, a terrible light on the conduct and character of the public men in England under the reigns of George IV and William IV. Its descriptions of those kings and their kinsfolk are never likely to be forgotten."—*New York Times.*

New York: D. APPLETON & CO., 1, 3, & 5 Bond Street.

BIOGRAPHY.

A JOURNAL OF THE REIGN OF QUEEN VICTORIA.
(Second Part of "The Greville Memoirs.") From 1837 to 1852.
By the late CHARLES GREVILLE, Clerk of the Council. 2 vols.
Large 12mo. Cloth, $4.00.

"Mr. Greville's Diary is one of the most important contributions which have ever been made to the political history of the middle of the nineteenth century. He is a graphic and powerful writer; and his usual habit of making the record while the impression of the events was fresh upon his mind gives his sketches of persons and places, and his accounts of conversations, great vividness. The volumes will be read with as much interest for their sketches of social life as for their political value."—*London Daily News.*

RETROSPECT OF A LONG LIFE, FROM 1815 TO 1883.
By S. C. HALL, F. S. A. With Portraits of Mr. and Mrs. S. C. Hall.
Crown 8vo. Cloth, $2.50.

MEMOIR AND CORRESPONDENCE OF CAROLINE HERSCHEL (Sister of Sir William, and Aunt of Sir John Herschel). By Mrs. JOHN HERSCHEL. 12mo. Illustrated with Portraits. Cloth, $1.75.

RECOLLECTIONS OF PAST LIFE. REMINISCENCES OF MEN, MANNERS, AND THINGS. By Sir HENRY HOLLAND, Bart. 12mo. Cloth, $2.00.

"A life extending over such a period, and passed in the most active manner, in the midst of the best society which the world has to offer, must necessarily be full of singular interest; and Sir Henry Holland has fortunately not waited until his memory lost its freshness before recalling some of the incidents to it."—*New York Times.*

LIFE OF SAMUEL LOVER. ARTISTIC, LITERARY, AND MUSICAL. With Selections from his Unpublished Papers and Correspondence, with Portrait. By BAYLE BERNARD. 12mo. Cloth, $2.00.

STRAY MOMENTS WITH THACKERAY: HIS HUMOR, SATIRE, AND CHARACTERS. Being Selections from his Writings, prefaced with a Few Biographical Notes. By WILLIAM H. RIDEING. 18mo. Paper, 30 cents; cloth, 60 cents.

BIOGRAPHY.

LORD MACAULAY: HIS LIFE—HIS WRITINGS. By C. H. JONES. 18mo. Paper, 30 cents; cloth, 60 cents.

LIFE OF CAPTAIN MARRYAT, R. N. By FLORENCE MARRYAT. 2 vols. 12mo. Cloth, $4.00.

RUSKIN ON PAINTING. With a Biographical Sketch. 18mo. Paper, 30 cents; cloth, 60 cents.

WILKES, SHERIDAN, FOX. THE OPPOSITION UNDER GEORGE III. By W. F. RAE. 12mo. Cloth, $2.00.

"An interesting, a truthful, and a wholesome book."—*London Athenæum.*
"A book which embraces vigorous sketches of three famous men like John Wilkes, Richard Brinsley Sheridan, and Charles James Fox, is truly worth having. The author is in evident sympathy with all three of his subjects."—*Chicago Tribune.*

LIGHTS OF THE OLD ENGLISH STAGE. BIOGRAPHICAL AND ANECDOTICAL SKETCHES OF FAMOUS ACTORS OF THE OLD ENGLISH STAGE. 18mo. Paper, 30 cents.

"The book treats of Richard Burbage and other 'originals' of Shakespeare's characters, the Cibbers, Garrick, Charles Macklin, 'Peg' Woffington and George Anne Bellamy, John Kemble and Mrs. Siddons. Cooke, Edmund Kean, Charles Young. Dora Jordan, and Mrs. Robinson. A more interesting group of persons it would be hard to find."—*New York World.*

ENGLISH MEN OF SCIENCE: THEIR NATURE AND NURTURE. By FRANCIS GALTON, F. R. S. 12mo. Cloth, $1.00.

McCLELLAN'S LAST SERVICE TO THE REPUBLIC, TOGETHER WITH A TRIBUTE TO HIS MEMORY. By GEORGE TICKNOR CURTIS. With a Map showing Position of Union and Confederate Forces on the Night of November 7, 1862. 12mo. Paper cover, 30 cents.

LIFE OF DANIEL WEBSTER. By GEORGE T. CURTIS. Illustrated with Steel Portrait and Woodcuts. 2 vols. 8vo. Cloth, $4.00; sheep, $6.00; half morocco, $10.00.

A most valuable and important contribution to the history of American parties and politics, and to the best class of our literature. It is a model biography of a most gifted man, wherein the intermingling of the statesman and lawyer with the husband, father, and friend, is painted so that we feel the reality of the picture.

New York: D. APPLETON & CO., 1, 3, & 5 Bond Street.

BIOGRAPHY.

THE LAST YEARS OF DANIEL WEBSTER. A MONO-GRAPH. By GEORGE T. CURTIS. 8vo. Paper, 50 cents.

REPRESENTATIVE NAMES IN ENGLISH LITERA-TURE. By H. H. MORGAN. 8vo. Cloth, $1.00.

THE NOVELS AND NOVELISTS OF THE EIGHTEENTH CENTURY, IN ILLUSTRATION OF THE MANNERS AND MORALS OF THE AGE. By W. FORSYTH. 12mo. Cloth, $1.50.

LIFE AND PUBLIC SERVICES OF SALMON PORT-LAND CHASE. By J. W. SCHUCKERS. Illustrated. 8vo. Cloth, $5.00; sheep, $6.00; half morocco, $7.50.

MEMOIRS OF GENERAL W. T. SHERMAN. New edition, revised, and with Additions. With numerous Maps and Portraits. 2 vols., 8vo. Cloth, $5.00.

This edition of General Sherman's memoirs has been thoroughly revised, and contains two new chapters and important appendices. Fifteen maps and several portraits, not given in the first edition, enrich the present issue. The portraits consist of engravings on steel of Generals Sherman, Thomas, Schofield, and McPherson, and a phototype group of corps commanders. The new chapter at the end of the work, entitled "After the War," throws light on recent controversies in regard to President Johnson's purpose in wishing to send General Grant to Mexico. The appendices contain numerous letters from army commanders bearing upon events of the war.

THE LIFE OF DAVID GLASGOW FARRAGUT, FIRST ADMIRAL OF THE UNITED STATES NAVY, EMBODYING HIS JOURNAL AND LETTERS. By his Son, LOYALL FARRAGUT. With Portraits, Maps, and Illustrations. 8vo. Cloth, $4.00; sheep, $5.00; half morocco, $6.00.

"The book is a stirring one, of course; the story of Farragut's life is a tale of adventure of the most ravishing sort, so that, aside from the value of this work as an authentic biography of the greatest of American naval commanders, the book is one of surpassing interest, considered merely as a narrative of difficult and dangerous enterprises and heroic achievements."—*New York Evening Post.*

FARTHEST NORTH; OR, THE LIFE AND EXPLORATIONS OF LIEUTENANT JAMES BOOTH LOCKWOOD, OF THE GREELY ARCTIC EXPEDITION. With Portrait, Map, and Illustrations. By CHARLES LANMAN. Small 12mo. Cloth, $1.25.

New York: D. APPLETON & CO., 1, 3, & 5 Bond Street.

BIOGRAPHY.

LIFE OF GENERAL ROBERT E. LEE. By John Esten Cooke. Illustrated with Portraits on Steel, Maps, and Wood Engravings. 8vo. Cloth, extra, $5.00; sheep, $6.00.

A BIOGRAPHY OF WILLIAM CULLEN BRYANT. WITH EXTRACTS FROM HIS PRIVATE CORRESPONDENCE. By Parke Godwin. With Two Portraits on Steel—one from a Painting by Morse, taken in 1825, and one from a Photograph, taken in 1873. 2 vols. Square 8vo. (Uniform with Memorial Editions of Prose Writings and Poetical Works.) Cloth, gilt top, $6.00.

Containing a full account, from authentic sources, of the poet's ancestry; of his boyhood among the Hampshire hills; of his early poems; of his ten years' life as a country lawyer; of his long editorial career in New York; of his intercourse with contemporaries; of his travels abroad and at home; of the origin of many of his poems; of his political opinions; of his speeches and addresses; and of the honors he received.

RALPH WALDO EMERSON: POET AND PHILOSOPHER. By A. H. Guernsey. (Published by arrangement with Messrs. Houghton, Mifflin & Co., publishers of the complete editions of Emerson's Works.) A companion volume to "Carlyle: his Life, his Books, his Theories." 18mo. Paper, 40 cents; cloth, 75 cents.

THE STORY OF MY LIFE. By the late J. Marion Sims, M. D. Edited by his Son, H. Marion Sims, M. D. 12mo. Cloth, $1.50.

Under the simple title of "The Story of my Life" Dr. Sims has in the most fitting terms narrated the origin and growth of those achievements in surgery which by the general judgment of enlightened men have stamped him as the benefactor of his race. The account of Dr. Sims's early struggle is of the deepest interest.

LIFE AND LETTERS OF FITZ-GREENE HALLECK. Edited by James Grant Wilson. Two Steel Engravings. Uniform with Halleck's Poems. 12mo. Cloth, gilt top, $2.50; half calf, extra, $4.50; morocco, $6.00.

The Same. Large-paper Edition. Illustrated. Cloth, $10.00; morocco antique, $15.

New York: D. APPLETON & CO., 1, 3, & 5 Bond Street.

BIOGRAPHY.

ESSAYS AND SPEECHES OF JEREMIAH S. BLACK. WITH A BIOGRAPHICAL SKETCH. By CHAUNCEY F. BLACK. With a Portrait on Steel. 8vo. Cloth, $3.75.

LIFE AND LETTERS OF EMORY UPTON, COLONEL OF THE FOURTH REGIMENT OF ARTILLERY, AND BREVET MAJOR-GENERAL U. S. ARMY. By PETER S. MICHIE, Professor U. S. Military Academy. With an Introduction by JAMES HARRISON WILSON, late U. S. A. With Portraits. 8vo. Cloth, $2.00.

"The subject of the following memoir was widely known by reputation in the military profession, and the story of his life would, at least to military men, have been a matter of passing interest. The tragic circumstances of his death seemed to demand some explanation in harmony with his established reputation and character. At the earnest solicitation of his nearest relatives, the author, although conscious of his own deficiencies, undertook the task of compiling a brief record of General Upton's life for his family and immediate personal friends."—*From Preface.*

LIFE AND LETTERS OF THOMAS GOLD APPLE-TON. Prepared by SUSAN HALE. With a Portrait. 12mo. Cloth, gilt top, $1.75.

Mr. T. G. Appleton, it is needless to say, was well known in social and literary circles in Europe and America, and distinguished as one of the best conversationalists of the day. The present work consists of a biographical sketch, selections from his letters, and some account of his different journeys.

LOUIS PASTEUR: HIS LIFE AND LABORS. By his SON-IN-LAW. Translated from the French by Lady CLAUD HAMILTON. With an Introduction by Professor TYNDALL. 12mo. Cloth, $1.25.

"Since the first studies of M. Pasteur on molecular dissymmetry, down to his most recent investigations on hydrophobia, on virulent diseases, and on the artificial cultures of living contagia, the author of these pages has been able, if not to witness all, at least to follow in its principal developments, this uninterrupted series of scientific conquests."—*From the Preface.*
"A record in which the verities of science are endowed with the interest of romance."—Professor TYNDALL.

MEMOIRS OF NAPOLEON: HIS COURT AND FAMILY. By the Duchess D'ABRANTES (Madame Junot). 2 vols. 12mo. Cloth, $3.00.

This book supplies many valuable and interesting details respecting the Court and Family of Napoleon, which are found in no other work. The author's opportunities for observation were excellent and long continued, and she has availed herself of them so effectually as to present us with a very lively, entertaining, and readable book, as well as to supply important materials for future historians and biographers.

New York: D. APPLETON & CO., 1, 3, & 5 Bond Street.

BIOGRAPHY.

MEMOIRS OF MADAME DE REMUSAT. 1802–1808. Edited by her Grandson, PAUL DE RÉMUSAT, Senator. In 3 vols., paper covers, 8vo, $1.50; also, in 1 vol., cloth, 12mo, $2.00; half calf, $3.50.

"These memoirs are not only a repository of anecdotes and of portraits sketched from life by a keen-eyed, quick-witted woman; but some of the author's reflections on social and political questions are remarkable for weight and penetration."—*New York Sun.*

"Madame de Rémusat's keenness of intelligence, and her intimacy with Josephine, to which she was not only admitted but welcomed, gave her those extraordinary opportunities which she has turned to so good account in these 'Memoirs.' The work, as a whole, is at once the most interesting and the most damaging commentary on the character of Napoleon that has ever been produced."—*Dr. C. K. Adams's Manual of Historical Literature.*

A SELECTION FROM THE LETTERS OF MADAME DE REMUSAT. 1804–1814. Edited by her Grandson, PAUL DE RÉMUSAT, Senator. Uniform with "Memoirs of Madame de Rémusat," 1802-1808. 12mo. Cloth, $1.25.

"'A Selection from the Letters of Madame de Rémusat to her Husband and Son' has been published by the Appletons. Coming closely upon the fascinating memoirs of that lady, they possess the same interest, and will add to the reader's knowledge of social and political life in France in the days of the first Napoleon."—*Boston Evening Transcript.*

VOLTAIRE. By JOHN MORLEY. 12mo. Cloth, $2.00.

CONTENTS.—Preliminary; English Influences; Literature; Berlin; Religion; History; Ferney.

FRENCH MEN OF LETTERS. Personal and Anecdotical Sketches of Victor Hugo, Alfred de Musset, Théophile Gautier, Henri Murger, Sainte-Beuve, Gérard de Nerval, Alexandre Dumas, fils, Emile Augier, Octave Feuillet, Victorien Sardou, Alphonse Daudet, and Emile Zola. By MAURICE MAURIS. Paper, 35 cents. cloth, 60 cents.

HISTORY OF GENERAL JAMES A. GARFIELD'S PUBLIC LIFE. (The Republican Text-Book for the Campaign of 1880.) By B. A. HINSDALE, A. M., President of Hiram College. 8vo. Paper, 50 cents.

LIFE OF WINFIELD SCOTT HANCOCK, MAJOR-GENERAL UNITED STATES ARMY. By Rev. D. X. JUNKIN, D. D., and FRANK H. NORTON. 12mo. Cloth, $1.50.

New York: D. APPLETON & CO., 1, 3, & 5 Bond Street.

BIOGRAPHY.

LIFE AND CORRESPONDENCE OF THEODORE PARKER, MINISTER OF THE TWENTY-EIGHTH CONGREGATIONAL SOCIETY, BOSTON. By JOHN WEISS. Portrait and Engravings. 2 large vols. 8vo. Cloth, $4.00; half calf, extra, $8.00.

THE LIFE, CORRESPONDENCE, AND WRITINGS OF ARCHBISHOP HUGHES. By JOHN R. G. HASSARD. 8vo. Moroeco, $4.50.

LETTERS OF LIFE. By Mrs. L. H. SIGOURNEY. 12mo. Cloth, $1.50; half calf, extra, $4.00.

LITERATURE IN LETTERS; OR, MANNERS, ART, CRITICISM, BIOGRAPHY, HISTORY, AND MORALS ILLUSTRATED IN THE CORRESPONDENCE OF EMINENT PERSONS. Edited by JAMES P. HOLCOMBE, LL. D. 12mo. Cloth, $2.00; half calf, $4.50.

"The sources of pleasure and instruction to be found in the private correspondence of eminent persons have never been fully explained; much less have they been rendered accessible to the bulk of the reading public. Our language abounds in letters which contain the most vivid pictures of manners, and the most faithful and striking delineations of character, which are full of wit, wisdom, fancy, useful knowledge, noble and pious sentiment."—*Extract from Preface.*

JOHN KEESE, WIT AND LITTERATEUR. A BIOGRAPHICAL MEMOIR. By WILLIAM L. KEESE. Small 4to. Cloth, gilt top, $1.25.

John Keese was a popular book-auctioneer of New York thirty years ago, whose witticisms were the town talk. "If John Keese should quit the auctioneer business, I should die of *ennui*," exclaimed one of his admirers. Mr. Keese was known to all the literary people of his day, and these memoirs contain reminiscences and anecdotes of literary circles in New York a generation ago that will be valued by those who like glances at past local conditions.

LIFE OF JAMES W. GRIMES. By W. SALTER. 8vo. Cloth, $3.50.

LIFE OF EDWARD LIVINGSTON. By C. H. HUNT. With an Introduction by GEORGE BANCROFT. Portrait. 8vo. Cloth, $4.00.

New York: D. APPLETON & CO., 1, 3, & 5 Bond Street.

BIOGRAPHY.

THE LIFE OF SAMUEL F. B. MORSE, INVENTOR OF THE RECORDING TELEGRAPH. By S. I. PRIME. Illustrated with Steel Plates and Wood Engravings. 8vo. Cloth, $5.00; sheep, $6.00; half morocco, $7.50; morocco, $10.00.

LIFE OF EMMA WILLARD. By JOHN LORD, LL. D. With two Portraits on Steel. 12mo. Cloth, $2.00.

RECOLLECTIONS AND OPINIONS OF AN OLD PIONEER. By P. H. BURNETT, First Governor of the State of California. 12mo. Cloth, $1.75.

Mr. Burnett's life has been full of varied experience, and the record takes the reader back prior to the discovery of gold in California, and leads him through many adventures and incidents to the time of the beginning of the late war.

"I have been a pioneer most of my life; whenever, since my arrival in California, I have seen a party of immigrants, with their ox-teams and white-sheeted wagons, I have been excited, have felt younger, and was for the moment anxious to make another trip."—*The Author.*

LIFE OF JOHN RANDOLPH, OF ROANOKE. By HUGH II. GARLAND. Portraits. Two volumes in one. 8vo. Cloth, $2.00.

ELIHU BURRITT: A MEMORIAL VOLUME, CONTAINING A SKETCH OF HIS LIFE AND LABORS. With Selections from his Writings and Lectures, and Extracts from his Private Journals in Europe and America. Edited by CHARLES NORTHEND, A. M. 12mo. Cloth, $1 75.

THE LIFE AND PUBLIC SERVICES OF DR. LEWIS F. LINN. FOR TEN YEARS A SENATOR OF THE UNITED STATES FROM THE STATE OF MISSOURI. By E. A. LINN and N. SARGENT. With Portrait. 8vo. Cloth, $2.00.

OUTLINE OF THE PUBLIC LIFE AND SERVICES OF THOMAS F. BAYARD, SENATOR OF THE UNITED STATES FROM THE STATE OF DELAWARE, 1869–1880. With Extracts from his Speeches and the Debates of Congress. By EDWARD SPENCER. 12mo. Paper, 50 cents; cloth, $1 00.

New York: D. APPLETON & CO., 1, 3, & 5 Bond Street.